D1130913

International Studies on Childhood and Adolescence 5

International Studies on Childhood and Adolescence (ISCA)

The aim of the ISCA series is to publish theoretical and methodological studies on the social, cultural, economic, and health situation of children and adolescents.

Almost all countries worldwide report increased risks and problems in the development of children and adolescents. Many pedagogic, psychosocial, and medical institutes as well as education and training centers are trying to help children and adolescents deal with problematic situations. They step in to help with existing difficulties (intervention) or to avoid problems in advance (prevention). However, not enough is known about the causes and backgrounds of the difficulties that arise in the life course of children and adolescents. There is still insufficient research on the effectiveness and consequences of prevention measures and intervention in families, pre-school institutions, schools, youth service, youth welfare, and the criminal justice system.

The ISCA series addresses these issues. An interdisciplinary team of editors and authors focusses on the publications on theoretical, methodological, and practical issues in the above mentioned fields. The whole spectrum of perspectives is considered: analyses rooted in the sociological as well as the psychological or medical and public health tradition, from an economic or a political science angle, mainstream as well as critical contributions.

The ISCA series represents an effort to advance the scientific study of childhood and adolescence across boundaries and academic disciplines.

Children, Cities, and Psychological Theories

Developing Relationships

Edited by
Dietmar Görlitz
Hans Joachim Harloff
Günter Mey
Jaan Valsiner

Walter de Gruyter · Berlin · New York 1998

Dietmar Görlitz, Ph.D., Professor of Developmental Psychology, Technical University, Berlin, Germany
Hans Joachim Harloff, Ph.D., Professor of Social and Environmental Psychology, Technical University, Berlin, Germany
Günter Mey, Department of Developmental Psychology, Technical University, Berlin, Germany
Jaan Valsiner, Ph.D., Professor of Psychology, Clark University, Worcester, Mass., U.S.A.

With 14 photos, numerous tables and figures

The frontispiece, *5th Avenue in New York*, and the final picture, *Little Girl at Play in a Hamlet of the Equadorian Rain Forest*, are reprinted with the kind permission of Niklas Görlitz.

♾ Printed on acid-free paper which falls within the guidelines of the ANSI to ensure permanence and durability.

Library of Congress Cataloging-in-Publication Data

> Children, cities, and psychological theories : developing rela-
> tionships / edited by Dietmar Görlitz ... [et al.].
>   p.   cm. − (International studies on childhood and
> adolescence ; 5)
>   Includes bibliographical references and index.
>   ISBN (invalid) 3 11 01460370 (alk. paper)
>   1. City children.   2. Child development.   3. Cities and
> towns − Psychological aspects.   4. Social ecology.
> I. Görlitz, Dietmar, 1937− .   II. Series.
> HT206.C444   1998
> 155.4−dc21   98-18583
>   CIP

Fine Arts

Die Deutsche Bibliothek − CIP-Einheitsaufnahme

> **Children, cities, and psychological theories** : developing rela-
> tionships / ed. by Dietmar Görlitz ... − Berlin ; New York : de
> Gruyter, 1998
> (International studies on childhood and adolescence ; 5)
> ISBN 3-11-014603-7

In memoriam
Joachim F. Wohlwill
(1928-1987)

To the genius loci
of the city of Herten
(Ruhr District)

Contents

B. Transactional, holistic, and relational-developmental perspectives on children in the cities

Part III The Finale

Appendix

Keynote

Roger Hart

With the poorer cities of most southern countries continuing to grow at rapid rates and the older cities of the northern hemisphere suffering from increasing alienation and violence, the problems of urban children seem so overwhelming that it is often difficult to imagine how academia can be useful. But seeing this impressive collection of theoretical papers feeds my optimism that psychologists may yet be able to address this most critical domain of concern for all societies. This volume is a remarkably broad and self-critical review of psychological theories on children's relationships to cities. It has long been needed. It sets the stage for what must be a dramatic reorientation of the attention of psychologists toward useful research on the pressing issues of planning and managing cities with children in mind.

Many psychologists would argue, of course, that their general theories are relevant to any setting and that it is up to practitioners to interpret them. But such responses are indicative of the problem. With the erosion of child study came a more theoretically oriented and abstract developmental psychology divorced from children's everyday life. Related to this has been the emphasis on cognitive development at the expense of a more wholistic view of children. More generally, psychology has been trapped by adherence to experimental methods that lead most psychologists to avoid the complexities of research on real problems of children in their environment. Without detailed study of children in the context of their everyday lives, social scientists are unlikely to generate the rich theory they need.

Empirical research and theory on the ecology of children in cities is in an impoverished state. When I look through my shelves for the books that inform readers about the lives and experiences of city children, I find so few that are by psychologists: Barker and Schoggen's (1973) analysis of the different behavior settings found in cities of different sizes in the United States and England; Muchow and Muchow's (1935/1978) ecological study of children in Hamburg; Newson and Newson's (1970 and 1977) longitudinal studies of social class and child-rearing in Nottingham, England. There has been a reliance upon the creativity of people outside psychology to write of the behavior and experience of children in cities; urban planners and designers such as Cooper (1975), Lynch (1977), Moore (1985), and Ward (1978) pop out of my bookshelves as the practical psychologists and social scientists of the city. Most sources are autobiographies or works by journalists and lack the systematic and comparative qualities needed for improving cities. Scientists probably know more about the natural history of other primates in the wild than about the everyday activities of children in cities.

To be fair, the situation is not only a reflection of the methodological orthodoxy of psychological research. It is also indicative of the orientations of other disciplines. Anthropologists, with some rare exceptions (e.g., Lewis, 1963, Whiting & Edwards, 1988) have until very recently focused almost entirely on adults and their child-rearing practices. Similarly, though there is now an incipient field of the sociology of children, sociologists used to focus narrowly on deviant youth (Chombart de Lauwe, 1976, Michelson, Levine, & Michelson, 1979; are important exceptions). A growing number of valuable interdisciplinary books are now appearing concerning children living in difficult circumstances in the cities of the Third World (e.g., Blanc, 1994; Boyden & Holden, 1991; Hardoy, Mitlin, & Satterthwaite, 1992; Myers, 1991). Unfortunately, they are largely limited to the reporting of large-scale survey and epidemiological data, illustrated by brief profiles of individual children, because of the same lack of detailed accounts of children's activities and experiences.

The broad theoretical sweep of this book is in part the fruit of interdisciplinary collaboration in the study of child-environment relations that was fostered in the 1970s. Unfortunately, this development seems to have slowed down and even regressed, probably as a result of the retreat of academic disciplines to the safe, protected confines of their home territories during times of economic cutbacks. Because this book illustrates the exciting and extremely important new questions and theoretical insights that can grow out of interdisciplinary work with children, I hope it will help challenge the straitjacketed world of psychology conferences and journals and spur a new interdisciplinary wave of integrated and socially relevant theory and research on children's lives in cities.

Having established through this book a clear picture of the state of relevant psychological theories, psychologists are now in a better position to join the broader theoretical debates on urbanization and the quality of urban life, which involve economists, sociologists, political scientists, geographers, anthropologists, and urban historians. By contributing psychological theory on children to these discussions we researchers will be better able to understand the impact of urbanization on human development. Social scientists need to understand how cities of different sizes, with different degrees of wealth, and in different cultures and political systems affect people who live in them and how these relationships change as a result of the global economy. Within cities, there is a need to integrate psychological theories with economic analysis in order to inform efforts to achieve social justice for children. The landscape of cities is structured to afford very different opportunities for different children. Some of these discrepancies are obvious. Suburbs, for instance, were created specifically to improve opportunities for middle-class families with children.

But other important environmental variations in quality lie outside the researcher's knowledge and await investigation.

An unstated assumption in much of this book is that policy-makers and planners will draw on the good research of psychologists and social scientists. This notion of rational planning is too limited. Though the planning process in some cities (in the Netherlands, for example) includes research, such as regular surveys documenting the *use* of city play and recreational facilities, this approach is the exception rather than the rule. But providing practical guidelines for planners is not the only role for child-environment research. The theoretical work of this book provides the bases for research at multiple levels. At the most local level, psychologists need to forge with communities a working relationship like that in the city of Herten, where this book was born. The "Children's Friends Committee" of Herten is a superb base for supporting communities in research and in the ongoing monitoring of environmental quality for children. That kind of socially relevant action research is what Kurt Lewin called for 50 years ago (Lewin, 1948). We should build upon Lewin's thinking by also incorporating children themselves into this research endeavor (Hart, 1997).

There is still a place for research that aids the traditional rational planning of large-scale services and facilities, but it is probably at the most local level that our research efforts on behalf of community planning and management offers the greatest opportunity for building cities that truly foster children's development. To this end there is a need for psychologists who can contribute their theoretical insights to the modest enterprise of countless local social experiments with communities in cities. In this way, theory on children's behavior and development can be better brought to bear on the real problems of communities, families, and children struggling to improve their lives. There should, of course, be a continuation of some strategic top-down research and planning, but this model for applying psychological theory cannot be the only standard in a world where the problems of children require the collaboration of all. Though there is a long way to go in constructing a comprehensive research agenda for children in cities, my colleagues in this book have created an important foundation of theory on which we can confidently build.

References

Barker, R. G., & Schoggen, P. (1973). *Qualities of Community Life*. Washington, DC: Jossey-Bass.

Blanc, C. S. (1994). *Urban children in distress: Global predicaments and innovative strategies.* Florence: International Child Development Centre of UNICEF and London: Gordon and Breach.

Boyden, J., & Holden, P. (1991). *Children of the cities*. London: Zed Books.

Chombart de Lauwe, M. J., Bonnin, P., Mayeur, M., Perrot, M., & Soudierre, M. (1976). *Enfant En-Jeu: Les pratiques des enfants durant leur temps libre en fonction dest types d'environnement et des ideologies* [The child at play: The activities of children during their free time as a function of types of environment and ideologies]. Paris: Centre National de la Recherche Scientifique.

Cooper, C. C. (1975). *Easter Hill Village: Some social implications of design.* New York: Free Press.

Hardoy, J. E., Mitlin, D., & Satterthwaite, D. (1992). *Environmental problems in Third World cities.* London: Earthscan.

Hart, R. A. (1997). *Children's Participation: The Theory and Practice of Envolving Young Citizens in Community Development and Environmental Care.* London: Earthscon / UNICEF.

Lewin, K. (1948). *Resolving social conflicts.* New York: Harper and Brothers.

Lewis, O. (1963). *The children of Sanchez.* New York: Vintage Books.

Lynch, K. (1977). *Growing up in cities: Studies of the spatial environment of adolescence in Cracow, Melbourne, Mexico City, Salta, Toluca and Warsawa.* Cambridge, MA: MIT Press.

Michelson, W., Levine, S., & Michelson, E. (1979). *The child in the city: Today and tomorrow.* Toronto: University of Toronto Press.

Moore, R. C. (1985). *Childhood's domain.* London: Croom-Helm.

Muchow, M., & Muchow, H. H. (1978). *Der Lebensraum des Großstadtkindes* [The life space of the urban child]. With an introduction by J. Zinnecker. Bensheim, Germany: päd. extra Buchverlag. (Original work published 1935)

Myers, W. (Ed.). *Protecting working children.* London: Zed Books.

Newson, J., & Newson, E. (1977). *Four years old in an urban community.* New York: Penguin Books.

Newson, J., & Newson, E. (1977). *Seven years old in the home environment.* New York: Penguin Books.

Ward, C. (1978). *The child in the city.* London: The Architectural Press.

Whiting, B. B., & Edwards, C. P. (1988). *Children of different worlds: The foundation of social behavior.* Cambridge, MA: Harvard University Press.

Foreword

Urie Bronfenbrenner

This book offers rich and variegated gifts to the thoughtful reader. Its commendable, but modestly unstated, aspiration is to present what is known, and what still needs to be known, about the role of cities in shaping human development. To be sure, what is already known is very little compared to what has yet to be discovered. Nevertheless, the knowledge gained thus far is substantial. Some of it goes back more than a century. For example, in a chapter tracing the history of studies of children growing up in urban environments, Dietmar Görlitz gives due prominence to two little known early investigations of the effects of neighborhoods on the content of children's concepts by the time they enter school. The first study was carried out by the Pedagogical Society of Berlin well over a century ago (Schwabe & Bartholomäi, 1870); the second, a cross-cultural replication, was conducted in Boston a decade later by the well-known American psychologist G. Stanley Hall (1883). Both investigations were remarkably ahead of their time in terms of theory and research design. As a result, they yielded unexpected findings that foreshadowed key contemporary issues. For instance, within neighborhoods both in Berlin and Boston, children who had attended kindergarten before entering school exhibited a richer store of concepts than those who had not. Even more instructive for today's scene, again in both cities, was a marked difference by gender, but in the reverse direction from what prevails in the United States today. In those days, boys outshone the girls. A clue to the turnaround is contained in the following prescient comment by the Berlin educators back in 1870: "It is plain, therefore, that the school must assume an attitude with reference to boys different from that assumed toward girls" (quoted in Bronfenbrenner & Crouter, 1983, p. 361).

Overall, however, the chapters in the present volume look more to the future than to the past, and, in doing so, they often break new ground. For example, Werner and Altman argue compellingly that neighborhoods cannot be viewed simply as static environments in which behavior and development take place; instead, they maintain, neighborhoods should be treated as dynamic contexts that generate changes over time. As a first step in moving from theory to research design, the authors propose a richly differentiated and dynamic taxonomy of neighborhood characteristics and activities posited as furthering the development of friendships, feelings of solidarity, territorial investment, and shared identity, both within and across successive age levels.

Werner and Altman's chapter is but one of many that could be cited as making significant contributions. However, their authors often draw upon different theoretical traditions and empirical work and, thereby, call attention to other influential factors, among them physical features of the environment, cultural traditions as sustainers of neighborhood life, cities and neighborhoods as objects of emotional attachment, and environmental features especially important to the development of young children (e.g., opportunities for exploratory behavior, reality testing, and learning from the feedback of their own activities). What is notable about these elements is not so much their diversity as their complementarity and, therefore, their capacity to be included, in combinations of two or three variables, within the same research design. An instructive example is Frieder Lang's chapter, in which he analyzes features of urban life that have different significance for the young and the old, and then looks at structures that can bring the age groups together, thus fostering intergenerational ties.

Paradoxically, one of the most distinctive and potentially promising features of this volume is its inclusion of chapters that have little to say about the specific characteristics of cities that influence human beings. The future potential nevertheless exists because the theories presented lie at the frontiers of contemporary developmental science. These formulations have certain features in common. All are multivariate systems-theories that cut across and integrate concepts and findings from different disciplines, ranging from comparative and evolutionary biology on one side through developmental psychology, sociology, and cultural anthropology to economics, political science, and both micro- and macroeconomics. A second defining property is the bidirectionality of processes and effects. A third distinctive characteristic, and perhaps the most elusive, appears under the rubric of "transactionalism." A succinct definition that has the additional virtue of including concrete examples is provided by Rolf Oerter:

Transactionalism, a concept that is sometimes used very vaguely . . . [refers] to the assumption that individuals change their environment through their own actions in such a way that personal ideas, designs, and goals are transported into the environment and 'materialized' there. As part of the human-made environment, however, these products have impacts on the individual. . . . Everyday objects like tools and cars may serve as examples. Using a tool means that the constructors' ideas that are imposed on the object are realized and transformed into action. (p. 253)

On a broader level, the book's editors have employed an ingeniously simple strategy to help readers understand, think critically about, and apply creatively these newly evolving theoretical models; namely, in the second half of the volume, the original authors change roles to become constructive critics of a theoretical position differing from their own. This procedure often has the additional advantage of providing a perspective from another culture or scientific discipline.

In conclusion, I turn to a theme appearing in this volume on which there is both division and emerging integration. I refer to the distinction frequently made in the social and behavioral sciences between the world as perceived, and so-called objective reality. The nature of the former is perhaps best conveyed in the Thomases' inexorable dictum: "If men define situations as real, they are real in their consequences." In a monograph published almost two decades ago, I referred to the foregoing statement as "perhaps the only proposition in social science that approaches the status of an immutable law" (Bronfenbrenner, 1979, p. 23) The qualifying "perhaps" turned out to be well-advised. Since that time, an analysis of accumulating theoretical and empirical writings, including my own, has led me to a second, complementary formulation that is no less immutable: "Situations *not* perceived as real are also real in their consequences." The inexorable realities to which I refer are the biological requirements and imperatives for the effective functioning and development of members of our own species: Homo sapiens.

The nature of these requirements and imperatives, their bases in research findings, and their implications for theory and social policy are set forth in several recent works[1] that specify the defining properties of what I now call the bioecological model. Their relevance to the present volume lies in the fact that violation of these biological requirements has been producing profound social changes in our own times.[2] I refer to this phenomenon as the mounting chaos in the lives of children, youth, and families. Today, it is occurring at an increasingly rapid rate in all postmodern societies at all class levels, and it is especially pronounced in large cities. Even if unwittingly, many of the chapters in the present volume shed light on this phenomenon, both in terms of the forces that produce it and those that have the power to turn it around. Here, once again, I see the promise of Kurt Lewin's classic maxim: "There is nothing so practical as a good theory."

Notes

1 Bronfenbrenner, 1992, 1993, 1995, 1996; Bronfenbrenner, McClelland, Wethington, Moen, & Ceci, 1996; Bronfenbrenner & Morris, in press.
2 These changes are documented in several of the publications cited above.

References

Bronfenbrenner, U. (1979). *The ecology of human development: Experiments by nature and design.* Cambridge, MA: Harvard University Press.
Bronfenbrenner, U. (1992). Ecological systems theory. In R. Vasta (Ed.), *Six theories of child development: Revised formulations and current issues* (pp. 187-249). London: Jessica Kingsley.

Bronfenbrenner, U. (1993). The ecology of cognitive development: Research models and fugitive findings. In R. H. Wozniak & K. Fischer (Eds.), *Scientific environments* (pp. 3-44). Hillsdale, NJ: Erlbaum.

Bronfenbrenner, U. (1995). Developmental ecology through space and time: A future perspective. In P. Moen, G. H. Elder, Jr., & K. Lüscher (Eds.), *Examining lives in context: Perspectives on the ecology of human development* (pp. 619-647). Washington, DC: APA Books.

Bronfenbrenner, U. (1996). Japanische Kindheit als Grundlage einer Lernkultur: Folgerungen für Forschung und Praxis [Japanese childhood as a foundation of a learning culture: Conclusions for research and practice]. In D. Elschenbroich (Ed.), *Anleitung zur Neugier. Grundlagen Japanischer Erziehung* (pp. 329-354). Frankfurt on the Main: Suhrkamp Verlag.

Bronfenbrenner, U. & Crouter, A. C. (1983). The evolution of environmental models in developmental research. In P. H. Mussen (Series Ed.) & W. Kessen (Vol. Ed.), *Handbook of child psychology: Vol. 1. History, theory and methods* (4th ed., pp. 357-414). New York: Wiley.

Bronfenbrenner, U., McClelland, P., Wethington, E., Moen, P., & Ceci, S. J. (1996). *The state of Americans: This generation and the next*. New York: The Free Press.

Bronfenbrenner, U., & Morris, P. A. (1998). The ecology of developmental processes. In W. Damon (Series Ed.) & R. M. Lerner (Vol. Ed.), *Handbook of child psychology: Vol. 1. Theory* (5th ed.). New York: Wiley.

Hall, G. S. (1883, January-June). The contents of children's minds. *Princeton Review*, 249-272.

Schwabe, H., & Bartholomäi, F. (1870). Ueber Inhalt und Methode einer Berliner Schulstatistik [On the content and methodology of a statistical description of Berlin schools]. *Berlin und seine Entwickelung: Städtisches Jahrbuch für Volkswirthschaft und Statistik, 4,* 1-76. Berlin: Guttentag.

How it all began – Background to this book

Dietmar Görlitz

This book arose from encounters; it lives on dialogue, on exchange and discussion. When Joachim Wohlwill was in Berlin for the first time, oppressed by the proximity to things German, he was intent on finding a way to move from research in environmental psychology back into developmental psychology. Our aim, with his aid, was to bring the everyday world into psychology (Fietkau & Görlitz, 1981). This contact nurtured confidence and grew into an extended stay for Wohlwill in the then still divided city. And developmental psychology spread into zones of everyday life, where it was infused by amazement at children and adults observed in situations that piqued their curiosity on the streets.

They were city streets, but not yet the city itself. Our fascination was with process models, with the putatively brief moment of time. Wohlwill, a native of Hamburg, was keen at that time (in the early 1980s) on seeing the city where Martha Muchow, as an associate of William Stern, had sought out other children and followed their activities through participant observation. Our research on play and exploration became an exploration by the researcher and an adventure for those accompanying him along the way. Wohlwill was always the advisor on the findings and on what was preserved for further reflection (Görlitz & Wohlwill, 1987), the purpose of which was to analyze the course of play and exploration in context. Their urban context was kept in mind but not elevated to a topic in its own right, let alone a complex topic, although the mentor was always aware of it. Wohlwill bequeathed American psychology new traditions by reminding us Germans of our own past traditions and helped us tie into them again (Wohlwill, 1985). What would Martha Muchow make of children's doings in the West Berlin of the 1980s? Which city would her methods allow us adults to see and experience?

In long discussions between the primary editor of this book and the researcher to whom this book is dedicated, the idea was born to look at the modern city as seen from the perspective of the children there, remembering that cities in today's world may have become more problematic, more menacing – or at least dubious – in the contribution they make to children's development. Beyond playing and exploring, what would children themselves want to do or even make possible in the first place if they were to participate in planning streets, dwellings, or larger units of the city?

Wohlwill's death in the initial stage of joint work with Germans suspended this project (Görlitz, 1989), as it did many others.

As strange as our viewpoint was to architects in Berlin, however, some of them liked it, and the adventure of engaging in the development of psychology by actually walking the streets and sharpening the focus on children acquired an interdisciplinary dimension. Among psychologists, Gerhard Kaminski's work group in Tübingen was particularly supportive of this orientation, which was soon expanded further by the contributions of town and regional planning. All this interest, however, still lacked a place where it could strike roots. The encounter with Herten, an average sized mining town in the northern part of Germany's Ruhr District, quite literally gave our project life.

This introduction is purposely written in a biographical and historical mode, for only enthusiasm or necessity drives psychologists onto the streets; as a research topic, curiosity can be confined to labs and left at that. Streets, by contrast, are a promising start, for they are "a primary ingredient of urban existence . . . [on which] the urban process never stops [. . . . They] are as mutable as life itself," as Çelik, Favro, and Ingersoll (1994, p. 1) wrote when they introduced their portrait of streets in major cities of the world. In Herten, in our small circle of psychologists, architects, town planners, and students – vulnerable in our lack of a model and in our effort to span disciplinary boundaries – there was the pioneer spirit of turning to a city whose patrons had a long record of pursuing child-oriented town planning and settlement design. "Go west!" From our vantage point in Berlin, that meant happily embracing Herten as a venue that augured well. The then three-year-old project of getting acquainted with children's perspectives on the city and becoming familiar with ways that children at different phases of their development can help design the settings of the settlements in which they live has been described elsewhere (Görlitz, 1993; Görlitz & Schröder, 1994; Schröder, 1995, 1996).

Upon successful completion of this initiative, it was logical for like-minded, experienced, and interested thinkers at home and abroad to be invited to Herten to exchange their views on the city as a framework for children's development. That dialogue took place at a four-day conference hosted in the town's renaissance castle in the summer of 1992 as planned by this book's four editors along with students and their partners in Herten, especially Richard Schröder, a graduate of the Technical University of Berlin who is currently the director of Herten's "children's friends" office.

Were we able to think in terms of development despite the impressive immobility of a city and its buildings amid the constant flow of traffic? It is true that Wohlwill had regarded the adaptations made by developing children as the true subject of psychology (Wohlwill, 1981, pp. 108-111), but when Jaan Valsiner joined the project it was through that younger author's serious reconsideration of the developmental subject matter (Valsiner, 1987, Wohlwill, 1973) that the Herten adventure found the way back to Wohlwill's disciplinary roots (see also Valsiner, 1988). It explicitly acquired the dimension of environmental psychology with Hans Joachim Harloff (Harloff, 1993; for a characteristically broad approach, see also Harloff, 1995), and the Herten planning staff gained Günter Mey from Heidi Keller's circle in Osnabrück, which, as Jean Paul might have put it, was one of the project's "preparatory schools" (Mey & Wallbrecht, 1988; Mey, 1989).

As the conference organizers, we wished to achieve what Gary Moore and Roger Hart had taught us and what Urie Bronfenbrenner had outlined as a developmental model. We wished to engage in an exchange between adults from the academic, administrative, and decision-making communities in order to sharpen our senses for and our knowledge about these purportedly so permanent artifacts – cities as "the greatest works of art that a culture can produce"[1] – and their formative and formable effects on the children growing up in them. Are cities "a work of art, a design to be controlled and orchestrated" (Kostof, 1994, p. 12), and "unendurable contradiction of itself and human life" (Barber, 1995, p. 33)? Can the voices of children in the city be detected amid all that is superimposed upon them? And what is taught about them by closely listening trained psychologists with their major theories? And how is it with the attempts to formulate objectives for thriving, fruitful development among children in the city as a framework and space for living? There is no "language" more piercing than the earth one treads upon; than the buildings with their windows, stairways, and doors that intermittently shelter us; than hard stone. In the same vein, we wanted the participants, who represented different backgrounds, countries and languages, to be in the right mood, so we walked, waited, and watched together in the host city.

As we did, conversation centered first on theories that could be considered important to developmental and environmental psychology focused appropriately on specific inner-city areas. Those discussions are not recounted here (see the excerpts in Görlitz et al., 1992). I note here only that the authors of the main theory chapters entered the desired frame of mind before even setting foot in Herten or composing their contributions. While still in their home countries, they were familiarized with the town through artistically edited videotaped clips, a medium as theoretical as their writings: which were kindly prepared for us by Tyrone Greene. Architects and city planners were the authors and target audience of the related publications that appeared after the conference. After all, much that is decided in their offices has a bearing on cities, and even more on children and their families (see Görlitz et al., 1993).

With theory understood today as "that explanation of the range of appearances that allows their control" (Gadamer, 1997a, p. 87), the following presentation of psychological theories about the development of children in the city would be more closely linked to the creative hand of the architect or city planner than might be generally presumed were the overriding characteristic of theories not the very antithesis of practical application (Gadamer, 1997a, p. 86). The reader should not expect a textbook presenting concise extracts of theory assessable according to detailed rules indicating how children actually live their lives and how to increase their developmental possibilities. Despite the focus on the city and physical structures, this book is not intended to be as fixed as they. The reader should see it as a process in which meaning is gradually clarified through constant contact with urban reality, be it that of a town or a major city.

The theoretical dialogue originated first in and with the work on this volume. Thus, the book lacks most of what would lend it utility, as shown by the confining images of New York's Fifth Avenue and a little scene in the tropical rain forest of Ecuador. If this book's quasi-musical structure succeeds, it will leave the reader more informed than we authors were, more serious and more proximate to the essence of what is urban, the main form of settlement inhabited by people and their children today. We were serious about the idea that the socially defined materiality of urban life worlds were highly salient for psychology theories emanating from their hard-to-differentiate subdisciplines, environmental and developmental psychology. We thank our colleagues that they joined us on this so promising yet so uncertain path. In this book science does not carry off her heroes to the Valhalla of theory-builders; she lives more from the flow and contention of contradiction. And I do not mean battling over moot property rights – an act reminiscent of the Scottish nobleman who, according to a travelogue by Prince von Pückler-Muskau (1832/1991, pp. 345-346) threw his severed hand upon unclaimed land before his brother could take possession of it. This book is about gaining and getting used to an unobstructed view of the city while still keeping one's footing on the bedrock of familiar theoretical positions and developing tradition further in a personal way as well (Elias, 1993, p. 140). Looking back, the nearly one-hundred-year-old teacher of one of the editors stated, "Controversy is always the thing. We erring humans should never forget that, and all our effort to overcome our prejudices are based on it" (Gadamer, 1997b, p. 285). In this culture of controversy, too, our topic and its presentation seems to be just a beginning, something capable of development. As it develops, fronts and horizons shift, movement that is considered and described in the final part of the book.

The volume is divided into three parts, the first being of an introductory and preparatory nature. In the first chapter of Part I, Dietmar Görlitz explores the subject matter and its structure, illuminating selected aspects of it and calling attention to the history of the topic by adding biographical experiences, which always articulate the predispositions and biases of urban researchers, too. Unfortunately, lack of time ultimately made it necessary to forego a closing chapter on the history of this subject in psychology by Jürgen Zinnecker, who deserves much of the credit for the current topical interest in Martha Muchow's work in Germany. Many German writings and traditions still await discovery by an international readership. In place of his concluding piece, Behnken, du Bois-Reymond, and Zinnecker (1989) is recommended. In the subsequent chapter, Hans Joachim Harloff, Simone Lehnert, and Cornelia Eybisch elaborate upon a systematic way to arrange children's living space in the city. Transcending Muchow's early efforts, they provide a structural outline in which environmental and developmental thinking in psychology are brought together. The authors especially emphasize the contribution and role of adults and the structure of networks in children's life worlds in the city. Harry Heft, a close research associate of Joachim Wohlwill in the latter's final years, ends the first part of the book by depicting Wohlwill's achievements in lending psychology a modern – environmental and developmental – orientation. He also points out overarching characteristics of Wohlwill's thinking, and readers who are relatively unfamiliar with Wohlwill's work are given a close look at his research and the wide range of topics he treated. The chapter is the most visible expression of the fact that we editors jointly dedicate this book to Wohlwill.

The main section of this volume, Part II, is an elaborate exposition of theoretical perspectives commonly taken in environmental and developmental psychology when it comes to the specific subject of children's development in urban living conditions. After initial treatment at the Herten conference in July 1992, many of them were discussed further and considerably elaborated upon and changed by their authors, to whom the editors owe special thanks for the willingness and patience they showed throughout that process. These presentations of theoretical positions are complemented by the contributions of colleagues who joined the project more recently. Nonetheless, the individual concepts are still not finished works but rather more like compact summaries in an ongoing conversation, a dialogue expanded in particular by the commentators of each theoretical position and, in many cases, by the rejoinders by the authors.

The structural principle of the theory section was to place three contrasting theories together, an approach that yielded four groups. After Günter Mey's general introduction to the theory section as a whole, the treatment of each group is introduced in turn by one of the four editors. The theories are then interrelated in the respective section's last contribution by one or more integrators, who come from widely different national backgrounds. Given such extensive texts, there is little need for further amplification here. The reader, who is certain to follow his or her own preferences or newly awakened curiosity when browsing through the book, may wish to use these special introductions to become attuned to the material, choose texts to digest, and eventually, as we may wish, to take in all of them. The editors themselves address the reader in a reflective intermezzo entitled "What has happened," a title chosen to capture as faithfully as possible the event-related, perhaps dynamic character of all that has been presented up to that point. The contribution is also an attempt to see which strategies we and the authors of this book have used against and learned from each other in considering children in the city, the ways in which psychology reaches children, and what may still be standing in the way.

A passionate discourse cannot be intensified; it is easier to subdue it. But instead of presenting a synopsis or an outline of an integrating theory, we offer perspectives complementing the theme of the book. In this vein the two chapters of Part III deal with additional facets of our interest. Building on some of Bronfenbrenner's early precepts, Richard Lerner and Alexander von Eye develop trains of thought in which discussion of a dense, richly patterned context is held up as a model for the development of children and adolescents. Their discourse brings in more than just the preoccupation of our book with children. They also present a developmental model as a multifaceted approach to developmental contextualism in which interindividual differences and the developing subject's changing relationships to his or her context are emphasized with recognition of the dynamic and plastic character of human development. The reader will recognize in this approach engaging links to earlier theoretical positions and will note at the same time the increased prominence given to developmental thinking as well as the attention devoted to ethnic differences and demographically important subgroups of children and adolescents that have been neglected in research.[2] To Lerner and von Eye, one of the implications that their approach has for policy and intervention is the need for research in real-world settings, cooperation between the disciplines, and harmonization between academic and community interests.

The modern version of an ecology of human development in Lerner and von Eye's chapter also touches on the prevailing practice of seeing development as a life-span phenomenon and taking it seriously as such, a position that acquires definite shape in the concluding chapter by Frieder R. Lang, who enriches the context of discussion about children and the city by bringing in the later periods of life – the phases of the aging and the elderly person – as elaborated by Paul B. Baltes and Margret M. Baltes. It almost seems as though the contours of our topic – childhood and children – will gain clarity especially through the eyes of an old person. But it is a comparatively young author who contrasts the "city of late life" with the "city of childhood," elaborates the aspects particular to each, and then concentrates on the area in which they overlap, "the urban zone of intergenerational contact." Wohlwill, in his day, had suggested that contrasting life worlds be selected in developmental psychology if it were not possible to represent or apprehend the entire continuum (see Wohlwill, 1981). Lang, however, selects contrasts to illustrate the mutual dependence of young and old in the city. The city, with its constraints and opportunities specific to developmental phases, becomes richer with people who interact. The city itself acquires "a face," and life-span oriented developmental psychologists find opportunity to test new theoretical models of their work in the urban context, find a chance for their scientific endeavor in the realm of the city, at least as far as social embedding and the costs and benefits of intergenerational relations are concerned. In a short chapter concluding section III, the editors reflect upon their path through the topic (guided by the insight and insistent questions of Bettina Koböck) commenting on what has been achieved and on the attempt to come to a structural outline of future theory on the development of children growing up in urban living conditions. Recommendations for planning supplement these proposals.

The clear summer days prevailing now as we editors close the work on this book are similar to those we had at the time of the Herten conference. It is a book on the way to the city. Only the reader will be able to judge how close we editors and the contributing authors have come to the city, the children living or merely surviving there, and his or her own idea of what *urban* means to psychologists. That is all this book can help with. Bringing a work to its end, however, affords the opportunity to thank the many people who assisted in its development and completion. The manuscript's final form in American English has profited from the gracious perseverance shown by our technical editor, David Antal, in his translations of the contributions originally written in German and his sentence-by-sentence review of the book. At the 1992 Herten conference, too, he greatly facilitated communication in English and German with his judicious and constant focus on the essence more than the form of every text passage. The institutional backing we received despite the difficult conditions confronting the academic community and the university in Germany since the country's unification was also encouraging and helpful. The research award that the Alexander von Humboldt Foundation conferred upon Jaan Valsiner, one of this volume's four editors, provided the basis for the work we had agreed to undertake on the book as its parts took shape. The close collaboration that blossomed from this mutual interest shows how felicitous and seminal his nomination had been. Its culmination in a book on this scale is due to our publisher, especially de Gruyter's Dr. Bianka Ralle, whose initial surprise at the presence of all the editors during most of the planning discussions soon gave way to astute and invaluable guidance. Her spirited involvement and confidence in our project was an abiding source of motivation, and her patient willingness to accommodate the length, content, and scheduling in de Gruyter's commercial realities were immensely appreciated, as were the efforts of her colleagues, particularly Ms. Elisabeth Abu Homos and Mr. Christoph Schirmer.

As only the first step of this project, Herten was no longer our only priority after the conference there in the summer of 1992. Nonetheless, the unbureaucratic assistance we continued to receive from Herten's officials during the periodic organizational difficulties we faced demonstrated the deep commitment that this community has to fostering child-centered urban planning and design not only as a practice but as a philosophy reaching beyond the city limits. We express our gratitude to all the offices and individuals who lent their support in Herten, a city that welcomed us, or better, the entire outlook on which our project was based. Special mention, though, must be made of "ProKids" and its director, Richard Schröder; former city director Friedhelm Hodde; Mr. Heinz Lauzeningks; and Mr. Hans-Jürgen Ahmann as the "fathers" of the agreement that enabled such productive cooperation between Herten and Berlin. The task of keeping the budget of this time-consuming and costly project within the realm of the possible – and during turbulent times at that – was entrusted to the Technical University of Berlin, which hosted one of this book's editors and employs the other three. The university's chancellor, Mr. Ulrich Podewils, and the heads of the administration have our sincere thanks for their dedication in meeting that challenge.

With this framework firmly in place, others in our immediate circle ensured that the book could take shape. Our department's teaching assistants in developmental, environmental, and social psychology compensated for our involvement in the book by assuming an increased part of our equally important teaching and research responsibilities. If this book achieves something, part of the credit goes to them. We are indebted to Heidi Pissoke-Wegner for the exceptional care and precision she invested in putting the edited texts into an inviting, legible form, in some cases more than once. Without her teamwork and sharp eye, it would not have been possible to document the contribution our authors have made. We also thank Stephan Felbermayr for his knowledgeable, essential, and ever-willing assistance with the frequently tedious text comparisons, corrections, and standardizations and the bibliographical research that were required to bring the book into line with the publication guidelines of the American Psychological Association. Working with us even after he completed his course work in psychology, he also took on the meticulous job of compiling the subject index. Sandra Geirhardsdottir, assisted by Sigrun Würfel, proofread much of the manuscript despite the pressures of finishing her degree, and Martin Mühlpfordt, who was responsible for the author index, layout, and the redrawing of figures, repeatedly proved his skill and creativity in electronic data-processing. Our team also benefited from Bettina Koböck, a graduate student in psychology who came to us from the work group on cognitive developmental theory in Darmstadt and who made us aware, through her own curiosity, of new facets of developmental psychology that this book explores. Elvira Valamanesh coordinated our activities, oversaw the correspondence, maintained a reassuring degree of order in the office, and constantly managed to keep an overview of things even during the adventure and complications of moving the entire institute to new, separate "islands."

The list of those involved in the creation of this book is so long that we inevitably risk failing to name many who were important to us. Among them are certainly our seminar students, who made it clear in correcting and encouraging us in their presentations, discussions, and project work that our hope of having developed a rather promising topic for psychology was not in vain, at least as far as university education is concerned. In addition to our partners in Herten's municipal administration, the group of key participants includes the close circle of bilingual students who helped our foreign guests with more than just language obstacles at the Herten conference.

If, as Leonardo da Vinci is said to have declared, all truth is in the picture (Schumacher, 1981), then the pictorial material included in this book reflects our conviction that we could not do without the truth conveyed in the way a city and its related themes are, or can be, presented. In this regard we are obliged to a variety of copyright holders, many of whom granted permission for the gratuitous reproduction of pictures the editors considered valuable for this volume. We express special thanks to Verwertungsgesellschaft Bild – Kunst in Bonn, Germany; the Oskar Reinhart Museum in Winterthur, Switzerland; Edition Lidiarte in Berlin; Tushita edition in Duisburg; the Verlag Kunst und Bild in Berlin; and all the other sources of this visual enrichment for their generous cooperation; to the de Gruyter publishing house for willingly allowing it to enhance the volume; and to Niklas Görlitz, the well-traveled son of one of the editors, for donating this book's opening and closing photographs, which de Gruyter agreed to reproduce in full size. Within that frame lies what moved us to invite similarly interested, often better informed, and always reflective colleagues to present their approaches and misgivings in the international forum provided by a book with wide circulation and to see the project through despite the often convoluted road it has traveled toward publication. We deeply thank them all once again for doing just that.

Gratefully acknowledging the many people who have carried this work forward for so long, I have reserved my final and highly personal thanks for my coeditors, who saw not only a frequently contentious privilege of seniority in having me write this introduction on their behalf. It speaks for all four of us. If the thinking person's state of mind tends toward melancholy (Böhme, 1989), just allow me to say that being centrally involved in this book's publication has truly been fun. We wish our readers a little of it, too.

Notes

1 As formulated by Cesar Pelli, an important modern Argentinean architect, in a television broadcast entitled "New York – Millennial Architecture" (Bavarian Broadcasting System, 29 July 1997, 8:15 p.m.).

2 Incidentally, it has been unjustifiably forgotten that this call to focus on marginal groups was made by Berlin urban researchers in Hans Ostwald's series *Großstadt-Dokumente* years before it was heard in the so meritorious urban research of the Chicago School of Sociology. Indeed, Jazbinsek and Thies (1997) have shown that the idea had a hitherto unknown influence on the Chicago School, as reflected by the work of Louis Wirth (information for which this author is indebted to Cornelia Eybisch and Hans-Joachim Fietkau). In the 50 titles published in Ostwald's series form 1904 through 1908, an impressive spectrum of topics related to cities, especially Berlin, are elaborated by 40 authors. Though none of them expressly touched on children of this city, the subjects of unwed mothers (vol. 27) and endangered and neglected youth (vol. 49) are examined (cited after Jazbinsek & Thies, pp. 2-6).

References

Barber, S. (1995). *Fragments of the European city*. London: Reaktion books.

Behnken, I., du Bois-Reymond, M., & Zinnecker, J. (1989). *Stadtgeschichte als Kindheitsgeschichte. Lebensräume von Großstadtkindern in Deutschland und Holland um 1900* [Urban history as childhood history: Life spaces of city children in Germany and Holland in 1900]. Opladen: Leske + Budrich.

Böhme, H. (1989). *Albrecht Dürer – Melencolia I. Im Labrynth der Deutung* [Albrecht Dürer – Melancholy I: In the labyrinth of interpretation]. Frankfurt on the Main: Fischer.

Çelik, Z., Favro, D., & Ingersoll, R. (Eds.) (1994). *Streets: Critical perspectives on public space*. Berkeley, CA: University of California Press.

Elias, N. (1993). Mozart. Zur Soziologie eines Genies [Mozart: Toward the sociology of a genius]. Frankfurt on the Main: Suhrkamp.

Fietkau, H.-J., & Görlitz, D. (Eds.) (1981). *Umwelt und Alltag in der Psychologie* [Environment and everyday life in psychology]. Weinheim: Beltz.

Gadamer, H.-G. (1997a). Über die Möglichkeit einer philosophischen Ethik [On the possibility of a philosophical ethic]. In J. Grondin (Ed.), *Gadamer Lesebuch* (pp. 86-99). Tübingen: Mohr. (Original work published 1963)

Gadamer, H.-G. (1997b). Dialogischer Rückblick auf das Gesammelte Werk und dessen Wirkungsgeschichte. In J. Grondin (Ed.), *Gadamer Lesebuch* (pp. 280-295). Tübingen: Mohr. (Original work published 1996)

Görlitz, D. (1989). *Winning and losing, or what abides: In memory of Joachim F. Wohlwill* (Technical Report Series No. 4, pp. 16-20). University Park, PA: Pennsylvania State University, Center for the Study of Child and Adolescent Development, College of Health and Development.

Görlitz, D. (1993). Es begann in Berlin – Wege einer entwicklungspsychologischen Stadtforschung [It began in Berlin – Paths of developmental urban research]. In H. J. Harloff (Ed.), *Psychologie des Wohnungs- und Siedlungsbaus – Psychologie im Dienste von Architektur und Stadtplanung* (pp. 97-120). Göttingen: Verlag für Angewandte Psychologie.

Görlitz, D., & Wohlwill, J. F. (Eds.) (1987). *Curiosity, imagination, and play: On the development of spontaneous cognitive and motivational processes*. Hillsdale, NJ: Erlbaum.

Görlitz, D., Harloff, H. J., Valsiner, J., Hinding, B., Mey, G., Ritterfeld, U., & Schröder, R. (1992). The City as a frame of development for children: The Herten conference. *Children's Environments, 9*, 63-64.

Görlitz, D., Harloff, H. J., Valsiner, J., Hinding, B., Mey, G., Ritterfeld, U., & Schröder, R. (Eds.) (1993, July). *Entwicklungsbedingungen von Kindern in der Stadt* [Developmental conditions of children in the city]. Nontheoretical papers presented at the Herten conference.

Görlitz, D., & Schröder, R. (1994). Urban development for children – Reexploring a new research area. In H. Keller, K. Schneider, & B. B. Henderson (Eds.), *Curiosity and exploration* (pp. 307-331). Berlin: Springer.

Harloff, H. J. (Ed.) (1993). *Psychologie des Wohnungs- und Siedlungsbaus. Psychologie im Dienste von Architektur und Stadtplanung* [Psychology of housing and settlement constructions: Psychology in the service of architecture and urban planning]. Göttingen: Verlag für Angewandte Psychologie.

Harloff, H. J. (1995). Der transaktionale Ansatz der Wohnungspsychologie – Transaktionen des Menschen in und mit seinem Wohnmilieu [The transactional approach of residential psychology – Human transactions in and with the residential milieu]. In E.-M. Weinwurm-Krause (Ed.), *Wohnen Behinderter – Behindertes Wohnen* (pp. 21-35). Aachen: Shaker.

Jazbinsek, D., & Thies, R. (1997). *"Großstadt-Dokumente". Metropolenforschung im Berlin der Jahrhundertwende* [Documents of "major cities": Metropolitan research at the turn of the century in Berlin]. Series by the research group on metropolitan research, FS II, Wissenschaftszentrum Berlin für Sozialforschung.

Kostorf, S. (1994). His majesty the pick: The aesthetics of demolition. In Z. Çelik, D. Favro, & R. Ingersoll (Eds.), *Streets: Critical perspectives on public space* (pp. 9-22). Berkeley, CA: University of California Press.

Mey, G. (1989). *Hyde Park – Ein Ort zum Schreien. Sozialisations- und Satisfaktionsraum Diskothek. Interviews und Beobachtungen in einem Freizeitbereich* [Hyde Park – A perfect scream: The discotheque as a space for socialization and satisfaction, with interviews and observations in a recreational area]. Unpublished project report, University of Osnabrück, Department of Psychology.

Mey, G., & Wallbrecht, G. (1988). *Hyde Park. Dokumente eines Wandels* [Hyde Park: Documents of change]. [Film]. Osnabrück.

Pückler-Muskau, H. Fürst von (1991). *Briefe eines Verstorbenen. Ein fragmentarisches Tagebuch geschrieben in den Jahren 1826-1829* [Letters of a deceased man: Fragment of a diary written in the years 1826 to 1829] (Vol. 1, parts 3 and 4). Frankfurt on the Main: Insel. (Original work published 1832)

Schröder, R. (1995). *Kinder reden mit! Beteiligung an Politik, Stadtplanung und -gestaltung* [Children's participation in policy-making, urban planning, and urban development]. Weinheim: Beltz.

Schröder, R. (1996). *Freiräume für Kinder(t)räume! Kinderbeteiligung in der Stadtplanung* [Latitude for children and their dreams! Children's involvement in urban planning]. Weinheim: Beltz.

Schumacher. J. (1981). *Leonardo da Vinci. Maler und Forscher in anarchischer Gesellschaft* [Leonardo da Vinci: Painter and researcher in an anarchic society]. Berlin: Wagenbach.

Valsiner, J. (1987). *Culture and the development of children's action.* Chichester: Wiley.

Valsiner, J. (Ed.) (1988). *Child development within culturally structured environments.* 2 Vols. Norwood, NJ: Ablex.

Wohlwill, J. F. (1973). *The study of behavioral development.* New York: Academic Press.

Wohlwill, J. F. (1981). Umweltfragen in der Entwicklungspsychologie: Eine kritische Betrachtung zu Repräsentanz und Validität [Environmental issues in developmental psychology: A critical assessment of representation and validity]. In H.-J. Fietkau & D. Görlitz (Eds.), *Umwelt und Alltag in der Psychologie* (pp. 91-111). Weinheim: Beltz.

Wohlwill, J. F. (1985). Martha Muchow, 1892-1933: Her life, work, and contribution to developmental and ecological psychology. *Human Development, 28,* 198-224.

Part I
Prelude and dedication

Themes in the relation between children and the city

Dietmar Görlitz

1   The others

"Children, cities, and psychological theories" and "developing relationships" are the subject of this book. By that is meant children, "perennially the others." Formulated as in the title of this volume, however, it is one that puts everyone in a quandary because of the expectations it raises and the many different ways there are of treating it. The reader can see it as a list of nouns that can be randomly sequenced and connected by "and" or, at the other extreme, made to interrelate variously, including the possibility of "children in cities, as shown and depicted in psychological theories" or "the naive theories that young urbanites formulate about cities and other living conditions affecting them." It will be easier to agree on a spectrum of specific children than on the concretion known as the city. One of the parties that "has" psychological theory in these two sophisticated versions of the title is specialized science, the other is children with their developing knowledge systems. These versions give a certain substance to relations imagined to be developing, be they ones blossoming wholesomely or initially underdeveloped ones awaiting *to be* shaped. It is easier for psychological theories, particularly those in developmental psychology, to be focused on developing children than on cities, not to mention cultures and regions, which themselves are places of change that figure in the myriad interrelations of developing individuals.

Turning to examine a more complex version of relations, one may ask what developmental theory does with naive, piecemeal theories or concepts that children form about the city in which they live. Furthermore, is there in developmental psychology also a systematic theoretical discussion (as called for in Kindermann & Valsiner, 1995) revolving more around the nature of and change in *relations* than around the agents that create, introduce, maintain, or disrupt those relations as child, adult, material artifacts, or traffic regulation? For example, do the structural elements, or rather the essential structural parts, of exchange relations engaged in by urban children in the course of their development differ significantly from those frequently favored or promoted in the life situations characteristic of small village communities or settlements widely scattered across a region? If so, which special features stem from the wider context of culture and history? Which overarching shared characteristics arise from participation in the surrounding media and news culture of modern times – as a way of balancing "the world in which we live" with "the world we know about, the one shown to us"?

In terms of a methodological and strategic research decision, these questions make relations the focus of interest, with less attention being accorded the children and urban things serving as the agents of those relations. But this de-emphasis, at least as far as the physical dimension is concerned, can also be due to historical and violent changes to which cities, city dwellers, and urban architecture fall victim – along with the supporting and controlling social systems. It can constitute hovering attachments that are no longer anchored to any existing urban reality. After moving or fleeing from a city, the bonds with it that a person has developed or maintained fade as it recedes from daily awareness. Conversely, those relations may be accentuated or may appreciate, as when a sick child must temporarily be denied access to the "outdoors," where "the others" are.

Lastly, relations are articulated in each component mentioned in the title of this book. Children develop and maintain their individual ranges of changing relations to others whom they know, like, admire, envy, imitate, or cooperate with. Does growing up in cities bring about special colorings? Does it interrupt common threads of destiny, making the mutual relations upon which adult villagers can rely (including the necessity of protecting themselves from each other) different even from those villagers who have become urbanites? Does "the air of the city" make one "free" in that sense as well? There are also relations, such as those between playmates "I" encounter, in which it may be important where the other comes if he or she is a stranger. The relation between the area from which the other child comes and "my" region may be important. Is that new child's home area one I have heard about in the media? Is he or she "from the country" or perhaps from the rival town whose fierce pride in its difference from my town is made clear to later teenagers and adults in sports and other arenas of life? Is the child possibly even a refugee or a son or daughter of asylum seekers? Some children, when it comes to their attractiveness in a game or to parental warnings against playing with them, will become more familiar with their urban surroundings and more inclined to outdoor activities than children who remain within the more confined, controlled space defined by disciplinary rules laid down by their parents. It may be remembered that in middle-class German families of previous decades children were to be kept from encounters with "dirty, grimy street children," who were actually envied.

In discussing the connections within each of the components in this book's title, one has to include relationships between cities, especially their regions, districts, and quarters. These relationships often covary with socioeconomic characteristics of which children become surer as they develop their socioenvironmental knowledge and come to value their own regional situation in their city. Children do so as both residents and waifs, as castaways in the manner practiced by street children in every city even of the modern world. Concluding this reflection, I wish to add relations in the sense of metatheoretical analyses. One may look for links between several psychological theories dealing with children in their urban environment. One may articulate an abundance of relations between these theories, ranging from mere unrelatedness, irreconcilability, mutual exclusiveness, and contrast to toleration, integration, or, better, shared basic concepts.

But it cannot be that I, in trying to make out all the configurations of relations between the parts of the topic, remain above it as though the background and development from which I come did not have a bearing, as though it did not matter which research strategies a scientist uses in treating the topic of child, city, and psychological theories. I am bound to attend to certain facets and not others. In this unsettling discipline, developmental psychology, one is always involved, one's own remembering always accompanies the memory of the field's history.

2   Oneself

As Alfred described his city – Berlin, from which he and his parents had been evacuated to rural areas during the first bombing raids – we six-year-old school beginners playing in the front and back yards of our homes in a town were amazed at everything his repeated comparisons told us we lacked. Older now, I remember only the frequent embarrassment, and defiance, I felt at having to counter his trumps with what was familiar to us. That exercise had its limits, as when it came to escalators, which we did not have and whose use always awed me for the dexterity with which cityfolk were able to ascend or descend as if on so many rolling logs. But telephones, which to me were miniature tubes barely suitable for talking through, were as familiar and commonplace in our small town as in Berlin. Besides, what *we* received direct from the sky was hailstones, which lay scattered in the yard, beckoning to be sought and gathered by us children after thunderstorms, lightening, and rain. Something else we had that was unknown to the Berliners, who sounded so strange when they spoke, was a magnifying glass, with which we could set newspaper alight and brand our bare hands in sunny weather. In burying dead mice, however, these other children did join us.

Children seldom live, develop, thrive, or waste away on an island. They are rarely confined to a circumscribed region that they hear older people refer to as "our city." In asserting themselves, knowing, experiencing, or comparing, children have more. The internal structure and specifics of the place where children are compelled to develop with others or to fend for themselves are articulated through inexpressible interrelations and contrasts, and probably even more through induced environmental change they have experienced and the related stories about what older people do (or plan to do). Only one facet of my story is touched on by recalling the middle-class European family custom of traveling "to the countryside" or to a little seaside resort during the hot weeks of summer, a well-known alternative for leisure among western teenagers and adults even today.

It seems that concepts as expressed in accepted words conveying a general idea concerning the nature or dimension of such things as "city," "metropolis," "world city," "my" town, or "our" village consist of many different comparative processes and contrasting direct and indirect experiences. Each person's position and perspective, along with the particular region and culture in which they are framed ("I come from," "I am headed for," or "I am talking to"), will have an important bearing on the substance and salience of such knowledge structures and their valuations, alternatives for action, and expectations of interaction.

3   Remembering some parts of history

3.1   Idleness and work in Goethe's notes on his journey to Naples

Perhaps the history of this book's focus did not begin with what is presented below, but in this part it is authenticated in especially lively terms. Johann Wolfgang von Goethe, who was the great figure among the German poets of the classical period and who was himself "a town child" (Boyle, 1991, p. 46), had theory "in his head" when he stopped off in Naples for two weeks in late May and early June of 1787 on his return from the south during his richly documented journey through Italy. If the meaning of "theory" includes the personal manner in which a given individual takes note of and comments on things, often by explicitly using and drawing on previous knowledge or previous expectations, then Johann Jakob Volkmann, whose book was the main work read by all people traveling through Italy in the late 18th century, shaped Goethe's expectations just as other texts shape the expectations of today's travelers (see pp. 819-820 of the stupendous commentary in the 1992 edition of Goethe's *Italian Journey* by Beyer & Miller).

Volkmann had put Goethe, the traveler, into the right frame of mind to encounter tens of thousands of idlers in Naples. It was this introduction that Goethe, before mightily contradicting it, examined in carefully formulated observations that he made on the streets of the city, beginning "early in the day" (according to his entry for 28 May 1787; see Beyer & Miller, 1992, pp. 404-410). These passages provide a superb basis for the microgenesis of an observational process in which from an initial "monstrous jumble" there emerge various familiar figures whose shabby, "vile" apparel stand out, but not their idleness. To him, they fall into categories of "form, clothing, conduct[, and] employment." In keeping with their vocations, it is not that they "are this" or "do that" but rather "are in the process of doing." In their own time frame of action, they can be either standing still or resting. When they pause in doing something, they do not turn the break into idleness.

In this vein, Goethe takes advantage of several opportunities to observe as the day wears on, believing himself able to observe ever more precisely the way each person does, or is about to do, something at particular places and, as Goethe saw it, in keeping with his or her station in society. Children variously preoccupied along the paths to kitchen gardens on the edge of town ensure the vitality and credibility of his account. It brings them to life in their myriad relations to the adult world as they walk, run, even crawl with the help of older children, in going about their chores of carrying water, gathering wood-cuttings, reselling the fruit they just bought from older people, or taking the garbage out on donkeys (not forgetting the animals' manure either).

Having taken in these many scenes of shopkeepers and secondhand dealers, sellers of ice water and lemonade, and those purveying other kinds of merchandise, the author soon begins to theorize, albeit it with self-critical circumspection, about why he finds the varied doings of the people he sees in Naples so different – so different the industrial development, the painting and scholasticism, and the sheer pleasure taken in working by these people intently observed one day in Naples. By nature, as Goethe says, they work "to enjoy" in intensely emotional colors, exchanging jokes and open-minded glances. As though unnoticed by the author, the upper classes are happiest passing the time by indulging themselves in idleness. For his attempt to develop a national character from southern climates in contrast to that in northern countries, children as highly vivid guarantors vanish completely from the picture. As active as they were, though not in play, they no longer find mention in the conclud- ing passages.

Nonetheless, Goethe's annals – except for the romantization of poverty – are widely and admiringly considered an accurate record that reveals more than "an army of social scientists," as the commentary by Beyer and Miller (1992, pp. 1070- 1071) add from recent assessments. Much later, incidentally, the impact that land- scape and climate have on the natures of their inhabitants is a basic question addressed in *Geopsyche*, by Willy Hellpach, a German psychologist working pri- marily in Heidelberg in the first half of the twentieth century. He is to thank for the first concepts (as of 1937) about the effect that urban settings, namely cities, have on the people who live in and move to them (see pp. 44-52 in this chapter). Goethe's work was an intense, inquisitive beginning in which the present topic develops out of and in contradiction to the basic assertions made in a travel guide intended for a talented, engaged person journeying to see things with his own eyes. (Incidentally, Goethe was a traveler to whom is attributed one of the first uses of the subsequently so momentous word *Umwelt* [environment], which appears in a passage he wrote early in his trip to memorialize the "magnificent images of the Umwelt" [Beyer & Miller, p. 22, line 37]). Out of historical and comparative interest in children in the city, one could flip through travel guides illustrating and telling about the same town and instilling anticipation, could "browse" through epochs to see how, if at all, the faces of children change (something that would perhaps not be possible for Naples but certainly for Rome and Paris, perhaps also Vienna).

3.2   The Pedestrian of Paris in prerevolutionary France (Mercier)

In occasional candid snapshots of everyday Parisian life, Louis Sébastien Mercier had earlier reported about things "that struck and occurred to him while strolling across the boulevards and in the lanes of Paris" (as Jean Villian wrote in the afterword to a 1979 German edition of selections from Mercier's work, p. 419).

These notes by a "pedestrian of Paris" (Villian) appeared in a two-volume edition in 1781 as a "tableau," the "true-to-nature and lively depiction of something, whether by means of the spoken word or the quill" (in a definition that Villian [p. 423] cites from the Académie française of 1694). During and after Mercier's years of exile, they were expanded into a 12-volume edition containing more than one thousand chapters and were published in the 1780s, the decade that saw the onset of the French Revolution. Mercier's "Tableau de Paris" still ranks (according to Villian) as a socially critical, literary commentary that strove to capture what was authentic and verifiable, an account of which only the 140 some-odd chapters chosen for inclusion in the small German edition can be used for my purposes here, without weighing and pondering the criteria that guided the selection ("the most interesting and amusing facets of this work," as stated on the dust jacket of the 1979 Insel edition).

There were children in the Paris of prerevolutionary France, perhaps not interesting or amusing enough, perhaps taken for granted too much, to acquire their own faces for today's anthologist or yesterday's reporter (Mercier). Those children are there, as is necessary for the continued existence of city and country (see the chapter entitled "About the Population of the Capital" [1979, pp. 22-24]), and as a part of a generally growing population whose sufficient fertility sustained it and its fragile balance between the number of births (mostly boys) and deaths (mostly men). For the living, Paris would have been a paradise to the women, purgatory for the men, and hell, no longer for the children mentioned earlier but rather for the horses, whereby Mercier in this regard initially uses a source from the first half of the 18th century (Count de Buffon), knowledgeably bringing in his own observations only in the factual description of the city. One reads of the "barbaric luxury of traveling around in carriages," an inexorable ill to whose danger almost all Parisian streets were succumbing and to which not only outstanding thinkers of their age fell victim, as happened with Jean-Jacques Rousseau when he was badly injured by a mastiff running ahead of his master's coach (cited from the chapter "Watch Out! Watch Out!" 1979, pp. 37-39). Despite the praise of broad and splendid thoroughfares ("Boulevards," 1979, p. 53), one also hears the complaint about "polluted air" in poorly laid-out lanes, and buildings that are much too high (1979, p. 39). Those observations turn the chronicler's attention to children, too, in this case to breast-feeding infants, to whose mothers he recommends rural wet nurses, for whom the "air of the countryside and balanced, quiet village life" had mitigated the damage to which urban mothers were exposed, quite apart from all the distractions of maternal responsibilities (1979, p. 226). Such hazards, at least as far as the use of streets and squares go, have their own diurnal rhythm. Mercier's exquisite chapter entitled "The hours of the day" allows the reader to glimpse the radiance of life and richly varied cast of characters in 24 hours of light and dark (1979, pp. 227-235), reveals what there is to see, hear, and smell, without explicitly mentioning children but rather delighting in the special circumstances, such as a clap of thunder or the slam of a carriage door at night (p. 231), that inspires their origin. As victims of robbery and mugging – say, by malicious women on the street who scolded children as if they were the proper guardians only to strip them of their jewelry and fine attire and garb them instead in burlap before fleeing (see the chapter by the same name, p. 132) – children do not figure much in the urban ensemble of everyday configurations. They do not stand in front of the diorama peep show surrounded by adults interested in history and stories, nor do they undertake "journeys around the world without mis-hap" (see the chapter entitled "The peep show," 1979, pp. 295-297). But in summer, enjoying their frothy licorice juice, they happily crowd, big and small, around the vendor, who especially frequents the major boulevards, plying his prosperous busi-ness as "consoler of the thirsty nation" in full regalia with silver mugs hanging from chains, and who is never sparing "with song, jokes, and licorice" (1979, p. 300) except when treating himself not to licorice but to the "fruity wine" in the cups dur-ing a break (1979, p. 300).

Endangered particularly by the distraction of the mothers and by breast milk that has been tainted by the city air, by the upper class's reckless use of carriages in the streets, or by outright highway robbery, children are nevertheless present in this city for Mercier, this passionately involved and curious diarist of urban life at the end of the 18th century. They are necessary for the continued existence of city and country-side but, in contrast to both, are more incidental, are demonstrably engaged in the more pleasurable aspects of everyday urban life after having grown up in a different manner than their rural counterparts. But these Parisian children do not yet give rise to a theory in terms of the social class, change, form, substance, and specific places of their activities. They are probably not especially meant when Mercier writes of "people," of "masses and throngs."

In a more detailed examination of the unabridged edition of *Tableau de Paris*, that assertion would have to be tested. It would also have to be clarified what was not written, what was not intended and not permitted to be written – the kind of consid-eration for the public that guided Heinrich Heine in his *Letters from Berlin* (1822, see the 1980 Insel edition of Heine's *Reisebilder*, p. 595). Furthermore, it would have to be corroborated that Mercier was more concerned with "children in the plu-ral," with "children in the plural of old and young" – to the extent that they appear at all – with that other, equally warranted (or indifferent) partner. That kind of focus was destined to change in novels of inner development, such as those standing in the tradition of Rousseau, the same Rousseau who, according to Mercier, had once stumbled in the streets of Paris. They were novels in which the already heralded threat posed by certain living conditions of civilization and society became the central theme, in which nature in all her richness of flora and fauna acquires a locally specific visage that could be looked in the eye.

3.3   Thriving far from cities (Bernardin de Saint-Pierre)

At the same time, the year before the gathering storm of the French Revolution, an author of almost unimaginable success in his epoch, Jacques-Henri Bernardin de Saint-Pierre, a trained military engineer (Kappler, 1987, p. 270) and Jean-Jacques Rousseau's faithful partisan (p. 272), published a novel about a utopia of the natural, of children's thriving in the attentive care of their mothers far from the cities and centers of power of their time. Read in more than 200 French editions and approximately 260 editions in other languages since its appearance in 1788 (Kappler, 1987, p. 285), the novel depicts and imagines the blossoming of Paul and Virginie, a pair of children bonded like brother and sister. Without a real upbringing in the middle-class sense of the word, they grow up learning with and from nature, falling back upon it, and gaining experience that nourishes and supports a Christian maternal code of values. Temporal knowledge based on nature is not the only thing that separates them from the clocks of the city (Saint-Pierre, 1789/1987, pp. 77, 177). Doors went unlocked and door locks were an object of amazement (p. 94). And despite one region's remoteness from another, the neighborly relations that the novel's fictive narrator observes make him think about how much streets and even simple walls in Europe's metropolises can prevent people from coming together (p. 21). These country people live happily in cottages they have built themselves. The old culture from which the protagonists fled does not invade until one of the mothers who comes from the higher classes begins thinking ahead about the development of her daughter, Virginie.

In writing letters to arrange for Virginie's future, she entangles herself in the ethics of the "old France." Piety and moral chastity nevertheless remain the key regulators of hope and fear (Saint-Pierre, 1789/1987, p. 49) in the basal praise of God-guided nature (p. 66). Far from the "calumnious stories of society," she is filled with delight and joy in nature (p. 63), which also encourages feelings of "not falling prey to unhappiness" (p. 84).

Jean-Jacques Rousseau, who claimed to be the first person to really bear in mind the natural state of the human being (Figal, 1989, p. 26), created all the same an anthropological conception rich in aporias, one against which the contrasting reality of urban living conditions cannot be measured, not even for children, that is, for humans in their development. The "originally assumed (construed) primitive human being is by no means the ideal of . . . humanity" (Fetscher, 1989, p. 4). Still, from Rousseau's approach, and as encouraged by Rousseau, there followed the condemnation of certain sociocultural conditions that destroy "the natural goodness" of the human being, making it desirable to create "pedagogical provinces" far removed from the city – for an *Emile*, for example – so that the stultifying impacts of urban society can be resisted later as well (pp. 5, 7). Perhaps these ideas can be demonstrated in the contrast between Plate 1 and Plate 2.

Figure 1: Paul et Virginie, dessin fin 19e siècle *[Drawing, late 19th century]* © *Imagerie d'Epinal 1997*

Figure 2: George Grosz (1893-1959): Widmung an Oskar Panizza *[Dedication to Oskar Panizza] (1917-18)* © *VG Bild-Kunst, Bonn 1997*

Nor is Anglo-Saxon culture the only one that seems to have "a deep and enduring tension between the image of the city and that of the countryside" (Saunders, 1981, p. 80), where the virtues of country life correspond to the burdens of the city. Indeed, the contrast between the urban and the rural goes back to classical antiquity (Williams, 1973).

This aspect of urban and nonurban upbringing, of development in harmony with nature, is treated by Bernardin de Saint-Pierre (1789/1987) in his positive idyll of Paul and Virginie's life in the bounded region of Ile-de-France, or the island of Mauritius as it is called today. The reality of the city and of class and court society, however, is always present – as a negative foil contrasting lucidly and positively characterized living conditions. Analyzing a city's negative components described by the author of this once highly esteemed source (which was even read by Napoleon in exile; see Kappler, 1987, p. 285) may even be one way of gaining an impression of the unique features (including threatening ones) of what makes a city a city. The pair of happy children, Paul and Virginie, blossomed in part because they knew nothing of the city. Upon returning from the city, Virginie was undone by the corset of shame and virtue.

To the author of this novel, the city figures more as a foil than detailed depiction of individual characterizations. He applies his art of description entirely to nature on Ile-de-France, whose vibrant colors were so remote from France that even Alexander von Humboldt believed that he could learn from this novel a good deal about describing nature when documenting his travels (see Humboldt's *Ansichten der Natur*, 1807/1986). The city thus came across as a cultural entity of high form and dubious values rather than a descriptive presentation of its characteristics, but, as seen by Mercier, it also figured as a space and framework that provoked no questions about children. It was not only the privilege of a few who took children "out" of the city in utopian novels of inner development, who kept them out of the city for the sake of child-raising ideals.

3.4   "The cry of the street" (Ariès)

Writing in the looser tone of the times in the field of history, Philippe Ariès (1994) stated: "In the past the child, with or without its parents, was quite naturally a part of the urban setting." And he added that "such a city really did exist, a city in which children lived and ran around, some outside their families, others without them" (p. 75). In other words, the changing presence of children in the urban setting of certain cultures is attributable not only to differing foci of research interests. Historically speaking, one not only finds a shift in interest of chroniclers, an interest I document with early sources; entities, too, and that includes cities, have their historicity in which the manner and frequency of use that children make of individual, structurally similar regions can change drastically. Ariès outlines this historicity as it applies to the network of urban streets – that significant place. It is not just that the city grows over time, that it has multiple layers, or that it teaches history and how to understand it. It shows historical change in the appreciation and use of its places and regions. It appears in such entities as rows of houses and streets, which, having been laid out with an eye to comprehensible use, embody what is known, demanded, expected, feasible, and (in the case of children, for instance) granted.

Asking about what entities were to people in the past is the job of historical anthropology, a theory that opens a way to the materiality and sociability of past living conditions. It makes use of something that has been physically preserved, passed on; something of which at least a trace has survived. According to Bachtin, as Gurjewitsch (1993) pointed out, only historical anthropology will be able to understand how to ask new questions in dialogue with the dead (in this context, meaning bygone texts and entities) and, paradoxically, will be able to find children precisely because it does not seek them and their physical living conditions. What remains for psychologists is the surface structure – what was said, witnessed, written, and built. But the fact that psychologists examine handed-down texts and other documents for information about children reveals psychology, too, in this "dual dialogue."

In a narrative and sometimes sweeping fashion, Ariès does help the reader remember history in a saliently different way, and that for very specific urban regions. In this case, it is streets of the city, which in his mind are interwoven with an air of regret about what has been lost to cities and their children (in the western world, particularly France). He believes he can document that urban streets remained fascinating to children for hundreds of years from medieval to early modern times (Ariès, 1994, p. 76); that the sociability of the street continued even into the twentieth century after life in society broke up into private, occupational, and public dimensions; that streets have only recently been changing from stopping places to thoroughfares, and that urban centers have been allowing themselves to change from cities to agglomerations interconnected by expressways. He asserts that the oft-lamented segmentation and impoverishment of functions – for city streets, in the present context – had its beginnings in 18th-century Paris; Paris, the lightning rod for his arguments, the city in which the streets are increasingly taken over by the poor as a hard, unsympathetic, yet common place to live, a place from which the private sphere of the middle classes shut themselves out more and more. Prior to that time, according to Ariès, children had no place of their own in the house, so they extended "their living space quite naturally to the street," and the houses of the better classes did not separate their "private" sphere from any others (p. 77).

What, then, is it in the value judgments about such regions that changes so that the "street clears"? Ariès (1994) is reminded of an earlier principle of his according to which the state does not like seeing areas of life move beyond its influence and control (p. 86). At least, so he says, the concern of pedagogical philanthropists was the origin of the tendency to lock up and keep children in the deurbanized space of house and school, to transplant them to the closed world of "privacy." What used to be common was, because it was dangerous, soon said to be no longer worth learning. Out of precautionary concern for their upbringing, children were taken off the street; middle-class children in particular were placed under restrictions. To Ariès, it was the "frightened philanthropists" since the 18th century for whom the streets (and taverns) became dangerous places against which children were to be protected and paupers were to be turned (p. 81) – with a cogent diptych of the urban street as seen by children themselves, for whom "an archaic image of festivities and familiarity" blend with a modern image "of insecurity and disquiet" (p. 82). And he points out how the street was replaced upon the advent of cafés and parks in the 18th and 19th centuries, but it remained a free zone into which children steal away and in which, according to the contemporary police reports cited by Ariès, they were also apprehended by the police who were pursuing them according to the laws of time. A painting of that period shows a "counterpart" of the space desired for middle-class upbringing (see Plate 3).

Figure 3: Jacques-Laurent Agasse (1767-1849): Der Spielplatz *[The playground] (1830), Museum Oskar Reinhart, Winterthur (reprinted by permission)*

It is Ariès's familiar, often sweeping rationales that deserve closer inspection (as Trefzer, 1989, offered on the basis of documents from the city of Basel that trace the "construction of middle-class man" at the end of the 18th century; see also Sennett, 1974, which is especially rich in sources on "the decline and fall of public life and the tyranny of intimacy"). But Ariès's arguments allow one to see that a city's squares, stones, buildings, and courtyards do not consist purely in materiality. There is more to them than that. To the person who uses them, "may" use them, or disobeys in order to do so, they are both witnesses and evidence of child-rearing ideology that admonish one to heed them. The city has pedagogically solicitous and arranged places as well as those that are off limits. Children on city streets therefore not only demonstrate the benefit of appropriating streets and other public regions without colliding with anything. Their activities may also reflect both the visible and obscuring expression of what the resultants of profound social friction can be. It has never been decreed for all places, times, and classes that children in such regions always do only what is "appropriate" for them – as Goethe wrote in the diaries quoted at the beginning of this chapter. The city as a framework also puts frames into the hands of active mediators, educators, planners, and designers. Identical regions can change from familiar to lost space or can be obstinately or secretively reacquired, which is Ariès's concern about children in the street as he gives free play to dreams after the "intentional death of the street."

3.5 Utopias of society

These reflections end the brief series of bygone ideals and counterparts relating to the child and the city. It remains to expand on and probe more deeply into the role that children play in the city in communal dreams, or dreams intermittently shared by the members of a society. To the extent that social utopias also take the city into consideration, do they have their own design specifications when children are the focus?

It may be that social reformers and utopian thinking in general has always been honest or self-critical enough never to want to project cities, the polity, upon children. At least the first narrative history (one told as a utopia of the past at that) – Plato's history of *Atlantis*, as discussed by Brentjes (1993) – contains a great deal about construction, irrigation, and fortifications, but nothing about children, except that they were in many cases conceived and born as twins, the future rulers. State, belief, power, and polity were handed down through them, through children. And the fact that they always grew did not violate any utopia (as exemplified in Renaissance paintings of cityscapes; see Plate 4). Even today's visions of "the new man" for an urban culture of modern times allow him to reflect upon "the real values" and keenly feel "experiences for himself," and yet tacitly he is always grown up (Lampugnani, 1995, pp. 100-102).

Why design utopias without feeling distress or suffering oneself? Has a new quality of concern (concern for *children's welfare*, for example) entered the projections of occidental thinking? It is the ideal state, as designed by others long after Plato's utopia had been forgotten, not necessarily the ideal city, or it must be founded on such cities. An ideal polity need not be established only in the form of urban living structures, although they were the preferred setting (as in Campanella's city of the sun). On the other hand, cities have often inspired ideal designs (see Kruft, 1989), and have even been the source of revolutionary movements (Zimmermann, 1996, pp. 106-107, 113). But all that had little or nothing to do with how *children* fit into these entities, be they niches or plateaus. It was as if only the grown-ups carried the cross of life's distress and the need to provide for daily existence (recalling medieval pictures of the Passion). The little ones and those growing up appear indifferent or unthreatened – progeny taken for granted. Child-centered urban planning (Görlitz & Schröder, 1994) would certainly be just that: a counter-utopia. To put it differently, theory-building, particularly that in psychology, is not the only mode in which one can relate child and city and have them interact. Another way to do so is to create utopias in which urban design that responds to the needs and desires of children would supplant the older utopian vision of a prospering, happy polity. As was made clear at a recent symposium (Bellebaum, 1992), a happy childhood and child-centered urban planning have not yet been placed on the agenda of research on happiness.

Figure 4: *School of Piero della Francesca (1480):* Vedute della città ideale. *Edition Lidiarte, Berlin (reprinted by permission)*

But that omission has not kept entrepreneurs, architects, and educators, even at the beginning of this century, from creating garden cities such as Hellerau outside Dresden in "reaction to the sprawl of filthy tenement cities and their desolate living conditions that characterized Germany's industrial revolution during the early years of the Second Empire" (Sarfert, 1993, p. 12). Based on the concept of public benefit, the intention there was for the contrast between city and country to be integrated into urban planning modeled on systematic precepts and initial architectural experience with a garden city (built in 1903 by Howard in Letchworth, outside London; see Sarfert, pp. 13-14). It was a matter not only for adults, for the workers in Karl Schmidt's workshops in Hellerau. It included their families as well, the children growing up there, for whom Hellerau was indeed intended, planned, built, and for whom it prospered, as a "pedagogical province" at the end of the first decade in this century (Lorenz, 1994, pp. 48-49). What Paul Claudel lauded as a "laboratory of the new man" (laboratoire d'une humanité nouvelle, Lorenz, p. 17) in an obituary on the founder, Wolf Dohrn, shortly before the outbreak of World War I was a brief developmental reality – given the visions of an apocalyptic city in the art of the fin-de-siècle and its poems about the end of the world (Hüneke, 1994, p. 18), given the crumbling city of corrosive human relations that Alfred Kubin's *Dream City* (1909) became (Hüneke, p. 20), until Europe's historical reality matched, and ultimately eclipsed, the horror of such visions.

3.6   What do children "know" about their cities? (Schwabe & Bartholomäi)

According to the daily reports of police commissioners, as Ariès (1994, p. 86) reminds us, officers began pursuing daylight vagabond juvenile thieves in Paris at the end of the 18th century. Children's action in outdoor regions, the streets, was vehemently challenged by officialdom, which soon legally sanctioned intervention based partly on educational concerns about the potentially criminal careers that "little tramps" could be developing. These actions were restricted to the child as a *user* of the environment, as an active participant in his or her city. But pedagogical concerns, the foresighted opinions of educators, lent our topic of child and city another dimension quite early, illuminated other epistemological interests. They, like the persuasions from which they sprang, are just as interesting.

   In the late 1860s an educational institution, the "Pädagogischer Verein in Berlin," commissioned a survey intended to document what children knew about their environment, about their city (Schwabe & Bartholomäi, 1870). Basically (for details, see Görlitz, 1993), the conviction was that living conditions in the city had a specific impact on the individuality of the children growing up there, at least impacts other than those that the living conditions of small towns had on their young inhabitants. Indeed, various inner-city districts were already contributing to such differentiation. To the clients of the survey, the theory ranked as "indisputable fact" (cited in Schwabe & Bartholomäi, 1870, p. 60), even without details about the directions of the effects and factors governing how it worked. That survey stemmed from the definition of purpose in applied psychology. Proceeding from the average individuality of city children as characterized by their urban environment, the idea was to help improve Berlin schools and compensate for shortcomings by offering appropriate curricula in the formal educational system. The survey was not concerned with school children in the course of their specifically urban development; it documented a cross-section of boys and girls who were beginning their education at any of 84 elementary schools in Berlin. A wide spectrum of topics elicited information about the city's specific squares, markets, streets, and monuments; the animals and trees in the forests and meadows; facts about the observable sky, and religious beliefs concerning the heavens. As seen by the authors of that day, this environmental knowledge in first-year school classes, a truly vexing, panoramic epistemological mosaic, was reliably framed in a kind of learning theory about the organization of environmental knowledge. The environmentally, urban "conceptual range [of children] at the outset of formal education in school" seemed a useful starting point for using its richness or gaps to put concomitant scholastic measures on the road in the conviction that environmental knowledge is regionally specific, that it contributes to the individuality of the cognizant child, and that it can be recorded by inquiry comprehensive enough to serve as a foundation for compensatory educational actions.

In this respect, too, but in very specific terms, in physical architectural details, one encounters the *city as an active agent* that builds individuality and makes it possible to differentiate children according to their regional background, all after just a few years of development, of growing up, although the researchers themselves (Schwabe and Bartholomäi) tended to see "social rank and property" as a greater part of what defined the essence of children's individuality (Schwabe & Bartholomäi, 1870, p. 20). That was in the stratified 19th-century society of the kingdom of Prussia.

3.7   But how can one know what children know? (Hall)

Referring explicitly to the issue addressed in the Berlin survey, Stanley Hall (1891) of Clark University pursued the thought that "[although] concepts from the environment were only one important cause of diversity of individuality, this cause once determined, inferences could be drawn to other causes" (p. 139). And he pointed out the supposition made by the Berlin researchers: By the time urban and rural children entered school, there was already a marked difference between them in that the former had a good deal of experience with moving things; the latter, with objects at rest (including scenic ones); and that each group dealt with corresponding questions with different degrees of ease. Confined to city schools as it was, the Berlin survey was unable to test this assumption on its own, of course. Hall took this supposition and the Berlin data into account when weighing educational measures (geography lessons) and ways to fill obvious gaps, for "few knew the important features of their city at large" (p. 139). At that time, as nearly a century later in the influential psychological studies by Roger Hart (1979), interaction in geography classes was what prompted, and benefited from, surveys on children's environmental knowledge, with

Hall praising the focus on specific local places that characterized the style of instruction in German schools (Hall, 1891, p. 144). His retrospective, rich in information and insight (e.g., about a comparative Saxon study of urban and rural children), could only serve as a reminder without solving the associated methodological problems for him. The knowledge children have of their environment became the center of occasional interest among educators (in Germany), but suitable survey methods did not. One interviewed children, relied on their answers, and documented them, but not the way in which the questions were asked.

In the hands of a psychologist like Stanley Hall, it is not just a matter of repeating questions in a different country. As he complained, "little is told of . . . methods (Hall, 1891, p. 145). Repeating questions cannot just be about learning what school beginners know about their environment, especially their city. Instead, researchers must also ask themselves in what ways *they* can know and learn what others, in this case, little ones, know about specific things, such as a city. One does not simply transliterate or translate batteries of questions; the issue itself has to be thoroughly and methodologically reconceived. It is not enough to ask, one has to consider "why that and why in that way." Interviews with the child should be so conducted that pondering and remembering can freely enter into play, although local knowledge in the microgenesis of the individual child's remembering did not become the subject for Hall. A tentative list of 143 questions for children entering the primary schools of Boston was compiled in test trials, with no answer seeming reliable enough to go without follow-up questions. Interviewed in very small groups, the school beginners showed and elaborated their conceptual, their local, knowledge in response to the questions, which were posed by interviewers trained to aim for agreement so that answers like a "cow" that is "blue" and is "the size of my fingernail" did not slip through as correct answers. Nonetheless, Hall indeed had the development of the elicited concepts in mind when he figured there would be a "process of gradual acquisition . . . in the mind of a child" (Hall, 1891, p. 147) and recorded the answers in the children's own words as much as possible. Hall at least intended the documentation of gaps to be authentic.

Linguistic labeling and words have always been the arduous and problematic path (as is still true according to Seiler & Wannenmacher, 1987) along which to get at conceptual thinking. In this case, among children, Stanley Hall had the reader take part in it, conceding the researchers' arbitrariness in attributing or not attributing conceptual knowledge. "Men's first names seemed to have designated single striking qualities, but once applied, they become general or specific names according to circumstances" (Hall, 1891, p. 147). Phylogenetically, or as far as the speaking adult is concerned, that viewpoint of 1891 maps out the course of semantic development in language without already attributing urban – as opposed to rural – children with their own, typically urban trajectories of concept development. That task is not considered feasible even in research today. Urban life certainly has its idiosyncrasies, but does it create its own concepts? Is urban knowledge organized differently than rural knowledge? What does "city" mean to the person who grows up there? What do "countryside and village" mean to those who live far away from cities? And which precepts does each unique culture determine? Concerned more about the representativeness of his findings, Stanley Hall documented and compared the knowledge gaps that questions about country and nature, animals and plants exposed among more than two hundred Boston and Kansas City school beginners. It was astounding what they did not know. Even more astounding were the differences between the ignorance levels of children in both cities or between white and non-white first-year schoolchildren in one of the cities. Documentable differences between the knowledge shown by boys and that shown by girls also surfaced.

In all there were 50,000 items that, taken as a whole, led Stanley Hall to formulate a law holding that human perceptual knowledge is guided by interests, that people do not see and know about what is near them but rather what their attention is drawn to when their interest has been aroused. Children bring "more or less developed apperceiving organs with them into school," organs on which classroom teachers can count and with which they must live, for "the mind can learn only what is related to other things learned before" (Hall, 1891, p. 154), an observation to which Hall appended detailed recommendations for classroom instruction with a heavy emphasis on "natural objects." In a peculiar reversal, knowledge gaps, which showed up in tables, made a case for using what was available, but what was available, be it Boston or Kansas City in their urbanness, did not need to be focused on. In fact, it did not even warrant follow-up questions, for nothing about cities appeared in the tables. As "knowledge of cities," the other things that had previously been learned (to the extent that children could learn them) were not asked about. It remained open as to when and how they would determine, even break through, the natural order in the sequence of concept acquisition, which varies "very greatly with every change of the environment," with each location determining the sequence of concepts uniquely and anew for the children developing there, "save within comparatively few concept-spheres" (Hall, 1891, p. 154).

3.8   What the city "makes" out of children (Tews)

In subsequent decades the city, particularly the large city, became a topic of its own as an actor both instructive and morally menacing in its public places. One of the aspects considered was how, in its eternal presence, the city shaped individuality and how it organized knowledge. Once again, it was an educator who tackled the subject. In nine lectures delivered before a lay audience at the Humboldt Academy in Berlin in 1911, Johannes Tews expounded on thoughts, observations, and demands relating to metropolitan education. He envisioned a kind of education located in and tailored to cities as well as a perspective in which the physical conditions of the city were taken seriously as a *pedagogical* element, as something that contributed to

rearing the children who grew up in the urban setting. To Tews, it was an auspi-
cious, thoroughly optimistic undertaking, for to him the big city had an entirely new,
unique life that demanded recognition. The city became a place for learning and was
taken seriously as such.

Tews taught first to look at the city, if the city was meant, no matter if it initially
raised more questions than were already being asked by this favorably disposed
defender of the city. He resolutely pursued a strategy of seeking out the life of children where it was lived, where it was visible. Those places were no longer in teachers' questionnaires handed out in classrooms. As Goethe did in the regions of
Naples, Tews went into the streets of Berlin in the interest of the metropolitan education he was calling for. He went into the many interlocking rear courtyards as well
as into apartments, describing what was in some cases a desperately wretched Berlin. He did not forget the institutional educators, the teachers themselves, but "the
things in the child's surroundings, life on the street, the display window" (Tews,
1911, p. 21, italics in the original deleted here) were more important to him in their
capacity as the city's educators. To him, the metropolis becomes the "great teacher"
that educates its people typically, that is to say, into types. The metropolis was the
teacher that steers everything, particularly all informal effects of metropolitan life,
toward a rather uniform type, the urbanite, starting as a child.

But that process begins in many different places and needs a suitable amount of
time, perhaps more than childhood offers. Martha Muchow's early experiences
showed that she, too, was impressed by such milieu-centered, city-oriented educational theory before she raised the awareness, through her own classical studies, that
children essentially act on their own in their life space of the city (Muchow &
Muchow, 1935). In Tews's thinking, the directions of impact are more unilateral,
more partial. To him, the urban setting is not particularly benevolent, but thorough,
in attending to a widely supported and probably also thwarted educational work,
starting at many different places whose contribution, however, is not yet specified. It
is the local tie of basic needs and their satisfaction with which his agenda begins,
with living, sleeping, and eating and the concomitant temporal structure of the day.
"In what way does the city child live and sleep? What does it eat and drink? How is
it dressed, where is its playground?" (Tews, 1911, p. 43, without the italics contained in the original).

That is a rich spectrum of interests; then come the trappings and decoration of the
dwellings. It is a spectrum that has not been exhausted even today. Not until Sennett
(1994) has anyone again turned, in historical comparison, from the city in its perceptibility, sensuality, and sensuousness to the feeling, sensing human being. In
Tews's work, children's dwelling and living in the big city begins in the most intimate, personal areas, whose imbalance and possibilities for compensation the public
space of streets and squares become the focus of attention. It is true that no dwelling,
especially an urban one, is an island. But neither does the city lie only *in front of* the

windows of buildings. To Tews, it begins and its effect continues in the most private of spheres, as private as the bed shared with others.

In this network of manifold and changing linkages between one's own space and the public regions of the city, Tews begins weaving theory here and there without reflecting upon it as such, still unconcerned about it. I focus here solely on that aspect (for further detail on Tews, see Görlitz, 1993, pp. 100-110) in saying that Tews's rather narrative lecture to the audience at the Humboldt Academy in Berlin in 1911 can be condensed into seven theses. Beginning with the urbanite, the city dweller, I call them the type-building rules of delayed effect experienced by a response-oriented person who develops according to his or her environmental conditions or who lives in such correspondence. This type of person is exposed in "herd-like receptivity" to the variegated educational work of the city, where places in particular, especially their range of material affordances, favor adaptation and conformance. Streets, the streets of the city in this capacity as places of education and training, acquire a value that cannot be compared to any other. In their additional functions, however, they also vary with the size of the settlement (town versus city), so some of their functions can be shifted into the domestic sphere of dwelling and family.

Let me now elaborate a bit on each of these theses (marked below by italics), which Tews himself did not formulate in precisely this manner. Tews saw the city as being active in the formation of types (as a *type-building rule* that had scant regard for individual manifestations and differences, see Tews, 1911, pp. 21, 23). To him, the typical city dweller seemed more tangible as an adult than as a child. Tews thought that children needed a certain period of incubation to become typical urbanites, as if all their development began in virtual villages, in local microsystems that do not initially anchor one or the other type of development explicitly to the city, as if a kind of sleeper effect governed one's development into an urban child or adolescent. It seemed to be a sleeper effect in two senses when the idea was taken up again and formulated by Jean Piaget late in his life, some 70 years after Tews: "Furthermore, I am . . . of the opinion that the child is closer to the origins of the human being than any adult is, including primitive man, . . . [even though] today's small child develops more rapidly" (Bringuier, 1977/1996, p. 142-143; translated here from the German edition). Tews spoke of the predominance of a generalized nature of children, as if the time it took to have an impact on city children was not long enough to make them sufficiently distinguishable from children from other life spaces, as if the "genuine" urbanite needed more time to live and develop (see Tews, p. 58).

And he sees the person more in terms of malleability than as an active shaper, more in terms of *resonance* with environmental conditions (Tews's second thesis so to speak), with which the person is so intimately intertwined that, according to Tews's *correspondence* thesis, the knowledge about the environment and its characterization also allow reliable statements about the children who live there, about the urban child in its intellectual and physical uniqueness. The person becomes a mirror, acquires from his or her documentable circumstances of life the nature of a type (Tews, 1911, p. 33), or, as it was called in the studies cited earlier in this chapter, the "typical individuality" acquired by a person from a particular city district. The person is the target of the city's wide-ranging pedagogical work, becomes the focus of the instructional function and intention of major cultural artifacts – the completely new kind of metropolitan education that Tews brings together in, as I call it, the *functionality of the city* (Tews, pp. 34-35).

Of course, professional educators themselves are involved, too, but it is mainly places and local things that provide for correspondence (which I refer to as *the rule of place effect*). In the physical realm, the "great educators" in this sense are not only buildings whose inhabitants often had to settle for the worst imaginable living conditions, as Tews speculates, not only the developed and undeveloped spaces in the suburbs, but primarily the streets of the city. To Tews, streets are a reflection of the widest possible forms of life in the "river bed" of the throngs, too (p. 105), animated by thousands of figures for whom or which everything "is calculated for its external effect, its appearance" (p. 107). Loss threatens, a life bereft of "its inner meaning," as a recurrence of the aforementioned ambiguities of the street. Abounding in display windows filled with arrays of real things (pp. 112-113), the street is nevertheless totally indispensable as a place for the "all-round spiritual and intellectual development of the child" (pp. 115-116). To the child, who participates in "the great community of passers-by," the street is primarily also "a school with a democratic and social world view," (Tews, 1911, p. 109). That role undoubtedly has more dimensions than the thesis of what I call the *ambiguous educational value of the street*. The street is irreplaceable as "one of the hardest working assistants" (pp. 115-116), although, as Ariès lamented, that was precisely why only a short period in history sufficed for it to be lost. Even at that time, however, the home had to absorb many of the social needs that public space still remaining on the streets of towns and in the countryside was able to meet – unlike the situation in the city (or, in brief, the thesis of *functional compensation and functional shift* of places as a function of settlement size).

There is much forgotten history that 20th-century psychology, oriented to the type of human that the city adapts and develops, could have tapped when it began work on the topic addressed in this chapter. Initial reflections on it reaching back to Tews's time were offered by Willy Hellpach, whose public lecture on "Mensch und Volk der Großstadt" (Man and the Population of the City) in Paris in 1937 marks the point at which the subject began to take shape in that author's work.

3.9   When the city is unavoidable (Hellpach)

What later (1939) came to distinguish urbanites and determine their social psychology and characterology (Hellpach, 1939/1952, pp. 67-112) – their *Reizsamkeit* (perhaps translatable as the keen awareness and processing of sensory stimulation) – had been the only topic important to Hellpach at the congress on international demography where he delivered the lecture cited above (Führ & Zier, 1987, p. 215). As early as 1904, in his *Fundamentals of a psychology of hysteria*, Hellpach praised Karl Lamprecht, the humanist researcher who discovered "the mental condition of *Reizsamkeit*" (Hellpach, p. 80), a frame of mind whose genetic (and historical) foundation Hellpach explained in terms of excessive mental demands and heavy pedestrian and other traffic. Reaching back even further, Zimmermann (1996, p. 35) has pointed out that "the growing nervousness of our time" was mentioned in a lecture delivered in 1893 by Wilhelm Erb, a Heidelberg physician, who attributed this characteristic to life in the big city. Perhaps the city, with its effects, was becoming remotely perceptible.

Not long afterward (1906), they were expressly given a name in Hellpach's more popular book, *Nervenleben und Weltanschauung* (Nervous life and world view), which built on advances in psychopathology such as the discovery of neurasthenia by an American physician named Beard (p. 45). Subsuming it etiologically under the heading "The problem of nervousness" (pp. 46-47), Hellpach attempted to unravel the "knot of causes" and delimit the group of those suffering from them. In so doing, he characterized "the new nervous life of the middle-class." Nervousness, he wrote, "is the historical psychosis of the advanced capitalistic bourgeoisie" (p. 49) stemming from living conditions that violate the normal alternation of emotional states, precipitating new tensions before the resolution of the previous ones has been brought to an end (p. 50). In Hellpach's view, this disorder was fed by modern undertakings, uncontrolled traffic, and the transformation of all consumption. The entire description reflects middle-class urban living conditions as opposed to those of the rural population and the working class, even of the gentry, and does not grant this one-sided metropolitan life much of a future (p. 72).

That was in 1906, written when Hellpach was still a Karlsruhe neurologist dealing with the "nervous collapse" of the middle class. But in Germany, the country to which he was referring, the cities continued to grow – indeed the 19th century was "decisive in the history of European urbanization" (Zimmermann, 1996, p. 13) – and the speed of the traffic he lamented increased "in its colossal development" (p. 51). From today's perspective, mobility is necessary . . . in order to take part in urban life at all," an observation of which Flade (1994, p. 5) reminded her readers. As Belschner (quoted after Flade, 1994, p. 5) said, the modern city is characterized by an "imperative of mobility."

The German poet Rainer Maria Rilke once prophesied that "the cities [were] . . . the lost and the dissolved . . . and their ephemeral time is passing" (quoted after

Hellpach, 1939/1952, p. 1), but there was a migration to urban centers around the turn of the 20th century – documentable with impressive statistics on Germany, for instance – that certainly made it sound to inquire about the features of these migrants, these "rural refugees," before characterizing cities. It was a subject with which Willy Hellpach (1939/1952) commenced the second edition of his monograph about the city (which he dedicated to the German Society for Psychology). Bismarck, in his own day, had believed he knew why even "quiet, orderly, and honest people" fled from the countryside to the city. In Bismarck's final speech in the German imperial parliament in May 1889, quoted by Hellpach, the city became the place "where there is music outdoors and where one can sit and drink beer at one's ease" (Hellpach, 1939/1952, p. 5), according to the admission of some of the similarly described, embarrassed farm hands from Varzin, Bismarck's estate. A picture of Berlin in those days may bring those words alive (see Plate 5).

Figure 5: Alt-Berlin mit dem Brandenburger Tor *[Old Berlin with the Brandenburg Gate] (Color reproduction of an old postcard), Kunst und Bild, Berlin (reprinted by permission)*

Focused on *Reizsamkeit*, the tenor of Hellpach's presentation soon loses this feeling for positionality, that is, for the specific situation from which the desired, probably also the feared – the life in the city – acquires its contours. It gets lost in the subsequent passages of the monograph on the city. At the beginning, however, it is still so pronounced that Hellpach interprets Bismarck's passages about the motives for fleeing the countryside to mean leisure that is personally freer and more agreeable.

Hellpach acknowledges that leisure as the desired goal of at least the socially dependent person living on the land and having to do hard, exhausting work, the person to whom the city promises greater personal discretion over his existence instead of entrapment in the feudal way of life (pp. 7-9). To Hellpach the flight from the countryside, this migration to the cities, had assumed such proportions that it was necessary to think in terms of more than *one* group of motives (a point that he [1939/1952, pp. 11-12] helps document with contemporary writings), but it is both impressive and amazing how, without realizing it, he allows this hope for leisure to shatter against the unforgiving surface of urban reality. As more of an emphatic than a precise observer of the city dweller's reality, Hellpach saw the urban tempo increasing to *haste* in every sphere, spreading from body movement and speech to the entire "mental demeanor" to become the dominant characteristic of urbanites (p. 30) regardless of whether the hope for limited, discretionary leisure had brought them there or whether they lived as urbanites without caring about the origins of, indeed the change in, their frame of mind.

It is odd how few traces this frustration of hope left in Hellpach's developed thoughts, which are often cited only in abbreviated form. Given the polarity between the leisure that is hoped for and the haste that is experienced, it is also peculiar how little this dashed hope prompts consideration of whether special places teach special ways of coordinating, scheduling, and experiencing time, as was common to the film settings of that era (see Plate 6).

But this lesson might change in the course of culture and history. The idea of city as a *polis* emerged in a culture that still demanded "time as a natural human treasure" for the stranger, a culture that experienced time in a different manner – and surely in different places, too, as in her groves of olive trees, whose very age made time tangible (a thought from Kästner's book on Greece, 1974, pp. 27, 222). And the lesson must be differentiated for earlier decades as well. More recent discourses on Berlin's cultural history show what became of such thwarted hopes, how the issue of poverty reached unprecedented dimensions in Berlin and other cities "through the migration of the countryside's pauperized and proletarianized strata" (Pokiser, 1995, p. 23). But let me return to Hellpach's questions.

Is it really that, once in the city, one becomes different "through and through" (Hellpach, 1939/1952, p. 34)? At least some questions remain: "*How* does the city change the person who lives in it" (p. 34)? "What does the city make out of the human being who lives in it" (p. 34)? And if it effectively changes that person, are the changes irreversible? After study of the type of human being represented by the urban population and by those drawn to such cities, these questions led Hellpach to his second group of topics: the investigation of the "psychophysics of urban existence" as a contribution to understanding the mutability of organisms (p. 35). He reminds the reader that mutability has its limits, for creatures perish under living conditions hostile to their species. He did not mean climatic conditions only, whose effects are often overrated (p. 37), and shortly thereafter (p. 39) he formulated a law of "Lebensraum" stating that "a species or subspecies of organisms . . . is fit for a location if it is able to develop viable *breeds*" (p. 39; spaced in the original). The city is an excellent location of this kind, a viewpoint that raises what to Hellpach was the legitimate and essentially scientific question of whether a city forms such a breed, "human breeds" of a special type that could be not only characterized as "special" in comparison to townspeople or the rural population but also – and in this regard Hellpach was thinking in very sociobiological terms – shown to possess undiminished powers of reproduction.

Figure 6: *Harold Lloyd in "Safety Last" (1923), Tushita edition, Duisburg (reprinted by permission)*

Much as Goethe in his own day had thought he could tell the structure of work processes on the basis of regional climate when he noticed the idleness in Naples, Hellpach pondered the urban climate as one of the "impositions" with which large cities burdened their inhabitants. Hellpach, who in his thinking and abundance of observations was curiously similar to Goethe in many respects, also contemplated "city-air bodies" and "urban climatology" as well as the contribution and particular aspects of the radiation that produces the light-deficient "existence of the urbanite" (p. 44), referring to the much higher proportion of artificial illumination experienced by the city dweller. According to Hellpach, the climate produced by urban lighting shifts from biactive to "psychologically stimulating" (spaced in the original). In addition to a tendency toward thermal attenuation and toward photic stimulation (pp. 49-50) as other possible components of *Reizsamkeit* caused by the urban environment, it is peculiar to the city that its ground surface is characterized almost everywhere by such closed structures as asphalted streets and other ways of sealing off the earth. Conscious that he was able only to hypothesize about the effects and directions of effects that these features had on the nature of urbanites, of "the" city dwellers, Hellpach shortened his list of potential agents more and more. His exposé increasingly became an argument for urban research, which, as he saw it in the early 1950s, was more impressive for its gaps in knowledge than for its store of insights.

But it is striking in these perceptive descriptions of place how little the city acquires its own physiognomy in terms of houses, windows, streets, and corners. The term metropolis communicates something more generic than specific. The city remains an entity that is largely unstructured, even from region to region, an unarticulated artifact in which a person is, incidentally, changed in a way that still needs to be studied. The person becomes a human breed but does not actually develop. Hellpach's metropolis has no children; at least he does not call them that. "Human breeds" form there, breeds whose ontogenetically earlier phases are altogether murky. He is deeply troubled by the question of what contributes to the urban population's lack of biological reproduction (Hellpach, 1939/1952, pp. 61-66). It is just that if the urban population ever were successful at biological reproduction, "the consequences" would not acquire a character of their own, unless it be acceleration in the sense of excessively early sexual maturity. But remember, what a long road urban childhood has before it reaches that point.

That emphasis comes across plainly in Hellpach's "characterology" of the urbanite, the core attributes of which are often cited. Hellpach began with what to him – and not only to him (see Simmel, 1903/1995, for example) – was a basic characteristic of coexistence in the cities, the fact of *quantity* (*Menge*) as distinguished from mass (Hellpach, 1939/1952, pp. 67, 142). Quantity is impressively and always palpable or visible in re-encounters with the city at its most congested places. Correspondingly, urban life is played out in unavoidably *close physical proximity* (*Enge*) characterized by inescapable motion or turbulence, by incessant and urgent change. Hurried change is simply the only way that the confines of the city can cope with the quantity imposed upon it. "The watchword breathlessness" thus belongs to the "mode of existence of urban street life" (p. 67) just as *haste* is "an integral part of urban existence" (p. 68) – though experience today shows that at least a Berliner can experience the peace of gently gliding through the Spree Forest on a skiff before returning to the busy metropolis.

That breathlessness indicates an altered way of dealing with time, to other forms of time in urban living reality. It is formulated according to a central psychological law of irradiation (extension) versus contrast. In this case, haste extends into the most private psychological spheres and feelings of humans in the city, which pushes people not only when they cross the street. Condensed into a sociophysical and sociopsychological haste in living, the impatience of city dwellers (through which children should actually have to be purged of their dreaming and dawdling) becomes part of their "nervousness," which Beard described in terms of the late-19th-century megalopolises of the U.S. east coast (see p. 44, in this chapter). But Hellpach sees nervousness more as the endpoint of a pathogenic sequence beginning with the more inclusive characteristic called *Reizsamkeit* (at this point in his text, he thus assesses Lamprecht more critically) and set apart from the more leisurely tempo of life in cities of intermediate size. In the large cities, "the stimuli crowding in upon the urbanite, . . . are much greater in number [and], above all, more diverse and rapid in sequence than those that townspeople and villagers have to cope with" (Hellpach, 1939/1952, p. 69). From this observation Hellpach derives a second main character-istic, the urbanite's increased *alertness* – a shifted, not broadened, process of per-ception that would lead city dwellers into hazardous situations on the street and elsewhere under other circumstances.

What, then, is the special, unique aspect of the excessive demands the city makes on its inhabitants, the impositions with which they must deal with and to which they must adjust? It is the city as a cramped, crowded, hurriedly changing environment (see Hellpach, 1939/1952, p. 70) to which the coping urbanite responds by devel-oping a "second nature" of not inconsiderable potential for conflict, a secondary per-sonality that forms around perceptual acuity, keen awareness and processing of sen-sory stimulation, and haste. Modern sociobiology, represented in this volume by Charlesworth, would find a fundamental ontogenetic rule that could be ramified and spelled out according to limits and risks of plasticity and environmental adaptability compatible with and specific to this species of human being. To Hellpach, the counterpole to the urban setting would be the villager's much less predictable, over-powering, yet more leisurely world of fields and stalls (Hellpach, 1939/1952, p. 70).

In biology today it is still believed that the most obvious ecological characteristic of cities is that they confront the human inhabitant with completely new kinds of environment:

The most obvious ecological characteristic of cities is that they present their human inhabitants with a completely new and altogether different environment to anything else found on Earth. They constitute as distinct an ecosystem as an entirely new biome. (Campbell, 1983, pp. 178-179)

In modern behavioral research, it is still doubted whether the human being's "first nature" is biologically in harmony with these environmental conditions of what is actually a "pathogenic environment" (Eibl-Eibesfeldt & Hass, 1985, quoted after Fischer, 1995, p. 6). As John Berger (1992) disconsolately stated about a position articulated in an earlier age, it could be countered that

life in the city . . . is apt to lead to a sentimental view of nature. One thinks of nature as a garden or as a window-framed vista or as a place of freedom. Farmers, mariners, and nomads know better: Nature is energy and struggle. She is what exists, with no promises of any kind. . . . Her forces are terrifyingly indifferent. (pp. 9-10; for earlier opinions, see this chapter, pp. 30-32)

Following Hellpach's train of thought, let me summarize at this point what the city demands of its inhabitants and those growing up in it. A basic law of biology is that a species can adapt to the "rigors" of its immediate environment in a wide variety of ways (though certainly not without consequences). Nevertheless, documentable contemporary adaptations to the demands of urban life are difficult to distinguish from previous selection brought about by immigration. Given this restriction, one can formulate the following rules based on Hellpach's ideas: (a) Confined space shared under the local urban conditions inevitably accelerates the rate at which persons and their locations get rearranged. (b) The greater and more rapidly changing range of stimuli arising from urban living conditions inevitably makes for keener and more flexible corresponding perceptual alertness. Accordingly, the city can be characterized as a living space that both compels and facilitates the adaptation of its fast-paced, alert, and highly responsive human inhabitants. These two rules lead to a third: (c) For the urbanite, successful adaptations constitute a "second nature" that can become an increasing, then probably pathogenic, contradiction of the human being's first nature as a nonarbitrary, at least not inconsequential, distortion of preadaptation. These rules pertain to city dwellers without spelling out models of development and effect over the human life span, without individualizing claimed effects or conceding that urbanites may have compensating (or other) strategies for actively reshaping their environment. It was not until Anselm Strauss and Richard Wohl that the urbanite was seen as more active and less suffering, that urbanites were considered to have the vigor to cope with the incomprehensible whole of the city by drawing on a variety of ingeniously analyzed personal strategies (see Strauss, 1976, pp. 5-17). As Graumann (1990, pp. 70-72) points out, though, Hellpach did in principle think about possibilities for regulating and intervening in the city-dweller's "sociopsychological system of constraints."

Hellpach teaches his readers how city dwellers see, feel, speak, deteriorate, how they get on in the world, in which form of time, with what degree of urgency, and with how much consideration for others this occurs with urbanites, born as they are of the perpetual squeeze of the teeming crowds. And he does so in a prose whose linguistic and conceptual flourish rivals that of Luther's tracts. All the while, he is actually also teaching how humans defer their hopes, make key decisions in their lives, create out of wretched childhoods an urban living experience that leads them to enter into partnerships more cautiously and to practice family planning, all the while not underestimating the pedagogical value of the urban environment as a limited phase in the life of the young adult.

Yes, Hellpach teaches all that, too, concerned as he is about the well-being of peoples, especially in their big cities. Paying tribute to the educational (assimilative) dynamics of the city in more global terms than Tews did from his perspective on metropolitan education, Hellpach considers its ineluctable power to absorb and assimilate those who move to the city in huge waves and encounter those who have long been living there already. To Hellpach, it is once again the urban life's fundamental characteristics of quantity and close physical proximity that offer liberally apportioned opportunities for the daily workings of Carpenter's law – as at least a rudimentary imitation of seen or imagined behavior, quite apart from desired assimilation (Hellpach, 1939/1952, pp. 94-95).

The city is thus presented to modern readers through idiosyncratic language describing experiences with earlier living conditions, an urban environment whose inhabitants live in strata of unequal positions, unequal desire to escape those conditions, and incessant variety of fleeting and indifferent encounters, including encounters with children (see Hellpach, 1939/1952, p. 96). All the while, these inhabitants remain subject to the "law of the city," according to which the pull toward assimilation, "the inescapable pressure to comprehend rapidly, and the interaction of quantity and close physical proximity, of haste and change," makes itself felt in more than just the differences between the language of the city and that of the countryside (p. 98). That law is rooted "in the city's peculiarity of gathering so many people in so close a space that it generates the power to largely *standardize* the appearance and gestures of these throngs" (p. 107). What distinguishes cities from each other is the localized variations they form in their populations, or as Hellpach put it, "cities are forming a new kind of regionally specific demographic species" (p. 106). In many different ways he illuminates what they do, but they are nonetheless artifacts for which he wishes no further growth. What remains is "the unnaturalness of the phenomenon called the city" (p. 108), for it lacks fresh air, fresh light, and fresh soil (quoted after p. 82) even after the reconstruction from the wastelands of debris left by times of war. To compound the problems, the city now also suffers from growing motorization and, literally, the "derailment" of technology. How hard it is to be a child swaddled in the fabric of all the possible derailments without being able to figure as a topic inherently worthy of interdisciplinary urban research – a science that Hellpach enthusiastically invokes. Though it sings no song of "woe about the cesspools of vice of the megalopolises" (p. 132), neither does it give a voice to the children who grow up there. Cities develop, it is true, but not the people living in them, although they *are* transformed "by the fact that so many *fellow humans* are gathered in so small a space." To Hellpach that fact is the crucial point of departure for everything that distinguishes urbanites from those who are probably happier, those in towns and villages (p. 73). But Tews's legacy passed to other hands, to researchers who eagerly and alertly inquired about urban children, seeking them out where one encounters them: on the streets, in the courtyards, and on the squares of the city. What remained of those precepts? What did they contribute to children, the city, and theory? Meanwhile, the second generation after Hellpach has kept the subject of urban research very much alive in Heidelberg (Graumann, 1990, and, now in Munich, Weinert, 1992).

References

Ariès, P. (1994). Das Kind und die Straße – von der Stadt zur Anti-Stadt [The child and the street--From the city to the anticity]. *Freibeuter, 60*, 75-94.

Bellebaum, A. (Ed.) (1992). *Glück und Zufriedenheit. Ein Symposion* [Happiness and satisfaction: A symposium]. Opladen: Westdeutscher Verlag.

Berger, J. (1992). *Das Kunstwerk* [The work of art]. Berlin: Wagenbach.

Bernardin de Saint-Pierre, J. H. (1987). *Paul und Virginie* [Paul and Virginie] (K. Eitner, Trans., revised by Arno Kappler). Munich: Winkler. (French original published 1789)

Beyer, A., & Miller, N. (1992). Kommentar [Commentary]. In J. W. Goethe, *Italienische Reise* (pp. 797-1210). Munich: Hanser.

Boyle, N. (1991). *Goethe: The Poet and the Age: Vol. 1. The Poetry of Desire. 1749-1790.* Oxford: Clarendon Press.

Brentjes, B. (1993). *Atlantis. Geschichte einer Utopie* [Atlantis: The history of a utopia]. Cologne: DuMont.

Bringuier, J.-C. (1996). *Jean Piaget. Im Allgemeinen werde ich falsch verstanden. Unterhaltungen* [Conversations with Jean Piaget: In general, I am misunderstood] (E. Heinemann & R. Tiffert, Trans.). Hamburg: Europäische Verlagsanstalt. (French original published 1977)

Campbell, B. (1983). *Human ecology: The story of our place in nature from prehistory to the present.* London: Heinemann.

Eibl-Eibesfeldt, I., & Hass, H. (1985). Sozialer Wohnungsbau und Umstrukturierung der Städte aus biologischer Sicht [Public housing and urban reorganization from a biological perspective]. In I. Eibl-Eibesfeldt et al. (Eds.), *Städte und Lebensqualität. Neue Konzepte im Wohnungsbau auf dem Prüfstand der Humanethologie und der Bewohnerurteile* (pp. 49-85). Stuttgart: Deutsche Verlags Anstalt.

Fetscher, I. (1989). Jean-Jacques Rousseau: Ethik und Politik [Jean Jacques Rousseau: Ethics and politics]. *neue hefte für philosophie, 29*, 1-23.

Figal, G. (1989). Die Rekonstruktion der menschlichen Natur. Zum Begriff des Naturzustandes in Rousseaus "Zweitem Discours" [The reconstruction of human nature: On the concept of the natural state in Rousseau's "Second discourse"]. *neue hefte für philosophie, 29*, 24-38.

Fischer, M. (1995). *Stadtplanung aus der Sicht der ökologischen Psychologie* [Urban planning from the perspective of ecological psychology]. Weinheim: Beltz – Psychologie Verlags Union.

Flade, A. (1994). Einführung [Introduction]. In A. Flade & K.-P. Kalwitzki (Eds.), *Mobilitätsverhalten. Bedingungen und Veränderungsmöglichkeiten aus umweltpsychologischer Sicht* (pp. 1-13). Weinheim: Beltz – Psychologie Verlags Union.

Führ, C., & Zier, H. G. (Eds.) (1987). *Hellpach-Memoiren 1925-1945* [Hellpach's memoirs]. Cologne: Böhlau.

Görlitz, D. (1993). Es begann in Berlin – Wege einer entwicklungspsychologischen Stadtforschung [It began in Berlin – Avenues of developmental urban research]. In H. J. Harloff (Ed.), *Psychologie des Wohnungs- und Siedlungsbaus. Psychologie im Dienste von Architektur und Stadtplanung* (pp. 97-120). Göttingen: Verlag für Angewandte Psychologie.

Görlitz, D., & Schröder, R. (1994). Urban development for children – Reexploring a new research area. In H. Keller, K. Schneider, & B. Henderson (Eds.), *Curiosity and exploration* (pp. 307-331). Berlin: Springer.

Goethe, J. W. (1992). *Italienische Reise* [Italian journey] (A. Beyer & N. Miller, Eds.). Munich: Hanser. (Original work published 1816/17 and 1829)

Graumann, C. F. (1990). Ansätze zu einer Psychologie der Großstadt [Approaches to a psychology of the city]. In G. Lensch (Ed.), *Möglichkeiten der Analyse von natürlichen und kultürlichen Regelsystemen und ihren Verknüpfungen im städtischen Lebensraum. Methodologisches Seminar: Vol. 1. Urban-industrielle Umweltforschung* (pp. 64-75). St. Ingbert: Röhrig.

Gurjewitsch, A. J. (1993). *Stimmen des Mittelalters – Fragen von heute. Mentalitäten im Dialog* [Voices of the Middle Ages – Questions of today: Mentalities in dialogue]. Frankfurt on the Main: Campus.

Hall, G. S. (1891). The contents of children's minds on entering school. *The Pedagogical Seminary, 1,* 139-173.

Hart, R. (1979). *Children's experience of place.* New York: Irvington.

Heine, H. (1980). *Reisebilder (1826-1831)* [Travel images (1826-1831)]. Frankfurt on the Main: Insel.

Hellpach, W. (1904). *Grundlinien einer Psychologie der Hysterie* [Fundamentals of a psychology of hysteria]. Leipzig: Engelmann.

Hellpach, W. (1906). *Nervenleben und Weltanschauung. Ihre Wechselbeziehungen im deutschen Leben von heute* [Nervous life and world view: Their interrelations in German life today]. Wiesbaden: Bergmann.

Hellpach, W. (1911). *Geopsyche. Die Menschenseele unterm Einfluß von Wetter und Klima, Boden und Landschaft* [Geopsyche: The human mind under the influence of weather and climate, soil and landscape]. Leipzig: Engelmann.

Hellpach, W. (1948). *Universitas Litterarum. Gesammelte Aufsätze* [University of literature: Collected essays]. Stuttgart: Enke.

Hellpach, W. (1952). *Mensch und Volk der Großstadt* [Man and people of the city] (2nd ed.). Stuttgart: Enke. (Original work published 1939)

Hüneke, A. (1994). *Franz Marc – Tierschicksale. Kunst als Heilsgeschichte* [Franz Marc – The fates of animals: Art as the history of salvation]. Frankfurt on the Main: Fischer.

Humboldt, A. von (1986). *Ansichten der Natur* [Views of nature] (expanded reprint of the 3rd ed. [1849]). Nördlingen: Greno. (Original work published 1807)

Kästner, E. (1974). *Ölberge – Weinberge. Ein Griechenland-Buch* [Olive groves – vineyards: A book about Greece]. Frankfurt on the Main: Insel.

Kappler, A. (1987). Nachwort [Afterword]. In J.-H. Bernardin de Saint-Pierre, *Paul und Virginie* (pp. 269-290). Munich: Winkler.

Kindermann, T. A., & Valsiner, J. (Eds.). (1995). *Development of person-context relations.* Hillsdale, NJ: Erlbaum.

Kruft, H.-W. (1989). *Städte in Utopia. Die Idealstadt vom 15. bis zum 18. Jahrhundert zwischen Staatsutopie und Wirklichkeit* [Cities in utopia: The ideal city from the 15th through the 18th centuries between state utopia and reality]. Munich: Beck.

Kubin, A. (1909). *Die andere Seite. Ein phantastischer Roman* [The other side: A fantastic novel]. Munich: G. Müller.

Lampugnani, V. M. (1995). *Die Modernität des Dauerhaften. Essays zu Stadt, Architektur und Design* [The modernity of durable: Essays about the city, architecture, and design]. Berlin: Wagenbach.

Lorenz, K. (1994). *Wege nach Hellerau. Auf den Spuren der Rhythmik* [Roads to Hellerau: On the trail of rhythmics]. Dresden: Hellerau-Verlag.

Mercier, L. S. (1979). *Mein Bild von Paris* [My picture of Paris]. Frankfurt on the Main: Insel. (French original published 1781)

Muchow, M., & Muchow, H. H. (1935). *Der Lebensraum des Großstadtkindes* [The life world of the city child]. Hamburg: Riegel.

Pokiser, A. (1995). Armut und Armenfürsorge in Berlin 1800-1850. Von den Schwierigkeiten im Umgang mit neuen Phänomenen [Poverty and public assistance to the poor]. *Neue Streifzüge in die Berliner Kulturgeschichte, Arbeitsbericht 1995* (pp. 19-85). Berlin: Luisenstädter Bildungsverein.

Sarfert, H.-J. (1993). *Hellerau. Die Gartenstadt und Künstlerkolonie* [Hellerau: The garden city and artists' colony]. Dresden: Hellerau-Verlag.

Saunders, P. (1981). *Social theory and the urban question.* London: Hutchinson.

Schwabe, H., & Bartholomäi, F. (1870). Ueber Inhalt und Methode einer Berliner Schulstatistik [On the content and methodology of a statistical description of Berlin schools]. *Berlin und seine Entwickelung. Städtisches Jahrbuch für Volkswirthschaft und Statistik, 4,* 1-76. Berlin: Guttentag.

Seiler, T. B., & Wannenmacher, W. (1987). Begriffs- und Bedeutungsentwicklung [Development of concepts and meaning]. In R. Oerter & L. Montada (Eds.), *Entwicklungspsychologie* (2nd ed., pp. 463-505). Munich: Psychologie Verlags Union.

Sennett, R. (1974). *The fall of public man.* New York: Knopf.

Sennett, R. (1994). *Flesh and stone: The body and the city in western civilization.* New York: Norton.

Simmel, G. (1995). Die Großstädte und das Geistesleben [Metropolises and mental life]. In O. Rammstedt (Chief Ed.) & R. Kramme, A. Rammstedt, & O. Rammstedt (Vol. Eds.), *Georg Simmel Gesamtausgabe: Vol. 7, part 1. Georg Simmel: Aufsätze und Abhandlungen 1901-1908* (pp. 116-131). Frankfurt on the Main: Suhrkamp. (Original published 1903)

Strauss, A. L. (1976). *Images of the American City.* New Brunswick, NJ: Transaction.

Tews, J. (1911). *Großstadtpädagogik. Vorträge, gehalten an der Humboldt-Akademie zu Berlin* [Metropolitan education: Lectures delivered at the Humboldt Academy in Berlin]. Leipzig: Teubner.

Trefzer, R. (1989). *Die Konstruktion des bürgerlichen Menschen. Aufklärungspädagogik und Erziehung im ausgehenden 18. Jahrhundert am Beispiel der Stadt Basel* [The construction of middle-class man: Education of the Enlightenment and child-rearing in the late eighteenth century as exemplified by the city of Basel]. Zürich: Chronos.

Villian, J. (1979). Nachwort [Afterword]. In L. S. Mercier, *Mein Bild von Paris* (pp. 383-440). Frankfurt on the Main: Insel.

Weinert, F. E. (1992). Ökopsychologie des Stadtlebens [The ecopsychology of urban life]. In Rundgespräche der Kommission für Ökologie der Bayerischen Akademie der Wissenschaften (Ed.), *Stadtökologie* (Vol. 4, pp. 113-121). Munich: Pfeil.

Williams, R. (1973). *The country and the city.* London: Chatto & Windus.

Zimmermann, C. (1996). *Die Zeit der Metropolen. Urbanisierung und Großstadtentwicklung* [The age of metropolises: Urbanization and the development of cities]. Frankfurt on the Main: Fischer.

Children's life worlds in urban environments

Hans Joachim Harloff, Simone Lehnert, and Cornelia Eybisch

1 Terms and Issues

This chapter may serve as a kind of introduction to the entire book. We wish to ask what children's life worlds are in the city. That is, what are the urban spaces in which children live, play, learn, and linger? We describe them and point out the significance they can have for children's development. In so doing, we largely set aside the historical aspect of this topic and confine ourselves to changes that have occurred since World War I. (For children's urban living conditions before that point, see Görlitz, in this volume, and Görlitz, 1993.) We present children's urban living spaces as a network of organism-environment units in which children participate (see section 3 for a definition of our concept of network).

The purpose of this chapter is threefold. First, we wish to show that there are as many such networks at any given moment as there are children in the city, that the network of every child changes according to that child's state of development, and that some parts of the network may compensate for other parts. Second, we stress that development can be conceived of as a life-long process of person-environment transactions in whose course both the cognitive and emotional-motivational structures of the person change. In this manner, the individual's knowledge of the city is modified, places and elements of the environment acquire new meanings, and the person's mental representation of the city is updated. Third, we intend to demonstrate that both the concept of home range (the area in which children are permitted to move about alone or in the company of persons other than their parents) and the "island-forming thesis" (the assumption that the places significant to children today are widely separated and that children must be helped to reach them) can be integrated into our conception of networks.

We need not take this chapter to review the research bearing on the theories about the relation between children on the one hand and urban spaces on the other, for those theories already constitute the core of this book, and the respective authors cite the most important results pertaining to them. But before we can describe children's urban life spaces and explore their potential significance for children's development, we must state our own theoretical position. First, however, we turn briefly to the two concepts of *child* and *city*. Actually, it seems they do not need to be defined. After all, everyone knows what a child and a city is. But even contemplating the seemingly straightforward job of counting up and describing the more or less important spaces in which urban children act and experience life makes one thing crystal clear: *The* child and *the* city do not exist, so one cannot speak of *the child in the city*. As trivial as that statement is, there are many different children (different in their abilities to experience and act because, say, they are handicapped; different in age or family background; different in the urban space in which they live, go to school, and so forth; and different in the strata to which they belong, just to mention a few of the aspects involved). Similarly, one city is not like another (differing, for example, in size, architecture, geographic location, state of economic development, and significance to the surrounding areas). To the environmental psychologist, the differences between cities may seem almost more numerous and weighty than those between children. Then there are also linguistic and cultural differences. For instance, the German visitor to the United States must first learn that the English word *town*, the equivalent of the German word *Stadt*, is used to refer even to settlements with perhaps fewer than 200 inhabitants, places that Germans would not even call a hamlet or a village, let alone a *Stadt*.

It goes without saying that this short chapter cannot even come close to treating the entire range of variety in the nature of cities and children. For precisely that reason, however, we find it important to make at least a few rough delimitations. In the following pages the kind of people we are speaking about are those of "normal ability" in the age span ranging from birth to 13 years. That is, we are speaking mainly about preadolescents, and we do not deal with the broad spectrum of different handicaps or special abilities. In terms of the city, our observations pertain to communities with at least 100,000 inhabitants.

Now to our theoretical position. As social and environmental psychologists, we consider ourselves committed to Altman and Rogoff's (1987) transactionalism, which we have gradually developed into a theoretical approach of our own. In our eyes, the subject of "child in the city" and the intent to work with planners to optimally shape urban spaces to meet the developmental needs of children requires the approach outlined below.

1. The units of analysis always consist of an organism, or of organisms, in addition to the milieu (e.g., a small child playing in a sandbox), whereby the organism and the milieu must not be seen as two independent, juxtaposed units but rather as two units that embrace each other, that are part of one another.

2. The organism and the milieu (both physical and social) do not interact in the sense of reciprocal response but rather act simultaneously with or against each other, transforming each other into new states. The child and the sandbox, for instance, change one another in mutual action (Harloff, 1995). In our eyes, the difference between the kind of activity engaged in by organisms and that engaged in by things is only a

matter of degree. It is true that the activity of things lacks intentions and emotions, that it is nontelic, but the physical milieu, through its affordances (Gibson) or valence (Lewin), "speaks" to the organism, invites certain action, and thereby contributes actively to transformation if an appropriate response is forthcoming.

3. Transactions, changes of state, occur over time, need time. In many cases they do not have a definite beginning and a clear termination but always have a before and after. Imagine a 3- or 4-year-old child who is awakened by its mother in order to get to church on time. Stretching and yawning, the child gradually wakes up, while the mother talks with him and a visitor. Transactions occur in and with the child, the mother, the visitor, and the physical milieu. It also becomes clear that the units (behavior episodes) later identified by the researcher overlap, that they can be grouped into larger units, and that they are interwoven and interlocked in several ways (Wright, 1967).

4. An additional idea is closely linked to point 3:

Human beings and things change over time. *Change is normal and generally needs no special explanation.* Humans and their environment take part and are the object of many different dynamic processes of change. Social, economic, biological, and physical forces are perpetually at work. They bring about changes in us, the environment, and under certain circumstances even without any conscious act by the individual. . . . Through intentional human intervention (or the activity of other living organisms), situations may change quickly and radically. Transactions, however, always take place between inanimate objects as well, sometimes very slowly, at a snail's pace, almost imperceptible to the human senses. Such is the case, say, with water that gradually seeps into the walls of an uninhabited house. . . . At other times, transactions between inanimate objects can be rapid and abiding as well, as when a storm blows the roof off a building. (Harloff, 1995, pp. 26-27)

5. Person-environment units vary in size and affect each other. Depending on the question posed in research or planning, the size that is selected depends on the question being addressed. When studying ways in which action is carried out in "household kitchens," one will form synomorphs (Barker, 1968), such as rinsing ingredients, preparing food on the cutting board, cooking on the stove, setting the table, and eating at the kitchen table, and will consider the ways in which they interrelate. When designing a housing estate, however, one deals with larger synomorphs such as apartments or even apartment buildings, playgrounds, preschools, schools, and grocery stores.

6. Larger units are composed of smaller ones. (Dwellings, for instance, consist of their individual rooms and the uses to which they are put.) Reciprocal impacts exist not only horizontally (that is, between the synomorphs of the same level, as in the kitchen example, above) but also vertically. What can happen at the kitchen table, and what under certain circumstances must happen there (as may be the case with school homework), depends on the overall layout of the dwelling and on the living concept of the family residing in it. Moreover, the same synomorph can be part of

very different patterns of relations, or "different authority systems," as Barker (1968) put it. Action sequences that take place in a child's bedroom are thus a function not only of living that is simultaneously going on in other rooms but also of what is happening on the playground, in the nursery, or in the school (before, after, and at the same time). In many ways, then, person-environment units are horizontally, vertically, and temporally interwoven and interlocked.

7. Human action must always be viewed in its physical (and social) milieu. The nature of and closeness of the reciprocal relations between person and environment varies greatly. For example, the weave

is strong, tight, and direct if the milieu is directly manipulated or if it is otherwise constitutive (as a bathtub is for bath). It is wide, open, and indirect if the milieu is rather a coincidental framework for the action (as a kitchen is for conversations between a household member and a visiting neighbor). (Harloff & Ritterfeld, 1993, p. 34)

The concept of synomorphy cited above in reference to Barker suggests that people deliberately often shape environments in a way that makes it possible to execute recurring actions or "standing patterns of behavior" (Barker) quickly, precisely, and easily. However, the relation between a milieu and a standing pattern of action is usually not so close that the milieu precludes action complementing or diverging from the intention of the planning that has been undertaken. Over time, both the patterns and the milieu are changed (Wicker, 1987).

We close this introduction with a brief explanation of our concept of development. (On a wide variety of developmental theories and on the development of the concepts of *development* and *developmental psychology*, see Trautner, 1991-1992; Moshman, Glover, & Bruning, 1987; Montada, 1995; Carlson & Buskist; 1997; Fernald, 1997.) Building on our theses of transactionalism, we understand development as an engaging, life-long process that takes place as transactions. The individual at the center of consideration and that individual's social and physical surroundings have a part in the process. Each of these three agents is both active and passive. (a) An individual, for example, acquires new cognitive and motivational-emotional structures. That person appropriates his or her physical setting, thereby "developing" in this sense (and simultaneously contributing to the "development" of other organisms and the physical environment). (b) At the same time, the individual is subject to, is affected and shaped by, the active influences exerted by the social and physical milieu through transactions. Development of that individual is *brought about*. (c) Lastly, person-environment units develop as such in the context of the dynamic processes of change that their parts or larger surrounding units go through. (Views of development such as those by Bronfenbrenner and Vygotsky come close to such a transactional concept.)

When describing and analyzing development, one can shift the focus from one element to another: from one individual to the next (e.g., from the child to the mother), from the individual to the group (e.g., from the mother to the family), from the group to the physical milieu (e.g., from the family to the dwelling inhabited by the family), and so forth. The segments of reality that are selected can and do differ in size, depending on the question being posed. One can look at a child's cognitive development in one case and at the development of a housing estate in the next. However, one must always be aware of the ways in which the part being focused on transacts with the other areas and must keep in mind the simultaneous activeness and passiveness of all the parts.

In the following pages, we first develop a system of urban living space, basing our ideas on the cultural area familiar to us, namely, Western Europe and North America. We describe parts of those spaces, identify their potential function in development, and critically examine the actual possibilities offered by the conditions prevailing today.

2   Spaces for children in the city: Spaces to "Grow Into"

2.1   The overall system of urban living space

In this section we identify the spaces that urban children inhabit and experience, the spaces in which they play, work, and otherwise spend time. We begin with an overview of the urban space at large, moving from the dwelling as the center of children's activities to areas ever further afield. As Table 1 shows, we distinguish between four ranges: the dwelling, the dwelling's immediate vicinity, the local neighborhood (places reachable by foot in 20 minutes or by bicycle in 10 minutes), and the greater metropolitan area. The dwelling's immediate vicinity and the local neighborhood demarcate roughly the area in which the child's so-called home range is located.

Remember that we use the term *city* to mean a metropolitan area of 100,000 people or more or an agglomeration (several overlapping cities). We presume that many different kinds of residential structures exist side by side, as in most major European cities (settlements with individual single-family houses or row houses, blocks with free-standing rows of apartment buildings, complexes of attached apartment houses with courtyards and side and rear buildings, as well as high-rise structures with tower apartments and slab houses). The spaces cited in Table 1 exemplify conditions found in such an urban setting and need not exist in the same way elsewhere in the world.

Table 1: System of the urban living space, by location and dominant user group

child-environment ranges	spaces primarily for children	general spaces	spaces primarily for adults
dwelling	children's room	hall, kitchen, living room, bathroom	study, parents' bed-room
immediate vicinity of the dwelling	sandbox in the court-yard	back courtyard, buil-ding entrance and lan-dings, drive-way, street	basement garage, par-king lot, cellar
local neighborhood (places reachable by foot within 20 min-utes)	playground, pre-school, kindergarten, elementary school, neighborhood club-house	park, little shops for daily needs	sex shop, beauty parlor
greater metropolitan area	zoo, youth center, ice-skating rink, recrea-tional swimming pool, athletics club, puppet theater	businesses, depart-ment stores	large parts of the "adult" world of work and leisure

After this overview we concentrate on different spaces within the four mentioned ranges in order to see how the discrete areas under consideration are structured in terms of the child living in them. We ask where boundaries for the children run, which spaces there are, and what the connections are like between spaces of par-ticular importance in the daily lives of urban children.

In the third and fourth sections, we describe how these structures are embedded, feeling our way through the rooms used by children and adults alike. We then localize taboo zones from which children are largely excluded. Spaces are not always unequivocally classifiable into one category or the other. In one family the parents' bedroom is allowed to be used and played in by the children and is clearly counted as one of the "general-purpose rooms"; in the next family, that room is off limits to the children and is thus a "space for adults." Our presentation is simultane-ously an attempt to integrate the concept of home range, which is considered out-moded by many scholars (see Flade, 1993, and the literature cited there), with the island-forming thesis proposed by Zeiher and Zeiher (1994).

2.2 Life spaces in brief: Description and potential meaning for children's development

2.2.1 The dwelling

The dwelling is considered the first and most important setting in a child's life. The external walls with their doors and windows that can be opened and shut define a place that usually consists of several rooms and connecting passages. Children generally spend most of their time there during the first three to five years of their lives. It is there that they live with their most important reference persons and have their most important objects for learning to grasp the world, both literally and figuratively. The dwelling is where the child's personality develops in all its facets. The child acquires social and spatial identity. In other words, varied processes of habituation and other sorts of mental development, an exploration of which would go beyond the scope of this article, contribute to the gradual awareness in children that they belong to the surrounding group (i.e., social identity) and place (i.e., spatial identity) and, vice versa, that both the group and the place are part of the children's own selves (Rivlin, 1987).

How the family's life is organized within these "four walls" called the dwelling, how immediate that life is felt to be or how it falls apart, is determined first by the square footage and the floor plan as well as by the existence or absence of discrete, functionally defined spaces (e.g., a child's room). In addition, the life of the inhabitants is structured by the way it is embedded in the urban surroundings. The distance to the place of work, for example, partly decides how much time the parents can spend in the dwelling with the child. Likewise, the time it takes to get to school, relatives, friends, stores, and other destinations in the city is a factor in scheduling activities within the dwelling. The way the dwelling is furnished is also related to the surroundings. For instance, a dwelling that has no access to a garden or courtyard in which a swing can be hung is more likely to have an indoor swing than will a dwelling that does have such outdoor space available to it.

How much time the child spends in the dwelling at all depends largely on its location within the local neighborhood and greater metropolitan area. For children who can play outside without having to be supervised of, the dwelling has other functions to fulfill than for peers who grow up, say, on a main street. Whereas the first setting offers sufficient possibilities for withdrawal and recreation, the second setting must offer chances to move about and romp around. If it does not, tensions can result in the family. That is not to say, however, that a dwelling with room to move around freely in it can replace a residential vicinity in which children can play. The reason is that children are under much closer adult supervision when inside than when outside. As Flade (1993, p. 185) stated, the dwelling is, for children, not only a "private zone, the nest offering security, protection, and support," it is also "the place of parental dominance and limitation imposed by the family" (see also Moore & Young, 1978).

The story on which one lives, occupant density, and noise are other factors affecting the potential social life and the emotional-motivational and cognitive input a child can give within a dwelling. It is known that high occupant density can be reflected in aggression within the family and that noise penetrating the dwelling from outside impairs children's cognitive performance. (For synopses of the relevant research, see Wohlwill & Heft, 1987, and Parke, 1978, for example.) In this way the social status and economic situation that a family can maintain in the city is indirectly mediated by the dwelling.

Toys and objects in the dwelling represent physical stimuli that can substitute for or complement a child's outdoor alternatives for play. The television is an especially potent example of the degree to which the use of things within the dwelling can affect activities outside it. It has been shown that TV programming structures children's schedules and that the content of TV broadcasts is incorporated in outdoor play. To put it another way, the impressions assailing children in the world of TV are processed and grasped by those young viewers by way of the real, tangible living environment. Electronic media such as computer games and telegames are also of growing importance in this regard. In fact, they rank as the preferred play activity among 8- to 13-year-old boys (Binger, Hellemann, & Lorenz, 1993). These "virtual worlds" may come to offer more and more of what is becoming ever harder to find in urban living environs bereft of function: direct feedback and interaction.

As far as potential significance for children's development is concerned, the dwelling, especially in the initial years of a person's life, serves not only as a place of learning in terms of the child's innumerable physical and intellectual abilities (Gifford, 1997) but also as the place where the child's social and spatial identity (see also Proshansky & Fabian, 1987) and ability to regulate privacy develops vis-à-vis close people such as parents, siblings, and others belonging to the household (Altman, 1975). After children are able to distinguish between themselves and the environment, they try to control the distance to another occupant according to their own emotional and motivational state and learn to employ the means appropriate for doing so (Parke, 1978; Wolfe, 1978). Lastly, the dwelling is the place where something like a cognitive map emerges for the first time from the child's knowledge about the disposition of the various rooms and the arrangement of the furniture in them. The cognitive map is an individual design, a mental picture of the real environment, and it goes through several stages of development. These stages proceed from unconnected landmarks to paths and then to an overview. Initial abilities to gain a spatial overview appear in 3-year-olds and improve over time (Rutland, Custance, & Campbell, 1993).

2.2.2 *The immediate vicinity of the dwelling*

Except for the dwelling itself, the most important place of development is said to be its immediate vicinity, or the adjacent terrain (Cooper, 1975). That area consists of the spaces that lie outside the dwelling but that still belong to it. It is the semipublic area beginning at the dwelling's entrance door and extending to the landings, the stairwell, and entrance to the building; to the courtyard; and to the garden or yard (if there is one). Depending on the traffic situation, it may also encompass the sidewalk and the street in front of the house, ending, say, at the first heavily traveled street after that. This range generally marks the boundaries of children's forays into the environment until they come of school age. Sometimes these spaces feature play equipment, sandboxes, or Ping-Pong tables. Many inner-city rear courtyards offer the typical wasteland of garbage cans and die-hard thorn bushes.

Children in the immediate vicinity of the dwelling are still within earshot of their mothers (and sometimes the neighbors) but find there a space in which they are monitored less than in the dwelling. Flade (1993) called it "the area featuring the absence of parental control and more casual, if any, adult supervision and thus demanding and fostering the child's independence" (p. 185).

Studying how preschoolers in a major German city use their living environment, Peek (1995) has written extensively on children's experience in this space between family and the public world. The children in his sample spent an average of 1¼ hours a day in the vicinity of their homes. On the whole, however, Peek found that only half of the children (52.6 percent) had access to such an area in the first place. In another study conducted in Germany, Flade (1993) confirmed that preschoolers "are in many cases children without a home range" (p. 192), especially if they are growing up in large 1960s- and 1970s-style settlements dominated by apartment buildings more than seven stories high. Motorized road traffic and the ugliness and social desolation of those residential areas are suspected as reasons.

Of course, the *actual* significance that a dwelling's immediate vicinity has for children's development is limited, too, if only one child in two has access to such space for personal experience and action. The *potential* significance, however, is high for all children. Depending on the physical articulation of the attendant spaces, a dwelling's immediate vicinity not only provides room for the additional acquisition of cognitive structures (including a cognitive map) and physical abilities but also facilitates the development of important social skills (Cooper, 1975; Cooper Marcus & Sarkissian, 1986). It is in the immediate vicinity of a dwelling that children encounter the neighborhood adults, and especially their children. It is there and in the local neighborhood that 1- to 5-year-olds begin to develop trust and distrust of persons who do not belong to the circle of those with whom the child lives. Basic privacy-management skills that the child has acquired in that group are developed further there and are transferred to relations with neighbors. In particular, it is in the dwelling's immediate vicinity and in the dwellings of the neighborhood that children make their first childhood friends. Social and spatial identity "grows" into that space (Rivlin, 1987).

2.2.3 The local neighborhood

The local neighborhood is understood to mean the areas around the dwelling that adults and children are able to reach by foot within 20 minutes or by bicycle within 10 minutes. Initially, children first become acquainted with this area when out with their parents, say, on the way to school, the store, the nearby park, or the playground. The local neighborhood, with its equipment and streets, represents the second extension of the child's experiential and action space (see Johnson, 1987, and the sources cited there). In addition to large playgrounds (large and varied in comparison to the play equipment provided for very young children in the dwelling's immediate vicinity), there are nursery schools and regular schools. Aside from being venues for focused play and learning instruction by educators, these places are ones at which children learn to fit into larger groups and obey authority figures (Weinstein, 1987; Wolfe & Rivlin, 1987). Further, close bonds with other children and groups form through the school and often last a lifetime. As concerns the regulation of privacy, it is in the local neighborhood (and the greater metropolitan area) that children learn to keep their distance to individual strangers and outside groups. Social and spatial identity extends to the local neighborhood, too, as the child comes to use it more and more.

Martha Muchow (Muchow & Muchow, 1935/1978) described the local neighborhood as a space for roaming and exploring, one that children come to appropriate. In those days it was still possible for her to speak of the street as an outdoor home and as a space lived in by children. But what was everyday experience for children in the city districts of Hamburg in the 1930s is no longer comparable to the modern living conditions facing children in major German cities today. As early as 1979, Jürgen Zinnecker stated that the conditions for a street culture among children were worsening:

> What with the flight of many families to the suburbs, the surplus of childless young families and single elderly people, the congestion of the streets by automobile traffic, [and] ethnic fragmentation among groups of inhabitants, street life is no longer possible for children and adolescents . . . because there are too few of them left. (p. 738)

For many children today, the point at which they can explore their surroundings on their own does not begin until they start attending elementary school. The heavily traveled street, which up to that moment marks the boundary for their independent explorations, is now becoming the link to new worlds of experience. Under certain circumstances, this "boundary-crossing" poses mortal danger, for statistics show that the accident rate is highest among 6- and 7-year-olds.

The way to school is not the only one that children walk in their residential quarter. Over time, they make friends whom they go to visit on their own. Children do their first shopping in nearby stores; they explore the vicinity. But the street offers more than just the transition from one location of children's action to the next. It also functions as a transition from the protected world of the child to public social life.

The local public life of children and adolescents is mediated by street space. On the street they learn to band together in groups without guidance by educators. It is there that they develop independent forms of play and social interaction, the foundation for a street-related culture of children and adolescents that is well guarded from the "pedagogical eyes" of adults. (Zinnecker, 1979, p. 738)

Decidedly juvenile gangs form especially in social "hot spots," meaning also dwellings that become too crowded. Those "independent forms of social interaction" can assume violent and criminal guises and thereby test the limits of the adult world's tolerance. The street is thus the place where young people can try out and practice their autonomy on the one hand and their "regular civic roles as buyers, consumers, and road users on the other" (Zinnecker, p. 744).

2.2.4 The greater metropolitan area

Unlike the context in Martha Muchow's era, urban spaces and facilities lying beyond walking distance play an important role for children today. These spaces are located within the greater metropolitan area, which is composed of highly dissimilar milieus. Depending on whether children are brought to a play group in the neighboring district or to a specialist clear across the city, they experience its entire range of social and spatial structures along the way. As they do, however, they have to rely on grown-ups, who must accompany the child to the "islands" in the sea called the city (Zeiher & Zeiher, 1994). Not until children are between 10 and 13 years of age do they learn to get around independently with public transport and face the situation of having to reach the needed child-environment units of the greater metropolitan area on their own. As Jacob (1987) stated, "given the changes in the urban environment, children [today] are, and have to be, highly mobile. This is shown by the high share of destination-oriented routes that about one third of all activities have meanwhile come to consist of" (p. 17). By the same token, the extension of the alternatives for experience and action in the greater metropolitan area coincide with both cognitive and socioemotional development, particularly in terms of identity formation.

Remember in this context that development is sometimes paraphrased as getting to feel at home in new settings (Bronfenbrenner, 1978; see also Oerter, 1995). Most individuals only partly manage to acquire this feeling in the greater metropolitan area of major cities, especially those with a million or more inhabitants. No one can know everything about a city measuring 28 miles in diameter (Berlin). There will always be white patches. The urbanite lives with a city map. Nevertheless, social and spatial identity with the city as a whole develops independently of the completeness of one's actual knowledge of the city in which one lives. This fact is especially true in relation to outsiders. One does not tell a person from Munich: "I am from Kreuzberg" or "I am from Charlottenburg" (two districts in Berlin) but rather "I am from Berlin."

2.3 Children's spaces in the city – Containment and exclusion

How do the four ranges presented above differ in the eyes of a child? Where are the spaces in which children should, can, and may spend time? How are those spaces connected, and where are children excluded? Let us first examine the spaces set up especially for children.

2.3.1 Children's spaces

The corners and niches, rooms and furnishings, and squares and grounds that are set up and maintained especially for children in the city must be regarded as outcomes of general urban specialization that has not only divided functions in separate areas of life in society (living, working, and leisure) but has also divorced the child's world from the adult's. There are recreational, care, and educational facilities, which signify protection for children and room for them to play but also mean control and exclusion from the world of grown-ups.

The child's room is a socialization space provided by parents. The social position and economic circumstances of the parents decide whether a child has this space at all. As shown by Keller (1993), the likelihood that it is actually available is significantly higher if the child lives in an area of single-family homes than if he or she lives in the city center. The parents decide how this space is furnished and arranged; they create the possibilities for their children's actions; and they decide on the objects and, hence, the affordances in it (Moore & Young, 1978). If they install slides and monkey bars, then actions that children customarily execute outdoors are brought indoors. In Keller's view, such parental design of the environment "curtails socialization in a major way. . . . The time for exploring the outdoor surroundings is reduced, and a variety of sensory experiences is precluded" (p. 125). It also restricts children's opportunities to choose social contacts on their own in public or semipublic space.

For most children, their room not only serves as a "play room" that must compensate for what in some cases is a vacuous, unattractive home range. It has a number of other functions to fulfill as well. In addition to toys, it houses the child's bed, desk, and school materials. The child's room is thus a place for playing, working, sleeping, and withdrawing all in one. Keller (1993) found it problematic that children's rooms were "overloaded with different functions": "Results of research on sleep, for example, clearly indicate that sleep is interfered with when the bedroom obviously prompts thoughts of daily obligations (school and homework) or arousal and stimulation (toys, materials relating to specific interests)" (p. 129).

The child's room in the private sphere has a great many counterparts in the semi-public and public sphere. The following examples suggest the spectrum of the urban infrastructure serving children (see also Table 1):

- Leisure: playgrounds, children's theaters, children's movie houses, children's restaurants, puppet theaters, amusement parks, ice-skating rinks, zoos
- Guidance and care: children's clubs, nursery schools, private preschool groups, daycare centers, youth centers
- Education: public and private schools for every pedagogical persuasion; children's books section in municipal libraries; and specific programs, classes, and activities (music schools, ballet schools, museum services)
- Spaces for children within adult domains: children's amusement centers in department stores, "play corners" in restaurants

What characterizes children's spaces in the semipublic and public urban realm? The city offers a range of facilities tailored to very special needs and interests of children. More precisely, it is again adults who plan these spaces for children and who see to it that the spaces are used and played in as intended. Whereas many spaces and squares in small localities serve a variety of functions (such as a gym successively being an auditorium, sports arena, theater, assembly room, and hall for mass medical examinations), the urban child is taken to a different place for each of these functions, so certain places are thus associated in the child's mind with specific actions intended for each place. An imaginative adaptation of space, a change, or a conversion is often not possible, so the spaces remain anonymous and do not permit as much place attachment as they would otherwise.

Unifunctional use of urban spaces by children is widely criticized in the literature (Hart, 1987). Assessing the fact that important urban life spaces of children are located far from where children live in the city, Sachs (1981) states:

Where preschool facilities, schools, friends – indeed, all the places where life teems – leave the neighborhood, children become less mobile. On their own, whether by foot or bicycle, they cannot reach some of the places attractive for them, and even many places to which they *must* go. The increasing use of cars has decreased their mobility. Their capacity, by virtue of their own physical effort, to become masters of the space important to them is impaired. Their autonomy is curtailed not [only] because they may not do so but [also] because they cannot. (p. 83)

2.3.2 General spaces

By general spaces we mean spaces that have not been provided especially for the needs and purposes of children but that are nonetheless also used by them. In the dwelling, such general areas include the kitchen, living room, and bathroom; they are used by children and adults alike. General spaces are often transitional spaces in both senses of the word. To many children, the stairwell and its landings, the street, and public transport are at first barriers that they cannot overcome alone. These spaces later become communications to the courtyard, the elementary school, and the neighboring part of the city, permitting the transition to new worlds of experience.

Children use these spaces differently than adults do. Whereas stairs and streets serve adults primarily as bridges between two locations, children turn them into something else for their own purposes.

Adults have divided up their world pretty definitively. In their world many things have their fixed meanings and functions. Children ascribe the things and places in their surroundings very different meanings and functions depending on the situation. . . . [T]his is precisely where a fundamental difference between children and adults surfaces, or seems to surface. It is imaginativeness. Children are able to create a completely new world, one in which objects can take on a completely new meaning. (Beekman, Bleeker, & Mulderij, 1985, p. 248)

Children and adolescents thus have their own way of appropriating space. Where ways to change spaces are absent, graffiti and tags (the felt-pen or lacquer markings scrawled so prolifically on public walls and seats, especially on public transport) bear witness to the need to record one's presence in the environment (Cooper Marcus & Sarkissian, 1986). Etching the windows of subway cars with a key, young people leave their mark on the normality and perfect functioning of the world created by adults.

Often, what makes general spaces outside the dwelling attractive to children is the absence of what characterizes children's rooms: the lack of intended specialized uses and the absence of persons who compel space to be used in a particular way. Children try to break through the specialized functions assigned to spaces where they can. Spaces that are especially suited to imaginative play outside adult control are those that have temporarily lost their social function or that allow for changes. Examples are undeveloped property, construction sites on which no work is being done at the moment, and buildings slated for demolition (Zeiher, 1983). General spaces make it possible for children to grow out of spaces they frequent and facilitate the gradual extension of their action into zones hitherto reserved for adults.

2.3.3 Spaces of adults
Lastly, we briefly examine the spaces from which children are explicitly excluded in the city. As shown in Table 1, those spaces include major parts of the working world and the leisure realm of adults. Unlike the picture that Kurt Lewin was able to convey in his 1931 film entitled *Die Lebenswelt des Großstadtkindes* (The life world of the city child), the situation today is such that children are largely shut out of the working world of adults.

The relocation of local crafts and industries from urban residential areas has reduced the possibilities for children to come into contact with work processes engaged in by adults. Today, experience in this sphere is determined by service businesses, shops, and construction and repair work on streets and houses. (Jacob, 1987, pp. 228)

Similarly, major segments of the urban leisure culture is reserved for adults in that children, especially in Germany, are excluded from the night life found in restaurants, pubs, and bars. Clubs, sports studios, and advanced training courses are also usually settings where adults are among themselves and where they are left unmolested by the sometimes quite headstrong methods children use to appropriate space.

Figure 1: Child in-line skating on a main street. (From "Platz da!" [Make way!], by S. Baumgarten, 4 September 1996, Brigitte, p. 146. Copyright 1996 by R. v. Forster. Reprinted with permission.)

Thoroughfares, too, are spaces that adults want to keep children away from. Adults do not always succeed, however, and conflicts erupt (see Figure 1). The attitude of many adults and the distribution of power in such competitive situations were expressed in a traffic warning heard on the radio in Hamburg on 13 April 1996: "Attention, all drivers, an urgent alert: Children are playing on highway 24!" Shortly thereafter the announcer updated the report, stating: "There is no longer any danger to drivers" (after Baumgarten, 1996, p. 146).

In summary, individual life spaces cannot be examined in isolation from each other. They affect and condition each other. To be able to estimate, for example, the effect that a 129 sq. foot (12 m^2) child's room has on the dwelling's occupants, one must have additional information, such as where the child spends time otherwise, what alternatives the child has, and how the child's everyday life is organized as a whole. These questions lead to the next section, in which we delve into the ways in which the individual life worlds are interlinked in the city.

3   Individual "Networks of Children's Life Worlds"

In the previous section we gave a general overview of the diversity of urban life spaces that children live in and experience. It became clear that the specific way in which a dwelling is integrated into its vicinity or quarter greatly contributes to the quality of residential conditions. In this section we discuss the relation between places frequented by children. The gradual extension of the child's action space, from the child's room as the central place to the dwelling's immediate vicinity, the local neighborhood, and greater metropolitan area, proceeds *individually* according to the personal interests of the children and their parents, developing out of necessity, situational factors, and chance. In this way there emerge many different individual "networks of children's life worlds" that are highly subjective representations of the city. The network concept we have chosen in this context is meant as a metaphor, with the separate places (islands) being the "knots" and the connecting paths, or communications, being the "threads." The different meanings that communications have can be affected, for example, by the frequency with which they are used, which does not mean, however, that rarely used paths and destinations necessarily make few enduring impressions on children. (The zoo is a prime example of a setting that is seldom visited but that nevertheless has a lasting impact.) The cognitive representation of these networks takes the form of cognitive maps. The nature and scope of the connected networks depend on a number of additional variables, such as the location of the dwelling within the city; the furnishings, facilities, and other resources of the dwelling's immediate vicinity and the local neighborhood; the accessibility of other milieus; the child's age, gender, and nationality; and the family's socioeconomic status.

In the rest of this section we attempt to describe the variables playing a major role in the origins of these networks and to present examples of conceivable networks of children's life worlds that differ in complexity and spatial dimension.

3.1   Urban living: Restriction or opportunity?

Trying to describe the city as a life space for children first brings to mind such restrictions and stress as the motorized traffic, air pollution, and noise that urban children are increasingly exposed to and that interfere with their outdoor explorations and play behavior. On the other hand, stress and the loss of opportunity to experience things are not the only characteristics of life for children growing up in cities today. The city also offers positive, specifically urban experiences. The depreciation of the area near the dwelling often goes hand in hand with the greater metropolitan area's wide range of leisure and cultural activities, which can broaden and deepen children's understanding of culture. By attending performances in puppet theaters, visiting the zoo, swimming in the municipal pool, and taking advantage of other urban leisure activities, even very young children become familiar with the expansiveness and diversity of life in the city. Older children, by going to such child-environment units as movie theaters, discos, exhibitions, and downtown, are able to move about with ever greater frequency on their own outside their parents' sphere of control and thereby gradually increase their autonomy. As places of socialization, urban life worlds thus provide a partly limiting and partly liberating framework for children's development. They require of the growing child an ever greater competence in actively dealing on their own terms with those symptoms of modern times called "isolation," "dependency on transport," and "keeping to time schedules." The skills needed are those of setting and organizing appointments, handling the exigencies of mobility and the hazards of traffic, becoming familiar with cultural diversity, and changing the use of urban space (e.g., in-line skating).

In mastering these demands successfully, urban children, as they age, actively begin molding their everyday world under the guidance of their parents. They are not just passive victims. In the ongoing process of child-environment transactions, the cognitive map of the city expands and changes, with places and environmental elements assuming new meanings and thereby updating the mental representation of the city. Basically, this process continues throughout adult life, whereby the stretching and changes that go with growing from a child into an adolescent and then into an adult correspond to other changes and limitations that are part of growing old.

3.2   Qualitative factors of children's networks

It is difficult to assess the quality of children's life worlds in terms of attributes that promote or impede development. It cannot be done without especially considering the different needs that older and younger children have. When evaluating built environments, one also needs to keep in mind that many of them serve certain communal functions and must meet the needs of other user groups as well, such as adults, the elderly, and the handicapped (David & Weinstein, 1987). At the level of places where children act, however, the point is not to judge individual segments of the environment for their quality. Instead, the focus is on the presence or absence of access to, and thus the freedom of choice between, the settings needed by the individual child and on ways to have parts of the network compensate for deficiencies in other parts. The reciprocal influence of interlocking child-environment units becomes especially clear in this function (see section 1, thesis 6). A number of variables determine whether the linked networks of life worlds have the overall tendency to promote and inspire, to compensate, or to limit action and development. For one, the physiospatial elements of the environment constitute the latitude for action; for another, social, socioeconomic, cultural, and personality factors partly determine whether and how that latitude can be used or overcome. The most important factors that shape networks are presented below.

The strata to which one belongs. In connection with their island-forming thesis, Zeiher and Zeiher (1994) compared two residential quarters located in different parts of West Berlin and found that the "degree of modernization" characterizing the parents' approach to education had a major impact on the way the child's everyday life was shaped and that the strata to which the parents belonged played a role. The more consciously the parents pursued an approach oriented to the needs of the child, the more developmentally supportive the networks of the provided contexts became. These networks included playmates who were not necessarily sought out in the immediate neighborhood; in certain cases they were specially chosen regardless of where they lived. By contrast, factors like "size of the action space" and "number of fixed appointments" are not explicable by differences in strata (Jacob, 1987). The phenomenon of appropriating islands of space pervades all strata. In urban spaces, bonds to one's own residential area are loosened, and social relations are viewed as less binding than they used to be in traditional life worlds (Zeiher & Zeiher, 1994).

The attractiveness of the dwelling's immediate vicinity. The furnishings, facilities, and other resources of the dwelling's immediate vicinity largely determine the degree of mobility children must have in order to seek out preferred places or playmates. For example, having one's own yard to play in or having playmates who live in the same building can tie a preschooler's circle of activity to the dwelling's immediate vicinity. This result is just as possible in a tract of single-family houses as in an area of high-rises with a large population of children. Conversely, an absence of places to play in the private and semipublic area around the dwelling set the stage for compensating measures, such as the installation of exercise and play equipment inside the dwelling or increased time spent at places away from the dwelling in order to offset the deficiency. In this context, too, the possibilities and initiative of the parents are the key to the quality of the networks involved.

Location of the dwelling. A dwelling's location within a building determines whether a child has access to the immediate outdoor vicinity, especially in the child's first years of life. Ground-floor dwellings permitting independent shifts from the private, indoor space of the dwelling to the semiprivate space outdoors offer the best possibilities for such access. The location of a dwelling or a building within a particular district also has profound implications for the play and everyday behavior of children. The degree to which a dwelling's immediate vicinity is suitable for play is often not apparent at first glance. For example, some studies in Germany indicate that the action space of children living in inner city areas that consist of buildings predating 1948 is larger than that of children living in more recently built residential areas situated on the outskirts. These results suggest, among other things, that the presumed diversity of experience provided in the former type of area often does not meet many of the needs and desires of children, for a host of restrictions and regulations evidently keep it from being used (Jacob, 1987). Children therefore withdraw into their own dwellings or venture to settings beyond the immediate vicinity of where they live.

Age and gender. Age is a key variable of the perception and use of urban space. To preschool children the immediate vicinity of the dwelling as an outdoor setting is highly important (Peek, 1995). As children age, their action radius expands (see above). In leisure behavior, the playing habits of girls and boys exhibit differences that are reflected by the size of the action radius. Among boys the space that is used independently is larger than that among girls (Flade, 1993).

Traffic safety and communications. Children face their greatest risk from traffic accidents between the ages of six and seven years, for at that point they are neither cognitively nor motorically able to cope with the traffic situation yet are beginning to cover short distances alone, as indeed they must when they enter school (Moore & Young, 1978). An important variable bearing on the quality of the networks is, therefore, the possibility the child has of reaching the desired island. It can be sufficient and safe only if a convenient connection to public transport is combined with traffic safety and a well-developed system of bicycle paths. As described above, parents or other adults can provide transportation, but it means that the child is dependent on them for mobility, that a car must be available, and that someone must have time to do the driving.

Personality factors and cultural influences. Personal interests, abilities, and preferences determine what a child needs and wants from his or her residential setting. The child will prefer very specific places in that setting and reject others, depending on what those needs and desires are. In this respect, Jacob (1987) notes differences from one nationality to another. Children representing dissimilar subcultures differ in the way they use space. In Germany, for instance, children of immigrants from Turkey or former Yugoslavia are said to play outdoors more often than children of German ancestry do. Gender differences, too, are more apparent among children of non-German ancestry.

3.3   Different networks of child-environment units

Combining the concept of home range with the island-forming thesis proposed by
Zeiher and Zeiher (1994), we now present fictional representative networks of children's life worlds. In a city there is any number of such individual networks, in principle as many as there are children. The examples presented below have been so
chosen that they differ in their range of conceivable complexity, scope, and orientation within the overall urban setting and could exist in this or a similar form at least
in Berlin or other major European cities. Besides the dwelling, action spaces can be
tied to the dwelling's immediate vicinity (the second range) and the local neighborhood (the third range) or can be widely distributed in the greater metropolitan area
(the fourth range) (see Figure 1). Exploration of the parents' dwelling itself can
likewise be described in terms of a changing network of child-environment units,
but in the following discussion we confine ourselves to the outdoor spaces.

Example 1

Living circumstances
Example 1 shows the setting of a 3-year-old girl who lives with her parents in a single-family house with a yard. It is located in a tract of such homes on the outskirts of
the city. The child's mother is not employed. There are a few neighbors in a similar
situation. A second car is available.

Urban spaces lived in outside the dwelling
In the immediate vicinity of the dwelling: the yard belonging to the house, the paths
leading into and out of the yard, and the adjacent yards of the neighbors
In the local neighborhood: playground, the houses and yards of the children living
nearby, green belt
In the greater metropolitan area: attractive public places for children, such as the
zoo, a lake and a public pool for swimming, children's theater or similar facilities,
the homes of friends or relatives (see Figure 2)

In this example the small child has optimal social and spatial conditions. Accordingly, the child's action space comes to be centered on the immediate vicinity of the
dwelling. In addition, specific child-environment units lying further afield are sought
out in the company of the mother or both parents. The network is shaped partly by
the fact that the child is cared for largely by her mother; the availability of a car,
which affords relative independence from the public transport system; the direct
access to private and public open spaces that meet the needs and desires of children;
and the presence of other children in the immediate neighborhood.

Such a network of child-environment units is not static. Its particular shape lasts only for a limited period and is subject to constant change as a matter of principle. The parents and other care-givers continually search the environment for new stimuli that correspond to the child's motoric and cognitive development. The changes may be barely noticeable, but they can suddenly entail a number of visible and tangible alterations (see section 1, thesis 4).

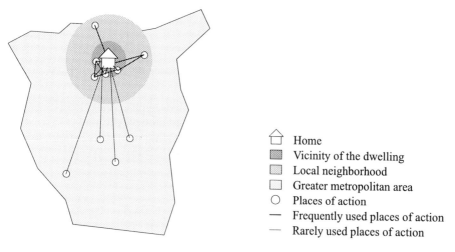

⌂   Home
▓   Vicinity of the dwelling
▒   Local neighborhood
☐   Greater metropolitan area
○   Places of action
—   Frequently used places of action
‒   Rarely used places of action

Figure 2: Network of child-environment units of a 3-year-old girl who lives with her parents in a suburban single-family house with a yard

The form of a network is affected especially by decisive events, such as those that arise when the child enters preschool or elementary school, when the family moves to a different part of the city, or when the child loses significant reference persons through illness or death. In the example described above, the child might attend a private preschool group in the greater metropolitan area a year later. Some of the child-environment units hitherto frequently used in the immediate vicinity of the child's home would then presumably become less central, and some, such as the yards of the neighbors, would no longer be sought out at all. Visits to the playground near the child's home would be less often, especially if the preschool group offered opportunities to play outdoors (see section 1, thesis 6). Some of the contact with neighborhood children might fade because new friendships would be made in the preschool group. The role of the mother, the main reference individual, also changes, as does her daily schedule as a result of the time she gains through such rearrangement. She has the chance to go shopping and do other errands by herself, allowing her and her child to spend the remaining time together more intensely. In Figure 2, such changes would mean that the knots of the net would shift more to the greater metropolitan area and away from the dwelling's immediate vicinity.

Example 2

Living circumstances
The second example is about a 12-year-old Berlin boy of Turkish background who lives with several siblings in an inner-city area of pre-1948 buildings. The parents have a car, and the mother remains at home, as in example 1. The boy spends a great deal of time outdoors with a peer group and knows his quarter of the city well (local neighborhood).

Urban spaces lived in outside the dwelling
In the immediate vicinity of the dwelling: the courtyard, the street in front of the building
In the local neighborhood: youth center in the district, shops, open spaces such as squares, and a small fenced-off soccer area belonging to the playground
In the greater metropolitan area: school, public swimming pool, soccer field, movie house, department stores, vacant lots, and public parks (see Figure 3)

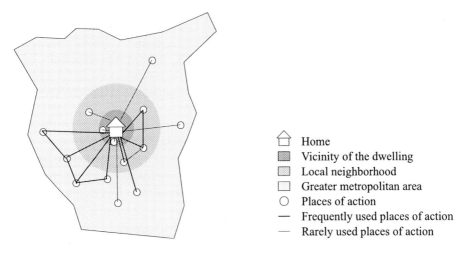

☖ Home
▨ Vicinity of the dwelling
▢ Local neighborhood
▢ Greater metropolitan area
○ Places of action
— Frequently used places of action
— Rarely used places of action

Figure 3: *Network of child-environment units of a 12-year-old boy of Turkish background who lives with his family in an inner-city area of apartment buildings from the first half of the 20th century*

This example illustrates the already advanced exploration of the local neighborhood and the greater metropolitan area. To be sure, there is still a strong tie to the vicinity of the dwelling and the neighborhood, but the appropriation of islands much further away is apparent. The use of public transport figures prominently in the exploration of the metropolitan area together with peers. The development of autonomy is fostered in this example by the fact that the boy usually spends his free time outside his parents' sphere of control, a circumstance that also always entails the risk of negative influences and experiences.

The described situation would change if, for example, the boy received a bicycle. His role as a road user would shift from that of a pedestrian and passive passenger in his parents' car or on public transport to that of a bicyclist responsible for himself and others. His relation to the street as a child-environment unit would be closer and more direct (see section 1, thesis 7). It is conceivable that other child-environment units, too, would be affected, such as the dwelling if he had to keep the bicycle in his room for lack of a secure place to put it in the courtyard. His room would simultaneously be a storage area for the bicycle and would lose some of its attraction as a room in which to play (see section 1, theses 1 and 2). By using the bicycle, the boy may become reacquainted with the local neighborhood in a new way, may come to know it in greater detail, discover new routes or shortcuts between two places. His personal network may expand.

Both of the following examples, too, are "snapshots" as it were in the life of an urban child. This version of them is only temporary.

Example 3

Living circumstances
This example is about an 8-year-old girl living in a high-rise of a new settlement built on the outskirts of the city. Her mother is single and has a full-time job. After school, the girl spends her time at a child-care facility or visits neighbor children in her apartment building. She knows the building's immediate vicinity well.

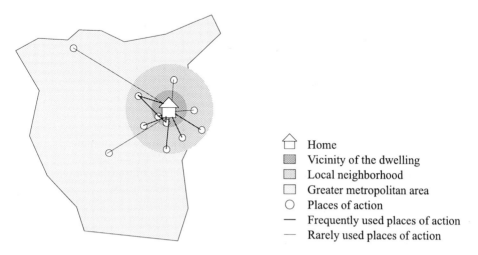

⌂ Home
▨ Vicinity of the dwelling
▨ Local neighborhood
□ Greater metropolitan area
○ Places of action
— Frequently used places of action
— Rarely used places of action

Figure 4: *Network of child-environment units of an 8-year-old girl living in a high-rise in a new suburban settlement*

Urban spaces lived in outside the dwelling
In the immediate vicinity of the dwelling: the playground in front of the building; the green space separating the buildings; the apartments of the neighbor children; the stairwell and its landings; the building's parking areas, where she skates
In the local neighborhood: the elementary school, the child-care facility, friends, relatives, shops in the vicinity of her apartment building, the gymnastics club
In the greater metropolitan area: the zoo, the swimming lake (see Figure 4)

In this example, the adequate physical and social setting of the local neighborhood facilitates social contact and regular leisure activities in that area. Dependency on public transport is minimal. The girl can structure her everyday life after school more or less as she wants. Children's spaces lying beyond the local neighborhood can be sought out only on weekends, usually with her mother. In this example, the numerous social contacts within the apartment building or its immediate vicinity are especially important as compensation for the absence of the girl's single mother when she is at her job.

Example 4

Living circumstances
The final example describes the circumstances of a five-year-old kindergartner who lives with his two-year-old brother, his parents, and other adults and children in a downtown commune. The parents are both students.

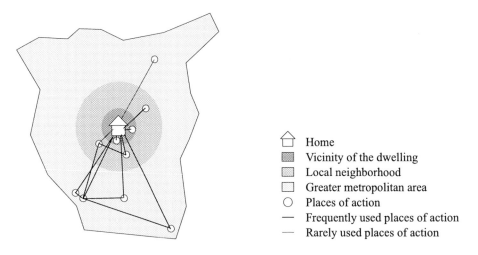

⌂ Home
▨ Vicinity of the dwelling
▨ Local neighborhood
☐ Greater metropolitan area
○ Places of action
— Frequently used places of action
— Rarely used places of action

Figure 5: Network of child-environment units of a 5-year-old boy who lives with his family on in a downtown commune

Urban spaces lived in outside the dwelling
In the immediate vicinity of the dwelling: the courtyard, shops
In the local neighborhood: a playground near the apartment
In the greater metropolitan area: the university daycare center, the university, the homes of friends he visits on the outskirts of the city, the children's theater, the private institution where he receives early musical training, municipal park, block parties, visits to friends (see Figure 5)

The daily life of the small child in this example revolves around the greater metropolitan area, a situation predicated by the parent's work setting. Aside from the apartment itself, the main center of interest is, hence, not the dwelling's immediate vicinity, as one would assume for children of this age. Because several children live in the apartment, the parents take little initiative to establish contact right in the area where they live. The communal child care provided by all adults in the household, and the fact that it entails no financial burden, is a major help to the parents.

In summary, the variability of the networks described in these four examples is due to the interaction of all relevant situational, interpersonal, and intrapersonal factors, and it is infinitely great. The examples give an idea of how much the weighting of individual qualitative factors differ in each of the age grades and of how "dependency" on access to other milieus is at least partially offset by well-endowed second and third ranges.

The first example depicts the rather rare case of young parents who enjoy an especially favorable socioeconomic status in which the small child not only finds optimal opportunity for play and exploration in the dwelling's immediate vicinity but, through regular activity, also becomes familiar with the setting beyond that sphere. In general, the economic circumstances of parents are fairly modest when their children are small. The way the children spend their daily lives is, therefore, highly affected by the characteristics of their home's immediate vicinity and external exigencies. At just five years of age, the child in example 4 is already highly mobile (with his parents) in the greater metropolitan area, whereas the 8-year-old girl in example 3 needs to look no further than her home's immediate vicinity and the surrounding milieu to find almost everything she needs for shaping her everyday world. The 12-year-old boy in example 2, who uses public transport and downtown bicycle paths more frequently and independently than any other child described above, has the most complex network.

4   Recommendations to parents, planners, and policy-makers

To portray children's life worlds appropriately, it appears worthwhile to join the home-range principle and the island-forming principle. We conceive of children's life worlds as networks linking knots, that is, person-environment units in which children spend time. Life worlds are thus individual linkages of child-environment units. They can be scattered across the entire city area (i.e., the four ranges mentioned in Table 1) and can also be more or less closely linked to each other in the dwelling's immediate vicinity, the local neighborhood, and, ultimately, in the dwelling itself (whereby the frequency with which one uses the routes between the knots is represented in figures 2 through 5 by lines of different thickness).

The structure of these networks is complex and constantly in flux. Its nature is decided by details of the infrastructure, by the parents, and increasingly by the child as he or she ages. From the many possibilities offered the child in the city, parents can select those that they consider conducive and can consciously shape the network that represents their child's life world.

The significance and impact that discreet units, or knots, have is determined essentially by the context created by all the knots. As suggested by the transactional approach, they can be complemented in different ways. Their effects can compensate for deficiencies in particular child-environment units or detract from special advantages of others.

If one thinks of development as a process of never-ending transactions within and between person-environment units – whereby the impulses of the process can emanate not only from the individual but also from the physical and/or the social setting and whereby these elements simultaneously change with each other at all times, albeit to different degrees (see section 1) – and if one sets children the developmental goal of "becoming fit" for adult urban worlds, then the network has to have certain characteristics, and parents, planners, and policy-makers have to behave in certain ways. The individual network should be structured at all times in such a way that it corresponds to and "grows with" the child's abilities and needs. That means it should consist of knots that always both protect and challenge children appropriately and thereby afford them the chance to develop and test their skills. Existing spaces and persons should promote the child's development, not hinder it. In addition, the network must be malleable. Elements of it can disappear and new ones can emerge, with the parents and other caretakers as well as planners and policy-makers providing opportunities but also giving the child a voice in selecting at least some units and ignoring others.

In many respects, a high degree of responsibility falls to parents and other caretakers in this constant process of transaction. First, they are the ones in the here and now who draw and must continually redefine the line between "guiding and protecting the child" and "letting go and allowing the child to take responsibility." Second, they must constantly anticipate their children's next steps of development and must provide the corresponding affordances (knots), keeping in mind the proper balance between "prompting, encouraging, and sometimes even pushing and demanding" on the one hand and "giving the child room to make his or her own decisions" on the other. This thinking ahead and anticipating can concern all parts of the network. The segment affected might be the "proximate" environment of the dwelling or its immediate vicinity, where the parents have more or less great power to act and shape. But it can also be the more "remote" units of the local neighborhood or the greater metropolitan area, where the parents have little influence, that is, where they must turn to planners and policy-makers and, under certain circumstances, must exert pressure on them by forming grass-roots initiatives to get what are regarded as needed child-environment units (e.g., a playground or preschool facility). After all, it is necessary to plan roads, transport, and travel times to units beyond the immediate neighborhood.

The third and perhaps most important aspect of parental and planning responsibility is the ratio between "spaces primarily for children," "general spaces," and "spaces primarily for adults" (see section 2). In other words, how is the available space to be divided between children and other persons or groups of users? Within the dwelling this decision lies with the parents. But where the layout of residential buildings and external spaces is concerned, architects, town planners, and landscape planners are called upon to keep the needs of various user groups in mind. Children congregate largely in the spaces set aside especially for them (see Table 1). However, those spaces promote children's development only to a limited degree. It is true that they should fulfill their function as a protected space for children to play in and withdraw to, but there must always also be the chance to leave these child-environment units, and there have to be points for crossing into the "general spaces" or one risks excluding children from parts of social life. The spaces set aside especially for children need to be integrated into an overall context that likewise offers sufficient security and stimulation. Planning and design should therefore be focused primarily on jointly used spaces, not on an effort to create even more spaces especially for children. If several people claim a right to use the same space, and if that space is limited, the question arises as to whose needs come first. Conflicts over use may break out between individual persons and groups. However, planning optimal networks for children cannot mean fulfilling their wishes at all costs and subordinating everyone else's interests. Instead, parents, planners, and policy-makers must try to arrive at optimal solutions for the family and larger social communities, an objective that always means constraints on everyone involved when resources are scarce.

A clear example of this viewpoint is a dwelling used by several persons, including children. The call to respect children's needs and to foster children's development certainly competes with at least some demands raised by adults, among whom may be an old, handicapped, or chronically ill person. In general, an attempt must be made to balance interests fairly. When it comes to the question of who should have which room in the dwelling, for example, "private" area to retire to should also be granted the parents if they so desire, not just to the children, meaning that two children may have to share space at home. Moreover, the development of children into people whose thinking and actions show consideration for others virtually requires them to experience social conflicts and learn that they must be resolved with everyone's interests in mind.

Similarly, outside spaces such as paths, roads, and squares could be designed so that they not only serve functional interests of adults but also provide settings that are both safe and flexible enough to be adapted by children for purposes of play. Specifically, this demand could entail the redesign of public squares or measures to reduce the speed and volume of traffic in the downtown area, steps that could be combined with the establishment of green belts and other green spaces to create niches for social life. The result could enrich children's life worlds, offer relaxation to other groups of users as well, and restore the quality of life for all of them. Such an organizational model for urban area planning would help diversify the uses of "general spaces," an organizational model for using urban space. It would mean moderating unilateral functionality and monotony, would prevent the spread of further specialization, and would smooth the way for children to enter the adult world.

References

Altman, I. (1975). *The environment and social behavior*. Monterey, CA: Brooks/Cole.

Altman, I., & Rogoff, B. (1987). World views in psychology: Trait, interactional, organismic, and transactional perspectives. In D. Stokols & I. Altman (Eds.), *Handbook of environmental psychology* (Vol. 1, pp. 7-40). New York: John Wiley and Sons.

Barker, R. G. (1968). *Ecological psychology: Concepts and methods for studying the environment of human behavior*. Stanford, CA: Stanford University Press.

Baumgarten, S. (1996, 4 September). Platz da! [Make way!]. *Brigitte*, pp. 146-150.

Beekman, T., Bleeker, H., & Mulderij, K. (1985). Kinder wohnen auch. Eine Orientierung in der niederländischen Kinderlandschaft [Children matter, too: A look at the children's scene in Holland]. In H. Hengst (Ed.), *Kindheit in Europa. Zwischen Spielplatz und Computer* (pp. 247-279). Frankfurt on the Main: Suhrkamp.

Binger, L., Hellemann, S., & Lorenz, C. (1993). *Kinderspielräume* [Children's play rooms]. Berlin: Transit Buchverlag.

Bronfenbrenner, U. (1978). Ansätze zu einer experimentellen Ökologie menschlicher Entwicklung [Approaches to an experimental ecology of human development]. In R. Oerter (Ed.), *Entwicklung als lebenslanger Prozeß: Aspekte und Perspektiven* (pp. 33-65). Hamburg: Hoffmann und Campe.

Carlson, N. R., & Buskist, W. (1997). *Psychology – The science of behavior*. Boston: Allyn and Bacon.

Cooper, C. C. (1975). *Easter Hill Village: Some implications of design*. New York: Free Press.

Cooper Marcus, C., & Sarkissian, W. (1986). *Housing as if people mattered*. Berkeley: University of California Press.

David, T. G., & Weinstein, C. S. (1987). The built environment and child development. In T. G. David & C. S. Weinstein (Eds.), *Spaces for children: The built environment and child development* (pp. 3-18). New York: Plenum.

Fernald, D. (1997). *Psychology*. Upper Saddle River, NJ: Prentice Hall.

Flade, A. (1993). Spielen von Kindern im Wohnviertel: das Home range-Konzept [Children at play in the residential setting: The concept of home range]. In H. J. Harloff (Ed.), *Psychologie des Wohnungs- und Siedlungsbaus. Psychologie im Dienste von Architektur und Stadtplanung* (pp. 185-193). Göttingen: Verlag für Angewandte Psychologie.

Gifford, R. (1997). *Environmental psychology: Principles and practice* (2nd ed.). Boston: Allyn and Bacon.

Görlitz, D. (1993). Es begann in Berlin – Wege einer entwicklungspsychologischen Stadtforschung [It began in Berlin – Avenues of developmental urban research]. In H. J. Harloff (Ed.), *Psychologie des Wohnungs- und Siedlungsbaus: Psychologie im Dienste von Architektur und Stadtplanung* (pp. 97-120). Göttingen: Verlag für Angewandte Psychologie.

Harloff, H. J. (1995). Der transaktionale Ansatz der Wohnpsychologie – Transaktionen des Menschen in und mit seinem Wohnmilieu [The transactional approach of residential psychology – Human transactions in and with the residential milieu]. In E.-M. Weinwurm-Krause (Ed.), *Wohnen Behinderter – Behindertes Wohnen* (pp. 21-35). Aachen: Shaker.

Harloff, H. J., & Ritterfeld, U. (1993). Psychologie im Dienste von Wohnungs- und Siedlungsplanung [Psychology in the service of housing and settlement planning]. In H. J. Harloff (Ed.), *Psychologie des Wohnungs- und Siedlungsbaus: Psychologie im Dienste von Architektur und Stadtplanung* (pp. 31-44). Göttingen: Verlag für Angewandte Psychologie.

Hart, R. A. (1987). Children's participation in planning and design: Theory, research, and practice. In C. S. Weinstein & T. G. David (Eds.), *Spaces for children: The built environment and child development* (pp. 217-239). New York: Plenum.

Jacob, J. (1987). *Kinder in der Stadt. Freizeitaktivitäten, Mobilität und Raumwahrnehmung* [Children in the city: Leisure activities, mobility, and spatial perception]. Pfaffenweiler: Verlagsgesellschaft.

Johnson, L. C. (1987). The developmental implications of home environments. In C. S. Weinstein & T. G. David (Eds.), *Spaces for children: The built environment and child development* (pp. 139-157). New York: Plenum.

Keller, H. (1993). Entwicklungspsychologische Überlegungen zur Funktion von Kinderzimmern [Developmental considerations concerning the function of children's rooms]. In H. J. Harloff (Ed.), *Psychologie des Wohnungs- und Siedlungsbaus* (pp. 123-130). Göttingen: Verlag für Angewandte Psychologie.

Montada, L. (1995). Einführung in entwicklungspsychologisches Denken – Fragen, Konzepte, Perspektiven [Introduction to developmental thinking – Issues, concepts, perspectives]. In R. Oerter & L. Montada (Eds.), *Entwicklungspsychologie* (3rd completely revised and expanded ed.) (pp. 1-83). Weinheim, Germany: Psychologie Verlags Union.

Moore, R. C., & Young, D. (1978). Childhood outdoors: Toward a social ecology of the landscape. In I. Altman & J. F. Wohlwill (Eds.), *Children and the environment* (pp. 83-130). New York: Plenum.

Moshman, D., Glover, J. A., & Bruning, R. H. (1987). *Developmental psychology: A topical approach*. Boston: Little, Brown and Company.

Muchow, M., & Muchow, H. H. (1978). *Der Lebensraum des Großstadtkindes* [The life space of the urban child]. With an introduction by J. Zinnecker. Bensheim, Germany: päd. extra Buchverlag. (Original published 1935)

Oerter, R. (1995). Einführung in entwicklungspsychologisches Denken: Kultur, Ökologie und Entwicklung [Introduction to developmental thinking – Culture, ecology, and development]. In R. Oerter & L. Montada (Eds.), *Entwicklungspsychologie* (3rd completely revised and expanded ed.) (pp. 84-127). Weinheim, Germany: Psychologie Verlags Union.

Parke, R. D. (1978). Children's home environments – Social and cognitive effects. In I. Altman & J. F. Wohlwill (Eds.), *Children and the environment* (pp. 35-73). New York: Plenum.

Peek, R. (1995). *Kindliche Erfahrungsräume zwischen Familie und Öffentlichkeit. Eine empirische Untersuchung zum Stellenwert der Wohnumwelt im Alltag jüngerer Kinder* [Spaces for children's experience between family and the public realm]. Münster: Waxmann.

Proshansky, H. M., & Fabian, A. K. (1987). The development of place identity in the child. In
    C. S. Weinstein & T. G. David (Eds.), *Spaces for children: The built environment and child
    development* (pp. 21-40). New York: Plenum.

Rivlin, L. G. (1987). The neighborhood, personal identity, and group affiliations. In I. Altman &
    A. Wandersman (Eds.), *Neighborhood and community environments* (pp. 1-34). New York:
    Plenum.

Rutland, A., Custance, D., & Campbell, R. N. (1993). The ability of three-to four-year-old chil-
    dren to use a map in a large-scale environment. *Journal of Environmental Psychology, 13,*
    365-372.

Sachs, W. (1981). Geschwindigkeit und Lebenschancen. Über die Schwierigkeiten, in einer
    automobilisierten Umgebung aufzuwachsen [Speed and chances of survival: On the difficul-
    ties of growing up with motorized traffic]. *Vorgänge, 53,* 83.

Trautner, H. M. (1991-1992). *Lehrbuch der Entwicklungspsychologie* (Vols. 1-2). Göttingen:
    Hogrefe, Verlag für Psychologie.

Weinstein, C. S. (1987). Designing preschool classrooms to support development: Research and
    reflection. In C. S. Weinstein & T. G. David (Eds.), *Spaces for children: The built environ-
    ment and child development* (pp. 159-185). New York: Plenum.

Wicker, A. W. (1987). Behavior settings reconsidered: Temporal stages, resources, internal
    dynamics, context. In D. Stokols & I. Altman (Eds.), *Handbook of environmental psychology*
    (Vol. 1, pp. 613-653). New York: John Wiley and Sons.

Wohlwill, J. F., & Heft, H. (1987). The physical environment and the development of the child.
    In D. Stokols & I. Altman (Eds.), *Handbook of environmental psychology* (pp. 281-328). New
    York: John Wiley & Sons.

Wolfe, M. (1978). Childhood and privacy. In I. Altman & J. F. Wohlwill (Eds.), *Children and
    the environment* (pp. 175-222). New York: Plenum.

Wolfe, M., & Rivlin, L. G. (1987). The institutions in children's lives. In C. S. Weinstein &
    T. G. David (Eds.), *Spaces for children: The built environment and child development*
    (pp. 89-114). New York: Plenum.

Wright, H. F. (1967). *Recording and analyzing child behavior.* New York: Harper and Row.

Zeiher, H. (1983). Die vielen Räume der Kinder [The many spaces of children]. In U. Preuss-
    Lausitz, P. Büchner, M. Fischer-Kowalski, D. Geulen, M. E. Karsten, C. Kulke, U. Rabe-
    Kleberg, H. G. Rolff, B. Thunemeyer, Y. Schütze, P. Seidl, H. Zeiher, & P. Zimmermann
    (Eds.), *Kriegskinder, Konsumkinder und Krisenkinder. Zur Sozialgeschichte seit dem zweiten
    Weltkrieg.* Weinheim: Beltz.

Zeiher, J., & Zeiher, H. (1994). *Orte und Zeiten der Kinder. Soziales Leben im Alltag von
    Großstadtkindern* [Children's places and times: Everyday social life of urban children].
    Weinheim, Germany: Juventa.

Zinnecker, J. (1979). Straßensozialisation. Versuch, einen unterschätzten Lernort zu thematis-
    ieren [Socialization on the streets: An attempt to focus on an underrated place of learning].
    Zeitschrift für Pädagogik, 25, 726-746.

Toward a functional ecology of behavior and development: The legacy of Joachim F. Wohlwill

Harry Heft

Over the last two decades, collaborations across the areas of developmental psychology and environmental psychology have been producing a theoretical and empirical literature addressing relationships between children and the environments they live in. The present volume is evidence of some of this exciting and important work that has been occurring in psychology and related disciplines. It is fitting that the editors chose to dedicate this volume to the memory of Joachim F. Wohlwill (1928-1987) because the growth of interest in children's environments can be attributed, to a great extent, to his efforts.

In examining some of Wohlwill's contributions in this chapter, my goal is more prospective than retrospective. A reexamination of the career contributions of notable scientists, such as Wohlwill, provides an additional opportunity for their body of work to inform and instruct us. What I hope will be revealed through this consideration of Wohlwill's career is his distinctive *style of thinking and discovery*. As will be seen, this feature of his work should prove to be especially valuable as the second century of research in the behavioral and social sciences begins. Because Wohlwill's approach can only be revealed through examination of his activities in a variety of areas, and in the interest of a fairly comprehensive look at his contributions, it will be necessary for me to go beyond considering only his work relating to children's environments.[1]

The years spanning Wohlwill's career coincide with the beginnings of significant changes in the configuration of the behavioral and social sciences – indeed changes to which he contributed. His career, when considered most broadly, reflects some convergences among areas of human study that have been taking place in the second half of the 20th century. Thus, an appreciation of Wohlwill's work will help to reveal some of the important changes over the past several decades among the disciplines directed toward understanding human phenomena. These disciplinary convergences are more than mere academic maneuverings because it may be that only through intra- and interdisciplinary collaboration can the behavioral and social sciences adequately address pressing human and social needs. Consequently, Wohlwill's orientation as a scholar, as well as his commitment to the welfare of people and the environment, can serve as a model for the kind of stance that will enable us to bridge intra- and interdisciplinary boundaries and take on significant global problems.

1 Historical context

An examination of the evolution of academic disciplines over the past two centuries reveals a process of gradual structural change among the social sciences. The 19th century was a time during which new areas of scientific specialization proliferated. New disciplines, such as psychology, sociology, and anthropology (not to mention subdisciplines within each of these areas) were carved out from Enlightenment moral philosophy. The result was a differentiation of newly founded, distinctive disciplines devoted to the scientific study of human phenomena.

One legacy of these events for the present century was the establishment of distinct and rigid boundaries between disciplines, as well as numerous distinct subspecialities within disciplines. Commenting 20 years ago on this "fragmentation by specialization" within psychology alone, Jaynes (1973) wrote:

Psychology has not only been expanding, it has been separating. ... One problem has led to another, moving psychology to newer subsciences at an ever-increasing rate. And with each new field, thousands of research titles soon make their appearance. Psychology has diverged beyond the scope of any one specialist, shattering into brilliant fragments by its own progress and causing areas to lose touch with each other in their very success. (p. xi)

Movements counter to this trend started to appear, albeit hesitantly, about mid-century. Research stimulated in part by attempts of scientists to address applied and social problems led to the emergence of several interdisciplinary areas of study. Over the past three decades, these tentative gestures toward the blurring of inter- and intradisciplinary boundaries seem to have increased, if only in fits and starts. Now as psychologists prepare to enter the 21st century, it appears certain that a reconfiguration of the behavioral and social sciences is underway.

It is in the context of these changes that Wohlwill's scientific contributions can be best assessed. As will be seen, his primary strength was to bridge issues and areas of study that are often treated separately. His impressive and often astonishing skill at creatively synthesizing apparently distinct issues advanced the study of several behavioral and social science problems in important ways. In some cases, and especially in the early part of his career, these efforts were directed at problems within developmental psychology. Later, Wohlwill made important conceptual connections between subspecialities in psychology, and between psychology and other disciplines. His efforts at constructing these conceptual bridges reveals his prescience as a scholar.

Wohlwill's interdisciplinary vision is built upon a specific theoretical approach or, as characterized earlier, a distinctive style of thinking, rather than on a coherent, unified theoretical system. The following section of this chapter examines the attributes of this approach. After this analysis, his interdisciplinary contributions are considered somewhat more briefly, with particular attention to his contributions to the study of children and the environment. It may seem odd, in light of the significance I am claiming for his interdisciplinary contributions that more attention is paid here to Wohlwill's theoretical perspective. However, a central thesis of this chapter – and one with which I am confident Wohlwill would have agreed – is the Lewinian claim that only by having a carefully thought out theoretical base can one truly do significant, applied interdisciplinary work. As we will see, Wohlwill's interdisciplinary activities follow naturally from his theoretical stance.

One final introductory comment is needed regarding the motivational impulses behind his work. Wohlwill was an individual with an ardent and wide-ranging intellectual curiosity that, among other things, created possibilities for his seeing connections among diverse ideas. Furthermore, much of his activities derived from his social and ethical ideals, which included a deep concern for the quality of human existence, particularly for the living conditions experienced by children; a dedication to promoting equality and freedom of expression among people; and a commitment to environmental preservation and environmental aesthetics.

2   A functional ecology of behavior and development

The range of topics that Wohlwill examined over the course of his career is remarkable. A partial list would include perceptual development, cognitive development, environmental aesthetics, exploration, play, creativity, aesthetic preference, developmental methodologies, adaptation to environmental stressors, residential density, and environmental planning. The variety of this list might suggest that Wohlwill was a dabbler or a dilettante. But nothing could be farther from the truth, as an examination of any of his writings clearly demonstrates. The depth and the care with which he examined a problem was extraordinary. Moreover, although the diversity of his research interests might suggest otherwise, as does his willingness to draw upon a variety of psychological theories, a common thread runs through his various contributions in the form of a *theoretical perspective* that unifies much of the work. I will characterize this perspective, following his own terminology (Wohlwill, 1973a) as *a functional ecology of behavior and development*.

2.1   The influence of Brunswik's functionalism

The roots of Wohlwill's functional ecology lie in his academic training. His graduate work at the University of California at Berkeley was carried out initially under the tutelage of the psychologist Egon Brunswik; and although Brunswik died not long after Wohlwill arrived in Berkeley, his influence can be clearly seen in much of Wohlwill's subsequent work. For the purposes of this chapter, three interrelated aspects of Brunswik's approach need to be identified.[2]

First, Brunswik's primary area of interest was perception, and more than any other perceptual psychologist (with the exception of James Gibson), he argued that the study of psychological processes requires a detailed analysis of the environmental conditions confronting the organism. The behavior of organisms is assumed to be functionally related to environmental conditions, for organisms adjust to the characteristics of their surroundings. With this functionalist perspective, Brunswik (1956) was concerned that psychological research considers too limited a range of stimulus conditions, particularly within the constraints of laboratory-based designs. For this reason, it is uncertain whether a pattern of results obtained with respect to one set of conditions would be generalizable to other conditions. This concern led Brunswik to argue for the representative sampling of environmental conditions as a counterpart to a representative sampling of subjects in experimental psychology. Although Wohlwill and others recognized numerous difficulties in carrying out Brunswik's representative sampling method (Leary, 1987), he was deeply impressed by Brunswik's general plea that researchers need to take seriously the environmental conditions confronting perceivers. We will see this to be an enduring theme in Wohlwill's work.

Second, Brunswik (1956) proposed a functionalist theory that examined environmental features and organisms' behaviors in a more global or molar manner than was typical during the early years of behaviorism. It was common then, and in many quarters still is today, for psychologists to adopt molecular, physicalistic analyses of stimuli and physiological analyses of behavior. Brunswik, by contrast, viewed the adaptive relationship between the individual and the environment as an adjustment of the entire organism to molar, large-scale environmental features. Wohlwill, too, viewed the relation between individual and environment as a functionally adaptive process at a molar, rather than a molecular, level of analysis. At the same time, his approach differed from Brunswik's in important ways, not the least of which was that Wohlwill placed considerably more emphasis on the potential significance of organisms acting on the environment – a reflection of Piaget's subsequent influence on his thinking.

Third, Brunswik was trained in the logical positivist tradition, and accordingly, he refrained from including unobservables in his framework. Foremost, he wanted to avoid the error of reification, which is so common in psychology. This error involves giving real, concrete status to entities that, at least initially, were intended at best as hypothetical. Although Wohlwill's career path coincided with the rise of cognitive psychology – and, hence, the return of mentalistic constructs to psychological theory – and although he himself contributed in important ways to the study of cognitive development early in his career, Wohlwill, too, generally avoided reifying psychological constructs.

2.2 Attributes of Wohlwill's theoretical perspective

Each of these characteristics of Brunswik's position can be seen in Wohlwill's work to varying degrees. An examination of Wohlwill's writings reveals several attributes that in part reflect these Brunswikian themes. These attributes of Wohlwill's theoretical perspective are a focus on environmental conditions, objective specification of environmental variables, avoidance of reifying psychological variables, emphasis on the functional relationship between environment and behavior, dimensional conceptualization of environmental variables, and a process orientation with regard to behavioral variables. After examining in turn each of these attributes of Wohlwill's theoretical perspective, I will be better able to present his interdisciplinary contributions generally and his approach to children in environments specifically.

2.2.1 A focus on environmental conditions

A recurring theme in Wohlwill's work is the need to consider the role of stimulus conditions when attempting to understand psychological processes. This issue can be traced from his second publication (Wohlwill, 1958) through to one of his last (Wohlwill, 1988) published thirty years later, even though these papers address very different topics. Let us trace this thematic arc by briefly examining these two papers.

In the earlier article, Wohlwill helped sharpen a significant psychological debate concerning alternative approaches to the nature of perceptual learning. The question concerned the processes by which individuals come to perceive new aspects or features of the environment. The two sides of this debate were articulated by, on the one hand, Leo Postman (who incidentally was nominally Wohlwill's graduate school adviser after Brunswik's death), arguing that learning to perceive environmental features occurs through the formation of new stimulus-response associations; and James and Eleanor Gibson, on the other hand, arguing that perceptual learning entails the perceptual differentiation of new qualities or dimensions of stimulus information. Wohlwill concluded that a clearer understanding of the mediating, organismic processes in perceptual learning was needed, and although this goal was not consistent with the intent of the Gibsons' information-based differentiation theory, it could best be attained by first following their suggestion of "specifying what aspects [of the stimulus] are discriminated as a result of learning" (p. 294).

In the later paper (Wohlwill, 1988), he critically examined the claim that the decline in creativity and interest in drawing during the early childhood years is attributable to cognitive developmental processes and reflects an increased concern to make realistic-looking representations (Gardner & Winner, 1982). Instead, Wohlwill suggested that this decline results from young children's attempting to cope with a task (e.g., creating a drawing with crayons and paper) that is too unstructured relative to their cognitive development. He offered empirical support for this claim by teaching children to draw via computer programming, which gave them greater control over their productions than more conventional means.

In these two papers, which essentially bracket Wohlwill's thirty years of highly diverse scholarly work, we see a central theme in his writings, namely, that psychological processes are best understood in relationship to the particular environmental conditions confronting the individual. With this point of view, Wohlwill brought a critical eye to the evaluation of experimental designs, especially in developmental psychology. For example, in an early paper (Wohlwill & Wiener, 1964), he and his coauthor demonstrated that empirical claims of young children's insensitivity to the orientation of visual forms are attributable to the kinds of tasks presented to children rather than to some generalized developmental constraint. Thus, echoing Brunswik's perspective, Wohlwill asserted that because psychological processes are quite malleable, within the limits of developmental status, one cannot adequately understand an individual's behavior unless it is viewed in relation to the specific environmental or task conditions at hand as well as those previously experienced. His early papers on perceptual development further explored these ideas (Wohlwill, 1960, 1963a, 1965). Although many psychologists give lip service to the seemingly obvious points that environments vary in psychologically important ways, and that these variations are reflected in behavior, Wohlwill took these matters to heart.

2.2.2 Objective specification of environmental variables

Wohlwill's commitment to the analysis of environmental conditions was expressed most clearly and forcefully during the second decade of his career, which he devoted primarily to the nascent field of environmental psychology. His efforts to call colleagues' attention to the need for objective specification of environmental conditions in psychological analyses were expressed initially in his paper entitled "The physical environment: A problem for a psychology of stimulation" (Wohlwill, 1966a), which was included in a collection of papers, "Man's response to the physical environment," that he coedited for the *Journal of Social Issues* (Kates & Wohlwill, 1966) and then in his notable *American Psychologist* article, "The emerging discipline of environmental psychology" (Wohlwill, 1970a), a paper that gave this growing area much needed visibility and credibility.

His arguments about the manner in which environmental conditions are to be specified were especially distinctive and somewhat controversial. He pointed out the tendency among environment-behavior researchers to adopt the paradoxical position of discussing the environment solely in mentalistic terms (that is, only in terms of the individual's phenomenological experience of the environment) to the virtual neglect of an independent analysis of its properties. To take a simple example, in the early years of environment-behavior research, investigators were prone to have subjects evaluate some sample of environments (usually in still-photograph or slide format) with reference to bipolar affective scales, (e.g., happy-sad, stimulating-dull).

However, further steps were not typically taken to determine what features of the stimulus displays accounted for a particular pattern of affective evaluations. This tendency seemed to be especially curious to Wohlwill in that this research was conducted supposedly for the explicit purpose of learning more about individuals' reactions *to* environmental features, yet the environment, considered in any independent sense, was notably absent from the analyses.

This ironic situation was the basis for several critiques of research in environmental psychology – papers with such revealing titles as "The environment is not in the head!" (Wohlwill, 1974a), "In search of the environment in environmental cognition research" (Wohlwill, 1976a), and "Up from psychogeography!" (Wohlwill, n.d.). The first of these essays was without question one of his most influential and hotly debated environmental psychology papers. The fact that this essay was so widely read and discussed (e.g., Evans, 1980), even though it appeared in a source that was not readily accessible, points out that Wohlwill identified with characteristic insight a critical problem that this new field had to address.

In a previous assessment of Wohlwill's contributions to environmental psychology (Heft, 1988a), I discussed some of the reasons that he adopted this position. It will be useful to reexamine those reasons here. First, when researchers address environmental concerns through a focus on subjective experience and thus define the environment solely in those terms, they are begging the question when it comes to explaining the relation between environment and psychological outcomes. In order to understand, for example, how successfully knowledge of environmental layout (e.g., a cognitive map) mediates behavior such as way-finding in that environment, it is logically necessary to know the structure of the environment in question. Similarly, examining perceivers' affective responses to environments in relation to their own evaluations of characteristics of those environments – and in the absence of an independent description – makes it impossible to account for these affective responses in terms of stimulus characteristics.

Second, because such a mentalistic focus leads researchers away from efforts to link behavior to environmental conditions, it precludes attempts to address applied, environmentally relevant problems, which are presumably unique contributions that environment-behavior researchers can offer. In other words, an emphasis on the environment, admittedly construable in theoretically different ways, is the *raison d'etre* of the environment-behavior area; thus, a mentalistic approach would work against any lasting contribution that environmental psychology might make. As Wohlwill (1974a)[3] stated:

To the extent that we fail to give proper attention to the definition and specification of the environmental variables to which we wish to relate behavior, to that extent we will be in danger of building an environmental psychology on a foundation of quicksand.

This orientation has contributed in part to the gap between empirical research and environmental design that has continuously plagued the environment-behavior field.

The preceding two points address the methodological implications of environment-behavior researchers' mentalistic tendencies. Wohlwill also objected to these tendencies on theoretical grounds. Adopting Brunswik's notion of "vicarious mediation," he argued that two observable instances of the same environment-behavior relations can be psychologically mediated in different ways. In other words, there is no necessary reason why identical intervening psychological operations are needed to achieve particular behavioral adjustments under similar environmental conditions. Indeed, the fact that individuals can accomplish the same behavioral outcome in a variety of ways (e.g., avoiding an obstacle in one's path) is presumptive evidence against such a view. This argument stems from the functionalist perspective that psychological processes entail an on-going attempt of the organism to maintain an adaptive relation to environmental conditions. Once one recognizes the possibility of vicarious mediation of participating psychological operations, it becomes clear that an analysis of mentalistic processes cannot in principle provide information *about the environment*. Consequently, an exclusively subjectivist approach cannot be usefully applied to the study of environmentally relevant problems.

2.2.3   Avoidance of reifying psychological variables

Consistent with his efforts to specify environmental variables objectively, Wohlwill was wary of reifying mental constructs. This position may seem surprising considering that he was an active developmental psychologist during the rise of cognitivism in the 1960s and 1970s, and that he pursued postdoctoral study in Geneva with Jean Piaget. But in Wohlwill's developmental writings one finds only occasional mention of cognitive structures, and then most often in his collaborative papers. This omission seemed to be due to his caution about invoking unobservable, mental processes that could not be empirically grounded. For example, although he greatly admired Piaget's analysis of the developmentally changing structure of intellectual processes, Wohlwill (1962) was also somewhat critical of this work. He points out:

[An] objection that is bound to be raised concerns the nonoperational, and at times frankly mentalistic terms [e.g. schemata, operations, centrations] used by Piaget which may seem to leave his analysis devoid of empirical, and perhaps even of theoretical significance. . . . Admittedly, Piaget does little to dispel this impression; . . . rigorous, systematic efforts at tying the empirical phenomena to his constructs are generally eschewed in favor of ad-hoc and post-hoc arguments. (p. 206)

Wohlwill was interested instead in exploring "functional relationships between antecedent conditions and developmental change," the latter considered in terms of changing "modes of utilizing stimulus information" that are reflected in behavior

(Wohlwill, 1987b). As a result, much of Wohlwill's early developmental work can be viewed as an effort to develop methods that elucidate psychological structure and to effect a reapproachment between Piaget's structuralism and a functionalist psychology (G. Weiner, personal communication, June 30, 1994).

2.2.4 Emphasis on the functional relation between environment and behavior

The view that most strongly and consistently characterizes Wohlwill's work is the adaptive relation between the person and the environment. We have already seen that this functionalist orientation was held by Brunswik, and taken broadly, it is a view adopted by most behaviorally inclined psychologists. However, Wohlwill's functionalism had several distinctive features. (a) As already noted, he urged an analysis of the specific character of the environmental conditions confronting an individual. (b) He was concerned not only with the moment-to-moment functional adjustments that individuals make to environmental conditions, but most significant, he was interested in the long-term developmental consequences of experiencing particular environmental conditions. (c) He recognized that environments vary not only in the amounts of stimulation and the kinds of stimulus information they present to developing individuals but also in the kinds of opportunities for action that they afford. (d) He was interested in identifying the environmental correlates of motivational processes, such as exploration and play, and of aesthetic experiences. The first of these points was considered above, but the last three points require further discussion.

2.2.4.1 The effects of environmental conditions on child development

Although all developmentalists acknowledge the role of both environmental variables and organismic processes in development, many tend to emphasize one factor in this relation with only a passing glance at the other side of this duality. However, Wohlwill's developmental approach was emphatically interactive. He was distinctive among developmental psychologists for his emphasis on the environment; conversely, he was distinctive among environmental psychologists for his emphasis on developmental processes.

Early in his career, Wohlwill's primary focus was empirical examination and theoretical extension of Piagetian theory. Some of this work concerned Piaget's views on cognitive development (Flavell & Wohlwill, 1969; Wohlwill, 1962, 1963b, 1966b; Wohlwill & Wiener, 1964), but some of it addressed Piaget's less-examined views on perceptual development (Wohlwill, 1960, 1963a). Wohlwill's differences from 'main-stream' Piagetians are revealed in a monograph examining perceptual and cognition processes:

[Piaget] has frequently emphasized the continual interaction between external and internal forces. Nevertheless, his biological orientation and interest in structure leads him to take external factors for granted and to regard the form which this interaction takes as largely predetermined from the start. The only problem, then, is that of specifying the successive stages through which the organism passes; little leeway is left for differential manifestations of external conditions. (Wohlwill, 1962, p. 216)

Wohlwill attempted to complement Piaget's theory by more thoroughly exploring "functional relationships between antecedent condition and developmental change . . . [in order to promote] a more explicit understanding of the processes at work in the interaction between environmental and organismic forces" (p. 216). But when he turned to the literature of more environmentally oriented psychologists, Wohlwill found little guidance:

One of the criticisms that environmentalists have been prone to level against those who would attribute a functional role to hereditary variables in human behavior is that they represent little more than a cloak for our ignorance . . . Whether or not one accepts this argument . . . it ignores the fact that the standard equation, B = f (H, E) is in fact an equation of *two* unknowns. The fact is that environmentalists have been woefully unspecific in their reference to the role of the 'environment' as a determinant of behavior . . . (Wohlwill, 1973a, p. 90).

And in those instances when developmental psychologists did more than merely acknowledge the importance of environmental variables in very global terms, only social factors such as maternal influences were typically considered in any detail.

There were only a few research programs in psychology that attempted to examine physical environmental variables systematically. Wohlwill explored two of these programs – that of Donald Hebb and of Daniel Berlyne – as possible starting points for a functional ecology of behavior. With respect to their concern for environmental versus organismic factors, these approaches were in some ways the mirror image of Piaget's in that they gave little more than a nod to intrinsic organismic processes. (Berlyne's work has less direct relevance for developmental issues, and it will be examined more fully below.)

Hebb (1949) was among the most prominent of a group of psychologists who examined the role of early perceptual experience for development (for a review, see Hunt, 1961). His approach emphasized the effects of varying *levels* of stimulation on the individual, with low levels of stimulation early in life found to affect adversely the development of a variety of psychological processes. One implication of this research, conducted primarily in animal laboratory settings, was that increasing levels of stimulation were positively related to developmental outcomes.

Although Wohlwill thought that this Hebbian approach could be profitably applied to a functional analysis of environment and development, he questioned the implied positive monotonic relation between levels of stimulation and developmental outcomes. Drawing on work by Berlyne (1960), Fiske and Maddi (1961), and others, he suggested that both low levels and high levels of stimulation in the environments children experience might have adverse developmental effects, with inter-mediate levels being optimal (Wohlwill, 1974b, 1975). This Hebbian-inspired analy-sis was subsequently elaborated by drawing two further distinctions. First, the level or amount of stimulation (quite apart from its meaning) having an impact primarily through its arousal-producing properties can be distinguished from meaningful stimulus information, which in abundance may place excessive cognitive demands on the individual. Second, one can distinguish between background environmental conditions (e.g., noise, activity levels) and potential focal features (e.g., toys, books, language), supported by evidence that intensive background levels could interfere with learning processes directed at focal features (Heft, 1979, 1985; Wachs, 1979; Wohlwill, 1983a; Wohlwill & Heft, 1977a, 1987).

Reflecting his early Brunswikian training, Wohlwill asked us environmental and developmental psychologists to consider the variety of early environments that young children experience rather than limit our attention to urban and suburban middle and upper-middle class environments. In his writings he examined a broad range of research of children's environments in North America and in some of the more socially isolated regions of Europe (Wohlwill, 1983a; Wohlwill & Heft, 1987). He argued that developmental outcomes would vary in the context of differing envi-ronmental conditions and that those variations would be indicative of children's adaptation to those conditions.

His ideas with respect to these developmental questions directly or indirectly served as an impetus for a number of studies looking at the effects of levels of stimulation on development and surely contributed to a richer conceptualization of the nature of environments experienced by children (for reviews, see Weinstein & David, 1987; Wohlwill & Heft, 1987; Wohlwill & van Vliet--, 1985).

2.2.4.2   The environment as a source of stimulation and as an opportunity for activity

In the paper "The concept of experience: S or R?" Wohlwill (1973a) further clarified the concept of the environment in the developmental literature by contrasting the differences between approaches represented by the Hebbian framework and those represented by Piagetian theory. On the one hand, a framework such as Hebb's tends to view the organism as having environmental conditions imposed on it, ranging from low to high levels of stimulation or from an absence to a surfeit of meaningful stimulus information (Milgram, 1970). Alternatively, there is a group of theories, such as Piaget's, that attributes psychological development to changes in activity, overt or symbolic, as actions become coordinated to stimulus conditions. In the lat-ter, more organismic theories, the role of the environment in development is con-ceptualized as providing opportunities for behavior or engagement. From this per-spective, one critical property of the environment becomes the responsivity of the environment to the child's actions. Thus, in this comparative analysis Wohlwill identifies two broad types of properties of the environment that may have relevance for child development.

The implication of this analysis is that the environment may be beneficial to the child to the extent that it provides (a) opportunity for voluntary selection and exploration of environmental stimuli for passive exposure, so as to allow the child a measure of control over rate of incoming information . . . as well as the intensity, diversity, and novelty of stimulation to which he is exposed, and (b) feedback to the child's own behavior, to foster environmentally adaptive and responsive behavior, as a foundation on which eventual autonomous behavior can develop.

In his later writings, Wohlwill (1983a, 1984a; Wohlwill & Heft, 1987) began to consider alternatives that go beyond this dichotomy between imposed environmental stimulation and behavioral adjustment to environmental conditions. He began to explore the theoretical utility of the concept of *affordances* (E. Gibson, 1982; J. Gibson, 1979), which are functionally significant properties of the environment that are perceived through the active detection of stimulus information. Because affordances are functional properties of features specified by information detected through exploring or otherwise engaging the environment, they are neither passively imposed on the individual nor are they changes in the individual's patterns of action. They are mutual properties of the person-environment relation that are neither exclusively in the environment nor "in" the organism; they cut across the objective-subjective dichotomy (J.Gibson, 1979; Heft, 1980, 1989). While affordances have been studied experimentally by developmental psychologists, there have been few attempts to apply this concept to the problem of environmental description (Heft, 1988b; Heft, 1997). Characteristically, Wohlwill was less concerned with resolving differences among these various theoretical camps than with determining more pragmatically how the insights offered by theorists such as Hebb, Piaget, Held, and the Gibsons might help to clarify thinking about environmental contexts for development.

2.2.4.3 *Environmental correlates of affect and exploration*
For much of this century, experimental psychologists have attributed the motivational basis for behavior to organismic factors, such as biological needs or more molar intrinsic tendencies (e.g., curiosity, achievement motivation, cognitive balance or equilibrium). In the work of Berlyne (1960, 1971), Wohlwill found a systematic attempt at linking the causes of epistemically related behavior to stimulus conditions of the environment. Berlyne made the assumption that stimulus features possessed arousal-producing properties and that organisms function best within some intermediate range of physiological arousal. These stimulus features, or *collative properties*, are stimulus complexity, incongruity, ambiguity, surprisingness, and novelty. A positive, linear relationship was posited to exist between degree of collative property present and level of physiological arousal generated.

From this starting point, Berlyne identified two types of stimulus exploration. In *diversive exploration*, organisms attempt to maintain an optimal level of arousal, by seeking out features that will elevate arousal if it is too low or reduce it if too high. That is, diversive exploration occurs when organisms freely explore features of their environment, and the motivational basis for this exploratory behavior is maintenance of arousal. Alternatively, *specific exploration* typically occurs when organisms confronted by, or happening upon, a stimulus feature with arousal-producing collative properties inspect or otherwise become more familiar with this feature in an effort to return arousal to an optimal level. In these cases, unlike the free exploration associated with the diversive type, specific exploration is directed from the outset toward a particular environmental object.

Wohlwill was attracted to this framework because it identified potential environmental correlates of exploration and preference. With regard to perceptual preference, because affective or emotional experience seems to be related to minor departures from an intermediate level of arousal, collative properties of stimulus features might also predict affect. For the most part, Berlyne limited his examination of preference to the perceptual exploration of visual patterns. Wohlwill attempted to determine whether Berlyne's framework could be usefully applied to preference for environmental scenes and more generally to environmental aesthetics. Accordingly, he designed a number of experiments to assess the utility of environmental properties such as complexity and fittedness or harmony (a modification of Berlyne's incongruity variable) as stimulus predictors of environmental preference (Wohlwill, 1968, 1976b; Wohlwill & Harris, 1980). His early work on this issue helped to launch one of the more important and fruitful areas of environmental psychology research, resulting in findings that have implications for environmental planning and design (for reviews, see Kaplan & Kaplan, 1982, 1989; Nasar, 1989).[4]

In some of his last writings, Wohlwill (1987a, 1987b) extended this approach to the development of curiosity, exploration, and play. His focus on these topics was intended to contribute to growing efforts to broaden the range of developmental issues examined by psychologists. The developmental literature throughout the 1960s and 1970s was dominated by research on cognitive development. Commenting on this orientation, Wohlwill (1987a) wrote that one comes away from this research literature "with the impression that what children do mostly is cognize, *ad infinitum*" (p. 2). Two psychological functions that had received scant attention by comparison were exploration and play, in spite of their ubiquity in the daily activities of children. Wohlwill suggested that one of the reasons exploration and play had not been studied more extensively is that analysis of spontaneous activities such as these requires the researcher to give up control over the stimulus features made available to children. Modifications such as these, which permit the investigation of spontaneous and self-directed actions, often go beyond usual experimental strictures. He wrote:

If we are to do justice to exploratory behavior in all of its facets, . . . it is clearly essential that we study the individual as he or she is engaged in such behavior – that is, without predetermining the stimuli to which the person will attend. It seems that psychologists have felt uncomfortable about undertaking such study, in part, undoubtedly, because it involves giving up a degree of control over behavior that the presentation of the pre-programmed series of stimuli affords. (Wohlwill, 1981)

His sympathies with studying children's exploration and play in everyday living environments are clear from this passage. In a related vein, researchers who have examined exploration and play did not usually differentiate among the various activities that are collectively called exploration because attention seems to have been limited primarily to behaviors that could be controlled by the experimenter.

In an effort to broaden the conceptualization of exploration, Wohlwill (1981, 1984a, 1987b) suggested two conceptual differentiations in considering exploratory behavior. The first is between (a) exploration involving free search of the environment in order to become familiar with its layout and its features, and (b) exploration directed at an object or feature with which one is confronted. This differentiation is similar to that between diversive exploration and specific exploration (see above), although here diversive exploration is viewed as entailing more self-directed search than Berlyne allowed. This self-directed exploration could be assessed by measures such as extent of exploration and pattern of movement through the environment. The second differentiation concerns two forms of exploration directed at a specific environmental feature that one has encountered: (a) inspective exploration refers to activities, such as information extraction, that lead to learning more about the feature in question, one result of this activity being perhaps the reduction of cognitive uncertainty; and (b) affective exploration refers to activities directed at familiar objects for the primary purpose of deriving affective satisfaction from interacting with them. In his analysis, Wohlwill suggested ways in which these modes of exploration could be differentiated with respect to behaviors of the child.

In what was perhaps his most innovative endeavor in this area, Wohlwill attempted to integrate these two exploratory processes by viewing them as successive phases of a temporal course of exploration. This behavioral circuit begins with diversive exploration leading to some environmental feature, continues with inspective exploration to reduce uncertainty, and concludes with affective exploration primarily for aesthetic pleasure. He was not suggesting that each phase necessarily occurred on every occasion. Indeed, depending on the situation encountered, some phases or even only one phase may occur. But by conceptualizing each form of exploration along a temporal dimension, one may be better able to conceptualize how these activities are functionally linked. Also, individual differences could be identified with respect to the dominant phase of exploration engaged in by an individual.

One direction in which Wohlwill seemed to be headed with this work was that of developing a framework that would integrate these modes of exploration with the development of imaginative and creative activity. The very beginnings of this work can be seen in Wohlwill's pioneering research of children's creativity using computer graphics (Wohlwill, 1988; Wohlwill & Wills, 1988). In addition, the writings by Wohlwill in the latter years of his career seem to reflect a growing interest in individual differences in exploration and play.

2.2.5 Dimensional conceptualization of environmental variables

Having discussed three ways in which Wohlwill addressed the functional relation between environment and behavior, I return to a consideration of two final and related attributes of his overall approach. A style of analysis that recurs in many of Wohlwill's writings is that of conceptualizing environmental variables along continuous dimensions. An example of this approach can be seen in his aesthetics research, in which he gravitated toward the study of stimulus variables such as complexity and fittingness (incongruity) that could be conceptualized dimensionally, varying from low to high levels of each property. This approach as applied to environmental variables has several positive features. Positing the existence of a particular stimulus dimension that increases incrementally, such as complexity, permits one to obtain ratings from different perceivers of an environmental scene along this dimension. Those ratings can then be examined for degree of interperceiver agreement, and positive intercorrelations can be taken as an objective indicator of the stimulus property in some relative amount. In other words, dimensional analysis of the environment provides one avenue for developing an objective description of the environment (Wohlwill & Kohn, 1976). In addition, having identified a way of differentiating environmental scenes along some dimension, one can selectively present a sample of these scenes to perceivers in order to explore functional environment-person relations (Wohlwill & Harris, 1980).

Thus, conceptualizing the environment dimensionally facilitates the sort of functional analysis Wohlwill sought. If environmental conditions and behavior are functionally related, then predictable changes in environmental conditions along a stimulus continuum should be accompanied by changes in behavior along some response dimension. A clear and important instance of Wohlwill's use of this functional approach is his insightful application of Helson's (1964) adaptation-level theory to several issues in environmental psychology (Wohlwill, 1975). An example of his creative use of adaptation-level theory is an impressive study on the effect that the size of a prior residential environment has on migrants' evaluation of their new environment (Wohlwill & Kohn, 1973).

2.2.6 Process orientation

The immediately preceding comments concerning dimensional analysis of environmental variables have their counterpart in the process orientation that is characteristic of much of Wohlwill's analysis of psychological variables, an orientation that grows out of his developmental perspective. This process perspective is firmly advocated in his book, *The Study of Behavioral Development* (1973b). Its thesis is that developmental psychology requires methodologies revealing developmental *change*. Consequently, importing methods wholesale from experimental psychology that do not capture change over time may obscure the processes most central to the developmental domain (see also Wohlwill, 1970b, 1970c).

This process-oriented conceptualization of psychological variables contributed directly to the conceptual integration that characterized much of his writings. For example, in an interesting monograph, Wohlwill (1962) conceptualized perceptual and inferential processes as the poles of a continuum along which one can trace developmental changes in the child's reliance on stimulus information for cognition. Thus, as one moves from the predominance of perceptual processes to that of inferential processes, there is a decrease in the need for informational redundancy, and an increase in the tolerable amounts of irrelevant information and the spatial and temporal separation (contiguity) of information. The relative dependence on perception or inference, and the associated stimulus conditions that support them, was posited to change developmentally.

A second example, which I have examined above, is Wohlwill's proposal to link exploration and play functionally along a temporal dimension. In this case as well as the preceding one, he saw this dimension as having developmental implications, with cognitive development leading to an increase in imaginative play relative to object exploration. Wohlwill (1980a) also examined the temporal course of aesthetic experience, and in an innovative application of this process approach, he applied developmental methodology to examine the impact over time that an introduction of amenities in natural recreation areas has on outdoor recreational behavior (Wohlwill & Heft, 1977b).

In general, it can be seen that Wohlwill's application of a dimensional conceptualization to environmental variables and a process conceptualization of psychological variables contributed directly to the conceptual integration that characterized much of his writings and, hence, was well suited to his functionalist goals.

2.3 Summary

Wohlwill's functional ecology of behavior and development is characterized by a focus on an objective specification of the environment in order to contribute to an understanding of the functional relation between dimensions of the environment and developmentally significant behavioral processes. In attempting to elaborate on such a functional analysis, he explored the long-term effects of experiencing particular environmental conditions, examined the environment as a source of stimulation and of opportunities for action, and considered the stimulus properties of the environment as a basis for motivation and affect.

3 Bridging boundaries: Wohlwill's integrative vision

In the process of examining the primary characteristics of Wohlwill's perspective, I have noted only in passing several ways in which he succeeded in bridging intra- and interdisciplinary boundaries. Having detailed his theoretical approach, I am now in a position to look more closely at these contributions.

3.1 Understanding person-environment relations by crossing theoretical and disciplinary boundaries

In order to develop a functional ecology of behavior and development, Wohlwill turned to a variety of sources. Within psychology, these sources included the neobehaviorist work of Berlyne and ecological theories of Gibson and of Barker. For example, in his work on environmental perception and aesthetics, Wohlwill drew heavily on the ideas of Berlyne. However, when offering an analysis of the stimulus information that differentiates features of the natural environment from those of the built environment, Wohlwill (1983b) based his discussion largely on Gibsonian considerations of stimulus information. Further, he fruitfully applied Helson's (1964) adaptation-level theory and Fiske and Maddi's (1961) analysis of sensory experience in several treatments of individuals' reactions to environmental conditions (Wohlwill, 1974b, 1975).

Wohlwill was certainly aware of the significant theoretical differences among these positions, but he defended his synthetic approach:

> Some may consider this juxtaposition of assorted . . . theories hopelessly eclectic, and unlikely to lead to significant advances at a conceptual level. If we recognize, however, that our task is not to build a new theory of behavior, but rather to arrive at as complete an account as possible of the varied forms of environmental-behavioral interrelationships, then such a synthetic strategy appears defensible. (Wohlwill & Kohn, 1973)

For this reason, in his writings he also drew upon relevant research literature in architecture, landscape architecture, planning, and environmental law, and in so doing, did much to bring this work to the attention of psychologists.

On the side of the organism, he seemed less concerned with finding support for particular theories of perception and cognition than finding a perspective that would contribute to his functionalist goals. Thus, Wohlwill avoided much comment on particular mechanisms of perception and cognition. Instead, he was content to view these processes as differing "modes of utilizing stimulus information" that are constrained by an individual's developmental level and influenced by current stimulus conditions. Even in his use of organismic-based concepts such as uncertainty, conflict, and adaptation level, Wohlwill employed these notions as vehicles for making predictions about systematic functional relations between environment and behavior. Thus, he was especially interested in accounts of perception, cognition, and motivation that contributed to a clearer understanding of environment-organism relations, and accordingly, he was drawn to those approaches that might help him achieve these ends.

3.2   The study of children in the environment as an interdisciplinary endeavor

Wohlwill's interest in the quality of children's environments necessarily led him to consider a range of disciplines and subdisciplines in which an interest is taken in this topic. In several papers and in conference settings, he encouraged a convergence of developmental and environmental psychology (e.g., Wohlwill, 1980b, Wohlwill & Heft, 1977a, 1987). For evidence of the impact of his efforts toward such a convergence, one needs to look no farther than the present volume.

In trying to gain a better understanding of the relation between environmental conditions and developmental change, Wohlwill examined the writings of a wide variety of psychologists and nonpsychologists who offered different ways of thinking about the environment. He valued the activity of numerous nontraditional psychologists who studied the relation between environment and behavior. For example, he held in high regard the work of ecological psychologists such as Barker, Schoggen, and Wright (Barker, 1968; Barker & Schoggen, 1973; Barker & Wright, 1955), who identified higher-order, extraindividual structures in the environment (i.e., behavior settings) that influence behavior in important ways. He integrated into his writings the work of geographers, sociologists, and anthropologists who explored environment-development issues at a more macrolevel of analysis than do most psychologists. He also looked toward and encouraged the work of educators and architects who had interests in the design of institutional settings for children, such as day-care centers and schools (Heft & Wohlwill, 1987; Weinstein & David, 1987; Wohlwill & Heft, 1987; Wohlwill & van Vliet--, 1985).

Approaching developmental issues from an interdisciplinary, environmental perspective can lead one to reformulate and extend empirical questions in interesting and potentially significant ways. For example, consider again Wohlwill's distinction between viewing the environment as a source of stimulation and seeing the environment as a source of opportunities for action. As mentioned previously, the conceptualization of the environment as a source of sensory stimulation and stimulus information had its origins in laboratory research. Wohlwill actively promoted the extension of this approach to analysis of children's home environments. In addition, this formulation of environmental effects could be extended more broadly to consider the possible consequences of growing up in cities or in geographically remote or culturally isolated settings. With respect to the latter locales, would relative social isolation be reflected in developmental outcomes, with amount and diversity of stimulation acting as the predictive variables? Or do the pervasive effects of media and mass-marketing, at least in mainstream segments of Western countries, tend to homogenize experience and thereby minimize such differences? Formulating the question of effects of sensory stimulation in this way led Wohlwill to draw on a broad research literature in his writings. He explored some of these questions in a preliminary manner by conducting research among the Amish, a culturally isolated group in the United States.

The view of the environment as a source of opportunities for developmentally significant actions is reflected in the works of researchers examining such variables as the availability of responsive objects and the opportunities for the child to freely explore in the home (e.g., Wachs, 1979) and to engage playground features (Ostro, 1977). These same questions can be applied to the environment in broad terms. What is the qualitative nature of environmental features in the neighborhood, within the child's territorial range? Are there impediments, either environmental or social, to the child's gaining access to these resources? For example, do busy roads act as a barrier to a child's mobility? Alternatively, are resources that facilitate extensive exploration of the environment, such as safe, inexpensive mass transportation, available to the child? Wohlwill's writings in environment and development are rich with such questions. Although these issues are potentially significant from a psychological standpoint, they also incorporate economics, sociology, communication, and design considerations.

Interdisciplinary activities are notorious for the impasses that grow out of differing conceptual frameworks, with their specialized terminology and diverging goals sometimes held by the participants. Wohlwill's efforts clearly indicate that progress in addressing significant human problems, such as the quality of environments for children, depends on researchers going beyond the parochialism of adhering to concepts and methods only within one's own academic discipline or subdiscipline.

Beyond his own theoretical and empirical work, Wohlwill as an editor concretely promoted his interdisciplinary approach to developmental issues. In the third volume of the *Human Behavior and Environment* series, which was devoted to "Children and the Environment" (Altman & Wohlwill, 1978), he assembled chapters by developmental psychologists as well as environmental psychologists and designers. The book *Habitats for Children: The Impacts of Density* (Wohlwill & van Vliet--, 1985) was the product of an interdisciplinary study group he organized to address the implications for child development of environmental conditions relating to residential density. Further, his generous efforts in resurrecting the pioneering research of Martha Muchow, who in the 1920s studied children's behavior in an urban environment, are yet a further indication of his commitment to the study of children's environments (Wohlwill, 1985a, 1985b). This work is especially poignant since

Muchow's tragic death in Hamburg is tied to the same set of political events of pre-World War II Germany that caused Wohlwill's family to flee this city of his birth.

3.3   Environmental quality and interdisciplinary research

Wohlwill's deep personal concerns about environmental quality led him to topics typically considered to be beyond the disciplinary boundaries of psychology. His research program in environmental aesthetics not only addressed several intriguing theoretical questions relating to perception and affect but also contributed to a growing research literature that offers an empirical basis for environmental decision-making (Wohlwill, 1976b), as did his research on development in natural recreation areas (Wohlwill & Heft, 1977b).

Wohlwill's (1979) investigation of attitudes toward the environment and related sociopolitical values, as these attitudes are reflected in voting patterns, is further evidence of how an issue of great personal concern to him, such as environmental quality, could shape his research activity. Although attitudinal research and political psychology were outside of the usual province of his psychological activity, he was willing to explore these issues if they might shed some light on important social and environmental questions.

Wohlwill saw psychological factors, such as attitudes, as one of a constellation of variables that play a role in policy-making concerning land use and environmental quality. Addressing an audience of landuse planners and policy-makers he wrote:

These psychological questions are not at the heart of the problem of land use in the larger, environmental sense. They do, however, merit a place in a comprehensive account of the system of forces that shape our use of the land. (Wohlwill, 1978, p. 36)

Thus, he not only attempted to broaden the purview of psychology, but also tried to convince nonpsychologists to incorporate psychological concepts and research into their work (also see Wohlwill, 1984b).

3.4   Psychology and the arts

Wohlwill's work in the psychology of the arts reveals yet another side of his inter-disciplinary orientation. In brief, his interest in perception led him to consider several problems concerning aesthetics in the arts and architecture. One issue that he found particularly interesting was how to reconcile the apparently competing claims that positive aesthetic experience is derived from perceived order, balance, harmony, congruity on the one hand, and from complexity, variety, diversity on the other (Wohlwill, 1976b, 1980a). In exploring this issue, he struggled with what he saw as some of the limitations of physicalistic analyses of variables such as complexity and incongruity. Also, as discussed previously, developmental aspects of aesthetic appreciation and aesthetic expression deeply interested him (Wohlwill, 1985c).

3.5 Interdisciplinary commitment and action

One can see Wohlwill's commitment to interdisciplinary work perhaps most concretely in his career choices. He left a prestigious developmental position at Clark University to join a fledgling program in environment-behavior studies at The Pennsylvania State University. In doing so, he expressed his interdisciplinary commitment in a very tangible way and in the process lent much credibility to environmental psychology in particular and to interdisciplinary endeavors generally.

This commitment can also be seen in his numerous projects as an editor, from his involvement in the seminal series *Human Behavior and the Environment*, which he initiated with Irwin Altman, coediting the first seven volumes, to several interdisciplinary volumes that he coedited (Kates & Wohlwill, 1966; Wohlwill & Carson, 1972; Wohlwill & van Vliet--, 1985; Wohlwill & Weisman, 1981). His participation in numerous committees and task forces, such as the U.N."Man-in-the-Biosphere" program, further attests to his active involvement as a scientist in efforts to address social and environmental problems.

4 Concluding remarks

Joachim Wohlwill possessed a breadth of intellectual vision that is unusual among scientists trained within a specific discipline. His interdisciplinary work was marked by a keen skill at synthesis, one that enabled him to recognize fruitful conceptual connections across diverse areas of scholarship. This interdisciplinary orientation was attributable, in part, to the fact that many of the problems to which he was intellectually committed and which grew out of his work toward a functional ecology of behavior could not be adequately addressed within the boundaries of a single discipline or subdiscipline.

Probing more deeply to understand the basis for his intellectual commitments, one finds that they often were derived from his humane concern for pressing societal and environmental problems, such as the provision of psychologically adequate environments for children and the preservation of environmental quality. For Wohlwill was a scientist who hoped that his work, and the work of behavioral and social science generally, would contribute in positive ways to the future well-being of humankind and nature. He directly participated in these efforts through his own writing and research and in his role as a teacher, helping prepare a significant number of students to work in both academic and applied settings. His life's work stands as an inspiration for social scientists preparing to enter the 21st century.

Acknowledgements

I am very grateful to the following individuals for their insightful criticisms and helpful suggestions on an earlier draft of this chapter: Louise Chawla, Gary Evans, Jack Nasar, Ted Wachs, Seymour Wapner, Jerry Weiner, and Fay Wohlwill.

Notes

1 Other discussions of Wohlwill's contributions are reflected in an edited volume of papers prepared for a conference held in his honor (Downs, Liben, & Palermo, 1991), a special issue of *Children's Environments Quarterly* (Wapner, 1988) dedicated to his work and based on an American Psychological Association symposium in his honor, an essay reviewing his contributions to environmental psychology (Heft, 1988a), eulogistic reflections from a former colleague (Wapner, 1987), and a collection of testimonials (Center for the Study of Child and Adolescent Development, 1989).

2 For a detailed examination of Brunswik's work, see Hammond (1966) and Leary (1987).

3 Here, and in other places in this chapter, page citations are not provided because I was often working from preprints rather than from the papers as they appeared eventually in print.

4 I cannot resist describing what I experienced as one of Wohlwill's more ingenious experimental arrangements, which was devised in the early 1970s, thus pre-dating by several decades advances in simulation such as virtual reality. Berlyne's typical measure of specific exploration was amount of voluntary exploration time. However, photographs or slides of scenes are used in all environmental aesthetic research. Thus, unlike everyday experience, where environments surround the perceiver, the experimental situation is one in which subjects view a delimited, bounded scene. In order to present environmental scenes in more "ecologically valid" ways (apologies to Brunswik here), slides of scenes were systematically taken by sequentially rotating a still camera on a tripod through 360 degrees. Wohlwill then constructed a rotunda or a "theatre in the round," and these slides were back-projected onto a series of panels adjoined in a circular configuration. A subject sitting in a swivel chair in the center of this rotunda could then freely turn to look in any direction at a scene that surrounded him or her. As the subject faced in any particular direction, microswitches were tripped causing automatic timers to record duration of viewing. The stimulus properties of each panel could then be compared to amount of voluntary exploration. Plans were also made to take the swivel chair – timer arrangement to various sites in the field to record exploration time there as well. To my knowledge, the results of this preliminary work were never published.

References

Altman, I., & Wohlwill, J. F. (Eds). (1978). *Human behavior and the environment: Vol. 3, Children and the environment.* New York: Plenum.

Barker, R. G. (1968). *Ecological psychology: Concepts and methods for studying the environment of human behavior.* Stanford, CA: Stanford University Press.

Barker, R. G., & Schoggen, P. (1973). *Qualities of community life.* San Francisco: Jossey-Bass.

Barker, R. G., & Wright, H. F. (1955). *Midwest and its children.* Evanston, IL: Row, Peterson, & Co.

Berlyne, D. E. (1960). *Conflict, arousal, and curiosity.* New York: McGraw-Hill.

Berlyne, D. E. (1971). *Aesthetics and psychobiology.* New York: Appleton-Century Crofts.

Brunswik, E. (1956). *Perception and the representative design of psychological experiments.* Berkeley, CA: University of California Press.

Center for the Study of Child and Adolescent Development (1989). *Joachim F. Wohlwill (1928-1987): Tributes and memories.* (Technical Report Series, No. 4). State College, PA: Pennsylvania State University.

Downs, R. M., Liben, L. S., & Palermo, D. S. (Eds.) (1991). *Visions of aesthetics, the environment, & development: The legacy of Joachim F. Wohlwill.* Hillsdale, NJ: Lawrence Erlbaum.

Evans, G. (1980). Environmental cognition. *Psychological Bulletin, 88*, 259-267.

Flavell, J. H., & Wohlwill, J. F. (1969). Formal and functional aspects of cognitive development. In D. Elkind & J. H. Flavell (Eds.), *Studies in cognitive development: Essays in honor of Jean Piaget* (pp. 67-120). New York: Oxford University Press.

Fiske, D. W., & Maddi, S. R. (1961). A conceptual framework. In D. W. Fiske & S. R. Maddi (Eds.), *Functions of varied experience* (pp. 11-56). Homewood, IL: Dorsey Press.

Gardner, H., & Winner, E. (1982). First intimations of artistry. In S. Straus (Ed.), *U-shaped behavioral growth* (pp. 147-168). New York: Academic Press.

Gibson, E. J. (1982). The concept of affordances in development: The renaissance of functionalism. In W. A. Collins (Ed.), *Minnesota symposium on child psychology: Vol. 15. The concept of development* (pp. 55-81). Hillsdale, NJ: Erlbaum.

Gibson, J. J. (1979). *The ecological approach to visual perception.* Boston: Houghton-Mifflin.

Hammond, K. R. (Ed.) (1966). *The psychology of Egon Brunswik.* New York: Holt, Rhinehart and Winston.

Hebb, D. O. (1949). *The organization of behavior.* New York: John Wiley.

Heft, H. (1979). Background and focal environmental conditions of the home and attention in young children. *Journal of Applied Social Psychology, 9*, 47-69.

Heft, H. (1980). What Heil is missing in Gibson: A reply. *Journal for the Theory of Social Behavior, 10*, 187-194.

Heft, H. (1985). High residential density and perceptual-cognitive development: An examination of the effects of crowding and noise in the home. In J. F. Wohlwill & W. van Vliet-- (Eds.), *Habitats for children: Impacts of density* (pp. 39-75). Hillsdale, NJ: Erlbaum.

Heft, H. (1988a). Joachim F. Wohlwill (1928-1987): His contributions to the emerging discipline of environmental psychology. *Environment and Behavior, 20*, 259-275.

Heft, H. (1988b). Affordances of children's environments: A functional approach to environmental description. *Children's Environments Quarterly, 5*, 29-37.

Heft, H. (1989). Affordances and the body: An intentional analysis of Gibson's ecological approach to visual perception. *Journal for the Theory of Social Behavior, 19*, 1-19.

Heft, H. (1997). The relevance of Gibson's ecological approach to perception for environment-behavior studies. In G. T. Moore & R. W. Marans (Eds.), *Advances in environment, behavior, and design* (Vol. 4, pp. 71-108). New York: Plenum.

Heft, H., & Wohlwill, J. F. (1987). Environmental cognition in children. In D. Stokols & I. Altman (Eds.), *Handbook of environmental psychology* (pp. 175-203). New York: John Wiley.

Helson, H. (1964). *Adaptation-level theory*. New York: Harper & Row.

Hunt, J. McV. (1961). *Intelligence and experience*. New York: Ronald Press.

Jaynes, J. (1973). Introduction: The study of the history of psychology. In M. Henle, J. Jaynes, & J. J. Sullivan (Eds.), *Historical conceptions of psychology*. New York: Springer.

Kaplan, S., & Kaplan, R. (1982). *Cognition and environment: Functioning in an uncertain world*. New York: Praeger.

Kaplan, S., & Kaplan, R. (1989). *The experience of nature: A psychological perspective*. New York: Cambridge University Press.

Kates, R. W., & Wohlwill, J. F. (Eds.) (1966). Man's response to the physical environment. *Journal of Social Issues, 22*.

Leary, D. E. (1987). From Act Psychology to Probabilistic Functionalism: The place of Egon Brunswik in the history of psychology. In M. G. Ash & W. R. Woodward (Eds.), *Psychology in twentieth century thought and society* (pp. 115-142). New York: Cambridge University Press.

Milgram, S. (1970). The experience of living in cities. *Science, 167*, 1461-1468.

Nasar, J. L. (Ed.) (1989). *Environmental aesthetics*. Cambridge: Cambridge University Press.

Ostro, J. M. (1977). *An examination of the indoor and outdoor play patterns of urban and rural preschool children*. Unpublished doctoral dissertation, Pennsylvania State University, University Park.

Wachs, T. D. (1979). Proximal experience and early cognitive intellectual development: The physical environment. *Merrill-Palmer Quarterly, 25*, 3-41.

Wapner, S. (1987). Joachim F. Wohlwill: 1928-1987. *Journal of Environmental Psychology, 7*, 209-213.

Wapner, S. (Ed.) (1988). Environmental psychology research: Essays in honor of Joachim Wohlwill [Special issue]. *Children's Environments Quarterly, 5(3)*.

Weinstein, C. S., & David, T. G. (Eds.) (1987). *Spaces for children: The built environment and child development*. New York: Plenum.

Wohlwill, J. F. (1958). The definition and analysis of perceptual learning. *Psychological Review, 65*, 283-295.

Wohlwill, J. F. (1960). Developmental studies of perception. *Psychological Bulletin, 57*, 249-288.

Wohlwill, J. F. (1962). From perception to inference: A dimension of cognitive development. In W. Kessen & C. Kuhlman (Eds.), *Thought in the young child, Monographs of the Society for Research in Child Development, 27*, 87-112. [Reprinted in J. Eliot (Ed.) (1971), Human development and cognitive processes (pp. 197-225). New York: Holt, Rhinehart and Winston.]

Wohlwill, J. F. (1963a). The development of "overconstancy" in space perception. *Advances in Child Development and Behavior, 1*, 265-312.

Wohlwill, J. F. (1963b). Piaget's system as a source of empirical research. *Merrill-Palmer Quarterly, 9*, 253-262.

Wohlwill, J. F. (1965). Texture of the stimulus field and age as variables in the perception of relative distance. *Journal of Experimental Child Psychology, 2*, 163-177.

Wohlwill, J. F. (1966a). The physical environment: A problem for a psychology of stimulation. *Journal of Social Issues, 22*, 29-38.

Wohlwill, J. F. (1966b). Piaget's theory of the development of intelligence in the concrete-operations period. In M. Garrison, Jr. (Ed.), Cognitive models and development in mental retardation [Monograph]. *American Journal of Mental Deficiency, 70*, 57-78.

Wohlwill, J. F. (1968). Amount of stimulus exploration and preference as differential functions of stimulus complexity. *Perception and Psychophysics, 4*, 307-312.

Wohlwill, J. F. (1970a). The emerging discipline of environmental psychology. *American Psychologist, 25*, 303-312.

Wohlwill, J. F. (1970b). The age variable in psychological research. *Psychological review, 77*, 49-64.

Wohlwill, J. F. (1970c). Methodology and research strategy in the study of developmental change. In L. R. Goulet & P. B. Baltes (Eds.), *Life-span developmental psychology* (pp. 150-191). New York: Academic press.

Wohlwill, J. F. (1973a). The concept of experience: S or R? *Human Development, 16*, 90-107.

Wohlwill, J. F. (1973b). *The study of behavioral development.* New York: Academic press.

Wohlwill, J. F. (1974a). The environment is not in the head! In W. F. E. Preiser (Ed.), *Environmental Design Research* (Vol. 1, pp. 166-181). Stroudsburg, PA: Dowden, Hutchinson, & Ross.

Wohlwill, J. F. (1974b). Human adaptation to levels of environmental stimulation. *Human Ecology, 2*, 127-147.

Wohlwill, J. F. (1975). Behavioral response and adaptation to environmental stimulation. In D. A. Damon (Ed.), *Physiological anthropology* (pp. 295-334). New York: Oxford University Press.

Wohlwill, J. F. (1976a) In search of the environment in environmental cognition research. In G. T. Moore & R. G. Golledge (Eds.). *Environmental knowing* (pp. 385-392). Stroudsburg, PA: Dowden, Hutchinson, & Ross.

Wohlwill, J. F. (1976b). Environmental aesthetics: The environment as a source of affect. In I. Altman & J. F. Wohlwill (Eds.), *Human behavior and environment* (Vol. 1, pp. 37-86). New York: Plenum.

Wohlwill, J. F. (1978). A psychologist looks at land use. *Environmental Review, 3*, 34-37.

Wohlwill, J. F. (1979). The social and political matrix of environmental attitudes: An analysis of the vote on the California Coastal Zone Regulation Act. *Environment and Behavior, 11*, 71-85.

Wohlwill, J. F. (1980a). The place of order and uncertainty in art and environmental aesthetics. *Motivation and Emotion, 4*, 133-142.

Wohlwill, J. F. (1980b). The confluence of environmental and developmental psychology: Signpost to an ecology of development? *Human Development, 23*, 354-358.

Wohlwill, J. F. (1981). Explorations into exploratory behavior: A reexamination of a problematical dichotomy. In H. Day (Ed.), *Advances in intrinsic motivation and aesthetics.* (pp. 341-364). New York: Plenum.

Wohlwill, J. F. (1983a). Physical and social environment as factors in development. In D. Magnusson & W. Allen (Eds.), *Human development: An interactional perspective* (pp. 111-129). New York: Academic Press.

Wohlwill, J. F. (1983b). The concept of nature: A psychologist's view. In I. Altman & J. F. Wohlwill (Eds.), *Human behavior and environment: Vol. 6. Behavior and the natural environment* (pp. 5-37). New York: Plenum.

Wohlwill, J. F. (1984a). Relationships between exploration and play. In T. D. Yawkey & A. D. Pellegrini (Eds.), *Child's play: Developmental and applied* (pp. 143-170). Hillsdale, NJ: Erlbaum.

Wohlwill, J. F. (1984b). Psychology and the environmental disciplines. In M. H. Bornstein (Ed.), *Psychology and its allied disciplines: Vol. 2. The social sciences* (pp. 123-161). Hillsdale, NJ: Lawrence Erlbaum.

Wohlwill, J. F. (1985a). Martha Muchow and the life-space of the urban child. *Human Development, 28*, 200-209.

Wohlwill, J. F. (1985b). Martha Muchow, 1892-1933: A tribute to a pioneer in environmental child psychology. In G. Eckardt, W. Bringmann, & L. Sprung (Eds.) *Contributions to a history of developmental psychology* (pp. 367-374). West Berlin: Mouton-de Gruyter.

Wohlwill, J. F. (1985c). The Gardner-Winner view of children's visual-artistic development: Overview, assessment, and critique. *Visual Arts Research, 11*, 1-22.

Wohlwill, J. F. (1987a). Introduction. In D. Görlitz & J. F. Wohlwill (Eds.), *Curiosity, imagination, and play* (pp. 2-20). Hillsdale, NJ: Erlbaum.

Wohlwill, J. F. (1987b). Varieties of exploratory activity in early childhood. In D. Görlitz & J. F. Wohlwill (Eds.), *Curiosity, imagination, and play* (pp. 60-77). Hillsdale, NJ: Erlbaum.

Wohlwill, J. F. (1988). The role of computer programming in school children's production of graphic designs. In G. Forman & P. Pufall (Eds.), *Constructivism in the computer age* (pp. 337-363). Hillsdale, NJ: Erlbaum.

Wohlwill, J. F. (n.d.). *Up from psychogeography! A comment on the state of environment-cognition theory and research.* Unpublished manuscript.

Wohlwill, J. F., & Carson, D. H. (Eds.) (1972). *Environment and social sciences: Perspectives and applications.* Washington, DC: American Psychological Association.

Wohlwill, J. F., & Harris, G. (1980). Response to congruity or contrast for man-made features in natural-recreation settings. *Leisure Science, 3*, 349-365.

Wohlwill, J. F., & Heft, H. (1977a). Environments fit for the developing child. In H. McGurk (Ed.), *Ecological factors in human development* (pp. 125-138). Amsterdam: North-Holland.

Wohlwill, J. F., & Heft, H. (1977b). The relationship between degree of development of natural recreation areas and attitudes toward development and wilderness on the part of their users. *Journal of Leisure Research, 9*, 264-280.

Wohlwill, J. F., & Heft, H. (1987). The physical environment and the development of the child. In D. Stokols & I. Altman (Eds.), *Handbook of environmental psychology* (pp. 281-328). New York: John Wiley.

Wohlwill, J. F., & Kohn, I. (1973). The environment as experienced by the migrant: An adaptation-level view. *Representative Research in Social Psychology, 4*, 135-164.

Wohlwill, J. F., & Kohn, I. (1976). Dimensionalizing the environmental manifold. In S. Wapner & B. Kaplan (Eds.), *Experiencing the environment* (pp. 19-54). New York: Plenum.

Wohlwill, J. F., & van Vliet--, W. (Eds.) (1985). *Habitats for children: Impacts of density.* Hillsdale, NJ: Erlbaum.

Wohlwill, J. F., & Wiener, M. (1964). Discrimination of form orientation in young children. *Child Development, 35*, 1113-1125.

Wohlwill, J. F., & Weisman, G. (1981). *The physical environment and behavior: An annotated bibliography and guide to the literature.* New York: Plenum.

Wohlwill, J. F., & Wills, S. (1988). Programmed paintings: Elementary school children's computer generated designs. In F. Farley & R. Neperud (Eds.), *The foundations of aesthetics, art, and art education* (pp. 337-363). New York: Praeger.

Part II
Exposition of theoretical perspectives

Introduction

Günter Mey

In a volume about the contribution of theories to the topic of children in the city, particularly in a volume dedicated not just to schematizing those theories but also to exploring what they mean for the design of children's environments, Kurt Lewin's assumption that "there is nothing so practical as a good theory" resonates implicitly or explicitly on every page. In this book we editors and authors are interested in asking which theory can offer which insights into children's developments in urban settings. In tackling this question, we agreed with Joachim F. Wohlwill that it is necessary to examine four issues, which he sketched at one of his last public talks, the meeting of the Society for Research in Child Development in April 1986. As recapitulated by Moore (1988, p. 5), they were (a) the "differentiation between social and physical environments"; (b) the question of "which aspects of the physical environment are more salient for child development at different ages and how . . . this evolve[s] . . . with development"; (c) the meaning of "different aspects of the physical environment in different spatial settings" that children encounter, use, or interact with; and, lastly, (d) the necessity of drawing also on theories from disciplines other than psychology in order to understand "the influences of the physical environment on human development."

These considerations served early as bearings for the conference entitled "City as a frame for children's development," which took place in the city of Herten in Germany's Ruhr District (see Görlitz et al., 1992, 1993; Mey, Hinding, & Görlitz, in press). In simplified terms, the idea of the conference was to ask how theories can be used to plan an environment that meets the desires and needs of children or to evaluate existing environments and make suggestions for their improvement if so desired. For this purpose, the characteristics of selected theories at the interface of developmental and environmental psychology were outlined by their authors and then applied to specific residential areas and spheres of life (the dwelling, the vicinity, and the street) in Herten. After the theories had been introduced, the strengths of each were elaborated upon by cospeakers before an interdisciplinary audience in order to open discussion about how to design a city that provides what children require. However, the impact that this confrontation with the realities of urban development was supposed to have on the theories themselves remained in the background. It is precisely that feedback loop that becomes the principle concern in this volume, a shift of emphasis marked in part II, "Exposition of theoretical perspectives."

Whereas the Herten conference was mainly an attempt to foster a dialogue between planners, decision-makers, and scholars from a variety of disciplines (architecture, sociology, and education as well as psychology), our aim in this book is not only to have theories presented by their authors but also to generate a scientific discourse among psychologists. In other words, we have sought to make the potentials of existing approaches fruitful for a development of *psychological* theories. Our goal is ultimately to learn more about children's development in cities. A mere series of monologues seems inadequate for this endeavor, so our decision as editors has been to ensure that the dialogic conception of the Herten conference is largely retained in the structure of this volume as well when it comes to conveying the theoretical perspectives.

The following chapters unveil a broad spectrum of developmental and environmental theories for describing and explaining children's development in urban environments. With the behavior-setting approach (Fuhrer; Cotterell), phenomenology (Graumann and Kruse), the ecological approach (Heine and Guski), contextualism (Wachs and Shpancer), transactionalism (Werner and Altman; Oerter), constructivism (Seiler), psychobiology (Charlesworth; Keller), a relational developmental theory (Overton), and a holistic systems-oriented perspective (Wapner), the relation between the individual and the environment ("person-in-environment") is conceptualized in vastly different ways. The authors were requested to explain their own theoretical points of view and to expand upon ways in which their theoretical ideas can further the study of children in urban contexts. Among other things, they were (a) to give a general account of the basic propositions of their theoretical stances, including the relevant traditions from the history of psychology (and/or other sciences); (b) to outline their notion of adequate methodology and show how that understanding guides one in devising or selecting specific methods for the study of children in urban environments; and (c) to give a brief description of some empirical use of their theoretical system.

We have been led by the hope that psychological theories, which are sometimes highly abstract, can be rendered useful for urban research questions. Another circumstance has also guided our thinking, however. Physical environments tend to be ignored in developmental theories, whereas in environmental theories, despite interactional and transactional viewpoints, development occasionally appears to be quite unitary and global. To help stress that processes of children's development in the city as a system are interwoven with that system's discreet elements, we have included both disciplines.

How much has such a distinction between theoretical approaches succeeded at defining their relevance to children's development in urban environments? And which additional explanations appear to be necessary? After each theory chapter, these two questions are addressed in comments written by one or more invited scholars. Every theoretical position is critically considered for its descriptive, explanatory, and/or prescriptive contribution to the issue of children's development in cities. The commentators also try to discuss the various approaches in terms of their explanatory scope in urban research. Their role thus differs from that of the cospeakers at the Herten conference, which was primarily to point out the strengths of the given approach and what it could contribute to the evaluation and design of children's environments. Instead, the commentators in this volume are to examine or elaborate succinctly and critically that theoretical approach. For approaches that tend to focus on the individual, the function of the commentators is thus to bring the theory to the city or, vice versa, to bring the city into the theory when considering the "developing relationships" aspect of the "children, cities, and psychological theories" theme. For theories that tend to stress the environment, it means bringing the theory to individuals/subjects, especially the individuals/subjects in the city. The idea is to show how every theory could be developed with children's environments in mind, to indicate where it is necessary to qualify or elaborate theoretical positions. At times, such dialogue requires an exchange that hones or expands on lines of reasoning, an opportunity for which is given in the brief responses that authors of the theory chapters have written as rejoinders to the comments.

To promote continued discourse between the authors about their theories and approaches, we then have each of the four theory groups considered as a whole. Our particular interest herein has been to determine if and how the theories are developing or can be developed. This task of integrating the various strands of thought found in each theory group falls to Hellgard Rauh, Hirofumi Minami, Tommy Gärling, and Isolda de Araújo Günther and Hartmut Günther. In order to identify similarities and differences between the theories and to determine both the individual and joint contribution the theories can make to the understanding of children's development in urban settings, these observers endeavor to show the extent to which each group of theories has managed to describe, explain, and/or deal normatively with urban living conditions with regard to children.

We have deliberately tried to broaden the perspective by reaching beyond the narrow circle of European and American psychologists laying out and commenting on the theoretical positions in this volume. After all, there is a difference between the developmental conditions of children in a European city (such as Buxtehude in Heine and Guski's chapter or a Swiss town as described by Fuhrer), U.S. cities and suburbs (as in Werner and Altman's chapter), and Brazilian or Japanese urban settings.

Because our aim is to look at psychological theories, their potential for development, and their strengths and weaknesses in terms of describing children's development in urban environments, our four groups of theories have dispensed with common, seldom wholly satisfactory classifications such as environmental and developmental theories, person-centered or environment-centered approaches, and approaches focused on the relation between the person and the environment. For the same reason we have avoided grouping them according to families (e.g., transactional approaches, contextual approaches). Instead, we have set up a comparative framework within which to contrast theoretical approaches that are as contrary as possible. By thereby revealing fault planes in theory-guided thinking in developmental and environmental psychology, our intention has been to help this exploration – and future ones – chart possible paths toward a synoptic theory of children's development in urban settings.

It is in the spirit of that abiding search that the exposition of theories in this book concludes with an interim thought, not a statement of results. Entitled "What has happened in treading the path toward a psychological theory of children and their cities," the final chapter offers a reflection upon what occurred during this exchange of views about children's development in urban environments and what it has meant for the theories and the scholars discussing them.

References

Görlitz, D., Harloff, H. J., Valsiner, J., Hinding, B., Mey, G., Ritterfeld, U., & Schröder, R. (1992). City as a frame of development: The Herten conference. *Children's Environments*, 9(2), 64-65.

Görlitz, D., Harloff, H. J., Valsiner, J., Hinding, B., Mey, G., Ritterfeld, U., & Schröder, R. (1993). *Entwicklungsbedingungen von Kindern in der Stadt. Praxisbeiträge der Herten-Tagung* [Developmental conditions of children in the city. Contributions on the practical nature from the Herten conference]. Berlin and Herten: Stadtverwaltung Herten.

Mey, G., Hinding, B., & Görlitz, D. (in press). Lebensraum Stadt. Ein Arbeitsbericht über die Herten-Tagung "Stadt als Rahmen kindlicher Entwicklung" [Urban living space: A report on the Herten conference, "The city as a frame of children's development"]. In M. Beck & S. Chow (Eds.), *Kinder in Deutschland. Realitäten und Perspektiven*. Tübingen: DGVT.

Moore, G. T. (1988). Theoretical perspectives on development and the environment. A paper in memory of Joachim F. Wohlwill. *Children's Environment Quarterly*, 5(3), 5-12.

A. Levels of relationship –
As they appear in different cultures

Introduction

Dietmar Görlitz

The presentation of the theories in this section begins with basics. In the chapter by Werner and Altman, a good deal of attention is devoted to philosophical orientation, an excursus that helps clarify the transactional world view. Silhouetted against concepts that confound that outlook with contextualism, the inseparability of actors and environments becomes a main topic for the authors. The focus of analysis is on the changing relationships among actors and contexts and on the facet specific to those relationships – the holistic perspective on phenomena that integrate temporal qualities and allow for both change and stability – all on the groundwork of a unique philosophy of science, especially with respect to causality. In the complex view of phenomena that results, actors, different psychological processes, social or physical context, and time take on reciprocally defining aspects.

This perspective is quickly made more explicit for young children and adolescents in a consideration of secondary territories, but not before the authors expand the transactional approach by adding three key characteristics of its dialectical complement. It seems as though the particular multifaceted phenomenon being observed acquires tension and dynamism primarily from this basic dialectical structure, without a hint that places, too, might owe their vividness to this tension with some other, unmentioned place and without a pronounced role for development in the ebbing and flowing of events and their contrasting qualities.

As a dialectical/transactional construct harking back to work by Altman, among others, secondary territories are then examined in greater detail, above all in relation to children in neighborhoods and communities. Secondary territories provide opportunities for the expression and management of dialectical processes that offer children clear, distinctive chances to develop individual skills and individual and social identities chosen by the children themselves. Werner and Altman thereby put their finger on a research gap. Urban space is shaped, is specially prepared. The line of reasoning is based on the activities of children themselves (e.g., particularly their play and exploration inside and outside structured play settings), along with a host of structural features that support the creation of secondary territories, with Werner and Altman pointing out the ever greater constraints imposed by modern urban life. Public gardens and such rituals as festivals and celebrations are called to mind as the authors examine supraindividual vehicles for the creation of secondary territories of which children are also a part as they develop. Community events are of special significance. These spheres make it possible to experience the city, with its local neighborhoods and familiar regions, for to Werner and Altman, society is based on personal relationships, on opportunity and challenge to find one's place in a community of manageable size. Secondary territories are keys to this experience. All development results from the dialectical tensions in them.

In the commentary on the chapter by Werner and Altman, Ritterfeld poses three main issues: the theoretical status of the underlying approach, the approach's consequences for the understanding of development, and the practical implications that the approach has for research and environmental design and planning. In distinguishing basic theoretical assumptions from philosophical views of the world, which are not as testable, she takes a somewhat skeptical view of the approach's aptness for developmental theory that can be inferred from it. She also considers the risks of monocausal statements in the creation of optimal person-environment relations to be minor if the authors' concept of dialectics is taken seriously. According to Ritterfeld, the contribution by Werner and Altman nonetheless contains explainable planning recommendations – not certainties – namely, a claim to design city environments that facilitate and enhance social relationships through the establishment of secondary territories. To Ritterfeld, the question remains whether that claim is specifically adapted to cities. In a brief response illustrating the dialectics of privacy regulation, Werner and Altman therefore discuss the problem of translating their transactional view into practical research and design principles.

The chapter by Wachs and Shpancer also revolves around a certain world view, and a popular one at that. To keep the approach from fragmenting and blurring, the authors summarize the basic tenets of contextualism, citing four fundamental emphases – fusion, change, openness, and scope – as main characteristics of each considered system and its scientific analysis. First, Wachs and Shpancer's view of phenomena as complex, emergent, and context-bound raises and feeds profitable expectations for developmental psychology. However, modern developmental psychology both substantiates and restricts that perspective. After all, there are many obstacles preventing basic contextualist assumptions from being adopted in toto in developmental thinking and research, one of them perhaps being that the process orientation of developmental psychology would completely "dissolve" in what tends to be an amorphous paradigm. At the very least, the deceptively flat reality of occurring phenomena turns into a multilevel surface, but without sustaining hope for stability, order, and clear definitions. In the opinion of the authors, that impression seems more resigned than is justified by the literature of developmental psychology, which offers many examples of the four principles being applied in practice. The authors' rather traditional line of reasoning holds that development (meaning children's development in the context of this book), bears out the fruitfulness of those principles, and not only for the basic one called change. Given the different kinds of organism-environment interaction involved, the reasoning also applies to the prin-

ciples of openness – a quality that emphasizes the probabilistic nature of development – and scope, that is, the diversity of systems operating in and within each other
at different levels as the multiple environmental layers that constitute the child's
world. Urban environments as a salient context for children's development are given
a great deal of attention in the discussion of ways to apply the principles, with the
stress being placed on social and demographic features in urban time and space as
well as on interindividual differences, application, and intervention.

In the subsequent commentary Hoppe-Graff recognizes the systematic analysis of
contextualism's implications in this purified presentation. However, he notes the lack
of specific implications for the study of child-environment relations in cities. To
him, that lack follows from the metatheoretical character of contextualism as Wachs
and Shpancer see it. Hoppe-Graff seeks to bridge the gap by including psychological
concepts in this view of contextualism being handled as a theory. He seeks to illustrate this strategy pars pro toto with the contextualist principle of fusion as applied to
child-city relations. He begins with the self, culture and society, developmental
tasks, and co-constructions as conceptual ingredients of psychology that are promising for this endeavor. To him, fusion becomes permeation more than an inability to
distinguish between phenomena. It becomes permeation expressly borne out in co-
constructive activities, including those that have to do with understanding the city.
But permeation also means shift and transposition, an aspect for which Vygotsky
formulated a law of development.

With this emphasis on development, Seiler follows up with a richly theoretical
contribution elaborating a constructivist viewpoint in post-Piaget tradition. He concentrates on the issue of development and developmental psychology's basic questions, inquiring specifically about causes and conditions of development and asking
why the developmental product is never only an effect of the external forces
impinging on the subject. To Seiler, explaining the true accommodation to cultural
conditions and the ever-existing discrepancy in the effect that all such influences
have on the developing individual is a problem that interlinks theories. After closely
examining alternative approaches, Seiler presents a constructivist model in which
subjects are conceived of as actively constructing their development. Basic theoretical assumptions are also presented: the position of an adaptive kind of constructivist
developmental theory illuminated by the priority of internal conditions and individual constructions.

Adaptiveness, however, is a variant according to which the emergence of such
constructions is neither arbitrary nor solipsistic but instead embedded in a complex
environment of socially arranged things. This activity begins with and is aimed at
structures, to which Seiler ascribes concepts as cognitive structures. He elaborates
on these two genealogies, the origin of new things, and new kinds of structures. He
also discusses effective social interactions and ecological conditions that are
regarded as indirect, exemplary causes and not as direct causal effects. In considering the scientific nature of explanations based on this theory, Seiler mentions urban

environments, too. Drawing on other theories as well, he concludes with observations about circumstances that foster children's development of concepts. He sees social discourses as particularly salient situations for such development, focuses on the concept of work in particular, and emphasizes multifaceted settings allowing for spontaneous activity, which are conducive to development. Things urban come up indirectly, and planning recommendations do not yet individualize or typify places, though they do individualize or typify children in their conceptual development and the relevant contribution by peers. Peers, too, convey something of the interpretations and valuations that are the perennially important, indeed the sole, basis on which an area's physical make-up is seen to be influential on development.

Hoppe-Graff addresses this latter aspect as a central point in his commentary when he proposes to express the emerging child-city relation in terms of social construction and pays tribute to Seiler's position in general as a rare, creative elaboration of Piaget's thought. The differences he notes between himself and Seiler are the evaluation of social construction, Seiler's distinction between different forms of causality, and the opportunities for and limitations on application of this theory to child-city relations. In this context, Hoppe-Graff discusses co-constructions and their genetic place and depicts some of the observable qualities they have in imitative interactions during pretend play. He ends his contribution with hints of how Neo-Piagetian thinking can be centered on the city.

Child-city relations then serve also as a point of departure and a red thread in the broad-ranging integrative contribution by Günther and Günther, which, for all its analytical focus on terminology, sensitizes the reader to aspects and restrictions of certain cultures. They take Brazil as their major example, even to the point of showing our partner in stunted growth, a partner who is also a desperate street child of the city.

A dialectical/transactional framework of social relations: Children in secondary territories

Carol M. Werner and Irwin Altman

This chapter explores implications of a dialectical/transactional world view for relationships involving children, adolescents, and their friends and families. We suggest that children's social relationships can profitably be examined as holistic unities that involve people, physical and social environments, and temporal qualities. This contrasts with approaches in which relationships are the sole focus of study, removed from social and physical contexts and without regard to temporal experiences. We argue that city life is integral to children's friendships, including the settings friends visit, the activities in which they engage, and their friendships both inside and outside of their immediate peer group. Our major focus is on secondary territories and how they can be nurtured and developed as a way to increase children's social opportunities and integration into their local milieu.

We assume that dialectic processes underlie all social relationships (B. B. Brown, Werner, & Altman, in press). That is, in contrast to perspectives that focus only on how children develop as individuals or as members of groups, our interest is in how children achieve *both* individual and social identities as natural and interdependent parts of relationship development and maintenance. We propose that children, in all aspects of their lives, ebb and flow between being unique individuals and being effectively functioning participants in groups. That is, they must be capable of developing as independent, self-interested individuals, but they must also be capable of becoming a part of, benefiting from, and contributing to social relationships and community activities.[1]

We illustrate these ideas with the concept of secondary territories and how they are promoted through rituals, play and exploration, and public gardens. In accord with a transactional/dialectic perspective, we will develop the theme that relationships are a whole system that contain both individuality and sociality and that these qualities are reflected in behaviors at multiple levels of functioning, involving various objects and settings, and containing intrinsic temporal qualities such as stability and change, familiarity and novelty, and other qualities.

The chapter begins with a general description of our philosophical orientation. The subsequent section illustrates these ideas by exploring how children can become more integrated into their cities by helping create secondary territories. We end with some thoughts on future research questions.

1 Philosophical orientation

1.1 *Transactional world view*

The transactional world view is an approach to science articulated most fully by Dewey and Bentley (1949) and Pepper (1942, 1967) and more recently advocated by a variety of psychologists, including Altman and Rogoff (1987), Campbell and Gibbs (1986), Fisher (1982), Lazarus and Folkman (1984), and Oerter (in this volume). There is considerable overlap between transactionalism and contextualism (Reese, 1991). Indeed, Altman and Rogoff drew on both contextual and transactional philosophies in their approach to transactionalism.

There is a long historical tradition in developmental psychology that is essentially transactional and that also guides our thinking. The Soviet version of activity theory as stated by Vygotsky (1930, 1933, 1935/1978) addressed the mutual involvement of the child and the social context. It also emphasized the analysis of change in studies of long-term individual development, transformation over short periods of time, phylogenetic studies, and studies of cultural history. Approaches by Riegel (1976, 1979) and those influenced by him (see, for example, Hardesty & Baltes, 1978; Laosa, 1979/1989) are also transactional in their focus on developmental changes and on development as an interplay of biological, psychological, sociocultural, and physical environmental processes. These approaches often adopt a dialectical approach, albeit one that differs somewhat from our own.

Most transactionalists agree that "transactions" involve an inseparability of actors and environments such that *changing relationships among actors and context* is the focus of analysis, not psychological processes separated from ongoing events (hence, the term *transaction*). However, transactionalists hold subtly as well as profoundly different positions on other features, especially their relative emphasis on the physical environment and their views of causality. In this chapter, when we refer to the transactional world view, we refer to that version developed by Altman and Rogoff (1987) (see also Werner, Altman, Oxley, & Haggard, 1987; Werner, Altman, B. B. Brown, & Ginat, 1993). The essential features of this view are that (a) phenomena are viewed holistically, which, in part, means that actors and their sociophysical context are interdependent and mutually defining, that neither can be understood without the other; (b) temporal qualities are integral to phenomena, and both change and stability are assumed; and (c) transactionalism has a unique philosophy of science, especially with respect to causality. We consider each of these in turn.

1.1.1 *Phenomena are composed of inseparable and mutually defining aspects*
The essence of transactionalism is that psychological phenomena should be studied as holistic unities. There are no separate parts to an event; children are not separate

from their actions or feelings, nor are they separate from other children or the physical, social, and temporal circumstances that comprise unfolding events. The different aspects of an event are mutually defining and lend meaning to one another. They are so interconnected that one aspect cannot be understood without the others. Indeed, in order to stress inseparability and mutual definition, Altman and Rogoff (1987) used the term *aspects* (as opposed to elements or entities) to refer to actors, psychological processes, social context, physical context, and time. This point is made eloquently by Campbell (1986), who said that children and settings

... cannot be conveniently pulled apart for the purposes of analysis, however much our social-science instinct tells us to partition the variance. People and situations are not logically independent of one another in the real world. For example a young male and a given street do not come together by happenstance. He is there because he lives there or because his friends do. His neighborhood and his streets have been part of the socialization process that has contributed to his personality. The street is not separable from its inhabitants. ... Without them the street is no more than concrete and tar. (p. 116)

As another example, Shaw (1987), in discussing playground design, emphasized the unity of children with their friends and play settings and argued eloquently that design should begin with the user and aim for an integrated unity of people and place.

1.1.2 Temporal qualities are inherent aspects of phenomena

In our transactional world view, temporal qualities are treated as an intrinsic part of the definition and character of phenomena. Transactional research is concerned with how events unfold, such as the sequences of events in rituals and celebrations (Werner, Haggard, Altman, & Oxley, 1988), and how the sequence and timing are triggered by aspects of the rituals rather than an external clock or timepiece. Similarly, transactional research is concerned with the natural ebbing and flowing of events, such as "sidewalk ballets" that develop on city streets as people go about their separate, but interconnected, daily routines (Jacobs, 1961, p. 50). As another example, Whyte (1980) used time-lapse photography to study the natural ebbing and flowing of activity in urban plazas. This careful monitoring of ongoing events allowed him to describe the subtle changes in people and activities that contributed to the rhythm and meaning of these places. Thus, in the transactional world view, events are described in terms of natural temporal units. This contrasts with other world views in which time is treated as a separate dimension that marks or locates the state of a phenomenon.

Another tenet is that temporal qualities contribute to the meaning of, and themselves acquire meaning from, events. Midnight may seem like an odd time to play basketball because adults are accustomed to daytime and evening basketball. However, in the United States, midnight basketball has become a device for reaching adolescents, giving them a structured activity as an alternative to drugs and violence. Holding the games at midnight contributes to their meaning by signifying that the community is reaching out to alienated youths. Simultaneously, the timing – midnight – acquires legitimacy as the success of the games grows over time.

A final fundamental assumption is that both stability and change are natural and important to study. Children need stability in their relationships; they need to develop trust and familiarity. But they also need novelty and stimulation, excitement, and the unexpected. As noted above, children's identities are also shifting and changing, sometimes being highly individualistic, other times being more communal and group oriented. The process of continuity and change is one focus of the present analysis, because we seek ways of building secondary territories that provide both stability and change in activities and identities.

1.1.3 The transactional world view has a distinctive philosophy of science

First, the transactual world view emphasizes Aristotle's *formal cause*, focusing on the description of the pattern and form of an event and giving less attention to efficient cause (i.e., antecedent-consequent relationships), material cause (i.e., cause residing in the phenomenon itself, such as "personality trait"), or final cause (i.e., predefined teleological goals) (Rychlak, 1977). This feature is one on which numerous transactional approaches diverge. Altman and Rogoff (1987), Campbell (1986), Ginsburg (1980), and Lazarus and his colleagues (Coyne & Lazarus, 1980; Lazarus & Folkman, 1984) accepted Dewey and Bentley's (1949) view that patterns and forms (formal causality) define transactionalism. Lerner (1992), Oerter (in this volume), Pervin and Lewis (1978), and Riegel and Meacham (1978) have advocated tracing cause-effect (efficient causality) relationships within unfolding events, much like organicist or systems theorists study reverberation and mutual influence in living systems.[2]

Thus, in our transactional world view, elements are not seen as pushing or causing one another, but rather as working together or fitting together as total unities.

[One tries] . . . to identify relationships among component parts and processes – but none of the components is 'caused' by the prior occurrence of another component; and even more important, none of the components 'causes' the action or act of which they are components. (Ginsburg, 1980, p. 307)

The idea of studying patterns rather than antecedent-consequent relationships differs considerably from traditional research approaches in which prediction and control of phenomena are the goals. In the transactional world view it is assumed that psychological events unfold in a purposeful and goal-directed fashion but that goals can be short- and long-term and can change with time and circumstances.

Fisher (1982) suggested combining formal with efficient cause such that formal cause is used to understand the meaningful patterns by which families operate, and efficient cause is used to understand how outside influences change the nature of those patterns. For example, families usually develop a morning routine by which they arise, get ready, eat breakfast, and go off to school or work. None of these aspects "causes" the next, but the total set forms a coherent pattern (albeit often more coherent in mind than in practice). Understanding these patterns and studying their organization is the domain of formal cause; how outside influences such as the presence of house guests or a change in the school schedule disrupts the pattern would be the domain of efficient cause.

A second feature of our transactional philosophy of science is that both unique events and universal principles are of interest. That is, in contrast to views that scientists should identify only general psychological principles, it is assumed that unique configurations of events may occur once but never again. At the same time, unique events may involve overarching principles. For example, Werner, Altman, Oxley, and Haggard (1987) suggested that individual families decorated their homes at holidays to express cohesiveness with neighbors and attachment to home and neighborhood, a general principle undergirding development of secondary territories. They noted, however, that details such as particular choices, amounts, and locations of decorations varied with neighborhood, time of year, presence and ages of children, and changing aesthetic values.

Two final features concern multiple perspectives and multiple levels of scale. In our transactional view, events can be seen from multiple perspectives, each of which contributes to an understanding of the total event. That is, unlike other world views in which it is assumed that phenomena can be studied by objective and detached observers, transactional approaches contain the assumption that phenomena are partly defined by the observer and partly by the observation process. Thus, events may be constructed in different ways by different participants, none of which is the single correct or best interpretation, and researchers should consider events from all of these perspectives. Furthermore, events can be viewed at many levels of scale, from micro- to macro-levels of analysis. No single level is either the only possible or the only correct one. And finally, no levels or perspectives are considered to be inherently better than the others, so that using multiple levels and perspectives provides a more holistic view of a phenomenon.

1.2 Dialectics

Recently, we have begun to integrate transactional and dialectical approaches that we view as complementary and overlapping perspectives. Our conception of dialectics is similar to many currently being developed by scholars of interpersonal relationships (Baxter & Montgomery, in press). It has the following key characteristics

based on Altman, Vinsel, and B. B. Brown's (1981) original analysis: (a) opposition
is fundamental to relationships; (b) change and continuity are assumed, but change
is not driven by teleological or homeostatic principles, and dialectic processes are
more likely indeterminate than transcendent; and (c) social units contain dialectics
and are connected to other social units through dialectic processes.

1.2.1   Opposition in relationships

This chapter focuses on individuals' unique identities and how they are in opposition
to individuals' social identities, that is, their identities as members of groups. We
assume that this opposition inheres in all relationships. The individual/community
identity dialectic is one of a family of dialectic opposites that flow from a general
autonomy/connection opposition, that is, opposites that describe waxing and waning
levels of connection among participants (B. B. Brown, Werner, & Altman, in press).
Several low connection/high connection opposites exist, including selfish/generous,
unique/common, competitive/cooperative, individualistic/communal, closed/open,
and public/private, although not all are salient or relevant to all phenomena at all
times. We focus on the individual/community identity dialectic because of its relevance to secondary territories and how the physical environment supports the
expression of personal and social identities (Gauvain, Altman, & Fahim, 1983).

Altman et al. (1981) drew on a number of sources in developing a perspective on
dialectic opposites and their qualities: (a) They noted that "not all opposites are
alike" (p. 119) and advocated using only pairs in which both poles are positive (e.g.,
open/closed), rather than considering contradictions (open/not open). (b) Although
dialectic polarities might partially exclude one another by definition, they also complement and define one another. For instance, one gains a fuller understanding of
"openness" by considering its opposite, "closedness"; of "harmony," by considering
"conflict"; of "cooperation," by contrasting it with "competition." (c) Both poles are
always present in the system, although their relative strengths vary with time and
circumstance. (d) Dialectic opposites are "components of a higher order system,"
meaning that dialectics do not operate in a vacuum but can only be understood in
relation to the people, their goals, relationship, and places of which they are a part.

The point that both poles are always present raises important considerations. First,
it is a fundamental assumption. If one pole is missing or is destroyed, the whole
dialectic is destroyed. In children's friendships, for example, each child needs to
develop as an autonomous individual, but the pair must also work on the relationship and their definitions as "friends." If they cannot conceive of themselves as
friends, the relationship is destroyed, and if each cannot develop separately, thereby
bringing new individual qualities to the relationship that help it grow and change,
the relationship stagnates and fails as well. Thus, both individual and collective
identities are needed for viable friendships. To use an analogy from children's play –
every team member needs to have excellent individual skills and a positive sense of

self, but each also needs the entire team to capitalize on those skills (no matter how talented, a goalie in hockey or soccer counts on other team members for defensive support). At the same time, the team is more than a collection of individuals. It needs to coalesce and function effectively as a unified team, to feel a sense of "teamness," but it cannot do that without the contributions and skills of individual players. Each side – individual player or collective team – is both different from and interdependent with the other. This is the essence of its dialectic tension.

1.2.2   Change and continuity

We assume that both change and continuity are needed for system viability and that neither change nor continuity is more important than the other. Furthermore, we do not assume that predetermined teleological forces draw relationships towards an ideal end state but rather that children pursue short- and long-term goals, that events ebb and flow in varied ways, and that children's unique and communal identities differ in salience with these changes. A related assumption is that balance, consistency, and homeostasis are not ideals towards which systems necessarily strive. As Baxter (1988, 1990) suggested, relationships that lack novelty can stagnate, and those that lack familiarity can disintegrate into chaos (see also Altman et al., 1981; Werner, Altman, Brown, B. B., & Ginat, 1993). Children adapt to, seek, explore, and create changing circumstances in their identities and relationships while at the same time benefiting from stability in these areas. As Altman et al. (1981) said:

Historically, dialectic philosophy has not always postulated an ideal state toward which systems strive. That is, dialectic systems do not necessarily move toward an equal 'balance' of polarities with respect to one another. Thus, equilibrium, in the form of equal and opposite forces ... is not, according to dialectic philosophy, necessarily a natural or desirable state of affairs. Nor do systems necessarily strive ideally toward any other relationship between opposites. The relationship between opposites can assume any of a series of relative strengths ... and none is inherently better than any other. (p. 121)

The present authors do not know how much change and how much stability systems, children, and relationships need, nor do we put precise numbers on when or under what conditions change or stability will be dominant. We simply view it as axiomatic that both continuity and change are necessary for viable relationships (and dialectic systems in general). Although many dialecticians endorse a view that oppositions are resolved through determinate processes (especially the Hegelian description of thesis/synthesis/antithesis), we have adopted an indeterminate view emphasizing unfolding events, the ebbing and flowing of oppositional qualities, and the reconfiguring of aspects of the system without a fixed and final goal or ideal end state (Altman et al., 1981; Werner & Baxter, 1994). In this regard, our views are similar to those of Adams and his colleagues (Adams, Day, Dyk, Frede, & Rogers, 1992; Adams, Ryan, Corville-Smith, Normore, & Turner, 1992) and Riegel (1976).

Consider a city neighborhood. It is everchanging and varied, not moving forward or ever achieving a predetermined or ideal homeostatic level. There are often different proportions of young and old, rich and poor, educated and uneducated, and members of different ethnic and religious groups. They draw from and contribute to the neighborhood "system" in varying ways and differing amounts. Activities and levels of participation vary across the day and over longer time spans. These events contribute to changing conceptions of the neighborhood and changing resident identities (both individual and communal). But the relative sizes of contributions and withdrawals do not remain the same as would be expected in a homeostatic system, nor is there a "perfect" neighborhood configuration, no single community identity. Outside pressures and internal changes require otherwise and provide opportunities for new configurations and new experiences that keep neighborhoods vital.

Our point is not that all neighborhoods function perfectly or provide adequate levels of safety, security, stimulation, and social contact. Indeed, there is growing evidence that many do not. We simply argue that there are many ways to achieve viable neighborhoods and that the ability to accept and manage changing circumstances is fundamental to viability.

1.2.3 Social units

The term "social unit" refers to the particular individuals or groups engaged in a relationship and managing dialectical opposition. Altman (1993) suggested that dialectics can operate inside the individual, within a dyad or family, between the dyad or family and other collectives, such as extended families, neighborhoods, and religious communities. In all of these cases, dialectic tensions exist between one social unit and another, such as children bonding with siblings but also distancing in order to find friends outside the family, families connecting to and separating from extended family members, or connecting to and separating from the surrounding neighborhood. Hinde and Stevenson-Hinde (1987), Maccoby (1990), and Maccoby and Jacklin (1987) also stressed the importance of embedding children's relationships in their larger social networks, and Hinde and Stevenson-Hinde especially stressed the need to consider the dialectic processes that connect the different groups.

Several authors have examined dialectic tensions involving different social units and how difficult it can be for the individual to manage these often conflicting loyalties (for overviews, see Altman, B. B. Brown, Staples, & Werner, 1992; B. B. Brown, Altman, & Werner, 1992; Montgomery, 1992). These tensions may be particularly salient to adolescents as they become increasingly autonomous from family and more interdependent with friends. Yet perhaps paradoxically, adolescents also need to remain a part of their family. These tensions can become quite severe, and one challenge for people who work with troubled adolescents and their families is to provide mechanisms by which family members can recognize each other's autonomy while simultaneously functioning as an effective social group (Imber-Black, Roberts, & Whiting, 1988). In a subsequent section, we will consider rituals as one mechanism by which children and families manage these tensions and create and sustain unique and collective identities.

In the next section, we review the concept of secondary territory, which has emerged as a dialectical/transactional construct. Then we consider play and exploration, rituals, and gardening as vehicles for expressing and enhancing individual and social identities and for contributing familiarity and novelty to relationships.

2   Children in neighborhoods and communities

2.1   Creating neighborhood territories

Altman and his colleagues (Altman, 1975; Altman & Chemers, 1980; B. B. Brown, 1987; B. B. Brown & Altman, 1981, 1983) developed detailed frameworks for understanding human territorial behavior, including children's territoriality. They distinguished between primary, secondary, and public territories along the dimensions of duration of occupancy, psychological centrality, degree and intentionality of marking behaviors, degree of control, and response to invasion (B. B. Brown & Altman, 1981). Primary territories such as homes are occupied for the longest periods, are psychologically central in meaning and significance, are well marked, under the owners' control, and are likely to be defended against intrusions. Public territories are areas that people can occupy as long as they follow norms and rules. Public territories have little psychological centrality, they are usually occupied for only a short time, control is limited, they are not marked in any permanent way, people exercise little control over their use, and intrusions are not always responded to with vigorous defense. Public plazas, shopping areas, and outdoor settings such as beaches and woods are typical public territories. The lack of defense does not mean that public places are not attractive to users but simply that users understand that these are spaces for sharing. Cooper Marcus and C. Francis (1990) described many public territories that were well occupied and seemed to give pleasure to people.

Secondary territories are between these two poles, and, in fact, it is more accurate to describe them as a range of possible forms or a continuum between primary and public territories rather than as a fixed point between the two. Some secondary territories for some groups are almost as meaningful and tightly held as a primary territory, whereas some secondary territories have less meaning, are shared readily with other groups, and are closer to a public territory. In general, secondary territories may be occupied for short or long periods, they are somewhat psychologically central to users, and groups often mark these areas to signify their attachment as well as their ownership, may exercise control over activities, and may defend the space against unwanted intrusions. The concept of territories is a holistic one and refers to the person/environment/temporal unity, not the physical area alone. Thus, secondary territories include physical settings, the groups that use them, and the meanings and actions that bind people with place. They have the potential to provide children with safe havens where they can develop individual skills as well as become integrated into the larger community.

Secondary territories often begin as public spaces that people use in casual ways and for which they begin to develop a sense of attachment. These spaces generally deepen in meaning over time as people occupy, control, use, play in, work in, decorate, and even build partial barriers around the areas. Earlier, we mentioned Jacobs' (1961) concept of "sidewalk ballets" and Whyte's (1980) observations of interactions and space usage in urban plazas. Both of these examples show how ongoing social behaviors begin at superficial levels but develop into the deeper meanings and attachments to people and setting that characterize secondary territories.[3]

Secondary territories develop through and provide opportunities for the expression and management of dialectic processes. That is, when people appropriate space by using, cleaning, repairing, and decorating, they express their individual and collective identities in concrete and lasting ways. Similarly, by using physical areas for play, relaxation, and adventure, people have opportunities to form friendships. Furthermore, they build individual and group memories and expectations that are part of the meaning of place. (For further discussions of space appropriation, see Korosec-Serfaty, 1976, and Werner, Altman, & Oxley, 1985.) Research and analyses indicate that residents who describe their neighborhood as a secondary territory know more of their neighbors, are more satisfied with the neighborhood, have more control over activities there, and are less vulnerable to disruptions such as burglaries, assaults, and inappropriate use by nonresidents (B. B. Brown & Altman, 1983; Werner, Altman, Oxley, & Haggard, 1987).

Although most analyses of secondary territories have emphasized group activities and group identity, as noted above, our dialectic approach suggests that they can simultaneously celebrate both group and individual identities (Altman & Chemers, 1980; B. B. Brown & Werner, 1985; Werner, Peterson-Lewis, & B. B. Brown, 1989). Thus, we extend to secondary territories Gauvain, Altman, and Fahim's (1983) analysis of individual and community identity in the primary territories of homes. Secondary territories are settings where neighbors can come together and establish a safe area for interacting, playing, and in general becoming a community. Simultaneously, they are areas where children can develop individual skills and identities and make choices about what to do and with whom to interact. In accord with the concept of social units, numerous groups and subgroups can form and develop distinct identities. By virtue of their membership in the larger neighborhood, these identities can be interrelated and can contribute to the larger whole.

Secondary territories have received considerable research attention because of their potential to support group cohesiveness and contribute to quality of life in urban outdoor areas. For example, Altman and Chemers (1980) likened Newman's

(1972) concept of defensible space to the effective development of local secondary territories. As noted above, the community ties can be so strong in some cases that the neighborhood can become almost a primary territory. This contrasts with observations about areas that lack secondary territories. Hayden (1984) and Louv (1990), for example, raised concerns about the isolation of children and families and the need to embed them in larger social systems. (In dialectic terms, the concerns describe a system suffering from overemphasis on the individual.) Hayden attributed part of the problem to single-family housing and other housing forms that isolate women and children from support groups. Louv described families as isolated from their neighbors, comparing the situation in many cities to a giant, but damaged, web. He discussed ways of repairing the web so that children and families can be integrated into a stronger society that provides collective safety as well as opportunities for individual growth and development.

It should be clear that secondary territories serve important functions for children, yet there has been little or no research explicitly showing that children use and define spaces as secondary territories. Many physical areas have the potential to become secondary territories, such as neighborhood parks (the entire park or sub-areas), recreation areas inside and outside planned developments, green spaces and other outdoor areas in an apartment complex, and even the yards and streets in a neighborhood. And there has been considerable research on related concepts among children, such as place identity (Proshansky & Fabian, 1987), environmental exploration and knowledge (Hart, 1979; Moore, 1986; Moore & Young, 1978; Saegert & Hart, 1978), and how children of all ages use and express satisfaction with playgrounds and neighborhoods (Brower & Williamson, 1974; Frost, 1992; Hayward, Rothenberg, & Beasley, 1974; Moore, 1989; Spencer, Blades, & Morsley, 1989).

Each of these research areas implicitly or explicitly considers how children become bonded to and feel a part of a setting as individuals and as members of groups. For example, both Hart's (1979) and Moore's (1986) young participants often described special places and the special activities that occurred there. Often they described private areas where they could be alone and develop as individuals, but often they described places enjoyed with friends where they developed relationships and a sense of belonging to a community. Spencer, Blades, and Morsley (1989) summarized a variety of studies that suggested that friendship and place attachment bonds grew simultaneously as youngsters enjoyed outdoor areas together. In a fascinating analysis of a Finnish housing development, Setälä (1984-1985) described how children of different ages used different kinds of areas as secondary territories. For example, the "backyard culture" was composed of young children (5-6 years old) who played in backyards and local streets, and the "corner culture" was composed of school-age children (7-12 years) who played farther away from home. The corner culture groups provide excellent examples of secondary territories. Each group in the corner culture maintained a constant membership, controlled a particular physical area, and developed special expertise that contributed to its unique collective identity. (Setälä did not consider individuals' unique identities.) Weinstein and Pinciotti (1988) involved parents, and Frost and Klein (1979) involved children and families in designing and building play areas. These activities not only involved families in creating places out of space, but contributed to the ongoing development of a sense of community among neighbors and an appreciation for each other's unique skills and contributions. So although it has not been specifically asked whether and how children "claim" secondary territories, existing research and observation suggest that the concept is relevant.

In accord with a social unit analysis, secondary territories can be considered at the level of the children alone (how one group of friends includes or excludes another, how a group uses physical space to manage intragroup relations), and they can be analyzed across age levels to see how children fit into the total fabric of a neighborhood. Anecdotes suggest that this latter view deserves attention because children are often ignored or excluded from adult society and that exclusion may alienate them. At the turn of the century, children on U.S. city streets were seen as troublemakers, and police harassment of children was followed by legislation designed to keep children off the streets – out of the realm of adults (Nasaw, 1985). Currently, more and more adult housing complexes in the United States have begun to exclude children and adolescents on the grounds of safety and noise reduction. A common concern is that young people may be troublemakers, intent on stealing from elderly persons, using graffiti to define a particular area as their territory while at the same time creating "incivilities" that undermine other neighbors' attachment to place and sense of secondary territory (Taylor, 1988). Yet, if children are not taught how to use physical settings in ways that serve their needs without interfering with others' activities, how can they grow up as responsible members of society? A relevant question, then, is how to integrate young members of the community into the secondary territory so that they can be real members rather than outside troublemakers.

One way is through architectural design, and a number of authors have described physical features of apartments and housing complexes that encourage people of all ages to spend time in public areas, interacting with other residents, playing and making friends with other children, and that provide opportunities for developing a sense of community as well as individual qualities (Bjorklid, 1984-1985; Cooper Marcus, 1975; Holahan, 1976; Newman, 1972, 1975/1976). Based on that literature, Table 1 provides a summary of design features that support individual skills, social involvements, and development of secondary territories by all age groups, but especially children. Notice in particular the design features that support both individual and group activities and identities, that create connections among subareas (i.e., an integrated whole), and that provide flexibility in seating and use during the day and across the seasons.

Of particular importance is creation of *behavioral focal points*, or areas that naturally draw people together and encourage interaction but do so in a way that also allows individuality and autonomy (Bechtel, 1977). Bechtel summarized four qualities that support behavioral focal points (this dialectical terminology is ours). These are (a) location close to other significant features to which people are already drawn; (b) design that allows visual access both in and out so that people can decide whether to remain alone or join the group; (c) position on a well-traveled route so that people can continue if they decide not to enter (i.e., not at a dead-end), a feature that also supports the dialectic tension between staying alone and joining in; and (d) comfortable, moveable seating that accommodates a range of group sizes, including solitary seating. Many observations of how people use the out-of-doors attest to the importance of these features (Carr, M. Francis, Rivlin, & Stone, 1992; Cooper Marcus & C. Francis, 1990; Holohan, 1976).

Table 1 describes a host of behaviors and activities that may contribute to creation of secondary territories. Not all of these behaviors and activities are discussed in detail in the present chapter but are described more fully in Altman (1975), B. B. Brown (1987), Newman (1975/1976), and Taylor (1988). Our focus is primarily on a small number of potentially territory-creating activities – children's play, rituals, and gardening. Let us now consider them.

2.2 Play and exploration and creation of secondary territories

There has been extensive interest in how children use the out-of-doors, especially among environmental psychologists and designers. Indeed, play is one mechanism by which children can appropriate space as individuals and as members of groups (Korosec-Serfaty, 1976; Werner, Altman, & Oxley, 1985), creating the potential for strong secondary territories. Playgrounds have received considerable attention and criticism in part because children spend much time there and because the potential is high for practicing important social and cognitive developmental skills (Moore, 1989). We argue that these skills contribute to children's development of individual and social identities. On the more social side, children learn how to cooperate and play with others, learn what skills are valued by their group, learn how to interact, and so on, by watching and interacting with other children, whether they are the same or different ages. On the more individualistic side, children have opportunities to hone and test their skills and learn about competition and how to handle winning and losing. Adults in roles as supervisors or participants are also an important part of play and can help children deal with these often conflicting goals.

Although research on play has not been explicitly dialectical, the criteria for evaluating playgrounds suggest that implicit value is placed on both individual and group play, both individual and group development (see, for example, J. G. Brown & Burger, 1984, and Weinstein & Pinciotti, 1988). There is also an implicit interest in whether people use playgrounds on a regular basis and begin to think of the settings as secondary territories. Observations of people in play areas show tremendous variety in responses and user groups and no clear guidelines for "ideal" types of

Table 1: Supporting creation of secondary territories for all age groups

---

Secondary territories are places that people occupy, use, and become attached to, often as groups of neighbors or friends. They may be occupied for short or long periods, they are somewhat psychologically central to users, and groups often mark these areas to signify their attachment as well as their ownership. They may exercise control over activities and may defend the space against unwanted intrusions. Secondary territories support dialectic tensions between individual and community identities.

A. Features that support secondary territories

1. Designs that encourage residents to identify with and take pride in the building and physical setting

   a. Attractive interiors, exteriors, and common areas
   b. Architectural appearance that does not stigmatize residents or identify them as "different"
   c. Buildings and grounds that are clean and safe
   d. Designs that enable (and rules that allow) residents to decorate both the inside and outside areas

2. Designs that allow residents to distinguish residents from nonresidents, thereby supporting a sense of group belongingness and identity and providing control over access

   a. Short halls and separate entrances for subgroups of residents
   b. Behavioral focal points: shared common areas inside and outside that allow residents to meet (see text for details; children's play areas and neighborhood gardens may be particularly useful)
   c. Locks for which only residents have keys or combinations

3. Designs that physically connect primary and secondary territories

   a. Natural flow inside to outside with "sittable" porches, chairs outside but close to building, and windows close to sidewalk for chatting with passersby
   b. Provision of a attractive outdoors that people want to use and can use as individuals and as groups of neighbors and children

4. Designs that separate secondary territories from public areas, providing long-term use and control

   a. Physical features: fences, gates, design elements that distinguish private from public property and that exclude from the secondary territory vehicular traffic and nonresident pedestrians
   b. Psychological/symbolic barriers: signs with name of building; design elements such as archways and decorative fences that welcome friends but let intruders know that this is private property

5. Designs that allow residents to monitor both inside and outside areas, thereby enhancing safety and providing control over intrusions

   a. Visual control from interior and exterior (especially important for families with young children)
   b. Outside seating that residents want to use (moveable, in the shade, in attractive areas, close to where children are playing, close to the action; see also behavioral focal point)

    c. Adequate opportunities for inside and outside surveillance (e.g., avoidance of bushes and structures that interfere with views)

6. Safe, varied play areas for children that allow friendships to form and place attachments to develop

    a. An array of opportunities: traditional playground structures, adventure playgrounds with supplies for building and creating, and undeveloped natural areas

    b. Playgrounds in which children build structures for short- and long-term use

    c. Avoidance of all age, ability/disability, and sex groups: Deliberate separation of the groups is unnecessary and may interfere with friendship and sibling-care responsibilities.

    d. Places for rest and adventure, complex but integrated arrangement of equipment and play settings

    e. Children and families involved in design and construction of play areas

B. Activities through which residents appropriate space, make it their own, and develop individual and social identities

1. Decorating in- and outside that establishes and expresses individual and group identities

    a. Decorations that residents invest with meaning and that display unique and neighborhood identities

    b. Competitions for decorative displays (even sanctioned graffiti) that express uniqueness and communality

2. Gardening by individuals and groups

3. Area clean-ups

    a. Events that involve all demographic groups (age, sex, ethnicity)

    b. Clean-ups that are held on a regular basis

    c. Emphasis on internal rather than external rewards for participation

C. Spontaneous and planned social activities that enable residents to get to know one another, thereby facilitating friendship formation as well as contributing to collective control over and defense of space

1. Neighborhood meetings and social events that encourage recognition and contact

    a. Balance of small and large groups for individual and social identities

    b. Games and other ice-breakers to span demographic barriers

    c. Friendly interneighborhood competitions and other "superordinate goals" to reduce local subgroup hostilities

2. Development of community-wide or neighborhood rituals and celebrations

    a. Celebration of established festivals, such as Halloween, Christmas, Valentine's Day

    b. Celebration of events unique to the neighborhood, such as ethnic festivals, summer parties, and dances

    c. Celebrations that span age groups and some that segregate by age group

3. User participation in design and other neighborhood decisions

Note: This table incorporates suggestions from a range of research and design literatures (see text for specific authors). We have adapted many ideas to fit our focus on secondary territories, especially the incorporation of people of all ages and ethnicities into those secondary territories.

playgrounds (see J. G. Brown & Burger, 1984; Hart, 1987; and Spencer, Blades, & Morsley, 1989, for reviews).

Additional research is needed to resolve questions about ideal types for particular circumstances. With our dialectical/transactional perspective, however, we emphasize people/place/time unities, suggesting that playgrounds should (a) be suitable for the local community and the natural context; (b) provide opportunities for people of all ages and especially avoid deliberately segregating children by age, sex, or ability; (c) provide opportunities for solitary as well as group activities to support both individual and group identities (Moore, 1989; Shaw, 1987; Spencer, Blades, & Morsley, 1989); (d) provide opportunities for both familiarity and novelty and both quietude and excitement – or as Moore (1989) said, diversity without chaos; (e) be designed from the users' perspectives, not the manufacturers'; and (f) involve children and parents in the design and construction so that they feel a sense of ownership and commitment (Baldassari, Lehman, & Wolfe, 1987; Hart, 1987; Weinstein & Pinciotti, 1988).

A great deal of attention has been paid to children's exploration in free ranges, outside structured play settings (Hart, 1979; Saegert & Hart, 1978). This research underscores the unity of people, place and behavior because the sizes and boundaries of children's home ranges vary with individual and situational features such as age, sex, and the availability of supervision (e.g., going to a distant friend's house if an adult is there) or other safety-providing features. Some of these areas fit our definition of secondary territories, or are secondary territories "in the making." They are close to home and interesting and safe enough to be visited often. Eventually, they may become favorite settings for interacting, working and playing with others. Other spaces are farther away and may require dangerous travel or present dangerous situations to unsupervised children. These are less likely to become secondary territories and may remain public territories that children enjoy visiting without making any territorial claim. Children often explore these environments as groups of friends, so exploration can become an opportunity to build individual skills, learn to coordinate skills as a group, and to develop deeper social bonds with peers.

Nasaw's (1985) analyses of urban children at the turn of the century showed a similar profile. Male and female children played in the street adjacent to their homes and benefitted from the protection and intervention of adults who lived or worked in the area. They were an integral part of their physical and social milieu, and their street was their secondary territory. Nasaw argued that these children were not abandoned to the streets, as reformists argued, but rather were bonding with neighbors and becoming a part of the very life of their neighborhood (e.g., supervising their siblings, running errands, playing and working on crafts). As they grew older, the males especially would explore outside their immediate block, although it was somewhat dangerous to do so because of traffic, other urban hazards, and attacks by other youths defending their own block as a secondary territory. On the other hand, some places were regarded as shared public territories (or a loosely held secondary territory), enabling children from across the city to interact amicably. For example, young adolescents from many city neighborhoods shared and felt ownership over a swimming hole without incident. Thus, much like the adults around them, children knew and were attached to their immediate neighborhood and more distant places, resulting in the development of an array of secondary territories that provided multiple opportunities for integration into many facets of the larger community.

In contrast to the freedom that Nasaw (1985) described for the beginning of the century, there are currently many factors that constrain children's access to cities, thereby reducing opportunities for developing secondary territories. These constraints include lack of appropriate settings, public or private-owners' policies that discourage use of settings, and current perceptions that many city neighborhoods are too dangerous for children to explore (Gaster, 1991, 1992). Many parents consider it unsafe to let their children explore any but their immediate neighborhood, and some parents may completely restrict their children to the home because of real and perceived dangers in the neighborhood (Gaster, 1991; Hayward, Rothenberg, & Beasley, 1974; Moore, 1989). These are the kinds of issues that concerned Louv (1990) and suggested to him that efforts to reclaim the streets are urgently needed in many cities. Researchers express concerns that these changes may have unknown consequences for children as individuals and as members of social groups. For example, the lack of opportunities to explore and expand the home range may be deleterious to development of both individual cognitive skills and interpersonal social skills (Berg & Medrich, 1980; Hayward, Rothenberg, & Beasley, 1974).

As suggested by territoriality theory, neighborhood efforts to reclaim the street show promise in reversing this trend. Design features such as the Dutch *woonerf*, in which streets are blocked off or vehicular traffic restricted, have increased use by young and old alike and provide opportunities for neighborhood bonding as well as individual exploration and development (M. Francis, 1988; Spencer, Blades, & Morsley, 1989). Behavioral changes such as "neighborhood watch" groups (not neighborhood vigilantes) and other forms of community organizing that encourage neighborhood participation could help build or rebuild a neighborhood's social fabric (Chavis & Wandersman, 1990; Florin & Wandersman, 1990; Perkins, Florin, Rich, Wandersman, & Chavis, 1990). This increased safety should, in turn, create opportunities for individual exploration and individual identity development, thereby supporting the identity dialectic.

2.2.1 Summary

This section reviewed opportunities for play in both structured settings and free ranges. We suggested that both of these areas could become secondary territories if they provide multiple kinds of experiences and opportunities for children and adults. Secondary territories support both individual and group identities by providing children opportunities to develop unique skills, to develop individual strength as a member of a group, and to contribute to group formation and stability.

2.3 Rituals as mechanisms for creating secondary territories

We use "ritual" as a general term to refer to an array of special occasions, such as festivals, celebrations, and holidays (Werner, Altman, B. B. Brown, & Ginat, 1993). In this section we review literature on how rituals support community identity and positive social relations and suggest that these can be used locally, in small-scale ways, to build secondary territories. Rituals are holistic events that nicely illustrate a transactional/dialectical perspective: they involve individuals and groups, physical places, and objects; they contain an array of temporal qualities such as novelty, rhythm, and relationship and identity change. Although Wolin and Bennett (1984) view different rituals as contributing to different kinds of identities (e.g., individual, family, neighborhood, or sociocultural), our view is that all rituals can contribute to multiple identities, although which identities are salient at any point in the ceremony can vary. That is, rituals support dialectic processes by serving as mechanisms for expressing multiple and competing identities and for managing changing identities and relationships. This chapter focuses on how children can be involved in community festivals and how these can contribute to their development as unique individuals as well as members of families and groups. In so doing, it also illustrates how rituals contribute to formation of secondary territories where these multiple identities can be expressed and affirmed.

One form of ritual celebrates the child and special events in that child's life. Examples are birthdays, graduation parties, bat and bar mitzvahs, and confirmations. We argue that these celebrations reflect the individual/society identity dialectic and can be used as part of a total neighborhood program to build local social bonds. Although the emphasis is on the individual, these celebrations also reflect ties to the larger social group, including family and friends, the larger society that sanctions and encourages such celebrations, and any religious groups involved in the ritual. Notice, also, how these celebrations illustrate the holistic transactional approach. They involve a total cluster of people, places, objects, and temporal qualities.

Consider birthday celebrations. At one level, they appear to be totally focused on the individual. The birthday child receives gifts acknowledging individual desires, enjoys favorite foods and settings, invites special friends, and is often given control over activities and events. Yet the celebration also enhances group and cultural identities. The presence of relatives symbolically links the group together as a unit and contributes to the sense of "family," and the presence of friends contributes to friendship bonds. Furthermore, birthdays are celebrated in socially sanctioned ways, with particular settings, clothing, people, and objects, thereby connecting the birthday child to the larger society (Werner, Altman, B. B. Brown, & Ginat, 1993).

Rituals are also being used as potentially effective therapeutic techniques for helping families through difficult transitions, such as a move to a new city (Imber-Black, Roberts, & Whiting, 1988). These are not culturally endorsed rituals; rather, they are developed for specific families with particular needs. For example, Imber-Black (1988) described how an immigrant family was in constant turmoil because the mother tried to adhere to values and behaviors of their country of origin, whereas her two adolescent children wanted to leave the past behind and become integrated into their new city. The therapist focused on this tension between the past and present and suggested that each needed to be respected by the entire family; the mother needed to come to accept the new, and the adolescents needed to accept the old. The family's therapy ritual consisted of weekly "story telling" in which each member told a story about, or engaged in, activities reminiscent of their country of origin and another about their new country, thereby affirming their commitment to both the past and present. Physical objects symbolized the old and new, such as one ritual that involved eating foods from each country. In undertaking the ritual, the mother could see that the children remembered and missed their former home, and the children could see that mother was embracing the new. So, even at a microlevel, rituals involve children and relationships, the physical environment, time and change, old and new, and they support family members' multiple identities.

These examples suggest that celebrations highlighting individuals' uniqueness simultaneous with group belongingness and identity can be part of community development. Hobby shows, sports events, ethnic celebrations, and the like can therefore provide opportunities for individuals to come together in particular places with particular objects, get to know one another, celebrate individual and group accomplishments, and foster individual and group identities (see these suggestions in Table 1).

Larger community-wide celebrations can serve similar functions. In describing a festival in one Canadian town, Farber (1983) argued that "festivals are about identity, whether personal or social, and they are the context and the process of creating links between children in the community, as well as between the community and the wider national and cultural environment" (p. 34). Roberts (1988) and Manning (1983) emphasized that rituals "hold" dialectical contradictions. That is, by allowing expressions of a community's past, present, and future, rituals allow individuals and groups to manage transitions, changing identities, and changing social relationships.

Many societies hold annual celebrations that serve one or more functions, such as reaffirmation of societal history and values, or release from strong social controls. Manning (1983) used dialectical concepts to describe communal celebrations from different societies and showed how several factors all contributed to the sense of community engendered by the celebration: who participated, what objects and symbols were encouraged or prohibited, what clothing was worn, and when events occurred. In many cases, children were invited to participate, indicating in both concrete and symbolic ways their membership in the society but also permitting them individuality in how they enacted their particular assignment. In some cases, children participated in ways that allowed them to step outside their normal roles and act out some of their frustration with their low status in society.

An example of the first type is the celebration of "Old Home Week," in Mount Forest, Ontario, Canada (Farber, 1983). Young people from the town are invited to participate in the parade where they wear clothing emblematic of the town's past, and they are active in planning and running the games and competitions central to events. In dialectical terms, communal identities are enhanced as the young people participate in events and contribute to the group's success, and individual identities are enhanced when the young people make decisions and receive recognition for particular contributions. Similarly, in Valencia, Spain, celebration of *Las Fallas* has emerged as a way to build and reaffirm local neighborhood as well as Valencian identity (Lawrence, 1992). Each neighborhood creates its own *falla* (large structures portraying scenes of political satire and commentary unique to each group) and holds its own celebration as part of the larger festival. Lawrence's description makes clear that the neighborhood is a secondary territory that residents protect and celebrate throughout the year but especially at this time. Children play a prominent role in the festivities, including helping raise funds to pay for the neighborhood's *falla*, producing their own separate children's *falla*, and participating in a children's parade.

We suggest that children's participation in these communal events contributes to their sense of individuality and uniqueness but also enables them to feel closer, more connected and identified with their sociophysical community. Indeed, Lawrence (1992) explicitly said that children were encouraged to participate in falla construction and other celebratory events in order to inculcate them into neighborhood and Valencian identity and values. Similarly, Farber (1983) described the four-day Canadian event as a family and community reunion, underscoring its potential for building involvement and identity at individual, family, and social levels. Taken together, these two festivals illustrate how children and adults participate in events that affirm and further develop neighborhood secondary territories.

An example of a celebration that allows children to step outside normal functioning, have excitement, and begin the transition towards adult identity is the Alikali Devils ceremony in Sierra Leone (Cannizzo, 1983). The Alikali Devils (boys between 8 and 12) dress up in particular costumes, each representing spirits or devils, and perform in public streets as parts of major Muslim or Christian festivals. The costumed youngsters are allowed (and even encouraged) to accost adults and berate and intimidate them, although this clearly would not be allowed in other times and settings. Cannizzo stressed that this celebration provides the children with an opportunity to reverse roles and temporarily exercise power over adults. It can serve simultaneously as a way for them to let off steam and allow them to experience adult power and authority, at least in this brief and structured situation. Cannizzo suggested that the celebration is particularly important currently because of rapid social changes and modernization that have begun to estrange children from their parents and the whole of traditional society. This example is in accord with our concern that, in many settings, children are increasingly isolated from larger society. It suggests that similar wild, but self-contained, festivals may help children make the transition to adulthood and help strengthen bonds between children and their community. Thus, even this unusual festival supports the dialectical tension between individual and social identities and the ongoing development of neighborhood secondary territories.

Halloween (short for *All Hallow Even*) provides opportunities for children to try on different roles, thereby serving functions similar to those of the Alikali ritual. In addition, it is a neighborhood festival and provides opportunities for neighbors to interact, express cohesiveness, welcome newcomers, and in general develop and affirm the neighborhood as a secondary territory. It is celebrated in the United States with perhaps more enthusiasm and vigor than in other countries. Especially in Utah, it has become a major event involving – in accord with a dialectical/transactional view – particular children, places, objects, timing, and identity expression. Many families plan elaborate and often home-made costumes and decorate their homes with extensive displays. It is not uncommon, for example, to see monsters sitting on a front porch with appropriate monster background music, greeting the trick-or-treaters, who come seeking candy. Children choose their costumes carefully, often in order to play out-of-character roles such as ghosts, monsters, fairy princesses, and movie or television characters.

B. B. Brown and Werner (1985) analyzed Halloween as an opportunity for residents to express a communal identity and strengthen ties with their neighbors, to affirm, and create a stronger secondary territory. In a holistic analysis in a large area of Salt Lake County, Utah, B. B. Brown and Werner (1985) found that the presence of Halloween-decorating was related to attitudes expressing a sense of connection and bonding with neighbors and a sense of commitment to their neighborhood, just as would be expected in a strong secondary territory. B. B. Brown and Werner reasoned that residents deliberately used decorations to express these sentiments as well as to make trick-or-treaters feel welcome at their homes. At the same time, Halloween is an opportunity for individuals to express their uniqueness through costumes and special decorations on the home and in the yard. Furthermore, by walking through the neighborhood and visiting every home, children improved their cognitive knowledge and deepened their understanding of the people and setting where they lived.

A follow-up study was designed to ask whether Halloween was a time for building individual and family identities as well as contributing to the residents' sense of community and the neighborhood as a secondary territory (Werner, 1989; Werner, B. B. Brown, & Harris, 1989). That is, we asked whether celebrating Halloween could highlight and reinforce these multiple identities and what roles people and physical environments played in this process. Responses to an extensive questionnaire indicated that people described connections between their Halloween-related behaviors and their self-concepts and attitudes to the neighborhood. For example, parents described Halloween as a celebration that they enjoyed because it was fun to see their children's special costumes and see how much their children enjoyed receiving candy and special recognition from neighbors. They also reported that participating in family Halloween activities, such as making decorations, shopping for candy and costumes, and trick-or-treating, contributed to the adults' as parents and spouses. And those who participated in neighborhood events also reported that those activities helped to build their sense of community identity and attachment to the neighborhood. At one level, then, Halloween is just an opportunity to dress in costumes, tour the neighborhood, eat candy, and act in unusual ways. At a deeper level, it provides children with opportunities to express and develop their multiple individual and social identities, to act out tensions between themselves and family, and to strengthen ties as members of families and larger social groups as well as attachment to the physical setting.

2.3.1 Summary
Many anthropologists and psychologists stress that rituals provide opportunities to establish and affirm identities, to manage dialectical tensions between conflicting identities, and to facilitate changing identities. They note that holidays are fun, providing a distraction from ordinary activities with opportunities for excitement and stimulation. These qualities underscore their potential for contributing to the development and maintenance of secondary territories. They draw people together in particular physical environments with particular people, objects, and temporal qualities. As suggested in Table 1, they can be used at opportune times throughout the year as mechanisms by which children and adolescents can be integrated into their community and further the development of secondary territories.

2.4 Public gardens

There is a small, but growing, interest in encouraging local residents to turn unused urban lots into private and/or public gardens. People clean up empty lots (including removing such unwieldy objects as abandoned automobiles, mattresses, and blocks of cement), prepare the soil, and then plant flowers and vegetables. These collective activities become the basis for stronger social relations in the neighborhood, supporting the social side of the identity dialectic and contributing to a sense that the neighborhood is a secondary territory. Gardens also support the individuality side. Gardeners may hold competitions to see whose garden is the most attractive or yields the best crop and may sell the flowers and produce around the neighborhood or at "farmer's markets." The land can be a part of the grounds around housing developments, it can be abandoned lots that are claimed formally or informally by residents, or it can be publicly owned land provided to citizens on a temporary basis (M. Francis, 1987; Goode, 1992; Lewis, 1978; Severson, 1990).

Numerous anecdotes attest that many of these gardens become very strong secondary territories, often verging on primary territories. Gardeners of all ages spend time in the gardens, working the soil and arranging their plantings in ways that emphasize their unique skills and preferences, building fences around their individual plots to protect them from animal (and perhaps human) intrusion, and becoming upset if their plot is disturbed or damaged. They take collective action if the entire garden is threatened, such as when a landowner decides to sell or develop the property (M. Francis, 1987).

For example, as part of an environmental design conference, conferees were invited on a tour of the housing development on Roosevelt Island, New York City, including the public gardens. Many of the garden plots were surrounded by fences (in a great variety of style and material). Some gardens were named or had signs indicating the gardener's name, and all contained a unique variety of flowers and vegetables. The gardens also supported social relationships and development of the whole area as a secondary territory. Residents talked about how the gardens fostered interaction and friendship as gardeners exchanged tips or won admiration for their special gardening skills. They also protected each other's plots and the whole area from intrusions, theft, and other damage, evidence that the group treated this as a secondary territory. As another example of such "territorial defense" of gardens, a public garden in Salt Lake City has been threatened with closure, and the gardeners are mounting a public fund-raising campaign to purchase the land and protect the garden.

Cooper Marcus and C. Francis (1990) also looked at individual plantings in a larger garden context. They showed how individual planting beds allowed personal expression but also contributed to and complemented the appearance of shared public areas. This example illustrates the tension between individual and social identities in that individual gardeners used their particular areas to express themselves and highlight their special skills, but they also "gave" their gardens to the community to share and enjoy. Furthermore, in these actions they contributed to their own and other residents' attachment and commitment to place, which are fundamental to a sense of secondary territory.

A common theme in anecdotes (and to some extent in research) about public gardens is that children and adolescents can be involved in these gardens or in gardens that are integrated into playgrounds (Hiss, 1992; Shell, 1994). Cooper Marcus and C. Francis (1990) explicitly recommended putting gardens into children's parks and playgrounds and providing adult supervision to help children develop effective gardening skills (in our terms, to develop this aspect of individual or social identity). In a study of one urban garden, by contrast, M. Francis (1987) found that only a small percentage of garden users were children or adolescents. However, he also noted that gardeners asked for a children's area inside the garden so that adults could work and supervise their children at the same time, perhaps enabling the children to learn this skill and become part of this community.

This idea is not new. Since the 19th century, Swiss and German cities or housing developments have provided public areas in which families cultivated private gardens, or *Schrebergartens* as a means of rearing neighborhood children in healthier settings (Lothane, 1992).[4] Some examples of children and adolescents in gardens exist in the current literature as well. For example, photographs accompanying Severson's (1990) account of a neighborhood garden showed young adolescents happily participating in heavy labor with shovels and hoes, suggesting that this space became a secondary territory, although Severson herself did not specifically discuss methods for involving youngsters in the activities. Lewis (1978) explicitly discussed how participating in gardening and gardening competitions had turned some youths around and made them a part of their neighborhood. Whereas they previously had been suspected of vandalizing their housing project's garden, once they had become involved in a gardening competition, some of them became the protectors of the area, and vandalism ceased. And a low-income support agency in Salt Lake City, Utah, has effectively connected children and adults in neighborhood gardening projects.

Although M. Francis (1987) echoed Kaplan's (1973) concern that gardening is too slow-paced of an activity to attract children, these examples suggest otherwise. At least for the age groups illustrated in the literature (late childhood to early adolescence), it seems to be an enjoyable and acceptable way to spend time, learn new skills, make new friends of multiple ages, and become part of the community.

2.4.1 Summary

Anecdotes and careful observations suggest that public gardens become secondary territories for people. People work in the gardens, become attached to them, protect and defend them, and use them as opportunities to develop and express their unique, individual skills and preferences, but they also use them as an opportunity to meet similar others and become part of a larger social group. Public gardens are also emerging as a setting where children can learn new skills, make new friends – especially with older neighbors – enjoy the out-of-doors, and contribute in material ways to their local neighborhood. Although gardening may not be appropriate for all youths, we encourage neighborhood groups to consider it as an additional mechanism for integrating residents of all ages into the community.

3 Recapitulation and questions for future research

Personal relationships provide the underpinnings of society. They are the glue that connect individuals to families and friends and connect these subgroups to the larger community and nation. Children's friendships have long been the focus of psychological research, but too often these relationships have been studied out of their larger social contexts and physical settings. In this chapter, we examined the concept of secondary territories, a holistic unity involving people, psychological processes, physical environment, and temporal qualities. We suggested that secondary territories provide opportunities for children to develop their unique and communal identities and proposed a variety of ways in which secondary territories could be encouraged in local neighborhoods.

We began this chapter with a description of our transactional world view and its defining qualities: (a) phenomena are holistic, composed of people, psychological processes, physical environment, and temporal qualities, all of which are mutually defining and inseparable; (b) temporal qualities are inherent to phenomena; and (c) this world view has a distinctive philosophy of science, including its emphasis on Aristotle's formal cause rather than efficient cause. It is the emphasis on formal cause that distinguishes our approach from many other contextual/transactional views, and we urge researchers to consider adding to their scientific repertoire an interest in the patterns and forms of phenomena along with more traditional interest in cause-effect relations.

We then coupled this world view with our perspective on dialectics, which we have described as an essential motor to interpersonal relations (Werner, Altman, B. B. Brown, & Ginat, 1993). Here, too, our views are both similar to and different from those of other dialecticians: (a) opposition is fundamental to relations; (b) both change and continuity are needed for viable system functioning; that is, homeostasis is not an ideal, nor are systems moving towards an idealized end-state; and (c) dialectic opposition involves social units in many combinations: individual with dyad, dyad with family, family with group, and so on.

We suggested that secondary territories – places that groups collectively occupy, use, and decorate, to which they become attached, and which they may defend against threatening intrusions – are transactional unities, composed of people, place, time, and psychological processes. Secondary territories support the dialectical tension between development, expression, and reaffirmation of both individual and community identities. We applied these transactional dialectical and territorial concepts to a variety of public and community settings and activities, such as gardens, play areas, rituals, and celebrations, as well as to some general design features of community sites. We believe that concepts of secondary territory, individual and community identities, and the dialectical/transactional world view, with its emphasis on holism and dialectic tensions, may be useful in future research and theory directed at creating better environments for children, families, and communities.

Table 1 provides a general introduction to design features and behavioral events that can support development and maintenance of secondary territories and integrate children into their communities. There are numerous places for children to develop secondary territories, places that they know and are attached to and where they meet and become friends with other youngsters. Although secondary territories among children have not attracted much research, studies of how children use their neighborhoods suggest that local parks, playgrounds, and home ranges have in many cases become secondary territories for children and their families. We proposed fostering these processes with the design and behavioral features laid out in Table 1, with particular emphasis on rituals, playgrounds and free ranges, and public gardens that provide safe, but stimulating, activities and involve participation by a wide spectrum of residents.

Acknowledgement

We thank the volume's editors and Barbara B. Brown and Sanford Gaster for their extremely helpful comments on an earlier version of this manuscript.

Notes

1 In our more extensive treatment of dialectics in relationships (B. B. Brown, Werner, & Altman, in press), we describe the identity dialectic (individual/social identity) as a subtype of a more general autonomy/connection dialectic. In the present manuscript, for clarity, we simply focus on the identity dialectic.

2 Naturally, a full understanding of phenomena would involve all forms of determinism and even all world views (Altman & Rogoff, 1987; Bates, 1979; Lazarus & Launier, 1978; Pepper, 1942, 1967).

3 There is considerable overlap between the ideas of territoriality and place attachment, a newly emerging construct in environmental psychology (Altman & Low, 1992). We have chosen to use territorial rather than attachment concepts because our own research had its origins in territoriality theory and because the physical-environmental features that may contribute to secondary territories and defensible spaces are more clearly articulated (B. B. Brown & Altman, 1981, 1983; Newman, 1975/1976).

4 We thank Regula Burki, M. D., for bringing *Schrebergartens* to our attention.

References

Adams, G. R., Day, T., Dyk, P. H., Frede, E., & Rogers, D. R. B. (1992). On the dialectics of pubescence and psychosocial development. *Journal of Early Adolescence, 12*, 348-365.

Adams, G. R., Ryan, B. A., Corville-Smith, J., Normore, A., & Turner, B. (1992). Dialectics, organicism, and contextualism: A rejoinder to Lerner. *Journal of Early Adolescence, 12*, 389-395.

Altman, I. (1975). *Environment and social behavior: Privacy, personal space, territory, and crowding.* Monterey, CA: Brooks/Cole. (Reprinted by Irvington Press, New York, 1981)

Altman, I. (1993). Dialectics, physical environments, and personal relationships. *Communication Monographs, 60*, 26-34.

Altman, I., Brown, B. B., Staples, B., & Werner, C. M. (1992). A transactional approach to close relationships: Courtship, weddings, and placemaking. In B. Walsh, K. Craik, & R. Price (Eds.), *Person-environment psychology* (pp. 193-241). Hillsdale, NJ: Erlbaum.

Altman, I., & Chemers, M. M. (1980). *Culture and environment.* Monterey, CA: Brooks/Cole.

Altman, I., & Low, S. M. (1992). Place attachment: A conceptual inquiry. In I. Altman & S. M. Low (Eds.), *Place attachment: Vol. 12. Human behavior and environment: Advances in theory and research* (pp. 1-12). New York: Plenum.

Altman, I., & Rogoff, B. (1987). World views in psychology: Trait, interactional, organismic, and transactional perspectives. In D. Stokols & I. Altman (Eds.), *Handbook of environmental psychology* (Vol. 1, pp. 7-40). New York: Wiley.

Altman, I., Vinsel, A., & Brown, B. B. (1981). Dialectic conceptions in social psychology: An application to social penetration and privacy regulation. In L. Berkowitz (Ed.), *Advances in experimental social psychology* (Vol. 14, pp. 107-160). New York: Academic Press.

Baldassari, C., Lehman, S., & Wolfe, M. (1987). Imaging and creating alternative environments with children. In C. S. Weinstein & T. G. David (Eds.), *Spaces for children: The built environment and child development* (pp. 241-268). New York: Plenum.

Bates, E. (1979). Brainerd versus Aristotle with Piaget looking on. *The Behavioral and Brain Sciences, 1*, 138-139.

Baxter, L. A. (1988). A dialectical perspective on communication strategies in relationship development. In S. Duck (Ed.), *A handbook of personal relationships* (pp. 257-273). New York: Wiley.

Baxter, L. A. (1990). Dialectical contradictions in relationship development. *Journal of Social and Personal Relationships, 7*, 69-88.

Baxter, L. A., & Montgomery, B. M. (in press). *Dialectical approaches to studying personal relationships.* Hillsdale, NJ: Erlbaum.

Bechtel, R. (Ed.). (1977). *Enclosing Behavior.* Stroudsburg, PA: Dowden, Hutchinson & Ross.

Berg, M., & Medrich, E. A. (1980). Children in four neighborhoods: The physical environment and its effect on play and play patterns. *Environment and Behavior, 12*, 320-348.

Bjorklid, P. (1984-1985). Environmental diversity in housing estates as a factor in child development. *Children's Environment Quarterly, 1*, 7-13.

Brower, S. N., & Williamson, P. (1974). Outdoor recreation as a function of the urban housing environment. *Environment and Behavior, 6*, 295-345.

Brown, B. B. (1987). Territoriality. In D. Stokols & I. Altman (Eds.), *Handbook of environmental psychology* (Vol. 1, pp. 505-531). New York: Wiley.

Brown, B. B., & Altman, I. (1981). Territoriality and residential crime: A conceptual framework. In P. J. Brantingham & P. L. Brantingham (Eds.), *Environmental criminology* (pp. 55-76). Beverly Hills, CA: Sage.

Brown, B. B., & Altman, I. (1983). Territoriality, defensible space and residential burglary: An environmental analysis. *Journal of Environmental Psychology, 3*, 203-220.

Brown, B. B., Altman, I., & Werner, C. M. (1992). Close relationships in the physical and social world: Dialectical and transactional analyses. *Communication Yearbook/15,* (pp. 508-521). Newbury Park, CA: Sage.

Brown, B. B., & Werner, C. M. (1985). Social cohesiveness, territoriality, and holiday decorations: The influence of cul-de-sacs. *Environment and Behavior, 17*, 539-565.

Brown, B. B., Werner, C. M., Altman, I., (in press). Choice points for dialecticians: A transactional/dialectical perspective on personal relationships. In L. A. Baxter & B. Montgomery (Eds.), *Dialectical approaches to studying personal relationships.* Hillsdale, NJ: Erlbaum.

Brown, J. G., & Burger, C. (1984). Playground designs and preschool children's behaviors. *Environment and Behavior, 16*, 599-626.

Campbell, A. (1986). The streets and violence. In A. Campbell & J. J. Gibbs (Eds.), *Violent transactions: The limits of personality* (pp. 115-131). New York: Basil Blackwell.

Campbell, A., & Gibbs, J. J. (Eds.). (1986). *Violent transactions: The limits of personality.* New York: Basil Blackwell.

Cannizzo, J. (1983). The shit devil: Pretense and politics among West African urban children. In F. E. Manning (Ed.), *The celebration of society: Perspectives on contemporary cultural performance* (pp. 125-141). Bowling Green, OH: Bowling Green University Popular Press.

Carr, S., Francis, M., Rivlin, L. G., & Stone, A. M. (1992). *Public space.* New York: Cambridge University Press.

Chavis, D. M., & Wandersman, A. (1990). Sense of community in the urban environment: A catalyst for participation and community development. *American Journal of Community Psychology, 18*, 55-81.

Cooper Marcus, C. (Ed.). (1975). *Easter Hill Village: Some social implications of design.* New York: The Free Press.

Cooper Marcus, C., & Francis, C. (1990). *People places: Design guidelines for urban open space.* New York: Van Nostrand Reinhold.

Coyne, J. C., & Lazarus, R. S. (1980). Cognitive style, stress perception, and coping. In I. Kutash, L. B. Schlesinger, & Associates (Eds.), *Handbook on stress and anxiety: Contemporary knowledge, theory, and treatment.* San Francisco: Jossey-Bass.

Dewey, J., & Bentley, A. F. (1949). *Knowing and the known.* Boston: Beacon.

Farber, C. (1983). High, healthy, and happy: Ontario mythology on parade. In F. E. Manning (Ed.), *The celebration of society: Perspectives on contemporary cultural performance* (pp. 33-50). Bowling Green, OH: Bowling Green University Popular Press.

Fisher, L. (1982). Transactional theories but individual assessment: A frequent discrepancy in family research. *Family Process, 21*, 313-320.

Florin, P., & Wandersman, A. (1990). An introduction to citizen participation, voluntary organizations, and community development: Insights for empowerment through research. *American Journal of Community Psychology, 18*, 41-54.

Francis, M. (1987). Some different meanings attached to a city park and community gardens. *Landscape Journal, 6*, 101-112.

Francis, M. (1988). Urban open spaces. In E. H. Zube & G. T. Moore (Eds.), *Advances in environment, behavior, and design* (Vol. 1, pp. 71-106). New York: Plenum.

Frost, J. L. (1992). *Play and playscapes.* New York: Delmar.

Frost, J. L., & Klein, B. L. (1979). *Children's play and playgrounds.* Boston: Allyn and Bacon.

Gaster, S. (1991). Urban children's access to their neighborhood: Changes over three generations. *Environment and Behavior, 23*, 70-85.

Gaster, S. (1992). Historical changes in children's access to U.S. cities: A critical review. *Children's Environments, 9*, 23-36.

Gauvain, M., Altman, I., & Fahim, H. (1983). Homes and social change: A cross-cultural analysis. In N. R. Feimer & E. S. Geller (Eds.), *Environmental psychology: Directions and perspectives* (pp. 180-218). New York: Praeger.

Ginsburg, G. P. (1980). Situated action: An emerging paradigm. In L. Wheeler (Ed.), *Review of personality and social psychology* (Vol. 1, pp. 295-325). Beverly Hills, CA: Sage.

Goode, E. (1992, August 31). A garden that grows people. *U.S. News & World Report*, p. 24.

Hardesty, F. P., & Baltes, P. B. (Eds.). (1978). The contributions of Klaus F. Riegel (1925-1977). *Human Development, 21*, 346-369.

Hart, R. A. (1987). Children's participation in planning and design: Theory, research, and practice. In C. S. Weinstein & T. G. David (Eds.), *Spaces for children: The built environment and child development* (pp. 217-239). New York: Plenum.

Hart, R. (1979). *Children's experience of place*. New York: Irvington.

Hayden, D. (1984). *Redesigning the American dream: The future of housing, work, and family life*. New York: W. W. Norton.

Hayward, D. G., Rothenberg, M., & Beasley, R. R. (1974). Children's play and urban playground environments: A comparison of traditional, contemporary, and adventure playground types. *Environment and Behavior, 6*, 131-168.

Hinde, R. A., & Stevenson-Hinde, J. (1987). Interpersonal relationships and child development. *Developmental Review, 7*, 1-21.

Hiss, T. (1992, October 26). An ecologist at large: Breaking ground. *The New Yorker*, pp. 101-102.

Holahan, C. J. (1976). Environmental effects on outdoor social behavior in a low-income urban neighborhood. *Journal of Applied Social Psychology, 6*, 48-63.

Imber-Black, E. (1988). Ritual themes in families and family therapy. In E. Imber-Black, J. Roberts, & R. A. Whiting (Eds.), *Rituals in families and family therapy* (pp. 47-83). New York: W. W. Norton.

Imber-Black, E., Roberts, J., & Whiting, R. A. (Eds.) (1988). *Rituals in families and family therapy*. New York: W. W. Norton.

Jacobs, J. (1961). *The death and life of great American cities*. New York: Vintage Books.

Kaplan, R. (1973). Some psychological benefits of gardening. *Environment and Behavior, 5*, 145-161.

Korosec-Serfaty, P. (Ed.). (1976). *Appropriation of space: Proceedings of the 3rd International Architectural Psychology Conference*. Strasbourg, France: Louis Pasteur University.

Laosa, L. M. (1989). Social competence in childhood: Toward a developmental, socioculturally relativistic paradigm. *Journal of Applied Developmental Psychology, 10*, 447-468. (Original work published 1979)

Lawrence, D. L. (1992). Trancendence of place: The role of *placeta* in Valencia's *Las Fallas*. In I. Altman & S. M. Low (Eds.), *Place Attachment: Vol. 12. Human behavior and environment: Advances in theory and research.* (pp. 211-230). New York: Plenum.

Lazarus, R. S., & Folkman, S. (1984). *Stress, appraisal, and coping*. New York: Springer.

Lazarus, R. S., & Launier, R. (1978). Stress-related transactions between person and environment. In L. A. Pervin & M. Lewis (Eds.), *Perspectives in interactional psychology* (pp. 287-327). New York: Plenum.

Lerner, R. M. (1992). Dialectics, developmental contextualism, and the further enhancement of theory about puberty and psychosocial development. *Journal of Early Adolescence, 12*, 366-388.

Lewis, C. A. (1978). Urban gardens: Landscapes for the soul. In G. Hopkins (Ed.), *Proceedings of the National Urban Forestry Conference* (Vol. 1, Session 1, pp. 54-62). Syracuse, NY: State University of New York, College of Environmental Science and Forestry.

Lothane, Z. (1992). *In defense of Schreber: Soul murder and psychiatry*. Hillsdale, NJ: Analytic Press.

Louv, R. (1990). *Childhood's future*. Boston: Houghton Mifflin.

Maccoby, E. E. (1990). Gender and relationships: A developmental account. *American Psychologist, 45*, 513-520.

Maccoby, E. E., & Jacklin, C. N. (1987). Gender segregation in childhood. In H. W. Reese (Ed.), *Advances in child development and behavior* (Vol. 20, pp. 239-287). Orlando, FL: Academic Press.

Manning, F. E. (1983). *The celebration of society: Perspectives on contemporary cultural performance*. Bowling Green, OH: Bowling Green University Popular Press.

Montgomery, B. M. (1992). Communication as the interface between couples and culture. In S. A. Deetz (Ed.), *Communication Yearbook/15* (pp. 475-507). Newbury Park, CA: Sage.

Moore, R. C. (1986). *Childhood's domain: Play and place in child development*. Dover, NH: Croom Helm.

Moore, R. C. (1989). Playgrounds at the crossroads: Policy and action research needed to ensure a viable future for public playgrounds in the United States. In I. Altman & E. H. Zube (Eds.), *Public places and spaces: Vol. 10. Human behavior and environment: Advances in theory and research* (pp. 83-120). New York: Plenum.

Moore, R. C., & Young, D. (1978). Childhood outdoors: Toward a social ecology of the landscape. In I. Altman & J. F. Wohlwill (Eds.), *Children and the environment: Vol. 3. Human behavior and environment: Advances in theory and research* (pp. 83-130). New York: Plenum.

Nasaw, D. (1985). *Children of the city: At work and at play*. Garden City, NY: Anchor Press/Doubleday.

Newman, O. (1972). *Defensible space: Crime prevention through urban design*. New York: Macmillan.

Newman, O. (1976). *Design guidelines for creating defensible space*. Washington, DC: U.S. Department of Justice. (Original work published 1975)

Pepper, S. C. (1942). *World hypotheses: A study in evidence*. Berkeley: University of California Press.

Pepper, S. C. (1967). *Concept and quality: A world hypothesis*. La Salle, IL: Open Court.

Perkins, D. D., Florin, P., Rich, R. C., Wandersman, A., & Chavis, D. M. (1990). Participation and the social and physical environment of residential blocks: Crime and community context. *American Journal of Community Psychology, 18*, 83-115.

Pervin, L. A., & Lewis, M. (1978). Overview of the internal-external issue. In L. A. Pervin & M. Lewis (Eds.), *Perspectives in interactional psychology* (pp. 1-22). New York: Plenum.

Proshansky, H. M., & Fabian, A. K. (1987). The development of place identity in the child. In C. S. Weinstein & T. G. David (Eds.), *Spaces for children: The built environment and child development* (pp. 21-40). New York: Plenum.

Reese, H. W. (1991). Contextualism and developmental psychology. In H. W. Reese (Ed.), *Advances in child development and behavior* (Vol. 23, pp. 188-230). New York: Academic Press.

Riegel, K. F. (1976). The dialectics of human development. *American Psychologist, 31*, 689-700.

Riegel, K. F. (1979). *Foundations of dialectical psychology*. New York: Academic Press.

Riegel, K. F., & Meacham, J. A. (1978). Dialectics, transaction, and Piaget's theory. In L. A. Pervin & M. Lewis (Eds.), *Perspectives in interactional psychology* (pp. 23-47). New York: Plenum.

Roberts, J. (1988). Setting the frame: Definition, functions, and typology of rituals. In E. Imber-Black, J. Roberts, & R. A. Whiting (Eds.), *Rituals in families and family therapy* (pp. 3-46). New York: W. W. Norton.

Rychlak, J. F. (1977). *The psychology of rigorous humanism.* New York: Wiley.

Saegert, S., & Hart, R. (1978). The play-world of children: The development of environmental competence in girls and boys. In M. A. Salter (Eds.), *Play: Anthropological perspectives* (pp. 157-176). New York: Leisure Press.

Setälä, M.-L. (1984-1985). Transmission of childhood culture in an urban neighborhood. *Children's Environment Quarterly, 1,* 15-18.

Severson, R. (1990). United we sprout: A Chicago community garden story. In M. Francis & R. T. Hester, Jr. (Eds.), *The meaning of gardens: Idea, place, and action* (pp. 80-85). Cambridge, MA: MIT.

Shaw, L. G. (1987). Designing playgrounds for able and disabled children. In C. S. Weinstein & T. G. David (Eds.), *Spaces for children: The built environment and child development* (pp. 187-213). New York: Plenum.

Shell, E. R. (1994, July). Kids don't need equipment, they need opportunity. *Smithsonian, 25*(4), 79-86.

Spencer, C., Blades, M., & Morsley, K. (1989). *The child in the physical environment: The development of spatial knowledge and cognition.* New York: Wiley.

Taylor, R. B. (1988). *Human territorial functioning: An empirical, evolutionary perspective on individual and small group territorial cognitions, behaviors, and consequences.* New York: Cambridge University Press.

Vygotsky, L. S. (1978). *Mind in society: The development of higher psychological processes* (M. Cole, V. John-Steiner, S. Scribner, E. Souberman, Eds.). Cambridge, MA: Harvard University Press. (Original works published 1930, 1933, 1935)

Weinstein, C. S. & Pinciotti, P. (1988). Changing a schoolyard: Intentions, design decisions, and behavioral outcomes. *Environment and Behavior, 20,* 345-371.

Werner, C. M. (1989, August). *Celebrations in family relationships.* Paper presented at the meeting of the American Psychological Association, New Orleans, LA.

Werner, C. M., Altman, I., Brown, B. B., & Ginat, J. (1993). Celebrations in personal relationships: A transactional/dialectic perspective. In S. Duck (Ed.), *Social context and relationships* (pp. 109-138). Newbury Park, CA: Sage.

Werner, C. M., Altman, I., & Oxley, D. (1985). Temporal aspects of homes: A transactional perspective. In I. Altman & C. M. Werner (Eds.), *Home environments: Vol. 8. Human behavior and environment: Advances in theory and research* (pp. 1-32). New York: Plenum.

Werner, C. M., Altman, I., Oxley, D., & Haggard, L. M. (1987). People, place, and time: A transactional analysis of neighborhoods. In W. H. Jones & D. Perlman (Eds.), *Advances in personal relationships* (Vol. 1, pp. 243-275). Greenwich, CT: JAI.

Werner, C. M., & Baxter, L. A. (1994). Temporal qualities of relationships: Organismic, transactional, and dialectical views. In M. L. Knapp & G. R. Miller (Eds.), *Handbook of interpersonal communication* (2nd ed., pp. 323-379). Thousand Oaks, CA: Sage.

Werner, C. M., Brown, B. B., & Harris, P. H. (1989). [Celebrations in family relationships]. Unpublished raw data.

Werner, C. M., Haggard, L. M., Altman, I., & Oxley, D. (1988). Temporal qualities of rituals and celebrations: A comparison of Christmas Street and Zuni Shalako. In J. E. McGrath (Ed.), *The social psychology of time: New perspectives* (pp. 203-232). Newbury Park, CA: Sage.

Werner, C. M., Peterson-Lewis, S., & Brown, B. B. (1989). Inferences about homeowners' sociability: Impact of Christmas decorations and other cues. *Journal of Environmental Psychology, 9,* 279-296.

Whyte, W. H. (1980). *The social life of small urban spaces.* Washington, DC: Conservation Foundation.

Wolin, S. J., & Bennett, L. A. (1984). Family rituals. *Family Process, 23,* 401-420.

Comment: Proving philosophy!?

Ute Ritterfeld

By definition, environmental psychology deals with person-environment relations. Of major importance for any theoretical or empirical approach is the understanding of the specific nature of these relations. Historically, they have been seen in a merely mechanistic way: the environment as unit on one hand and the person as unit on the other, each with the potential of having an impact on the other. From that viewpoint, for example, climatic conditions affect the mood of people, or human behavior destroys natural resources. This mechanistic view has been criticized fundamentally (overview: Altman & Rogoff, 1987). First, the implicit idea of final causality cannot be applied to complex units like environments. Second, the impact of humans and the environment is not unidirectional, but multidirectional. And third, the dynamics of the relation between the two should be considered a quality in itself.

In recent years transactionalism has gained popularity as an alternative to conceptualizing nonseparable person-environment units with inherent temporal qualities. Werner and Altman (in this volume) have even expanded the transactional perspective by using a dialectical framework within which to describe the ebbing and flowing of psychological acting, experiencing, and developing between such poles as individuality-society, excitement-boredom, and novelty-stability.

The following commentary focuses on three questions for discussing the possibilities and the boundaries of the proposed dialectical/transactional framework: (a) What is the theoretical status of the dialectical/transactional framework in general? (b) What consequences does this approach have for the understanding of development? (c) What practical consequences for research and for environmental design and planning can be derived from the approach?

1 The theoretical status of a dialectical/transactional framework in general

Werner and Altman use the term "philosophical view" to describe the theoretical character of their framework. Philosophical views can be defined as models of human beings or (in environmental psychology) as models of the person-environment relation. In the analytical philosophy of science ("Analytische Wissenschaftstheorie"), it is pointed out that every theory is based on models. It is also the

view that inherent assumptions of these models are basically axiomatic and, therefore, not empirically provable. This position is called the nonstatement view
(Stegmüller, 1973).

While theories may be evaluated on the basis of empirical data, axiomatic
assumptions can only be more or less *useful*. Unfortunately, these assumptions are
often implicit, a status that protects them from critical reflection about their usefulness. Werner and Altman are exceptional in that they *explicitly* point out what, in
their opinion, should be a philosophical background for theoretical and empirical
work in environmental psychology.

The discussion about philosophical views in psychology is not only legitimate but
necessary for two important scientific intentions. First, the views allow one to
structure the theoretical field and to identify similarities and differences between
different theories. Second, they set priorities about what is important for the development of theories. The latter intention makes the philosophical views prescriptive.
For example, the mechanistic model implies the view of an individual who is under
the direct influence of the environment. Accordingly, that person is not seen as
being able to moderate the effects of the world or even to play an active role within
it. A transactionalistic view, however, implies an active and reflective individual
who is as much influenced by the surrounding world as it is by her or him.

Since the status of transactionalism is metatheoretical, theories have to be developed on its basis. Given the subject of the present volume, these theories ought to
explain how the development of a child transacts with the sociophysical world of his
or her hometown. The theoretical concept that Werner and Altman propose is called
dialectics. In that they focus two different aspects, identity and motivation. The
authors argue that a child's oscillation between the poles of private and public or
individuality and society helps build up his or her identity. The motivational aspect
of the dialectics deals with the level of arousal that children seek. Although the
dimensions in which the dialectical processing oscillates are well known, Werner
and Altman propose an alternative to the common idea of homeostatics. They give
up the necessity of an ideal state of arousal effected through, for example, moderate
familiarity or novelty of a sociophysical environment. Instead, they assume that a
person needs the experience of both sides of the dimension, familiarity as well as
novelty.

In other words, the status of the transactional model is metatheoretical, whereas
the status of the proposed dialectical processes seems to be theoretical. This differentiation does have consequences for the evaluation criteria to be adopted. As mentioned above, metatheoretical assumptions cannot be rejected by empirical evidence,
they have to convince by being useful. Furthermore, their status is normative, for the
axioms set priorities on what should be important for research and investigation. The
theoretical status of the dialectics, however, can be descriptive or explanatory,
depending on the underlying axioms. Since the axioms of transactionalism explicitly
require holistic units and convincingly reject the idea of efficient causality, an

explanation of phenomena on the basis of probabilistic laws is not possible. Instead of, descriptions of phenomena could take place.

2 Consequences for the understanding of development

I turn now to the question of whether the axiomatic assumptions of the dialectical/transactional framework are useful for further research. Axiomatic models are not intended to reflect reality. They are intended to constitute the object of investigation (Herzog, 1984). In other words, if the philosophical model implies temporal qualities, as the transactional view does, the derived theories, too, have to take them into account.

Whereas the former mechanistic model may be described as atomistic (phenomena are considered to be understood and explained as soon as every element has been discovered, and development or change may therefore only occur by a recombination of elements), the dynamic view of transactionalism seems to be highly innovative because it allows one to conceptualize qualitative change.

These qualitative changes are what developmental theories are focusing on by definition. The question arises as to whether a dialectical/transactional framework naturally takes a developmental perspective. One can argue that it does, because the framework's temporal qualities are considered to be intrinsic. It still has to be emphasized that the concept of change or development from the transactional perspective is not comparable to what is called an organismic model (Herzog, 1984), which underlies most developmental theories in psychology. In Piaget's approach, for example, changes are due to the fundamental process of adaptation. The organism changes biologically and thereby provokes new schemata for interacting with the environment. The environment sets constraints for the development, and the individual's determinism is a consequence of this relation.

A dialectical/transactional framework, on the other hand, tries to overcome such a deterministic view. Changes are seen to emerge from a person-environment unit, which is embedded between other person-environment units and which, together with them, belong to larger units. That is, transactionalists do not try to localize the initiation of development in either the person or the environment. In their view, development occurs if the relation between the actor and his or her sociophysical context changes. However, this framework does not focus on developmental aspects, so the conditions under which the relation might change have not yet been explicated. In that regard, transactionalism may not work as a developmental theory, although the potential for a dynamic perspective is emphasized in its metatheoretical view.

3 Practical consequences for research and for environmental design and planning

As mentioned above, philosophical views such as the dialectical/transactional framework cannot be evaluated in terms of right or wrong. They have to convince the scientific community by their usefulness. This usefulness primarily relates to research goals, such as to elaborate theory and to derive methodological implications. Transactionalism seems to have its biggest impact on the definition of the *unit* of research. Werner and Altman use the word *holistic* to describe the complexity of the unit, which encompasses people, the physical and the social environment, and its temporal qualities. There is no doubt that the complexity of the unit determines progress in research. The less complex the unit, the easier it is to investigate a problem. But it is also true that the less complex the unit that is conceptualized, the more aspects are missing. Empirical researchers should therefore try to exclude as little as possible, but at the same time their research should remain practical in order to derive empirical hypotheses.

The approach of identifying efficient causality, which underlies most psychological understanding, is rejected by the authors. Instead, they propose description as a kind of formal causality. Considering an example, this argument seems plausible: An observer watching a person enter a room through a door easily accepts the impact of the environment on this action. But the door does not *cause* that person to pass through (efficient causality). Rather, the person's intention to move from one room into another *corresponds* with the environmental affordances. Does this mean that the idea of antecedent factors in environmental psychology is obsolete? I would not go that far. Surely, the environment does not play an antecedent role for psychological phenomena, for individuals do not only *re*act; they act *intentionally* (see also Graumann & Kruse, in this volume). The environment can only make for possibilities. A person's walking through the door is not caused by the door; it is caused by the person's intention to walk through the door. Efficient causality in environmental psychology seems only to be a contradiction if the environmental and the psychological units are conceptualized as being mutually independent. At the psychological level, however, it is still legitimate to take an empirical perspective, for empirical work always requires the splitting of units. However, antecedents and consequences alike must be conceptualized at the psychological level.

Werner and Altman claim a multiperspective and multilevel approach in environmental psychology. None of the single perspectives is considered to be superior to another. Theoretically, so they argue, it is the combination of all the perspectives and all the levels that provides a holistic view of the phenomenon. This model of a holistic view implies the assumption that each perspective or level contributes some part of the truth. From a nonstatement view the inherent character of models (as opposed to theories) is metaphoric. Models pretend to be *like* the truth, but they do not claim to be it. As in physics, the question is not whether light really behaves like waves or like particles. Each of the two models has its advantages in explaining some of the observed phenomena.

Some arguments forwarded by Werner and Altman therefore seem to be derived from a statement view. In that case the philosophical view would actually become the status of a theory. That status would imply that one would have to accept an empirical criterion to test the superiority of specific perspectives, that is, the idea of falsification.

An innovative contribution by Werner and Altman is the dialectical understanding of development. They understand dialectics in the sense of processes oscillating between two opposite poles. The authors refer to the more abstract dimensions of individual-society, autonomy-conformity, freedom-determinism, more psychological ones such as selfish-generous and competitive-cooperative, and to social psychological ones such as low connection-high connection in social groups. Rituals seem to manage the transactional/dialectical opposition. While celebrating festivals and holidays, people can express and enhance their individual and social identities, experience continuity and change, familiarity and novelty, public and private, and so forth. Children in particular are considered to oscillate between these various dimensions, for changes are essential parts of their lives.

As mentioned above, the dialectic processing, described as an ebbing and flowing of the scoring on a specific dimension, provides an alternative to the homeostatic theories still popular in psychology. With those theories it is assumed that people tend toward moderate arousal, gained by reducing arousal or arousal-seeking. The individual level of optimal arousal is implicitly conceptualized as a trait. Werner and Altman's idea of dialectical processing, however, is compatible with a state position, where individuals transpose quite different levels of activation in different situations.

One problem with these polarities can be demonstrated by the dimension of familiarity-novelty. Familiarity-novelty deals with the perceived information quality of environments. But from that information quality neither the psychological experience nor the value for the person can be inferred. Depending on a person's preliminary status, the experience can be positive or negative. A familiar setting could be boring, mundane, or relaxing; a novel setting could be exciting, stimulating, or confusing. In other words, plausibility in language opposition does not necessarily imply a psychological reality.

Technological thinking is usually based on the concept of the needs and motives of persons on one hand and environmental effects on the other. In this view psychologists must investigate what people need and which kind of sociophysical environment meets their needs most. Design and planning should use this knowledge to build environments that facilitate social activities and result in an optimal person-environment relation. With the concept of dialectics, however, such monocausal statements are not compatible. Does the person's dialectical ebbing and flowing between polarities mean that there is in principle no "perfect" sociophysical environmental configuration to be defined? That ideas of environmental fit, congruence, and so forth are obsolete? If so, the answer for design guidelines would be to provide for as much variation as possible. In calling for diversity without chaos, Werner and Altman take a noncommital position while setting some constraints for variation.

This stance leads to the second part of the question raised above, that about the practical consequences that the dialectical/transactional framework has for environmental design and planning. From a developmental perspective, cities can be defined as a sociophysical frame for child development. They offer opportunities for social interaction, for expression and the building of identities. The underlying message of Werner and Altman is a claim to design city environments that facilitate and enhance social relationships. The features proposed by them focus on the establishment of secondary territories and rituals. Secondary territories are seen to allow children to regulate their experiences between familiarity and safety (but also boredom) at home, and novelty and danger (but also excitement) in public. The literature, however, shows that secondary territories cannot be defined a priori. They emerge if spaces are used in a specific way. In addition, it seems impossible to predict which places might become significant for specific groups of people. This circumstance is surely quite a paradox for environmental design because the intended occupancy might not occur at all.

Rituals as social activities should enhance neighborhood connections, should establish individual and group identities in the periodic rhythm of time. Since the rituals follow established rules, they might be important and valuable for some groups of people, whereas they are useless for others. It should not be forgotten that adolescents in particular are eager to break with traditions, develop their identities, and establish their own rules and rituals outside their neighborhoods.

All the proposals for environmental design and planning summarized by Werner and Altman seem plausible and will probably help establish connections between neighbors, nurture home identities, increase safety, and integrate children in their hometowns. However, they are not specifically adapted to cities. They can easily be generalized to each kind of environment where people live together.

Nevertheless, the question arises as to whether these proposals require an elaborated transactional philosophical view as a background. *Meta*theoretical approaches are supposed to help develop, compare, and analyze theories. But they do not facilitate technology. Yet technology requires prognoses about which kind of sociophysical environment would probably be best. Since prognoses require explanations, it is not possible to deduce technological recommendations from transactionistic axioms. Instead, theories are required to serve as mediators. The proposed dialectical processing approximates a theoretical status, including important aspects of motivation and identity. Further research could strengthen the inherent developmental perspective of change and continuity and investigate the development of dialectics: How do dialectics change in children when they grow up? How can neighborhood conditions be improved to adopt oppositions in relationships? How can families and communities use rituals to encourage children to be autonomous, to grow and change while contributing to continuity and community membership?

In sum, the dialectical/transactional approach introduced by Werner and Altman has metatheoretical as well as theoretical components. The transactional perspective, which has the status of a metatheory, offers an interesting philosophical view in environmental psychology. It does not limit itself by focusing on the physical environment and playing the counterpart to social psychology. Instead, it concentrates on vivid units that encompass the social and the physical worlds alike. The proposed dialectical process appears as an innovative theoretical framework that refers to motivation and identity. Both aspects play an important role in the development of children. Environmental psychology is called upon to investigate the specific dialectical processing that growing children experience at home, in school, on streets and playgrounds, alone, and with others.

References

Altman, I., & Rogoff, B. (1987). World views in psychology: Trait, interactional, organismic, and transactional perspectives. In D. Stokols & I. Altman (Eds.), *Handbook of environmental psychology* (pp. 7-40). New York: Chichester.

Herzog, W. (1984). *Modell und Theorie in der Psychologie* [Model and theory in psychology]. Göttingen: Hogrefe.

Stegmüller, W. (1973). *Probleme und Resultate der Wissenschaftstheorie und Analytischen Philosophie: Vol. 2.2. Theorienstrukturen und Theoriendynamik* [Problems and results of scientific theory and analytical philosophy: Vol. 2.2. Theoretical structures and theoretical dynamics]. Berlin: Springer.

Authors' response: Translating a world view

Carol M. Werner and Irwin Altman

Ute Ritterfeld's insightful commentary raised a number of important issues for both researchers and practitioners. This brief note focuses on only one of those issues: how a philosophical world view is translated into practical research and design principles. Please note, however, that our experience is as researchers and theorists; we have not had extensive opportunities to design built environments.

For convenience, we distill our fundamental premises into the following watchwords: (a) holism, (b) dynamism and change, (c) patterns of relationships, and (d) dialectic dimensions that address specific psychological processes (see pages 124 through 131 for specific details). Our general strategy is to focus on a particular dialectic dimension or family of dimensions and study how people manage those processes in holistic ways. In general, we propose that the most successful environments are those designed or used so as to support both sides of a dialectic, either simultaneously or over time.

In our translation strategy, we begin with the dialectic dimensions because they define the psychological processes of interest. We next ask how *people* use the *physical environment* in *coordinated ways* to support these dialectic *processes*. In framing our questions in this way, we adopt a dynamic and holistic approach. Similarly, we assume that designs that are congruent with human activities; that support multiple, coordinated patterns of behavior; and that enhance growth and change will be most successful.

Much of our own work has examined the dialectic of privacy regulation, defined as the "selective control of access to the self or group" (Altman & Chemers, 1980, p. 77). That is, we examine how people open up to or closeoff from others, whether physically or psychologically. The next step is to define the holistic unit of analysis – whether to focus on a home, block, neighborhood, or community as a confluence of people, place, behaviors, feelings, and time. We try not to break these wholes into constituent parts but rather to study them as total dynamic entities. Similarly, we could recommend design decisions that address the whole rather than single aspects of behavior or space.

For example, in one project, Gauvain, Altman, and Fahim (1983) studied how, in traditional homes, two cultural groups supported openness and closedness processes. In each culture they found complex and diverse mechanisms for controlling who could enter the home, where visitors could go, and what actions were appropriate. These mechanisms included holistic patterns of verbal and nonverbal behaviors and physical design features. Gauvain et al. showed that when these mechanisms were disrupted by changes in physical design or social context, personal relations suffered and people struggled to restore their desired levels of openness and closedness. Similarly, Harris, Brown, and Werner (1996) found that residents were most satisfied with their apartments if the apartments provided adequate opportunities to both seek out and avoid family members. And as noted in our chapter, we suggested a variety of behavioral and design features that might support creation of secondary territories where people can regulate privacy by joining together in various groups or finding places to satisfy desires for aloneness and solitude.

In general, then, by anchoring research and design analyses around particular substantive dialectics, designers may be guided to think in terms of behavior and environmental features that serve particular psychological processes. If this approach is pursued with an eye towards holism, then coordinated patterns of behavior, multiple levels of scale, and continuity and change may result in both creative design solutions and new research questions.

References

Altman, I., & Chemers, M. M. (1980). *Culture and environment*. Monterey, CA: Brooks/Cole.

Gauvain, M., Altman, I., & Fahim, H. (1983). Homes and social change: A cross-cultural analysis. In N. R. Feimer & E. S. Geller (Eds.), *Environmental psychology: Directions and perspectives* (pp. 180-218). New York: Praeger.

Harris, P. B., Brown, B. B., & Werner, C. M. (1996). *Privacy regulation and place attachment*. Manuscript submitted for publication.

A contextualist perspective on child-environment relations

Theodore D. Wachs and Noam Shpancer

Just over 50 years ago, Pepper (1942) listed contextualism as one of the four viable "world hypotheses" that may be used to understand the nature of knowledge itself. Since then, there has been a growing interest in the application of contextualist principles to both science in general (Hayes, Hayes, Reese, & Sarbin, 1993) and human development in particular (Lerner, 1993; Reese, 1991). As often happens when theories become popular, the increased interest in contextualism has led many to adopt the contextualist label even when there is only a weak connection between an individual's work and contextualist principles. Part of the confusion arises because all metatheories (Chandler, 1993) and many experimental paradigms (Capaldi & Proctor, 1994) include some aspects of context as part of their frame of reference. Contextualism is easily confused with conventional situationist and main effect approaches that focus on how environmental stimuli determine behavior (Jaeger & Rosnow, 1988). However, just as studying behavior does not necessarily make one a behaviorist, so taking into account the context of the experiment does not necessarily make one a contextualist (Sarbin, 1993).

In this chapter we first briefly summarize the basic tenets of contextualism, indicating the unique aspects of the approach as applied to the study of development as well as the problems associated with the application of pure contextualism to the study of development. We then discuss the methodological and theoretical aspects of contextualism that are most profitably applied to developmental topics, with specific reference to the question of children's development in urban settings.

1 The basic principles of contextualism

Four fundamental emphases define "pure" contextualism as outlined by Pepper (1942).

a. An emphasis on fusion
Contextualism holds that a phenomenon cannot be investigated or understood properly – indeed, does not functionally exist – apart from the context in which it is embedded. For our purpose context is defined as the set of circumstances surround-

ing and influencing an event. Context, however, is not viewed as external to the event but rather as an integral part of it (Rosnow & Georgoudi, 1986). The root metaphor of contextualism is the historical event, an event "alive in the present" (Pepper, 1942, p. 232), in which objects and actions exist and become meaningful only in a dynamic, specific context of time and space. Any attempt to decompose or reduce the "fusion" of phenomena to separate objects, individual actions, or temporal elements is considered futile (Jaeger & Rosnow, 1988), akin to an attempt to unbake a cake to recreate its ingredients. In a contextual framework organisms and their environments actively influence each other (Lerner & Lerner, 1986). The object-context relationship is characterized by plasticity and reciprocity. The boundaries between object and environment are themselves viewed as permeable and elastic and their integrated and interdependent nature is emphasized.

b. An emphasis on change
Contextualism views events as active, dynamic, and changing – "an open process of becoming" (Rosnow & Georgoudi, 1986, p. 3). Constant change is the norm, and phenomena are viewed as "change processes" (Lerner & Busch-Rossnagel, 1981, p. 8). In the contextualist universe, multiple levels of both organism and context may exist simultaneously, change continuously, and interact actively and dialectically to shape the course of development. In contrast to both mechanism and organicism, which treat unexplained events or changes as merely random variability or gaps in knowledge to be explained away, contextualism allows for the possibility that novel, unexplained, emergent change is a real and inherent characteristic of phenomena (Reese, 1991).

c. An emphasis on openness
To the contextualist, "there is no final or complete analysis of anything" (Pepper, 1942, p. 249). Contextualists reject the deterministic position that views development as essentially prescribed to follow rigid, biologically based paths that are at best speeded or delayed by environmental influences. Contextualism emphasizes instead the probabilistic nature of development. The complex, emergent, and context-bound nature of phenomena renders the notion of "finished" or set facts useless. Rather, facts are considered in themselves "events," i.e., dynamic and context-dependent. Ultimate, complete knowledge is thus impossible; facts are better described in relative, probabilistic terms, and the course of individual development with regard to general norms is neither inevitable nor invariant.

d. An emphasis on scope
Central to contextualism as outlined by Pepper (1942) is the emphasis on scope over precision. A contextual analysis moves from the "event" outwards (Pepper, 1942) and assumes an expanded present, reciprocity of relationship, and the embeddedness of phenomena. Contextualism is thus inherently predisposed to sacrifice precision,

control, and the characteristically mechanistic preoccupation with a reductionist, inward-oriented probe for the elusive "essential elements" in favor of attempting to capture more fully the complex web that enables, affects, and defines phenomena. For contextualism, the essence of any phenomenon does not lie in its exact, detailed, and stable finality – as such finality or completeness is nonexistent and unknowable. Rather, the essence of events lies in the fact and process of their embeddedness in a potentially infinite array of multilevel contexts. Any attempt to approach a clear vision of the workings of phenomena necessarily entails enlarging the scope of the investigation.

2   Contextualism in developmental psychology

Many aspects of the contextualist agenda have been incorporated into the research and theory of developmental psychology (see also the chapter by Wapner, in this volume). Developmentalists have quite readily embraced several central features of contextualism, such as the notion of *multiple levels of analysis* (Parke, 1988), the *plasticity of development* (Brauth, Hall, & Dooling, 1991; Brim & Kagan, 1980), *the probabilistic nature of developmental outcomes* (Gottlieb, 1991; Horowitz, 1987), and the *transactional or reciprocal nature* of developmental processes (Bell & Chapman, 1986; Sameroff & Chandler, 1975).

Further, contextualism is congruent with a growing trend in developmental research toward *multidisciplinary cooperation* in the investigation of psychological phenomena (Plomin, 1993; Wachs, 1993a) and toward more *ecologically valid and cross-cultural research* (Bornstein, 1991; Bronfenbrenner, 1986; Szapocznik & Kurtines, 1993). The contextualist position as applied to developmental psychology is also congruent with an emphasis on the *role of individual differences* in influencing developmental outcome (Thomas & Chess, 1977; Wachs, 1992).

The contextualist influence also clearly underlies the *social interactionist perspective* in developmental psychology (Cairns, 1979; see also Fuhrer, in this volume), which has focused on the interactions between sets of individual responses and the social context in which they occur (e.g., Patterson & Reid, 1984). Finally, contextualist ideas underlie the move toward *life span orientation* in the study of development (Dixon, 1986; Lerner, 1990; Reese, 1991; see also Lerner & von Eye, in this volume).

The contribution of contextualism to developmental psychology has not been to promote a single research design, a specific research area, or a new methodology. Rather, contextualism's major contribution so far has been mainly to challenge and offer alternatives to some of the field's traditional assumptions, point to new questions, and offer a new frame for the underlying debate over the nature of developmental processes.

3   Why contextualism was not wholly incorporated by developmentalists

Although developmental psychologists have incorporated pieces of the contextualist vision into their research questions, designs, and attitudes, most have nevertheless found it difficult to swallow contextualism whole (Reese, 1991). There are a variety of reasons why the day-to-day practical and conceptual work of developmental scientists does not easily lend itself to a wholesale embrace of pure contextualism.

First, in pure contextualism, the number of potentially relevant variables is infinite. However, few developmentalists assume that all aspects of the context are equally salient with regard to particular behavioral outcomes (Stokols, 1987). Hence, researchers need to choose which aspects of the context will be most salient and need to decide in what way potentially relevant contextual variables should be incorporated into the research. In this regard contextualism is a rather amorphous paradigm, providing few clear guidelines and rules for explanation and inquiry (Dixon, 1986). Within a pure contextual framework the decision criteria for relevance and inclusion are, at best, slippery.

Further, even if one is able to identify the most salient contextual variables and decide how to incorporate them, obtaining the required sample size needed to reach adequate statistical power to test for the operation and nature of contextual moderating and mediating processes may be almost impossible. This is particularly true if one is dealing with higher order interactions (Wachs & Plomin, 1991). For example, in a contextually driven study investigating the role of parenting microprocesses upon adolescent adjustment as a function of ethnicity, socioeconomic status, and family structure, a sample size of 10,000 adolescents was insufficient to provide the needed power to adequately test some of the critical hypotheses under investigation (Steinberg, Mount, Lanborn, & Dornbusch, 1991). This state of affairs has led to a call for developing alternative approaches to data analysis in contextually derived studies (e.g., Bronfenbrenner, 1991). However, for the moment, such alternative approaches are in the potential rather than the applicable stage. As a result, in the scientific "real world," carrying out a full-fledged contextualist project – a multi-level, multivariate, ecologically valid investigation – is likely to become a daunting task in organizational and budgetary terms as well as in terms of statistics and methodology.

In addition, pure contextualism with its "horizontal cosmology" (Pepper, 1942, p. 251), affinity for inherent disorder, and its explicit rejection of the traditional notion of progress itself understandably seems at odds with – if not ultimately antithetical to – the traditional concepts of both "development" (Chandler, 1993; Kaplan, 1983) and "science" (Overton, 1984). For example, Lerner and Kauffman (1985) have argued that "dispersion, as a key feature of contextualism, means that the sort of changes depicted in a 'pure' statement of this position represents the antithesis of what is needed to forge a scientifically useful concept of development" (p. 318). Though not all developmental contextualists would agree with this argument (for example, Reese, 1991, notes that contextualism does not demand constant flux and novelty but rather allows for it, such that both order and disorder are accepted as possible), pure contextualism's emphasis and insistence on constant change is not easily reconciled with data suggesting the existence of stability and continuity with regard to some developmental phenomena (Reese, 1991). For example, available evidence suggests that there is lawful continuity for both cognitive characteristics (Bornstein & Sigman, 1986) and individual personality characteristics (Kagan, Reznick, & Snidman, 1989). Hence, the potential indeterminacy of prediction inherent in contextualism is troublesome to many developmentalists.

Finally, the contextualist cause is not helped by the fact that experimentation, still the hallmark of science, is difficult to adjust to pure contextualist specifications. Contextualism emphasizes the uniqueness of any event (Hayes, 1993) and denies any final causality (Reese, 1991), thus undermining the search for cause-and-effect contingencies and for generalizability, which are at the heart of experimentation.

While developmental scientists have not assimilated all aspects of the contextual framework into their research or theoretical schemata, some aspects of this framework have been shown to be particularly useful for developmental research. In the next section we use the four principles of contextualism discussed earlier as a framework for assessing specific examples of contextualism that may be particularly relevant to the study and understanding of children's development. In the final section we relate both results and examples to the question of children's development in urban settings.

4   Principles of contextualism and children's development

4.1   Fusion

As previously noted, contextualism emphasizes the fusion of individuals and contexts across time. The linkage of the contextual principle of fusion to processes influencing child development is best seen in the operation of two specific principles: the covariance between organism and environment and the operation of this covariance across both historical and individual time.

4.1.1   Covariance
Organism-environment covariance refers to the fact that the different environmental contexts children encounter are not randomly distributed across children; rather children with certain characteristics are more likely to encounter certain types of environmental contexts than are children with different characteristics. To understand covariance it is critical to recognize that we are talking about a probabilistic and not a deterministic relation between individual and contextual characteristics.

Certain individuals are more likely to encounter certain types of environments, but this view in no way means that individual characteristics alone are responsible for certain types of encounters. An excellent example of the probabilistic nature of this process is seen in studies looking for relations between children's temperament and parental rearing practices.[1] Though there are a variety of theoretical reasons to predict relations between children's temperament characteristics and parent rearing-styles, such predicted relations do not always appear (Crockenberg, 1986). One major reason why is that other factors such as caregiver preference for certain temperamental patterns, child gender, and parental stress can act to moderate relations between child temperament and parent rearing-strategies (Slabach, Morrow, & Wachs, 1991). The probabilistic nature of the processes governing organism-environment covariance are thus very much in tune with the contextual principles described above.

Three types of organism-environment covariance have been identified (Plomin, DeFries, & Loehlin, 1977). *Passive covariance* refers to the degree to which children receive both common biological influences and environmental features from their parents. Though the concept of passive organism-environment covariance appears most often in behavioral genetic studies (e.g., intelligent parents are more likely to pass along both "intelligent" genes and enriched environments for their children than are less intelligent parents), the operation of passive covariance is not necessarily restricted to genetics alone. As one nongenetic example, young infants whose mothers are malnourished are more likely to encounter nutritional deficiencies, based on less-than-adequate amounts of critical nutrients in the mother's milk, as well as less adequate parenting from their malnourished mothers (McCullough et al., 1990).

Reactive organism-environment covariance occurs when children with certain behavioral or biological characteristics are more likely to *elicit* certain reactions from their caregivers than are children without these characteristics. For example, children with higher rates of physical illness are more likely to receive more physical contact stimulation from their caregivers than are children with lower illness rates (Wachs et al., 1992). Similarly, children with insecure attachment histories are more likely to elicit rejection both from grade-school teachers and peers than are children with histories of secure attachment (Sroufe & Egeland, 1991).

Finally, there is *active organism-environment covariance*. In this case children with certain biological or behavioral characteristics are more likely to *seek out* certain contexts or settings than are children without these characteristics. For example, children having a higher degree of biomedical risk have been described as less likely to seek out cognitively stimulating activities than children who are not at biomedical risk (Breitmeyer & Ramey, 1986). Similarly, children with inhibited temperaments are more likely to avoid novel interpersonal situations than are children who are temperamentally uninhibited (Gunnar, 1993).

In addition to the three types of organism-environment covariance described above, it also is important to recognize that contexts themselves may covary. For example, children in lower quality daycare are more likely to encounter less parental involvement (Howes & Olenick, 1986) and greater parental stress (Howes & Stewart, 1987). Similarly, high levels of noise and crowding in the home are associated with less adequate patterns of parental caregiving (Wachs, 1989, 1993b). Thus, the contextual principle of fusion, as expressed in covariance processes, involves not only the fusion of individual and environment but also fusion across contexts (for a detailed discussion of the operation of covariance processes in children's development, see Wachs, 1992).

4.1.2 Temporal fusion

The operation of the contextualist principle of fusion can also be seen in regard to temporal processes. Current developmental processes do not function in isolation from processes that occurred earlier in the life span. Certainly, there is ample evidence demonstrating how previous psychosocial (Elder, 1995) or biological (Pollitt, Gorman, Engle, Martorell, & Rivera, 1993) experiences in the life histories of individuals can have an impact upon their current functioning. For example, measures of the quality of the child's early home environment predict later school functioning, even when one statistically controls for the impact of intervening home and school events (Sroufe, Egeland, & Kreutzer, 1990). The age at which the individual encounters specific events may be particularly critical, as seen in Elder's work illustrating different developmental paths for individuals who experienced the Great Depression of the 1930s at different time periods in their childhood (Elder, 1979). Alternatively, current events can also override the impact of earlier stressors. For example, mothers who were rejected during their own childhood are less likely to show inappropriate parenting behavior if they are currently receiving adequate levels of social support (Crockenberg, 1987).

Even more dramatically, available evidence indicates that prior historical events can play a role in development, even when the individual does not directly encounter these events. *Intergenerational transmission* of both biological (Galler & Propert, 1981a, 1981b) and psychosocial influences (Dell & Rose, 1993; Denenberg & Rosenberg, 1967) have been previously demonstrated at the infrahuman level, even when the offspring has not directly encountered the biological or psychosocial experiences of their parents. Though only limited evidence of such intergenerational effects is available at the human level, a number of interesting hypotheses have been proposed in this regard. For example, Ogbu (1990) has proposed that the current school difficulties shown by children of certain minority groups may be a function of whether previous generations in these groups were either voluntary or involuntary migrants to the United States.

Covariance and temporal processes may themselves be fused in the sense that previous events may influence the types of covariances that occur later in the lives of individuals. For example, longitudinal studies have demonstrated that women who are reared in disorganized circumstances in childhood have a greater probability of both later conduct disorder and early marriage. The covariance of conduct disorder and early marriage is, in turn, associated with a higher probability of marrying deviant spouses, which leads to even more problems for these women (Rutter, Champion, Quinton, Maughan, & Pickles, 1995). Higher order fusion of past events with current covariances may be an important mechanism for understanding variability in human development across the lifespan.

4.2 Change

The issue of change is central to developmental psychology (Brim & Kagan, 1980) and contextualism (Baltes, Reese, & Lipsitt, 1980). In both developmental psychology and contextualism change is regarded as a continuous process unfolding throughout the lifespan and involving reciprocal organism-environment transactions. Where the two viewpoints differ is with regard to the change processes they emphasize. Developmental psychology places greater pemphasis on "lawful" change, as contrasted with the contextualist emphasis on the salience of novel or incidental change. However, this difference is one of degree rather than opposition, given that contextualism allows for novel or incidental change but does not require that it occur (Reese, 1991).

Examples of lawful change phenomena are seen in many areas of developmental psychology (Brim & Kagan, 1980; Wohlwill, 1973). For example, Baumrind (1989) has argued that development is inherently unstable throughout the childhood years because the individual self-concept, which is central to personality organization, does not emerge in it's mature, reflective, internalized form until adolescence. The contextualist emphasis on the reciprocal nature of change processes is well reflected in the developmental literature. A number of studies have reported significant changes in maternal behavior toward the same child across the first several years of life. These studies also indicate that the changes in maternal behavior are, at least in part, elicited by the children's own developmental changes (Dunn, Plomin, & Daniels, 1986; Kindermann, 1993; Maccoby, Snow, & Jacklin, 1984). For older children, Stipek & MacIver (1989) have shown how changes in children's cognitive ability, such as the acquisition of conservation, interact with changes in ecological conditions, such as evaluation practices or teacher-students relationships, to produce changes in children's assessment of their own competence.

Research has further documented that within a system, a change in one level entails a ripple effect through other levels. For example, Bertenthal and Campos (1990) have shown how the emergence of self-produced locomotion leads to a reorganization of emotional, social, and cognitive functioning. Further, change can occur even within relatively restricted boundaries. For example, Matheny (1983) assessed the temperament of identical and fraternal twins using factors derived from Bayley's Infant Behavior Record. He concluded that even within a genetically induced range sufficient change occurred resulting in "idiosyncratic features which, for each infant, preclude strong predictions of test-taking behavior from one age to the next" (p. 358). Similarly, Kagan et al. (1989) reported changes in temperament over a six-year span, even within a biologically driven sample of extremely inhibited and uninhibited children.

For the most part developmental researchers have attempted to explain seemingly novel or incidental changes using a mechanistic framework, looking for the lawful efficient combinations of small behavioral units that underlie all complexity. For example, Thelen (1984) showed how the sudden emergence of independent walking in children necessitates a complex interaction between a multitude of immediate and distal components from the physiological, neurological, psychological, and environmental domains. Some of these necessary components are nonobvious and may appear long before the walking behavior emerges. However, the seemingly sudden appearance of walking behavior occurs only when all necessary components are present and interacting. Similarly, Gratch (1976) showed that changes in the emergence of object permanence, as illustrated by the AB phenomenon,[2] are affected by a variety of factors including visual contact with the object, time delay before the start of the search, and the infant's prior experience with searching for hidden objects.

In spite of this preference by developmentalists for mechanistic explanations of change, even if the causes are nonobvious, references to processes resembling incidental or novel change have sometimes appeared in the developmental literature. For the most part, discussion of incidental change centers on the role of chance events in changing individual developmental trajectories (McCall, 1983). Examples of the potential relevance of chance events can be found at the individual, cultural, and even the species level. For example, at the individual level studies have documented changes in children's development as a function of sudden natural disasters such as flooding (e.g., Burke, Moccia, Borus, & Burns, 1986) or drought (McDonald, Sigman, Espinosa, & Neumann, 1994). Changes in family and cultural patterns as a function of the introduction of outside influences, such as missionaries, have also been documented (Super & Harkness, 1986). At the species level Gottlieb (1987, 1991) has argued that evolutionary change in species-specific behaviors may result from exposure to nonnormative experiences.

Evidence for the operation of novel developmental change – change that would not be predicted and seems almost contraintuitive – while scarce, has also been presented. Perhaps the clearest example for novel developmental change is seen in the case of idiot savants – individuals with very low IQs who display remarkable talents in a specific area. As noted by O'Connor and Hermelin (1988): "One of the very notable features of the occurrence of talents in the idiot savant is that they frequently emerge unbidden, usually between the age of 5 and 8 years, often on the basis of no detectable genetic influences and in the complete absence of training" (pp. 393-394). While rare, such examples do illustrate that the concept of novel change is not unknown to developmentalists.

4.3   Openness

The linkage of the contextual principle of *openness* to processes influencing children's development is best seen in the operation of *organism-environment interaction*. Organism-environment interaction refers to differential reactivity to similar environmental or biological input by individuals with different biological, individual, or environmental characteristics (Wachs & Plomin, 1991). Congruent with the contextual principle of openness, organism-environment interaction means that rarely is there a single direct, predetermined path from genes, nutrition, biomedical status, or experience to developmental outcome. Rather the influence upon development of individual genotypes, nutritional status, and biomedical history will be moderated by the context within which genetic (Gottlieb, 1991), nutritional (Pollitt, 1988), or biomedical influences (Sameroff & Chandler, 1975) are expressed. Similarly, the influence of macro- and microcontextual processes upon individual development will be moderated by both individual and biological characteristics (Wachs, 1992). As a result the course of individual development is probabilistic, based on the joint operation of multiple determinants of development, all of which are necessary but none of which are sufficient (Wachs, 1995). While organism-environment interactions are often not easy to detect, the difficulties in detection appear to be primarily methodological-statistical in nature rather than due to a paucity of such interactions (McClelland & Judd, 1993; Wachs & Plomin, 1991; Wahlsten, 1990).

Rutter (1983) suggested that there are a number of different forms of organism-environment interaction. For our purposes we consider two of the interaction types noted by Rutter, namely *synergy* (making a bad situation worse or a good situation better) and *buffering* (minimizing the impact of a bad situation). Examples of synergistic interactions are seen in studies indicating that the negative consequences of having a biological predisposition to mental illness (Tienari et al., 1985) or criminality (Cloninger, Sigvardsson, Bohman, & VonKnorring, 1982) are substantially increased if children with these predispositions are reared in inadequate or inappropriate environments. The detrimental impact of illness upon development has been shown to be markedly increased if illness is accompanied by malnutrition (Pollitt, 1983), while the detrimental impact of inadequate nutrition is substantially increased by exposure to either general or specific contextual risk factors (Rahmanifar et al., 1993; Sigman, McDonald, Neumann, & Bwibo, 1991; Wachs et al., 1993). Similarly, the greater vulnerability of children with difficult rather than easy temperaments has been shown to be accentuated when such children are exposed to a variety of environmental stress factors such as noise (Wachs, 1987), maternal anger (Crockenberg, 1987), maternal emotional unavailability (Lumley, Ables, Melamed, Pistone, & Johnson, 1990), or family stress (Hetherington, 1989). What these data show is that the negative consequences of biological or psychosocial risk factors may be even more detrimental than would be predicted if we looked at these risk factors only in isolation.

On the other hand, risk status need not necessarily have long-term developmental consequences if buffering (protective) organism-environment interactions occur. For example, subsequent exposure to high-quality psychosocial rearing conditions has been shown to minimize or even eliminate the later developmental risk associated with abnormal EEG patterns in infancy (Beckwith & Parmelee, 1986), low apgar score (Breitmayer & Ramey, 1986), preterm birth (Bradley, Caldwell, Rock, Casey, & Nelson, 1987), malnutrition (Grantham-McGregor, 1993), or a family history of schizophrenia (Asarnow, 1988). Similarly, the impact of current stresses can be minimized or reduced as a function of the operation of protective factors that occurred earlier in the life span. For example, evidence illustrates how securely attached children show greater adaptation to later environmental stress than do insecurely attached children (Sroufe & Egeland, 1991), or how a history of frequent and positive mother-child interaction patterns can buffer children against the negative effects of maternal work stress (Moorehouse, 1991). (For more a detailed review of human studies illustrating the operation of organism-environment interactions, see Rutter & Pickles, 1991, or Wachs, 1992.)

The probabilistic and open nature of development as a function of the operation of complex organism-environment interactions is perhaps best illustrated in the case of so-called resilient children – children who have been repeatedly exposed to multiple biological and psychosocial risk factors but who show far fewer adverse developmental consequences than would be expected given their background. In a noncontextual universe one would expect essentially all these children to show long-term, serious developmental deficits. In fact, available evidence indicates that a surprising number of these children both cope with and even transcend the multiple and repeated stressors in their lives (Masten, 1989; Radke-Yarrow & Sherman, 1990), ultimately developing into "competent and autonomous young adults who worked well, played well, loved well and expected well" (Werner & Smith, 1982, p. 153). Resilience appears to be governed by sets of complex multidimensional interactions operating across time (Werner & Smith, 1982).

4.4 Scope

The linkage of the contextual principle of *scope* to children's development is best illustrated through existing structural models of the environment, which clearly delineate the hierarchical and multilevel nature of the contexts within which children function. Particularly as seen in the writings of Urie Bronfenbrenner (1989, 1993), children's contexts are best understood as a multidimensional dynamic system, which operates across multiple levels. For example, research on the effects of economic hardship on children has documented how sudden economic stress affects adult-child interactions, which, in turn, influence child behavior (Conger et al., 1992). An example of this type of system is shown in Figure 1. Variability in children's development is directly tied into characteristics of the microsystem. The characteristics of the microsystem that influence children's development are what Bronfenbrenner and Ceci (1994) call *proximal processes*: "progressively more complex reciprocal interactions between an active evolving biopsychological human organism and the persons, objects and symbols in its immediate environment. To be effective, the interaction must occur on a fairly regular basis over extended periods of time." However, as is also shown in Figure 1, the operation of microsystem proximal processes is both directly and indirectly influenced by contextual characteristics, both at the microsystem level and at higher levels of the system. In a non-contextual approach to development, these other layers would be either ignored or minimized, with the focus being only on immediate transactions between the child and the microsystem. In a contextual approach, by contrast, emphasis is on the importance of focusing on the whole contextual system and its operation if the nature of variability in children's development is to be understood.

Available evidence demonstrates a variety of ways in which higher order contextual dimensions are important in influencing both the nature of the microsystem and relations between microsystem proximal processes and children's development. Relations between higher order contexts and the microsystem may be *indirect*, in the sense that higher order contextual dimensions can influence caregiver beliefs or values that, in turn, can relate to how caregivers rear children. For example, the level of community violence can act to influence parent beliefs about the appropriateness of children's fighting and the role of parents in controlling children's aggression. These beliefs then influence the degree to which parents actually act to discourage children from fighting (Fry, 1988). Similarly, cultural beliefs about what skills are important for children and when children should display these skills can have a direct influence on how and when children are trained (Goodnow, 1988; LeVine, Miller, & Richman, 1991). Higher order contextual conditions such as degree of social support to the caregiver (Belsky, 1984), economic disruption (Conger et al., 1992; McLoyd, 1990), or characteristics of the parents' work environment (Kohn, 1995) can also *directly* influence the characteristics of parent's behavior patterns. Direct and indirect chains of influence across contextual dimensions can also be demonstrated. For example, Cotterell (1986) has shown how paternal working conditions influence the extent of the mother's social support network, which, in turn, influences the quality of the rearing environment provided by the mother (see also the chapter by Cotterell, in this volume).

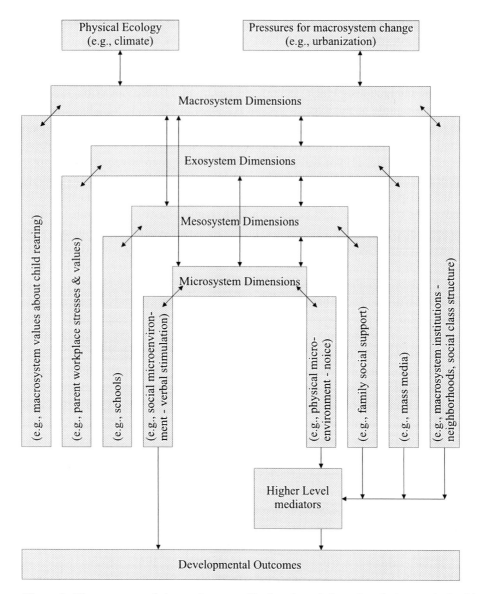

Figure 1: The structure of the environment (freely adapted from Bronfenbrenner). Double headed arrows refer to bidirectional levels of influence across the environment. Single headed arrows refer to direct or mediating influences of the environment upon development

In addition to structuring the nature of the microsystem, higher order contextual dimensions also can act to moderate the nature of relations between microsystem characteristics and children's development. That is, relations between specific micro-system characteristics and children's development will vary depending on the char-acteristics of higher order contextual dimensions. For example, relations between parents' rearing strategies (authoritarian, authoritative) and adolescent achievement vary as a function of the ethnic group to which the adolescent belongs (Steinberg et al., 1991). Cultural value systems, such as the importance of effort or education, can act to reduce the potential detrimental consequences associated with overcrowded school classrooms (Stevenson & Lee, 1990). Similarly, the impact of family socialization practices upon children's adjustment will vary as a function of whether the child is in daycare (Howes, 1990). (For a review of evidence on higher order moderation and mediation of the microsystem, see Wachs, 1992.)

The above pattern of findings does not in any way negate the importance of the microsystem in children's development or the relevance of studies that narrowly focus upon microsystem parameters. However, the contextual emphasis upon scope suggests that a better understanding of variability in children's development, and of the nature of the processes that underlie such variability, will be facilitated by increasing the scope of our investigations to include the multiple environmental layers that constitute the child's world.

5 Implications for research and intervention

The contextualist emphases discussed above seem to provide a particularly apt framework for the study of children in urban environments. Levine, Michelson, Spina, and Hodgson (1979) used the term "the environmental mosaic" (p. 484) to characterize the unique aspects of the urban environment that combine to influence urban children's lives. The city offers a complex social context – dynamic and immediate – with diverse formal and casual forms of cultural, ethnic, and class friction and cross-fertilization, multiple recreational and entertainment options, and the intensity and ambiguity of surrounding stimuli in the form of street advertisements, clothing styles, and so forth. City life also involves unique spatial and physical environments: diverse architectural styles, high-rise and apartment living, traffic, noise, crime, pollution, population density, and the sheer population mass. The urban context, with its multiple dimensions, provides unique opportunities and challenges for developing children – and for those who attempt to study and aid them. In the following sections we discuss the implications of contextualist principles for research and intervention efforts, with specific reference to the issue of their application in urban contexts.

5.1   Research implications

5.1.1   Fusion

The principle of fusion illustrates the importance of looking at the nature of the relations between the different macrocontexts that simultaneously impinge upon the
child. It seems clear that different urban contextual risk factors covary. For example,
chronic poverty in urban settings is an umbrella term encompassing a variety of
covarying risk factors, including level of neighborhood resources, ethnicity, quality
of schools, level of control of family activities by external agencies, family structure,
family stress, and punitive or inconsistent discipline patterns within the family
(McLoyd, 1990). How may the researcher deal with this contextual covariance? The
traditional approach has been to partial out "extraneous" variables statistically so as
to isolate the impact of the specific variables of interest to the individual researcher.
Traditionally, for example, studies on the impact of family density upon parent-child
relations statistically control for factors such as parental education level, parental
occupation level, and ethnicity (e.g., Booth & Edwards, 1977). In contrast, contextual researchers would argue that statistical partialling leads to an overly simplified
set of results that seriously misrepresents the nature of processes underlying developmental variability (Bronfenbrenner, 1993).

   Rather than partialling, a contextually driven research strategy would take account
of the fusion between the multiple settings within which the child functions. This
could be done through systematic comparisons of predictor-outcome relations across
different contexts or across different populations, as seen in studies illustrating how
the impact of nutritional supplementation (Pollitt et al., 1993) or more adequate
mother-child interactions (Bronfenbrenner & Ceci, in press) varies as a function of
the degree of family socioeconomic disadvantage. An alternative strategy would be
to treat multiple predictors as a *composite*, rather than studying them in isolation. An
excellent example is seen in the work of Sameroff, Seifer, Baldwin, and Baldwin
(1993), who were able to predict both current intellectual performance and stability
of intelligence of urban children using a cumulative index integrating 10 risk factors
(e.g., maternal behavior and mental health, family social support, family size, stressful life events, and parental occupation). The use of a cumulative risk index may be
particularly relevant for studying children in urban environments, where multiple
risk and support factors typically tend to be highly fused.

5.1.2   Change

The principle of change takes the researcher one step further in terms of emphasizing how context operates in time as well as in space. Temporal changes in parameters such as neighborhood quality, family poverty, or the status of ethnic groups
within society may be critical for understanding the contextual processes that influence children's development in an urban environment. For example, economic reces-

sion may result in urban neighborhoods changing from primarily working poor to primarily nonworking poor; neighborhoods that move in this direction are more likely to show increased social disruption and violence, which, in turn, have an impact upon the families living within these changing neighborhoods (Wilson, 1995). Similarly, while perceived social support can act to buffer individuals against the detrimental impact of high-density living conditions, high-density living conditions can eventually erode individual perceptions of social support (Evans, Palsane, Lepore, & Martin, 1989; Lepore, Evans, & Schneider, 1991). The impact of change can also interact with contextual characteristics. For example, school transitions (e.g., from elementary to junior high school) may be particularly problematical for disadvantaged urban children (Seidman, Allen, Aber, Mitchell, & Feinman, 1994).

Ideally, researchers would target such change processes through the use of longitudinal research strategies. However, contextual realities, such as the lack of available funding for longitudinal research, may make longitudinal strategies unfeasible. But even when actual longitudinal research is precluded, estimates of change processes can still be obtained. One approach is through the use of demographic information, such as changes over time in the percentage of regularly employed adults in a given neighborhood. One can also obtain this information at an individual level by assessing how long family members have lived in high density conditions, or by eliciting family members' perceptions of whether their neighborhood has gotten better or worse over a given span of time. Alternatively, researchers can target their investigations at critical transition points for families and children, such as when urban children move from preschool to elementary school, or when there are potential changes in the level of family or neighborhood organization as a function of factors like urban renewal, job loss, or new employment opportunities.

5.1.3 Openness

Evidence showing the operation of openness, as exemplified in individual differences in reactivity to contextual factors, has already been documented in this chapter. In addition, previous research has identified child or family characteristics that can act as moderators of contextual influences, such as individual differences in temperament, nature of past experience, and family risk factors (Wachs, 1992). The contextual principle of openness carries two implications for researchers who wish to study the development of children in urban contexts. The first implication involves research strategy and the question of the researcher's ability to detect individual differences in children's reactions to a given urban context. Previous reviews have documented the types of research strategies that are necessary to maximize the chances of detecting existing individual differences in reaction to specific contexts, including the use of theory- driven studies, the use of aggregated data, the tailoring of the statistics used to the nature of moderating processes that are hypothesized as occurring (Wachs & Plomin, 1991), and oversampling for extreme groups (McClelland & Judd, 1993).

The second implication involves evaluation of intervention projects designed to enhance the development of young children living in high-risk urban settings. For the most part, evaluation of the outcomes of these types of intervention has been based on assessing mean differences between treated and control children. What is typically missing in these evaluations is assessment of the degree of *intraprogram variability* in reaction to intervention. Significant differences between the cognitive or behavioral development of treated and untreated children can occur as a function of many children showing moderate gains or only a few children showing major gains. In a more complete assessment of the effectiveness of intervention strategies used with high-risk urban children, one would not only consider whether there were group differences but also examine the degree of variability within the treated groups in terms of the number of children who actually gain after intervention and of the distribution of existing gains (Wachs, 1990).

5.1.4 Scope

The contextual principle of scope emphasizes the importance of going beyond the child's microenvironment when attempting to understand the nature of contextual influences upon children's development. For example, Bronfenbrenner (1993) has argued that contextual research designs should always include at least two different macrocontexts. For the researcher, the critical question is what macrocontexts should be chosen for inclusion and how they should be measured. We argue that the choice of macrocontext measures depends upon the research question being asked. If the research question involves assessing *generalizability* of findings across contexts, then relatively broad and easily obtainable *demographic* macrocontextual measures can be utilized, such as neighborhood concentration levels of poverty families or the degree of violence in different neighborhoods. However, if the research question involves investigation of the *nature* of higher order contextual influences, then more detailed contextual measurements must be utilized. For example, a researcher may wish to answer questions involving the degree to which family and neighborhood or cultural institutions and processes are mutually reinforcing or mutually antagonistic. In the latter case, rather than simply contrasting urban neighborhoods in terms of income or violence levels, researchers would need to assess neighborhood residents' *perceptions* of the nature and salience of social networks within neighborhoods; the extent of personal and collective responsibility for neighborhood issues felt by neighborhood residents; or the nature of strategies used by parents, school person-nel, and other caregivers to help neighborhood children cope with chronic violence (e.g., Garbarino, Dubrow, Kostelny, & Pardo, 1992; Wilson, 1995). Similarly, researchers can use demographic information to answer questions on the generaliza-bility of findings from one social class or ethnic group to another (e.g., Steinberg,

Lanborn, Dornbusch, & Darling, 1992). However, researchers also can utilize more detailed individual measurement procedures that assess how members of different ethnic or social class groups view the nature of the society they live in and which strategies they feel are appropriate to use in dealing with the larger society (e.g., Ogbu, 1990).

5.2 Implications of contextualism for intervention

5.2.1 Fusion

The principle of fusion implies an emphasis on individual-environment *relations*. Research has shown that a lack of "fit" between individuals' needs and their environment may lead to adjustment difficulties. Providing such fit may be an appropriate goal of intervention. For example, Eccles et al. (1993) argued that the difficulties of many young adolescents in the junior-high-school years may be due to a poor fit between the adolescents' changing needs and capacities and the opportunities afforded them by the school environment. The authors point out that junior high schools tend to be more restrictive, less personal, and less cognitively challenging at a time when adolescents are developing a greater need for autonomy, participation, personal attention, and a greater capacity for higher order thinking. Research has shown how adolescents' behavioral and motivational problems can be effectively reduced in those middle and junior high schools that address this gap by emphasizing teacher efficacy and higher order thinking skills and by providing opportunities for warm student-teacher relations and for student participation in class decision-making (Eccles et al., 1993).

Another implication of this idea for intervention is that once implemented, the intervention program itself becomes a context with which the child is actively engaged. Interventors should take into account the interaction of the intervention-as-context with other contexts of the child's life. For example, once a child is assigned to a special education class, that class becomes one of the child's contexts. Mere affiliation with such a class may be negatively labeled by other kids and by teachers and thus adversely affect the child (Lazar, Darlington, Murray, & Snipper, 1982). Woodhead (1988) has proposed that preschool intervention programs such as Head Start may function to steer at-risk children away from early special education programs and grade retention, thus replacing the cycle of negative labeling and low expectations with a process in which early success (i.e., positive school experience, positive teacher expectations) breeds further, long-term school success.

5.2.2 *Change*

Periods of instability are an integral and necessary part of any organism's adaptation mechanisms (Futterweit & Ruff, 1993). Different dimensions of the organism-context interface may become more amenable to change at various times and should thus be appropriately emphasized in the intervention process. For example, the Conduct Problems Prevention Research Group (1992) identified the transition into school as a developmentally appropriate time for intervention because the children are then most at risk and their families most receptive. Similarly, looking at first grade outcomes for urban, low SES minority children, Reynolds (1989) suggested that the time periods prior to or during kindergarten are particularly amenable to intervention efforts because motivational and school behavior patterns are still forming. Interventions at this time may be particularly critical because they are more likely to trigger positive achievement expectations in children that may help maintain the impact of the intervention over time (Woodhead, 1988).

Along the same lines Schweinhart and Weikart (1987) argued that, generally, intervention is best initiated immediately prior to the time an individual is scheduled to enter into a new setting. Intervention should focus on promoting patterns that will enhance the individual's adaptation to the new setting. For example, a preschool program occurring shortly before the child's entry into school may focus on training the child in the intellectual skills and social behaviors that will be required in the school environment (Schweinhart & Weikart, 1987).

5.2.3 *Openness*

The contextualist emphasis on openness implies that one aim of intervention and prevention efforts should be to identify and provide "buffering" experiences for at-risk children. For example, research on resilience in urban children has identified a triad of protective factors separating resilient from stress-affected children. The triad consists of (a) positive child temperament, (b) a supportive family milieu, and (c) the availability of a supportive extended family and other adults (Garmezy, 1983; Wyman, Cowen, Work, & Parker, 1991).

Given this research, we argue that urban intervention programs should be structured to include all three domains. First, programs should identify the child's temperament and educate the parents about the behavioral implications of different temperaments. For example, parents of children with difficult temperaments could be taught to relax their demands and expectations regarding the behaviors that are characteristically difficult for these children, such as early establishment of regular sleep and feeding schedules, early self-feeding and self-dressing, and easy adjustment to new situations and people (Chess & Thomas, 1984).

Second, programs should incorporate a parent education and training component emphasizing both parent-child and interparental communication and problem-solving skills. For example, the behavior patterns of children with biological (e.g., prematurity) or biosocial risk factors (e.g., difficult temperament) may elicit inappropriate or inadequate caregiving patterns from their parents, particularly if parents are faced with other stresses characteristic of urban environments. Parent-training programs designed to enhance the responsivity of parents, increase their sensitivity to the unique needs of their child, and reduce the levels of parental emotional crisis have been described and have shown some degree of success in achieving these goals (e.g., Nurcombe et al., 1984; Seifer, Clark, & Sameroff, 1991).

Finally, programs should work to facilitate "cluster-building," establishing an informal network of neighborhood families who share information and resources, provide a mutually supportive atmosphere, and work to affect positive changes in the neighborhood. One such approach is seen in the work of Cochran (1987).

Openness also refers to the importance of individual differences in shaping developmental outcomes. This implies the need for customizing interventions to the characteristics of individuals. For example, in the classroom, teachers may need to tailor their interactions and expectations to the different behavioral tendencies of children with different temperaments, in order to promote optimal child functioning. Thus, slow-to-warm-up children should not be evaluated early in the school year, for their performance can be expected to suffer during the first weeks after the transition. Distractible, low-persistence children may not benefit from a demand for long periods of concentration (Chess & Thomas, 1984).

A related notion is that similar results may be achieved by different means or processes. This means that different intervention approaches may prove effective for different populations. For example, Culbertson and Schellenbach (1992) have described a variety of models for intervention programs with maltreated children, including outreach, hospital, and center-based programs. In choosing a program model, interventors should consider the unique nature, needs, and demands of the particular population and problem they attempt to address. Thus, outreach programs sending interventors into the home or neighborhood to prevent child maltreatment may be more suitable for high-risk, isolated parents, whereas center-based programs may be a better match for mobile, motivated parents (Culbertson & Schellenbach, 1992). Similarly, center-based interventions may provide a better intervention setting then home-based interventions for children coming from noisy, crowded home situations (Wachs, 1990).

5.2.4 Scope

Contextualism assumes that both macro- and microprocesses interact to produce developmental outcomes. Thus, intervention programs should include both proximal and distal contexts. For the most part urban intervention research has mostly been characterized by a narrow focus – aiming the intervention at one behavioral component or at a single contextual level (e.g., Comer, 1976; Gottesman, Croen, Cerullo, & Nathan, 1983; Kagitcibasi, 1989). Research has shown that the impact of intervention is maximized when multiple dimensions are incorporated into the program (e.g., Grantham-McGregor, 1993; Kaufman & Zigler, 1992; Seitz, Rosenbaum, & Apfel, 1985). Further, in a contextualist approach, effective interventions would emphasize the relations between children and the multiple layers or dimensions of their environment. For example, Olds, Henderson, Chamberlin, and Tatelbaum (1986) developed a longitudinal outreach program for child maltreatment prevention in single, low-income expectant mothers. The program included three components: parent education about child development and care, enhancement of family support, and creation of a link between mothers and formal health and human services in the community. The program resulted in better home environment, less child abuse, and improved life conditions for mothers at 24 and 46 months postpartum (Olds, 1987).

6 Summary

Attempts to integrate contextual principles into the conceptualization of research and intervention programs have been increasing in the past decade (e.g., Bradley et al., 1987; Futterweit & Ruff, 1993; Peters & Kontos, 1987; Woodhead, 1988). The implications of contextualism for research and intervention, as outlined above, amount to a call for inclusion. On the research front, contextualism calls for incorporating multiple dimensions of the child's life into the design and analysis. For urban research, this idea implies a need to look carefully both within and beyond the urban context to identify and include the relevant macrocontexts within which urban life happens. It also implies a need to look at the microlevel variables that may underlie the differences between children within the same urban context. On the intervention front, contextualism implies devising programs that would incorporate multiple levels and methods and regard participants as active agents in the change process. Adaptation of the contextualist view implies a greater complexity, given that contextual research will combine both a larger scope as well as increased attention to individual characteristics. However, along with the daunting aspects incorporating contextualist principles into research and intervention programs comes the promise of a new and more penetrating insight into what it must take to better understand, and affect, the development of children in the city and beyond.

Notes

1 Temperament refers to relatively stable, early appearing, biologically based, observable personality traits (e.g., mood, sociability, activity).
2 The AB phenomenon refers to an error in object search exhibited by infants, in which the infant looks for a hidden object in a location in which the infant has previously found the object rather than in a different location in which the infant now sees the object being hidden.

References

Asarnow, J. (1988). Children at risk for schizophrenia. *Schizophrenia Bulletin, 14,* 613-631.

Baltes, P. B., Reese, H. W., & Lipsitt, L. P. (1980). Life-span developmental psychology. *Annual Review of Psychology, 31,* 65-110.

Baumrind, D. (1989). The permanence of change and the impermanence of stability. *Human Development, 32,* 187-195.

Beckwith, L., & Parmelee, A. (1986). EEG patterns of preterm infants, home environment and later IQ. *Child Development, 57,* 777-789.

Bell, R., & Chapman, N. (1986). Child effects in studies using experimental or brief longitudinal approaches to socialization. *Developmental Psychology, 22,* 595-603.

Belsky, J. (1984). The determinants of parenting: A process model. *Child Development, 5,* 83-96.

Bertenthal, B. I., & Campos, J. J. (1990). A system approach to organizing effects of self-produced locomotion during infancy. In C. Rovee-Collier & L. P. Lipsitt (Eds.), *Advances in infancy research* (Vol. 6, pp. 1-60). Norwood, NJ: Ablex.

Booth, A., & Edwards, J. (1977). Crowding and family relations. *American Sociological Review, 41,* 308-321.

Bornstein, M. (1991). *Cultural approaches to parenting.* Hillsdale, NJ: Erlbaum.

Bornstein, M., & Sigman, M. (1986). Continuity in mental development from infancy. *Child Development, 57,* 251-274.

Bradley, R., Caldwell, D., Rock, S., Casey, B., & Nelson, J. (1987). The early development of low birth weight infants. *International Journal of Behavioral Development, 10,* 301-318.

Brauth, S. E., Hall, W. S., & Dooling, R. J. (1991). *Plasticity of development.* Cambridge, MA: MIT Press.

Breitmayer, B., & Ramey, C. (1986). Biological nonoptimality and quality of post-natal environment as codeterminants of intellectual development. *Child Development, 57,* 1151-1165.

Brim, O. G., Jr., & Kagan, J. (1980). Constancy and change: A review of the issues. In O. G. Brim, Jr., & J. Kagan (Eds.), *Constancy and change in human development* (pp. 1-26). Cambridge, MA: Harvard University Press.

Bronfenbrenner, U. (1986). Ecology of the family as a context for human development. *Developmental Psychology, 22,* 723-742.

Bronfenbrenner, U. (1989). Ecological systems theories. *Annals of Child Development, 6,* 187-249.

Bronfenbrenner, U. (1991, July). *The ecology of human development.* Paper presented to the International Society for the Study of Behavioral Development, Minneapolis.

Bronfenbrenner, U. (1993). Ecological system theory. In R. Wozniak & K. Fisher (Eds.), *Specific environments: Thinking in contexts* (pp. 3-46). Hillsdale, NJ: Erlbaum.

Bronfenbrenner, U., & Ceci, S. (1994). Nature nurture reconceptualized in developmental perspective. *Psychological Review, 101,* 568-586.

Burke, J., Moccia, T., Borus, J., & Burns, B. (1986). Emotional distress in 5th grade children 10 months after a natural disaster. *Journal of the American Academy of Child Psychiatry, 26,* 536-541.

Cairns, R. B. (1979). *Social development: The origins of plasticity of interchanges.* San Francisco: W. H. Freeman.

Capaldi, E., & Proctor, R. (1994). Contextualism: Is the act in context the adequate metaphor for scientific psychology? *Psychonomic Bulletin and Review, 1,* 239-249.

Chandler, M. J. (1993). Contextualism and the post modern condition. In S. C. Hayes, L. J. Hayes, H. W. Reese, & T. R. Sarbin (Eds.), *Varieties of Scientific Contextualism* (pp. 227-247). Reno, NV: Context Press.

Chess, S., & Thomas, A. T. (1984). *Origins and evolution of behavior disorders.* New York: Brunner/Mazel.

Cloninger, C., Sigvardsson, S., Bohman, N., & VonKnorring, A. (1982). Predisposition to petty criminology in Swedish adoptees. *Archives of General Psychiatry, 39,* 1242-1249.

Cochran, M. (1987). Empowering families. In K. Hurrelmann, F. Kaufmann, & F. Lösel (Eds.), *Social intervention: Potential and constraints* (pp. 105-120). New York: Walter de Gruyter.

Comer, J. P. (1976). Improving the quality and continuity of relationships in two inner-city schools. *Journal of the American Academy of Child Psychiatry, 15,* 535-545.

Conduct Problems Prevention Research Group (1992). A developmental and clinical model for prevention of conduct disorder: The FAST Track Program. *Developmental and Psychopathology, 4,* 509-528.

Conger, R. D., Conger, K. J., Elder, G. H., Lorenz, F. O., Simons, R. L., & Witbeck, L. B. (1992). A family process model of economic hardship and adjustment of early adolescent boys. *Child Development, 60,* 1015-1024.

Cotterell, J. L. (1986). Work and community influences and the quality of child rearing. *Child Development, 57,* 347-362.

Crockenberg, S. (1986). Are temperamental differences in babies associated with predictable differences in caregivers. In J. Lerner & R. Lerner (Eds.), *Temperament and psychosocial interaction in children* (pp. 55-74). San Francisco: Jossey Bass.

Crockenberg, S. (1987). Predictors and correlates of anger toward and punitive control of toddlers by adolescent mothers. *Child Development, 58,* 964-975.

Culbertson, J. L., & Schellenbach, C. J. (1992). Prevention of maltreatment in infants and young children. In D. J. Willis, E. W. Holden, & M. Rosenberg (Eds.), *Prevention of child maltreatment: Developmental and ecological perspectives* (pp. 47-77). New York: Wiley.

Dell, P., & Rose, S. (1993). Differential maternal environmental experience prior to pregnancy: Effects across two generations. *Medical Science Research, 21,* 75-77.

Denenberg, V., & Rosenberg, K. (1967). Nongenetic transformation of information. *Nature, 216,* 549-550.

Dixon, R. A. (1986). Contextualism and life span developmental psychology. In R. L. Rosnow & M. Georgoudi (Eds.), *Contextualism and understanding in behavioral sciences* (pp. 125-146). New York: Praeger.

Dunn, J. F., Plomin, R., & Daniels, D. (1986). Consistency and change in mothers' behavior toward young siblings. *Child Development, 57,* 348-356.

Eccles, J. S., Midgley, C., Wigfield, A., Buchanan, C. M., Reuman, D., Flanagan, C., & MacIver, D. (1993). Developing during adolescence. *American Psychologist, 48,* 90-101.

Elder, G. (1979). Historical change in life patterns and personality. In P. Baltes & O. Brim (Eds.), *Life span development and behavior* (Vol. 2, pp. 117-159). New York: Academic Press.

Elder, G. (1995). The life course paradigm. In P. Moen, G. Elder, & K. Luscher (Eds.), *Examining lives in context* (pp. 101-140). Washington, DC: American Psychological Association.

Evans, G., Palsane, M., Lepore, S., & Martin, J. (1989). Residential density and psychological health. *Journal of Personality and Social Psychology, 57,* 994-999.

Fry, D. (1988). Intercommunity differences in aggression among Zapotoc children. *Child Development, 59,* 1008-1019.

Futterweit, L. R., & Ruff, H. A. (1993). Principles of development: Implications for early development. *Journal of Applied Developmental Psychology, 14,* 153-173.

Galler, J., & Propert, K. (1981a). Maternal behavior following rehabilitation of rats with intergenerational malnutrition. I: Persistent changes in lactation related behavior. *Journal of Nutrition, 111,* 1330-1336.

Galler, J., & Propert, K. (1981b). Maternal behavior following rehabilitation of rats with intergenerational malnutrition. II: Contributions of mothers and pups to deficits in lactational related behaviors. *Journal of Nutrition, 111,* 1337-1342.

Garbarino, J., Dubrow, N., Kostelny, K., & Pardo, C. (1992). *Children in danger.* San Francisco: Jossey-Bass.

Garmezy, N. (1983). Stressors of childhood. In N. Garmezy & M. Rutter (Eds.), *Stress, coping and development in children* (pp. 43-84). New York: McGraw-Hill.

Goodnow, J. (1988). Parents' ideas, actions and feelings. *Child Development, 59,* 286-302.

Gottesman, R. L., Croen, L. G., Cerullo, F. M., & Nathan, R. G. (1983). Diagnostic intervention for inner-city primary graders with learning difficulties. *Elementary School Journal, 83,* 239-249.

Gottlieb, G. (1987). The developmental basis of evolutionary change. Special issue. Comparative psychology: Past, present, and future. *Journal of Comparative Psychology, 101,* 262-271.

Gottlieb, G. (1991). The experiential canalization of behavioral development. *Developmental Psychology, 27,* 4-13.

Grantham-McGregor, S. (1993). Assessments of the effect of nutrition on mental development and behavior in Jamaican studies. *American Journal of Clinical Nutrition Supplements, 57,* 303-309.

Gratch, G. (1976). On levels of awareness of objects in infants and students thereof. *Merrill-Palmer Quarterly, 22,* 157-176.

Gunnar, M. (1993). Psychoendocrine studies of temperament and stress in early childhood. In J. Bates & T. D. Wachs (Eds.), *Temperament: Individual differences at the interface of biology and behavior* (pp. 175-198). Washington, DC: American Psychological Association.

Hayes, S. C. (1993). Analytic goals and the varieties of scientific contextualism. In S. C. Hayes, L. J. Hayes, H. W. Reese, & T. R. Sarbin (Eds.), *Varieties of scientific contextualism* (pp. 11-27). Reno, NV: Context Press.

Hayes, S. C., Hayes, L. J., Reese, H. W., & Sarbin, T. R. (Eds.). (1993). *Varieties of scientific contextualism.* Reno, NV.: Context Press.

Hetherington, M. (1989). Coping with family transitions. *Child Development, 60,* 1-14.

Horowitz, F. (1987). *Exploring developmental theories.* Hillsdale, NJ: Erlbaum.

Howes, C. (1990). Can the age of entry into child care and the quality of child care predict adjustment in kindergarten? *Developmental Psychology, 26,* 292-303.

Howes, C., & Olenick, M. (1986). Family and child care influences upon toddler's compliance. *Child Development, 57,* 202-216.

Howes, C., & Stewart, P. (1987). Child's play with adults, toys and peers: An examination of family and child care influences. *Developmental Psychology, 23,* 423-430.

Jaeger, M. E., & Rosnow, R. L. (1988). Contextualism and its implications for psychological inquiry. *British Journal of Psychology, 79,* 63-75.

Kagan, J., Reznick, S., & Snidman, N. (1989). Issues in the study of temperament. In G. Kohnstamm, J. Bates, & M. Rothbart (Eds.), *Temperament in childhood* (pp. 133-144). New York: Wiley.

Kagitcibasi, C. (1989). Child rearing in Turkey and intervention research. Council of Europe workshop on the educational problems of immigrant children. *Psychology and Developing Societies*, *1*, 37-52.

Kaplan, B. (1983). A trio of trials: The past as prologue, prelude and pretext: Some problems and issues for a theoretically oriented life-span developmental psychology; Sweeny among the nightingales – A call to controversy. In R. M. Lerner (Ed.), *Developmental psychology: Historical and philosophical perspectives* (pp. 185-230). Hillsdale, NJ: Erlbaum.

Kauffman, J., & Zigler, E. (1992). The prevention of child maltreatment: Programming, research and policy. In D. J. Willis, E. W. Holden, & M. Rosenberg (Eds.), *Prevention of child maltreatment: Developmental and ecological perspectives* (pp. 269-296). New York: Wiley.

Kindermann, T. (1993). Fostering independence in mother-child interactions. *International Journal of Behavioral Development*, *16*, 513-535.

Kindermann, T., & Skinner, E. (1988). Developmental tasks as organizers of children's ecologies. In J. Valsiner (Ed.), *Child development within culturally structured environments*. (Vol. 2, pp. 66-105). Norwood: Ablex.

Kohn, M. (1995). Social structure and personality through time and space. In P. Moen, G. Elder, & K. Luscher (Eds.), *Examining lives in context* (pp. 141-168). Washington, DC: American Psychological Association.

Lazar, I., Darlington, R. B., Murray, H., & Snipper, A. S. (1982). Lasting effects of early education: A report from the consortium for longitudinal studies. *Monographs of the Society for Research in Child Development*, *47* (195, Serial Nos. 2-3).

Lepore, S., Evans, G., & Schneider, N. (1991). Dynamic role of social support in the link between chronic stress and psychological distress. *Journal of Personality and Social Psychology*, *61*, 899-909.

Lerner, R. M. (1990). A developmental contextual critique of evolutionary epistemology. In G. Greenberg & E. Tobach (Eds.), *Theories of the evolution of knowing*. The T. C. Schneirla conference series (Vol. 4, pp. 29-45). Hillsdale, NJ: Erlbaum.

Lerner, R. M. (1993). Human development: A developmental contextual perspective. In S. C. Hayes, L. J. Hayes, H. W. Reese, & T. R. Sarbin (Eds.), *Varieties of scientific contextualism* (pp. 301-316). Reno, NV: Context Press.

Lerner, R. M., & Busch-Rossnagel, N. A. (1981). Individuals as producers of their development: Conceptual and empirical bases. In R. M. Lerner & N. A. Busch-Rossnagel (Eds.), *Individuals as producers of their development* (pp. 1-36). New York: Academic Press.

Lerner, R. M., & Kauffman, M. B. (1985). The concept of development in contextualism. *Developmental Review*, 5, 309-333.

Lerner, R. M., & Lerner, J. (1986). Contextualism and the study of child effects in development. In R. L. Rosnow & M. Georgoudi (Eds.), *Contextualism and understanding in behavioral science* (pp. 89-104). New York: Praeger.

LeVine, R., Miller, P., & Richman, A. (1991, April). *Influence of culture and schooling on mothers' models of infant care*. Paper presented to the Society for Research in Child Development. Seattle: Washington.

Levine, S., Michelson, W., Spina, A., & Hodgson, S. (1979). Emergent themes and priorities. In W. Michelson, S. Levine, & A. Spina (Eds.), *The child in the city* (pp. 478-490). Toronto: University of Toronto Press.

Lumley, M., Ables, L., Melamed, B., Pistone, L., & Johnson, J. (1990). Coping outcome in children undergoing stressful medical procedures. *Behavioral Assessment*, *12*, 223-238.

Maccoby, E. E., Snow, M., & Jacklin, C. N. (1984). Children's disposition and mother-child interactions at 12 and 18 months. *Developmental Psychology, 20*, 459-472.

Masten, A. (1989). Resilience in development. In D. Cicchetti (Ed.), *Rochester Symposium on developmental psychopathology* (pp. 261-294). Hillsdale, NJ: Erlbaum.

Matheny, A. P. (1983). A longitudinal twin study of stability of components from Bayley's infant behavior record. *Child Development, 54*, 356-360.

McCall, R. (1983). Environmental effects on intelligence. *Child Development, 54*, 408-415.

McClelland, G., & Judd, C. (1993). Statistical difficulties of detecting interaction and moderator effects. *Psychological Bulletin, 114*, 376-390.

McCullough, A., Kirksey, A., Wachs, T. D., McCabe, G., Bassily, N., Bishry, Z., Galal, O., Harrison, G., & Jerome, N. (1990). Vitamin B-6 status of Egyptian mothers: Relation to infant behavior and maternal infant interactions. *American Journal of Clinical Nutrition, 51*, 1067-1074.

McDonald, M., Sigman, N., Espinosa, M., & Neumann, C. (1994). Impact of a temporary food shortage on children and their mothers. *Child Development, 65*, 404-415.

McLoyd, V. (1990). The impact of economic hardship on black families and children. *Child Development, 61*, 311-346.

Moorehouse, M. (1991). Linking maternal employment patterns to mother-child activities and children's school competence. *Developmental Psychology, 27*, 295-303.

Nurcombe, B., Howell, D., Rauh, V., Teti, D., Ruoff, P., & Brennan, J. (1984). An intervention program for mothers of low birth weight infants. *Journal of the American Academy of Child Psychiatry, 22*, 319-325.

O'Connor, N., & Hermelin, B. (1988). Low intelligence and special abilities. *Journal of Child Psychology and Psychiatry, 29*, 391-406.

Ogbu, J. (1990). Cultural models, identity and literacy. In J. Stigler, R. Schweder, & G. Herdt (Eds.), *Cultural psychology* (pp. 520-541). New York: Cambridge University Press.

Olds, D. (1987, April). *Long-term impact of nurse home visitation: Time and risk factors as conditioners of program effect.* Paper presented at the biennial meeting of the Society for Research in Child Development, Baltimore, MD.

Olds, D., Henderson, C., Chamberlin, L., & Tatelbaum, R. (1986). Preventing child abuse and neglect: A randomized trial of nurse home visitors. *Pediatrics, 78*, 65-78.

Overton, W. F. (1984). World views and their influences on psychological theory and research: Kuhn-Lakatos-Laudan. In H. W. Reese (Ed.), *Advances in child development and behavior* (Vol. 18, pp. 191-226). New York: Academic Press.

Parke, R. D. (1988). Families in life-span perspective: A multilevel developmental approach. In E. Mavis Hetherington, R. M. Lerner, & M. Perlmutter (Eds.), *Child development in life-span perspective* (pp. 159-190). Hillsdale, NJ: Erlbaum.

Patterson, G. R., & Reid, J. B. (1984). Social interactional processes within the family: The study of moment-by-moment family transactions in which human social development is embedded. *Journal of Applied Developmental Psychology, 5*, 237-262.

Pepper, S. C. (1942). *World hypotheses: A study in evidence.* Berkeley, CA: University of California Press.

Peters, D. L., & Kontos, S. (1987). Continuity and discontinuity of experience: An intervention perspective. *Advances in Applied Developmental Psychology, 2*, 1-16.

Plomin, R. (1993). Nature and nurture: Perspective and prospective. In R. Plomin & G. McClearn (Eds.), *Nature, nurture and psychology* (pp. 459-486). Washington, DC: American Psychological Association.

Plomin, R., DeFries, J., & Loehlin, J. (1977). Genotype environment interaction and correlation in the analysis of human development. *Psychological Bulletin, 84*, 309-322.

Pollitt, E. (1983). Morbidity and infant development. *International Journal of Behavioral Development, 6*, 461-475.

Pollitt, E. (1988). A critical view of three decades of research on the effects of chronic energy malnutrition and behavioral development. In B. Schurch & N. Scrimshaw (Eds.), *Chronic energy deficiency* (pp. 77-94). Lausanne: IDECG.

Pollitt, E., Gorman, K., Engle, P., Martorell, R., & Rivera, J. (1993). Early supplementary feeding and cognition: Effects over two decades. *Monographs of the Society for Research in Child Development, 58*, (17, pp. 1-99).

Radke-Yarrow, M., & Sherman, T. (1990). Hard growing: Children who survive. In J. Rolf, A. Masten, D. Cicchetti, K. Neuchterlein, & S. Weintraub (Eds.), *Risk and protective factors in the development of psychopathology* (pp. 97-119). Cambridge: University Press.

Rahmanifar, A., Kirksey, A., Wachs, T. D., McCabe, G., Bishry, Z., Galal, O., Harrison, G., & Jerome, N. (1993). Diet during lactation associated with infant behavior and caregiver infant interaction in a semi-rural Egyptian village. *Journal of Nutrition, 123*, 164-175.

Reese, H. W. (1991). Contextualism and developmental psychology. In H. W. Reese (Ed.), *Advances in child development and behavior* (pp. 187-230). New York: Academic Press.

Reynolds, A. J. (1989). A structural model of first-grade outcomes for an urban, low socioeconomic status, minority population. *Journal of Educational Psychology, 81*, 594-603.

Rosnow, R. L., & Georgoudi, M. (1986). The spirit of contextualism. In R. L. Rosnow & M. Georgoudi (Eds.), *Contextualism and understanding in behavioral science* (pp. 3-24). New York: Praeger.

Rutter, M. (1983). Statistical and personal interactions. In D. Magnusson & V. Allen (Eds.), *Human development: An international perspective* (pp. 295-320). New York: Academic Press.

Rutter, M., Champion, L., Quinton, D., Maughan, B., & Pickles, A. (1995). Understanding individual differences in environmental risk exposure. In P. Moen, G. Elder, & K. Luscher (Eds.), *Examining lives in context* (pp. 61-96). Washington, DC: American Psychological Association.

Rutter, M., & Pickles, A. (1991). Person environment interaction: Concepts, mechanisms, and implications for data analysis. In T. D. Wachs & R. Plomin (Eds.), *Conceptualization and measurement of organism-environment interaction* (pp. 105-141). Washington, DC: American Psychological Association.

Sameroff, A., & Chandler, M. (1975). Reproductive risk and the continuum of caretaking causality. In F. Horowitz (Ed.), *Review of child development and research* (Vol. 4, pp. 187-244). Chicago: University of Chicago Press.

Sameroff, A., Seifer, R., Baldwin, A., & Baldwin, C. (1993). Stability of intelligence from preschool to adolesence. *Child Development, 64*, 80-97.

Sarbin, T. R. (1993). The narrative as the root metaphor for contextualism. In S. C. Hayes, L. J. Hayes, H. W. Reese, & T. R. Sarbin (Eds.), *Varieties of scientific contextualism* (pp. 51-65). Reno: Context Press.

Schweinhart, L., & Weikart, D. (1987). Problem prevention by early childhood education. In K. Hurrelmann, F. Kaufmann, & F. Lösel (Eds.), *Social interventions: Potential and constraints* (pp. 87-104). New York: de Gruyter.

Seidman, E., Allen, L., Aber, L., Mitchell, C., & Feinman, J. (1994). The impact of school transition and early adolescence on the self system and perceived social context of poor urban youth. *Child Development, 65*, 507-522.

Seifer, R., Clark, G., & Sameroff, A. (1991). Positive effects of interaction coaching on infants with developmental disabiliites and their mothers. *American Journal of Mental Retardation*, *96*, 1-11.

Seitz, V., Rosenbaum, L., & Apfel, N. (1985). Effects of family support intervention. *Child Development*, *56*, 376-391.

Sigman, M., McDonald, M., Neumann, C., & Bwibo, N. (1991). Prediction of cognitive competence in Kenya children from toddler nutrition, family characteristics and abilities. *Journal of Child Psychology and Psychiatry*, *32*, 307-320.

Slabach, E., Morrow, J., & Wachs, T. D. (1991). Questionnaire measurement of infant and child temperament. In J. Strelau & A. Angleitner (Eds.), *Explorations in temperament* (pp. 204-235). Plenum: New York.

Sroufe, A., & Egeland, B. (1991). Illustrations of interaction from a longitudinal study of development. In T. D. Wachs & R. Plomin (Eds.), *Conceptualizations and measurement of organism-environment interaction* (pp. 68-86). Washington, DC: American Psychological Association.

Sroufe, A., Egeland, B., & Kreutzer, T. (1990). The fate of early experience following developmental change. *Child Development*, *61*, 1361-1373.

Steinberg, L., Lanborn, S., Dornbusch, S., & Darling, N. (1992). Impact of parenting practices on adolescent achievement. *Child Development*, *63*, 1266-1281.

Steinberg, L., Mount, T., Lanborn, S., & Dornbusch, S. (1991). Authoritative parenting and adolescent adjustment across varied ecological niches. *Journal of Research in Adolescence*, *1*, 19-36.

Stevenson, H., & Lee, S. (1990). Contexts of achievement. *Monographs of the Society for Research in Child Development*, *55*(221), 1-107.

Stipek, D., & MacIver, D. (1989). Developmental change in children's assessment of intellectual competence. *Child Development*, *60*, 521-538.

Stokols, D. (1987). Conceptual strategies of environmental psychology. In D. Stokols & I. Altman (Eds.), *Handbook of environmental psychology* (pp. 41-70). New York: Wiley.

Super, C. M., & Harkness, S. (1986). The developmental niche: A conceptualization at the interface of child and culture. *International Journal of Behavioral Development*, *9*, 545-569.

Szapocznik, J., & Kurtines, W. (1993). Family psychology and cultural diversity. *American Psychologist*, *48*, 400-407.

Thelen, E. (1984). Learning to walk: Ecological demands and phylogenic constraints. In L. P. Lipsitt & C. Rovee-Collier (Eds.), *Advances in infancy research* (Vol. 3, pp. 213-260). Norwood, NJ: Ablex.

Thomas, A. T. , & Chess, S. (1977). *Temperament and development*. New York: Brunner-Mazel.

Tienari, P., Sorri, A., Lahti, I., Naarala, M., Wahlberg, K., Ronkiko, J., Pohjla, J., & Moring, J. (1985). The Finnish adoptive family study of schizophrenia. *Yale Journal of Biology and Medicine*, *58*, 227-327.

Wachs, T. D. (1987). Specificity of environmental action as manifest in environmental correlates of infant's mastery motivation. *Developmental Psychology*, *23*, 782-790.

Wachs, T. D. (1989). The nature of the physical micro-environment: An expanded classification system. *Merrill-Palmer Quarterly*, *35*, 399-420.

Wachs, T. D. (1990). The development of effective child care environments. *Children's Environments Quarterly*, *6*, 4-7.

Wachs, T. D. (1992). *The nature of nurture*. Newbury Park, CA: Sage.

Wachs, T. D. (1993a). The nature nurture gap: What we have is a failure to collaborate. In R. Plomin & G. McClearn (Eds.), *Nature nurture and psychology* (pp. 375-391). Washington, DC: American Psychological Association.

Wachs, T. D. (1993b). Nature of relations between the physical and social microenvironment of the two-year-old child. *Early Development and Parenting, 2,* 81-87.

Wachs, T. D. (1995). Genetic and family influences on individual development: Both necessary, neither sufficient. *Psychological Inquiry, 6,* 161-173.

Wachs, T. D., Moussa, W., Bishry, Z., Yunis, F., Sobhy, A., McCabe, G., Terome, N., Galal, O., Harrison, G., & Kirksey, A. (1993). Relations between nutrition and cognitive performance in Egyptian toddlers. *Intelligence, 17,* 151-172.

Wachs, T. D., & Plomin, R. (1991). *Conceptualization and measurement of organism-environment interaction.* Washington, DC: American Psychological Association.

Wachs, T. D., Sigman, M., Bishry, Z., Moussa, W., Jerome, N., Neumann, C., Bwibo, N., & McDonald, M. (1992). Caregiver child interaction patterns in two cultures in relation to nutrition. *International Journal of Behavioral Development, 15,* 1-18.

Wahlsten, D. (1990). Insensitivity of the analysis of variance to heredity-environment interaction. *Behavioral and Brain Science, 13,* 109-161.

Werner, E., & Smith, R. (1982). *Vulnerable but invincible.* New York: McGraw Hill.

Wilson, W. (1995). Jobless ghettos and the social outcome of youngsters. In P. Moen, G. Elder, & K. Luscher (Eds.), *Examining lives in context* (pp. 527-544). Washington, DC: American Psychological Association.

Wohlwill, J. F. (1973). *The study of behavioral development.* New York: Academic Press.

Woodhead, M. (1988). When psychology informs public policy: The case of early childhood intervention. *American Psychologist, 43,* 443-454.

Wyman, P. A., Cowen, E. L., Work, W. C., & Parker, G. R. (1991). Developmental and family milieu correlates of resilience in urban children who have experienced major life stress. *American Journal of Community Psychology, 19,* 405-426.

Comment: Clarifying fusion

Siegfried Hoppe-Graff

Contextualism in Pepper's sense is a general world hypothesis. Therefore, it may be applied to the social and life sciences as well as to the physical sciences. In psychology, contextualism comes in many varieties, sometimes even as hybrid approaches that preserve some contextualist principles but cancel others. Thus, Wachs and Shpancer's presentation of the contextualist perspective starts with a definition of *pure* contextualism. It is defined (and distinguished from other world views) by four fundamental emphases: fusion, change, openness, and scope (see Wachs & Shpancer for details).

For the most part, the chapter by Wachs and Shpancer is an explication of these criteria. Consequently, they promise in the introductory section to "discuss the methodological and theoretical aspects of contextualism that are most profitably applied to developmental topics, with specific reference to the question of children's development in urban settings" (p. 164). A careful reading of the chapter led me to the conclusion that the authors indeed delineate a very systematic, fine-grained analysis of the methodological and content-free theoretical implications of contextualism. But their presentation lacks content-specific theoretical implications that apply specifically to the psychology of child-environment relations. I propose that this lack is a necessary consequence of the very nature of contextualism as a metatheory or world view. My commentary is a proposal for the theoretical advancement of Wachs and Shpancer's contextualist perspective through the inclusion of psychological concepts and propositions. I will start with a short analysis of their use of the term *theoretical* and then go on to present my own position. Both the analysis and the presentation are carried out *pars pro toto* for the contextualist principle of fusion. Lastly, I suggest implications that my elaboration on the concept of fusion has for the child-city relation.

1 What is "theoretical" about the theoretical implications of contextualism?

What are the "methodological and theoretical aspects of contextualism" that are included by the key idea of fusion? According to Wachs and Shpancer, fusion includes the notion that "a phenomenon cannot be investigated or understood properly – indeed, does not functionally *exist* – apart from the context in which it is embedded. . . . Context, however, is not viewed as external to the event but rather as an integral part of it" (p. 164). When defined in this way, fusion may be observed in two principles or processes of child development: the covariance between organism and environment, and the operation of this covariance across historical and individual time. In addition, these processes may themselves be fused in the sense that previous events may influence the types of covariance that occur later in the lives of individuals.

Are the principles of covariance and temporal fusion, as explained by Wachs and Shpancer, theoretical or methodological notions, or both? To find out, I quote the authors once more: "Organism-environment covariance refers to the fact that the different environmental contexts children encounter are not randomly distributed across children" (p. 168). I agree that the proposition about the nonrandom distribution of environmental contexts that children encounter might be called a theoretical assumption. But it is *theoretical* in a sense different from propositions that are called theoretical in terms of psychological theories. I will call the latter type of theoretical statements that are embedded in or derived from psychological theories, *substantive* or *psychological* statements. The principle that different contexts encountered by organisms are not randomly distributed across organisms also applies to lower level animals and to plants. Indeed, it is a general ecological principle.

One of Wachs and Shpancer's research implications of fusion is "the importance of looking at the nature of the relations between the different macrocontexts that simultaneously impinge upon the child" (p. 178). Another implication is the necessity of "a contextually driven research strategy [that] would take account of the fusion between the multiple settings within which the child functions" (p. 178) instead of statistical partialling. As concerns implications for intervention, Wachs and Shpancer emphasize the need to study "individual-environment relations" and the perspective that the intervention program itself becomes a context within which the child is actively engaged. From my point of view, all these implications are methodological and not theoretical: They tell us where to look, which strategy to choose, which phenomena to focus on, and how to conceptualize intervention in methodological terms. Again, the proposals are general and not content-specific and would apply equally well to the contextualist approach in the fields of clinical psychology, ecology, or general biology, for example.

2   The contextualist principle of fusion in the process of human development: A proposal

I propose that developmental psychology has already created conceptual ingredients that are needed for a substantive interpretation of the contextualist notion of fusion.

2.1 The self

Humans are distinct from other organisms because they begin to understand themselves early in ontogeny. The self (or self-understanding) is a conceptual system that encompasses "all the considerations that an individual uses to define the self and distinguish the self from others" (Damon & Hart, 1988, p. 1). It was William James who divided the self into two components, the *Me* and the *I* aspect. Whereas the *Me* encompasses all characteristics (material, social, spiritual) that identify the self as a unique configuration of personal attributes, the *I* stands for the awareness of the core features of individuality.

2.2 Culture and society

The context of human development is broader than the immediate environment. It is also more comprehensive than the material culture and includes all immaterial creations of culture and society that the self may use in the process of constructing and reconstructing him- or herself. For example, it includes the varieties of roles, relations, attribution patterns, values, moral rules, and ethical principles that exist as cultural and societal concepts (hereafter: sociocultural concepts) on a supraindividual level.

2.3 Developmental tasks

From a psychological point of view, the principle of fusion leads to a perspective on the process of development that emphasizes the interdependence of the evolving self and culture/society. Developmentalists have already created theoretical categories to conceptualize the "self-culture encounter," among them the concepts of a developmental task and of co-construction.

Havighurst (1948/1972) proposed the concept of developmental task as the link between the individual and those facets of the sociocultural context that are of foremost age-specific importance. To illustrate, for the period of middle childhood and adolescence he described eight tasks: getting along with age mates, learning an appropriate masculine or feminine role, developing basic intellectual skills, choosing and preparing for an occupation, developing attitudes towards social groups and social institutions, becoming independent of parents and other adults, developing conscience and moral judgment, and forming a system of ethics and a scale of values. According to Havighurst, some developmental tasks are "practically universal," whereas others are "peculiarly defined by the culture of the society" (p. 37). From my view, each task denotes a significant age-specific facet of the relation between the individual and culture/society.

Developmental tasks are two-sided coins. One side consists of cultural expectations, social values, systems of ethics, and so on; the other side, the child/adolescent's "appropriation" of the task. Even a child or adolescent who ignores the task of preparing for an occupation or who rebels against the fulfillment of this task, unavoidably acts in relation to the developmental task – in that case, by *not* fulfilling it, or by creatively trying to make his or her own way, and so on. Furthermore, the explicit refusal to resolve a developmental task may become central to a girl's or boy's self-understanding (see Erikson's theory of identity formation). In a similar way, the treatment of that task may become a central topic for the child's social relations. In other words, the idea of a developmental task actualizes the process of fusion between the self-defining individual and his or her sociocultural context because it relates at the same time to the self-concept of the child *and* to the sociocultural expectations of the child's environment.

2.4 Co-construction

Although Vygotsky did not use the term fusion, one of the central topics on his agenda was in fact the study of the fusion of the individual child and his or her sociocultural context. He argued that the process of individual development is at the same time a process of the individual's acquisition of culture. Thus, he suggested that the processes of development and enculturation are two sides of the same coin (they are fused). The fusion is made possible by a level situated between the cultural and the individual: the level of the developing individual's interactions with significant others (parents, teachers, friends, and so on):

Any function in the child's cultural development appears twice, or on two planes. First, it appears on the social plane, and then on the psychological plane. First, it appears between people as an interpsychological category, and then within the child as an intrapsychological category. ... We may consider this position as a law in the full sense of the word, but it goes without saying that internalization transforms the process itself and changes its structure and functions. Social relations or relations among people genetically underlie all higher functions and their relationships. (Vygotsky, 1981, p. 163)

It has become common within the social constructivist movement in developmental psychology to call these important interactions *co-constructions* or *joint constructions*. Co-constructive interactions take different forms, depending on the age level of the child, the psychological function that is observed, and the specifics of the child-partner dyad. In the studies that my colleague and I have conducted on the role of social construction in the emergence of symbolic play, we are able to demonstrate that imitative interactions between one-year olds and their parents figured as joint constructions in the Vygotskian sense. We observed a transitional step in the acquisition process: the cooperative acts of children and parents create new symbols that later become part of individual competence (Hoppe-Graff & Engel, 1996). In the social constructivist paradigm, fusion thus has the meaning of specific forms of joint action between the individual and others.

3 Implications for child/adolescent-city relations

To grasp the importance of urban environments for the rising generation, one has to understand that the child/adolescent-city relation (hereafter: child-city relation) is part of the all-embracing fusion of the processes of the development of the self and acquisition of culture. It is constructed through interactions between the child and his or her partners in the same way that all other concepts, rules, and standards are co-constructed. One should also take into consideration the possibility that the developing child-city relation is connected to the mastering of developmental tasks.

Children who live in cities *inevitably* acquire representations (concepts, naive theories, appraisals, and so forth) of urban environments for different reasons. First, they experience the environment permanently and intensely, and the experiences may become topics of explicit discussions. To illustrate, the surroundings may restrict the fulfillment of the child's wishes to run and to play, and child and mother may debate why there is no space for those activities. Second, the conditions of urban life are sometimes implicit and explicit topics of child culture, although they do not relate to the child's immediate experience. For example, some of the most popular books for kindergarden children in Germany are about the changes in nature and landscape that have been brought about by urbanization. The examples demonstrate that the image a child has of city life in general and of *his* or *her* city in particular is strongly influenced by significant others: parents, friends, picture books, media, and so on, at least in early and middle childhood. Thus, the concepts and appraisals of urban life are socially constructed in a very strict sense. And even for many adolescents, the concepts of urban life depend as much on indirect experiences (through others) as on direct experiences of city life. Take, for example, discussions of our way of life in the media; or consider how important public opinions are about what is "in" or "out." To conclude, when one wishes to improve predictions about the effects of changes in the urban environment, then the conceptual background of the children and the opinions of their personal and impersonal guides through city life should be taken into consideration.

But guidance by other people is not the only influence on the child's representation of cities and changes in the urban environment. The relation of the environment to the developmental tasks that the child has to tackle is also of tremendous importance. For example, an environment that includes *niches* (such as youth clubs) where elder children and adolescents can meet undisturbed by adults would be valued much more positively than surroundings that are experienced as controlling and coercive, and it might be unimportant how comfortable those *niches* are from an architect's point of view. In the preceding paragraph I pointed out that developmental tasks are represented on both the cultural and individual levels. The same may be true for changes in the city environment. Sometimes municipal authorities introduce changes with the explicit goal of helping children find space of their own, and adolescents may interpret changes in the environment as public attempts to solve youth problems.

The development of the self includes the organization of the child's world, and therefore it lays the ground for the child's sense of identity. The construction of personal identity has cognitive underpinnings – concepts and theories, which may be used to locate the self. The acquisition and continuous elaboration of the concept that the child has of his or her hometown is among those candidates for inclusion in the feeling of personal identity. But whether it really becomes part of identity depends on affective processes that go beyond the concepts. And again, the affective bond may depend more on the experiences that children have in the process of co-constructing their view of the hometown than on their experiences in the physical surroundings.

References

Damon, W., & Hart, D. (1988). *Self-understanding in childhood and adolescence*. Cambridge, Eng.: Cambridge University Press.

Havighurst, R. J. (1972). *Developmental tasks and education*. New York: McKay. (Original work published 1948)

Hoppe-Graff, S., & Engel, I. (1996, September). *The emergence of pretend symbols in infancy: Piagetian assumptions, Vygotskian predictions, and longitudinal data*. Paper presented at the 2nd Conference for Socio-Cultural Research, Geneva.

Vygotsky, L. S. (1981). The genesis of higher mental functions. In J. V. Wertsch (Ed.), *The concept of activity in Soviet psychology*. New York: Armonk.

Child development and environment: A constructivist perspective

Thomas Bernhard Seiler

1 The issue of development

Theories of development deal with at least four main issues. The first concerns the object of development and the question of what it is that is developing. The second issue revolves around causes and conditions of development. It has mainly to do with the question of whether they lie within the subject or outside it. The third issue centers on the beginning, end, and goal of development. The fourth pertains to the form of development. That is, is it smooth or abrupt? Are there transition states? Does it occur in alternative, but continuous and coherent, sequences of change or does it go through characteristic universal stages?

Theories of development differ with respect to the answers they give to these questions. Constructivist theories are primarily concerned with the second problem, for they conceive of development as a process of construction conducted by the subject itself. Their answers, however, also have consequences for the other three issues. Because constructivism began as a theory of cognition and science, it is not surprising that it focuses on cognitive development, particularly the origin and transformation of cognitive structures.[1]

What are the phenomena involved in causes of development, what are the current theoretical positions on this question, and what is the state of the related discussions today? Two fundamental assumptions figure in nearly all modern developmental theories. The first is that the origin and course of development, specifically human development, have a genetic basis. The second assumption is that genetic programs exclusively and completely determine neither the structure and content of development nor its speed and intensity, much less the steps of change it passes through.

In this sense, development is defined as the fact that a subject acquires new potentialities and new structures that he or she did not possess before but that are not predetermined in the genes. What causes them and in what way are they generated? On this question, too, some unanimity exists today among developmental theorists who hold that internal and external causes and conditions work together in each case. No psychologist today would deny that external facts and conditions influence the emergence of new psychological and cognitive capacities in some way. The problem then becomes more subtle, however, for theorists have to explain how internal conditions presuppose external influences, that is, how they function and work together. When, why, and in what way do external influences and conditions have an effect? Is it by virtue of their own activity and power, or is it necessary for the subject to have acquired specific capacities and to have reached a specific level before the external actions can interact with them to produce developmental effects?

There is no question that cognitive development, especially concept development, is dependent on sociocultural determinants. But there is a troubling problem in that the developmental product is never only an effect of the forces and influences impinging on the subject and that it is never completely the same as its models. In fact, if the equivalence between cause and effect were total, no theoretical problem would exist. The theoretical difficulty results from the fact that there is always both similarity and discrepancy between external causes and developmental effects, for one would expect that discrepancy would be minimal if the external forces could directly and completely determine their effect.

The same thing seems to be true of the relation between personality development and educational influences, but in an even more obvious and striking way. Nobody would contest that persistent educational practices and models applied over long periods have a massive effect on a developing person's attitudes, capacities, and motivations. But everybody knows also that human beings cannot be formed at will. They never develop completely according to given intentions and goals. The attitudes and actions of human beings always differ from the intended ones, at least in terms of their intensity. This fact cannot be explained only by the multiplicity of heterogeneous influences to which a person is subject in a complex society with highly diverse values.

One is often inclined to assume that such diversity is not possible in the domain of conceptual development and the development of meaning, for human subjects no doubt must – if they are to survive – adopt the same common concepts and conventional meanings of words that are important for communicating with other human subjects. Moreover, the members of a society unanimously stress the uniformity of educational goals and the identity of meanings. All parents and teachers go to great length to transmit these necessary and identical means of communication and understanding to young children. And certainly it must be agreed that they largely succeed, at least on a relatively superficial level. But a close look at the level of idiosyncratic comprehension and meaning, including simple, everyday words, reveals great discrepancy to the conventional implications of meaning that are explicitly taught by the social environment and school. Perhaps more astonishing are the frequent misunderstandings even among scientists working in the same area and using the same concepts.

Studies on several common concepts such as work, money, partner, and friend have found striking variations not only in emotional connotations and evaluations but also in central aspects and cognitive implications. They are found even in sociologically and demographically equal groups (see, for instance, Claar, 1990, and Seiler, 1988).

The fact that mutual understanding is achieved fairly well in most everyday situations follows from the practice of restricting intended meaning to global references and contenting oneself with only a very superficial understanding of the objects and actions about which one's interlocutor is speaking. Such understanding is sufficient for practical goals and often lets interlocutors forget that they have missed each other's specific content, implied relations, and intended evaluations. The more one intends to communicate above the level of concrete and immediate action and aims to grasp the finer and more subtle intentions and evaluative implications of the meaning conveyed by one's interlocutor, the greater the risk that mutual understanding will break down. Beyond concrete referential meanings, the danger of crass misunderstandings always exists.

In my view, then, theories of development must, above all, explain this fundamental fact of true accommodation to cultural conditions and social overtures on the one hand and the ever-existing discrepancy between all such influences on the other. Moreover, theories of development must account for the evident condition of external influences necessary for developmental change, but at the same time they have to conceive of and elaborate upon the conditions prerequisite in the subject and the subject's activity that modulate these influences. Most psychologists will object that this stance is not new, that all modern theories of development assume a kind of interaction between the subject and its environment. This is certainly true, as expressly affirmed above. As will be seen, however, merely supposing interaction is not enough. Interaction is a vague category that explains little. There are several kinds of theory that explain this interaction differently. Some of them do so with the concepts and logic of evolution. Others are based on cognitive reflexivity. I outline on a very abstract level their most fundamental assumptions and compare them before turning to a consideration of constructivist models.

2 Alternative explications of development

2.1 Interaction

In the concept of interaction, which is a notion in almost all textbooks, it is supposed that there are at least two sources or agents and that both of them must be active to bring forth a change or a new product. Development as interaction cannot be reduced to the activity of one of the factors alone. Its effect, that is, developmental transformations in general and the generation of new capacities in particular, require the combined activity of both agents. Only their coaction can function as a cause. Furthermore, the concept of interaction does not imply any distinction between them in terms of activity or causal role. Both factors are conceived of as being equally important and necessary, and their contribution to the production of the effect is regarded as being of equal kind.

However, it is evident that neither social influences nor external conditions are of the same nature as internal conditions and activities. Cognitive activities cannot be affected, touched, and directly transformed by external objects and material actions or by any kind of agents external to the person. To have an effect, external objects and conditions, social influences, and communicative offers must first be transformed into inner reality. Their content must be extracted by cognitive activities of the subject. Their effect depends entirely on such internal reconstruction. For this reason, explaining developmental processes in terms of interaction is insufficient because this concept is too vague; it leaves unconsidered the different kinds of role and reality that both agents have.

In psychology the term interaction is often used in a conditional sense. In that context it signifies that a cause for having an effect presupposes another cause or other causes. This type of interaction is usually conceived of in purely statistical fashion and is not determined by content. This type of interaction must therefore also be considered an insufficient concept inconsistent with true developmental explanations.

2.2 Evolution

Explicating development in terms of evolution supposes that the developing subject and its environment are active and interact in every instance of transformation and learning. But this time, the action of the subject and of the environment is thought to be different. The two kinds of activity are not regarded as being of equal nature. These theories contain two assumptions. First, the activity of the subject (or its genes) varies spontaneously. Second, these variations are not all of the same adaptive value with respect to environmental affordances. In other words, some variations are favored and reinforced by environmental conditions. That is, the subject endures them or masters them through new activities. Other variations are prevented or even extinguished. That is, the subject or its new forms of action do not survive. In the language of these theories, development and learning happen through environmental selection of spontaneous variations that conform to given environmental conditions and affordances. As far as the subject is concerned, one could speak of a kind of blind causation as chance (casual) variations come to subsist successfully. As for the environment, one could speak of an indirect determination as providing favorable conditions.

Almost all explanations that reduce development to learning and that revolve around the concepts of reinforcement (based on operational or classical conditioning) have this evolutionary touch. They may be adequate in very simple transformations of sensomotoric actions. But as general explanations of ontogenetic development, they are deficient on two counts. The first has to do with the assumption of purely chance and spontaneous variations of actions; the second, with the assumption of blindness and mechanical functioning. Both cases neglect the fundamental fact that human actions and their variations are intended and goal oriented.

2.3 Reflexivity

Explications of development in terms of reflexivity are reactions against the shortcomings of behaviorist and reinforcement models (see, for instance, Groeben, 1975). They enhance the role of insight and willfulness in human action. In reflexivity-based explanations of development, human subjects are self-aware and act and perceive consciously. This ability enables them not only to perceive their environment consciously but also to reflect on their own action, knowledge, needs, and emotions. Persons are not conceived of by theorists of reflexivity as reacting in a blind and mechanical manner to external conditions and social influences but as consciously triggering their actions and cognitions by simultaneously taking into account their own situation and needs and the environmental circumstances. Whereas evolutionary explanations of development fail to account for human cognitive capabilities, extreme reflexivity models exaggerate them, for they neither distinguish between different kinds and degrees of consciousness nor take into consideration that many developmental processes, especially in infancy, are not accompanied by true reflexivity or second-order consciousness.

There is an interesting parallelism between theories of cognition and theories of development. According to Piaget, who first worked it out, both classes of theories are fundamentally concerned with the same contrast between heterodetermination and autodetermination. Cognition on the one pole is seen as being determined by objective experiences; on the other, by its own activity. The first case is an empirist or realist position, according to which experience is an effect of external objects and their properties. The second case represents idealistic or rationalistic positions. Constructivist theories are somewhere between these two poles (Piaget, 1936).

2.4 Construction

Constructivist theories of development are closely akin to reflexivity theories. Constructivist theories, too, hold that the main cause of development lies in the subject, for subjects are conceived of as actively constructing their development. Another similarity may be seen in the fundamental role that both theories attribute to cognition in developmental processes. As already mentioned, constructivist theorists take cognition as an essential property of human action. Moreover, ontogenetic processes, in addition to their biological make-up, have intrinsic cognitive aspects that certainly imply some kind of awareness.

Constructivist and reflexivity theories also diverge in important ways. A main difference may lie in the place accorded consciousness. All cognitive acts imply some kind of awareness, whereas reflexive awareness, that is, consciousness in the strict sense, is not part of all cognitive acts, for reflexive awareness is a late construction supposing second-order cognitive structures by which humans become able to reflect on their own activity. Therefore, constructive activity generating new properties and new solutions is not necessarily conscious. Reflexivity and self-awareness do not exist originally, nor do they function as general causes of development. They result from development. When finally constructed, they may assume some causal force, but the power of that causal force remains limited. Within these confines, then, reflexivity and self-awareness become important agents that can influence and direct further developments in many situations by selecting and aggregating appropriate acts for setting new goals and attaining new objectives. However, these facts do not constitute the general nature of developmental processes. They are special and rare cases that tend to be realized in later instances of human development and learning. They are a culminating point of constructive developmental processes. Another dissimilarity, at least between some reflexivity and constructivist theories, may consist in an assumption made especially in structural genetics (see below) that constructive activity is not a uniform ability but rather something based on the activity of the multiple structures that the subject has acquired.

However, constructivism is not uniform. There are many different versions of it. I see a main difference in the role attributed to environmental conditions. Radical constructivism minimizes this role. All forms of adaptive constructivism hold that social influences and environmental conditions are just as necessary and important as the activity of the subject (see Rusch & Schmidt, 1994). Hence, the main task for all such conceptions is to explain how such adaptation can be performed by the subject and what the nature and the respective role of subject and environment are in this construction. Before these questions can be answered, it is necessary to investigate some of the fundamental implications entailed by the adaptive kind of constructivist theories on development for which I argue in this chapter.

3   Common implications of constructivist theories

3.1   Cognition as construction

Constructivism is the usual term for theories of cognition and science that reject any kind of empiricist or realist conceptions in scientific explanations. The fundamental principle of constructivism implies that knowledge is not directly and actively determined by objects that actually exist and that one does not passively perceive those objects as they are. On the contrary, they suppose an active role of the knowing person. For constructivist theorists, then, knowledge is not detected. Nor is it the effect or product of a mechanistic information-processing device. Living beings in general, and humans in particular, produce their knowledge themselves by interacting with their environment.

3.2 Development as construction

Transferring their ideas from cognition to development, constructivist theorists have two goals in mind. They either intend to elaborate general laws of development on the basis of their constructivist principles or they aim to explain and describe the development of knowledge itself as their immediate objective. These two approaches clearly have much in common and are sometimes combined. In either case, development is conceived of as a construction realized by the developing person or the evolving species.

Knowledge development is investigated by constructivist theorists on a phylogenetic or a human level. Phylogenetic considerations are found in the work of Konrad Lorenz, Rupert Riedl, and others (see Riedl & Wuketits, 1987). On the human level the investigations may aim at either reconstructing the origin and development of cultural or scientific knowledge (see, for instance, Damerow, 1993; Damerow & Freudenthal, 1986) or examining the ontogenesis of idiosyncratic knowledge. Without doubt, the main figure among constructivist theorists who apply their assumptions to human cognitive development is Jean Piaget (1896-1980).

It follows from such philosophy that cultural and individual knowledge as well as scientific knowledge and scientific work in all disciplines intrinsically have a constructive character. To constructivists, in other words, neither idiosyncratic knowledge nor scientific theories are abstracted or extracted from observations; they logically precede the observations. Only by virtue of them are theorists able to make relevant observations with which they can confront their ideas. The same is true for everyday idiosyncratic knowledge. With respect to the ontogenesis of what individuals know, the intention behind constructivist theories is, first, to identify the general laws of knowledge formation and transformation and, second, to reconstruct structures and content of common knowledge at different ages and stages of ontogenetic development.

Finally, construction never is closed and self-sufficient according to most constructivists. Those theorists admit or claim that all construction of knowledge is in some way dependent on the environment of the knowing subject and is the result of an interaction – an interaction, however, in which the internal conditions have some kind of priority.

3.3   Individual construction or social co-construction?

Among modern authors following Vygotsky in this respect, it is a widely held opinion that human development has to be characterized as the effect of a social co-construction rather than of a construction by an individual. They present this view as an antithesis to Piaget's constructivism. The term social co-construction certainly has high descriptive value, for it rightly emphasizes sociocultural factors in development. As with the term social interaction, however, co-construction is merely descriptive and lacks any true explicatory value.

First, common or conventional knowledge can legitimately be described as a genuine product of social co-constructions, for the construction of individual or idiosyncratic knowledge necessarily presupposes social interactions at all times. But that does not mean that the persons interacting have the same role in this construction. Descriptions in terms of co-construction do not analyze the different modes or stipulate the specific nature of the knowing person and his or her social partners in the process of constructing individual knowledge. Such descriptions confound necessary and sufficient conditions and fail to offer an adequate concept of their respective role, conditions, and limits. The main shortcoming in my view is that descriptions of knowledge that are based on co-construction neglect the fact that the subject constructing his or her means of action and knowledge is never completely at the mercy of cultural standards, social models, educational influences, and interpersonal discourses. Whether, which, and to what degree social offers are to be accepted is decided by the subject alone, consciously or unconsciously, on the basis of his or her possibilities of action, perception, and conception. As claimed at the beginning of this chapter, the necessary omnipresence of social models and meanings is only one aspect of developmental situations and processes. Another, equally important aspect of them is the fact that the imitation of these models and the transmission of these meanings is always limited and that many social interactions do not have an effect at all.

Hence, the problem does not consist only in the fact that the developing individual in many cases does not perceive everything a model or utterance contains, or misinterprets them, or even refutes them altogether. It is much more important to know, first, what cognitive means the developing individual has at his or her disposal for an effective imitation or reconstruction. Second, it is important to know whether that individual is able to activate and, if necessary, modify and accommodate these means in a given situation. Postulating co-construction does not answer these questions.

4   The emergence of cognitive structures as construction

4.1   Construction and adaptation

Constructivist theories of development, especially the approach presented in this chapter, go back to the genetic epistemology of Jean Piaget (see, for instance, Piaget, 1936). These theories primarily concern the origin and growth of cognitive structures and processes, but their principles simultaneously contain the logic of general developmental processes, for they attribute a fundamental cognitive aspect or nature to all actions and dispositions. They basically conceive of human beings as active subjects who themselves construct their cognitive instruments and contents. In the adaptive variant of constructivism at least, this construction is neither arbitrary nor solipsistic. Developmental transformations are therefore not considered entirely predetermined by genetics and maturation. They are understood as an epigenetic process in which it is postulated that previously acquired structures are reactualized in a specific situation and confronted with complex environmental circumstances, including natural objects and natural laws as well as cultural norms and social meanings.

In the light of such theories, human development must, first, be seen as a constructive and simultaneously adaptive process resulting from the activity of idiosyncratic structures. These structures initially consist of dispositions with which the neonate is stocked. At the same time, these dispositions are the final product of a phylogenetic construction. Second, as already stated, this constructive activity is constantly embedded in a complex environment of socially arranged things and meanings and cultural norms by means of which the individual deals with the other persons. Third, developmental constructions generally proceed by small, slow steps and are subject to invariant laws inherent in the nature and activity of the given cognitive structures themselves.

4.2   Structures and their dynamic nature

As previously noted, a constructivist view of development that bases the force of its explanation on the activity of idiosyncratic structures – I would like to call it structural genetic constructivism[2] – holds that developmental processes (a) begin with and are initiated by structures the subject already has at his or her disposal and (b) have new structures as their goal and product. But what is meant by structures? Before one deals with the origin of cognitive structures, the notion of structure must be explicated.

The term "structure"[3] in its idiosyncratic and ontogenetic sense is used in this theory for different reasons. First, every action, perception, and concept is composed of several interacting elementary parts, such as sensory impressions and motor innervations. Second, they can be reactualized by the subject upon a suitable occasion. In other words, cognitive structures have a dispositional character. This is also why it is unnecessary to postulate a separate memory for storing skills and knowledge. Instead, the structures must be regarded as the basis and the elements of human memory. It would be wrong, however, to see structures as static systems, for they also have an operative character and are almost virtual actions. For this reason one can say that they are the instruments by which humans perceive, know, and think and, when reactivated, are real actions aiming directly at the environment or, as internal actions, representing some of the objects and aspects of it.

A cognitive structure is never completely isolated from others. It is always linked to others and can be more or less systematically united with them. In addition, they are all embedded in the total organization of all structures. The emergence or transformation of a structure depends on other structures acting on it. Moreover, the activity and interaction of structures is always influenced by the overall organization of the cognitive structures in which it is embedded. The importance and the special causal role of external factors are discussed later in this chapter.

Apart from their cognitive nature and representational character, structures have motivational and emotional qualities. Motivation and emotion are not abilities and activities independent of and separated from cognition. Each cognitive structure, by its very nature, constitutes a motivational need and possesses an emotional load. These motivational and emotional qualities of cognitive structures are important aspects determining their power. The reactualization and intensity of a structure depends on the structure's motivational tendency and its emotional load. Hence, cognitive structures are at the same time and by their very nature motivational and emotional systems, too.

Moreover, the development and transformation of a structure is triggered primarily by its inherent motivational tendency and is reactivated when a suitable situation arises. Such reactivation is modulated by the emotional load investing this structure. A situation is suitable when its aspects evoke at least some of the structure's substructures or subroutines. If the situation is partially new, however, the structure has to be transformed and adapted to the new aspects. This adaptation, Piaget calls it accommodation, is realized and directed by a goal structure. In some cases the adaptation requires the activation of other structures, which are then combined with it or with some of its parts so as to form a new and more complex system.

The more an individual's conceptual system is ontogenetically developed, the more it begins to generalize and differentiate and the more its parts become interrelated and able to interact. Inherent in all structures, especially in their perceptual subroutines, is a kind of awareness or primary consciousness. Secondary consciousness, or reflexivity, however, is a late construction depending on the reconstruction of some structures by others.

4.3 Concepts as cognitive structures

Dealing mainly with concept development and its environmental conditions from a constructivist point of view, I must explain what theorists of structural genetics mean by "concept." In a wide sense, these theorists use the terms concept and cognitive structure identically, and conceptual development has, to them, the same extension as cognitive development. But in a more restricted sense, they use the term concept for referring to internalized cognitive structures, which are conceived of as units of knowing and thinking. These units, like all cognitive structures, have a double nature. On the one hand, they are products of cognitive processes; on the other hand, when reactualized they are themselves active processes of representation and thought.

In such use, the term concept signifies idiosyncratic and individual pieces of knowledge. It follows from the previous discussion that these concepts, which are the sole object of the present analysis, are formed by internalized systems of actions and perceptions. These internalized action systems represent objects and aspects acted on by them. They interact together, activating and regulating each other so as to create new concepts under the guidance of cultural and social models. Moreover, these systems, as I have already contended, do not have a cognitive nature and function only. They possess affective and dynamic qualities as well. Cognitive, dynamic, and affective aspects are inseparable qualities inherent in the nature of conceptual structures.

But when trying to describe and explain such idiosyncratic pieces of knowledge, a theorist necessarily idealizes them by abstracting their essential aspects. This theoretical work starts always from conventional concepts and conventional meanings of words. No theoretical reconstruction of idiosyncratic concepts is ever identical to knowledge structures present in the mind of an individual person. For instance, the concept of "school" that adolescents may have in mind greatly differs from the notion of school that parents or educational researchers hold. But when parents and researchers try to understand and investigate the thinking of adolescents, they must start from the conventional meaning of school and related terms and build on this basis a conceptual network of all possible meanings, aspects, and relations. Without such a hypothetical network, it is impossible to investigate and reconstruct the concept entertained by a sample of individuals, let alone find out its origin, conditions, and course of transformations.

Therefore, other distinctions are fundamental for constructivist and structurally based explanations of cognitive development. First, idiosyncratic knowledge must be distinguished from conventional or common knowledge, the latter essentially being combined into verbal concepts or meanings. Second, with respect to verbal concepts and the meanings of words and language in general, an individual kind of knowledge must be distinguished from a common or conventional kind. On the other hand, idiosyncratic meaning of verbal expressions and individual use of language in general always presuppose idiosyncratic concepts, that is, pieces of knowledge, that the person unites with the linguistic signs. Common or conventional knowledge and meaning in some way is knowledge frozen and objectivized in linguistic expressions by convention and culture or created and defined for theoretical needs by the scientific community. Only by virtue of such conventional determination is communication and the transmission of knowledge possible. However, it is important to see that this is done exclusively by individual subjects discoursing together and using their double kind of knowledge, their own interpretation of meaning and the interpretation they attribute to others or to the community in general, for there is no knowledge and no meaning if there are no subjects to have them.

Several other assertions must be mentioned for a thorough explication of the developmental psychologist's constructivist notion of concept. With respect to their extension, concepts are not classes of real objects, and their meaning cannot be conceived of as a simple list of properties and relations. They do not have to be taken as real categories of objects with similar and common properties, either. It is more exact to conceive of them as kinds of mental theories about objects, events, and their properties. Like scientific theories, these naive and subjective theories of individual persons are formed by implicit and explicit assumptions about the objects, their conditions and causes, as well as their multiple relations, goals, and functions. Finally, concepts not only refer to concrete objects and actions but also consist of abstract constructions about them and even represent internal and external human actions and their conditions.

Over and above these assumptions of constructivist theorists, the content of one's concepts is not present as such in reality. It is constructed by the concepts themselves. Even the distinction between objects and their properties is work done by concepts. Most important, the separation of intension and extension, the presentation of concepts as lists of objects and properties, is theoretical work and has to be interpreted as a kind of simplified formal representation for the goal of analysis.

4.4 Genealogies, sequences, and stages

As explained above, structural genetics distinguishes between different kinds of cognitive structures that mark different levels of cognition. The first level is that of sensomotoric or action knowing, part of which, in the course of development, is transformed into forms of knowing that are not acted out. Internal knowledge, initially, has an intuitive and figurative nature and is, later only, slowly transformed into conceptual or operative knowledge in the strict sense. These developmental forms of knowing and thinking imply different and characteristic levels of consciousness, with concepts in the strict sense being invested with higher degrees of consciousness and logic.

However, such distinctions of developmental levels are not the first objective of constructivist analyses. The logic and primary objective of structural genetics is to suppose the laws of developmental processes in the individual. The first line of theoretical analysis and empirical reconstruction is therefore to discern individual genealogies of idiosyncratic cognitive structures. This task is not only difficult but usually impossible because the path of these constructions is not known directly unless the subject can and actually does consciously guide or follow his or her own constructions. An external observer never has more than minimal knowledge about the concepts of an individual person and owes even that knowledge to the subject's actions and verbal communications. Even more critical is the fact that the observer must then always interpret both the actions and, perhaps more so, the words. Some of these methodological problems are discussed in Seiler and Wannenmacher (1983).

Whereas complete reconstruction of individual genealogies is generally precluded, other possibilities remain. First, one can derive developmental sequences, which are kinds of idealized (i.e., abstract and purified) idiosyncratic genealogies. They record neither every detail nor multiple interindividual variations but rather retain only the main steps and essential characteristics occurring in all, or at least most, individuals of a special group or population.

When this process of idealization and reduction is even more intensified and when the analysis rests not on specific content but on some abstract common aspects, neglects finer differences and minimal transition steps, and retains only the main general properties of at least the most important transformations in a field, it is no longer a matter of sequences but of stages of development. Stages do not represent idiosyncratic constructions or sequential transformations. They either express some general and essential properties of them or reconstruct only static aspects and characteristic performances that are possible for persons who have reached a certain level of development.

4.5 Origin of new structures and of new kinds of structures

In the view of structural genetics for which I argue in this chapter, concepts are neither automatically formed nor transformed by an invariable procedure or mechanism. They are not products of a computer-like device or program of the human being's cognitive apparatus. Concepts are constructed in active intercourse with all kinds of objects and situations that the subject can perceive or act on. This construction is essentially and continually conditioned by the sociocultural interpretation of those objects and situations. This interactive construction, however, is guided and determined by the concepts (even imperfect and vague ones) that the subject has at his or her disposal and is able to activate in a given situation. That is, not reality as such has an effect, but only reality as perceived. This condition is also fundamental for social influences to have an effect and for social discourses to be understood. In other words, every formation and transformation of a concept not only presupposes contrastive and conflictual intercourse with reality guided by the perceptions and concepts of the person but necessarily and constantly also demands discursive inter- actions with social partners, thereby taking on cultural rules, conventional meanings, and normative perspectives. Through such interactive processes, concepts gradually adapt to real affordances and sociocultural models and expectancies.

From those principles it follows that concept formation and concept development are slow and always partial adaptations to real objects and situations with which the subject is confronted but are also a continuous and incessant approximation to con- ventional concepts or meanings held by the surrounding culture and science (which, it is true, have their own history). Society takes an active and necessary part in this process by systematically arranging optimal conditions, transmitting information, and giving cues but cannot thereby acquire a causal role. Its offers serve only as models and have an indirect and exemplary function. Nevertheless, idiosyncratic concepts are clearly oriented to and influenced by cultural knowledge transmitted by social actions and language, but even in their presumably final state, idiosyncratic concepts do not become identical to them in all aspects. They especially do not encompass and express all corresponding conventional knowledge and meanings. Quite the contrary, they often break through their regulating power and surpass the lines they set out.

Explanations based on structural genetics also imply that concepts are not acquired in an all-or-nothing fashion but in a gradual way and that they pass through some kind of genealogies or sequences while developing. Concepts initially consist of loosely integrated sets of poorly differentiated aspects. Frequently, concepts in this state even combine contradictory aspects based on simple experiences and rather superficial perceptions. In a certain sense they are like prototypes at first. But as concepts develop, they slowly lose this character and begin to generalize. Through simultaneous differentiation they become more and more abstract; through acquisi- tion of new aspects and relations they resolve into multiple, mutually compensating components. In the final state, these components are combined into increasingly ordered and logically structured systems, which constitute the necessary basis for logical reasoning. The more an idiosyncratic concept is developed, the more its parts are combined and interrelated and the more the subject is able to be consciously aware of its components and its structure. Another consequence is that advanced concepts enable a subject to use them more and more consciously for giving words figurative, metaphorical, or metonymic senses. However, stringently structured sys- tems are rare, even with mature concepts of adults (Seiler & Claar, 1993).

To approach these ends of logic and conscience in the development of concepts, the subject must always be able to actualize concepts that approximate a new situa- tion or the meaning of a word closely enough to assimilate it, even if only in a super- ficial manner. Often, this process is directed by superordinated concepts and conscious strategies. But there are never strategies so sophisticated that they make this process a regular and conscious construction. There always remains great latitude for improvized and spontaneous accommodations in which hazard also plays an important role. In other words, the formation of new concepts is a complex and creative act that cannot be depicted as a regular and quasi-deductive process. Even less can it be conceived of as a progressive addition of further aspects and elements. Piaget calls it a dialectical[4] equilibration process.

I believe, as did Piaget, that it is useful and sound to distinguish preoperational and operational conceptual structures. Preoperational structures are kinds of internal representations that have a figurative character and that are fully dependent on immediate actual actions and perceptions that they internalize. Operational structures are system-like concepts with logical properties consisting in fully reversible systems of internalized actions. These distinctions have a built-in developmental logic, for preoperational structures are thought to be the precursors of operational structures in the course of cognitive ontogenesis.

Cognitive structures therefore seem to be causes and agents of ontogenetic construction as well as its products. New cognitive structures are not built in, not even in rudimentary form, in the genetic aptitudes of human nature. They are brought forth by assimilative and accommodative activities of "old" structures (those the subject already has at his or her disposal) that are activated when new objects are being processed in the actual situation.

Developmental transformations of structures presuppose the immanent or connatural tendency of those structures to "revive" when their proper object, a similar one, or a corresponding word is present. Owing to this dynamic tendency, which is modulated by their intrinsic emotional qualities and properties, structures generalize more and more. In this way the representational reference is extended to new objects, situations, and aspects. But such extensions become possible only when the structures are modified by adaptation to the new circumstances and properties. Thus, generalization is naturally accompanied by differentiation, and the generalized and differentiated structures can be reintegrated on a higher level in new steps. These complex activities are continuously directed by structures giving them goals. At the same time they presuppose other structures that deliver the means for causing transformations and overcoming obstacles.

The multiple kinds of confrontation with reality (see below) and the transformation and adaptation of the structures caused by them require two contrary, but compensatory, processes that Piaget calls assimilation and accommodation. They are not to be considered univocal mechanisms but analogue processes having a similar nature and function that require special forms and conditions of realization from one situation to the next. (For a more detailed discussion, see Seiler, 1978, 1991, 1994b.)

4.6   The role of social environment and ecological conditions

As explained above, developmental transformations of structures are elicited and determined by their mutual interaction, but the activation of a structure necessarily presupposes immediate and actual contact with external reality or physical signs representing it. This reality is not restricted to the natural environment and does not consist only of immutable objects and their properties and laws. First, this environment and its objects are largely formed or arranged by social activities and cultural norms. Second, and perhaps much more important, it also consists of a world of sociocultural signs offering a specific view of the surrounding world. For this reason cognitive development, especially the development of concepts, must also be characterized as a slow and step-by-step reconstruction of sociocultural knowledge.

A very frequent and widely held objection to constructivist theories, especially the theory of Jean Piaget, used to be that such explications of development ignore social and cultural influences. Some authors even claimed that Piaget would reduce development to pure maturational processes. Although such criticism is no longer heard, it remains a common opinion that explanations based on the dynamic of internal structures exclude or minimize social and cultural conditions. In his empirical research, though not in his theoretical discussions, Jean Piaget indeed seldom considered and analyzed social conditions. His research interests and intentions centered almost exclusively on demonstrating the essential role of internal structures and their self-determining activity. However, the logic of his theoretical explication and many of his fundamental texts accord a key place to external conditions, especially to social interactions.

Hence, cognitive development must be simultaneously and equally both an auto-construction by the subject's structures themselves and a sociocultural transmission or, better, an individual reconstruction of sociocultural constructions. How can these contradictory principles be reconciled into a coherent theoretical system? In particular, what role do cultural conditions, social models, educational instructions, and interpersonal discourses have in a structural and constructivist explication of cognitive development? Do they have a direct causal effect on cognitive constructions? I argue that their causal role is not direct but indirect only in the sense of Aristotelian exemplary cause.

4.7   Exemplary cause and effective cause

The conclusion drawn thus far is that mental and developmental adaptations, although performed by the structural system of the individual, necessarily presuppose incessant confrontations with a double external reality in the form of objects perceived and knowledge expressed by words and other signs and transmitted by social interactions and intercourse. But this external reality does not have the function of an effective, or direct, cause or influence. Objects and meanings of signs are thus not effective by themselves but only insofar as they are able to evoke in the subject structures by which they can be assimilated. It would be better, then, to call them offers rather than inputs.

Take verbal input, for example. The meaning of verbal signs and linguistic expressions is not inherent in their physical basis. Meaning requires a cognitive attribution or interpretation by the person using or understanding the signs and expressions. On the one hand, this meaning has been prepared by a long cultural process and is united by convention to the linguistic signs. On the other hand, in every act of social discourse and understanding a listener has to interpret the strings of sounds received by the ear. To do this, the listener must grasp at least some part of the cultural and conventional meanings as well as the additional pragmatic and situation-specific meanings of the linguistic exchanges by reconstructing it according to his or her proper available knowledge. As previously shown, however, this knowledge is subjected to the slow and complex development of conceptual structures.

The question to ask is, then, what kind of causality are these external objects and socially transmitted meanings and information when they are not directly transmitted? In my view the answer can be found in a distinction going back to Aristotle, who distinguishes between two different kinds of real causes, the exemplary and the effective. Their functions differ. Effective causes exert a direct and transformative influence. In the cognitive domain these are objects or actions that provoke a structure to be active or to be transformed. Such a direct transformation can result only if the cause is of the same nature as the object acted on. Therefore, only internal cognitive structure can directly influence other cognitive structures in terms of their cognitive content. External objects and social meanings, however, must, first, be assimilated and interpreted by the subject's own conceptual structures. Thus, all kinds of external (with respect to a subject's cognition) conditions, such as physical objects and their properties, linguistic signs, social actions and discourses, and educational influences, are certainly necessary for the transformation of structures, but their causality is exemplary or indirect only, for in order to be effective they have to be transformed and translated into knowledge structures of the subject.

The origin and growth of conceptual structures depends entirely on the cognitive activity of the subject. To the extent that environmental situations and events are objects perceived and known, and insofar as the meaning and challenges of the multiple signs presented by the surrounding society are extracted by the structures that the person is actualizing, these structures can, then, form and transform cognitive structures of the person. The external conditions form, so to speak, an indirect causality, depending on the content and meaning attributed to them.

The fact that external realities, cultural knowledge, social rules, and verbal communications have an indirect and exemplary causality can explain why they never completely determine the form and content of new structures. It is wrong to say that they are produced by communicative means or didactic instructions or that they are directly and simply internalized.

To perceive the material aspects of an object or situation or to comprehend at least the referential meaning of the means and signs that the social environment presents and offers, a person must meet certain conditions. For direct perception and cognition of external objects and events, the subject must possess appropriate sensomotoric schemes and cognitive structures. When it is cultural and social signs that are presented, the subject first needs structures suitable for perceiving the physical conditions of those signs (e.g., the clusters of phones and phonetic distinctions). Second, the subject must have developed the cognitive structures necessary for grasping at least part of the cultural and social meanings of the objects or signs. Third, the subject must be able to activate those structures in the actual situation and must in fact do so. Finally, full understanding is possible only when the subject possesses and actualizes all the structures necessary for assimilating the entire conventional and situation-specific meaning of the actions and signs offered. Because this condition is seldom met, the outcome of this process is highly variable, and the exact result of environmental conditions, social examples, and didactic instructions can never be predicted with certainty.

4.8 The scientific nature of explications based on structural genetics

For an adequate appreciation of the theoretical as well as the practical value of constructivist theories of development (and for all other theories), their scientific nature and status must be considered.

As concerns theoretical value, constructivist principles stipulate necessary conditions of development, but they generally do not state sufficient ones. They enable developmental researchers to reconstruct the course of transformations a posteriori but not to predict it except in a very limited fashion only. Moreover, every developmental analysis and its theoretical reconstruction are based on abstract concepts and general principles, so by their very nature they do not account for all conditions specific to a developmental process or performance.

This state of affairs must be kept in mind in scientific work aimed at constructing developmental sequences. Construction of new structures by an individual person is a creative and dialectical (Piaget, 1980; see also Seiler & Wannenmacher, 1983) process implying multiple degrees of freedom, especially personal decisions. The steps a person will take next cannot be compellingly deduced from the developmental state that a person has reached; only previous states can be deduced. Such sequences, even when scientifically constructed for specific abilities and contents, will rarely be unique, exclusive, and universal. In most cases one must conceive of alternative courses. One must be also aware of the fact that so-called logical implications based on conceptual content tend to be dialectical in nature, that the logical implications are consequences of the development, not its causes. In other words, their deductive character comes after the construction, not before it. There are even more limitations for the assumption of general stages. Very abstract conceptions of stages may be highly general, even universal, but this generality has to do with the abstractness of the merely descriptive notions of which they are constituted.

With respect to the practical value of constructivist theories of development, even greater restrictions must be made. Because theoretical laws and implications of any kind consist of abstract and idealized concepts, they cannot be used for directing and fostering developmental processes of individuals without further investigation of real-life situations. They always need to be carefully complemented by detailed observation and analysis of all relevant situation-specific conditions. Virtually no one will ever be able to predict with certainty whether and under what conditions a person will comprehend instructions, solve a problem, or take advantage of some hints. As will be discussed later in more detail, theoretical considerations alone are therefore never sufficient when one tries to describe and explain the role and influence of urban environments on cognitive development. It is obvious that modern cities are very complex worlds not only with respect to their physical environments but perhaps more so with respect to the social and cultural conditions that they present.

5 Development of concepts as guided construction

Because of the severe restrictions that follow from the scientific nature of every theory in general, and of genetic explications in particular, the best thing to do when trying to apply them for shaping environmental conditions and optimizing educational practice seems to be to deduce from them a kind of general set of guidelines for arranging more suitable environments, stating sensible developmental norms, and planning educational or therapeutic procedures. However, these norms and procedures will never acquire the status of deterministic rules and will never guarantee their effect with certainty and universal validity.

5.1 Environmental and social influences on conceptual development

It is not my intention here to present and discuss all problems and consequences for conceptual development that result from the conception of constructivism and structural genetics presented above. Instead, I analyze only the role of environmental conditions in general as they follow from the aforegoing theses and illustrate them with empirical findings of my research on conceptual development.

Drawing on Piaget, I have defended the idea that concepts in the strict sense consist of transformed, internalized, and economized forms of external actions and perceptions. From this and the other principles of structural genetics, one can deduce that an optimal development of conceptual thinking in the young child requires an environment that offers multiple possibilities of perceiving and acting in a systematic and intensive way. But in this respect, one also has to be aware that the objects, situations, colors, and other aspects of the environment that the researcher finds interesting and exciting may not be the best ones for the child. Each child, by virtue of its specific structural genetic history, may have its own preferences. However, there may exist more-or-less probable rules, at least for children with similar cultural and socioeconomic environments.

When a child's proximate environment is cleared of hazards and enriched with objects and situations affording multiple motor activities and high incentive value, it gives the child material to perceive and act on, material known to be essential to cognitive development. Perhaps even more important from the viewpoint of structural genetics is that possibilities for creative symbolic play be arranged, enhanced, and encouraged. The most important thing of all for conceptual development, however, is uninterrupted social discourses and social interpretations in all situations, though the restricted role of all external offers and conditions must not be forgotten.

In this latter respect my team and I (Claar, 1990; Seiler, 1988) have recorded many results clearly demonstrating that environmental circumstances, social discourses, and educational instruction always have an effect but that such effects are fundamentally limited because children are able to assimilate only those aspects for which they have already acquired suitable structures. Initially, they notice external aspects and purely referential meanings only. If they do not have the structures required for grasping the essential basis of new information, they will not be able to grasp its deeper sense. For instance, they may miss the meaning of *interest* entirely in a certain stage (Claar, 1990).

Certainly, the answers of the children at all ages reflect events they have observed and utterances they have heard in their everyday and familial context. At later ages the role of educational instruction becomes more and more evident. At the same time, it is striking that children and adolescents grasp only isolated aspects offered by their environment, never its integral whole. One may argue that parents and teachers discoursing with young children restrict their explications to these aspects. In part, they do, and where this is the case, it shows that most educators have an intuitive knowledge of their children's cognitive development and its logic. However, such insight is not general. Frequently, children are confronted with explanations they are unable to assimilate because they do not possess appropriate structures for grasping their meaning.

In the development of the concept of work, for instance, my team and I found an effect we never expected (Seiler, 1988). Only in late adolescence do juveniles begin to realize that work is not an exclusively individualistic activity subjected to biological needs only and mainly serving personal interests but that it is also subjected to intrinsic social and economic goals and conditions and regulated by conventional rules and norms. Even among the oldest adolescents (19 years) we have interviewed, these ideas remain rudimentary and are generally not integrated in a holistic understanding. Such relatively differentiated aspects are virtually never spontaneously named but only professed as answers upon further questioning. Only when an adolescent is explicitly asked the respective questions does he or she generally agree that every task involves and causes work by other people, that most work is done in company and with the aid of others, that the process of work has a societal function and is regulated by social norms, that economic production requires and brings about divisions of labor, and, finally, that this division entails manifold professions and specialized training. It seems that such knowledge in most adolescents remains rather vague and global. It has the status of isolated conceptual structures that are minimally integrated with the conceptual system of work.

Two other results are interesting as transition stages conforming to the consequences Jean Piaget implies with formal thinking (Inhelder & Piaget, 1958) and to the stage theory of cognitive complexity (see Seiler, 1973b). Adolescents from about 12 years of age on begin to bother with grasping the deeper sense of work. Initially, they tend to construct idealistic conceptions of self-fulfillment, of following their fundamental desires and realizing their dreams. Accordingly, external requirements and social expectations tend to be conceived in a negative way at first.

What are possible causes of these ways of thinking? Are the above-mentioned fundamental aspects and implications of the concept of work not part of social intercourse with children and are they not taught in school? If official curricula can be believed, then all these aspects, conditions, goals, and norms of work are explicitly assumed and expressed by educational objectives that teachers must meet in school from at least second and third grade on. Before undertaking this study, my team and I analyzed various instructional media that teachers have at hand and found that the conceptual system of work is systematically expanded and constructed in all its aspects and relations. But most of them do not play an active and explicit role in the ways adolescents think about work. Why? In terms of structural genetics, my answer would be that oral instruction is often not adapted to the cognitive structures the children have at their disposal. It is, therefore, not assimilated and integrated in the conceptual system of the child, or only the referential meanings of the respective words are assimilated, thus making for very superficial understanding.

To recapitulate the fundamental principle of a constructivist view, development of concepts is a reconstruction of external conditions, of cultural signs, social discourses, and educational instructions, but this reconstruction is a construction carried out on the subject's own terms. The culture-specific forms and content of concepts and their constructive and self-determining power are both necessary and indissociable aspects of conceptual development.

5.2   *Fostering conceptual development: Fundamental principles*

For reasons just explained, the new conceptual construction that a concrete environmental situation or verbal offer can elicit in a person depends not only on the
offer itself but even more so on the concepts the person can and actually does activate. Such fundamental limitations aside, profitable environmental conditions and
continuous social intercourse are always necessary. In this respect, too, the theory of
structural genetics and the research of Jean Piaget are important sources of guidelines and principles for conceiving and arranging an optimal environment and for
planning and directing favorable interactions and offers. I would like at this point to
distinguish, on the one hand, general conditions necessary for facilitating development and removing obstacles and, on the other hand, specific measures for directing
developmental processes toward special goals.

The general conditions I have in mind are rather external, but they are nonetheless
fundamental for conceptual development because they intimately affect its motivational and emotional state and quality. They concern the physical and psychological
well-being of persons, the absence of grave threats, and of limitations on sensomotoric actions. They encompass a vast range of ecological conditions, of environmental arrangements necessary for stimulating reasonably free, interesting, and
spontaneously exploratory activities. In this respect constructivist theories do not
seem to differ from other psychological theories, all of which in recent decades have
elaborated a number of physical and psychological conditions that must be met if
those conditions are not to diminish the possibility of normal development and
threaten serious disruption and deficiencies. The kind of environment and the type
of resources children have for arranging space, their possibilities for movement, the
objects they have to play with, the social contact necessary for their well-being and
growth – all these things constitute a stock of knowledge that all psychologists agree
on.

But when it comes to fostering development of personality, motivation, and cognition, the special measures that psychologists propose and the rationales given for
their efficacy differ greatly. In the spirit of constructivist theories, several authors
(see, for instance, Hunt, 1961, 1965) have deduced from Piaget's theory what they
call a principle of optimal distance or pairing. It states that there is an optimal discrepancy between external offers and internal structures and that if such a state is not
arrived at the person will not start effective attempts to do assimilative and accommodative work. If the activities one intends to stimulate by verbal discourses or the
creation of specific environmental conditions are too usual or too familiar to the person, if they do not present a new aspect but rather imply a simple extension to a new
situation, the resulting intensity of activation and interest will be low. If, by contrast,
the new activities required are completely outside the person's possibilities to act and
think, then the person will not be prompted to assimilate the offer, for he or she will
not possess structures suitable for accommodation. To create successful educational

measures and arrange an effective environment, it is first necessary to make a minute assessment primarily of the individual's cognitive abilities and structures and to take their emotional qualities and motivational dynamics into account.

Clearly, cognitive structures are the immediate focus of this rule. In my view, however, this principle is not only relevant to conceptual development but is fundamental to all kinds of socialization praxis and all fields of human development, personality, and social interaction. It therefore provides important criteria for finding and discerning optimal environmental conditions. Moreover, it results from considerations of structural genetics, according to which it is not enough to take the general developmental level into account. Even considerations of the concepts attributed to the persons who are to be influenced are insufficient. One must also inquire about the domain specificity of such theoretically conceived idiosyncratic structures (see Seiler, 1973a; Seiler & Claar, 1993).

5.3 Limits, restrictions, and consequences

The preceding thoughts about the nature and status of developmental theories in general and the explanations and principles based on structural genetics in particular lead to severe restrictions. Important conditions need to be considered when the attempt is made to apply them in practice and to foster conceptual development.

First, every developmental analysis and its theoretical reconstruction necessarily consists of abstract concepts and general principles. For this reason alone there is no theoretical principle accounting for all conditions specific to an individual and the concrete situation he or she is engaged in. Hence, a measure can make sense and prove to be successful for one person but not for another, or even for the same person under different circumstances. For instance, special procedures and arrangements that prove optimal in initial language development may be much less conducive to language development and linguistic competence in later phases and even less so for conceptual development. They can even be harmful. Language and thinking compensate and sustain each other in many respects but can conflict with each other as well (see Cromer, 1992; and Seiler, 1994a).

Second, the efficacy of the specific causal function of the kinds of external realities and social offers discussed above essentially depends on the internal cognitive structures the subject has hitherto developed. Hence, it is necessary for parents and teachers to know and remain constantly aware of the limits inherent in all their activities and rhetorical intercourse. Only then will they be flexible enough to vary and adapt their offers to the comprehension of the child and the affordances of the situation.

Third, every cognitive construct of an individual in a specific situation, as pointed out earlier, has a highly creative character in which spontaneous and accidental conditions play an important role.

For all these reasons there is no kind of environment that optimally fits the development of every human individual in the same way. In social intercourse and in all educational interaction, the knowledge structures that one's partners have at their disposal and actually activate must therefore be taken into account. If educational measures, instruction, and social discourses are to have an effect, they have to be adapted to each person's own level of understanding, interests, needs, and emotions.

But just as a subject's action and knowledge structures can be approached only by vague guessing and interpretation at best, and just as age norms do not preclude great variation from person to person, it is perhaps a sound strategy to create a broad and multifaceted offer while taking care not to impede intensive assimilation with excessive variation. Broad and optimal variation is one condition only. Another important rule inferable from structural genetics is that educators must give broad latitude for the spontaneous activities and interests of school children.

For the same reasons, logically sequenced instructional devices are seldom optimal for a class. Not only does the structural base line vary broadly across learners, quickness, solidity, and strength of construction does, too. In this respect knowledge about developmental sequences and stages is certainly extremely useful, although it does not apply in exactly the same way from one person to the next. Drawing on it can avoid frustrations and excessive demands.

Perhaps the considerations of structural genetics discussed here suggest that rather indirect instruction, rather unspecific hints, and simple encouragement are more effective than direct training. One surmises as much from an experiment I once designed to produce concepts of invariance in children. It showed that indirect interrogative verbal cues had a breakthrough effect on children's conceptions if they were already in a transitional state, whereas direct instruction was not comprehended and taken in (Seiler, 1968).

The more the concepts of a child grow and progress, the more important it is for social persons to engage the child in reflective dialogue and encourage that individual to consider, reflect, and reconstruct his or her own understanding, thinking, and feeling so that he or she will become able to use such conscious reflections for new conceptual constructions.

More important is the fact that conceptual systems are also need systems with emotional load. If it is accepted that structures have a power to optimize development, then it is important for nascient structures to have a positive emotional load. This condition is not directly manageable from the outside, but social educators have two ways to influence it at least indirectly. First, they can embed educational intercourse in a friendly and agreeable climate. Second, activation tendencies of the learner can be enhanced if the level of task difficulty is optimally adapted to the level of the structures involved.

Values and emotional factors have great importance for other reasons, too. While concepts idiosyncratically reconstruct the content, structure, and aesthetic aspects of the world views expressed in verbal utterances and intercourse, they also take on the emotional quality of those views and, even more so, the intrinsic and implicit values they convey. For instance, it is not astonishing that children and adolescents growing up in a world where urban planning and transport give priority to cars internalize this value in their conceptual worlds if it is not counteracted by other values and principles.

More difficult, perhaps, is that other central structures and needs of the subject must be duly respected at the same time. They are especially such competing needs as the need for protection, the need for freedom, and the need for given limits in the face of the need for wide latitude for self-determined action.

A last principle intrinsically connected with the theory of structural genetics concerns the role of peers in conceptual development. Conceptual understandings and interpretations are generally more similar between peers than between young people and adults. The same is true of peer motivational and emotional values. A very important consequence is that peer intercourse provokes conflicts that are more profitable than those with parents, teachers, and other adults because the discrepancy in understanding between peers is optimal whereas that between peers and older interlocutors is not. Thus, an optimal configuration of environment and living space for young people must provide, first, for multiple possibilities, occasions, and incentives for communicative exchanges among them, for planning and realizing socially relevant activities and common games. Schools, too, could certainly pay greater regard to this condition than is currently the case.

Neither this last rule nor the others are to be taken as unidimensional or unidirectional, clear-cut principles. They always require educational agents to find a compromise between two poles, between that which is optimal for the people involved and that which is optimal for the situation. In climax situations such a position can be found only when the situation and the possibilities of the person are thoroughly analyzed with theoretical sagacity and personal benevolence.

I conclude these considerations by reemphasizing three fundamental principles expressed here in various terms. First, from the stance of structural genetics, it is not the physical make-up of the living space that is important but rather its interpretation and the value attached to it in social discourse and everyday interaction. This interpretation alone is progressively taken over by the concepts available to the child at a given moment. Second, even more important than having a rich, familiar, and unfamiliar physical configuration of living space and its aesthetic make-up is to arrange it so as to facilitate multiple social activities and interactions. Lastly, in terms of forces and processes promoting conceptual development, I have shown that the social esteem that social partners express while and by arranging objects and situations is one of the most important factors determining the emotional and motivational load of cognitive structures.

Notes

1 For a general introduction to constructivist theories of development, see Rusch and Schmidt (1994) and Edelstein and Hoppe-Graff (1993), where multiple other references can be found.
2 In this chapter, the term "structural genetics" is generally used for this kind of constructivist explanation of development.
3 The term "structure" is frequently used in these theories, especially by Piaget, in still another, very different and more abstract sense to mean a complex system of possibilities for acting and thinking that all have similar characteristics and that are common to all persons of a certain developmental level (see below, the concept of stage).
4 Piaget uses this term to characterize a process whose nature is not deductive and whose product cannot be logically deduced from its starting point because many heterogeneous conditions play a role, especially hazard, indetermination, and spontaneity. Therefore, it is impossible to conceive of it as of a form of algorithm possessing a regular mechanism that always functions in the same way.

References

Claar, A. (1990). *Die Entwicklung ökonomischer Begriffe im Jugendalter. Eine strukturgenetische Analyse* [The development of economic concepts: A structural genetic analysis]. Berlin: Springer.

Cromer, R. F. (1992). A case study of dissociations between language and cognition. In H. Tager-Flusberg (Ed.), *Constraints on language acquisition: Studies of atypical children.* Hillsdale, NJ: Erlbaum.

Damerow, P. (1993). Zum Verhältnis von Ontogenese und Historiogenese des Zahlbegriffs [The relation between the ontogenetic development of the concept of number and its historical construction]. In W. Edelstein & S. Hoppe-Graff (Eds.), *Die Konstruktion kognitiver Strukturen. Perspektiven einer konstruktivistischen Entwicklungspsychologie* (pp. 195-259). Bern: Huber.

Damerow, P., & Freudenthal, G. (1986, May). *Quantification and concept development: Conceptual relations between force and motion in early modern physics.* Paper presented at the workshop "Context of dialogue in the formation of quantitative concepts," Tel Aviv and Jerusalem.

Edelstein, W., & Hoppe-Graff, S. (Eds.). (1993). *Die Konstruktion kognitiver Strukturen. Perspektiven einer konstruktivistischen Entwicklungspsychologie* [The construction of cognitive structures]. Bern: Huber.

Groeben, N. (1975). *Vom behavioristischen zum epistemologischen Subjektmodell: Paradigmawechsel in der Psychologie?* [From a behavioristic to an epistemological model of the human subject: A paradigmatical change in psychology?] Berichte des Psychologischen Instituts der Universität Heidelberg, Nr. 1.

Hunt, J. McV. (1961). *Intelligence and experience.* New York: Ronald Press.

Hunt, J. McV. (1965). Intrinsic motivation and its role in psychological development. In D. Levine (Ed.), *Nebraska Symposium on Motivation* (pp. 189-282). Lincoln: University of Nebraska Press.

Inhelder, B., & Piaget, J. (1958). *The growth of logical thinking from childhood to adolescence.* New York: Basic Books.

Piaget, J. (1936). *La naissance de l'intelligence chez l'enfant* [The origins of intelligence in children]. Neuchâtel: Delachaux et Niestlé.

Piaget, J. (1980). *Les formes élémentaires de la dialectique* [Elementary forms of dialectics]. Paris: Gallimard.

Riedl, R., & Wuketits, F. M. (Eds). (1987). *Die evolutionäre Erkenntnistheorie. Bedingungen, Lösungen, Kontroversen* [Evolutionary cognitive theory: Conditions, solutions, and controversies]. Berlin: Paul Parey.

Rusch, G., & Schmidt, S. J. (Eds.). (1994). *Piaget und der Radikale Konstruktivismus* [Piaget and radical constructivism]. Frankfurt on the Main: Suhrkamp.

Seiler, T. B. (1968). *Die Reversibilität in der Entwicklung des Denkens* [The role of reversibility in the development of thinking]. Stuttgart: Klett.

Seiler, T. B. (1973a). Die Bereichsspezifität formaler Denkstrukturen. Konsequenzen für den pädagogischen Prozess [Domain specificity of formal cognitive structures: Consequences for instructional processes]. In K. Frey & M. Lang (Eds.), *Kognitionspsychologie und naturwissenschaftlicher Unterricht* (pp. 249-283). Bern: Huber.

Seiler, T. B. (1973b). *Kognitive Komplexität, Theorien, Analysen, Befunde* [Cognitive complexity, theories, analyses, and findings]. Stuttgart: Kohlhammer.

Seiler, T. B. (1978). Grundlegende Entwicklungstätigkeiten und ihre regulative, systemerzeugende Interaktion [Basic developmental activities and their regulatory, systems-generating interaction]. In G. Steiner (Ed.), *Piaget und die Folgen. Die Psychologie des 20. Jahrhunderts* (Vol. 7, pp. 628-645). Zürich: Kindler.

Seiler, T. B. (1988). Thesen und Befunde zur Entwicklung des Arbeitsbegriffs [Development of the concept of work: Theses and results]. In I. Oomen-Welke & C. von Rhöneck (Eds.), *Schüler: Persönlichkeit und Lernverhalten* (pp. 108-128). Tübingen: Narr.

Seiler, T. B. (1991). Entwicklung und Sozialisation: Eine strukturgenetische Sichtweise [Development and socialization: From the viewpoint of structural genetics]. In K. Hurrelmann & D. Ulich (Eds.), *Handbuch der Sozialisationsforschung* (4th ed., pp. 99-119). Weinheim: Beltz.

Seiler, T. B. (1994a). Zur Entwicklung des Verstehens, oder wie lernen Kinder und Jugendliche verstehen? [On the development of understanding, or how do children and adolescents learn to understand?] In K. Reusser & M. Reusser (Eds.), *Verstehen. Psychologischer Prozess und didaktische Aufgabe* (pp. 69-88). Bern: Huber.

Seiler, T. B. (1994b). Ist Jean Piagets strukturgenetische Erklärung des Denkens eine konstruktivistische Theorie? [Is Jean Piaget's structural genetics of thinking a constructivist theory?] In G. Rusch & S. J. Schmidt (Eds.), *Piaget und der Radikale Konstruktivismus* (pp. 43-102). Frankfurt on the Main: Suhrkamp.

Seiler, T. B., & Claar, A. (1993). Begriffsentwicklung aus strukturgenetisch-konstruktivistischer Perspektive [Conceptual development from the viewpoint of structural genetics]. In W. Edelstein & S. Hoppe-Graff (Eds.), *Die Konstruktion kognitiver Strukturen. Perspektiven einer konstruktivistischen Entwicklungspsychologie* (pp. 107-125). Bern: Huber.

Seiler, T. B., & Wannenmacher, W. (1983). How can we assess meaning and investigate meaning development? Theoretical and methodological considerations from an epistemological point of view. In T. B. Seiler & W. Wannenmacher (Eds.), *Concept development and the development of word meaning* (pp. 320-340). Berlin: Springer.

Comment: Constructivist potentialities and limitations[1]

Siegfried Hoppe-Graff

> Cultural development does not create anything over and above that which potentially exists in the natural development in the child's behavior. Culture, generally speaking, does not produce anything over and above that which is given by nature. But it transforms nature to suit the ends of man.
>
> Vygotsky, 1929, p. 418 (quoted by Moll, 1994, p. 333)

Although *construction* and *constructivism*[2] have become the key concepts in almost all discussions about the nature of cognitive development, the traditional constructivist perspective in the field, namely, the genetic-structuralist approach by Piaget, has become outdated. Many publications still take some of his statements or the phenomena he discovered as starting points, but only very few would agree with his general theoretical framework (i.e., with stage theory and equilibration theory). Bernhard Seiler's chapter is an exception to the rule. His "constructivist perspective" on child development and environment is a coherent and creative elaboration of Piaget's cognitive-developmental approach that explicitly stays within the tradition of genetic structuralism. Thus, the widely misused label *Neo-Piagetian* would precisely apply to Seiler's chapter. It is to his credit that he expands traditional Genevan thought by introducing new ideas, such as the distinction between individual genealogies, developmental sequences, and stages of development – and at the same time integrates them into the propositions of genetic structuralism.

My own perspective on the fundamental principles of child development corresponds to most of Seiler's assumptions. However, as I do not want to be redundant in my comment, I do not elaborate on the lines of agreement but rather focus on those assumptions and arguments I do *not* agree with. My presentation is set out in three steps. It starts with a critical consideration of two of Seiler's central ideas. In the first step, I debate his presentation and evaluation of social construction. In the second step, I focus on the distinction between different forms of causation and causality. Lastly, I discuss the potentialities and limitations of the cognitive-developmental approach to the understanding of the child-city relation.

1 Constructionism: Individual and/or social?

Imagine you participated in a quiz and had to guess which approach to developmental psychology is illustrated by the following quotation:

In other words, every formation and transformation of a concept not only presupposes ... but necessarily and constantly also demands discursive interactions with social partners, thereby taking on cultural rules, conventional meanings, and normative perspectives. Through such interactive processes, concepts gradually adapt to real affordances and sociocultural models and expectancies. ... Society takes an active and necessary part in this process by systematically arranging optimal conditions, transmitting informations, and giving hints.

A good choice would be social constructivism. When arguing with the quizmaster about alternative choices, you would hardly consider genetic structuralism in the Piagetian sense. As a matter of fact, though, the quotation describes Seiler's cognitive-developmental approach to "[the] origin[s] of new structures and new kinds of structures" (Seiler, p. 211)! What makes things even more confusing is the fact that the following quotation is also taken from Seiler's chapter (p. 206):

Among modern authors following Vygotsky in this respect, it is a widely held opinion that human development has to be characterized as the effect of a social co-construction rather than of a construction by an individual. ... The term social co-construction certainly has high descriptive value, for it rightly emphasizes sociocultural factors in development. As with the term social interaction, however, co-construction is merely descriptive and lacks any true explicatory value.

Evidently, there are some irritating elements – at least, *prima facie* – in Seiler's characterization of construction by an individual, or genetic-structuralist constructivism, on the one hand and "social co-construction" or "social co-constructionism,"[3] on the other. Thus, the first aim of this section is to clarify these positions. I argue that Seiler's outline of social constructionism is different from Vygotsky's original ideas (when read carefully) and from "everyday research work" of today's social constructionism. The second aim is integrative. Starting with Seiler's elaboration of genetic structuralism, I point out that substantive progress in developmental psychology depends on new concepts and methods for the integrative study of individual *and* social construction processes.

1.1 Reading Vygotsky carefully

Seiler's presentation of genetic structuralism includes his emphasis on the "social element" in Piaget's theory: "However, the logic of [Piaget's] theoretical explication and many of his fundamental texts accord a key place to external conditions, especially to social interactions" (p. 214). But as well as Piaget was aware of the social side of the two-sided coin of development, so was Vygotsky of the internal side. This fact has been convincingly documented by Moll (1994). From the very beginning, Vygotsky's perspective included an *explicit* awareness of the internal prerequisites of all developmental changes, as is illustrated by the following quotations:

One must recognize a natural basis for cultural forms of behavior. Culture creates nothing (Vygotsky, 1981, p. 166, quoted by Moll, 1994, p. 339); Any new form of cultural experience does not simply come from outside, independently of the state of the organism at a given point of development (Vygotsky, 1981, p. 168, quoted by Moll, 1994, p. 340).

Vygotsky and Piaget share the basic assumption that development is by definition an interactive affair. Development takes place *within* an individual that has reached a certain state of internal potentials; at the same time the individual interacts with his or her environment, particulary the social environment. Probably because of his training in biology, Piaget had an inclination to the mechanism of self-regulation, especially of an internal kind. But as some of his scholars (Chapman, 1988; Youniss & Damon, 1992) have demonstrated, "Piaget's ideas about social construction are integral to his general epistemology and have important implications . . . for his theory in general" (Youniss & Damon, 1992, p. 268). Particularly in his early writings, Piaget was aware of the fact that "the knowledge process entails co-constructive exchanges between children and other persons as much as between children and physical objects" (p. 268). Vygotsky always emphasized the very interactionist nature of development by framing the cultural construction of the higher mental processes within the constraints and possibilities that the developing individual brings to social construction.

There are, however, at least two more similarities between the two giants of developmental psychology. First, despite their explicit interactionist orientation, both have been used as historical references in "simplified" variants of either individual or social constructionism that simply excluded the other side of the coin of development. Second, although they were aware of both "directors of development" (Okagaki & Sternberg, 1991), they *concentrated* either on the internal conditions and processes (Piaget) or the external (social) conditions and processes (Vygotsky). These different emphases had the positive effect that we owe to Piaget's ingenious insights into internal construction processes (e.g., assimilation theory and equilibration model) and to Vygotsky's creative concepts about social construction processes like mediation or the zone of proximal development. However, they also led to a theoretical and methodological neglect of the other side of the coin. Take Vygotsky, for example. Although he was aware of the fact that ontogenetic change depends on *necessary* internal conditions, he was much less explicit and precise about these developmental prerequisites. To conclude, Piaget and Vygotsky convincingly argue for the necessity of the integration of intraindividual and social construction processes, but I do not find in their work the concepts and methods needed to study the interdependence of external and internal construction empirically.

1.2   Descriptive or explanatory studies of social construction processes?

What does it mean that a concept is "merely descriptive"? And how could it be changed to have "explanatory value"? Seiler characterizes the concept of co-construction as "merely descriptive" but does not explain that categorization. I do not agree with him, and I explain my disagreement by demonstrating how processes of co-construction are studied in the research conducted by my colleagues and me.

In an ongoing longitudinal project we are examining whether the emergence of pretend symbols at the end of the first year of life is co-constructed by parent and child (for preliminary results, see Hoppe-Graff, 1993; Hoppe-Graff & Engel, 1996a; for final results, see also Hoppe-Graff & Engel, 1996b). Parents and their children were videotaped during solitary and social play when the children were 9, 10, 11, and 12 months old.[4] We assumed that the root metaphor of co-construction has consequences both at the interpersonal (social) and the intrapersonal (individual) level. We proposed that (a) co-construction includes specific modes of parent-child interactions that can be directly observed, and (b) although co-construction is only the first step and necessary prerequisite to the internal construction of new structures, progress in the child's acquisition of pretend symbols should be related to preceding co-constructive interaction.

In our case, we made the assumption that, among other kinds of interaction, *imitative interactions* between parent and infant are the "locus" where co-construction takes place. Imitative interactions are defined as sequences of reciprocal imitations instigated either by the parent or the child. In most cases, the introductory imitation acts as a model to be imitated by the partner, whose imitative act may, in turn, be imitated by the first partner, and so on. Thus, imitation in pretend play typically does not take place as a single act but as "packages" of prolonged imitation sequences. We classified imitative acts into four categories according to their similarity to the model's act:

- *Imitative acts in the strict sense:* Included are actions that look very similar to the model's act.
- *Attempts to imitate:* Included are actions where the imitator (typically the child) obviously attempts to imitate the model's act but does not succeed for one reason. For example, the child attempts to imitate a pretend act but in fact carries out a manipulative act.
- *Elaborations:* The imitator's act (typically the mother) unquestionably refers to the model's act but also elaborates the act. For example, the child takes an empty spoon into her mouth (without any sign of pretending to eat), and the parent, in turn, also directs a spoon to her own mouth but in an affectionate and superficial manner that demonstrates that she pretends to be eating.
- *Otherwise imitative acts:* Included are actions that are evidently imitations of a preceding action of the partner but that do not fit into the other categories.

Of special interest for the social construction assumption are imitative interactions that include sequences of *attempts* by the child and *elaborations* by the parent. These interactions are *co-constructive interactions* in the strict sense.

In empirical research, psychologists are always restricted to a small sample of observations from everyday interactions. Nevertheless, as part of the test of the social construction hypothesis, Hoppe-Graff and Engel (1996a, 1996b) assumed (a) that *some* co-constructive interactions should occur even in a reduced observation sample. We also assumed (b) that the occurrence of co-constructive interactions should be at least moderately correlated to subsequent acquisitions in the child's capacity to carry out pretend acts. By and large, our data indicate that pretend symbols are co-constructed during imitative interactions between parent and child play. First, even within samples of 15 minutes of parent-child play we observed many instances of imitation sequences, some of them being of the co-constructive kind (as defined above). Second, the number of imitative interactions was significantly correlated to the complexity of the child's pretend symbols in solitary pretense one month later. (To be precise, this relation exists only for imitative interactions instigated by the child. For more details, see Hoppe-Graff & Engel, 1996a; 1996b).[5]

The aforementioned results may be interesting in themselves, but in the context of this commentary it is necessary to decide whether they are "merely descriptive" or have "true explicatory value" (to use Seiler's terms again). Obviously, the answer depends on one's concept of description and explanation, and this brings me to the next section, where I discuss Seiler's "metatheory" of scientific causality and explanation. For two reasons I claim that we have in fact examined the *explanatory value* of the co-construction paradigm.

First, the seemingly clear-cut distinction between description and explanation cannot be applied to the study of developmental processes. Rather, I propose that the explanation of developmental processes partly consists of precise, step-by-step (or stage-by-stage) descriptions of transition processes and that social interactions, from the social constructivist perspective, form a neccessary (though not suffficient) part of the transition process. An explanation that has a stage law at its core is called a *developmental explanation*. It has "to explain why a system is in a certain stage of development by reference to a developmental 'law' which describes an orderly sequence of stages which systems of that kind go through" (Woodward, 1980, p. 443). In the philosophy of science, the status of developmental explanations is controversial (see Kitchener, 1983; Woodward, 1980), but I suppose that Seiler would agree that developmental explanations are "true" explanations, for he argues in favor of explanation-by-reconstruction.

Second, I assume that our approach is explanatory because my colleagues and I have demonstrated not only that an interactive process actually leads to a qualitative shift in pretend competences but also that this interactive experience covaries with subsequent progress in solitary pretense.

2 On causation and causality in developmental and environmental psychology

Although Seiler is not explicit on the relation between causal concepts and the distinction between description and explanation, I suspect that his classification of research as descriptive or explanatory is closely tied to questions of causation and causality. Therefore, I now turn to conceptions of causality in developmental theories.

Right from the start, Seiler states his position on causation in human development both precisely and vaguely: "Constructivist theories ... conceive of development as a process of construction *conducted by the subject itself*" (p. 199, my emphasis). This statement is precise because it is clear-cut about the source and force of development: It is the subject itself that creates ontogenetic progress. One could conclude that *the* causal factor for human development lies *inside* the person.

But how could internal causality be compatible with a basically interactionist position on human development? Seiler himself takes up this issue when he argues that it is the theorist's task "to explain how internal conditions presuppose external influences, that is, how they function and work together" (p. 199). His solution is the distinction between *direct* and *indirect* causality. Social influences – social models, instructions, discourses – are prerequisites for development, but they are only indirect causes because they are "not effective by themselves but only insofar as they are able to evoke in the subject structures by which they can be assimilated" (p. 215). By contrast, internal cognitive structures are direct causes because they "can directly influence other cognitive structures in terms of their cognitive content" (p. 215). To put the distinction in another framework, Seiler paraphrases it in Aristotelian terminology: *effective* vs. *exemplary causation.*

Seiler's metatheoretical analysis clarifies a dimension of developmental theorizing that is usually under the surface. It is a note of caution against prematurely equating influence with causal assumptions in psychological theories. In both lay psychology and academic circles, one often finds the erroneous argument that variable X is a causative factor to a process because X has an influence on that process. For instance, women reared under disorganized circumstances in childhood have a higher probability of both later conduct disorder and early marriage. Another example is the statement that a healthy and intact family and environment fosters the development of efficient coping strategies (see Wachs & Shpancer, this volume). But *from a psychological point of view*, do disorganized circumstances in childhood or intact families effectively *cause* development?

It is important to analyze why Seiler rejects the category of *effective* causality for these examples. I suppose that his distinction between effective and exemplary causation (or direct and indirect causation) is based on the locus of the causative force. Factors or influences from outside the individual are only effective after they have been transformed to some internal consequence: "only insofar [effective] as they are able to evoke in the subject structures by which they can be assimilated" (p. 215).

Thus, Seiler's argument is implicitly founded on the fact of *conditional effectivity*: An indirect or exemplary cause is effective only under the condition that its content (in this case, meaning) can be assimilated by the individual. But does not the same "conditionality" exist for the influence of internal factors? Could language development proceed without social input from the outside? Could the acquisition of pretend play proceed without play themes derived from the child's social experience? Could the corresponding assimilative structures be active and growing without experiences? From this point of view, the direct/effective internal cause is dependent on external inputs. These arguments lead to the conclusion that the distinction between *direct/effective* and *indirect/exemplary* causes can be based only on location: internal influences or conditions seem to be closer to developmental progress (which is, of course, *internal progress*!) than influences from the outside are.

As a fertile alternative to the distinction between direct/effective and indirect/exemplary causes, I suggest the return to von Wright's (1971) proposal of replacing the task of explanation by the analysis of necessary and sufficient factors of development (see Hoppe, Schmid-Schönbein, & Seiler, 1977; Hoppe-Graff, 1982).

So far I have discussed only the metatheoretical issues of causation and causality in the field of developmental psychology. I doubt that the arguments could be generalized with regard to environmental psychology; the perspective on the child-environment relation and the theoretical aims of this branch of psychology are quite different. The scope is still the child interacting with the environment. Of major interest, though, are the reciprocal effects of environments and developmental progress and the effects of child development on the environment. In this context, Seiler's analysis of causality has an important function as a reminder. It reminds one that, although some environmental variation might have an effect on the developing child, it is not the environment per se that is influential. The environment is effective only after it has evoked transformations in the subject's internal processing of environmental experiences.

3   Applying the cognitive-developmental approach to the child-city relation: Potentialities and limitations

Scientific theory A is never "better" (more correct, more appropriate, and so on) than scientific theory B in an absolute sense. The potential advantage of A depends on one's aims and goals. It is necessary to be aware of this qualification when considering the appropriateness of Seiler's cognitive-developmental approach to the understanding of the child-city relation. Genetic structuralism was created by Piaget (and elaborated by his students, such as Seiler) in order to improve understanding of the very nature of human knowledge and its emergence and transformations during the human life course. This approach conceptualizes the precursors, prerequisites, and effective factors in the growth of human knowledge *at a very general level* and locates them primarily *inside* the individual (see section 2). Seiler's genuine contribution consists in widening the genetic-structuralist horizon to include the growth of such social concepts as work and money and the idiosyncratic element of development in terms of the reconstruction of individual genealogies.

Seiler's chapter convinced me that substantive progress in understanding the nature of cognitive development has to include his line of research. I doubt, however, that the approach will go very far toward increasing comprehension of the influences and effects of different kinds of urban environments or specific aspects of urban environment. Genetic structuralism, as it stands, includes only very general ideas about the influence that environmental conditions have on the child's cognitive development. Seiler's principles of fostering conceptual development can be taken as illustrations of this fact. They are necessarily stated in very global terms. Even the single specific principle he proposes, the "principle of optimal distance or pairing" (p. 220), is a very general rule of thumb for supporting children's cognitive development. It states "that there is an optimal discrepancy between external offers and internal structures, and if such a state is not arrived at the person will not start effective attempts to do assimilative and accommodative work" (Seiler, p. 220). Research by A. L. Brown and her group (Brown & Campione, 1984; Brown & Palincsar, 1989; Palincsar & Brown, 1984) has demonstrated that the principle of optimal distance is by no means specific to genetic structuralism, for similar, if not identical, consequences – such as the principle of reciprocal teaching – can be derived from social constructionism.

In sum, there exist biases in traditional genetic structuralism that are in conflict with the scope and aims of environmental child psychology: its focus on "internal causality"; its neglect of differential effects of specific environmental conditions on the child's experience and behavior; and the absence of any specific conceptualization of the structure of the environment as experienced by the child. Although these shortcomings are unavoidable, given the *traditional* propositions of genetic structuralism, there is no reason why the structuralist framework itself should not be changed. Thus, one route to a more fertile model of the child-city relation could consist in the revision of some of Piaget's ideas, and it could take Seiler's thoughtful interpretation of genetic structuralism as a starting point.

Notes

1 I thank Susanne Drescher for her help in improving the final draft.
2 In this article *constructivism* and *constructionism* are used synonymously (although in other contexts it might be useful to make a distinction).
3 I speak of *social construction* or *co-construction*. *Social co-construction* seems to be redundant because the term *social* includes "*co-*", and vice versa.
4 To be precise, the study also included a follow-up observation at 18 months.

5 Our study demonstrated that imitative interactions are effective processes in the co-
construction of the earliest play symbols. As I have detailed in my commentary on the Wachs
& Shpancer chapter (in this volume), I propose that the emerging child-city relation has to be
conceptualized in terms of social construction. Perhaps imitative interactions are included in
the joint construction of the preschool child's rudimentary ideas of urban life. Sociodramatic
play in the preschool sometimes includes scenes and scripts of city life.

References

Brown, A. L., & Campione, J. C. (1984). Three faces of transfer: Implications for early competence, individual differences, and instruction. In M. Lamb, & A. L. Brown, & B. Rogoff
(Eds.), *Advances in developmental psychology* (Vol. 3, pp. 143-192). Hillsdale, NJ: Erlbaum.

Brown, A. L., & Palincsar, A. S. (1989). Guided, cooperative learning and individual knowledge
acquisition. In L. Resnick (Ed.), *Knowing, learning, and instruction: Essays in honor of Robert Glaser* (pp. 393-451). Hillsdale, NJ: Erlbaum.

Chapman, M. (1988). Constructive evolution: Origins and developments of Piaget's thought.
Cambridge, MA: Cambridge University Press.

Hoppe, S., Schmid-Schönbein, C., & Seiler, T. B. (1977). *Entwicklungssequenzen*
[Developmental sequences]. Bern: Huber.

Hoppe-Graff, S. (1982). *Bedingungsanalysen zur Genese der Klasseninklusion* [Conditional
analysis of the development of the class-inclusion concept]. Unpublished doctoral dissertation, Technical University of Darmstadt.

Hoppe-Graff, S. (1993). *Die Emergenz des Als ob-Spiels* [The emergence of pretense]. Unpublished manuscript, University of Heidelberg.

Hoppe-Graff, S., & Engel, I. (1996a, September). *The emergence of pretend symbols in infancy:
Piagetian assumptions, Vygotskian predictions, and longitudinal data.* Paper presented at the
2nd Conference for Socio-cultural Research, Geneva (CH).

Hoppe-Graff, S., & Engel, I. (1996b). *The emergence of pretense as social construction: Evidence from a longitudinal study.* Research report, University of Leipzig.

Kitchener, R. F. (1983). Developmental explanations. *Review of Metaphysics, 36,* 791-817.

Moll, I. (1994). Reclaiming the natural line in Vygotsky's theory of cognitive development.
Human Development, 37, 333-342.

Okagaki, L., & Sternberg, R. J. (Eds.). (1991). *Directors of development: Influences on the
development of children's thinking.* Hillsdale, NJ: Erlbaum.

Palincsar, A. S., & Brown, A. L. (1984). Reciprocal teaching of comprehension fostering and
comprehension monitoring. *Cognition and Instruction, 1,* 117-175.

von Wright, G. H. (1971). *Explanation and understanding.* Ithaca, NY: Cornell Press.

Vygotsky, L. S. (1929). The problem of the cultural development of the child. *Journal of
Genetic Psychology, 6,* 415-434.

Vygotsky, L. S. (1978). *Mind in society: The development of higher mental processes.* Cambridge, MA: Harvard University Press.

Vygotsky, L. S. (1981). The genesis of higher mental functions. In J. V. Wertsch (Ed.), *The
concept of activity in Soviet psychology.* Armonk, NY: Sharpe.

Woodward, J. (1980). Developmental explanations. *Synthese, 44,* 443-466.

Youniss, J., & Damon, W. (1992). Social construction in Piaget's theory. In H. Beilin & P. B.
Pufall (Eds.), *Piaget's theory: Prospects and possibilities* (pp. 267-286). Hillsdale, NJ: Erlbaum.

Author's response: Following Aristotle

Thomas Bernhard Seiler

Siegfried Hoppe-Graff's commentary on my chapter is very fair. I believe that he really picks up on the critical points of my position and perspicaciously expands some of the arguments that could be misunderstood and that demand greater differentiation.

Concerning the theoretical framework, I believe we slightly differ in the conceptual evaluation of social causality. Hoppe-Graff insists that some at least very general explanatory assumptions are contained in every description. He is certainly correct, and I do not maintain that the social part of coactivity, that between subject and environment has no causal role. The scope of my argumentation is intended to affirm that using the same notion to describe and explain the activity of both sides does not do justice to their respective roles and conditions. Such global and undifferentiated treatment does not define their specific limitations.

Siegfried Hoppe-Graff further emphasizes, as I did, that the activity of both partners is necessary and that it is sufficient only when it occurs jointly as true interaction. But I believe that characterization in terms of necessary and sufficient conditions does not resolve the problem. One can and must deepen the characterization by differentiating more finely between the causal role of one part and that of the other.

From my theoretical perspective, one can do so by following Aristotle in assuming different kinds of causation, namely, effective and exemplary. In the spirit of this distinction, the internal structures of the subject exert direct influence and directly bring about transformation, whereas cultural conditions, social models, educational instruction, and interpersonal discourses have a merely exemplary, or indirect, causal effect on cognitive constructions. In other words, provided that environmental situations and events are objects perceived and known and that the meaning and challenges of the multiple signs presented by the surrounding society are extracted by the structures that the person is actualizing, those structures can form and transform cognitive structures of the person. Conditions that are external (with respect to a subject's cognition) therefore form an indirect causality as it were, depending on the content and meaning attributed to them. This indirect causality is of an exemplary nature and depends on the perception and interpretation of the subject. It thus explains the fact that social impacts never completely determine the form and content of new structures and that it is wrong to say that these structures are produced by communicative means or didactic instructions or that they are directly and simply internalized.

I do not agree with Siegfried Hoppe-Graff when he attributes the distinction between these two kinds of causality (effective and exemplary) to their different locations, internal or external. In my view, the distinction is essential and results from the necessity of transforming "external" data into "internal" data, that is, of assimilating or interpreting them.

As for Vygotsky's theory, I have further differentiated my interpretation in a separate work (see Seiler, 1996).

References

Seiler, T. B. (1996, September). Concept development: In what respect can Piagetian and Vygotskyan views be complemented? Paper presented at the conference entitled Piaget and Vygotsky, Geneva.

Vygotsky, L. S. (1964). *Denken und Sprechen* [Thinking and speaking]. Trans. G. Sewekow. Berlin: Akademie Verlag. (Original work published 1934)

Integration: What environment? Which relationship?

Isolda de Araújo Günther and Hartmut Günther

Our charge is to integrate the various strands of thought dealing with the child-city relation presented by Werner and Altman, Wachs and Shpancer, and Seiler, as well as comments that Ritterfeld and Hoppe-Graff have offered on these contributions.

What makes the child-city relation an important object of investigation? For an ever increasing number of children, the urban setting is the stage where the "all-embracing fusion of the processes of the development of the self and acquisition of culture" (Hoppe-Graff, p. 197) is taking place. The child-city relation is of both theoretical and practical importance. From an academic and research perspective, it can be studied on the basis of a number of theoretical orientations, as the present volume attests. Hence, the child-city relation becomes an example of the richness of interdisciplinary approaches to a given problem and has the intradisciplinary potential for critical experiments.

From a practical perspective, the child-city relation is the focal point of interdisciplinary effort and a challenge for cooperative problem-solving by people of diverse inter- and intradisciplinary orientations. At yet another level, the degree to which this challenge is being met may become the object of further study.

The papers in this volume have a common origin: the streets of Herten, Germany. In Werner and Altman's terms, the book has turned into the environmental context within which authors establish their individuality as researchers and their sociability as practitioners as they develop in their concern for the child-city relation. This reflection leads us to focus our task. Rather than integrate various elements or strands of thought into some superordinate unity, we attempt to inquire into the potential of a joint approach to the child-city relation in a concrete cultural context.

To this end we highlight a few concepts from each text in terms of differences and commonalities. As a second step, we try to examine the possibilities of a joint application of the approaches in research and intervention. For this purpose, we selected a particular cultural context, Brazil. Within that context, we consider three psychological concepts from developmental psychology – attachment, social support and competence – and connect them with three environmental themes from the Herten conference: the dwelling, the neighborhood, and the street. We propose to use the Brazilian cultural context not simply because we happen to live and work there. Some social scientists call Brazil *Belíndia*, a country where the wealth of Belgium cohabits with the poverty of India, in other words, a country with considerable economic contradictions and, hence, variability in the human condition. At the same time, Brazil is the world's largest country with essentially only one language and culture. Regional variations and remnants of the colonial past constantly challenge the notion of psychological homogeneity.

1   A question of definition

From the outset, it appears necessary to clarify some terms. What environment, what relationships are the authors talking about?

1.1   Basic assumptions about development

Werner and Altman concentrate on the changing relation between person and sociophysical environment. Development happens to the extent that this relation changes. Their research strategy is to *describe* the pattern and the form of an event rather than look for antecedent-consequent relations.

The contextualist approach, as presented by Wachs and Shpancer, emphasizes fusion, change, openness, and scope. The course of the individual's development is probabilistic, based on the operation of multiple determinants. A phenomenon does not exist, and cannot be studied, apart from its context. Fusion implies that there is no differentiation between individual and context across development. The course of development is shaped by change, a process that supposes multiple coexisting and interacting levels of organism and context. Furthermore, the notion of finish or completion is without meaning because "there is no final or complete analysis of anything" (p. 165). Thus, the process of development is open-ended. Lastly, emphasizing the importance of going beyond a given microenvironment, or scope, raises the question of which macrocontext should be chosen for inclusion and measurement in a given study.

Seiler focuses on cognitive development, that is, on the origin and transformation of cognitive structures. Development is a process of construction accomplished by the individual. It involves the acquisition of new potentialities and new structures not predetermined in the genes. Assuming a genetic base for the origin and course of such development, he studies their causes and conditions. Whereas internal (person-centered) and external (environment-centered) causes and conditions work together and cannot be reduced to the action of one of these factors alone, internal aspects of the individual have priority.

Thus, a first answer to the question 'Why study the child-city relationship?' might be summarized as follows: From an environmental perspective, studying this relation can be seen as yet another instance of the reciprocal relation between person and environment. From a developmental perspective, it provides one more example of how a particular environment contributes to the development of the individual. Lastly, psychologists may welcome this topic as one more way to advance their ability to understand, predict, and intervene in human behavior.

1.2 Environment

If Ritterfeld finds it important to recall that "by definition, environmental psychology deals with person-environment relations" (p. 155) in commenting on a chapter written by environmental psychologists, how much more necessary it is to clarify the term 'environment' after reading the texts by Wachs and Shpancer and by Seiler.

Concentrating on secondary territories, Werner and Altman clearly talk about the sociophysical context from a specific environmental perspective. The environment involves the diversity of persons, objects, and settings, including temporal qualities, surrounding the individual.

Wachs and Shpancer do not use the word environment, but 'context'. The individual is fused with the context, constituting an event that can be studied. Their environment is more concrete, yet less physical and immediate, than the one considered by Werner and Altman. Not only is it more concrete, but they are clearly concerned with the possibility of predicting behavior and intervention.

Seiler, on the other hand, appears to use the term environment more in the sense of the nature-nurture controversy. To him, the construction of knowledge is dependent on the environment yet is the result of interaction in which the internal conditions of the person have priority.

In trying to use these three approaches to the study of the child-city relation, consider the image of an onion: Seiler deals with the very proximal and circumscribed surroundings of the child, the inner core. Werner and Altman are concerned with multiple levels of the somewhat more distal surroundings (of which Seiler's could be any one aspect). Wachs and Shpancer, for their part, remind us that the inner core and the multiple levels, the 'onion', are embedded in an even larger context.

1.3 Relation

Equally vexing is the question regarding the nature of the child-city relation expressed in the preceding chapters. Considering the titles of the three chapters might be helpful: "A dialectical/transactional framework of social relations: *children in secondary territories*" (Werner and Altman, our italics), "A contextualist perspective on *child-environment* relations" (Wachs and Shpancer, our italics), "Child *development* and environment: A constructivist perspective" (Seiler, our italics). The emphasis in the first two chapters appears to lie on the relation between persons and their environment, whereas the emphasis in the third instance is on the developmental process as such, an acknowledgment that it takes place in some environmental context.

Werner and Altman begin their chapter by affirming that "children's social relationships can profitably be examined as holistic unities" (p. 123). A little further on they cite Campbell, who argues that children and settings "cannot be conveniently pulled apart for the purposes of analysis, however much our social-science instinct tells us to partition the variance" (p. 125). In other words, what is related are children and any kind of setting (i.e., social, physical and/or temporal environments). Rather than constituting elements, these items are what Werner and Altman call aspects of a whole, aspects that relate in a dialectical manner but that are not subject to a traditional analysis of their relation. Werner and Altman list neighborhood secondary territories, their exploration, rituals that mark temporal aspects of these territories, and, specifically, neighborhood public gardens as examples of unities. They examine these unities by means of case studies, which may or may not provide replicable data.

This position contrasts sharply with that taken by Wachs and Shpancer, who conceptualize children and their settings as the elements of a larger context. They talk about measures of relations in terms of covariance between the phenomena studied. From a contextualist perspective, environment and object are integrated and interdependent, characterized by plasticity and reciprocity. Stressing the probabilistic nature of the continuous process throughout the life span, the contextualist approach allows for traditional social science analysis, including the partitioning of variances. Given the requirements of multivariate analysis, however, Wachs and Shpancer do point to the need for additional methods of data analysis.

The relation that Seiler focuses on is the interaction between individuals and their environment on a more circumscribed level. He analyzes the process of seizing control, a process through which the person constructs both self-knowledge and knowledge of the environment. Seiler appears to be more removed from the child-city relation as an object of study and seems more interested in the potential use of this particular research context to study the question of how cognitive structures change. Methodologically, he appears closer to Werner and Altman than to Wachs and Shpancer in that he, too, argues against deterministic rules and the ability to predict future behavior on the basis of current environmental conditions.

The diversity of the concepts of relation presented by the authors suggests the use of both a multimethodological and a multitheoretical approach to studying the complexity of the child-environment relation.

1.4   An attempt at integration

A Brahman friend and natural scientist once commented that 'Everything is true –
including its opposite'. Given the complexity of social phenomena, the transactional
position of not looking for a specific causal relation among the many elements, or
aspects, of a given situation is very attractive. It might be likened to what in architectural circles has been called the 'grand-gesture' style of construction, a style that
people in Brasília are more than familiar with: beautiful to look at, generous in its
integrative conception, especially from afar, yet not always easy to actually live with
and function in.

   Although Werner and Altman's secondary territories constitute a principal context
within which the child-city relation should be studied, we think that, from a practical
point of view, one needs to take sides every so often. Thus, at the outset, Wachs and
Shpancer's language is comforting in that covariance points in a direction beyond
description, though not necessarily implying an effective causal prediction. Furthermore, it might well be argued that it is important to know the antecedents of successful intellectual development in children, just as, from another point of view, the
same child-city constellation, even the same research context, may furnish information about the impact that certain children have on their environment. It should be
noted, though, that both equations – intellectual development as a function of a
given environment, as well as characteristics (constructed or not) of a certain environment as a function of the stage of intellectual development (in children) – have
the potential to furnish information for answering the question of how individuals
construct their knowledge of the world.

   In an attempt to integrate the three chapters, one might see Werner and Altman's
as the superordinate, philosophical position to the extent that the child's setting constitutes a unit of study. However, for practical purposes (in both research and intervention), these unities have to be broken down to allow for a contextual analysis. At
an even more subordinate level, the constructivist approach might constitute one
way to analyze a specific interface between the child and the setting. But whereas
the reciprocal nature of the relation between child and setting is a given as far as the
environmental perspective is concerned, it is necessary to demonstrate empirically
that the constructivist approach can provide a comprehensive explanation for, precise prediction of, and/or beneficial intervention in the behavior of children.

2   Implications for research and intervention

For social scientists working in developing countries, there is no need to emphasize
the contextual nature of their research or justify the necessity for intervention. Even
those trying to ignore the social context of their work do so in reactance to the same.
The educational context in Brazil is as follows: 38.8 percent of the population is

below age 18, 10 percent of the 10- through 14-year olds are illiterate, and only 15.4 percent complete high school and continue to higher education.[1] Any research dealing with the child-city relation, including such seemingly universal questions as cognitive development (from whatever perspective), is embedded in an all-determining macroenvironment and is largely beyond the reach of social scientists in their role as scientists. What, then, is the potential of joining the theoretical positions presented in this volume and applying them to developmental topics (attachment, social support, and competence) and environmental topics (residence, street, and neighborhood) of Brazilian society in all its diversity? As mentioned above, this question is predicated on the extreme economic variability and, hence, human condition in a large country that may not be as culturally homogeneous as it seems to be. The child-city relation reflects this economic-cultural variability starkly: Living within sight of each other are children who know Disneyland's *Main Street* better than the main street of their own hometown and children who know nothing but the main street because that is where they subsist.

2.1 Research strategies

Using our own cultural context, Brazil, as a point of departure, we first raise a series of hypothetical questions regarding research strategy. Although the following concerns would have to be addressed by researchers working in this context, similar concerns must be addressed *within* any one country or culture, not to mention within studies with cross-cultural perspectives.

Given the interdisciplinary implications of the child-city relation, we argue in favor of a multimethod research strategy, in which more than one research technique is applied to a given question in an attempt to arrive at convergent results. Even so, given the size of Brazil and the variability of the human condition therein, several decisions about the selection of research topics and strategy would have to be taken.

Should one select topics that are equally relevant to all regions of the country?[2] Or would one hope to arrive at results that could be generalized or might even be considered universal? And if so, how should one go about this? Should geographic region be treated as one more variable of a given study, or should studies conducted in different regions be combined by means of some subsequent meta-analysis? Or should one suppose that there are no universals in studies on any of the aspects of the child-city relation, with every geographic region therefore to be treated separately?

Besides the geographical division, the principal sociodemographic differentiation in Brazil is economic. Recent data[3] indicate that the top 10 percent of the population accounts for 48.2 percent of the declared income, whereas the bottom 10 percent receive 1.1 percent of the declared income, with 80 percent of the population competing for the other half. Obviously, results of studies with children from any one of these segments cannot readily be extended to any other. Should studies privilege one group rather than another? Should one try to compare groups? Should studies be conceived as representative studies or as case studies?[4]

Similar strategy considerations apply to the principal elements of the child-city relation. What kind of groups of children should be studied – children that are part of a family or extended family unit, of a given age cohort, or a group of playmates or friends? Is it relevant to ask which part of the city the children live in, or how large an urban area is to be regarded as the child's physical surroundings? The home range, no doubt, changes with age, as demonstrated more than sixty years ago (Muchow & Muchow, 1935). The appropriateness of the research strategy (or strategies) selected would depend on whether a given study's thrust is more theoretical and research-oriented or applied and intervention-oriented.

Given the concerns expressed above, the initial question about the possibility of joining different theoretical approaches may be answered in the following terms: The very complexity of the phenomenon studied is responsible for the multiplicity of theoretical approaches. At the same time, the way to deal with the complexity is to use both a multimethodological and multitheoretical strategy. This appears to us important, for the child-city relation occurs on many levels – some of which are mentioned below. Thus, we think it advantageous to consider the theoretical approaches presented in the preceding chapters not simply as alternatives, but, even if not purposefully, as possibilities for addressing different levels.

2.2 Defining territories

Studying the child-city relation necessarily implies defining the research territory. While the dwelling, the neighborhood, and the street may be considered examples of primary, secondary, and public territories, respectively, this classification is far from clear-cut. Werner and Altman's chapter deals specifically with secondary territories, that is environments of the neighborhood, which include streets. The dwelling generally is considered an example of a primary territory, whereas the street is also an example of public territory. The quality of the child-city relation varies considerably in these three territories and can be assumed to have distinctly different influences over the developmental process, especially from the constructivist level of analysis.

However, one needs to recall that perceived and conceded control over a given physical area are important elements in the definitions of territoriality. To the extent that actors involved in the social relation implicit in such control share the same value system, such division of territory will be relatively consistent. If no such common value system exists among them, the natural action of one actor may be conceived by another as invasion or undue appropriation.[5]

Besides (and as a consequence of) perceived and conceded control, *relative* size helps distinguish between primary, secondary, and public territory, especially when age cohorts are compared. As the child grows, not only does the home range (i.e., total area) expand, but more of the public territory turns into secondary territory (i.e., a larger proportion of the total area turns into secondary territory). Even primary territory may undergo changes in absolute size. Such changes in the proportion (and size) of territory, that is, of relevant environment, appear to have a direct bearing on the level of analysis possible in terms of the onion simile above. Furthermore, we understand that this expansion of relevant territory is not simply a question of home range or the territory in which the child is free to roam, but a question of control of territory, especially when dealing with marginalized children such as those in gangs.

2.2.1   The dwellings – a primary territory?

As mentioned above, a residential unit is generally considered an example of primary territory. Dwellings are inhabited by various combinations of individuals with biological links, such as nuclear or extended families, and individuals without such links, such as servants. In Brazilian families, it is usually the children who, from a very early age, set the pace of the home.

But, what is home? Given the economic diversity in Brazil, on the one extreme, home may be the street, or the permanently 'temporary' housing in the slums. At the other extreme, it might be sheltered within the modern version of the 'manor house and slave quarters',[6] an area sufficiently large to aggregate elements that normally would only be found in secondary and public territories (e.g., a playground or a movie theater). Furthermore, this shared residential unit constitutes the primary territory for the owner's family and the secondary territory for the servants. This division is not restricted, however, to one extreme of the economic spectrum. Even relatively modest two-bedroom apartments have a maid's room and bath, and building codes for certain single-family residences even require those facilities. The way this territory is experienced by the children in this residential unit depends on who they are: child of the owner or child of the maid. During an initial phase in life, they may explore the territory jointly as playmates. Later, depending on age and gender, different parts of the dwelling may become off-limits, some parts for the child of the maid, other parts for the child of the owner. Lastly, it must be noted that over the course of the last 20 years, with ever increasing urbanization and inflation, the prevalence of this manorial life style has been declining, though it continues to exist in the phantasy world of soap operas.

Besides considering the spacial arrangements in the home, one must reflect on the developmental importance of the composition, structure, and morphology of the dwelling. If growth depends on interactions, it is in the home where attachment, the feeling of being loved and liking others, first unfolds. It is there where construction and understanding of self, others, the world, and patterns of activity begin to take shape.

In summary, it is clear that the primary territory presents a far-from-homogeneous physical environment. Furthermore, the psychological environment can vary broadly in terms of the number and quality of caregivers. For this reason, even if one were to follow a primarily constructivist analysis of the person-environment interactions within the primary territory, which is a microlevel, it would have to be understood that (a) many microanalyses will have to be undertaken, and (b) they are embedded in a larger, multivariate context.

2.2.2 Neighborhood – a secondary territory?

Ever since the classic studies of the Muchows, it has been known that the extension of neighborhoods, that is home range, changes with age. We argue that an expanded home range frequently implies an expanded secondary territory within which the person-environment relation changes. Part of this changing relation is constituted, no doubt, by a change in the size of this territory. A larger territory need not mean simply a larger contiguous area; it may just as well signify access to and connectedness with a larger number of distinct parts of the city, such as a school, club, beach, park, local hangout, or shopping center. Depending on the overall size of the city, these territories may be spread out all over town. This constellation suggests several research questions: What is the process by which children extend their neighborhood(s)? Who are the persons involved in this process – Peers? Older sibling? Adults? Who provides support and advice about both hidden and explicit rules of the new environments? How is confidence enhanced so that more parts of the city become secondary territories? In what manner does the developmental impact of the secondary territories differ? In Werner and Altman's terms, they vary not only physically but also socially and temporally. In other words, one may say that different subsets of secondary territories are salient for different groups of children at different times, without necessarily specifying whether the territory defines the group or the group selects the territory.

One important variable in the number, kind, and location of secondary territories is their accessability in terms of children's ability to traverse public territories (that is, public for them but possibly secondary for another group of children). Whereas the children at the one extreme of the economic continuum are taken to shopping centers or other places considered safe by the parents, children from the other extreme stay outside – not being cared for, but taking care of such things as cars, that is, the means of transport used by the former group.

In summary, for some children, the expansion of their territory begins with the explicit support and supervision of their families, whereas other children depend much earlier on peer support. This arrangement suggests the task of investigating levels and sequences of competencies of the children as their home range and, consequently, their secondary territories grow.

2.2.3 Streets – public or territory?

The street constitutes the most complex environment for children. It is there that different groups of people compete for space to engage in activities, which many times are mutually exclusive: driving, playing, buying and selling, loitering, and strolling, to name but a few. As concerns children, streets serve two broad functions: providing access to secondary territories and being secondary territory itself. Among children, knowledge about and the significance of the street can be quite different from one social segment to the next. When certain public territories (e.g., shopping centers) are inaccessible as secondary territory (see above) to some (e.g., street children), the space to be traversed to reach it becomes secondary territory to them. 'Guarding' cars in public parking areas or on the streets constitutes a mean of support for oneself and one's family as well as a primary play activity. Frequently, these parking areas have 'owners', who concede to the children part of the territory in which to take care of cars. The children keep relatively little of what they receive from the owners of the cars. Instead of assuming the role of support, the 'owner' of the area exploits the children. Even the distinction between primary and secondary territory becomes difficult because dwelling, neighborhood, and street are becoming one.

At the other social extreme, parents of upper-class children may go so far as to consider streets and many other public spaces of the city unsafe and undesirable, trying to make them all but inaccessible, yet desirable, to their children. The street no longer is a place where one interacts, plays, explores, exercises curiosity, develops common bonds, and becomes competent in dealing with individuals different from oneself.

In terms of cognitive and social competencies, this segregation might imply a developmental impoverishment for the economically better-off children, without constituting significant gains in self-worth for the others.

3 Conclusion

We selected a concrete cultural context to reflect on the possibilities of integration and application of different approaches to the child-city relation. The three chapters we were to integrate do not, in our perspective, allow for a kind of amalgamation into a superordinate unity. However, to the extent that they deal with different features of developmental processes within complex social and physical environments, one may join the approaches presented in them in view of a common object of study, for each contributes to the comprehension of the city-child relation as a whole.

Notes

1 These data are from the 1995 National Census of Household Samples. Complete data are available through the Internet, www.ibge.gov.br. The study covered 334,263 persons in 102,787 households in 793 *municípios* (which correspond approximately to counties). Rural areas of the Northern Region of Brazil, about 0.2 percent of the population, were not included in this National Census of Household Samples.

2 In order to contextualize these reflections, compare the area and population of Brazil, Europe (minus the Commonwealth of Independent States), and the continental United States. The areas are approximately 8.5 million, 5 million, and 8 million square kilometers, respectively; the populations, 153 million, 515 million, and 260 million inhabitants. Whereas one hardly speaks of a European national characteristic, there is still some tendency not to differentiate among *the* Americans, and even less so among the Brazilians. What is largely a geographical differentiation in Brazil becomes a question of national identity in Europe and becomes confounded with ethnic distinctions in the United States.

3 The data are from the 1995 National Census of Household Samples, available through the Internet, www.ibge.gov.br.

4 Again, these questions apply to Europe and the United States as well.

5 In short, perception and concession of control depend on such larger contextual variables as the socioeconomic status of the individual or groups.

6 'Manor house and slave quarter' is the exact translation of the title of Gilberto Freyre's book *Casa Grande e Senzala*. This book describes the relationship of masters and slaves in colonial Brazilian society, including the spacial arrangements. Reference for the original is Gilberto Freyre, *Casa Grande e Senzala* (Rio de Janeiro: Maia Schmidt, Ltda, 1933). In the English translation, the title of the book became *The masters and the slaves* (1st edition, New York: Knopf, 1946).

B. Transactional, holistic, and relational-developmental perspectives on children in the cities

Introduction

Hans Joachim Harloff

It is fascinating to see how quickly new insights take over today, how soon recently created concepts are then occupied by the community of scholars, and how quickly their own older theories are retailored accordingly. However, the practice gives rise to quite different interpretations, which are used as foundations for the associated ideas. Ten to twenty years ago it was the concept of *action* that was juxtaposed with the older *behavior*. The human being did not behave in such and such a manner but rather acted (in a goal-directed and/or object-related way). Immediately, a wide variety of action theories arose. It is similar today with the word *transaction*, which is juxtaposed with what was called *interaction* in earlier theories. Humans do not interact with the environment; instead, the human being and the environment act jointly, operating together in events, generating new products and states, with both the human being and the environment changing and being changed (see Harloff, Lehnert, & Eybisch, in this volume; Werner & Altman, in this volume).

Of the theoretical contributions for which this introduction is to prepare the reader, two are called transactional (Oerter and Wapner). Granted, Wapner emphasizes the attributes *holistic*, *developmental*, and *systems-oriented* in the title of his chapter, but as soon as one begins to read the text it becomes clear that transaction is the key word in his theory. Through transactions (by which Wapner means experience and action), persons and the environment become linked in a person-in-environment unit. In Oerter's theory the same thing happens through *action*, the corresponding expression. Moreover, for theories that initially seem to diverge, one is astonished to find how similar they are after eliminating differences in terminologies. I am not saying the theories of these authors would then become identical, but a good part of the difference between Oerter's approach and Wapner's vanishes when one registers that the key theoretical concept Oerter calls *action* is what Wapner refers to as *transaction*. By contrast, Oerter speaks of transaction only in a very specific sense to mean that humans occasionally or frequently change the environment through their action. To Oerter, then, transactions constitute a subclass of actions. (Adding yet another concept of transaction to those discussed in this book, Hellgard Rauh, who integrates the three theories in this part, follows Leont'ev in taking transaction to mean the intergenerational transmission of cultural knowledge.)

The question remains, however, whether any of the three theories deserves the attribute *transactional*. Lang, the commentator for Oerter's chapter, shows that the word is not appropriate, at least for that contribution. Nor is Overton's theory the only one that is subject-centered. As Rauh's integrative comments demonstrate, Oerter's and Wapner's are, too. The environmental side of the person-environment relation remains underrepresented. None of the theories has what transactionalism calls for – the formation of person-environment units, with the individual and the environment (both social and physical) being equally warranted in the sense that transactions within a unit and between units can originate with both the individual and the milieu (e.g., a gust of wind makes one grab and hold one's hat).

Rather than delve deeper into the different contributions, I would like to make suggestions about the order in which to read them. If a certain amount of structuring is desired first, one should begin with the integrative comments by Rauh. She gives an excellent overview of the three theories, paying tribute to each before providing a synopsis of them. It seems especially fitting to begin with Overton, whose approach clearly revolves around the individual (the researcher or the developing child) and whose "world-out-there" is only an undifferentiated background. Building on Overton's theory, Rauh is able to show which important additions and corrections are gained through the approaches proposed by Wapner and Oerter, both of whom emphasize the environment, but in quite different ways. Readers who prefer instead to come to their own judgments without being influenced in any way should quickly forget this introduction and enjoy the theoretical contributions and the respective commentaries in the given order. These readers may formulate their own synopses and then compare them with that by Rauh.

Before leaving the reader with this decision on the sequence in which to digest these essays, I must expressly point out the commentaries. Each has a value of its own. That assessment is as true for A. Lang's fascinatingly stringent epistemological critique of Oerter's chapter as for the commentaries by Görlitz (on Wapner) and Deutsch (on Overton), both of which add something new. Specifically, Görlitz asks whether Heinz Werner's orthogenetic principle of development, which Wapner builds into his theory, is sufficient for explaining the development of children in the city. If I understand correctly, Görlitz leaves the question open but cautiously indicates a need for modification and expansion. Deutsch's commentary on Overton is persuasive primarily for the observation that Overton's kind of deductive theories must be contrasted with *inductive* theories (William Stern is singled out in this context) and that a discourse between the two lines of inquiry must be opened.

Transactionalism

Rolf Oerter

1 What is transactionalism?
An action-theory approach and its implications

Developmental and personality psychology long ago abandoned the theoretical causal model of unidirectional cause and effect. The reason for this change in view was the attempt to consider the exchange between the individual and the environment. In more recent explanations of mutual causal effects between the individual and the environment, two terms have come up: interactionism and transactionalism. Interaction refers in general to the relation between the person and the environment, particularly the social environment, in the sense of reciprocal influence. That is, the person and the environment are seen to have effects on each other, but those effects are often confined to social interaction between partners.

Transactionalism, a concept that is sometimes used very vaguely in ways that confound it with interactionism, is used in the following presentation to refer to the assumption that individuals change their environment through their own actions in such a way that personal ideas, designs, and goals are transported into the environment and "materialized" there. As part of the human-made environment, however, these products have impacts on the individual. The individual's action is determined by objects, ideas, or human beings. Everyday objects like tools and cars may serve as examples. Using a tool means that the constructor's ideas that are imposed on the object are realized and transformed into action. Using a car means a more or less total transformation of human action: flexibility in reaching places, a feeling of power and speed, working to earn money in order to purchase a car and so forth.

Hence, transactionalism focuses on action theory and considers interaction in a specific way. In transactionalism the emphasis in the term interaction falls on "action." While the special approach toward action theory will be elaborated below, a general reason for the crucial role of the concept of action is its function in connecting the individual to the environment. Action becomes the link between the individual and the environment and has bidirectional effects. On the one hand, action transfers ideas and goals into the environment. An example is the production of a tool or of goods in general. On the other hand, action transforms the ideas inherent in the objects into individual knowledge about the action possibilities of the objects. Thus, driving a car requires the acquisition of knowledge about the car, that is, its action possibilities, and every driver possesses at least some knowledge of cars in general and of his or her own car in particular. In summary, transactionalism attempts to explain the mutual transfer of cause and effect between the individual and the environment.

If one applies this view of transactionalism to the relation between the urban environment and the child, the advantage of this approach becomes clear. The city as a life-space (Lewin, 1936) offers a host of action possibilities for the child. Conversely, children contribute by their actions to a minor or major change of urban areas. Road traffic is a special case of action formation with children. As soon as the children leave the family home, they can survive only if they have at least some knowledge of the dangers of traffic. Their actions must be adapted to the traffic situation. Conversely, if one assumes a residential area with little traffic and specific traffic rules and precautions such as speed bumps, the playing child controls the traffic to a certain degree because drivers will watch the street more carefully and move more slowly. The perspective of transactionalism can therefore be used as an evaluation criterion of the child-environment relation. Whenever the bidirectionality of action is equalized, the child-environment ecological system is balanced.

To summarize the theoretical position of transactionalism, interaction from the perspective of action theory links the individual and the environment. Action works in both directions, toward the environment and toward the individual. Action, therefore, is the crucial explanatory concept of the ecological system that integrates the individual and the environment into a functioning whole.

The perspective of transactionalism reveals immediately the present existing imbalance in urban environments. In most cases children are unable to change their environments. On the contrary, they have to adapt continuously and unilaterally to situations that are structured for action goals other than those conceived to enhance the quality of life for children. Children are expected to avoid interfering with traffic. Therefore, planning an urban environment for children and for other age groups means achieving a more balanced state of action that enables the individual to control both sides, the environment and the self.

2 Action and object-relatedness

2.1 The evolution of action

Action is considered a specific human form of behavior. Its dynamics and structure can be conceived at best by deriving it from human history. Deducing the origins of action in terms of phylogeny and human history makes qualitative leaps apparent. Holzkamp (1983) saw such a qualitative leap in the transition from a purely cooperative to a societal preservation of life. A societal preservation of life provides alternatives for action that no longer have to serve the immediate survival. Rather they can be performed independently of actual needs. This liberation of action endows human beings with an action capacity that can be characterized by two criteria: goal-directedness and object-relatedness.

Actions are directed to a goal; that is, they pursue an intention that exists before the action starts. When action no longer serves only to preserve life, the distance between goal-setting and action performance can become very large, a circumstance that can provide opportunities for planning and coordinating single actions. The second criterion, object-relatedness, is more important for the present issue. The object-relatedness of action has been elaborated in the psychology of activity (Leont'ev, 1977), which holds that action is always directed at something and that this something becomes an *object*, that is the focus of human behavior.[1] As a general formula, object-relatedness can be expressed as

$$I \longrightarrow O,$$

whereby I symbolizes the individual; O objects; and the arrow, the direction of action.

It is important to note that object-relatedness is not identical with goal-directedness. Action may use objects for quite different goals and purposes. Goal directedness depends on both the *affordances* (see Heine & Guski, in this volume) of the object and the specific intentions of the individual. However, goal-directedness is imbedded in the mutual relationship between the individual and the environment that is described by objects. Goals can only be striven for within individual-object relations that are provided in the individual's environment. Applied to urban life, all activities in a city are thus necessarily object-related: shopping (goods as objects), driving (destination, street, and vehicles as objects), games (playgrounds and play equipment as objects), and so forth. The child's action in the urban environment is determined by objects. The bicycle, the seesaw, the trees, the meadow, the side-walks, and thousands of other things are objects in the above sense and shape the child's action. Vice versa, there is no action without an object. The analysis of child-environment relation can thus be pursued by analyzing action possibilities and action restrictions of an urban environment.

2.2   Shared object-relatedness

Object-relatedness is always a shared relatedness. That is, an object is a point of reference for more than one person. If a person acts upon an object, usually other individuals are also related to the object. Children play with each other, whereby the link between them consists of objects, be it toys, parts of the environment, or a common theme of play. Thus, every activity in urban life can be described as forms of shared object-related actions. Participating in traffic means relating one's activity to shared objects such as streets, traffic signs, and traffic rules. Even private life is governed by shared object-relatedness. For example, a typical action in everyday urban life is shopping. The customer who is choosing and buying goods is simultaneously in a systemic relation to the cashier and the persons who have produced and delivered the merchandise. Citizens of urban communities not only act within a given frame of objects but also produce new objects and object-relations.

Cities provide the life-space for cultural development, which, in terms of object-relations, means the production of cultural objects such as goods, works of art, and values. The negative effects of cities, often described as a Moloch who devours his inhabitants or as the loss of individual initiative, can be explained as a disturbance of shared object-relations and of the destructive function of objects. An illustrative example of disturbed common object-relations is the traffic jam; an example of the destructive function of objects is gambling that addicts the individual to indefinite loops of action. In general, action relates actors to shared objects and thereby becomes social action or social interaction.

Conversely, mature social interaction can usually be described as the production and maintenance of joint object-relatedness. Joint relatedness exists even when the subject makes strictly personal use of an object, say, a tool. The actor is in communication with the toolmaker, whose ideas have been reified in the tool. The tooluser must understand and internalize the toolmaker's ideas in order to use the tool appropriately. The functions of the tool can be explored by the actor him- or herself or can be explained by competent partners. In each case, however, this means indirect communication with the toolmaker. All objects are thus social in nature. Hence, the third constituent feature of action is its social and societal character.

Joint object-relatedness can be expressed in the general formula

$$I_1 \longrightarrow O \longleftarrow I_2.$$

Two or more individuals relate themselves to the same object, be it a material thing, a set of things, a knowledge item, or a value. Simultaneously, individuals relate themselves to each other in intending an effect with the partner and experiencing the effect of the partner via his or her action upon the object. Thus, the formula can be extended to read

$$I_1 \longrightarrow O \longleftarrow I_2.$$

The gaze to the partner during the shared object relation occurs rather early. Camras and Sachs (1991) presented evidence that infants tune their approach to objects according to the emotional reaction of the adult partner. In general, infants from an early age on alternate their attention between the shared object and the partner (Power & Parke, 1983).

3   Transactional processes

Transaction can be described and explained in terms of two dialectical pairs of concepts: reification – internalization, and subjectivation – objectivation.

3.1   Reification

The essence of reification is the production of objects. This process constitutes the core of human activity whose results are preserved as culture or serve, at least in most cases, the maintenance of culture. Reification, however, also includes all goal-directed activities that change the environment, activities such as the usage and alteration of objects. Control awareness, and the feeling of power arise as *basic emotional states of reification*. Lastly, reification is symbolized in the myth of the world's creation by God "in His image, after His likeness" (Genesis). Reification is, therefore, a central process of identity formation. It mediates the experience of self-efficacy (Bandura, 1977), which is a crucial component of a secure identity.

The construction of the urban environment is a prime example of reification. In a balanced system of town and inhabitants, each individual should participate in the process of urban reification in one way or another. Such a process provides stability and meaningfulness for the inhabitants because their identity is co-defined by their influence on the environment. Therefore, children, too, should be given more opportunities to help structure their environments. This idea is sometimes practiced, such as when children participate in planning playgrounds, kindergartens, and school environments. Children should also be encouraged to make suggestions for the improvement of the traffic system. At least their opinions about the traffic in their city should be heard and respected. In some cases families are involved in planning new residential areas. They therefore come to have the feeling of controlling their environment – if one accepts the assumption about the basic emotion connected with reification. The need for shaping the environment is also expressed in structuring the layout of one's own apartment.

3.2   Internalization

I shift attention now from the object to the individual. Internalization is the opposite process of reification. The individual appropriates the object by integrating it into his or her subjective structure. In terms of constructivism, it is a matter of reconstructing the object, which thereby becomes available for action (for the term *construction*, see Seiler in this volume). Similarly, perceiving and learning as well as enjoying and consuming goods are processes of internalization. The *basic emotional state* produced by internalization is self-security, for internalization makes the objects of the environment part of a person's identity structure. An environment that is known and liked by a person becomes a "home" for him or her. Thus, internalization develops a second component of identity: self-confidence and self-assurance.

Children's basic activity of internalization is exploration, which makes new things familiar. In the modern urban setting, children use opportunities for exploration in department stores, game centers, parks, rear courtyards, museums, movies, libraries, and so forth. Urban planning should provide positive environments for exploration and avoid negative settings that would be explored in the same way by children.

Reification and internalization appear in two different forms, subjectivation and objectivation. These two components of action shall be described in the following.

3.3 Subjectivation

Subjectivation orients action toward the individual's personal needs, ideas, and goals. This orientation exists with both internalization and reification. Subjectivation is the core process of forming consciousness and identity. Only that which can be integrated into one's own cognitive structure and harmonized with one's own needs becomes a part of personal identity. This idea is expressed directly in the formula "I can [cannot] identify with it." Subjectivation discovers and/or constructs similarities between the environment and the individual. It protects the actor from the feeling of alienation in a world with features different from those of the acting person. Processes of subjectivation have the effect of strengthening and improving identity. The *basic emotional state* of subjectivation is familarity, feeling at home, and feeling sheltered.

Subjectivation, too, can be illustrated by our topic of urban planning and living. Children's main subjectivizing activity is play. In play, things and actions are adapted toward a reality constructed by the child according to his or her personal needs and themes (Vygotsky, 1966; Oerter, 1993). Therefore, providing opportunities for play of every kind in urban scenarios means stimulating subjectivizing processes.

A possibility for subjectivizing reification beyond play consists in the opportunity of rearranging rooms by changing walls in the cellar or attic. Some urban planners take those opportunities into consideration in providing a flexible division of rooms in houses and apartments. Since the needs of families change during the life course, they can rearrange the size and number of rooms and adapt them to new requirements.

3.4   Objectivation

Objectivation, as the opposite process of subjectivation, refers to the orientation of action toward reality that exists independently of the individual (but is socially construed nevertheless). Reality is guaranteed through objects, that is, all things in the individual's surrounding such as tools, toys, goods, buildings, streets, and cars. In the process of both internalization and reification, the individual can thus deal with objects whose reality can be tested. Acting upon objects forces the actor to adapt to laws of action inherent to the object. Thus, the correct usage of a tool is only possible if physical laws are considered. The effect of the leverage of a hammer, for example, can only be realized when the actor seizes the hammer at the end of its handle und uses it as an extended arm (for the development of tool usage in childhood see Hetzer, 1931, and Lisina & Nevorovich, 1971). Lastly, every action has to be adapted to laws of reality that exist independently of the individual's knowledge and attitudes. Objectivation, as a *basic emotional state*, thus mediates the consciousness of the existence of an outer world, that is, of a reality that exists independently of oneself. This consciousness about reality simultaneously provides the basis for the awareness of one's own existence as an objectively given entity in an objectively given world.

Applying the concept of objectivation to children in urban scenarios, one sees that children have to objectivate by adapting to the traffic system, acquiring a cognitive map of their district, and learning the scripts of the specific urban settings (e.g., shop, library, and school). However, this form of objectivation belongs to processes of internalization, whereas processes of reification are far less possible. Components of objectivizing reification can be stimulated for children when they are encouraged to contribute to the construction and/or change of settings in which they live. Those settings include the kindergarten, school, home environment, streets, playgrounds, and parks. The main component of objectivation, however, is the experience of making products that are useful independently of one's own present needs. In this way, children learn that their work possesses value for the whole community, especially when the settings for which they had been productive are used by other children at a later age.

The four processes of action and transaction are linked. Subjectivation and objec-tivation occur either as internalization or as reification. Figure 1 illustrates the four-field combination of the two pairs of concepts as four components of an acting individual. They complement each other to form an integrative whole of human action. Each of the four components is involved in any action contributing, with different weights, to the process and outcome of the action. From this perspective a very general definition of mental health can be derived. Mental health is a state and a process in which the four basic components of human action are in balance.

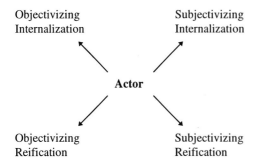

Objectivizing   Subjectivizing
Internalization   Internalization

Actor

Objectivizing   Subjectivizing
Reification   Reification

Figure 1: Four basic components which are involved with different wights in every action

Culture in general and settings in specific sometimes have constraints that restrict basic action components. Thus, in western cultures internalization prevails over reification because the economy is based on consumption. The dominance of consumption in everyday life suppresses processes of reification. People often try to compensate for this lack by productive leisure activity. Urban settings are attractive mainly because of their entertaining affordances discouraging initiative and reification, whereas productive activity is at best restricted to some occupational branches. Nevertheless, if one applies the four-field combination of reification-internalization and subjectivation-objectivation, examples of each of the four combinations can be found. Table 1 presents examples of living conditions in urban environments.

Table 1: The four-field combination of the two pairs of processes underlying the concept of transaction as demonstrated by examples of the living situation in urban environments

	Objectivation	Subjectivation
Internalization	Adapting to the traffic conditions in cities, learning to go safely from home to school	Exploring playgrounds and rear courtyards, choosing according to one's own needs
Reification	Considering physical laws and weather conditions in the planning and construction of dwellings	For parents and children, participating in building and decorating dwellings according to their wishes and needs

It is worth noting that Piaget's classification of assimilation and accommodation can be related to the four-field combination in Figure 1. Assimilation corresponds exactly to subjectivizing internalization; accommodation, to objectivizing internalization. Piaget (1977) was only marginally interested in reification processes, and even then he used them only as a vehicle for developing the epistemology of the young individual. His main interest focused on processes of internalization in the sense of cognition and knowledge acquisition (see also Seiler, in this volume).

4   Culture and the individual

For the most part, transactional effects have thus far been described from the perspective of the individual. This perspective is incomplete because larger structures, including life conditions in a city, do not come systematically under consideration. I therefore examine the perspective of transactionalism in terms of the relations between the individual and culture. First, it is necessary to describe culture in terms of action theory. Second, the individual as a member of the culture has to be related to culture in a systematic manner.

Herskovits (1948) was the first person to present a short and convincing definition of culture: It is "the man-made part of the environment" (p. 17). Culture shapes the typical human ecosystem. It is something that is positioned between the human being and the natural environment. Unlike most recent definitions (e.g., Camilleri, 1985; Kroeber & Kluckhorn, 1952; Segall, Dasen, Berry, & Poortinga, 1990), the definition of culture within the context of transactionalism is explicitly conceived of as the typical human environment produced by human beings. In order to use the concept of culture within an action-theory approach, it is additionally necessary to relate it to the term object, the counterpart of the actor linked by action. This connection is possible if culture is defined as the universe of objects created by human beings. As already pointed out, the term *object* refers to a broad range of entities. On the basis of Popper's three-world theory, material, mental, and psychological objects can be distinguished (Popper, 1973).

Material objects are utensils and thus primarily tools of all kinds. In the framework of the present topic all facilities, buildings, roads, stores, physicians' practices, playgrounds, and so forth belong to this class of objects. *Mental objects* include the accumulated knowledge, culturally established norms, and cultural products stemming from literature, art, and music. In cities, more than in rural areas, great value is attached to the availability of this knowledge, which is made accessible in libraries, museums, theaters, and schools. Mental objects are mediated by material vehicles such as books, videos, and discs. Hence, children in particular, and many adults, are not even consciously aware of the existence of mental objects unless the objects are tied to material substrata such as books and recordings. For this reason, the plain and prominent representation of mental objects is especially important in urban communities, where those objects can be provided more easily than in rural areas. In a way, relatively costly libraries, theaters, and other cultural facilities are the guarantees that mental objects will continue to exist. Nevertheless, analysis of the two classes of objects cited thus far shows that Western culture is a material culture with an infinite number of goods and utensils.

Psychological objects encompass the concepts of cognitive and emotional conscious states as well as psychological traits that explain behavior. Thus, achievement performance is explained by intelligence and achievement motivation; social behavior by social motivation and social competence; and so forth. Psychological objects are defined by the culture. They differ from culture to culture much as material objects and mental objects do (Oerter, 1994; for Japanese culture see, for example, Kojima, 1986; Markus & Kitayama, 1991). Therefore, psychological objects are constructs that the culture offers for the description and explanation of human needs and human behavior. Special types of psychological objects are demons, ghosts, and gods, all of whom possess psychological traits that have impacts on the life of the members of the culture.

Within the framework of urban planning, emotional states of a satisfaction, of feeling at home, as well as of excitement and of special atmosphere become important. If the whole community experiences the same feelings about its city, psychological objects exist as shared knowledge and received cultural reality. They become "objective," that is, they are shared among a large group of residents and exist objectively, so to speak. A city's "atmosphere" and "flair" is an example of such objective psychological terms.

Culture thus emerges as the structure of objects to which one's action is related. This structure can be called *objective structure*. Because subjects who could take action stand concealed behind every object, cultural objects can be symbolized as

$$[I \longrightarrow] O.$$

The environment appears as a structure of objects that exist independently of the individual's action. Actually, however, individuals are related to these objects, even when they are not acting upon those objects momentarily.

The above formula can be demonstrated nicely by the urban environment. It appears, in fact, as a system of objects, with buildings, streets, subways, parks, playgrounds, and so forth as material objects. The "culture" that is presented in the architecture of buildings, the masterpieces of museums, and the music in the opera and concert hall is a set of mental objects. These objects are connected with psychological categories of evaluation of urban living qualities and with the feeling of belonging to the city. Many people identify themselves with the city, expressing feelings of pride and happiness as residents.

What about the individual that lives within the universe of objects? Individuals appear to exist independently of these objects that have cognitive/affective structures per se. From the perspective of action theory, however, these structures are always related to something. There is no cognition and feeling without an object (defined broadly as described above). Individuals who have developed a cognitive/affective structure through enculturation can therefore be defined through the formula

$$I [\longrightarrow O].$$

The individual's cognitive/affective structure can be described as a system of object relations. Nevertheless, the individual appears as a separate entity; his or her object relations and embeddedness into the culture are hidden. Therefore, the relation to the objects of the culture are placed in brackets.

If one attempts to combine individual and culture into an integrated whole, the human ecosystem can be conceived as the interaction between culture (universe of objects) and the individual (system of action competences of handling cultural objects). The formula expressing this is

$$I \longrightarrow O.$$
$$\longleftarrow$$

It seems restrictive to describe the cultural ecosystem as relations of actions between individuals and objects. Actually, however, it is a very broad and general conception because the term object refers to everything at which action is directed. The goodness-of-fit between the individual and culture results in a structure of action that matches possibilities that have been provided for action, that is, the range of affordances offered by the culture (see also Heine & Guski, in this volume). The individual acting in the culture achieves a two-fold result. He or she internalizes the culturally provided action possibilities as the "subjective structure" but, through reification, also contributes to enriching or changing the culture, that is, the "objective structure." Perhaps the most impressive example of such a transaction is the invention of the automobile, which changed the world as no other object had before. In the present, computer technology is changing the cultural system of modern societies dramatically.

As a consequence of the goodness-of-fit relation between the individual and the culture, transactionalism demands the assumption of isomorphism between objective structure and subjective structure. The individuals of a society form their culture according to their own cognitive structure. Culture as the objective structure therefore possesses structural features of the individuals. Conversely, this means that the culture as a human-made environment can be easily acquired by individuals living in that culture because its structure is made by the human species. The individual as a member of the culture takes on that objective structure, thereby acting in a way that fits the possibilities of the cultural objects. If the individual fails to adapt to the possibilities for cultural action, he or she is labeled as deviant, mentally ill, or "inhumane."

Given the principle of isomorphism, where do freedom of action and creativity come in? They can develop only within the limitations and latitudes defined by culture. Whenever children produce something new, a tiny, at least temporary cultural change takes place. If culture tolerates and accepts those contributions, it provides freedom for individual development and acquires new impetus, it becomes enriched through the activity of its members. If a culture resists changes, it prevents new individual initiatives. But even in the most restrictive culture there is no complete concordance between culture and the individual. The whole system is dynamic and needs continuous regulatory activity. In complex cultures such as those of modern, highly industrialized societies, specific regulatory institutions are necessary, particularly systems of administration and bureaucracy. Hence, isomorphism is a regulation principle that coordinates the relations between individual and culture but can (and should) never be fully reached.

I shall now apply the idea of the cultural ecosystem to the urban environment from an action-theory perspective. In the history of the human race, town cultures have been the roots of the development of advanced civilizations (beginning with Ur in Chaldea and continuing with Babylon, Athens, and Rome). To this day, art and science as well as entertainment are represented best in modern cities. Therefore, urban residents can profit from the cultural affordances provided in cities. Children experience cognitive stimulation in urban environments and are offered better chances of development there than in rural areas.

On the other hand, the city is slandered as Moloch, as something that attracts, seduces, and finally devours its inhabitants. Modern urban environments encompass both positive and negative affordances. As is generally the case in modern cultures, urban environments favor internalization and offer few opportunities for reification. Children should receive more opportunities to shape their environment actively, whether as a planning activity or as an immediate contribution to rearranging urban living conditions. Only the opportunity for reification enables the individual to become creative. Therefore, the process of creatively rearranging the environment should become permanent. The possibilities for altering dwellings, say, the basement and attic, according to changing needs is an example of flexible planning that allows for reification.

5 Summary and conclusion

The approach of transactionalism does not compete with other theoretical perspectives as they are presented in other chapters of this volume. Rather, it is a framework that encompasses a broad range of views from an action-theory perspective. In the version presented here, some basic concepts have been introduced that combine the individual and the environment into an integrated system. The general formula of $I \longrightarrow O$ stands for the fundamental process by which the human ecosystem is transformed from a pure natural environment into the typical human environment: the culture. Contrary to a merely mentalistic understanding of culture as internalized cultural knowledge and norms, the present definition of culture also includes the material environment and emphasizes culture as a system that exists independently of the individual (but not independently of human beings in general).

Therefore, this approach is fruitful for a better understanding of the relation between urban environments and their residents. In particular, children who develop in urban environments can be described by means of the process of enculturation in the urban ecosystem. Introducing the concept of urban culture avoids a one-sided view. Cities are settings, media, and contexts of development. They offer affordances. But cities are more than that because they are complex systems determined by their urban culture.

The analysis of action in urban environments reveals an imbalance in favor of processes of internalization. This imbalance is simultaneously a general danger for human development in modern cultures. It jeopardizes the mental hygiene of children and other residents and blocks creativity. Furthermore, through this imbalance in urban life, people lose control over their life. Therefore, every resident should receive opportunities for reification. Children can require them through participation in the planning of playgrounds, schools, streets, parks, dwellings, and public buildings and through concrete reification by working with layouts in the family home, the kindergarten, and the school. Beyond these examples a host of suggestions are conceivable, many of them to be presented in the following chapters.

At their best, urban environments are the nourishing soil for new cultural developments; at their worst, they are settings for the destruction of human life. It is a major responsibility to help in determining where the future of urban development will lie between these two poles.

Note

1 The term *object* is used here in a philosophical sense and comprises all that becomes a focus of human conscious awareness. In terms of action theory, an object is the entity toward which a specific action is directed.

References

Bandura, A. (1977). Self-efficacy: Toward a unifying theory of behavioral change. *Psychological Review, 2*, 191-215.

Camilleri, C. (1985). La psychologie culturelle [Cultural psychology]. *Psychologie francaise, 30*, 147-151.

Camras, L. A., & Sachs, V. B. (1991). Social referencing and caretaker expressive behaviour in a day care setting. *Infant Behavior and Development, 14*, 27-36.

Herskovits, M. J. (1948). *Man and his works: The science of cultural anthropology.* New York: Knopf.

Hetzer, H. (1931). *Kind und Schaffen* [Child and creation]. Jena: Fischer.

Holzkamp, K. (1983). *Grundlegung der Psychologie* [Foundations of psychology]. Frankfurt on the Main: Campus.

Kojima, H. (1986). Japanese concepts of child development from the mid-17th to mid-19th century. *International Journal of Behavior Development, 9*, 315-329.

Kroeber, A. L., & Kluckhorn, C. (1952). *Culture: A critical review of concepts and definitions* (Vol. 47, No. 1). Cambridge, MA: Peabody Museum.

Leont'ev, A. N. (1977). *Tätigkeit, Bewußtsein, Persönlichkeit* [Activity, consciousness, personality]. Stuttgart: Klett.

Lewin, K. (1936). *Principles of topological psychology*. New York: McGraw-Hill.

Lisina, M. I., & Nevorovich, Y. Z. (1971). Development of movements and formation of motor habits. In A. V. Zaporozhets & D. B. Elkonin (Eds.), *The psychology of preschool children* (pp. 128-167). Cambridge, MA: MIT Press.

Markus, H. R., & Kitayama, S. (1991). Culture and the self: Implications for cognition, emotion, and motivation. *Psychological Review, 98,* 224-253.

Oerter, R. (1993). *Psychologie des Spiels. Ein handlungstheoretischer Ansatz* [Psychology of play. An action-theory approach]. Weinheim: Beltz.

Oerter, R. (1994). Persons' conception of human nature: A cross-cultural comparison. In J. Valsiner (Ed.), *Child development within culturally structured environments* (Vol. 3, pp. 210-242). Norwood, NJ: Ablex.

Piaget, J. (1977). *The development of thought: Equilibrium of cognitive structures*. New York: Viking.

Popper, K. R. (1973). *Objektive Erkenntnis. Ein evolutionärer Entwurf* [Objective cognition: An evolutionary design]. Hamburg: Hoffmann & Campe.

Power, T. G., & Parke, R. D. (1983). Patterns of mother and father play with their 8-month-old infant: A multiple analyses approach. *Infant Behavior and Development, 6,* 453-459.

Segall, M. H., Dasen, P. R., Berry, J. W., & Poortinga, Y. H. (1990). *Human behavior in global perspective*. New York: Pergamon Press.

Vygotsky, L. S. (1966). Play and its role in the psychological development of the child. *Voprosy psikhologii, 12,* 62-76.

Comment: Transactionalism – What could it be?

Alfred Lang

"Transactionalism" – like most goods thrown onto the intellectual market by modern psychology – comes in various versions. In order to comment upon Rolf Oerter's rendition, I shall first attempt to condense it to its essentials. To be fair to Oerter's transactionalism, it should be compared with notions given to that term by other transactionalists, contemporary and earlier ones,[1] and I think it would compare favorably with many. Unfortunately, lack of space prevents that approach. I also have to resist the temptation to sketch a simpler and more comprehensive version of the ecological situation (see Lang, 1988, 1992, 1993). Instead, I limit myself to an evaluation of some of Oerter's essential points in relation to general conceptual elements and thereby perhaps further elucidate the potential of a transactional perspective. To some degree I must rely on inferences about implications hidden in Oerter's view. I might well err in that attempt, but it is my hope that this approach will help everyone toward an adequate understanding of humans in culture, both in general and in view of children in the city. I write deliberately in the spirit of constructive criticism of a set of ideas, not of the persons having presented them. For I am convinced that psychology as a science suffers from too many publications not as carefully read as they are written and from a scatter of ever new constructions advanced without a solid enough foundation.

1   Oerter's transactionalism condensed

In the chapter I was asked to comment upon, I can discern 14 manifest assumptions. Obviously, they have to be thought of by the reader as forming a system, whereas I have to present them one after the other. I make liberal use of quotations and paraphrases without explicit markings. I also use catch-terms and bracketed numbers for easy identification of each assumption.

[1] *Ecosystems.* Individual subjects and their environment(s) as collections of objects (in a wide sense) together constitute ecological systems, in particular the human ecosystem integrating people and culture.

[2] *Action.* Action as the specifically human form of behavior is the crucial explanatory concept; it integrates the individual and the environment into a functioning whole. Action is what subjects do to the environment; action also has effects back on the subject.

[3] *Reification.* By their actions, individuals produce, change, and use "objects." Objects comprise all that can become a focus of human conscious awareness. By acting, subjects transport their personal ideas, designs, and goals into their environment.

[4] *Internalization.* By his or her acting, the individual also transforms the ideas inherent in environmental objects into his or her own knowledge and action possibilities.

[5] *Transaction.* Cause-and-effect transfer between individual and environment is called transaction in the ecosystem. Transactionalism has the task of explaining this bidirectional or mutual transfer, that is, of specifying its conditions and consequences.

[6] *Subjectivation.* Consciousness and identity are formed by rearranging parts of the environment in a personal way and thus integrating and harmonizing aspects of reality into any individual's cognitive structure and providing for his or her emotional security.

[7] *Objectivation.* In view of the fact that most of the world exists independently of oneself, any person's actions must ultimately be adapted to the laws of reality, both physical and logical.

[8] *Fourfold transaction.* Internalization and reification can both operate in the service of objectivation and subjectivation. Transactions can thus be grouped into four types: objectivating reification, subjectivating reification, objectivating internalization, and subjectivating internalization.

[9] *Inclusively psychological.* The four types of transactional processes include self- or identity-related perspectives and emotional ramifications as well as cognitive-factual structures and events.

[10] *Bidirectional balance.* Mutual, or bidirectional, transactions can be more or less balanced. Good balance is required for the integration of individuals and the environment in a functioning whole.

[11] *Isomorphism.* Objective (cultural) and subjective (personal) structures demand a minimal degree of isomorphism.

[12] *Action theory.* Transaction and isomorphism are best explained in terms of action theory. Its key notions are *object-relatedness* (i.e., intentionality) and *goal-directedness* (i.e., the actor, while incited by the objects, will eventually dominate them within the constraints of their reality).

[13] *Social (inter-)action.* Objects to which individuals relate themselves through their actions are largely shared among people interacting socially. By relating themselves to shared objects (things, knowledge, values), people are relating themselves also to each other.

[14] *Culture.* Transaction cannot be fully understood exclusively in terms of individual and social interaction. Culture, or the "human-made part of the environment," is the typically human ecosystem positioned between human beings and the natural environment. Culture comprises material objects (things and settings), mental objects (ideas and norms), and psychological objects (individual cognitive and emotional conscious states and traits).

2 Some implications

My above condensations are explicit in Oerter's article. His view evidently also includes a set of implications that might be quite important for understanding his transactionalism. Let me venture three of them.

[I] *Development.* Oerter construes his transactionalism only implicitly in the context of development. That context might seem to him to be self-evident. Unfortunately, it leaves the reader uncertain as to what notion of development Oerter adopts. Whether he follows, say, a Vygotskian or a Piagetian approach, makes a big difference. If he follows Vygotsky, primal causes of everything, to abridge radically, are assumed to reside within this world; if he follows Piaget, they are assumed to reside beyond it. It is also necessary to know what exactly, in Oerter's view, develops and in what respect. Is it individual subjects or the people together with their cultural environment? When individual subjects are seen as primarily given, is their being of a biotic or a cultural character? Can it be gained and lost? When humans act goal-directedly, is their development a realization of their plans? Is culture as the product of their action the realization of their plans? Of whose plans? When goals are attained, why does development not stop? What is the relation between the evolutions on the biotic, the individual, and the cultural level?

[II] *Dualism.* Oerter's notion of transaction evidently is of a dualist character. For example, Oerter includes traditional Cartesian thought, according to which subjects and objects are of essentially different nature [1, 2, 9, 12, 14], but he also postulates them to be isomorphic [11]. In addition, this dualism has counterparts in every one of the four bidirectional transaction types [3, 4; 6, 7]. Action or cause and effect [2, 5] generally are conceptions of the dyadic form "B follows from A." The ideal of modern sciences is to explain everything on such a basis, and it has accepted chance as one kind of it. Yet evolution cannot be accounted for this way. Dyadic systems based on oppositions generally are candidates for either overstatic fixation (as in dichotomic concepts and contradictory oppositions) or vulnerable instability (insofar as the dividing line or middle field in contrary oppositions is usually uncertain or relative). As a consequence, Oerter has to take care of balancing the system [10, 11]. Indeed, one might say that this whole transactional system between subject and object is but an attempt to unite or integrate [2, 5, 10, 13, 14] what had been separated in the first place [1, 12]. It is my contention that a reasonable understanding of the human condition is never gained as long as the essentials of human nature are presupposed rather than investigated. Although the claim that human nature essentially differs from the rest of nature is common in the history of ideas in the Western cultures, it is hard to reconcile with the known course and openness of bioevolution.

[III] *Primacy of System Elements.* Speaking of ecosystems constituted by subjects and their environments [1] seems to imply that subjects and environments precede their ecosystems at least in a logical sense, although it is obvious that organism-environment ecosystems of various kinds have a phylogenetic history and are a precondition for the emergence of the human-culture systems under discussion. In addition, on the ontogenetic level, sociocultural ecosystems must be present for persons and cultural objects to transact. The question arises whether the idea of an ecosystem should be considered a synthetic or an analytic concept, that is, whether ecosystems are composed of separate and preexisting entities (of an essentially different nature) or whether they are parts and qualities of one emerging whole. Whereas Oerter appears to favor the former, I argue for the latter and thus for the primacy of the organization constituting its parts [III']. In this view culture is neither a thing created by a priori given persons nor in any way an a priori itself, but rather an aspect of a system wherein both persons and their cultural environment reciprocally create each other when communities of symbolizing animals live together on the basis of collective environmental memory in addition to their instinctual and individual memory functions.

3 Is Oerter's transactionalism going beyond?

It appears essential, then, to have concepts for this process of mutual generation of entities in the course of history on several levels. Presupposed entities interact in influencing each other; in order to constitute each other, entities must have effects beyond the immediately given. In other words, they must change each other in such a way that they change the developing conditions of all entities involved. The effects of their acts must go beyond. It is the basic function of memory in the broadest sense of being capable to have effects at a later time. Whether memory within organisms takes the form of phylogenetic stream or ontogenetic organization or, among people, the form of culture is of secondary importance. The prefix "trans" is perhaps a suitable term to indicate the genetic connectedness of everything as part of one evolutive stream.

Let me begin my specific comments by commending Oerter for this carefully elaborated design of a system of ideas. Nevertheless, I find Oerter's transactionalism wanting because it does not do justice to both the bonds and freedoms of the evolving human condition. His article also suffers from not explicating something that might seem self-evident to the author but that the reader absolutely needs in order to make transactionalism fruitful: the pertinence of transaction for constituting development. On the other hand, Oerter relies without reflection, in my opinion, on something that appears natural to nearly everybody and yet that needs to be critically thought through: Do humans really have an absolutely special place in the whole of the world?

In its overall disposition, Oerter's transactionalism reminds one of Ernst E. Boesch's cultural psychology, which is also rooted in action theory (e.g., Boesch 1980, 1991). Boesch has not ordinarily used the term "transaction," yet what he has dealt with in terms of "subjectivation of the objective" and "objectivation of the subjective" in the double sense of changes in both the subject and the environment could have been a model to Oerter's internalizing and reifying processes in the double perspective of objectivation and subjectivation. On the other hand, Boesch's Symbolic Action Theory is a comprehensive approach to humans in culture. Boesch (1980) also has extended a Piagetian perspective by introducing a more bi-directional person-environment relation. Culture, however, has been understood by Boesch essentially as the Subject-Object relation itself, whereas in Oerter's transactionalism transaction and culture appear as added features or levels [14] rather than as an intrinsic constituent of the human condition. Oerter thus rightly sees in culture a human achievement, but he disregards its constituting character as creating humans out of members of the biotic species *homo sapiens*. Once in culture, human beings cannot live otherwise than culturally.

The fact that autonomous subjects act is seen to be basic by both authors. Boesch conceives of an intimate connection between persons, things, and symbols, whereas Oerter proceeds by adding social interaction with other humans as a first enhancement [13], transaction with objects as a second [5, 8, 14]. Transaction thus appears as instrumental in serving the self-realization of humans [12; Boesch 1991]. Whereas Boesch's understanding seems at times both to gain and suffer from fluid boundaries between subject and object, while there remains no doubt about their fundamental difference, Oerter evidently has them separate in principle and thus in need of coordination [10, 11]. As a consequence, both Boesch and Oerter fail to explicitly give a central place and role to open evolution of the human-environment system as a whole on either the individual or cultural level. Oerter, although aware of shortcomings of modern psychology, hesitates to adopt a perspective that takes human culturality and historicity as seriously as the traditional physical, biological, and logical foundations of this science. One needs to understand what Oerter means by "cause-and-effect transfer between individual and environment" [5].

In "my" fourteen essentials of Oerter's transactionalism, I can discern structural [1, 11, 13, 14], process-oriented [2 to 9], and regulative [10 to 12] statements. So a potential for explaining evolutive history is present, even though the regulative aspects are weak and one-sided. From the beginning, the ecosystems are introduced by Oerter as too asymmetric in nature, and their parts have characters defined by fixed polarity rather than by their mutual becoming. He sets the stage in a Cartesian backdrop by supposing subjects to be the only active agents, and objects to be passive with respect to subjects. Yet he also supposes objects to behave according to laws of their own. Thus, the question remains how objects can at the same time follow their own laws and be subject to the influence of actions of independent subjects. As a consequence of Oerter's view, objects should have to follow double lawfulness, a circumstance that takes them out of the material realm; and subjects should have to be endowed with magic or similar capabilities for manipulating objects, including their own bodies. If human individuals are supposed to be specifically endowed – they alone are said to act, they alone are declared object-related and goal-oriented, and it is even asserted that they eventually dominate their environment while also adapting to its constraints – it must be explained how such dispositions can fit into a lawful material world. Oerter seems to imply that human subjects can at the same time behave according to and go beyond the physical world and its laws. Nothing is said as to how they have gotten to be so different from the rest of the world.

I do not have enough space here to analyze Oerter's several allusions and claims to going beyond the given. It remained unclear to me in what respect and to what degree his understanding of transaction approaches an evolutive character. He remains strangely bound to the Cartesian presuppositions so dear to most modern psychologists and in large parts of social science. However, intensive discussions among hesitating and radical transactionalists, perhaps, will further the common cause best.

I think it to some extent helpful to investigate Oerter's presumable rationale for a fixed asymmetry and his hesitation of questioning it. Do any of those essentials also pertain to animals, especially large-brained animals? I do not ask this question for the sake of preserving or denying any distinction between animal and humans but simply in order to find out about the generality of the stated principles, for Oerter's action concept is claimed to be specifically human [2]. Animals in general are certainly environment-related, and they pursue goals such as finding and selecting food and mates and searching or avoiding various circumstances of living, even anticipating certain regularities of their future. Claiming a specifically human action type thus requires specification. Oerter, like many action theorists, points to some qualitative evolutionary leap without really giving proof. I do not deny a difference between instinct-based and planned action, yet both kinds of action are object- or situation-related and purposive in the sense that they can serve functional ends. Indeed, the probability of an instinct attaining its goal is normally much higher than that of planned action; failing instincts are a problem only under changed circum-stances.

By introducing an objective cultural realm [3, 11, 13, 14] in addition to the sub-jective mental [4, 6, 9, 11, 14] and material ones [1, 3, 4, 7, 14], Oerter appears to mirror Popper's worlds 3, 2, and 1, respectively. He also seems to presume that individuals are basically single, atomized entities that happen to live multiple, but separate, existences in one material world (Popper's world 1) and, hence, have to find ways to overcome the separateness of their individual inner worlds. For living together would necessitate explicitly learning to understand the consciousnesses or inner worlds of the others (Popper's world 2). One could imagine that task of learning as dealing with that common world in the common terms of a social system. So people subsequently might have invented and constructed the world of culture (Popper's world 3), the human-made environment, both the materially incorporated and the ideational mental world of "knowledge without a knowing subject" (Popper). This notion is in line with Oerter's view of the human ecosystem's being an achievement of transactions among subjects, that is, of their object-related and goal-directed actions in a common social system. Another question is the status and the relation of this world vis à vis the rest of the universe and the role that world transactionally plays on the subject or object side or beyond.

As plausible as this view may appear, it implies that the sociality of human cul-tural beings is in essence different from the sociality of animals and thus makes humans doubly separate: as a species from other species and as individuals from other individuals. As much as this separation of human individuals from the rest of the world is one crucial and consequential assumption of the enlightenment tradition and the modern world view, it has proven essentially wrong, not only against the background of the facts of bioevolution but also in view of the essentially social nature of higher animal life. Are humans not part of that nature and emergent from it? What does the phylogenetic step to humans add and how does cultural evolution arise out of all previous emergence? Is the individual subjective world genetically prior, simultaneous, or posterior to the objective mental or cultural world? Without saying it, Oerter seems to claim priority for the subjective mental world. Culture comes about, he says, because human individuals are capable of acting, because they are object-related and goal-directed.

I counter this stance with the claim that animals without language, but with a large forebrain and skillful hands to rely upon in their interactions with their environment, are apt to go beyond and change that environment, as with stone axes and other tools as well as with huts and clothes made from animal skins. Sooner or later their gestures and utterances go beyond their inborn coordination with their internal states and important locations and peculiarities of their environment and then really start to explode in scope and usefulness when coordinated with the cultural objects created in a community. In addition to the symbolic character of the things among the people living together, oral language serves an amplifying function in their use and their creative development. Language thus largely increases both the coherence and diversity of the intercourse that those people engage in. Culture, or the changed and enriched environment in the function of a common memory, is neither a precondition of human acting nor its simple offshoot but the very process of transaction changing transactants, and it cannot escape being object-related.

A reinterpretation of one of Oerter's examples might illustrate my contention that the majority of cultural and personal innovations are mostly by-products rather than, and at best, attainments of goal-directed actions of individuals. Take children in the urban environment endangered by traffic. Would they and their parents object to crossing streets and do more than verbally protest the inhumane living conditions in the cities? Not usually beyond the point at which such protest would inflict problems upon themselves. As a rule, children and their parents in hazardous urban environments adjust in favor of whatever advantage they expect from their living conditons. Would the parents go for the goal of protecting their children, the kind of reasonable regulative reaction one might expect? That response is precisely what would render their children incapable of moving independently. Some parents do indeed act in this way, but the majority do not accept being incapacitated by the human-generated environment. When children are repeatedly hurt or killed at a certain crossing, local authorities will eventually act to change that peculiar part of the environment if they do not prefer to institute traffic education programs to train the children. Probably little of observable human history is the direct result of planned action by human agents as goal-achieving subjects, yet the change of the world brought about by human activity is enormous, and so is the ensuing change in the people of the industrialized regions of the planet.

Note

1 In addition to the references cited by Oerter, the interested reader might consult the following sources giving the term "transaction" a salient role: Adalbert Ames (see Heider, 1983; Kilpatrick, 1961); Altman (1990); Altman, Brown, Staples, and Werner (1992); Altman and Rogoff (1987); Berne (1961); Dewey and Bentley (1949/1975); Proshansky (1976); Stokols and Shumaker (1981); Wapner (1990; see also Wapner's chapter in this volume). While these authors present quite various notions of transaction, the most intriguing and fertile among them, in my opinion, is still that of John Dewey (see also Deledalle, 1966). Psychologists would do well to study one of their best informed early critics who had started his career as a professor of psychology and then gone beyond.

References

Altman, I. (1990). Toward a transactional perspective: A personal journey. In I. Altman & K. Christensen (Eds.), *Environment and behavior studies – emergence of intellectual traditions*. New York: Plenum.

Altman, I., Brown, B. B., Staples, B., & Werner, C. M. (1992). A transactional approach to close relationships: Courtship, weddings, and placemaking. In W. B. Walsh, K. H. Craik, & R. H. Price (Eds.), *Person environment psychology: Models and perspectives* (pp. 193-241). Hillsdale, NJ: Erlbaum.

Altman, I., & Rogoff, B. (1987). World views in psychology – Trait, interactional, organismic, and transactional perspectives. In D. Stokols & I. Altman (Eds.), *Handbook of environmental psychology* (pp. 7-40). New York: Wiley.

Berne, E. (1961). *Transactional analysis in psychotherapy – A systematic individual and social psychiatry.* New York: Grove.

Boesch, E. E. (1980). *Kultur und Handlung: Einführung in die Kulturpsychologie.* [Culture and action: Introduction to cultural psychology]. Bern: Huber.

Boesch, E. E. (1991). *Symbolic action theory and cultural psychology: Recent research in psychology.* Berlin: Springer.

Deledalle, G. (1966). *L'idée d'expérience dans la philosophie de John Dewey* [The idea of experience in the philosophy of John Dewey]. (Thèse de Doctorat) Paris: Presses Universitaires de France (PUF).

Dewey, J., & Bentley, A. F. (1949). *Knowing and the known.* Boston: Beacon Press. (Reprinted 1975, Westport, CT: Greenwood)

Heider, F. (1983). *The life of a psychologist.* Lawrence, KS: University of Kansas Press.

Kilpatrick, F. P. (1961) *Explorations in transactional psychology.* New York: Holt.

Lang, A. (1988). Die kopernikanische Wende steht in der Psychologie noch aus! – Hinweise auf eine ökologische Entwicklungspsychologie [Still waiting for the Copernican turn in psychology! Ideas towards an ecological developmental psychology]. *Schweizerische Zeitschrift für Psychologie, 47,* 93-108.

Lang, A. (1992). Kultur als 'externe Seele' – eine semiotisch-ökologische Perspektive [Culture as "external soul" – A semiotic-ecological perspective]. In C. Allesch, E. Billmann-Mahecha & A. Lang (Eds.), *Psychologische Aspekte des kulturellen Wandels* (pp. 9-30). Vienna: Verlag des Verbandes der wissenschaftlichen Gesellschaften Österreichs.

Lang, A. (1993). Non-Cartesian artefacts in dwelling activities – Steps towards a semiotic ecology. *Schweizerische Zeitschrift für Psychologie, 52,* 138-147. (Reprinted in: Quarterly Newsletter of the Laboratory of Comparative Human Development (UCSD 15(3), 1993, 87-96.)

Proshansky, H. M. (1976). Environmental psychology and the real world. *American Psychologist, 3,* 303-310.

Stokols, D., & Shumaker, S. A. (1981). People in places: A transactional view of settings. In J. H. Harvey (Ed.), *Cognition, social behavior, and the environment* (pp. 441-488). Hillsdale, NJ: Erlbaum.

Wapner, S. (1990). One-person-in-his-environment. In I. Altman & K. Christensen (Eds.), *Environment and behavior studies – Emergence of intellectual traditions* (pp. 257-290). New York: Plenum.

Author's response: Is Lang going beyond?

Rolf Oerter

While Lang's commentary is a thoughtful analysis of my approach, it contains serious misinterpretations that should be corrected. I start with Lang's vision of the individual in culture as 'a system wherein persons and their cultural environment create each other'. Lang contrasts the definition with my conceptual distinction between subject and object. Actually, there is no contradiction between the two notions but rather a distinction in the analysis. Psychology is an empirical science and needs approaches that allow for empirical testing. A vague notion of 'system' needs further elaboration in order to test empirically what it means. One such possibility that I proposed was the subject-object relation. Objects in a person's culture can be described and analyzed, and the individual's action toward the object can be observed.

The second point concerns the 'dualism' between subject and object. Lang did not follow the main idea of my approach, namely, that 'action', not 'subject' and 'object' is the theoretical starting point. As Goethe's Faust says: 'Am Anfang war die Tat' ('In the beginning was the action'). I propose to start with the explanatory concept of action in order to avoid the very dualism that Lang attributes to my approach. If one follows this idea, the action produces the subject and the object through its characteristic mutual directions. It creates the subject through both internalization and reification. Conversely, the object is created and maintained through reification but also through its utilization by the subject. This change in thinking does not seem easy, but it is necessary in order to dispense with naive realism, which is also shared by Lang. That is, Lang's ecosystem is based on a sophisticated, but still 'naive', realism in which the dualism is not overcome.

That kind of realism might be also the reason why Lang does not see that my approach is developmental in its basic nature. Because action is a dynamic concept, it explains creation and development of culture as well as creation and development of the individual. Through action, culture and the individual are connected with each other. Development is explained fundamentally as enculturation, cultural maintenance, and change at the same time. Thus, many points made by Lang are in accordance with my approach.

To mention only two of them, I briefly note the problem of memory and the distinction between animals and human beings. In my approach cultural memory is located in the object. This viewpoint seems to me an elegant solution to the question of what memory means. The object contains the idea of the producer (constructor) as well as its possibilities of action. But this kind of cultural memory is partially or completely lost if there is no actor available who is able to use those possibilities of action. Many prehistorical objects are certainly misinterpreted because it is no longer known what they were used for. Again, the mutual definition of object and subject is necessary in order to explain memory.

The second point, the distinction between animals and human beings, is more marginal. Starting with a biological distinction, one can claim that human beings are animals who are genetically able to produce culture. In terms of my approach this statement means that human beings share a special kind of action that is not only goal-directed, as with higher animals, but also object-related, a feature specific to human beings. In this respect my approach seems clear, and it is not necessary to struggle with the animal-human distinction as Lang does.

On the whole, Lang is not going beyond my approach; he points to the frame in which this approach is embedded.

A holistic, developmental, systems-oriented perspective: Child-environment relations

Seymour Wapner

The present approach to the more general study of the transactions of persons-in-environments is an outgrowth of Heinz Werner's (1940) seminal work on a comparative and organismic analysis of mental development and of the variety of theoretical and empirical advances made by Werner and his colleagues over the years (e.g., Kaplan, 1983; Wapner, 1987; Wapner, Cirillo, & Baker, 1969, 1971; Wapner & Kaplan, 1983; Wapner & Werner, 1957, 1965; Werner, 1940, 1957; Werner & Kaplan, 1956, 1963; Werner & Wapner, 1952). Because of its formal, organizational nature, its broad conception of development, and its systems orientation, the present elaboration (e.g., Wapner, 1981, 1987; Wapner & Demick, 1990, 1991) has applicability to a wide variety of content areas and subfields of psychology as well as a number of aspects of transactions of persons-in-environments. In this chapter, the perspective is described by characterizing its assumptions and illustrating them with examples of research, methodology, and issues related to child development and linked to the theme of child-centered urban planning.

1   The holistic, developmental systems-oriented perspective

The approach is synoptically characterized in Figure 1. This complex figure depicts the Transactions (Experience and Action) of the Organism (Person [P], Agent [A], and Respondent [R]) with the Environment (World [W], Habitat [H], and Ambience [A]) in terms of the organism's Instrumentalities (Conceptual systems [C], Tools [T], and Inherited body parts [I]), and Ends (long-term values [L], episodic motives [E], humoral states [H]). It also includes a listing of analytic categories of Experience (its cognitive [sensorimotor action, perception, conception, and so on], affective, and valuative features), Planning, and Action. The figure depicts progressive (and regressive) development in terms of the orthogenetic principle, that is, progressive change from de-differentiation to differentiation and hierarchic integration or vice versa (regressive change) as applied to group differences, temporal changes, and conditions of functioning. There follows an elaboration of these features of the perspective and its underlying assumptions.

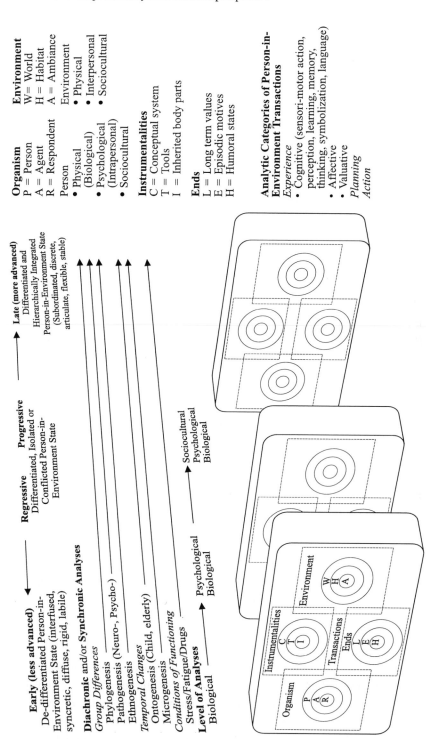

Figure 1: *A holistic, developmental, systems approach to person-in-environment functioning (adapted from "An organismic-developmental systems approach to the analysis of experience and action," by S. Wapner, paper presented at the conference on Holistic Approaches to the Analysis of Experience and Action, University of Catania, Sicily, Italy, November 1986)*

1.1   Theoretical assumptions

1.1.1   Transactionalism/Unit of analysis

In contrast to other perspectives where the organism or person is the unit of analysis, basic to this approach is the transactionalist assumption that the *organism-in-environment system* or more specifically, as restricted in this article, the *person-in-environment system* is the unit to be analyzed (cf. Altman & Rogoff, 1987; Dewey & Bentley, 1949). As already implied, organism-in-environment is further differentiated in terms of levels of integration (Wapner, Kaplan, & Cohen, 1973). As shown in Figure 1, at the least complex level, the organism-in-environment is a *respondent-in-ambience* (e.g., fixed reflexes-like responses of the whole organism [moth] to ambient stimulation [directional light]). At the next level, there is the *agent-in-habitat* (e.g., a chimpanzee solving a problem). At the most complex level, one finds the *person-in-world* (acculturated human being transacting in an environment that includes sociocultural objects, rules, regulations, and so on) (see Wapner & Demick, 1990). Here, the unit to be analyzed will be restricted to the *person-in-environment system*.

This unit of analysis is somewhat complex insofar as it includes various mutually defining aspects of the person and of the environment. The person features include: (a) physical/biological aspects (e.g., physical change, growth, health, and the onset of puberty); (b) his/her psychological state (e.g., body percept, body concept, self concept, self reliance, and intelligence); and (c) sociocultural aspects (e.g., role as infant, child, and young adult). The environmental features, include: (a) its physical aspects (e.g., dwelling, playground, street, neighborhood, city, country, and school); (b) its interpersonal aspects (e.g., relations with family, including parents, siblings, relatives and with peers in the neighborhood, playground, street, and classroom); and (c) its sociocultural aspects (e.g., school rules, governmental restrictions on use of streets, regulations, mores, and laws). The ultimate goal would be to conceptualize the person, the environment, and the relations between them in their total complexity.

Now, it is important to note that transactions with the environment include action and experience. Experience in turn is comprised of affective, valuative, and cognitive functions. Cognitive functions include sensorimotor action, perception, conception, symbolization, language, memory, and so forth.

1.1.2   Structural and dynamic analysis

The transactions of the person with the environment are teleologically directed, that is, the person transacts with the environment in terms of long-term goals or ends that are achieved by a variety of instrumentalities or means. Transactions are analyzed structurally (i.e., in terms of part-whole relations, how the parts are organized to produce the whole); and dynamically (i.e., with respect to means-ends relations, the instrumentalities by which a goal is accomplished). A structural analysis can be exemplified by the analysis of developmental changes in sketch map representations made over a 6-month period after entry into a small, university environment (Schouela, Steinberg, Leveton, & Wapner, 1980). The descriptive structural analysis assessing microgenetic changes over time used a number of indices including differentiation of the environment into parts, congruence of the representation of the parts with the actual physical arrangement of those parts, and the manner in which the parts were integrated into the total representation.

The same situation can also be used to exemplify a dynamic, means-ends analysis of *how* the sketch map representation is produced. To assess this process, subjects were questioned on how they went about producing their sketch maps. It was found that they fell into such patterns as: (a) projecting themselves in imagination into the environment at the location of their anchor point (base of operations or locale that serves as the basis for the cognitive organization of the new environment) and then sequentially adding parts as they are encountered on an imagined route; (b) entering parts of the environment closest to the anchor point first, then elaborating parts of more distant regions; and (c) independently treating juxtaposed environmental subregions.

Moreover, though this example is restricted to cognition, analogous modes of analysis are employed to assess affective and valuative aspects of experience as well as action. For example, subjects may be asked to describe their feelings about the place being represented and how important that place is to them or how much they value it. The descriptions given to such open-ended questions are analyzed by phenomenological methods (see Watkins, 1977).

Such a phenomenological method has been used in a study on retirement (Hornstein & Wapner, 1985) and a study on use of automobile safety belts (Rioux & Wapner, 1986). In these studies an open-ended question (e.g., What is retirement like? What are your thoughts about wearing an automobile safety belt?) is presented in an interview that is tape recorded. The interview is transcribed in written form. After becoming familiar with the transcript through multiple readings, the researcher breaks it down into "natural meaning units" representing single aspects of the subject's experience. Next, the "central theme" dominating each unit is identified and given a psychological interpretation. Then the themes are tied together in the form of a narrative description that characterizes the qualitative pattern of experience of the individual. The separate narrative descriptions may then be compared for similarities and differences and used in constructing a final description of the defining properties of the experience of the phenomenon under investigation.

Descriptions of feelings and of valuations may touch on aesthetic experience. Relevant to the discussions in this volume are studies on children's aesthetic experience of the environment (see Engel & Franklin, 1991). For example, Olwig (1991) and Hansen-Møller and Taylor (1991), show how active exploration of a park followed by writing poems, mimicking sounds of nature, and so forth, transforms the park for children from a wasteland subject to vandalism to a part of nature with which they can interact, play, enjoy and value. The shifts in attitude through the activities of mimicking sound, writing a poem, and representing a scene artistically are presumed to be linked to (a) changes from a passive relation of rootedness, to a sense of place that "implies a certain distance between self and place that allows the self to appreciate a place" (Olwig, 1991, p. 4); and (b) the development of self-esteem (see Engel, 1991). Thus, in keeping with the principle of functional equiva-lence (Werner & Wapner, 1952), alternative means can be used to accomplish the same end. That is, a change in the perception of an area can be brought about by writing poetry about a place as well as by bulldozing tenements (see Olwig, 1991).

1.1.3 Constructivism

The approach is constructivistic insofar as human beings are assumed to structure their environments actively. That is, the individual is *not* a passive recipient of incoming stimuli. Instead, the individual shapes or structures the environment rather selectively, depending on his or her state (Lavine, 1950a, 1950b). An example is a study, to be described more fully below, by Dandonoli, Demick, and Wapner (1990), which required 5-7, 8-10, 11-13 year-old children and adults to view a furnished university common room and then reconstruct it using a miniature model. Though exposed to the same physical environment, adults structured it in terms of socially relevant, meaningful wholes while the young children structured that physical environment by grouping similar parts together, that is, a piling together of similar items as in a stock room. This points to the role of the cognitive status of the individual in organizing, representing, and experiencing the physical environment to which the individual is exposed.

1.1.4 Multiple intentionality

Active structuring of the environment is linked to *multiple intentionality;* that is, the person transacting with the environment has the capacity to focus on or to direct him/herself to constructing different objects of experience, such as the self (e.g., I am proud of how I handled that situation), the environment (e.g., Herten is a very beautiful city), and self-environment relations (e.g., I feel very comfortable in Herten). As Schütz (1971, Vol. I) characterized the product of active structuring "the intentional object of my preserved perception is 'the chair *as I have perceived it*,' the *phenomenon* chair *as it appears to me*, which may or may not have an equivalent in the bracketed outer world" (p. 106). Moreover, Schütz (1971) assumed that human beings live in different, yet related, experiential worlds, or spheres of activity, such as the multiple worlds of family, work, school, recreation, community, and so forth. Relevant here is Werner's (1940) notion of "spheres of reality" and Muchow's characterization of the child's world in parallel terms (see Muchow & Muchow, 1935; Wapner, 1985).

1.1.5 Spatiotemporal nature of experience

Multiple worlds and spheres of reality are abstracted from everyday life, which is characterized by the ongoing flow of events. Over the course of an ordinary day, the ordinary person is constantly carrying out various activities while moving from one place to another, namely, bedroom, kitchen, school, and city streets and is in contact with different people at different places, and so forth. Though this ongoing flow of events is continuous, it is usually experientially structured into a succession of discrete units – for example, being at school, playing with friends – that are separated from preceding and subsequent units by temporal boundaries (Wapner & Lebensfeld-Schwartz, 1976). The abstraction from continuous spatiotemporal change may be *temporally* bounded units independent of spatial objects (e.g., an event described with respect to its duration independent of changes in people and/or objects) as well as *spatially* bounded units independent of temporality (e.g., a park that represents a spatial figure abstracted from the flow of everyday spatiotemporal events).

1.1.6 Directedness and planning

The person-in-environment system is assumed to exhibit *directedness* toward goals. That is, transactions are not simply random and chaotic but are directed toward some goal; the person-in-environment system exhibits directed change from some initial state of functioning to some end state. Such directedness is linked to the capacity to plan. Planning, the verbalized plotting of a future course of action, is viewed as one of a number of means by which the person-in-environment systems move from some initial state of functioning to some new end state; such movement involves transactions of the person with the environment (Wapner & Cirillo, 1973). For example, relative to college students without plans for the future, those with highly articulated plans for the future experience *greater* "self-world distance" (e.g., the current environment is represented in a distanced aerial view in map-like objective terms) from the university environment in which they are located. Moreover, with a change from plans to no plans there is a shift back to *lesser* self-world distancing (e.g., the current university environment is represented three-dimensionally and with links to others in that environment) from that environment (Wofsey, Rierdan, & Wapner, 1979).

1.1.7 Holism

In contrast to interactional approaches that focus on partitive analyses the perspective presented in this chapter is characterized by a *holistic* assumption that implies that the person-in-environment system operates as an integrated whole and that a perturbation to any part of the system has an impact on the whole. The focus is on relations between parts of the total system. In the context of child development, the approach suggests that an appropriate unit is the relation between the child and another person (parent or some other peer), and the relation between the child and some object.

Here, consideration is given to the approach of Vygotsky (1978) and more recent followers who have advanced his ideas with respect to the notion of the "zone of proximal development" (ZPD), that is, divergence between the existent level of development of the child and the level reached in collaboration with another (Rogoff & Wertsch, 1984). Valsiner (1984, 1985, 1987, 1988a, 1988b) and others have elaborated the concepts of the "zone of free movement" (ZFM) and the "zone of promoted action" (ZPA); these concern the limits that the parent places on the child, thereby affecting the development of the child (see Gärling & Valsiner, 1985, on accident prevention). In this conceptualization, which is linked to what is called the co-constructionist approach (Lightfoot, 1988; Valsiner, 1984, 1985, 1988a, 1988b; Wozniak, 1986), it is assumed that understanding is a function of the joint action of interacting individuals. The conceptualization is consonant with the holistic assumption of the theoretical approach presented in this chapter. However, the holistic assumption implies that an analysis restricted to the interpersonal relationship between two interacting people is limited. In keeping with the holistic principle, it is necessary to give consideration to the interrelations among all levels of person (physical/biological, psychological, sociocultural) and environment (physical, interpersonal, sociocultural) functioning and thereby come closer to the everyday life situation.

Another aspect of the holistic assumption is the *pars pro toto* principle, by which it is assumed that the part stands for the whole, that each part belongs to the whole and has a reciprocal effect on the totality. Studies conducted in Worcester, Massachusetts, required one group of students living in two colleges in high socioeconomic neighborhoods and another group living in two other colleges located in low socioeconomic neighborhoods to draw a pictorial representation and write a verbal description of the city as a whole. Relative to students residing in colleges in low socioeconomic neighborhoods (one part of the city), those residing in high socioeconomic neighborhoods (another part of the city) affected their experience of the city as a whole, that is, they were more positive of, and knew more about the city as a whole (Demick, Hoffman, & Wapner, 1985).

1.1.8 Development: Orthogenetic principle

A central feature of the perspective is its developmental assumption, which stands in contrast to those perspectives that are restricted to child and life-span development. Components of the person-in-environment system as well as part processes are assumed to be developmentally orderable in terms of the *orthogenetic principle*. This principle, which characterizes development with respect to an ideal, or telos (Werner & Kaplan, 1956), states that development involves a shift from a de-differentiated toward a differentiated and hierarchically integrated person-in-environment system state. The developmental ideal is characterized by control over self-world relations; subordinated rather than interfused functions; discrete rather than syncretic mental phenomena; articulate rather than diffuse structures; stable rather than labile, and flexible rather than rigid, modes of coping. Such an advanced state of organization is assumed to involve greater salience of positive affective states; diminution of isolation, anonymity, helplessness, and depersonalization; coordination of long-term and short-term planning and goals; and movement toward a unity of overt and covert actions (Wapner, 1987). This postulated ideal is of marked significance for viewing the issues of concern here. It represents an optimal person-in-environment system state towards which child-centered efforts on urban planning might be directed.

A significant feature of the perspective, because of its focus on formal, organizational modes of analysis, is the breadth and applicability of the orthogenetic principle. Developmental ordering, from less advanced de-differentiated person-in-environment system states to more advanced differentiated and hierarchically integrated states includes changes from: early to later stages of a percept, thought or a concept (*microgenesis*); the individual's status at birth to adulthood (*ontogenesis*); the status of the aged compared with the middle aged adult; the status of persons suffering from neuro- or psychopathology (*pathogenesis*) compared with those functioning normally; and individuals operating under drugs or fatigue as compared with those under optimal conditions of functioning.

1.1.8.1 Microgenesis and Ontogenesis

Very important for the issues discussed in this volume are the developmental progressions of microgenesis and ontogenesis. An example of a part-whole analysis involving both microgenesis and ontogenesis is evident in a pilot study on four American children (ages 4½, 6½, 9, and 10 years) who accompanied their parents to an unfamiliar environment and drew sketch maps immediately after entering the new environment and after 2 months and 6 months of residence. Microgenetic changes were evident in the sketch maps of all four children. In the initial map of the 4½-year old, global undifferentiated blobs are used to represent some objects like cows. There was no evidence of the coordination of spatial regions and transactions within the scene were not depicted. In the intermediate map, the form of the objects constituting the scene was more articulated with a few connecting links between regions. In the sketch map drawn after six months of residence, there was much greater articulation and integration of objects constituting the scene. Similar microgenetic changes took place for the 6½-year old, who started at a more advanced level than the 4½-year old and then progressively articulated, differentiated, and integrated the scene well beyond the level reached by the younger child. The same was true for the 9-10 year-old children as compared with the 6½-year old. Thus, both microgenetically (separately for each of the four children) and ontogenetically (comparing differences between children differing in age), sketch-map representations of an environment show progressive differentiation of a scene into distinct objects with their spatial interrelations more integrated (Wapner, Kaplan, & Ciottone, 1981).

Three other studies are of interest. The first (Dandonoli, Demick, & Wapner, 1990), briefly mentioned earlier, was concerned with the physical aspect of the environment. The authors assessed age differences (5-7, 8-10, 11-13 years and adults) in representations of the same room biased in two ways: (a) furniture placed in a "part-quality" manner (similar objects placed near each other) and (b) furniture placed in an "integrated" manner (parts arranged into socially relevant groupings, e.g., chairs and sofas in a rectangle facing each other). Through verbal recall, drawings, classification, and memory reconstruction, it was found that: (a) adults' representations were characterized by an integration of parts into a socially relevant, meaningful whole (e.g., on verbal recall they characteristically stated "there is a lounge area that includes coffee tables, chairs, and sofas"), while children produced representations consisting of groupings of isolated, fragmented parts (e.g., "There are tables, there are chairs, there are photographs"); (b) even when exposed to a part-quality room, adults represented the room in terms of socially relevant, meaningful wholes.

The second study, restricted to microgenetic change over time, dealt with interpersonal as well as physical aspects of the environment. To examine individual's affective involvement with people in their interpersonal environment, a *Psychological Distance Map (PDM)* was employed (see Wapner, 1977). The procedure involved the use of a piece of paper whose center bore a small circle labeled "me." The subject, told that "me" stands for him/her, was asked to add other circles, each one standing for "*someone important in his/her life*," so that "those people who are close to you are placed closer to the circle that stands for you." After drawing each circle, note was made of the person it represented and the sequence of entry (Wapner, 1977; see Minami, 1985, for further development of the method). There are many interesting uses for this technique. The relevant study dealt with microgenetic changes in social networks of students over the course of their stay in the university (Wapner, 1978; Minami, 1985; Thom, 1991). With respect to microgenetic change it was found that with time, the interpersonal networks of first-year college students become increasingly dominated by college friends and that there is a shift of sources of support from home to college networks. .

The third study was confined to age differences in relations between physical and interpersonal aspects of the environment (Wapner, Demick, & Mutch-Jones, 1988). Two PDMs were used, one for "people" and one for "places." The PDM for "places" was the same as the PDM for "people" except that subjects were requested to enter "places" rather than "people" important in their world. Subjects differed in age (5½ , 11½ , 17, and 22 years). On the PDM for people, the 5½-year olds entered fewer people, more relatives, and fewer friends than the older groups did. On the PDM for places the 5½ -year olds entered fewer places than the older groups; the 11-year olds represented the distance associated with home as closer and the distance associated with school as further than did the 5½ -year olds and the two oldest age groups.

Although it is quite clear that ontogenetic change in children's perception, judgments, needs, capacities (cognitive, affective, valuative), instrumentalities and transactions (experiences and actions) with all facets of the environment (physical, interpersonal, and sociocultural) are critical in attempts to optimize child-centered urban change, there must also be concern with microgenetic change. Having knowledge about (a) the course of microgenetic changes in person-environment relations as exposure to the newly constructed features of the urban environment increases, and (b) how those changes relate to the ontogenetic changes that are also occurring will make it possible to help judge when and what new opportunities might best be made available in the urban environment.

1.1.8.2 Progression/Regression

It should also be noted that the formal, organizational characterization of development is viewed as regressive as well as progressive. In studies of critical person-in-environment transitions – a paradigmatic problem that derives, from the transactional, holistic as well as from the developmental assumptions underlying the perspective – it is assumed that a perturbation in any part of the person-in-environment system (physical/biological, psychological, sociocultural aspect of the person; physical, interpersonal, sociocultural aspect of the environment; means; ends; transactions) has impact on all parts of the system and may make for developmental regression of the system state, which may be followed by developmental progression to a developmentally advanced state. A large variety of critical person-in-environment system transitions have been studied over the years, covering perturbations induced by change at each of the three levels of organization of the person, of the environment and the relations between them (for summaries, see Wapner, 1980, 1985, 1987). When a change is introduced in one aspect of the environment, it has impact on other parts and the relations between them.

1.1.9 Underlying process

There is interest not only in characterizing the developmental status before and after a perturbation to the system but also in understanding underlying process and/or specifying the conditions under which developmental transformation is reversed, arrested, or advanced (Wapner, 1987). This process is shown in the previously described study on the representation of a university environment by Schouela et al. (1980) where a *physical* and/or a *social* anchor point operated to facilitate knowledge of adaptation to the new university environment.

Analysis of underlying process is also exemplified in a study of transactional conflict (Apter, 1976) where undergraduates recalled specific events in the physical, interpersonal, and academic/sociocultural aspects of the university environment where actuality fell short of expectation. They were to describe the situations and the ways in which they coped with those conflicts. In keeping with the orthogenetic principle, the following means of handling conflict were found:

(a) *accommodation* (going along with or accepting status quo – this response represents a *de-differentiated* person-in-environment system state);

(b) *disengagement* (distancing oneself from the situation by laughing, becoming cynical – this response represents a *differentiated and isolated* person-in-environment system state);

(c) *nonconstructive ventilation* (exhibiting an aggressive act toward a source of conflict, without suggesting constructive ways of remedying the situation – this response represents a *differentiated and in conflict* person-in-environment system state); and

(d) *constructive assertion* (recommending planned action and different, creative alternatives for achieving a goal – this response was interpreted as a *differentiated and hierarchically integrated* person-in-environment system state).

Here one sees individual differences in modes of coping with conflict relevant to transactions with the environment, a problem of central concern, analyzed from the perspective employed here in terms of the orthogenetic principle.

1.1.10 Relations between experience and action

Lastly, another aspect of the approach is linked to the assumption that transactions include experience as well as action of persons-in-environments. It is assumed that some aspects of the relation between experience and action can be understood by identifying (a) general experiential factors that are preparatory toward action, and (b) events that precipitate, or trigger, action.

The relation between experience and action was first analyzed with respect to the use of automobile safety belts. In Massachusetts, where there was no seat belt law, phenomenologically oriented, open-ended interviews eliciting descriptions of the experience of using automobile seat belts were conducted with people self-proclaimed as nonusers, variable users, or committed users (Rioux & Wapner, 1986). Committed seat belt users are triggered by and maintain usage through a salient imagination of accident situations, through fear of personal injury, memories of accidents involving significant others, perception of potential accidents as dependent on external circumstances, and the desire to be a "responsible citizen" or a good "role model" for children. Nonusers, in contrast, distance themselves from the potential end-state of an accident and/or injury by perceiving themselves able to avoid potential accidents, by psychologically minimizing the risks involved, particularly of personal injury. Variable users are context oriented. The trigger to wearing a seat belt depends on such factors as weather, size of car, with whom they are driving, familiarity with area, and so forth.

This study was followed by cross-cultural studies in Japan, the United States, and Italy prior to and following introduction of a seat belt law. Simply put, the Japanese showed that more than 95 percent use following passage of the law; Italians showed an increase following passage of the law and marked dropping off 2½ years later (Bertini & Wapner, 1991); in Massachusetts, there was adherence to the law after its passage, and this was followed by a large number of citizens voicing concern that the mandatory seat belt law was an invasion of privacy and an infringement of human rights. When the law was put on the ballot again, it was voted out of existence (Demick et al., 1992). Thus, the efficacy of legislative change in the immediate environment must, in turn, be assessed with respect to the encompassing sociocultural context in which such legislative change occurred. It is hoped that such analyses as the use of automobile seat belts, the start of a weight loss diet, and the cessation of alcohol and cigarette consumption, for example, directed towards uncovering precipitating events or triggers underpinning change in action will throw light on the significant issue of "What we know and what we want to do in relation to what we, in fact, do."

1.2 Methods

From our perspective, method (means) should be subordinated to the problem (end) (see Maslow, 1946). This is coupled with the belief in (a) using human science methods (including qualitative, phenomenological analysis) as well as natural science methods (laboratory experiments, and so forth), depending on the nature of the research problem; (b) using person-in-environment system units (e.g., including the focal subject as well as members of his/her support system; (c) recognizing that the experimenter is part of the environmental context for any subject (see Wapner & Alper, 1952); (d) using both idiographic and nomothetic methods; and (e) focussing on process analysis. In this connection, it is noteworthy that Muchow, an associate of Heinz Werner at the University of Hamburg during the early 1930s, in her ground breaking work entitled *The life space of the urban child*, utilized "a variety of methods for assessing [the child's] experience, including blocking out (with crayon) well-known and less well-known areas on a map of the city, verbal report, interview, surveys, written essays, and graphic records, as well as observation of action" (Wapner, 1985, p. 210).

1.3 Summary

The world view of the approach is both organismic and transactional. It is organismic insofar as it is "the study of dynamic and holistic psychological systems in
which person and environment components exhibit complex reciprocal relationships
and influences" (Altman & Rogoff, 1987, p. 19). It is transactional, insofar as
Altman & Rogoff (1987) describe it as a "synthesis of Pepper's (1942, 1967)
contextualist and selectivist orientations and Dewey & Bentley's (1949) transactional perspective," and define it as "the study of the changing relations among
psychological and environmental aspects of holistic entities" (Altman & Rogoff,
1987, p. 24). The unit of analysis of the perspective is the person-in-environment
system state, a holistic entity where person and environment are defined with respect
to levels of integration, including their physical, psychological, and sociocultural
features. Its philosophical underpinning includes the notion of constructivism or
interpretationism (Lavine, 1950a, 1950b). Its developmental conceptualization,
viewed as a mode of analysis, is characterized by the orthogenetic principle, which
portrays development as a change from a de-differentiated state toward the ideal of a
differentiated and hierarchically integrated person-in-environment system state. The
formal, organizational features of the approach permit applicability to such developmentally ordered series as microgenesis, pathogenesis, as well as ontogenesis and
other series defined with respect to developmentally orderable conditions of
functioning. With this unit of analysis, adaptation is viewed in terms of optimal
relations between person and environment achieved by change in either, or both
poles, and one is concerned with the problem of relations between experience and
action. Structural (part-whole relations) and dynamic (means-end relations) modes
of analysis are employed. Methodology varies depending on the level of organization and the nature of the problem under scrutiny. Accordingly, the approach utilizes
experimental, naturalistic observational as well as phenomenological methods. Its
orientation is both idiographic and nomothetic insofar as generalizations are drawn
from representative samples as well as from a given sample regarded as a prototype.
The goals of the perspective include achieving a qualitative understanding of
context-specific psychological events and applying the findings in a practical way in
order to move the person-in-environment system to an equilibrial state of more
optimal functioning.

2 Implications for shaping a child-centered environment

Given the main assumptions of the holistic, developmental, systems-oriented
perspective, one may briefly consider a number of issues that bear on the ways this
approach is applicable to help shape a child-centered urban environment. Before
proceeding with such issues, it is to be noted that Werner (1940) influenced and

collaborated with Muchow (see Wohlwill, 1985a) on infant research and had a deep interest in and first publicized her work on the life space of the urban child. As Wohlwill (1985b) noted,

Muchow emphasized the environment as it is perceived, cognized and experienced by the child, at all levels from sensation to action. Indeed, in the conclusion of the monograph [cf. Muchow & Muchow, 1935], where the far-reaching differences between the children's and adult's experiences of the same environment are detailed, Muchow appears to foreshadow more recent transactional perspectives on the environment-behavior relationship, such as those of Ittelson [1976] and of Wapner and his colleagues at Clark [e.g., Wapner et al., 1973]. (p. 205)

Muchow's work touches on the very issues and questions that are central to this volume.

What are the specific goals toward which urban design for children might be directed?

1. Most generally, urban design for children might be directed to providing more optimal environmental conditions (physical, interpersonal, and sociocultural) matched to the needs of the child for promoting his/her physical, mental, and social development.

2. From the perspective taken in this chapter, one goal would be to optimize the transactions (experience and action) of the child with the physical, interpersonal, and sociocultural aspects of the environment. More specifically, this goal would involve providing conditions that foster development of the ideal differentiated and hierarchically integrated person-in-environment system state, which is assumed to involve control over self-world relations; greater salience of positive affective states; diminution of isolation, anonymity, helplessness, and depersonalization; coordination of long-term and short-term goals and planning; and movement toward a unity of overt and covert actions.

3. Another goal would be to protect the child from accidents in the home and in the city.

In attempting to achieve these goals through design of urban environments, what features of the focal child must one take into account?

1. In general, several features of the perspective appear relevant. Among them are the views that (a) the child is an active, rather than passive organism who constructs a psychological, behavioral environment that is distinguished from the physical, geographic environment; (b) the child has multiple intentionality, that is, the capacity in his/her experience to make focal one's "self," an object out-there, or the relation between them; (c) the child lives in multiple worlds, or spheres of reality; and (d) the child has a variety of means or instrumentalities (conceptual systems, tools, body parts) to accomplish ends.

2. More specifically, one should consider a variety of features of the focal child that are derived from the assumption that the person-in-environment is the unit to be analyzed. With respect to the characteristics of the person, one should take into account: (a) *Physical/biological status*, such as children's needs that vary depending on health of the child, (e.g., whether he or she is afflicted with cerebral palsy or is mentally retarded) and sex and age differences; (b) *psychological status*, such as developmental status with respect to cognitive, affective, and valuative aspects of experience; and (c) *sociocultural status*, such as the role and status of children in different environmental contexts. As an extreme example, children in Japan are catered to and overprotected, put on a pedestal, and given all kinds of privileges, at least until the age of 11 years. This status is not characteristic of American society; thus, the role of the child in the two cultures must be taken into account.

This point on the implications that the characteristics of the focal child have on design of the environment has been treated systematically by Pollowy (1977). She did this by characterizing "physical growth and activity development", "personal and social development," and "intellectual and perceptual development" of three groups of children: infants (up to 24 months); preschoolers (up to 5 years); and children of middle childhood (5 to 11 years). Then she described her notion of the design implications of these aspects of child development. What is still needed is an understanding of the adolescent's development and its implications for experimental design.

Regarding physical growth and activity during infancy, for example, she noted that "children develop from helpless, fragile newborns to relatively competent and self-sufficient toddlers" (p. 8). Regarding personal and social development, "attachment behavior emerges in most children during the sixth or seventh month and increases in intensity until twenty-four months" (p. 8). During this period, Pollowy's (1977) suggestions on design implications were linked to two predominant themes, namely, attachment and sensorimotor play. One suggestion was to avoid a gate at the door of a bedroom. Such a barrier may make for anguished crying. Another was to recognize that children confined to a playpen are not going to be able to develop skills in running. Lastly, for optimal development to occur, an appropriate location is required.

According to Pollowy (1977), physical growth and activity development are significant during the preschool period. The child becomes a good walker, climbs up and down stairs, uses simple play equipment, enjoys sliding using self-propelled vehicles, makes playthings, begins to explore the near environment, and runs, climbs, uses stilts, and roller skates. "There is a need for differentiation and affirmation of the self. Attachment behavior is still strongly exhibited" (p. 15), but children accept mother's temporary absence, have a secure home base, engage largely in associative play in small groups, and, by the fifth year, spend more than half of their time with peers. Pollowy further stated that the design implications during the preschool period are focused on two major themes, namely, exploration and social play. The preschoolers need activity space close to the dwelling because they cannot yet roam freely. There is a need for socialization opportunities and for engaging in joint activities.

In the middle childhood period, Pollowy (1977) reported that physical growth permits practice of complex skills such as bicycling, roller skating, skiing, and the use of tools and realistic implements become more important. Six-year olds are involved in hide and seek, swinging, swimming, baseball, cops and robbers, playing house. By the end of the seventh year they explore the far environment of the dwelling, and by the eighth year, they are involved in simple organized games, baseball, soccer, skating, jumping, swimming, collections, roller skating. By the ninth year they explore the far environment, using public transportation (depending, of course, on the particular sociocultural context). Their personal and social development is characterized by spending more and more time away from home, play becomes more important, and they are members of informal peer groups. From the 11th year on they organize formal, structurized peer groups, develop adult distance perception, auditory acuity, better discrimination, and rapid information-handling.

According to Pollowy (1977), the design implications for the middle childhood period focus on the themes that this is a period of relative independence, socialization, and exploration. There is need for accessibility of public transportation. The presence or absence of public transportation depends, of course, on the particular sociocultural context because economic conditions, size, and other factors may play a role in the particular mode of transportation available. Children in middle childhood are capable of riding their bicycles to distant points and need the appropriate physical/spatial arrangements and interpersonal and sociocultural contexts to carry out these activities.

One further point to be noted is that Pollowy (1977) adopted Thomas, Chess, and Birch's (1970) analyses of individual differences in temperament and characterized each of the three developmental stages in terms of their nine dimensions: *activity level* (high; low); *quality of mood* (positive; negative); *approach/withdrawal* (positive; negative); *rhythmicity* (regular; irregular); *adaptability* (adaptive; nonadaptive); *threshold of responsiveness* (low; high); *intensity of reaction* (intense; mild); *distractibility* (distractible; not distractible); and *attention span and persistence* (long; short) (see Thomas & Chess, 1977). It is of significance that these individual differences should be clearly taken into account in the design of physical spaces and that such design should provide the physical, interpersonal, and sociocultural environments that permit optimal development for a broad range of individual differences.

What features of the environment must be taken into account when attempting to optimize the urban environment for children?

An array of physical environments (e.g., Michelson & Roberts, 1979; Pollowy, 1977) must be taken into account. For example, consideration should be given to the interior space in the multiple family dwelling; the immediate exterior; the school; the playground (both formal or adventure playgrounds); the street corner; the shopping center; the back alley; the garage; the roof; nearby building sites; vacant lots; projects; the neighborhood; the city sector; the city and its structure; and larger territories conducive to physical, mental, and social development. Though these physical aspects of the environment are listed separately, it is important to note, as Heidmets (1985) has indicated, that the physical features of an environment that serve as a mediator of social relationships and as a means of fostering physical, cognitive, affective, and valuative development.

This approach is consonant with Moore's (1985) concern about the relations among the physical environment, children's play behavior, and subsequent development. In considering the state of the art in play environments, he not only reviewed research relevant to this issue but also provided data on the impact that adventure playgrounds, as opposed to neighborhood play settings, have on a variety of types of play related to child development. Moreover, Moore offered some principles for planning and design, including: (a) consideration of the total environment of play rather than a focus on playgrounds; (b) provision of possibilities for "interaction of children with older siblings, adults and significant others" (p. 15); and (c) "improve the whole fabric of children's play in urban, suburban and rural environments" (p. 16). Special treatment is given to the relevance of these and other principles to "latchkey" children, that is, children who arrive home to an empty house (Moore, Chawla, & McGinty, 1986).

Indeed, Gehl (1986, 1987, 1991) has focused on "the importance of creating 'soft edges' by way of frontyards/forecourts/porches in order to provide better opportunities for staying in the public places for residents of all ages" (Gehl, 1991, p. 140). Gehl (1987) commented that "social development of children is largely based on observations of the surrounding social environment" (p. 23); that "children stay and play primarily where the most activity is occurring or in places where there is the greatest chance of something happening" (p. 27); that in contrast to a lifeless city, one "with multistory buildings, underground parking facilities, extensive automobile traffic, and long distances between buildings and functions" (p. 33), a lively city is one "with reasonably low, closely spaced buildings, accommodations for foot traffic, and good areas for outdoor stays along the streets and in direct relation to residences, public buildings, places of work, and so forth" (p. 33).

Michelson (1991) intensively studied, through surveys and observational methods, the impact that the design of Swedish housing has had on social contact among neighbors, child care, household work, and intergenerational contact, finding "that the design and organization of residential areas can play an essential role in helping behavioral objectives materialize" (p. 107).

Accordingly, consider the interpersonal aspects of the environment. Relevant to the child's physical, personal, social, intellectual, and perceptual development are the availability and characteristics of friends, peers, and family (including parents, grandparents, siblings, and cousins) and the ways in which these various people inhibit or promote the development of the focal child.

Again, consideration must be given to the sociocultural features of the environment. There must be concern for creating and maintaining the mores, rules, and regulations of government, schools, and so forth, which are conducive to the physical, mental, and social development of the child.

What relations between the focal child and the environment should be taken into account?

Given individual differences, it is important to recognize that there is no univocal environmental setting that will maximize growth and development. Rather, the potential for growth and development can occur in different environmental contexts, and growth and development should be made variable enough to encompass a large variety of individual differences in children of different ages.

In contrast to those who consider adaptation as adjustment to an unvarying, fixed environmental condition, the notion of the person-in-environment as a unit of analysis implies a different concept of adaptation. It implies movement toward an optimal relation between person and environment, movement that can come about by change in the organism, change in the environment, or change in both. Moreover, a holistic attitude should underpin features of design. For example, while it might be of value to develop and use defensible space (Newman, 1972), that is, provide space within the sight of others, one has to remember that such an arrangement may be disturbing to older people. The overall, more holistic, picture must be taken into account.

3   Conclusion

The holistic, developmental, systems-oriented perspective, its mode of formulating problems, and methods of inquiry and analysis have both theoretical and practical value for shaping environments that foster child development. The heuristic value of the approach in attacking this problem is evident, for instance, in a number of its assumptions, including the person-in-environment as the unit to be analyzed. This assumption points to a system for categorizing persons and environment that has been effective in designing environments that can foster child development. This system of categorization includes three levels of organization characterizing the *person*, namely, the physical/biological aspect (e.g., his/her age and condition of health), the intrapersonal/psychological aspect (e.g., his/her cognitive, affective, and valuative status and concerns), and the sociocultural aspect (e.g., his/her role, such as whether the child is a member of an intact or broken family). It further includes three aspects of organization characterizing the *environment*, namely, the physical environment (e.g., the population and terrain of the physical locale), the interpersonal environment (e.g., the plans and action of the immediate family, friends, and members of the community), and the broader sociocultural context (e.g., the existing and proposed regulations, mores, and economic status of the particular urban community; the goals and plans of its urban planners and political leaders for community development). Ideally, these factors of the person-in-environment system state should be considered holistically in relation to one another and in relation to the overall goal of designing environments to foster child development.

To illustrate other examples of the heuristic value of the approach, consider its developmental features. As already noted, the developmental status as well as the needs of the focal person, namely, the cognitive, affective, and valuative status of the growing child must be taken into account in the planning and in the action taken. But consideration might effectively be given also to the microgenetic development of the plan and to use of the newly constructed environment as well as to the rules and regulations associated with it. The action taken may be de-differentiated at early stages and may be differentiated and isolated and differentiated and in conflict at later stages, but the ultimate goal is one of achieving a differentiated and hierarchically integrated person-in-environment system state. This system state provides choice conditions for the developing child and is expected to be characterized by salience of positive affective and cognitive states as well as values that constitute optimal human functioning. Hopefully, the heuristic value and implications for theory and practice of the holistic, developmental, systems-oriented perspective described in this chapter can help in achieving optimal human functioning through establishment of more effective child-centered environments.

References

Altman, I., & Rogoff, B. (1987). World views in psychology: Trait, interactional, organismic and transactional perspectives. In D. Stokols & I. Altman (Eds.) *Handbook of environmental psychology* (pp. 7-40). New York: Wiley.

Apter, D. (1976). *Modes of coping with conflict in the presently inhabited environment as a function of plans to move to a new environment.* Unpublished master's thesis, Clark University, Worcester, MA.

Bertini, G., & Wapner, S. (1991). *Automobile seat belt use in Italy prior to and following legislation.* Unpublished study, Clark University, Worcester, MA.

Dandonoli, P., Demick, J., & Wapner, S. (1990). Physical arrangement and age as determinants of environmental representation. *Children's Environments Quarterly, 7*(1), 26-36.

Demick, J., Hoffman, A., & Wapner, S. (1985). Residential context and environmental change as determinants of urban experience. *Children's Environments Quarterly, 2*(3), 44-54.

Demick, J., Inoue, W., Wapner, S., Ishii, S., Minami, H., Nishiyama, S., & Yamamoto, T. (1992). Cultural differences in impact of governmental legislation: Automobile safety belt usage. *Journal of Cross-Cultural Psychology, 23*, 468-487.

Dewey, J. & Bentley, A. F. (1949). *Knowing and the known.* Boston: Beacon.

Engel, S. (1991). The world is a white blanket: Children write about nature. *Children's Environments Quarterly, 8*(2), 42-45.

Engel, S., & Franklin, M. (1991). Children's aesthetic experience of the environment. *Children's Environments Quarterly, 8*(2), 2-3.

Gärling, T., & Valsiner, J. (1985). *Children within environments: Toward a psychology of accident prevention.* New York: Plenum.

Gehl, J. (1986). "Soft edges" in residential streets. *Scandinavian Housing and Planning Research, 3*, 89-102.

Gehl, J. (1987). *Life between buildings: Using public space.* New York: Van Nostrand Reinhold.

Gehl, J. (1991). "Soft edges" in residential streets. In T. Niit, M. Raudsepp, & K. Liik (Eds.), *Environment and social development. Proceedings of the east-west colloquium in environmental psychology* (Tallinn, Estonia, May 16-19, 1991, p. 140). Tallinn, Estonia: Tallinn Pedagogical Institute.

Hansen-Møller, J., & Taylor, G. (1991). Creative nature interpretation for children. *Children's Environments Quarterly, 8*(2), 30-37.

Heidmets, M. (1985). Environment as the mediator of human relationships: Historical and ontogenetic aspects. In T. Gärling & J. Valsiner (Eds.), *Children within environments: Toward a psychology of accident prevention* (pp. 217-227). New York: Plenum.

Hornstein, G. A., & Wapner, S. (1985). Modes of experiencing and adapting to retirement. *International Journal on Aging & Human Development, 21*, 291-315.

Ittelson, W. H. (1976). Some issues facing a theory of environment and behavior. In H. Proshansky, W. H. Ittelson, & L. Rivlin (Eds). *Environmental psychology: People and their settings (2nd ed.)* (pp. 246-288). New York: Holt.

Kaplan, B. (1983). Genetic dramatism: Old wine in new bottles. In S. Wapner & B. Kaplan (Eds.), *Toward a holistic, developmental psychology* (pp. 53-74). Hillsdale, NJ: Erlbaum.

Lavine, T. (1950a). Knowledge as interpretation: An historical survey. *Philosophy and Phenomenological Research, 10*, 526-540.

Lavine, T. (1950b). Knowledge as interpretation: An historical survey. *Philosophy and Phenomenological Research, 11*, 80-103.

Lightfoot, C. (1988). The social construction of cognitive conflict: A place for affect. In J. Valsiner (Ed.), *Child development within culturally structured environments. Vol 2: Social co-construction and environmental guidance in development* (pp. 28-65). Norwood, NJ: Ablex.

Maslow, A. H. (1946). Problem-centering vs. means-centering in science. *Philosophy of Science, 13*, 326-331.

Michelson, W. (1991). Built environment as a mediator of human intentions. In T. Niit, M. Raudsepp, & K. Liik (Eds.), *Environment and social development. Proceedings of the east-west colloquium in environmental psychology* (Tallinn, Estonia, May 16-19, 1991, pp. 98-107). Tallinn, Estonia: Tallinn Pedagogical Institute.

Michelson, W. & Roberts, E (1979). Children and the urban physical environment. In W. Michelson, S. V. Levine, A. Sina, & Associates (Eds.) *The child in the city: Changes and challenges* (pp. 410-477). Toronto: University of Toronto Press.

Minami, H. (1985). *Establishment and transformation of personal networks during the first year of college: A developmental analysis.* Unpublished doctoral dissertation, Clark University, Worcester, MA.

Moore, G. T. (1985). State of the art in play environment. In J. L. Frost & S. Sunderlin (Eds.), *When children play* (pp. 171-192). Wheaton, MD: Association for Childhood Education International.

Moore, G. T., Chawla, L., & McGinty, T. (1986). Neighborhood play environments: Design principles for latchkey children. *Children's Environments Quarterly, 3*(2), 13-23.

Muchow, M., & Muchow, H. H. (1935). *Der Lebensraum des Großstadtkindes.* Hamburg: Riegel (reprinted 1978).

Newman, O. (1972). *Defensible space: Crime prevention through urban design.* New York: Macmillan.

Olwig, K. (1991). Childhood, artistic creation, and the educated sense of place. *Children's Environments Quarterly, 8*(2), 4-18.

Pepper, S. C. (1942). *World hypotheses.* Berkeley: Univ. of California Press

Pepper, S. C. (1967). *Concept and quality: A world hypothesis.* LaSalle, IL: Open Court.

Pollowy, A.-M. (1977). *The urban nest.* Stroudsberg, PA: Dowden, Hutchinson & Ross.

Rioux, S., & Wapner, S. (1986). Commitment to use of automobile seat belts: An experiential analysis. *Journal of Environmental Psychology, 6*, 189-204.

Rogoff, B., & Wertsch, J. V. (Eds.). (1984). *Children's learning in the "zone of proximal development."* San Francisco, CA: Jossey-Bass.

Schouela, D. A., Steinberg, L. M., Leveton, L. B., & Wapner, S. (1980). Development of the cognitive organization of an environment. *Canadian Journal of Behavioural Science, 12*, 1-16.

Schütz, A. (1971). *Collected papers* (Vols. I-III) (M. Natanson, Ed.). The Hague, Netherlands: Nijhoff.

Thom, F. (1991). *Relationship between people and places important in the freshmen's and senior's experiential world.* Unpublished manuscript, Clark University, Worcester, MA.

Thomas, A. T., & Chess, S. (1977). *Temperament and development.* New York: Brunner/Mazel.

Thomas, A. T., Chess, S., & Birch, H. G. (1970). The origins of personality. *Scientific American, 223*(2), 102-109.

Valsiner, J. (1984). Construction of the zone of proximal development in adult-child joint action: The socialization of meals. In B. Rogoff & J. V. Wertsch (Eds.), *Children's learning in the "zone of proximal development"* (pp. 65-76). San Francisco, CA: Jossey-Bass.

Valsiner, J. (1985). Theoretical issues of child development and the problem of accident prevention. In T. Gärling & J. Valsiner (Eds.), *Children within environments: Toward a psychology of accident prevention* (pp. 13-36). New York: Plenum.

Valsiner, J. (1987). *Culture and the development of children's actions.* Chichester, CT: Wiley.

Valsiner, J. (1988a). *Child development within culturally structured environments. Vol 1: Parental cognition and adult-child interaction.* Norwood, NJ: Ablex.

Valsiner, J. (1988b). *Child development within culturally structured environments. Vol 2: Social co-construction and environmental guidance in development.* Norwood, NJ: Ablex.

Vygotsky, L. S. (1978). *Mind in society.* Cambridge, MA: Harvard University Press.

Wapner, S. (1977). Environmental transition: A research paradigm deriving from the organismic-developmental systems approach. In L. van Ryzin (Ed.), *Wisconsin Conference on Research Methods in Behavior Environment Studies Proceedings* (pp. 1-9). Madison: University of Wisconsin.

Wapner, S. (1978). Some critical person-environment transitions. *Hiroshima Forum for Psychology, 5*, 3-20.

Wapner, S. (1980). Toward an analysis of transactions of persons-in-a-high-speed society. In *Reports on Man and a High Speed Society, the IATSS Symposium on Traffic Science* (pp. 35-43). Tokyo: IATSS.

Wapner, S. (1981). Transactions of persons-in-environments: Some critical transitions. *Journal of Environmental Psychology, 1*, 223-239.

Wapner, S. (1985). Martha Muchow and organismic-developmental theory. *Human Development, 28*, 209-213.

Wapner, S. (1987). A holistic, developmental, systems-oriented environmental psychology: Some beginnings. In D. Stokols & I. Altman (Eds.), *Handbook of environmental psychology* (pp. 1433-1465). New York: Wiley.

Wapner, S., & Alper, T. G. (1952). The effect of an audience on behavior in a choice situation. *Journal of Abnormal and Social Psychology, 47*, 222-229.

Wapner, S., & Cirillo, L. (1973). *Development of planning.* (Public Health Service Grant Application). Clark University, Worcester, MA.

Wapner, S., Cirillo, L., & Baker, A. H. (1969). Sensory-tonic theory: Toward a reformulation. *Archivio di Psicologia, Neurologia e Psichiatria, XXX*, 493-512.

Wapner, S., Cirillo, L., & Baker, A. H. (1971). Some aspects of the development of space perception. In J. P. Hill (Ed.), *Minnesota Symposia on Child Psychology* (Vol. 5, pp. 162-204). Minneapolis: University of Minnesota Press.

Wapner, S., & Demick, J. (1990). Development of experience and action: Levels of integration in human functioning. In G. Greenberg & E. Tobach (Eds.), *Theories of the evolution of knowing: The T.C. Schneirla Conference Series, Vol. 4* (pp. 47-68). Hillsdale, NJ: Erlbaum.

Wapner, S., & Demick, J. (1991). Some relations between developmental and environmental psychology: An organismic-developmental systems perspective. In R. M. Downs, L. S. Liben, & D. S. Palermo (Eds.), *Visions of aesthetics, the environment & development: The legacy of Joachim F. Wohlwill* (pp. 181-211). Hillsdale, NJ: Erlbaum.

Wapner, S., Demick, J., & Mutch-Jones, K. (1990, March). *Children's experience of people and places.* Paper presented at the Eastern Psychological Association Meetings, Philadelphia, PA.

Wapner, S., & Kaplan, B. (Eds.). (1983). *Toward a holistic developmental psychology.* Hillsdale, NJ: Erlbaum.

Wapner, S., Kaplan, B., & Ciottone, R. (1981). Self-world relationships in critical environmental transitions: Childhood and beyond. In L. S. Liben, A. Patterson, & N. Newcombe (Eds.), *Spatial representation and behavior across the life span* (pp. 251-282). New York: Academic Press.

Wapner, S., Kaplan, B., & Cohen, S. B. (1973). An organismic-developmental perspective for understanding transactions of men in environments. *Environment and Behavior, 5*, 255-289.

Wapner, S., & Lebensfeld-Schwartz, P. (1976). Toward a structural analysis of event experience. *Acta Psychologica, 41*, 308-401.

Wapner, S., & Werner, H. (1957). *Perceptual development.* Worcester, MA: Clark University Press.

Wapner, S., & Werner, H. (1965). An experimental approach to body perception from the organismic-developmental point of view. In S. Wapner & H. Werner (Eds.), *The body percept* (pp. 9-25). New York: Random House.

Watkins, M. (1977). *A phenomenological approach to organismic-developmental research.* Unpublished manuscript. Clark University, Worcester, MA.

Werner, H. (1940). *Comparative psychology of mental development.* New York: Harper. (2nd ed., Chicago: Follett, 1948; 3rd ed., New York: International Universities Press, 1957)

Werner, H. (1957). The concept of development from a comparative and organismic point of view. In D. Harris (Ed.), *The concept of development* (pp. 125-148). Minneapolis: University of Minnesota Press.

Werner, H., & Kaplan, B. (1956). The developmental approach to cognition: Its relevance to the psychological interpretation of anthropological and ethnolinguistic data. *American Anthropologist, 58,* 866-880.

Werner, H., & Kaplan, B. (1963). *Symbol formation.* New York: Wiley.

Werner, H., & Wapner, S. (1952). Toward a general theory of perception. *Psychological Review, 59,* 324-338.

Wofsey, E., Rierdan, J., & Wapner, S. (1979). Planning to move: Effects on representing the currently inhabited environment. *Environment and Behavior, 11,* 3-32.

Wohlwill, J. F. (1985a). Martha Muchow, 1892-1933: Her life, work and contribution to developmental and ecological psychology. *Human Development, 28,* 198-200.

Wohlwill, J. F. (1985b). Martha Muchow and the life space of the urban child. *Human Development, 28,* 200-209.

Wozniak, R. H. (1986). Notes towards a co-constructive theory of the emotion/cognition relationship. In D. Bearison & H. Zimilies (Eds.), *Thought and emotion; Developmental perspectives* (pp. 40-64). Hillsdale, NJ: Erlbaum.

Comment: Werner augmented

Dietmar Görlitz

1 Claim and structure of the approach

Wapner's contribution is striking. The approach has a number of attributes that characterize it not only as developmental but also as holistic and systems oriented. Drawing on Heinz Werner and his theory, Wapner states that his own concept delineates only one aspect that throws light on part of the complex subject called child-oriented urban planning.[1] Does it provide an intellectual tool for professionals responsible for urban planning that benefits children as well as others? Does it at least help planners consider the special nature of children and their needs? Perhaps. But when the planner is meant and not also children as planners and designers in their own right, the aims of that user take a back seat, and Wapner expands the scope of his approach to deal with more than a single aspect – application and user.[2] Indeed, the formal, rather than the substantive, peculiarities of the theory he presents can be applied to a broad range of areas in psychology. The theory focuses on an aspect whose broad applicability largely divests it of its allegedly modular nature. This aspect relates to a unit that is not confined in monad-like isolation to the complex present of exchange relations, to the activity of individuals and what they experience, but rather points primarily to transactions emanating from the more complex unit of *persons-in-environments*. Upon closer reading, however, one finds that these transactions are the very essence of the unit in the two poles that feature in persons-in-environments.

Even before Figure 1[3] summarizes Wapner's theory, the basic assumptions of which are clearly illustrated (as will be shown in a moment), questions to ponder are raised by the architecture of the entity, by the transactions and their corresponding unit. Are those transactions only the dynamic glue holding together a unit that could not exist without them? Or does the persons-in-environments unit remain intact even without the transactions, and does it trigger higher-order transactions in order then to focus retrospectively or prospectively on other spatiotemporal regions? The synoptic scheme of theory ties it into present events without forging such relations, simultaneously changing each of these persons-in-environments from plural to singular, into a *person-in-environment* unit whose two poles are divided into phylogenetic and microgenetic strata for both the actor and his or her assigned environment.

Wapner differentiates the actor into respondent, agent, and person, initially as centers in a phylogenetic sequence. On the environmental side, they correspond to ambiance, habitat, and the world of cultural settings, rules, and works. In doing so, Wapner oscillates between presenting[4] a purely formal, categorical inventory of what the actor and the environment could embody and showing how they are reflected in different levels of access to the individual, whose embedding in the environment makes it possible to map out three corresponding aspects – also manifested in the environment – as physical-biological, as psychological (intra- or interpersonal), and as sociocultural ways of viewing the poles in the person-in-environment unit. These aspects even determine the specific sequence of organizational steps, or levels of analysis, in which three levels corresponding to the above-mentioned differentiations are focused upon (the biological, psychological, and sociocultural), whereby each succeeding level includes the previous one.

2   Basic unit of analysis

Having presented these many possible combinations, Wapner confines his unit of analysis to person-in-environment. He loses nothing in focusing the analysis this way, but much that is decisive about the structure of this unit, with its layered, double-poled centers, is left open. In the list of environmental features, for example, socioenvironmental aspects appear only as *relations* to others,[5] without systematically including these persons or groups of persons and their respective unit of person-in-environment. Merely formal relatedness to one another leaves no chance for anything to occur interpersonally. What remains is what burdened classical conceptions of the life space in a similar way early on – the difficult world of the other and that which I share with it, that which it inflicts upon me or gives me. Not only this "with whom" remains too pale and bald, so does the "where" as a physical aspect of what happens. It remains too much a stringing of localities for it to become apparent as distinguishable by their structures – say, as playground, street, or big city. Children have not yet turned up, if you will. More precisely, they have not been named; but neither have they been excluded as one of the possible persons in the person-in-environment unit, a concretion of which can be a city.

3   On the contribution of transactions

Transactions in that context are the dynamic link between the person and that which constitutes the person's environment. Persons are party to them in everything they do and experience without actually becoming creative or seminal, productive, without plainly signaling to others that "I was there" or experiencing one's own traces and doings retroactively. With their preferred source *in* the person – after all, they are transactions of *the person* with the environment (my italics)[6] – transactions are enacted in relation to goals by means of an abundance of instrumentalities. But it seems as if their role consists in linking the person with the environment, be it for long-term goals or quickly satisfied needs, as if these transactions constitute *the* unit actually already premised by person-in-environment.

The spatiotemporal omnipresence of the "I am here now," the fact of being in a certain situation if you will, of suddenly doing useful errands in the midst of business activity on a metropolitan shopping street before Christmas, for example, is more presumed than explained. The figure illustrating the approach (see Wapner's Figure 1) may be more instructive and productive in this sense, for it shows not only layers of the individual (as a person) and the environment but also strata upon which they are superimposed as it were – as open systems in exchange. They contain further areas of depth that are sharply and consistently delineated. A person may acquire different scopes of environment through his or her transactions, may process it affectively, evaluatively, and cognitively, confined only by the sharp boundaries remaining in the directional, temporally ordered continuation when the person-environment units are repeated at a higher level.

Repeated or not, these large-scale change sequences are still progressively directed at differentiated and hierarchically integrated person-in-environment units in a manner assessable according to a target criterion (the orthogenetic principle of development from Heinz Werner's theory of development). There is a large developmental trajectory as it were, true geneses (as a generic term for all kinds of development) ranging from the sequence of brief actions to phylogenetic change, all of which can be progressive or temporarily even regressive. For a given person-in-environment system, that is true almost more in the sense of something that happens to the unit, for the active, goal-oriented, transacting person-in-environment continues to be a goal-setting agent precisely in that unit, lets its transactional activity be analyzed in various ways (structurally and dynamically). Such modes of analysis instruct the graphically nonrepresented researcher but do not enable the actor to follow the great directional line containing the smallest and the greatest forms of development. It is possible, if one is so inclined, to see therein a flaw in the system's weave: It is not that *I* develop (in the sense of the great, temporal trajectory of development) without really wanting to (in terms of the goals guiding my transactions in this or that person-in-environment unit). Instead, it is as if long-term transactions are already used up, consumed, for the situation presented as a basic unit; they are no longer available as "microgenesis" to constitute a subcase of temporal changes on the great developmental trajectory stretching from "early" to "late."

4   Modes of analysis

The structure of this transactional activity in the person-in-environment unit is itself subjected to a microgenetic analysis; that is, it *may* be subjected, if I correctly understand the author's distinction between a structural and a dynamic analysis, both of which are applicable to transactions. *Structural* analysis concerns the overall part-whole relations of this complex exchange process between person-in-environment and an environment, its environment. However, the author's chosen example of "sketch-map" representations focuses less on a person's analyzable action than on the possibility of taking what the person produces (the person's products, e.g., completed drawings) and analyzing it in terms of ontogenetic sequences (i.e., structures of known and remembered "environment"), with microgenesis not being understood in this context as brief sequences in time. By contrast, *dynamic* analysis, illustrated by the remembered course of environmental drawings and the strategies used to create them, is much more the context in which the process of action over time is discussed. The discussion, however, revolves around transactionally engaged persons-in-environment who focus on the *imagined* "environment" of their particular knowledge and report on means or strategies that helped them remember.

After the reported basic unit and its inherent transactions, the *second* pillar of Wapner's sequenced, theoretical assumptions consists in means-ends analyses and part-whole analyses – as representing what is real and the researcher's possibilities for analyzing that reality. In such person-in-environment units there are goal-oriented, overt or covert transactions that can be analyzed structurally or dynamically. According to Wapner, transaction in the sense of acting or experiencing involves cognitive processes and has emotional and evaluative dimensions that can also be subjected to structural or dynamic analyses and complemented by phenomenological descriptions. Every facet of transaction would therefore have to admit of such description of phenomenological orientation as well as these other modes of analysis by a researcher. But the empirical evidence mustered to illustrate this point is not encouraging. Instead, it renders the subject of transaction complexly ambiguous, as is apparent in the open question of whether remembered and present feelings about places are proof of the affective side of transactions, including aesthetic experience.

5   Constructing activities of changing orientation

According to what has been explained thus far, transactions are directed processes that take place in a "person-in-environment" unit. Including action and experience alike, they originate in the person and have cognitive, affective, and evaluative aspects upon which a researcher can focus in two modes of analysis (structural and dynamic) and in the mode of phenomenological description. If the researcher does so, he or she can use additional interpretive and focusing procedures to build up an ever denser picture of the material being described. But the experiencing person embedded in the environment can also change the structure, or organizational level, of existing attitudes (arrested, or frozen, transactions with regions of the person's environment, so to say) through a variety of interpolated activities (including functionally equivalent ones). In a microgenetic sense, that person thereby almost conforms to the orthogenetic principle. The *third* basic assumption in Wapner's approach is that persons do so actively, constructively, something that should actually further characterize transactions, at least as far as the subject is concerned. In the examples offered, however, this activity does not go beyond reconstructions of remembered experiences of space. It remains open whether transactions in this context acquire an additional aspect or whether Wapner discusses an additional person-in-environment activity related more to ways of dealing with what is remembered, with representations of earlier experiences. In either case, persons would be active in reconstructing what earlier transactions had brought about. While doing so, persons would also be free to engage alternately in the different, inter-twined poles of their basic unit. According to the principle of multiple intentionality, Wapner's *fourth* basic assumption, there are many orientations upon which the person can alternately center: the person himself, his environment, or the relation in which he lives in that environment.

This view touches on Heinz Werner's implied basic idea of "spheres of reality," which is far richer, for he meant the intertwining of realities in each subject's own world, the unique, idiosyncratic things that occur there. Those things definitely can lose their identity, indeed will not even have acquired it yet if the spheres of reality or their respective regions in the child's pragmatic and concrete world are segregated by boundaries, be they fluid or rigid. After all, it is the personal salience of things, not their objective quality, that characterizes them in the world of children. The informed reader knows that, but in the presentation of the fourth assumption it is not clear enough. Other readers not familiar with this idea are made acquainted only cursorily with a rather valuable principle of earlier Hamburg psychology, Werner's psychology, as the possibility that the perceiving, acting subject has of relating to something in a number of ways (see Werner, 1961, pp. 379-402).

6   What continuities structure and what planning does

The reader encounters multiple intentionality in the person-in-environment system more in the iridescent, oscillating linking of the poles than in the quiet centering on the position of each actor with his or her perspective on whatever circumstances obtain at the moment. After all, children (according to Werner, 1961, p. 383) are intensely interested in what they "can do" with something as they move along the way to "what one does with it." They act, embedded in a continuous stream of experience in which the change of places or the incisions of time make discrete units emerge, if the reader may pin down Wapner's *fifth* basic assumption by relating it to children in this way. If the reader may do so, then the question remains open as to whether these units – removed from the flow of space-time – correspond to the sequential figures of person-in-environment systems. More specifically, *are* these systems over a microgenetic period not rather an individual's developmental levels in the course of his or her ontogenesis? The latter understanding may lie even closer to the interest of Werner's psychology.[7]

Actors in the system have varying degrees of contact with the environmental side of their worlds. They can transcend the given environment and engage in worthwhile person-in-environment configurations, for their transactions in directed planning are effective in promoting development, as formulated in Wapner's *sixth* basic assumption. In abandoning and foregoing such planning, such orientation to goals, these transactions are open for regressions, for developmental relapses. All the way to mother? Into the hands of a child playing with others? Yet in all this goal-setting and goal-renouncing action, the doing proceeds from the person-in-environment system as a whole, as is wont in a psychology beholden to holism, according to which an impact on a part of the system effects the entire system. From whom, then, and from which system, does this impact come? Is it, say, from the recurrently forgotten researcher?

7   Creative analysis and boundaries of the whole

Wapner's *seventh* basic assumption follows Heinz Werner's (1961) earlier maxim that the synthesis toward, say, a new whole (as Wundt predicated) is not what is creative but rather the *analyses* of an already existing whole. It is a maxim – particularly for a psychologist, like this commentator, who has been brought up to esteem the whole – that promises more than it delivers. How far flung are the *boundaries* of each thematic whole, which "spheres of reality" does it encompass, and how many of them? In terms of the basic unit, the person-in-environment systems, is it the totality of the present, not also the totality of what each "I" had allegedly promised or set out to become? Is it also the distant beat of a butterfly's wings or that in which others move their worlds or discuss me in my world? Is it what their action incidentally or occasionally provides each "me" with, as workers do when digging ditches for a municipal drainage system in front of a child's home? Where is whose totality solid? And who determines the boundaries? Improving on Wundt and thereby expanding on Werner, perhaps one should work toward providing the researcher with a *principle of creative unit formation* that demarcates the "claims" within which life teems. In the present context, such "claims" would be the city, in which, knowingly embedded, each person consciously lives with others, even in distinguishing, special relations to which Wapner calls the reader's attention.

Despite the multilevel analysis that he recommends, however, and for all the creation of what Valsiner refers to as developmentally salient zones for each child, the "others" who are active in each child's world recede to the pale fringes of "environment" in Wapner's scheme of things. It seems to me more psychological and thus more straightforward to proceed instead from the idea of a *polycentric entity* – humans in their particular cities – than from a multilevel analysis of the individual. Only humans in such a polycentric entity are significant parts of conflicting or balancing assignment to the city as a whole, in which they develop. What seems to me to be the real contribution of Wapner's approach is that this view of the developing person, expanded as I propose, is essentially comprehensible according to a principle that, after creative analysis (in Werner's sense), holds for the whole of a given system as well as its parts. The system lies on the ordering and ordered path of proper becoming. Whose or what's becoming? That of the system's organization as a whole and as parts.

8   Levels of developedness

Heinz Werner (1961) considered the orthogenetic principle, which he stressed and which he drew from ideas in Goethe's *Morphology* (pp. 40-41), as the fundamental law of development (p. 44). Wapner presents it as his *eighth* basic assumption. By that point much has plainly happened, the operating of the person-in-system that he highlights has constructed and directed a good deal. It is then accorded what Wapner sees as an ideally tailored, overarching objective, one that makes it possible to mark on this trajectory levels of development that can be characterized by the polarities formulated by Werner, for whom "the wholesome organism . . . [constitutes] a well-integrated entity" (p. 56). The key position that the nervous system of living systems plays in Heinz Werner's thought is exchanged by Wapner – a modernization consistent with the topic of this book – for the actor in his or her system, who is linked to and effective in the environment in many ways for which the orthogenetic principle provides a tool for descriptive and *normative* measure. It turns development into a topic.

9   What major cities teach

9.1   Structures and perspectives

Cities, particularly major ones, teach thinking – perhaps beyond this principle that orders actors so variously. They teach one to think, for example, of the figure-ground principle handed down from gestalt psychology. Cities as a ground provide an abundant variety of regulated routines: the figures treated by the researcher, beginning with partners walking or driving by each other without colliding as they go about obeying signs of known rules or strategies of coordination, all in structures decaying in the day's fickle luminosity and tangible weather. In this cosmos of richly executed, even colliding, processes that stem from different juxtapositions accompanying each individual's changing perspectives in front of and with others – herein one can single out processes of what happens by drawing on the orthogenetic principle. That means not only traffic jams and gridlocks on the unexpected icy patches on urban streets or the straightforward routine with which a grocer arranges his fruit while others look on. Cities teach thinking. Amid the many things that come to pass in the city, I always see "masters" of their activities and see "apprentices" on their way in life next to, in front of, and with each other with things, objects, apparatuses, and machines, whether indifferently or actively engaged in related, relatable, or individual time structures.

9.2   Developments of the principle

If the development of biological forms is expressed in increasing differentiation of their parts and their increasing subordination and hierarchization, as postulated by Heinz Werner (1961, p. 41), but if those growing up in a city live in an ecosystem with historically new demands and challenges, can the purely formal orthogenetic principle then hold entirely unaltered for the city, for the people living in it? Does it formulate, say, ideal developmental processes that hit their limits here? Does it reveal a failure of development at precisely that point? Or does it make clear in which direction cities must be overcome, must change, if they are to be livable developmental environments for many people in all cultures and not just for the birds of the air and rodents of the earth? I repeat, cities teach thinking, teach one to consider new things. This orthogenetic principle diversifies and variegates on its own into hierarchies upon impact with the multilayered imponderability of man-made metropolises in the courses of their histories. Upon the ground of a variety of processes taking place against the greater constancy of things and the mobility of conveyors as figures, it allows one to single out special processes upon which masters act, with some of them failing and perishing.

A commentary of this nature cannot present the orthogenetic principle's "development" that would be appropriate for the city. It can only suggest that the solution for the abiding, sheltering, and guiding self-containment through things is prepared by Wapner himself when he recommends thinking in new units containing persons-in-environments of the person-in-environment, always being in front of others. So, "the modern city, with its multistory buildings, plants and factories, and so forth, with its two- or three-story shopping zones, streetcars, automobiles, the three-dimensional neon signs, ocean liners, airplanes," has not only "changed a few things about the traditional psychology of perception," as Rodtschenko wrote back

in 1928 (cited in Züchner, 1994, p. 4) in praise of photography as the only appropriate procedure for depicting large cities. The city can also prompt reflection – to learn
by further developing Wapner's position – about *city*-specific systems (units),
system limits, and transactions of the residents acting in those systems. Goethe, "the
child of the city" (Boyle, 1995, p. 360), lived and worked in Weimar, not in the New
York of modern times.

9.3   The uniqueness of large cities

There is probably no entity in the world in which there gather as many active, indifferent strangers intertwined in a wider variety of orthogeneses and observing each
other at a wider range of angles – from the street to the top of high-rises – as in the
large city, with the virtual presence of others behind innumerable windows, in a
maze of constantly shifting configurations that foreshortens what is given to an often
fleeting, always selective, visual, perceptual impression. The city teaches at least
that. "The great educator" (Tews), the urban setting, fittingly challenges the person
developing in the city to adopt unique perceptual habits and puts strangers (visitors)
up to their necks (and eyes) in this hyperspace (Jameson, cited in Hauser, 1990,
p. 1), where familiar dimensions of spatial conception such as perspective and
volume can be initially lost. This change in perceptual situations has always been
noted in the literature on the great cities (Hauser, 1990) and perhaps also shapes
urbanites through that literature as part of a self-fulfilling prophecy.

   In this respect, city life and the city as an alternative way of living explodes the
simple, internally directed centering of the traditional orthogenetic principle into
many scattered, colliding, mutually supporting or restricting orthogeneses of
mutually indifferent, unconcerned, or even mutually committed partners. To what
degree has human perception been changed in the history of the city? And which
individual paths of development are nevertheless conceivable?

9.4   Further developments

Discussion of the orthogenetic principle brings out not only the city's ideal forma-
tions more than it otherwise might. At every turn, whether normative, descriptive, or
explicative, it also makes places visible along with others who are always or
temporarily there, linked by a weave of ways and means to reach them from
wherever "I call home," from a growing abundance of the unknown or only by its
familiar name as "that region of the city over there." Not until a cultural and
developmental view is gained of the *historical* change in cities, of the
"development" of cities – which, like descriptions of them (Kauffmann, 1994),
usually change over longer periods and do not always vanish "as completely as

flowers" (Lawrence, 1932/1992, p. 13) – not until that point can one test (see Hofmeister, 1991) the degree to which this overarching principle of development is profitable for the historical change of *urban* structures as well. But it is not just the city that changes. It is also that "today's city dwellers are different than the first residents of Jericho" (Berndt, 1978, p. 7), to bring urbanites back into the picture.

Figure 1: Andreas Feininger (1906): Traffic on Fifth Avenue (New York, 1950) © Time Life Syndication, 1997

For *each* of them, more than anything else, it is true "that stability of behavior requires a flexibility of response in order to preserve the functional equilibrium of the organism in the face of mutable situations" (Werner, 1961, p. 55). It requires "mutable situations," an abundance of which the young city dweller encounters in big cities, differing as they do from region to region and in the hierarchy of their importance. If the orthogenetic principle itself "develops" – toward the conflicting, familiar adjacency of the incompatible – for children in their urban ontogeneses, a preliminary plane of the developmental levels that Wapner points out for an individual may consist of or embrace "the here and there in my city, where I live with others of my family, tied in many different ways, where my home is; and the special places I already know, would like to know, or be allowed to know on my own, or must use in recurring routines (a route to school, for instance)." This preliminary plane can extend to "living with others in the shared temporal and local world, in which the *I* in each case reckons with the changing positions of the *others* in it and with each person's own perspective on it" – sometimes interrupting the person's separate lines of development, scattering them through diffraction in which the seeds of the new are laid or the loss of the old is prepared.

So much for sketches accompanying commentaries intended to broaden the ortho-genetic principle. In its traditional version, it would lose nothing if cities had never been founded in human history or if children had been forbidden to grow up in them. It would lose as little as it would gain by its very existence.

10 Possibilities for further developing microgeneses

As a theme, getting to know cities in their regions, works, and paths is nicely documented by Wapner himself when, as a *ninth* basic assumption, he presents the distinction between microgenesis and ontogenesis. Both are said to be subject to the orthogenetic principle previously discussed, though microgenesis and its *aktual-genetische* experiments on the construction and deconstruction of shapes has not really been uppermost in developmental psychology ever since the days of holistic psychology in Leipzig. Microgenesis is concerned with small stretches of time.[8] In Wapner's empirical example of it, the scale is measured in years of life; for this commentator, in the courses of shorter observable or hypothetical processes in which one can document development, too, by comparing microgenetic processes over a life span in ontogenetic sequence just as one would compare products. It would be completely consistent with Werner (see Werner, 1937) not to level out or run these small stretches of time together as stages of ontogenesis. The emphasis on microgenesis is especially exciting for the big city, for observations of microgenesis were precisely what the city's earliest critics (see pp. 44-52 in this volume) drew on when, in praise of rural life, they attacked urban living conditions by asserting that humans in that environment often failed to experience satisfying closure to their emotional reactions and engaged, detailed perception processes. Borrowing from Freud, Benjamin argued that humans suffered "Chocks" (shocks) that were not without consequence for the process of adaptation. In this respect a noble good pales in Wapner's presentation, a good that is reconcilable with theoretical assumptions only to the extent that its course is said to conform to certain structural principles, as is the case for ontogenesis and pathogenesis. Wapner thinks in microgeneses but does not present them properly – as the old wholists would see it – as the valuable topic that even he acknowledges them to be (see, for example, Wapner, pp. 285-287 in this volume).

The *tenth* basic assumption, which is oriented less to constructing developmental theory than to clarifying the formal organization of development, also seems to show an appreciation for microgeneses; it recommends being aware of progressions and regressions. Accordingly, the formation of impressions in the person-environment system are also subject to the orthogenetic principle. To Wapner, microgeneses shaped in that manner, too, formulate normative standards for planners – if, and probably only if, children growing up in the city acquire a reliable, articulated image of their city (as the structured readability recommended by Lynch, 1960). But microgeneses are also involved when a given individual's childhood becomes the subject of autobiographical retrospective, as captured with such artistic insight by Benjamin (1966) and expressed in Hessel's (1929/1984) lament that the first glimpse of an unfamiliar city and its streets is irretrievable. How much the microgeneses of well-preserved impressions are destroyed by an observer's changing position in the flow of traffic, by a rapid elevator as opposed to a paternoster of olden days! How much these impressions are reshaped in the din of the large city, for they are not unlike the video clips of modern television or the modern TV viewer's channel surfing.

11 Too firmly set?

The system can regress through impoverishment or, more precisely, through functional impoverishment of city regions. Developmentally supportive transitions to geographically other regions as well have a somewhat unfortunate role in this context. According to Wapner's figure, the system moves to a different place; upon transactional reintegration, the person moves to new regions, settles in them, and only the system's continuation along the established main axis can instruct the researcher and the developmental partner whether there is progression or degeneration or whether regression as a temporary stage is operating in preparation for further development at a higher level. Seen in this way, it would be stylistically cleaner to take the main axis, with its parallel bundle of analytical lines, and split it into a primary continuum of the evolving person-in-environment system toward which the different aforementioned analytical aspects can be applied in more orthogonal than parallel placement. Berliners in their modern environment know what effects passing or profound impacts can have on a city, including temporary regression in one's personal embeddedness and orientation. It is again the case that the basic unit is operating with boundaries that are much too fixed. A person leaving a system of that kind falls into the abyss to the side or into a fathomless future to the fore, beyond the reach of anyone's aid or menace. It is odd that the subjects in the empirical study reported by Wapner patiently sat on chairs, "eyeing" what they imagined and remembered rather than actually reshaping streets and embankments, as Muchow's city children did. But even they, upon request, can tell of strategies that help them cope with imposed transitions into regions that are new to them. Let them

move personally and handle the world of real city environments, real for children –
with all the opportunities and risks of development offered.

Notes

1 This observation is based on earlier drafts of the chapter and on discussions at the Herten
  conference.
2 This shift is an inconsistency only if one considers the first subheading of Wapner's article as
  "[a] perspective for child-centered urban planning" and if the sentence introducing an
  "approach to the more general study" is seen to be as important as the basic conviction that
  the author makes clear in the opening passage. This addendum and the following ones have
  profited from a discussion with the author.
3 Most of my further comments in the text are keyed to this synoptic pictorial presentation of
  Wapner's theory.
4 Or, as Wapner sees it, he presents both the following aspects.
5 The preceding critical discussion of environmental features calls for a more detailed
  discussion. The presence of the others and their view of the world is, to Wapner, conveyed in
  the list of relations to others, albeit only implicitly.
6 As perhaps in this case, one is still apt to misunderstand transactional researchers whose use
  of language occasionally does not do justice to their intentions when they link persons, too, to
  transactions as a source while meaning the complex system consisting of person-in-
  environment, a construction that calls for further clarification.
7 For somebody introduced to psychology by the Leipzig wholists, as is the case with this
  commentator, microgeneses always have something immediate about them, the becoming and
  transience of gestalt here and now. Given that background one finds it difficult to see how
  microgenesis and ontogenesis can be distinguished solely on the basis of seconds and minutes, though such brief chronometric units – themselves also building blocks of ontogenesis –
  are surely documented in individual events of managable temporal proportions. As an even
  more complex task, the researcher can track these two types of geneses when looking for
  changes in microgeneses in the course of ontogenesis.
8 See note 7.

References

Benjamin, W. (1966). *Städtebilder* [Images of cities]. Frankfurt on the Main: Suhrkamp.
Berndt, H. (1978). *Die Natur der Stadt* [The nature of the city]. Frankfurt on the Main: Verlag
  Neue Kritik.
Görlitz, D. (1993). Es begann in Berlin – Wege einer entwicklungspsychologischen Stadtfor-
  schung [It began in Berlin – Avenues of developmental urban research]. In H. J. Harloff
  (Ed.), *Psychologie des Wohnungs- und Siedlungsbaus – Psychologie im Dienste von
  Architektur und Stadtplanung* (pp. 97-120). Göttingen: Verlag für Angewandte Psychologie.
Hauser, S. (1990). *Der Blick auf die Stadt. Semiotische Untersuchungen zur literarischen
  Wahrnehmung bis 1910* [View of the city: Semiotic studies on literary perception until 1910].
  Berlin: Reimer.

Hessel, F. (1984). *Ein Flaneur in Berlin* [A stroller in Berlin]. Berlin: Das Arsenal. (Original work published 1929 as *Spazieren in Berlin*)

Hofmeister, B. (1991). *Die Stadtstruktur. Ihre Ausprägung in den verschiedenen Kulturräumen der Erde* [Urban structure: Its manifestation in the different cultural regions of the earth]. Darmstadt: Wissenschaftliche Buchgesellschaft.

Kauffmann, K. (1994). *"Es ist nur ein Wien!" Stadtbeschreibungen von Wien 1700 bis 1873. Geschichte eines literarischen Genres der Wiener Publizistik* ["There's only one Vienna!" Descriptions of Vienna from 1700 to 1873 – The history of a literary genre of Viennese journalism]. Vienna: Böhlau.

Lawrence, D. H. (1992). *Sketches of Etruscan places and other Italian essays* (Simonetta de Filippis, Ed.). Cambridge, Engl.: Cambridge University Press. (Original work published 1932)

Lynch, K. (1960). *The image of the city*. Cambridge, MA: M.I.T. Press.

Werner, H. (1937). Process and achievement – A basic problem of education and developmental psychology. *The Harvard Educational Review, 7*, 353-368.

Werner, H. (1961). *Comparative psychology of mental development*. New York: Science Editions.

Züchner, E. (1994). *Fotografie am Bauhaus. Materialien zum Bauhaus* [Photography as taught at Bauhaus: Materials about Bauhaus] (No. 5). Berlin: Museumspädagogischer Dienst.

Relational-developmental theory: A psychological perspective

Willis F. Overton

1   Introduction

The goal of this chapter is to further the continuing dialogue that operates – often implicitly – in the field of developmental psychology concerning the concept of development. But dialogue cannot occur without the explicit recognition of the fact that each participant in a dialogue necessarily operates from a particular point of view. Thus, I argue for a particular point of view or narrative concerning the nature of development (see Overton, 1998). The narrative to be described is one that attempts to overcome splits in thinking about development and doing empirical work in developmental psychology. This is not the only narrative available on the contemporary developmental scene. Indeed, a survey of the field would probably reveal that the narrative I present is not currently – at least not on the North American continent – even a terribly popular one. The popular contemporary narrative on the North American continent is one that implicitly celebrates splits into either/or thinking about virtually all of the fundamental problems and issues of development. However, I believe that if the story I present were adequately understood it would offer major advantages to scientists, educators, and practitioners over ways that they currently think about development and over ways they currently employ the idea of change in their work. I believe that if this narrative were adequately understood, not only would we have a powerful way of integrating knowledge about evolutionary change, changes in individual organisms across the life span, and changes in those special developmental spaces called education, and therapy, but we would also have a better way of understanding the function of change agents, whether these be parents, educators, or therapists.

The narrative that I want to present is currently being called relational-developmental theory. When it is presented as a theory of mind it has been called embodiment theory (Overton, 1994a, b, c). Because at some fundamental level this narrative asserts that framing or context is as central to understanding as is content, I want to start by describing a kind of bullet list of what this relational-developmental theory implies and what it does not imply. In other words, I want to provide the reader with some abstract frames of reference that form the framing context for a relational-developmental perspective:

2   Frames of reference for a relational-developmental perspective

1. Relational-developmental theory is a narrative that takes as its primary focus the description and explanation of change (transformational change and variational change; expressive change and instrumental change; universal change and individual change) across the life span. Broadly, it defines development as the changes in the form and function of expressive and instrumental features of behavior (see Overton, 1998). However, while such changes are the focus, it is also asserted that the description and explanation being offered is relevant for other change series, including evolutionary change and therapeutic change. The idea here is that the pattern of change discovered in ontogenesis can, with benefit, be seen as isomorphic with the pattern of change found in these other change series and, hence, that developmental inquiry is inherently comparative.

2. In this narrative on the nature of development, the *disavowal of all ontological and epistemological splits is fundamental*. That is, "either/or" statements about the nature of the world, the nature of knowing or the nature of organisms, are disavowed. "Avoid all splits" is the marching banner of this point of view. Thus, for example, the world is not to be broken into the either/or of matter and form; subject and object; and knowing is not to be broken into the either/or of reason and observation, deduced and induced. The contrastive terms described here enter the present narrative as alternative, but interrelated, points of view.

3. As a consequence of the disavowal of "either/or" ontological-epistemological thinking, all classical references to the nature-nurture issue (or biological determinism vs. social determinism) are considered misleading. This also holds for those supposed conventional "interactionist" positions that would claim that a behavioral outcome is to x degree determined by nature and to y degree determined by nurture (e.g., sociobiology theory, in which a split-off set of genes is identified as the cause of response variation, and a split environment is identified as the cause of the selection of some response variant). All this latter sort of "How much?" approach does is make the "either/or" ontological-epistemological splits tinier, it does not move to the disavowal of splits.

4. In this narrative, the concept of "level of analysis" or "recursive level of discourse" is taken seriously. Thus, for example, whereas splits are avoided at the ontological level of discourse (which defines what one accepts as the real), it is quite reasonable to take a biological, psychological, or social *perspective* when one moves to the epistemological level of discours (which defines how a person will know). Taking a perspective is an epistemological act, and it differs in *level* of discourse or analysis from taking an either/or ontological position (see Figure 1). Taking a biological *perspective* entails a background recognition that biology can have meaning only in the context of the social. Taking a social *perspective* entails a

background recognition that the social can have meaning only in the context of the biological. In other words, *biological* and *social* are contrastive or bipolar concepts that can have meaning only as they define each other (see Figure 2).

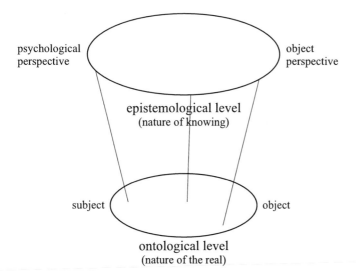

Figure 1: Ontology and epistemology: A relational perspective

5. In the relational-developmental narrative, *relational* means dialectical in character. A dialectical system is any system that moves toward integration through cycles of paradox (i.e., contradiction and self-reference) and differentiation (see Overton 1991a, b, c; Overton & Horowitz, 1991).

6. In the relational-developmental narrative, paradox is celebrated as a necessary feature of understanding (knowing). Paradox implies circularity, and circularity is one necessary mode of understanding. This mode of understanding stands in relationship to a second mode of understanding called the *analytic mode*. Thus, positions that attempt to split paradoxically circular understandings and analytic understandings into "either/or" segments are disavowed (see Overton 1991c; 1994a, b). For example, definitions of science that claim that "scientific explanation" must avoid *all* circularity is understood as a split position and is disavowed. As an illustration, a set of behaviors may be the observational base from which to infer a latent mental structure, whereas the mental structure may then be said to explain the behaviors. This is a circular argument that a positivistic definition of science disparages. From a relational point of view (e.g., see the work of Kuhn, Lakatos, and Laudan esp. in Overton, 1984, 1991b), this circularity is a scientifically appropriate explanation to the extent that the circle is not completely closed. That is, to the extent that the mental structures explain more than simply the initially observed

data, the circle avoids viciousness and constitutes scientifically acceptable explanation.

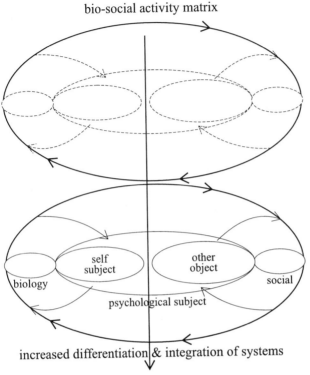

bio-social activity matrix

increased differentiation & integration of systems

Arrows = Activity Patterns = Assimilation (integration)/Accommodation (differentiation).
Note: If arrows are viewed from the left side of the figure (i.e., the biological and self/subject side) the arrows pointing toward the right represent assimilation and the arrows pointing to the left represent accommodation. If arrows are viewed from the right side of the figure (i.e., from the social and other/object side) then arrows pointing toward the left represent assimilation and arrows pointing to the right represent accommodation.

Bio-social Activity Matrix = The matrix from which both the biological and the social worlds differentiate, and from which the psychological subject also differentiates.

Psychological Subject Matrix = The matrix from which both subject and objective consciousness differentiate, and from which the bio-social activity matrix also differentiates.

Figure 2: The differentiating bio-social-psychological relational matrix

7. Because relational means dialectical, it is not a narrative where relational necessarily means two-person as opposed to one-person. Any attempt to give absolute priority or absolute privilege to a two-person or to a one-person psychology involves an "either/or" ontological split. From a relational point of view, a one-

person and a two-person psychology are alternative perspectives on the same psychological whole. Here, both the intrapsychic and the interpersonal are legitimate perspectives, but it is the relation of the two that defines the whole.

8. In the relational-developmental narrative, pattern takes precedence over cause as the primary vehicle of explanation (i.e., relation takes precedence over isolated elements). As a consequence, explaining development, as distinguished from explaining some individual differences in development, involves the rational interpretative search for principles that identify patterns of change. The explanation of development is not found in observable causes.

9. Finally, perhaps to help pin down this very abstract set of contextual features that frame the relational-developmental narrative, let me just say that this narrative is compatible with the biological evolutionary narrative presented by Gerald Edelman; the cognitive developmental narratives presented by Heinz Werner and Jean Piaget; the psychosocial developmental perspective presented by Eric Erikson; the dynamic personality developmental perspective described by people like Melanie Klein, W. R. D. Fairbairn, John Bowlby, Donald Winnicott, and Thomas Ogden; and some recent perspectives on the nature of psychotherapeutic change, such as those described by Merton Gill, Irwin Hoffman, and Arnold Modell.

To this point I have described some abstract contextual features of this relational-developmental perspective and presented some names to hang some of these features onto. Now let me be a bit more precise about the developmental relational narrative.

3   A closer look at relational-developmental narratives

First, note again that this is fundamentally a theory about the *psychological* development of the organism. I emphasize this point to establish perspective. If this were a theory about culture, for example, then cultural concepts would be the figure against a ground of psychological concepts. Or if this were theory about biology, then biological concepts would be the figure against the ground of cultural concepts. It is exactly these figure-ground relations that constitute the relational nature of the relational-developmental perspective. These figure-ground relations identify "point-of-view." Because I propose to describe a sketch of a theory about the development of psyche (i.e., a psychological theory) biological and social concepts remain as ground to the psychological figure. Again, note that there is no ontological split here. It is simply that if one is going to have a theory about the psychological, then the psychological subject becomes the figure to biological and sociocultural concepts that constitute the ground (see Figure 2). An example can be found in at least one reading of the relation between the Piagetian approach (psychological-cultural) and the Vygotskian approach (cultural-psychological). This is a reading suggested by Van der Veer and Valsiner (1994), who – in contrast to contemporary Marxist split interpretations – maintain that Piaget and Vygotsky do not differ about the idea of "the developing personal-cognitive (and affective) structures" (p. 6). Further, there is an "actual closeness of the basic personalistic standpoints of both . . [that] has gone without attention" (p. 6).

As a theory about psychological processes or a theory of an embodied mind (where mind is understood as cognitive/affective understanding [expressive feature] and the instruments that serve to access and apply this understanding [instrumental feature]), relational-developmental theory of the person starts from an ontological point of view that identifies and describes the human organism as an organized activity matrix that becomes differentiated from the biocultural or biosocial field through its action (see Figure 2). Thus, mind in this narrative is neither a disengaged subjective concept that emerges from an isolated and reified biology nor a set of equally disengaged cultural and linguistic norms. To borrow a term from Charles Taylor (1991), mind is "dialogical" in character. Mind emerges out of embodied practices (action) that both constitute and are constituted by the phenomenological world. Or to put this idea into another contemporary context, the organism is viewed as a self-organizing system, an open system operating far from equilibrium (Overton, 1994a).

4   Understanding developmental change

With this base as a narrative platform for understanding, how then is developmental change understood? What are the processes of change, the mechanism of change? Let me here repeat a warning from my earlier bullet list. The traditional narrative is that developmental change is something that must be caused, and thus the search in the traditional narrative is focused on either those biological elements or those social elements or the combination of both elements that are understood as causing change to occur. From the relational-developmental perspective, however, there are no independent elements that cause change, and from this perspective there is no separation of energy (activity) and structure (organization). From the relational-developmental perspective change occurs through the organized action that defines the organism qua organism.

4.1   Action as change mechanism

But to say that change occurs through the mechanism of action is, at best, a first approximation to a process understanding of development. How does one charac-terize this action? Frankly I can think of no better way of making such a characteri-zation than in terms of Piaget's (e.g., 1952, 1954, 1985) familiar notions of the activity of assimilation/accommodation. However, it is critical here that assimilation/accommodation be specifically understood as a dialectical cycle and specifically not understood as independent processes (see Figures 2 and 3).

increased organized complexity

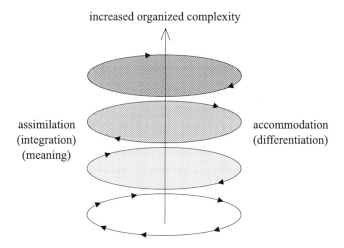

assimilation
(integration)
(meaning)

accommodation
(differentiation)

Figure 3: Dialectical activity cycles of change: Assimilation and accommodation

Assimilation is the primary phase of the activity cycle that necessarily involves accommodation. Assimilation is primary because the perspective presented in this chapter is a theory of the psychological subject rather than a theory of the social or biological world. Assimilation from a perspective of the psychological subject is the action of expressing the fundamental psychological organization that is attributed to the organism. In that assimilation, at any given time, is an expression of the current state or organization of the organism, it is conservative in nature. As an expression of the current state of organization, assimilation is an act of integration, it defines continuity. Assimilation projects the current structure of the organism outward. Assimilation projects meaning. Assimilation is the affirmation of the system. Assimilation imposes necessity. But all assimilation encounters resistance, and in encountering resistance new possibilities are opened. By resistance, I here mean that the assimilation is never completely successful. If this activity were to simply run itself out, it would be the purest of play, without constraint. Assimilation bumps into what from the sociocultural point of view one would call a "world" of other people, other objects and this bumping statically defines constraint, but dynamically it defines the activity of modifying the organization to accommodate the partial failure. This phase of the activity cycle is accommodation. Accommodation is the action of change that occurs in the context of continuity or stability. It is the act of differentiation that occurs in the context of integration, and it returns the organism to a novel integration. Figure 3 illustrates the cycle of assimilation and accommodation, but an accurate appreciation of the process involved entails thinking of the circle as an open cycle that never returns to its starting point and thus leads progressively to novel organizations, as suggested by Figure 4.

Figure 4: Dialectical activity cycles of change: A direction emerges

4.2   The self-organized activity matrix

So, as a theory of psychological development, the relational-developmental narrative proposes that the functioning of the self-organized activity matrix called the human organism be characterized as action cycles of systems that differentiate, integrate, and, thus, develope (transforms themselves through cycles of variational activity) through the resistances the action encounters. This resistance can be thought of as bumping up against what would be generally defined and described from a biological or social perspective as the surrounding environment. Or the resistance can be thought of as a partial failure of complete expression of an underlying competence (i.e., activity organization).

Action – whether it be sensory, motoric, or representational – necessarily encounters resistance. As a consequence, the action cycles back to redefine and, thus, transform, the organization of the action. Success or affirmations of action (i.e., assimilation) are conservative and insure continuity of the cycle. Resistance or negations are progressive and ensure differentiation of the action, and hence, transformational change. Affirmations and negations, however, are complementary, not radically separate processes.

If the focus of inquiry were to move from a psychological theory about the psychological subject to the sociocultural perspective of the bio-socio-cultural activity matrix, the encountered resistance would be more specifically described as cultural and linguistic contexts. Thus, from this perspective questions may readily be raised and empirically addressed about the role of, for example, urban settings in providing contexts for both competencies and strategies. Relational-developmental theory is an embodiment theory that proposes that psychological change necessarily occurs through the partial successes or – which amounts to the same thing – partial failures of any organized action as this action functions in both a biological and a sociocultural context. This perspective stands in radical opposition to the idea presented in some contemporary information-processing analyses that suggest that change or learning occurs through either total failure or total success (e.g., Siegler & Munakata, 1993).

4.3 Dialectical cyclic action

Relational-developmental theory, like other theories of self-organizing systems, further asserts that the cyclic action that constitutes the mechanism of developmental is dialectical in character and, thus, directional and nonreversible. As already suggested, each cycle of action is not a closed circle that returns to its precise point of departure. Instead, each cycle opens new possibilities, so each resistance that is overcome, or each partial failure, moves the system forward toward greater complexity. In this regard development cycles forward as an Arrow of Time (see Figure 4; see Overton, 1994a).

Complexity in this narrative of the Arrow of Time is understood as increased differentiation, integration, and flexibility of the system under examination and not simply an additive acquisition of elements. *Development*, here, ultimately becomes explained by some general principle of pattern that captures the dialectical progression of the system's activity and not by split-off causes. For example, Heinz Werner's orthogenetic principle is such an explanation. This pattern principle of explanation (see Overton, 1991b) asserts the rule that the development of all systems begins from an initial state of relative globality and relative (never absolute) lack of differentiation and proceeds through activity to increasingly complex states of articulation, differentiation, and hierarchic integration. Piaget's equilibration process is virtually an identical pattern explanation but it adds greater specificity to Werner's principle by identifying the functional processes involved. The equilibration principle asserts the rule that organisms as psychological systems cycle according to the active process of adaptation (i.e., assimilation/accommodation) toward increasingly complex dynamic states of equilibrium, where *equilibrium* is defined as a dynamic balance between assimilation and accommodation, and *complex states* are defined in terms of both the cognitive territory covered and the flexibility and mobility of the underlying cognitive organization. In passing, I also note that Erikson's epigenetic principle is another such pattern explanation of developmental relational change. In all of these cases, causes do not explain the principle. The principle becomes the context within which causes may be identified as parts of the relational whole (see Overton 1991b, c).

5   General principles of pattern explanation

5.1   Examples of the pattern explanation of development

Because this idea of the pattern explanation of development is quite abstract, a couple of concrete examples are needed for illustrative clarity. The first example, the development of attachment, is drawn from the social-affective arena. The second example, the development of logical reasoning, is from the cognitive arena. As an introductory note, it is important to understand that what is being explained in each case is the developmental trajectory or developmental function of some cognitive/affective system rather than the individual differences that may occur in that system. Individual differences are variations that cycle around an imaginary point. As these variations cycle, they form the arrow of a developmental trajectory (see Figure 4). The trajectory is *explained* by pattern explanation; the rate at which the arrow accelerates (i.e., rate of development in any arena) or the specific individual variation from the trajectory (i.e., individual differences) may be explained according to biological or social change agents. If this position were articulated in methodological terms, the developmental trajectory would be indexed by mean levels of a variable across a temporal series, and individual differences would be the correlations among individuals at each mean level.

5.2   The development of attachment

Consider Bowlby's description of the formation of that strong psychological social affective bond between infant and primary caregiver that we psychologists call attachment. Attachment behaviors (e.g., turning toward, turning away, crying) are considered the outer manifestation of an underlying attachment system that moves in a trajectory across four phases. These phases describe a universal developmental function that begins with (1) The Initial Preattachment Phase, which is characterized by "orientation and signals without discrimination of figure." Following this first phase, development moves to (2) The Phase of Attachment-in-the-Making, beginning around 8 to 12 weeks of age and characterized by "orientation and signals directed towards one (or more) discriminated figure(s)." Next is (3) the Phase of Clear-cut Attachment, usually beginning after 6 months of age, is characterized by the "maintenance of proximity to a discriminated figure by means of locomotion as well as signals." Thereafter comes (4) the Phase of a Goal-Corrected Partnership, beginning in the second or third year, which is characterized by emerging representational models of the caregivers. Finally, there may be a fifth phase of attachment that begins in the late adolescent years characterized by reflective transformations of the representational models.

In searching for an explanation for this trajectory one might take a split position and think of infant and caregiver as two isolated and independent entities. If this perspective were adopted, one would look for the causal factors that come to glue these two individuals together. The questions raised then would be something like: To what extent do fundamental biological factors and to what extent does direct social instruction determine the attachment trajectory? On the other hand, from a relational-developmental perspective there is initially no psychological infant and no psychological caregiver; there is only the infant/caregiver activity matrix. Hence, from the beginning, the fundamental problem is how the psychological emerges out of the nonpsychological; how two (infant and caregiver) can emerge out of one (infant/caregiver); how the newly emerged two can reintegrate at this novel (psychological) level; and how further transformations in the system take place. The general solution to this problem is given by the Wernerian/Piagetian pattern rules. At birth there is no psychological subject. What from an external point of view is called "the infant" is from a psychological point of view an organization of sensori-motor actions. Initially, (Phase 1) there is little differentiation in the activity matrix that will ultimately become the psychological self (infant) and other (mother). The initial bond – that from a social perspective called the mother-infant bond – is an action bond, not a psychological bond. The infant may behaviorally orient to signals but these are not the symbols that reference an independent person or psychological other. A "figure" means that the child has differentiated a – however primitive – "me" from a "not me", and that this level of differentiation has not yet been attained in Phase 1 of the attachment trajectory. As the child's activities are satisfied (assimilation, integration) and encounter resistances (accommodation, differentiation), the *psychological* subject differentiates from the activity matrix, a change that entails the further differentiation of the psychological subject into self and other (see Figure 2). Here, the organism has constructed a primitive psychological sense of "me" and "not me." Thus, the infant has constructed a figure, a psychological object (Phase 2). With progress to a fully differentiated, but instrumental (not representational) sense of self and other (marked cognitively by Piaget's "concept of the permanent object"), signals move to a psychological plane and become clearly identified with the constructed figure. As this degree of differentiation is attained, reintegration of the two, now psychologically separate, individuals defines the continuing dialectical process. The reintegration is articulated by the traditional attachment behaviors (e.g., separation protest, locomotion toward the caregiver, reuniting behaviors) of Phase 3. As the trajectory continues, the psychological subject – as an open self-organizing system – attains a sufficient level of complexity that results in a structural reorganization, and consequent novel systemic properties come to characterize its activity. Chief among these characteristics is representation, and at this point there begins a novel style of attachment organization along with its attendant behaviors (Phase 4). Finally, in adolescence a further structural reorganization takes place, and a level of complexity is attained that is characterized by the capacity to reflect upon and, hence, transform earlier representations.

While this pattern account is sufficient to explain the universal attachment developmental trajectory, it is not sufficient to explain the individual differences that occur at each point in this trajectory. These differences, which represent variations around a point in the trajectory – identified as the categories of the Type A (Anxious/Avoidant), Type B (Secure), and Type C (Anxious/Resistant) infants – require a specific accounting in terms of the covariation of observed biological and sociocultural factors. In this context it is possible to conceive, for example, of temperament as a biological-context-setting variable and the responsiveness and availability of the mother as a sociocultural-context-setting variable. Obviously, the latter have particular relevance for the child living in the city, where group childcare is often an important feature of child-rearing practices. Thus, pattern explanations on the one hand, and what are traditionally referred to as "causal" and correlational explanations on the other hand, articulate yet another bipolar dimension that is needed in any relatively complete relational-developmental theory.

5.3   The development of logical reasoning

A second example of the use of pattern explanation pertains to the domain of logical reasoning. Here, the traditional split position designed to explain progression toward an adult level of reasoning competence revolves around the question of whether logical reasoning processes are *either* biologically determined *or* socially determined, *or* the result of some additive combination of the two causal factors (see Overton, 1990). From a relational-developmental perspective, on the other hand, logic emerges out of differentiations in the original activity matrix according to the Wernarian/Piagetian pattern rules. Logic refers to a coherence of action or a coherence of argument. With the emergence from the initial activity matrix of the psychological subject and the differentiation of a primitive sense of "me" and "not me," the fundamental contextual form for a logical system is attained. There are three fundamental rules or laws of Aristotelian logic (the law of identity: $A = A$; the law of contradiction: not $[A = not A]$; and the law of excluded middle: A must be either A or not A), and each of these is an extension of the instrumental sense of "me" (A) and "not me" (not A). Thus, in infancy, the child comes to attain a logic, but it is a psychological logic of action, an instrumental logic.

Reasoning involves thought and thus requires symbols. But the symbolic capacity or representational level is an emergent level of complexity that differentiates out of the instrumental. With the attainment of this differentiation, the earlier instrumental logic becomes transformed (across a lengthy series of assimilation/accommodation cycles) into a representational logical reasoning competence. Further differentiation and reintegration ultimately advances the system to the level of organized complexity at which the representational logic becomes transformed into the reflective logical reasoning competence characteristic of hypothetical deductive reasoning or formal reasoning (see Overton, 1990).

As with the attachment example, this pattern account is sufficient to explain the universal developmental trajectory toward adult competence in the domain of logical reasoning. It is not, however, sufficient to explain individual differences in rate of attainment or individual differences in the access to and expression of this competence. As with attachment, these questions, in turn, require a specific accounting in terms of the covariation of observed biological and sociocultural factors. For example, it might well be the case that there is a greater demand to express a reflective deductive understanding in certain urban settings (e.g., in Overton, 1990, there is the illustration of highly technical skills that require deductive reasoning moving from a general principle to specific disconfirming instances). Thus, an empirical prediction can be made that performance on tasks assessing *preference* for deductive vs. inductive solutions would yield higher deductive scores for urban than for other children. On the other hand, for tasks that preclude preferences and tap only deductive competence, predictions concerning differential performance among urban and other children would not be made.

6   Role and function of social change agents or interpersonal relations

6.1   A constructivist perspective

Before continuing with a few other points concerning the development of various intrapsychic processes, I want to move briefly from a primary focus on the psychological subject and say something about the complementary focus on interpersonal functioning. More specifically, I want to say something about the role and function of social change agents or interpersonal relations in this relational-developmental narrative. In other words, I want to say something about the more specific role of sociocultural factors that I have mentioned in the last two examples.

First, it should be quite clear that the perspective being offered is a constructivist perspective. That is, given that the theory is about (i.e., is from the point of) the psychological subject, the organism constructs the world it knows, as it constructs itself as known, through its embodied action (sensory activity, motor activity, instrumental activity, representational activity, linguistic activity, reflective activity). But once this is said, the question that tends to jump to the lips of those who take a split "either/or" position concerning development is, "is this a biological constructivism or is it a social constructivism?" That is, is it the case that biology first produces the organism that then constructs its known world, or is it the sociocultural that first produces the organism that then constructs its world? The answer is that it is neither because each of these approaches leads back to the split between nature and nurture. According to the relational position, this split is disavowed, and the terms *biological* and *social*, like *subject* and *object* enter understanding as bipolar, contrastive terms (see Figure 2). Each defines the other, and at the ontological level the splits that would make them independent elements that could cause the individual to construct anything is rejected.

6.2   Facing a paradox

Aside, however, from the false issue concerning type of constructivism, there still remains the meaningful question of the relation between individual organism and other organisms. To understand this relation, however, we must face a paradox (i.e., a case of self-reference and contradiction). This paradox is one that delighted Donald Winnicott and in a sense formed the basis for his system of understanding both normal and pathological development (see Overton & Horowitz, 1991). For Winnicott (1971), the paradox that he asked us to appreciate and not to try to resolve too quickly was the following: "The baby creates the object, but the object was there waiting to be created" (p. 89). Or, to put this paradox in terms of change agents or significant others: "The child constructs the mother, parent, friend, therapist, or whomever, but the mother and so on is waiting there to be constructed." This paradox is illustrated in Figure 5 in general terms as creating the world in the face of a preexisting world.

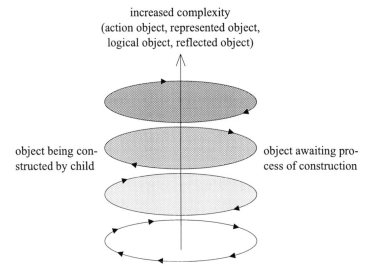

Figure 5: *Dialectical activity cycles of change: The relational paradox*

The paradox, in whatever specific form, has several important implications. First, consider that this is a paradoxical statement. To claim that the child constructs the world contradicts the notion that there is a preexisting world, as a claim to a preexisting world contradicts the claim that the child constructs the world. Further, the claims are circular, self-referencing claims. This would become even clearer if the paradox were phrased to read "The child constructs the world and the world constructs the child." Here the terms bend back upon themselves. How, then, is one to resolve this seemingly vicious circularity?

Winnicott suggests, there should not be an attempt to resolve the paradox at the level of the paradox itself, for resolution at this level could only involve splitting the relation and then trying to determine which side of the equation is cause and which is effect. Thus, at the ontological level of discourse the split would be to suggest that it is *either* the case that biology creates the psychological person who creates the culture *or* that culture creates the person who creates biology, and this split is, of course, again simply another variation of the nature/nurture split itself. Similarly, to claim that either the intrapsychic leads to the interpersonal or the interpersonal leads to the intrapsychic is an attempt to provide a split solution to the same paradox.

6.3 Resolution of the paradox

Successful resolution entails preserving the relational nature of the paradox by moving to another level of understanding. Thus, in this case, by moving above the paradox to the epistemological level of discourse (see Figures 1 and 5), one finds that the child constructing the world or constructing mother is one *knowledge perspective* (within which resides the earlier discussion of the development of the psychological subject). The mother waiting to be constructed, on the other hand, is another knowledge perspective.

Each of these interrelated knowledge perspectives contributes to the whole (which, in the present context, is intrapsychic and interpersonal development). However, each provides a unique point of view. The knowledge perspective of the preexisting world (which can, of course, be thought of as changing – i.e., the mother waiting to be constructed) articulates various attitudes, orientations, and techniques of the mother (or primary caregiver or culture) that will facilitate the child's construction of the mother and, indeed, of the world. In other words, the actual mother, educator, or therapist's primary task is to provide contexts for a constructive process (actually within this narrative, a co-constructive process) that maximizes growth opportunities. Or to say this another way, the change agent's fundamental task is to provide what Winnicott termed a "facilitating environment."

It should be clear that this facilitating environment is not designed to shape the child. The notion that the caregiver, educator, or therapist is somehow like a potter ready to shape the organism belongs to the narrative of the split cause/effect model.

In the present relational model when the focus is on the individual's psychological development, caregiver, educator, or therapist must operate to facilitate the organism's self-initiated development. At the beginning of each of several epochs in this process, the most immediate task for the change agent is to avoid splits or ruptures in the relational matrix. This is accomplished by creating a holding environment characterized by availability, responsivity, and empathetic attunement. It is then, within this holding environment, or what Winnicott called the "playground," that the change agent gradually allows the developing organism to experience the resistances that are fundamental to the developmental processes.

7   Additions to a psychological theory of individual development

While there is, of course, much more to say about the specific role of change agents and interpersonal functioning in this relational-developmental narrative, I now return to the focus on the psychological theory of individual development in order to make a few additional points.

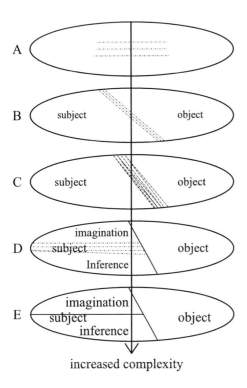

Figure 6: Dialectical activity cycles of change: The differentiation of mind

As the arrow of relational development cycles forward (Figure 4), new patterns that exhibit novel, emergent systemic properties are differentiated and coordinated. Two basic and simultaneous ontogenetic differentiations of mind that have already been alluded to in the examples require further detail in even this schematic description (see Figure 6).

These differentiations consist of the differentiation of the initial psychological matrix into (a) subject and object poles of consciousness and (b) divisions of the subject pole itself into *modalities* of subjective experience.

7.1 Subject and object poles of consciousness

This narrative stance, on the basis of which it is proposed that mind (where mind is understood to be a web of cognitive/affective understanding [expressive feature] and the instruments that serve to access and apply this understanding [instrumental feature]) initially differentiates into a subject and an object pole, in part reflects the narrative's deep commitment to a radical constructivist or interpretationist stance. The development of mind is not understood as the acquisition of representations from a detached world, nor from an isolated biology (see Taylor, 1995). The mind is not a camera, and the brain is not photographic film. Representations entail the re-presentation of action at whatever level this re-presentation is codified – from sensorimotor images to consciously reflective abstract linguistic categories. Similarly, the traditional categories, which from an objective side of the subject-object relation are understood as defining "reality" – space, time, number, causality, and object itself – are, from the subject side of the relation, as already stated several times, the directional developmental outcomes of the dialectical cycles of activity.

With the differentiation of the psychological activity matrix into subject and object poles of consciousness, there simultaneously occurs a differentiation of the subject pole into modes or spheres of experience. The principle initial differentiation is the prototype of what will be called the sphere of the *imagination* and the sphere of *inquiry or inference* with respect to the adult mind. These modes of experience have also been contrasted as the relational spheres of the aesthetic and the theoretic, the intuitive and the analytic. When they have been applied to the interpretation of early forms of ontogenetic differentiation, they have been primarily described by psychoanalytically oriented theorists and have been conceptualized as primary and secondary processes modes by Freud (1915/1957), paranoid-schizoid and depressive modes by Klein (1975), prototaxic-parataxic and syntaxic modes by Sullivan (1953), and object relations and object use modes by Winnicott (1965). Each initial bipolar term (primary process, paranoid-schizoid mode, prototaxic-parataxic, object relations) is conceptualized as the sphere of the nonlinear where action, affect, and impulse are minimally regulated, consciousness is unmediated, categories have permeable boundaries and flow, and a dialectical logic prevails. The latter terms of each pair (secondary process, depressive mode, syntaxic mode, object use) constitutes the sphere of lineary regulated understanding constituted by the rules of inductive and deductive logics.

7.2 Modalities of subjective experience

Further differentiations of mind occur along both a vertical and a horizontal axis of the whole activity matrix. Of particular importance for this embodied relational-developmental perspective are differentiations in the subject pole itself (see Figure 7). Here differentiations along what can be called the vertical axis or the temporal axis define emergent developmental levels, from a level of consciousness (or instrumental knowing), to self-consciousness (or representational-linguistic knowing), to reflective self-consciousness (reflective knowing). Differentiation along the horizontal or synchronic axis further articulates and coordinates the imagination and the inference as they are constrained by novel levels of consciousness. Thus, the imagination and the inference entail different qualities as they operate at the instrumental level of consciousness than they operate at the representational level or at the self-reflective level.

Further, the subjective pole itself differentiates according to a core-peripheral dimension. The core represents the individual's imaginative/inferential understanding or character, and the periphery represents the strategies, procedures, defenses, and other instrumentalities that access, express, and disguise the central core. If, for instance, an object relations theory of personality development were being discussed, the core might be termed the "true self," or "central self," and the periphery might be called the "false self" to follow Winnicott's example (see Overton & Horowitz, 1991). If the development of attachment were being discussed further, the core might be called the "attachment behavioral system"; the periphery, "working models of attachment" (see Overton, 1991b). Or, if the development of logical reasoning were the topic of further discussion the inferential core might be called logical "competence," and the periphery might be called "procedures" for accessing that competence (see Overton, 1990).

A relational-developmental theory of optimal adult functioning in any specific domain, or for the person as a whole, would require the flexible interplay of each sphere of experience as well as differentiated and coordinated subspheres (e.g., the inductive as contrasted with the deductive subsphere of the analytic) forming a core competence and operating in relation to a set of instrumental procedures. However, in composing a detailed theory of any phenomenological domain such as a detailed theory of cognitive development or a detailed theory of a less inclusive cognitive domain such as formal deductive thought, some spheres would for analytic epistemological purposes necessarily be less accented.

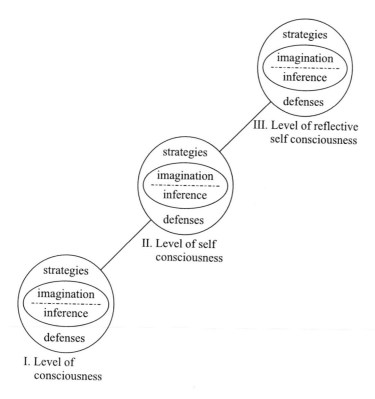

Figure 7: Dialectical activity cycles of change: The emerging person

8   Conclusion

In conclusion, in this essay I have presented in broad outlines a relational-developmental narrative of the development of the psychological individual. This narrative represents an inclusive alternative to traditional split narratives. In split narratives some feature of developmental interest (the biological, the psychological, the cultural) is elevated to a privileged ontological position, and other features of the whole are excluded as mere appearances or minor players in the developmental drama. The inclusive relational narrative asserts that there are no minor players, there are only alternative figure-ground relations. The specific story told in this essay is about the development of the individual psychological subject, and as a consequence it is the psychological that is the figure against a broad activity ground that differentiates into the spheres of biological ground and sociocultural ground. Within this context there is no conflict between the intrapsychic, and the interpersonal and traditional change agents (biological, social, cultural) offer opportunities, for better or worse, to the organizing activity of the individual agent.

References

Freud, S. (1957). Instincts and their vicissitudes. In J. Strachey (Ed. and Trans.), *The standard edition of the complete psychological works of Sigmund Freud* (Vol. 14, pp. 111-140). London: Hogarth. (Original work published 1915)

Klein, M. (1975). *Envy and gratitude and other works.* London: Hogarth.

Overton, W. F. (1984). World views and their influence on psychological theory and research: Kuhn-Lakatos-Laudan. In H. W. Reese (Ed.), *Advances in child development and behavior* (Vol. 18, pp. 191-226). New York: Academic Press.

Overton, W. F. (1990). Competence and procedures: Constraints on the development of logical reasoning. In W. F. Overton (Ed.), *Reasoning, necessity, and logic: Developmental perspectives* (pp. 1-32). Hillsdale, NJ: Erlbaum.

Overton, W. F. (1991a). Historical and contemporary perspectives on developmental theory and research strategies. In R. Downs, L. Liben, & D. Palermo (Eds.), *Visions of aesthetics, the environment, and development: The legacy of Joachim Wohlwill* (pp. 263-311). Hillsdale, NJ: Erlbaum.

Overton, W. F. (1991b). The structure of developmental theory. In H. W. Reese (Ed.), *Advances in child development and behavior* (Vol. 23, pp. 1-37). New York: Academic Press.

Overton, W. F. (1991c). Metaphor, recursive systems, and paradox in science and developmental theory. In H. W. Reese (Ed.), *Advances in child development and behavior* (Vol. 23, pp. 59-71). New York: Academic Press.

Overton, W. F. (1994a). The arrow of time and cycles of time: Concepts of change, cognition, and embodiment. *Psychological Inquiry, 5,* 215-237.

Overton, W. F. (1994b). Interpretationism, pragmatism, realism, and other ideologies. *Psychological Inquiry, 5,* 260-271.

Overton, W. F. (1994c). Contexts of meaning: The computational and the embodied mind. In W. F. Overton & D. S. Palermo (Eds.), *The nature and ontogenesis of meaning* (pp. 1-18). Hillsdale, NJ: Erlbaum.

Overton, W. F. (1998). Developmental psychology: Philosophy, concepts, methodology. In W. Damon (Chief Ed.) & R. M. Lerner (Vol. Ed.), *Handbook of child psychology. Volume 1: Theoretical models of human development* (5th ed., pp. 107-188). New York: Wiley.

Overton, W. F., & Horowitz, H. (1991). Developmental psychopathology: Differentiations and integrations. In D. Cicchetti & S. Toth (Eds.), *Rochester symposium on developmental psychopathology* (Vol. 3, pp. 1-41). Rochester, NY: University of Rochester Press.

Piaget, J. (1952). *The origins of intelligence in children* (M. Cook, Trans.). New York: W.W. Norton. (Original French edition published 1936)

Piaget, J. (1954). *The construction of reality in the child* (M. Cook, Trans.). New York: Basic Books. (Original French edition published 1937)

Piaget, J. (1985). *The equilibration of cognitive structures* (T. Brown & K. J. Thampy, Trans.). Chicago: The University of Chicago Press. (Original French edition published 1975)

Siegler, R. S., & Munakata, Y. (1993, winter). Beyond the immaculate transition: Advances in the understanding of change. *SRCD Newsletter,* pp. 3-13.

Sullivan, H. S. (1953). *The interpersonal theory of psychiatry.* New York: W. W. Norton.

Taylor, C. (1991). The dialogical self. In D. R. Hiley, J. F. Bohman, & R. Shusterman (Eds.), *The interpretative turn: Philosophy, science, culture* (pp. 304-314). Ithaca, NY: Cornell University Press.

Taylor, C. (1995). *Philosophical arguments.* Cambridge, MA: Harvard University Press.

Van der Veer, R., & Valsiner, J. (1994). Reading Vygotsky: From fascination to construction. In R. Van der Veer & J. Valsiner (Eds.), *The Vygotsky reader* (pp. 1-7). Cambridge, MA: Blackwell.

Winnicott, D. W. (1965). *The maturational process and the facilitating environment*. New York: International Universities Press.

Winnicott, D. W. (1971). *Playing and reality*. New York: Basic Books.

Comment: From the general to the individual or from the individual to the general?

Werner Deutsch

Textbooks on developmental psychology usually commence with the sentence "Development is ..." No science without definitions; without definitions, no science. Commentaries, however, may start differently – with a painting, for example (see Figure 1). The one I have in mind was painted in the middle of the 17th century in the Dutch city of Haarlem and can be found today in the Museum Haus Koekkoek, Kleve (de Werd, 1974). It is not clear who executed the painting. Initially, it was attributed to Pieter Jansz Post, who was employed by the governor, Johann Moritz von Nassau-Siegen, but this attribution did not catch on. This work, an oil on canvas, has a motif that at that time was rarely ever seen in paintings but quite often seen in print.

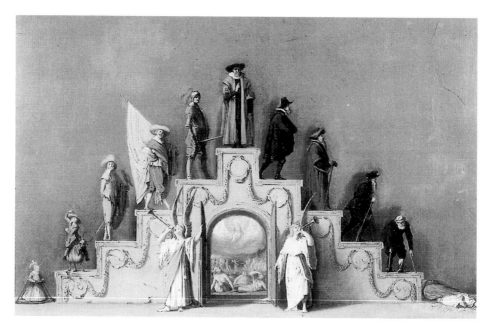

Figure 1: The Staircase of Life, *Museum Haus Koekkoek, Kleve (reprinted by permission)*

The staircase of life deals with developmental psychology at a time when such a discipline did not exist at universities. As with psychology in general, developmental psychology did not rise to scientific honors until the 19th century. What kind of image does the staircase of life convey about prescientific developmental psychology? Does it perhaps represent a naive theory of what development is or should be? The staircase of life is a model of the human life course organized into ten stages. Each stage consists of 10 years, resulting in a life span of 100 years. The first stage is reached at 10 years of age; the last stage ends with the ninth decade of life. The center and climax of the symmetrically composed staircase is the fifth decade of life. At each stage of the staircase of life, there is a male individual depicted at different elevations and in different postures and clothing, depending on his age. As long as the staircase ascends, the colorfully attired person is turned toward the viewer. As the staircase descends, the figure's gaze diverts from the viewer, and somber tones dominate. At the end of the staircase lies a corpse veiled in white garments and lying on straw. Does the human being's life course end in this manner? In the foreground two angels, who are sounding trumpets, have opened a huge arched gate beneath the apex of the staircase, allowing the viewer a glimpse of the Last Judgment, the moment at which it is decided what the future will look like.

When this staircase of life was painted and many others were circulating as prints, the life course did not take place as depicted in them. Child mortality was high, average life expectancy was low, and upper positions in society were reserved for a few male individuals. In other words, the staircase of life does not depict facts. Rather, it expresses the ideal of a completely fulfilled life course, which, according to the facts, was (and still is) the absolute exception. At the same time, the staircase of life conveys a warning. The life course has two parts: one in the here and now, the other in the hereafter. At the Last Judgment people must account for their deeds in the here and now. One is well advised to be oriented to the hereafter while still in the here and now.

Like the wheel of life, the staircase of life is a prescientific model, a naive theory, of the changes that occur in human ontogenesis. To what extent did modern, scientifically oriented developmental psychology break from its past? This past reappears, albeit in abbreviated form, whenever the description and explanation of age differences is made the center of developmental research. As Karmiloff-Smith (1981) stated, these attempts often lead to statistically significant differences, which, however, are insignificant from the perspective of developmental theory. It is still rare to find extensive documentation that captures commonalities and differences of individual developmental courses in periods of life that are relevant for development processes. Such documentation requires a high personal input and seldom receives the recognition it deserves.

Willis F. Overton presents the foundation of an ontogenetic developmental theory that is anything but naive. He does not endorse a normative developmental theory for defining stages in terms of age. Neither is he interested in making a name by listing many statistically significant differences between different age groups. Overton does theoretical developmental psychology by asking what kind of mechanisms trigger ontogenetic developmental processes and move them toward goal states. Overton does not start from scratch, and it is only fair to name the pioneers whose approaches he elaborates: Heinz Werner, Jean Piaget, Lev Vygotsky, and Donald Winnicott. His pioneers come from two directions. In one, the active constructive role the individual plays in his or her own development is emphasized. In the other direction, attention is drawn to the dialogical interaction between the developing individual and his or her developmental partners. For Overton, neither direction excludes the other. In his conception they belong together, although not in the sense that one direction is the stopgap for what is missing in the other. Overton claims that forces do not combine in additive, linear fashion in developmental processes but that development is pushed forward by polar forces creating tensions. From this theoretical perspective, it is clear why Overton rejects those developmental theories that included the either-or in their program.

Is Overton's approach still up-to-date? The big domain-general developmental theories such as Piaget's cognitive developmental theory are heavily criticized. In light of a growing number of domain-specific theories, does Overton try to protect developmental psychology from fragmentation into different thematic domains? Does he try to develop a unifying supertheory? Certainly not. The relational-developmental theory is a building based on postmodern architecture. Whereas the classics of developmental theory found their place in the interior, the postmodern Zeitgeist influences its external appearance. The building has many entrances. No single entrance is more important than any other. The entrances open changing perspectives on different – psychological (subject-oriented), biological, sociological – aspects of developmental processes. When one perspective is stressed, the others do not disappear; they constitute the ground upon which the chosen perspective is elaborated. The perspectives are not claimed to have a monopoly on truth. Instead, they are offered as possibilities for gaining and extending knowledge. Overton's impressive design does not stand alone in developmental psychology. It is striking how much Overton builds his postmodern conception on tradition and how little he discusses peers: Bischof, Bruner, Karmiloff-Smith, and Valsiner. These peers also try to solve important problems in developmental psychology. Let us hope that the peers will initiate a dialogue with Overton. And what better means are there for prompting a dialogue than contradiction?

In the hope of hitting a core problem and not just a marginal one, I limit myself to only one point of Overton's theoretical conception. For the psychological perspective of the theory, the human organism who becomes a psychological subject in the course of development plays an important role. What kind of subject is it? How does Overton understand that subject generically? It is not an individual subject but a general subject that, however, achieves this status only in and through its development. It is not enough to be a member of the human species to possess the status of psychological subject. Rather, Overton offers a detailed list of necessary qualifying criteria specific to development. The possibility of becoming a subject is universalized. This possibility does not depend only on the specific spatiotemporal conditions under which an organism grows up. In adopting a universalistic perspective on this and other core elements of human development, Overton follows pioneers of the past such as Piaget. The general precedes the particular, and the particular is understood as a deviation from the general, a deviation in need of an explanation. As Overton points out, the general occurs as a variation, say, in different types of human attachment that have been distinguished. Moreover, the types and distribution of interindividual variation in different cultures is by no means the same. Overton does not ignore the facts and does not start looking for variables to explain the emergence of this or that type of attachment. He obviously sees no reason to integrate individual traits (characteristics) and resulting individual differences into his general concept of ontogenetic development, which is directed toward universals. His theoretical proposal receives an extension (annex), in which Overton explains interindividual differences – here the independent variable X and there the dependent variable Y – that had been banned from the main building.

For my taste, Overton's theoretical proposal loses the bite it had at the outset of the chapter. Instead of postulating a universal organism or a universal subject, would it not be more appropriate to proceed from an individual organism or subject when dealing with ontogenesis? Early in this century, one person chose this route, William Stern. He did not care about the opinion, which has its origin with Aristotle, that $N = 1$ is unscientific and that inductive generalizations are taboo in science. Together with his wife, Clara, Stern documented the development of his three children, Hilde, Günther, and Eva (see Behrens & Deutsch, 1991; Stern & Stern, 1907, 1909). He suggested a similar approach to studying the person (theory of personality; see Deutsch & Hoppe-Graff, 1996; Lamiell, 1982).

Clara and William Stern did not stop at analyzing developmental processes – which were not a priori but only ex post organized into thematic domains – in small samples ($n = 1$ or $n = 3$). They watched for other valid data sets in order to assess the possibilities for and limits of generalizations. Of course, these generalizations could not capture a universal, developmental individual but only more or less numerous subclasses of individuals.

During the second year of life, for example, almost all children begin to designate themselves or other people linguistically. Children growing up in a German-speaking environment differ in terms of whether their first self-designation consists of a name or a pronoun. Clara and William Stern discovered that their firstborn (a daughter) first designated herself with a name, whereas her two younger siblings started designating themselves with a pronoun.

Ninety years later, this sibling effect, first discovered in case studies from just one family, has been replicated in large samples taken from different cultures and languages (e.g., Oshima-Takane, Goodz, & Derevensky, 1996; Wagner, Burchardt,

Deutsch, Jahn, & Nakath, 1996). Moreover, after having designated themselves at first with either a name or pronoun, most children, whether or not they have siblings, use both the nominal and pronominal forms of self-designation. The use of one or the other form depends on its function. Descriptions of states are connected with nominal forms; desired (or undesired) changes of state, with pronominal forms. This finding can, at least in language development, illustrate an important universal principle that William Stern called "convergence." Convergence is the interaction of inner dispositions and external conditions (nature-nurture). Children do not only imitate the language spoken in their environment, as a parrot does. Neither do they create a completely new language. Rather, conservative and innovative processes interact in such a way that children bypass developmental intermediary stages and reach goal states that remain stable over an extended period of time.

I have mentioned the developmental work of the Sterns for several reasons. It waits to be rediscovered. That rediscovery will be possible only when their major publications are accessible in English. Furthermore, there are both parallels and differences between the Sterns's work and Overton's conception of development. Both approaches progress beyond controversies (e.g., the nature-nurture debate) that were more harmful than useful to developmental psychology. Both approaches embrace a developmental optimism, stemming from the 19th century, by focusing mainly or even exclusively on mechanisms that initiate and advance development. Development, however, can also be connected with standstill, decrease, and regression, processes that are largely neglected by Overton and the Sterns. Finally, a reminder about the research methodology of the Sterns may help improve the solution to a basic problem of developmental psychology. The primacy of the general developing subject, acknowledged by Overton, entails priorities that will lead to empirical difficulties. Taking the Sterns seriously means rehabilitating the individual subject as the point of departure for research. And the point of departure does not mean endpoint when the boundaries between the individual and the general become fluid – for that fluidity will promote the understanding of the relation between nature and culture in the ontogenesis of human individuals.

Acknowledgement

I thank Ulrich Müller, Bill Overton's present collaborator and a previous student of mine, for his help in translating this commentary from German into English. Thanks also go to Guido de Werd, the director of the museum in Kleve, for his permission to reproduce the painting *The Staircase of Life*.

References

Behrens, H., & Deutsch, W. (1991). Die Tagebücher von Clara und William Stern [The diaries of Clara and William Stern]. In W. Deutsch (Ed.), *Über die verborgene Aktualität von William Stern* (pp. 19-37). Frankfurt on the Main: Lang.

Deutsch, W., & Hoppe-Graff, S. (1996). Eingrenzen, Begrenzen, Ausgrenzen: Anmerkungen zu Asendorpfs Neubestimmung der Persönlichkeitspsychologie [Delimiting, defining, and circumscribing: Comments on Asendorpf's redefinition of personality psychology]. *Psychologische Rundschau, 47,* 161-163.

Karmiloff-Smith, A. (1981). Getting developmental differences or studying child development? *Cognition, 10,* 151-158.

Lamiell, J. T. (1982). The case for an idiothetic psychology of personality: A conceptual and empirical foundation. In B. A. Maher and W. B. Maher (Eds.*), Progress in experimental personality research* (Vol. 11, pp. 1-64). New York: Academic Press.

Oshima-Takane, Y., Goodz, E., & Derevensky, J. L. (1996). Birth order effects on early language development: Do secondborn children learn from overheard speech? *Child Development, 67,* 621-634.

Stern, C., & Stern, W. (1907). *Die Kindersprache* [The speech of children, 1st edition; 4th edition]. Leipzig: Barth.

Stern, C., & Stern, W. (1909). *Erinnerung, Aussage und Lüge in der ersten Kindheit* [Remembrance, testimony and lies in early childhood]. Leipzig: Barth.

Wagner, A., Burchardt, R., Deutsch, W., Jahn, K., & Nakath, J. (1996). Der Geschwistereffekt in der Entwicklung der Personreferenz [The sibling effect in the development of personal reference]. *Sprache & Kognition, 15,* 3-22.

de Werd, G. (1974). *Städtisches Museum Haus Koekkoek Kleve. Katalog Gemälde, Zeichnungen, Skulpturen und Kunstgewerbe* [Municipal museum, Koekkoek Kleve House. Catalogue of paintings, drawings, sculptures, and industrial art]. Kleve: Boss.

Author's response: General and individual – A relation

Willis F. Overton

Werner Deutsch's commentary delights me both in its thoughfulness and in the fact that he focuses exactly on a core point that advances the dialogue. Before I address this core point, let me agree with Deutsch that I did, indeed, slight many peers in not discussing their work in relation to my proposal. In defense, yet trying not to sound defensive, I must state that the editors of the book imposed significant page restrictions, and it was impossible to go into many facets of the proposal at the depth I would have liked. I believe that my chapter in the 5th Edition of the *Handbook of Child Psychology* (Overton, 1998) corrects this problem. I would ask the interested reader to look there for a much more complete elaboration of a number of the features of the present chapter, including the referencing of peers.

The core point for dialogue is Deutsch's concern that my focus on the universal stands in opposition or contradiction to the individual. For Deutsch, my focus on the general subject precludes or limits the individual organism, the individual subject. Deutsch suggests that "instead" of my focus it would be "more appropriate" to "proceed from an individual organism" (p. 339). For me, the problem here is that in making this "instead of" proposal Deutsch falls back into a split discourse. It is *either* my universal *or* his particular that constitutes the correct, or best, way to proceed. But this is exactly the either-or stance that I have tried to argue is unnecessary and unproductive.

My relational proposal is that universal and individual define and are defined by each other. In my chapter, I did indeed take a universalistic *perspective*, but this is a "point of view" or "line of sight," and its complement is the individualistic perspective. The two are like Escher's famous drawing entitled *Drawing Hands,* where two hands draw, and are being drawn by, each other. The two hands represent, in Hegel's terms, "an identity of opposites." Piaget did not suggest, nor have I suggested, that "the general precedes the particular, [that] the particular is understood as a deviation from the general, a deviation in need of an explanation" (p. 339). Such a statement would be an anathema to Piaget's work and to mine. General and particular are complementary and alternative moments of knowing, not split-off adversaries in a debate.

On turning to the individual line of sight, I would certainly agree with Deutsch that William Stern's personalistic psychology is both underappreciated and highly significant as a source of specific ideas and methods. It is a complement to the broad principles that I articulated in my chapter. However, Stern himself did not cast the general-specific issue into an either-or frame. One need only read Stern's (1938) *General Psychology*, especially Chapter 4 on foundations, to realize that his own individual subject was contextualized by broad principles, just as the broad principles were contextualized by his appreciation of the individual subject. I suspect that Stern himself might not agree when Deutsch suggests that the particular split off from the universal constitutes an absolute "point of departure for research" (p. 340).

Reference

Stern, W. (1938). *General psychology: From the personalistic standpoint.* New York: The Macmillan Company.

Integration: Dimensions of a conceptual space – But for what?

Hellgard Rauh

It is an ambitious task to write a synopsis of the three theoretical positions presented by Overton, Wapner, Oerter, and their commentators. I do not discuss the theories in their epistemological status as theories; some of the commentators have already done so. Instead, I reflect on these positions, as I have understood them, in terms of

1. how the respective authors conceptualize urban environment for a developing child,
2. how they conceptualize the developing child in an urban environment,
3. how they explicate the concept of development with respect to children in urban environments, and
4. what suggestions they could offer to people of other disciplines, such as city planners, architects, or politicians.

The first three questions are interrelated; they focus on the three dimensions of the conceptual space fundamental to all contributions in this volume. The last question emphasizes the instrumental relevance of each position for practical issues. In the following pages, I try to highlight both the commonalities and the differences of all three positions with respect to these issues.

1 Figure-ground phenomena

Overton's focus is the researcher and the child. In his theory, both "relate" to the world that consists of persons, objects, and symbols, and both take points of view.

There is, first, the adult researcher. He or she can take a biological, psychological, or social perspective when looking at children and their worlds. Alternatively, the researcher could take a sociopolitical or aesthetic perspective, that is, the perspective of a city planner or an architect. In each role, he or she would see something different, even when looking at the "same" world. Overton describes this aspect-based relating as a figure-ground phenomenon.

The relations that human beings have to the "world-out-there" are multifaceted and have undergone evolutionary and ontogenetic changes. For the fly or the wood tick (examples from von Üxküll), perspectives are instinctive and very simple. Only light and some contour or a particular smell are highlighted, whereas all other aspects of the world-out-there are nondifferentiated background. Humans are, of course, biologically much more complex, and their relations change dramatically with ontogeny, primarily because of development (especially cognitive development), socialization, and specialized learning.

Human beings not only relate to the world, they also construct or reconstruct their perspectives of the world mentally. This reconstruction process also undergoes developmental changes. Accordingly, reconstructions can occur or can be achieved at different levels of abstraction. Furthermore, the same person can take several different perspectives on the same phenomenon and can switch between them (for instance, from a social to a psychological perspective). In this case, one point of view becomes the figure, the other(s) return(s) to the background. With development, several aspects can obtain simultaneously and can be coordinated within a single more general perspective, thus constituting a dynamic system, as Overton says.

In this sense, the psychologist as a researcher can coordinate the biological, social, and psychological perspectives on a person (a child), or an interpersonal and an individual perspective. The open question is whether these three perspectives are sufficient for the psychological researcher to conceptualize the developing child in an urban setting, and, if not, which other aspects of the world-out-there should become developed and integrated.

The other focus in Overton's approach is the child as a subject and perspective-taker. Again, Overton as a researcher takes two perspectives: (a) How does the child develop an understanding of him- or herself as a person, as an active agent and one pole in the conceptual system, and how does he or she simultaneously construct the other dynamic pole, that of social or physical objects and of the world? (b) Which tools does the child use to relate to the world, and how do they develop? The tools are called *embodied activity* (sensory, motor, instrumental, representational, linguistic, and reflective activity).

Overton concentrates on the subjective pole of the child's mental constructions, and he describes its development as a transformation, first from consciousness to self-consciousness, and then to reflective self-consciousness. Subject and object become differentiated at ever more abstract levels. There has been more research on the subjective pole, and Overton alludes to it by mentioning theory-of-mind debates, that is, how children develop their concepts of their own psychological experiences and processes (such as feelings, motivation, and memory).

The child's constructions of the world remain largely unconceptualized in Overton's presentation. To illustrate how children construct and differentiate social objects as a result of their relating to persons, he refers to research on the mother as an attachment figure, and to illustrate how children construct and differentiate object characteristics in the physical world, he points to research on the conservation of liquid. Unfortunately, Overton cites no accounts of how children construct and differentiate the environs of their dwellings and how they conceptualize other areas of their urban world. This gap is partly filled by Kahn (1997), a report on how urban children of African-American background and how urban, as opposed to rural, children in Brazil appreciate and relate to plants, animals, and parks; how they feel about air and water pollution or garbage dirtying their urban landscape; and how they morally judge polluting behavior.

Overton describes the developmental course of the child's tools for relating to the world. He does so by differentiating two polar (dynamic) kinds of understanding or modes of experience: inferential understanding (or logic) and imaginative under-standing (a further explication of Piaget's figurative thinking). He also differentiates between (a) competencies that children feel (and that the researcher infers) as core characteristics of themselves as agents and (b) peripheral strategies, procedures, working models, and defenses that characterize children's relations particularly to the social world. Changes in the mental system of a child occur when his or her concepts or the instrumental psychomotor or mental activities encounter "resistance," presumably either by relating to the world-out-there or when trying to coordinate different perspectives (the child's own perspectives or interpersonal ones).

In Overton's account, the conceptual systems of the subject are conceived of as open systems – but open to what? How do they relate to the pre-existing world-out-there? Is there a developmental sequence or hierarchical order of basic aspects – such as social, physical, psychological, biological, or thematic (e.g., security and trust, initiative and achievement, peer relations and friendship) aspects – that a child will develop, differentiate, and integrate? Is there a limit to the number of aspects or perspectives that a child at a given age or developmental level can handle? Are there aspects characteristic for children of one gender or the other, for children living in today's industrialized (e.g., digital and electronic) world, or for children of particular cultures? How do children learn to switch and coordinate aspects? There has been research on children's coordination of interpersonal perspectives on such topics as friendship or moral decisions, but to my knowledge there has been none on the coordination of knowledge areas or other perspectives. How do children at different developmental levels coordinate the perspectives of the street as a thoroughfare and the street as an adventure ground for children? As Deutsch proposed, research could start from descriptions that individual children give of their perspectives. The next step would be to use inductive-deductive cycles to map (a) the aspects children construct of how they relate to their urban world and (b) the changes in these aspects as development continues. Some of these aspects could be safety or exploration, the latter of which could include seeking adventure and coping with danger, particularly for children beyond preschool age and into adolescence; meeting peers; and learning about adult living. Other aspects are conceivable as well. Do developmental changes in the subjective pole imply specific changes in conceptions that children have not only of their social worlds but also of their life spaces, urban space, and city dwellers with whom they do not interact directly?

If one were to follow Overton's theoretical approach strictly, it would be necessary for architects, city planners, politicians, traffic experts, economists, landscape gardeners, psychologists, and so on to try to coordinate their respective perspectives on urban settings and on children in these settings. It would be also necessary for them to try to coordinate their perspectives with the perspectives that children and adolescents apply (and vice versa). Is it easier for professionals, or for children and adolescents, to relate to the world-out-there via aspect-based conceptualizations already developed by fellow humans than via aspect-based conceptualizations developed by individual, original activity? How much direct experience would be necessary?

There is some fascination about Overton's approach. The world-out-there is obviously not physical, chemical, biological, social, or whatever. Humans actually cannot even know what it is, really, for they can only relate to the world through human potentialities and limitations and can develop only typically human aspects of it.

2   Processes of relating

Wapner's approach is in many respects similar to that of Overton, although episte-mologically it is less rigorously conceived. Whereas for Overton a "relation" is a mental perspective that a person has on some object, Wapner's concern is how children (or adults) enter into a psychological "relation" to their environment. He tries to venture into this *process* of relating. If only a short stretch of time is involved, this process is described as microgenesis; if it occurs over extended periods of a person's lifetime, it is known as ontogenesis.

The process can be prestructured into the future by the subject's plans. What develops is a meaning structure, the person-in-environment system, and the development of this structure follows Werner's orthogenetic principle from undiffer-entiated (he writes "de-differentiated") to differentiated, articulate, and integrated. The orthogenetic principle, therefore, is a normative measure of where a person stands developmentally (micro- or ontogenetically). Similarly, emotional states can signal the developmental position. As positive feelings, feelings of control are supposed to signal successful achievement.

According to Wapner, one can facilitate this process of relating in specific ways, such as by starting with an anchor point of orientation or by engaging in diverse exploratory activities, including reading or writing a poem about the location. Pursuing these various activities would, in Overton's conception, be equivalent to coordinating several perspectives on the same object. Wapner seems to differentiate not only orthogenetic states in the process of relating but also styles, calling them "modes of coping with conflict" (accommodation, disengagement, nonconstructive ventilation, and constructive assertion). In so doing, Wapner introduces individual differences into his conception.

As Görlitz has rightly pointed out, many theoretical features of Wapner's approach remain unclear. Where do these conflicts come from? What theoretical, epistemo- logical status does Wapner's concept of environment have? Sometimes, it seems to be the world-out-there; at other times, the person's conceptions. Does he describe several, perhaps even competing or conflicting, person-in-environment units within one personality, or is his approach the perspective of the researcher who conceives of several persons-in-complex-environments units?

Overton's approach and his theoretical vigor, I believe, can be nicely supple- mented by Wapner's process approach of examining how children psychologically conquer parts of the world around them, that is, how children give meaning to those parts and how children develop their identities by including those parts in their personal mental maps. For Wapner this process differs for children at different points in their ontogenesis (toddlers, young children, adolescents), and it differs across personalities. But how would the two authors integrate different mental levels of reality (e.g., fantasy play) into their respective theoretical models?

Both approaches, however, leave the real environment and its influence more or less untouched. When, in the process of relating, do children start molding their actual environment according to their own conceptions? Which features of the world-out-there are particularly amenable to the child or adolescent? Which features foster or block their creative activity? Is it important for the child's psychological well-being to pass through the full dimension of the orthogenetic principle (from de- differentiation to articulation), or should that genesis be foreshortened or acceler- ated? Is the final state that is described by the orthogenetic principle the thing that makes people happy, or does such happiness derive from the way in which the final state is achieved from the degree to which the individual's own activity was invested?

3   Transmitting culture

Another dimension of my synthetic model is added by Oerter: the culture. Culture is conceived of as a feature of all human environments, as that part of environment made by human beings. It includes material, mental, and psychological objects and their structures. Urban environment can certainly be well characterized as an expression of human culture. How is culture transmitted in an urban setting? Oerter refers in his theoretical model to Leont'ev and to the concepts of appropriation and reification via action. When trying to use or act upon cultural objects appropriately, the person indirectly interacts with the producer of those objects in his or her ideas, even if the producer is remote in either space or time.

There are many epistemological questions to this conception and to Oerter's model, some of which have been addressed in Lang's commentary. I would like to highlight the notion of *transaction* with regard to cultural transmission. For Oerter, transaction differs from interaction in that interaction is confined to social partners, whereas transaction is also possible with objects and includes a change of environment. For Lang, transaction additionally involves the generation of new structures and alters the conditions for further interaction. For both authors, then, producing something, changing something, becomes an important feature of persons in a human environment, and this propulsive activity is said to have major impact on a person's psychological well-being. Both Oerter and Lang, regret that children in urban settings have too few opportunities to influence their environment. Because objects of actions (environment in more general terms) are shared by many people, the adult members of a culture's population tend to regulate and restrict major alterations to the objective structure of their culture. (I hesitate, however, to follow Oerter's ideas and evaluations of positive or negative affordances in urban environments, the characterization of individuals who fail to adapt to the possibilities for cultural actions, and the necessity of regulatory institutions. These ideas could lead to dangerous consequences.)

If I read Leont'ev (1977) correctly, then *transaction* could mean something different but valuable for this discussion: How are aspects or perspectives (Overton), or meaning structures (Wapner), or cultural knowledge (Oerter) transmitted from generation to generation?

According to Leont'ev (1977) and, less directly, to Wapner, human beings can react as animals do in their *ambulance* or *habitat* (terms Wapner used) but also as persons in a sociocultural world. I can stumble on a staircase but can also experience it as the border between home and street or even use it as a bench and watch people strolling by. Oerter restricts his view solely to this sociocultural world.

If culture is not transmitted directly by personal interaction, it is, according to Leont'ev and Oerter, mediated by real or symbolic objects used either jointly in social interaction (as in early childhood) or in virtual interaction. Tools are cultural material objects that seem to express most clearly the ideas of their constructors and previous users. Language and cultural artistic products are other examples presented by Leont'ev. One could add architectural products (buildings), traffic systems, city landscapes, or parks as such cultural products. Transaction would be the transfer of a cultural idea from one mind to another, particularly a mind remote in time. Cultural knowledge is mediated (appropriated) through action with these cultural products. And because human beings are somewhat similar in their biopsychological make-up, it is highly probable that the newly appropriated idea is similar (though not necessarily identical) to the original idea.

I do not agree, however, that the interaction with objects devoid of their cultural contexts is sufficient for picking up the cultural ideas built into cultural objects. If the culture that produced the object is too strange for people, too remote from their thinking and feeling, the object will probably be treated in a manner quite different from the original use. On the other hand, the transmission of cultural features of the urban environment to the inhabitants (cultural memory formation, as Lang terms it), including children, can create deep feelings of belonging, a sense of feeling at home, as well as a feeling of responsibility. How can the cultural-historical dimension be added to the developing life spaces of urban children in such a way that those children can integrate this aspect into their developing personal identities?

The other side of the coin is more difficult: the impact of children and adolescents on urban settings. Conflicts can occur when settings or objects transformed or changed by children are already cherished cultural objects of adult citizens or members of other subcultures. How can the ideas of children and adolescents be transmitted to and appropriated by the adult world, particularly when the adults, for some reason, are not able to adopt the ideas through more or less isomorphic actions (such as in-line skating or tram-hopping). Cultural learning by members of the adult generation from their adolescents was suggested similarly by Mead (1970). Dialogue problems between generations and subcultural groups in larger cities could be described within this model.

Whereas Leont'ev tried to explain how culture is transmitted from the past, Oerter and Lang try to explain how culture is created and produced for the future and how important it is for the individual to be an active producer (even if it is only building one's own house). But are persons and cultures really out of equilibrium, as Oerter and Lang assume, when appropriation (learning) is not counterbalanced by production and change of the environment? What about traditional cultures?

4   Theories and the world-out-there

All three theoretical approaches use similar terms (e.g., open or dynamic systems, transactions, setting, holistic ideas, and accommodation and assimilation) but with minor or major modifications that make it difficult to transfer the concepts from one model to the other. Also, their epistemological points of view differ in that Overton would, for instance, call Oerter a dualist. For his part, Oerter referred more explicitly to a world-out-there that is simultaneously the object of many different subjects whose psychological life spaces or environments could either harmonize or conflict. In contrast, this world-out-there remained underconceptualized by Overton.

Furthermore, "reality" in Oerter's account includes a historical-cultural dimension separate from the actual individual. In Wapner's presentation, the "real world" remains more or less untouched, but he explicates the ways in which an individual can relate to the world and build up a more or less harmonious person-in-environment or life-space unit. Overton ponders the subject side of this unit and the way in which children ontogenetically develop mental representations of themselves relative to their conceptions of environment. At the same time, he reflects on the researcher's perspectives on the observed child-in-environment units. Whereas Overton considers biological, social, and psychological aspects as perspectives of the researcher, Wapner prefers to see them as aspects of the units themselves.

All three approaches demonstrate a preponderance of interest in the subject side of the unit and major difficulties in describing the environmental side in terms that transcend individual psychological relations. Although all three authors and their commentators have attempted to adorn their ideas with examples relating to children in urban settings, their examples and concrete suggestions neither appear to be systematically related to their theories nor contain novel information for city planners or architects. However, Overton's approach can stimulate research on children's mental reconstructions of parts of their urban world relative to their developing conceptions of self and modes of embodied activities. One can expect suggestions on how to coordinate differing professional perspectives. Wapner's approach may lead to research on the ways or styles by which children can become familiar with new settings and develop setting-identity. It may also lead to ideas on how to facilitate and evaluate this process. Oerter's conception, finally, can stimulate investigation into the processes of appropriating and reifying urban culture as historical transmission and active contribution, into the impact of these processes on individual personality development, and into communication between contemporaneous generations and subcultures in an urban setting.

All three main authors and commentators would probably agree that theoretical conceptions in developmental psychology need greater precision in the way they delineate conceptions of the environmental side of the child-in-context and that the interdisciplinary discussion in this book has been a challenge and a major step in that future task.

References

Kahn, P. H., Jr. (1997). Developmental psychology and the biophilia hypothesis: Children's affiliation with nature. *Developmental Review, 17*, 1-61.

Leont'ev, A. N. (1977). *Probleme der Entwicklung des Psychischen* [Developmental prob-lems of the psychological realm]. (2nd ed.). Kronberg in Taunus, Germany: Athenäum.

Mead, M. (1970). *Culture and commitment*. Garden City, NY: Natural History Press and Doubleday.

C. Modern versions of Barker's ecological psychology and the phenomenological perspective

Introduction

Günter Mey

The following contributions on phenomenology (Graumann and Kruse) and the behavior-setting approach (Cotterell, Fuhrer) can be classified as ranging somewhere between environmental and person-centered perspectives. To various degrees, each of them either does or could claim to be what Carl F. Graumann and Lenelis Kruse state about the phenomenological approach they present – "neither subject-centered nor object-centered."

Graumann and Kruse see the phenomenological approach, which originated in philosophy, as an orientation in solving psychological problems. In terms of children's development in the city, it is notable that this perspective focuses on the intentional relationship between person and environment, with the authors drawing on four basic principles: the bodily subject, the material and spatial environment, historicity, and the sociality of the situation. Along these dimensions the authors outline the possibilities for shaping children's environments, especially the possibility of appropriation. After discussing the basic principles and grappling with the terminology used by Graumann and Kruse, Katja Mruck and I center our commentary on the significance that the phenomenological approach, particularly the concept of intentionality and perspectivity, has for strengthening subject-oriented research. Given what we stress as the need to avoid or counter potential biases of environmentalism, we elaborate on a few methodological implications.

John L. Cotterell is concerned with making the behavior-setting approach fruitful for the study of planning problems in public environments. He first points out some shortcomings in the conception and then elaborates on how the behavior-setting theory can be used to conceive of environments in terms of systems. He proposes borrowing associated concepts from other fields, such as the concept of place from geography and architecture, and the concept of situation, which is linked more to social psychology. Cotterell continues by mapping out a methodological procedure that permits a topological analysis, a component analysis, and an intersetting analysis, and he illustrates this procedure with examples from the World Expo in Brisbane, Australia, and other public places such as museums, zoos, and theme parks. In the subsequent commentary, Barbara Hinding identifies some terminological ambiguities in Cotterell's attempt to broaden the behavior-setting theory. A positive aspect to which she draws attention is that Cotterell's expansion of behavior-setting theory has made development easier to discuss than has been the case with Barker's original concept. According to Hinding, however, the real strengths of Cotterell's approach, the intention of which is to offer an interface for psychology and planning, lie primarily in its implications for the design and analysis of places, for it is in that realm that suggestions are made for evaluating architecture and analyzing the living conditions of children and adolescents.

Urs Fuhrer's contribution is based on two lines of tradition. Fuhrer, who is committed to Lewin's tradition, orients himself to Barker's behavior-setting approach while keeping Simmel's cultivation theory in mind as well. After delineating the concept of cultivation and Barker's research program, Fuhrer attempts to reformulate the behavior-setting approach in terms of cultivation and to show how behavior settings, individuals, and their development are to be understood as interrelated processes. Fuhrer then accentuates the active role of the individual and speaks of variability and openness as relevant dimensions for environments, illustrating his point with a study he has conducted in a rural Swiss town. In the commentary to the chapter, Hans Joachim Harloff takes a genuinely environmental perspective on Fuhrer's approach. He confronts Fuhrer's statements with the traditional understanding of the behavior-setting approach, inquiring, for example, about the relevance that standing patterns of behavior have and about multisetting synomorphs. Harloff concludes that Fuhrer has overemphasized the actively controlling role of the child and has given too little heed to the formative character of behavior settings. Harloff maintains that attention must be directed not only to behavior settings chosen by a given individual but to all behavior settings surrounding the child. By the same token, he states that setting-dependencies (e.g., between public settings and dwellings) should be given greater consideration than Fuhrer grants them.

In the final integrative contribution in this part of the book, Hirofumi Minami points out that the phenomenological approach and both versions of behavior settings each have heuristic power when it comes to understanding children's transaction with urban environments. Although the respective thrusts differ and can be plotted along the dimension of microscopic - macroscopic and the dimension of environmental setting - individual experience, Minami does see common ground and new dimensions. As he indicates, they arise because Cotterell's modifications, and especially Fuhrer's sociocultural turn, make it possible to forge links to the phenomenological perspective in the effort to understand children's experiences.

Children's environments:
The phenomenological approach

Carl F. Graumann and Lenelis Kruse

1 A conceptual clarification

Outside philosophy, its original field, the term *phenomenological* has many meanings. For this reason and because it is a popular attribute in psychological discourse,
a preliminary conceptual clarification may be helpful. A delimitation is required also
because the field of interest in this chapter is ecological psychology (also called
environmental psychology), not the whole and diversified area of the human sciences (see Herzog & Graumann, 1991).

Phenomenology refers to philosophical thinking associated with the names of
Husserl, Pfänder, the early Heidegger, Merleau-Ponty, the early Ricoeur, Schütz,
and Gurwitsch. But we do not present or discuss their systems in this chapter. We
only cite their names because they are representatives of a current of thought that, in
its variety and dynamism, has been a movement rather than a school (see Spiegelberg, 1960). The use of the attribute *phenomenological* does not refer to a school in
psychology, either, or even to a subdiscipline. It is an approach, an orientation, in
solving psychological problems (Graumann & Métraux, 1977).

The main features of this orientation are the basic assumption of intentionality, the
structural analysis of horizonal situations, and the identification of some methodological consequences of this situation-centered approach. The underlying assumption is that the person-world relationship must be analyzed in terms of its intentionality. Phenomenologically, intentionality is an essential characteristic of all human
experience and behavior, so the term must not be restricted to the everyday usage of
the word *intention* to mean having something in mind as a plan or design that may
be considered a special volitional case of intentionality. In the phenomenological
sense, this intentionality means that any human experience or action has an object
that is meant (or posited) to be independent of this experience or action. The tree
that I see I believe to exist independently of my seeing it. I know it to be there even
if I turn away, and I still remember it as a real tree after it has been cut down. The
pain I feel I experience as raging in my sick tooth despite all mental efforts to ignore
it. An ideal object like the Pythagorean theorem, if I hold it to be true or valid, will
not cease to be valid if I divert my attention from it. The same holds true for action.
Action always takes place with respect to some state of affairs, such as a purpose or

goal that one either attains or fails to attain. Or one replaces it with something easier to attain. In any case, a goal is something one strives for as something that exists independently of one's attempts to reach it.

The fact that each of these intentions and intentional states is assigned a correlate object to which the intending subject or person relates as independent of each state or act gives intentionality an objectifying function. Hence, intentionality is the word denoting an active relationship whose terms – called person and environment – must in principle be treated as coexisting within a dynamic unit. That is why the phenomenological approach is neither subject-centered nor object-centered; the emphasis is on the situation as the intentional relationship between person and environment (Graumann, 1988; Graumann & Métraux, 1977). If, for some specific research purpose, interest is primarily in persons (individuals, groups, or classes of persons), they shall be considered in their experiential and behavioral relationship to their present environment. If the concern is primarily with environments, they will be treated exclusively and exactly as the lived correlates of the persons whose environments they are.

These are the main reasons why intentional analysis, which deals only with intentional environments (Taylor, 1964), always results in situational analysis. The person as the intentional subject is, in principle, situated.

Following Linschoten, who, belonging to the former Dutch group of phenomenological psychologists (see Kockelmans, 1987), defined psychology as "the scientific study of the situated person" (Linschoten, 1953, p. 246), we differentiate the structural analysis of situations into at least four essential and interrelated themes. These themes are ideally suited to demonstrating the phenomenological approach to ecological psychology (see Graumann, 1990a; Kruse, 1974).

2   The phenomenological approach to ecological psychology

In the phenomenological perspective, the environment must be conceived of as intentional environment. The world must be accounted for as it is, within the limits in which it is experienced and acted upon by a given individual or group of persons. In a closely related approach, von Uexküll (1909, 1957, 1982) introduced the term *Umwelt* as the concept for the species-specific environment. In its two main functions, that is, as sensory environment (*Merkwelt*) and as motor environment (*Wirkwelt*), it is a strict correlate of the structure and functions of an organism. Structurally different organisms (species) have different *Umwelten*.

Generalized to the human level by von Uexküll himself, *Umwelt* has now become the technical term for the subjectively meaningful surroundings of an individual or group. As the ensemble of meanings that a surrounding may have for a person or a group of persons, *Umwelt* coincides with what we have introduced as intentional environment.

2.1 The bodily subject

Though we prefer to speak of themes of the intentional analysis of situations, we do *not* deal with separate entities (like organism, person, or environment). We emphasize terms of an interrelationship merely for analytical purposes.

Starting from the relationship between the structure of the intentional environment and the structure of the intentional subject, we have to account for the subject's body. The meanings of things, even their appearances, are contingent upon a subject's gendered bodily structure and condition. They will be different for the healthy, the sick, the pregnant, the athletic, the overweight, the small, the tall, the physically handicapped, the bedridden, the aged, and so forth. They will be culturally different for boys and girls, men and women; hence, one may speak of *gendered environments* (Kruse, 1992). To the degree that these bodily states apply to whole categories of people, such as children, patients, or the elderly of either gender, it is their intentional environments that must be considered, never the environment per se. The identity of a person must be sought not in a mental or cognitive, but in an *incarnated self*.

There is one trivial, but fundamental, feature of the human's physical being to be considered. It is the basic perspectivity of a person's cognition. Whatever one perceives is seen from a given viewpoint, and whatever object one perceives is seen in aspects, that is, *pars pro toto*. The fact that objects are seen in aspects implies, as Husserl's analyses have demonstrated (Husserl, 1973; cf. Graumann, 1960), that the immediately given aspect of what one perceives always refers one to further viewpoints and aspects of it and, ultimately, to the horizon of one's experience. This continuous transition from the actual to the potential constitutes the horizonal structure of the situation.

From the perspectival structure of situations, which is founded in the incarnation of human subjectivity, one can infer that *Umwelten* (in the phenomenological sense of the term) are not limited but horizonally open. That is, the world in which one lives, experiences, and acts is lived not only in its actuality but also in its potentiality.

2.2 The material and spatial environment

In terms of the fundamental person-environment relation, the correlate of the subject's bodily nature is to be found in the materiality and spatiality of the intentional environment. The world that is experienced and acted upon presents itself spatially as tangible and reachable by some mode of locomotion (e.g., by foot, car, or plane) or as unreachable (e.g., at one or more points in one's life cycle, as for a baby, a toddler, or an aged person). Creeks and ditches are too broad to be jumped over, walls and fences are too high to be scaled, or both are just broad and high enough to challenge one's skill or courage. Objects are experienced as rough or smooth, hot or cold, solid or fragile, edible or inedible, repulsive or attractive. In other words, the spatiality as well as the materiality of the intentional environment must be described in strictly experiential and behavioral terms, that is, always with regard to the sensory and motor capacities of the subject under consideration. Lewin (1935) took a basically phenomenological approach when he introduced the term *valence* (*Aufforderungscharakter*) for those experiential qualities of things that correspond to a person's needs or intentions. So did Tolman (1967) when he described an organism's environment strictly in the behavioral (not behavioristic) terms of manipulanda, discriminanda, and utilitanda. Because manipulation, discrimination, and utilization both develop and have to be appropriated, the capacity and skill-specific qualities of the intentional environment change during the life cycle.

To generalize, we can propose that it is the human qualities and valences of the world of bodies, things, and spaces through which both the kind and measure of one's appropriation and alienation show. The world of things in which one lives (Graumann, 1974) is a world of meanings (for personal objects, see Habermas, 1996; for material possessions, see Dittmann, 1992; for objects in the domestic sphere, see Csikszentmihalyi & Rochberg-Halton, 1981).

2.3   *The historicity of the situation*

If the person-environment relationship is conceived of as horizontal, both the spatial and the temporal character of situations are accentuated because perspectivity implies the continuous transition from the present to the future (thereby transforming the present into the past), from the actual to the possible. The overarching concept conjoining the different and changing pasts, presents, and futures is the historicity of situations. It is not only one's own biographical experience and expectancies that are carried into every situation. Others, with whom one interacts or whom one merely remembers or expects, also have biographies and histories of their own. So have things, buildings, landscapes, cities, many of which show their true or feigned age (see Bertels & Herlyn, 1990; Kruse & Graumann, 1998).

These different histories interact. It is mainly between persons that histories become mutually entangled (see Schapp, 1976). People meeting in the same situation inevitably become part of each other's history. Being in each other's story presupposes the all-embracing power of language by means of which humans constitute, construct, and deconstruct the meaning of situations.

2.4 The sociality of the situation

Mutual entanglement in histories and the constitution of situations through the use
of language are not all that is involved in the basic sociality of the person-
environment relationship. Being physical subjects also means being objects of others' perceptions. One is seen and evaluated as beautiful or ugly, fat or skinny, adroit
or clumsy, and so forth. From the moment of birth, one is with others, interacting,
communicating, being part of their history. From them one learns what the world is
like and what things are called. One learns about others who had been here before
and learns to anticipate others who will be here after one has left (Schütz, 1953).

Most important for one's own way of life is that one learns the norms and rules of
how to interact and how to deal with the physical and social environment. Spaces,
places, and objects as well as motion, speed, and rest have social meanings and
valences (Graumann & Kruse, 1978). Whether some part of one's environment or
some environmental activity is dangerous or harmless, recommendable or unrecom-
mendable, or good or bad is largely, if not exclusively, a matter of social convention
and symbolically mediated meanings. Goals and barriers in the modern environment
are conventional symbols rather than physical attractions and obstacles, and it is
through language and other symbols that these meanings are communicated. The
increasingly symbolic character of one's intentional environment emphasizes the
discursive sociality of a world of human-made, or at least human-ordered, objects.

3   The intentional environment of children

3.1 The perspective of the child

One important methodological implication of a phenomenological approach to the
study of the person-environment relationship is to describe and assess a given environment strictly from the perspective of the child, or rather of children of different
ages, but children who are members of, and who communicate with, families and
other social groups that include adolescents, grown-ups, and the aged. Hence, the
perspective of the child in a given society or community does not mean the environment as an adult expert (architect, planner, or educator) thinks that a child sees it,
but the given setting just as the child experiences it.

The fact that it is possible to describe and assess an environment in this way was
demonstrated more than sixty years ago by two psychologists who tried to capture
the perspective of the child. One was Martha Muchow, whose study of the life space
of the city child differentiated phenomenologically between the "space in which the
child lives," the "space that the child experiences," and "the space that the child
lives" (Muchow & Muchow, 1935/1980; see Wohlwill, 1985). Mainly the latter, the
child's lived space, was shown to be child-specific, that is, different from the urban

space adults live. The child's lived world, a kind of second (exterior) home, is mainly the street with its entrance gates and backyards. Urban children feel at home there and, in fair weather, spend most of their free time there if the street permits some of their favorite activities, such as romping about and playing ball games, hide-and-seek, and cops and robbers. Such affordances are not the ones adults look for when they use their street. They either do not notice them or they experience them as aggravating or inhibiting circumstances of their daily activities. The wooden slatted fence, if perceived at all by adults, may limit the pavement. For the younger child, however, it allows climbing, sitting upon, jumping from, hiding behind. As for the pavement itself, do adults perceive that it is covered with square tiles? For the young child this design is a challenge to avoid stepping on the lines or to step only on the lines, and there may be rules and penalties regulating the action.

The other psychologist to take a child's perspective on the immediate environment was Kurt Lewin, who tried to introduce the film as a scientific instrument (see Lück, 1984, 1985; Bulgakowa, 1992). In a film entitled *The child and the world*, released in 1931, Lewin followed children from birth to the age of eight years, recording their everyday situations by means of a "candid camera" technique and thereby producing a vivid account of historicity in person-environment relationships. Lewin's ingenious approach for shooting this film on the changing life space of the child was to take all pictures from the child's perspective, at least as closely as possible. Hence, the viewer at first sees the world as it looks from inside the crib. It is not much more than light and sound and mother's rather huge smiling face bending over the crib; later the world passes by when the baby is pushed around in a baby carriage. Perhaps the most fascinating film documentation is of what Lewin called "the gradual conquest of space." Through the eyes of the crawling baby, the viewer discovers a world that consists mainly of legs, be it of persons or of furniture, something to look up to, to hold on to, to creep through. But those legs also separate the crawler, who, unless picked up, remains attached to the floor, away from all the attractive, but inaccessible, things on tables, cupboards, and cabinets. The discrepancy between the sphere of vision and that of reach is a distinctive feature of the crawler's lived space.

Lewin followed ontological development through the child's perspectively changing environments. But one can just as well change sides and follow the biography of a piece of furniture: the table under which the creeping baby and the toddler live as under a roof that perhaps provides a sense of territory to be defended against intruders. For the schoolchild the same table, now looked at from above, may become the unloved place for the daily chore of doing homework. For the adolescent the same table as the obligatory dinner place may symbolize the constraints of family life from which he or she is trying to become emancipated.

3.2 Designing with children in mind

Such biographies of children's spatial conquests of pieces of furniture, things (such as toys or tools), rooms, buildings, streets, sidewalks, and places could serve as starting points for planners, designers, and architects when designing "with children in mind" (see Perin, 1970). Eventually, however, children's participation is called for in planning and design, in the creation of settings that reflect the ideas, meanings, and values that make up children's intentionalities. As indicated by Baldassari, Lehman, and Wolfe (1987), Hart (1987), and approaches documented in the *Childhood City Newsletter* (1981a and b) and the *Child City Quarterly* (1982/1983), children's participation in designing environments is no longer a utopian ideal. But because most environments for children will eventually be designed by professional planners and designers, it is crucial that these experts deal with relevant information about children-environment relationships.

Phenomenologically oriented research has treated a number of important facets of this relationship, such as the experiences of place or being-at-home (Dovey, 1985; Graumann, 1989; Korosec-Serfaty, 1985; Seamon & Mugerauer, 1985), the problem of inside-outside or privacy (Kruse, 1980, 1987, 1991; Wolfe, 1978), and of children's experience of nature (Tuan, 1978). Other research has focused on children's behavior outdoors, issues of spatial knowledge and representation, and patterns of locomotion and activity (e.g., Hart, 1979; Moore, 1986; Moore & Young, 1978; Rauschenbach & Wehland, 1989; Spencer, Blades, & Morsley, 1989).

Researchers working in a phenomenological tradition not only try to create concepts of children's lived space, such as home, dwelling, place (see Kruse, 1974; Relph, 1976; Seamon, 1979, 1987; Seamon & Mugerauer, 1985). They also make an effort to develop methods and techniques that enable children to present and represent their life worlds in verbal language, forms of play, drawings, or scale models (see Hart, 1979; Ziegler & Andrews, 1987). In principle, any method that accounts for the intentional environment of "users," whether children or adults, substantiates the phenomenological approach. Lastly, there have been attempts to translate phenomenological concepts into design processes. Examples subsumed under the term *place making* (Seamon, 1987) are Norberg-Schulz's (1985) approach to the design of dwelling or Alexander's (1977) approach to development of "pattern language," which identifies elements that, far beyond aesthetic or functional requirements, are meant to contribute to a sense of place.

Applying the principles of a phenomenological analysis of situations to the understanding and design of children's environments, one must accept that the intentional environments of children vary with their developing physical and mental makeup. That makeup, in turn, is stimulated, incited, or challenged or is subdued, inhibited, or even paralyzed by appropriate or inappropriate environments.

Learning from the first and from the last theme of the situational analysis sketched above, one should try to differentiate between (a) the direct physical impact and

(b) the symbolic message of a given environment (David & Weinstein, 1987). If, for example, educators, planners, and architects are resolved to build an environment that is child-friendly rather than indifferent or even unfavorable, the dual impact should be considered. It is advisable to supply a rich variety of material and spatial qualities to be experienced and appropriated by the developing child, such as high and low walls, rough and smooth surfaces, round and angular shapes, dull and sharp edges, mobile and immobile objects, hard and soft material, and solid and fluid substances. The richer in qualities an environment is, the more suitable it will be for appropriation by children.

Moreover, in a rich, variegated, stimulating, and safe setting, perceptual and motor experiences will give to children (maybe more than to adults) the feeling that they are worthy human beings and that they are cared about, a feeling they certainly will not develop in the cheap, bleak environment epitomized by many educational and (even worse) correctional institutions. David and Weinstein (1987, pp. 8-10) have listed five major functions that an environment may have for a child's development: (a) to foster personal identity, (b) to foster the development of competence, (c) to provide opportunities for growth, (d) to foster a sense of security and trust, and (e) to provide opportunities for both social contact and privacy. It is not easy, but possible, to correlate and complement these tendencies and intentions with a variety of environmental qualities that children of different ages and temperaments are ready to enjoy and utilize. Utilizing the environment, however, must never be synonymous with consuming it as it actually is but must include the construction of a potential world. In other words, children's naturally creative intentionality should be challenged by appropriate features of the environment.

All the above functions that an environment should have are as essential for adults, including seniors, as they are for children and adolescents. Hence, an environment consisting of such qualities and functions is what we consider a *human habitat* rather than a merely child-centered environment.

The reality, however, of "the space in which the child lives" (Muchow & Muchow 1935/1980) is far from what has been postulated by planners and architects with children in mind. The history of urban reconstruction in postwar Germany exemplifies this discrepancy between what is and what ought to be. As shown by Zeiher (1983), who sketched the change of spatial living conditions for urban children after 1945, interior living space at home in the largely destroyed and damaged cities of Germany at that time was initially too scarce and too limited to permit playing. Outside, there were large areas of ruins and rubble, which were dangerous and, hence, forbidden, but which were ideal for adventurous games. They also served as shelters, substitutes for real homes. The streets, many of which had little or no traffic, were suitable for running, chasing, racing home-made soapbox cars, and so forth.

As urban reconstruction progressed, however, space became functional and specialized again, with more and more space for automobiles and shopping and less and less space for children. Families gradually moved into new suburban satellite towns, frequently into high-rise buildings surrounded by parking lots and neatly trimmed (and sometimes well-guarded) lawns, cut off from where parents and other adults work and shop. Playing grounds, almost exclusively for the little ones, were designed and constructed by specialists, but more often than not they were not accepted by the children, who resented being insulated, even isolated, in children-only territories. They refused to be constrained and to allow their playing activities to be dictated by specialized constructions. Even where nurseries were provided, high-rise buildings did not have enough interior space for children to play together. Although occasionally planned with children in mind, neither the interior nor exterior new environment available for children's play was really designed and constructed from children's perspectives. Hence, playgrounds were frequently "reinterpreted" and used for other functions (see Forsch, 1980) or even forcefully "reconstructed."

3.3   An environment to be appropriated

One of the most significant features that a human environment must have for children and adults alike is its challenge and necessity to be appropriated instead of merely being experienced or consumed. *Appropriation (Aneignung)*, as the term was introduced into ecological psychology in the 1970s (Graumann, 1976; 1990b), refers to the active, or interactive, components of the person-environment relationship. Its dialectical conception, which was originally Hegelian-Marxian, emphasizes that, on the one hand, it is only through human mental and physical activities that the world becomes a truly human habitat, that objects and events become human things and affairs. On the other hand, the conception also stresses that it is objective features of the material physical world that arouse, incite, foment, and afford environment-related human intentionality.

Within the framework of the cultural-historical school of psychology (Vygotsky, Leont'ev, Luria), the role of the sociocultural and interpersonal context of all appropriation is emphasized. What a person knows things to be, what they are called, how they are to be dealt with is learned from others either by instruction or, more often, by doing as others do. Those others, in turn, have appropriated the world by means of and in interaction with others who acquired their knowledge from predecessors and contemporaries. It is therefore possible to speak of a dual sociality of appropriation; it is societally and interpersonally situated. How to use a spoon, a ladder, an oar, must be learned by each individual through trial and error, but the resulting sensorimotor coordination (of eating, climbing, rowing) need not be invented anew; it is handed down to each person by others who instruct, correct, and reinforce the learner. This dual sociality holds for the appropriation of both object and language use (Graumann, 1990b, p. 124). If we are right in assuming that both work and discourse are the major constituents of what Merleau-Ponty (1967, p. 162) called "the human dialectic," which brings forth the "proper milieu of man," then the play of children ought to be acknowledged as the playful appropriation of the world of work and language, of the material and the cultural environment.

For the design of an environment that is appropriate for children as well as adults, the concept of appropriation makes for environments that are shaped as challenges. In other words, human environments should be designed and constructed not as surroundings merely to be experienced, passively received, or even consumed in terms of commodities, but as a world of objects (things and spaces) that have to be interacted with, acted upon, shaped, and reshaped by creative physical and mental efforts that presuppose the play of imagination.

References

Alexander, C. (1977). *A pattern language.* New York: Oxford University Press.

Baldassari, C., Lehman, S., & Wolfe, M. (1987). Imaging and creating alternative environments with children. In C. S. Weinstein & T. G. David (Eds.), *Spaces for children: The built environment and child development* (pp. 241-268). New York: Plenum.

Bertels, L., & Herlyn, U. (Eds.). (1990). *Lebenslauf und Raumerfahrung* [Life course and the experience of space]. Opladen: Leske + Budrich.

Bulgakowa, O. (1992). Sergej Eisenstein und Kurt Lewin. In W. Schönpflug (Ed.), *Kurt Lewin: Person, Werk, Umfeld* (pp. 161-171). Frankfurt on the Main: P. Lang.

Childhood City Newsletter. (1981a). *Participation one: An introduction.* New York: City University of New York Graduate Center, No. 22.

Childhood City Newsletter. (1981b). *Participation two: A survey of projects, programs, and organizations.* New York: City University of New York Graduate Center, No. 23.

Childhood City Quarterly. (1982/1983). *Participation three: Techniques.* New York: City University of New York Graduate Center. Double Issue, 9(4) and 10(1).

Csikszentmihalyi, M., & Rochberg-Halton, E. (1981). *The meaning of things.* Cambridge, MA: Cambridge University Press.

David, T. G., & Weinstein, C. S. (1987). The built environment and children's development. In C. S. Weinstein & T. G. David (Eds.), *Spaces for children: The built environment and child development* (pp. 3-18). New York: Plenum.

Dittmann, H. (1992). *The social psychology of material possessions.* Hemel Hempstead: Harvester Wheatsheef.

Dovey, K. (1985). Home and homelessness. In I. Altman & C. M. Werner (Eds.), *Home environments* (pp. 33-64). New York: Plenum.

Forsch, B. D. (1980). Spielplätze – Spielangebot ohne Nachfrage? [Playgrounds – Play supply without demand?]. In N. Kluge (Ed.), *Spielpädagogik* (pp. 120-134). Bad Heilbrunn: Klinkhardt.

Graumann, C. F. (1960). *Grundlagen einer Phänomenologie und Psychologie der Perspektivität* [Foundations of a phenomenology and psychology of perspectivity]. Berlin: de Gruyter.

Graumann, C. F. (1974). Psychology and the world of things. *Journal of Phenomenological Psychology, 4,* 389-404.

Graumann, C. F. (1976). The concept of appropriation (*Aneignung*) and modes of appropriation of space. In P. Korosec-Serfaty (Ed.), *Appropriation of space*. (Proceedings of the Strasbourg Conference) (pp. 113-125). Strasbourg: Université Louis Pasteur.

Graumann, C. F. (1988). Phenomenological analysis and experimental method in psychology – The problem of their compatibility. *Journal for the Theory of Social Behaviour, 18*, 33-50.

Graumann, C. F. (1989). Towards a phenomenology of being at home. *Architecture et comportement/Architecture and Behaviour, 5*, 117-126.

Graumann, C. F. (1990a). Der phänomenologische Ansatz in der ökologischen Psychologie [The phenomenological approach to environmental psychology]. In L. Kruse, C. F. Graumann, & E. D. Lantermann (Eds.), *Ökologische Psychologie. Ein Handbuch in Schlüsselbegriffen* (pp. 97-104). Munich: Psychologie Verlags Union.

Graumann, C. F. (1990b). Aneignung [Appropriation]. In L. Kruse, C. F. Graumann, & E. D. Lantermann (Eds.), *Ökologische Psychologie. Ein Handbuch in Schlüsselbegriffen* (pp. 124-130). Munich: Psychologie Verlags Union.

Graumann, C. F., & Kruse, L. (1978). Sozialpsychologie des Raumes und der Bewegung [The social psychology of space and movement]. In K. Hammerich & M. Klein (Eds.), *Materialien zur Psychologie des Alltags. [Kölner Zeitschrift für Soziologie und Sozialpsychologie, Sonderheft 20]* (pp. 177-219). Opladen: Westdeutscher Verlag.

Graumann, C. F., & Métraux, A. (1977). Die phänomenologische Orientierung in der Psychologie [The phenomenological perspective in psychology]. In K. A. Schneewind (Ed.), *Wissenschaftstheoretische Grundlagen der Psychologie* (pp. 27-53). Munich: Reinhardt.

Habermas, T. (1996). *Geliebte Objekte* [Cherished objects]. Berlin: de Gruyter.

Hart, R. A. (1979). *Children's experience of place: A developmental study*. New York: Irvington.

Hart, R. A. (1987). Children's participation in planning and design: Theory, research, and practice. In C. S. Weinstein & T. G. David (Eds.), *Spaces for children* (pp. 217-239). New York: Plenum.

Herzog, M., & Graumann, C. F. (Eds.). (1991). *Sinn und Erfahrung. Phänomenologische Methoden in den Humanwissenschaften* [Meaning and experience: Phenomenological methods in the human sciences]. Heidelberg: Asanger.

Husserl, E. (1973). *Experience and judgment*. Evanston, IL: Northwestern University Press.

Kockelmans, J. J. (1987). *Phenomenological psychology: The Dutch school*. Dordrecht: Nijhoff.

Korosec-Serfaty, P. (1985). Experience and use of the dwelling. In I. Altman & C. M. Werner (Eds.), *Home environments: Human behavior and environment* (Vol. 8, pp. 65-86). New York: Plenum.

Kruse, L. (1974). *Räumliche Umwelt. Die Phänomenologie räumlichen Verhaltens als Beitrag zu einer psychologischen Umwelttheorie* [Spatial environment: The phenomenology of spatial behavior as a contribution to a psychological theory of the environment]. Berlin: de Gruyter.

Kruse, L. (1980). *Privatheit als Problem und Gegenstand der Psychologie* [Privacy as a problem and topic of psychology]. Bern: Huber.

Kruse, L. (1987). Personale und interpersonale Sphären und Grenzen der Person [Personal and interpersonal spheres and boundaries of the person]. In E. R. Lampe (Ed.), *Grundrechte aus der Sicht der Sozial- und Verhaltenswissenschaften* (pp. 60-71). Opladen: Westdeutscher Verlag.

Kruse, L. (1991). Privatheit als öffentliches Problem [Privacy as a public problem]. In M. Herzog & C. F. Graumann (Eds.), *Sinn und Erfahrung. Phänomenologische Methoden in den Humanwissenschaften* (pp. 197-210). Heidelberg: Asanger.

Kruse, L. (1992). Environments for women – Environments for men? In B. Wilpert, H. Motoaki, & J. Misami (Eds.), *22nd International Congress of Applied Psychology Kyoto, Japan 1990. Proceedings* (Vol. 2, pp. 367-371). Hillsdale, NJ: Erlbaum.

Kruse, L., & Graumann, C. F. (1998). Metamorphosen der Umwelt im Lebenslauf [Metamorphoses of the environment in the life course]. In A. Kruse (Ed.), *Psychosoziale Gerontologie* (Bd. I: Grundlagen) (Jahrbuch der Medizinischen Psychologie, pp. 51-64). Göttingen: Hogrefe.

Lewin, K. (1935). *Dynamic theory of personality.* New York: McGraw-Hill.

Linschoten, J. (1953). Naaword [Afterword]. In J. H. van den Berg & J. Linschoten (Eds.), *Persoon en wereld – Bijdragen tot de phaenomenologische Psychologie* (pp. 224-253). Utrecht: Bijleveld.

Lück, H. E. (1984). *Kurt Lewin: Video and accompanying text.* Hagen: FernUniversität.

Lück, H. E. (1985). Der Filmemacher Kurt Lewin [Kurt Lewin: The film maker]. *Gruppendynamik, 2,* 131-141.

Merleau-Ponty, M. (1967). *The structure of behavior.* Boston: Beacon.

Moore, R. C. (1986). *Childhood's domain: Play and place in child development.* London: Croom Helm.

Moore, R. C., & Young, D. (1978). Children outdoors: Toward a social ecology of the landscape. In I. Altman & J. F. Wohlwill (Eds.), *Children and the environment: Human behavior and environment* (Vol. 3, pp. 83-130). New York: Plenum.

Muchow, M., & Muchow, H. H. (1980). *Der Lebensraum des Großstadtkindes* [The life space of the urban child]. Bensheim: päd.extra. (original work published 1935)

Norberg-Schulz, C. (1985). *The concept of dwelling: On the way to figurative architecture.* New York: Rizzoli.

Perin, C. (1970). *With man in mind: An interdisciplinary prospectus for environmental design.* Cambridge, MA: MIT Press.

Rauschenbach, B., & Wehland, G. (1989). *Zeitraum Kindheit. Zum Erfahrungsraum von Kindern in unterschiedlichen Wohngebieten* [Time-space childhood: The experienced space of children in various living areas]. Heidelberg: Asanger.

Relph, E. (1976). *Place and placelessness.* London: Pion.

Schapp, W. (1976). *In Geschichten verstrickt* [Entangled in stories]. Wiesbaden: Heymann.

Schütz, A. (1953). Common-sense and scientific interpretation of human action. *Philosophy and Phenomenological Research, 14,* 1-37.

Seamon, D. (1979). *A geography of the life world.* London: Croom Helm.

Seamon, D. (1987). Phenomenology and environment-behavior research. In E. H. Zube & G. T. Moore (Eds.), *Advances in environment, behavior, and design* (Vol. 1, pp. 3-27). New York: Plenum.

Seamon, D., & Mugerauer, R. (Eds.). (1985). *Dwelling, place and environment: Towards a phenomenology of person and world.* Dordrecht: Nijhoff.

Spencer, C., Blades, M., & Morsley, K. (1989). *The child in the physical environment.* New York: Wiley.

Spiegelberg, H. (1960). *The phenomenological movement: A historical introduction.* 2 vols. The Hague: Nijhoff.

Taylor, C. (1964). *The explanation of behaviour.* London: Routledge & Kegan Paul.

Tolman, E. C. (1967). *Purposive behavior in animals and men.* New York: Appleton-Century Crofts.

Tuan, Y. F. (1978). Children and the natural environment. In I. Altman & J. F. Wohlwill (Eds.), *Children and the environment: Human behavior and environment* (Vol. 3, pp. 5-32). New York: Plenum.

von Uexküll, J. (1909). *Umwelt und Innenwelt der Tiere* [Environment and the inner world of animals]. Berlin: Springer.

von Uexküll, J. (1957). A stroll through the worlds of animals and men. In C. H. Schiller (Ed.), *Instinctive behavior*. New York: International Universities Press.

von Uexküll, J. (1982). The theory of meaning. *Semiotica, 42*, 25-82.

Wohlwill, J. F. (1985). Martha Muchow and the life-space of the urban child. *Human Development, 28*, 200-209.

Wolfe, M. (1978). Childhood and privacy. In I. Altman & J. F. Wohlwill (Eds.), *Children and the environment: Human behavior and environment* (Vol. 3, pp. 175-222). New York: Plenum.

Zeiher, H. (1983). Die vielen Räume der Kinder. Zum Wandel räumlicher Lebensbedingungen seit 1945 [The many spaces of children: The change of spatial conditions since 1945]. In U. Preuss-Lausitz, P. Büchner, M. Fischer-Kowalski, D. Geulen, M. E. Karsten, C. Kulke, U. Rabe-Kleberg, H. G. Rolff, B. Thunemeyer, Y. Schütze, P. Seidl, H. Zeiher, & P. Zimmermann (Eds.), *Kriegskinder, Konsumkinder, Krisenkinder. Zur Sozialisationsgeschichte seit dem Zweiten Weltkrieg* (pp. 176-195). Weinheim: Beltz.

Ziegler, S., & Andrews, H. F. (1987). Children and built environments: A review of methods for environmental research and design. In R. B. Bechtel, R. W. Marans, & W. Michelson (Eds.), *Methods in environmental and behavioral research* (pp. 301-336). New York: van Nostrand.

Comment: Don't forget the subjects –
An approach against environmentalism

Katja Mruck and Günter Mey

The objective of the chapter by Carl F. Graumann and Lenelis Kruse is to outline a phenomenological approach to research on children's environments. Starting from the key concept of intentionality, which characterizes the dynamic unity of the person-environment relationship, the authors sketch the four main categories of intentional analysis, or situation analysis – bodily subject, material and spatial environment, historicity, and sociality – in terms of their significance for ecological psychology. Assuming that there is a "basic perspectivity of a person's cognition" (p. 359), Graumann and Kruse afterwards draw conclusions about the appropriation and shaping of children's environments.

Our commentary is guided by three questions: (a) What are the basic assumptions and categories of a phenomenological research approach? (b) What does its application mean in ecological psychology and, specifically, for the study of children's environments? (c) What are the methodological implications of a phenomenological approach? In discussing these questions, we have tried to solve what we consider a fruitful problem partly associated with the very conception of this book. Because one of the main concerns is not only to present psychological theories about children and environment but also to interrelate them and integrate the different theoretical approaches where possible, we further accentuate some of the special features of a phenomenological perspective by drawing on other works of the authors. With an eye to the contributions of the integrators, we do so by using our *relative expertise*, for as qualitative social researchers we find it particularly important to stress the necessity of considering "meaning and experience" (Herzog & Graumann, 1991) in ecological psychology. The phenomenological research approach is practically the only one in the present volume that tackles this difficult, but essential, task of psychological investigations. Compared to the authors, however, we are not really experts in the field of phenomenology. Our knowledge is confined to a few more or less fleeting encounters stemming from our affiliation with qualitative social research and with our more private predisposition to philosophy.[1] In this respect we hope our *relatively lay background* can help us use both our understanding and our interpretative difficulties as possible springboards for further explication and clarification of a phenomenological perspective on the study of children's environments.

1   What are the basic assumptions and categories of a phenomenological research approach?

Graumann and Kruse point out three main aspects of a phenomenological research approach: (a) the embedding or delimitation of different phenomenological lines of tradition, (b) the fundamental phenomenological assumption of "intentionality," and (c) the "structural analysis of horizonal situations." As the authors state, a phenomenological approach is not a philosophical or psychological school, but rather – "in its variety and dynamism," especially in psychology, "an orientation in solving ... problems" (p. 357). This point seems all the more important because mainstream psychologists in particular continue to regard and reject phenomenology as a philosophical tradition of thought, and an outmoded one at that (on these "prejudices," see Graumann, 1991, pp. 22-23, for example). Unfortunately, however, the authors fail to define or explicate *their* understanding of a phenomenological orientation. It remains unclear whether their stated position consists in the common elements remaining of a phenomenological approach after differences have been sifted out or whether it consists in highly specific stances of the authors. A clarification seems necessary if only because the aforementioned diversity of phenomenological approaches entails equally diverse epistemological positions, views of the world, images of human beings, and attendant ideas about whether they can be studied scientifically.

What distinguishes a phenomenological view of knowledge in psychology? What are its premises about the object of its consideration? Graumann and Kruse introduce two terms, intentionality and structural analysis of horizonal situations. Both are used vaguely in the text at times, and for lack of further explanation they are likely to be a source of confusion to nonphenomenological readers. Intentionality is initially defined as the "essential characteristic of all human experience and behavior" (p. 357) and as a subject's "intentional *state*[ ]" (p. 358; these and the following italics are ours). But it also refers to the "active *relationship*" with the "terms ... person and environment" (p. 358). It is thus additionally identical with the authors' understanding of "situation," which, defined as the "relationship between person and environment" (p. 358), is characterized by intentionality. Similar problems arise with the structural analysis of horizonal situations. The dictum of the authors is that the person-environment relationship "must be analyzed in terms of its intentionality" (p. 357). This is supposed to be accomplished through the *structural analysis* of horizonal situations, or "*intentional analysis*," which only deals with intentional environments and thus "always results in *situational analysis*" (p. 358).

Because intentionality and intentional analysis are key concepts of a phenomenological approach – elsewhere, intentionality in particular is called the "heart," "axiom," and "lowest common denominator" of a phenomenological orientation (see Herzog & Graumann, 1991) – at least a note about the range of the term seems warranted. Unlike the connotations of intentionality in everyday language or other psychological approaches, the sense of the word the way the authors use it extends "from prereflective awareness to processes of reflection and voluntary actions to habitual and misguided actions" (Graumann & Métraux, 1977, p. 43). By embracing the concept of intentionality, a phenomenological research approach turns against the predominant way of viewing objects of psychological study, which is based on the Cartesian distinction between subject and object and centers on consciousness, behavior, or cognition whether in associationistic, behavioristic, or cognitive terms. From a phenomenological perspective, psychological studies do not start from isolated functions or features of the subject but rather from the person "as the intentional subject" who "in principle [is] situated" (p. 358). It is situated in an environment that likewise does not represent itself as environment in itself but always only as environment *for the subject*, an environment that must be reconstructed from the subject's perspective. (The research implications of the premise that there are situated persons and intended environments are discussed below.)[2]

2 What does the use of a phenomenological research approach mean for ecological psychology and the study of children's environments?

Unfortunately, the authors' promised clarification of what a phenomenological research approach means for ecological psychology is rather implicit. The difference between human and physical environments – especially the idea that, unlike "the perception of things, the perspectivity of one's perception of persons is reciprocal" (Graumann & Métraux 1977, p. 46) – is not spelled out explicitly and remains vague throughout the chapter. For example, the chapter's description of the "historicity of the situation", one of the four categories of structural analysis that Graumann and Kruse explain in connection with the Utrecht school of phenomenological psychology, focuses the interaction with other persons. The historicity of objects, buildings, or cities intentionally related to by the subject, who, in turn, is socially mediated, is merely noted in passing.

Other main categories, and the actual starting point of intentional analysis, are the "bodily subject" and its correlate, the intentional "material and spatial environment." As explained in the chapter by Graumann and Kruse, the intentional subject as bodily subject focuses almost solely on physical features (though understood as socially mediated ones), or the "sensory and motor capacities of the subject under consideration" (p. 360). It would certainly have been helpful at this point, as done elsewhere, if the authors had stressed, say, "the broadly conceived *Leiblichkeit* (corporeality) discussed in phenomenology, embracing sensuousness, historicity, affectivity, expression, and behavior" (Graumann, 1990, p. 99). The concept of corporeality also represents a semantic shift in the development of a phenomenological research approach, a shift in which "the concept of intentionality is liberated from its original mentalistic version with Husserl and transferred to the *bodily* subject" (Herzog, 1993, p. 49).

The conceptual problems, which are only indicated here,[3] are not confined to the approach expounded by Graumann and Kruse, however. In our opinion, they always arise when researchers try to gain an interactionist understanding on the one hand while having to resort to traditional concepts on the other. For if a phenomenological approach has been adopted, the subject is always situated and the environment is always an intended environment, yet the concepts that have been handed come from a period and a way of thinking in which subject and object were thought of as being separate (and, as Graumann and Kruse stress, not just temporarily differentiated for analytical purposes).

Lastly, the presentation of the fourth basic category, the "sociality of situations," seems misleading in its description of other persons as reference points – "that one learns the norms and rules of how to interact" (p. 361). The same is true of the reference to learning "by doing as others do" (p. 365). In contrast to a concept of sociality and society that has been reduced to unidirectionality and normativity (a concept that these descriptions seem to suggest under certain circumstances), a phenomenological research approach has, in our opinion, repeatedly and justifiably rejected "the alternative of interiority and exteriority, private and public, internal . . . and external" (Graumann & Métraux, 1977, p. 35). And it has taken it upon itself to uncover and articulate "simplistic 'biases' such as mechanization, genetization, social determinism, environmentalism, and the theories and models arising from them" (p. 29). To that extent it seems important for the intimate interplay of "social convention and symbolically mediated meanings" (p. 361) to be emphasized more than they are in the present chapter.

In summary, the special potential of a phenomenological approach for ecological psychology and the abiding productive tension between the two is to be stressed. There are ties to ecological psychology because Graumann and Kruse's phenomenology is an attempt to describe the person in situ. The special nature of a phenomenological research approach lies in the endeavor to work "*with* the individual to glimpse and record what constitutes his world" (Graumann & Métraux, 1977, p. 44). Or, more clearly in terms of ecological psychology, it lies in the quest to elaborate "the subject-relatedness and, hence, the personal and social relevance of buildings and things, squares, and landscapes" (Graumann, 1990, p. 99). It is essential to include subject-relatedness, sociality, and historicity as relevant dimensions of analysis in ecopsychological work if only because they counteract the aforementioned danger of environmentalism. True, the assumption that person-environment or organism-environment units closely interact is meanwhile no longer confined to a phenomenological perspective. Its particularity and salience, however, is that it offers alternatives to simplistic conceptualizations of this interaction, as found primarily in radical constructivist conceptions as well as in the majority of more narrowly ecopsychological approaches. Thus, one not insignificant contribution of a phenomenological orientation would be its "critical function" (Graumann & Métraux, 1977) of trouble-shooting for pointing out possible tendencies toward an ecological psychology ultimately more or less bereft of subject, sociality, and time.

In line with their premise that situated persons and personal environments should be taken as the starting point for psychological studies, Graumann and Kruse treat the more specific question of children's environments by seeing children not as a homogeneous age group but as individuals that differ in their motor and cognitive state of development. Children (as a broadly defined age group) also differ from adults in the way they perceive, experience, and use their environment. (In terms of psychological analysis, it seems puzzling that the authors speak only of groups of persons – babies, toddlers, adolescents, grown-ups.)

According to Graumann and Kruse, children's development proceeds in what they understand to be a dialectical relation between changing individuals in a changing environment (whereby it is not only the child's perspective on the environment that changes but also the environment's function for the growing child). The motor moving this process along is a ludic appropriation of material and cultural environments, some of which is accomplished through "trial and error," and some of which is "learned from others either by instruction or, more often, by doing as others do" (p. 365). As with the historicity of situations, Graumann and Kruse tend to marginalize questions concerning the appropriation of spatial environments.[4] When they do treat them, they do so in a manner that seems at odds with their own program. After all, statements like "human environments should be designed and constructed not as surroundings merely to be experienced, passively received, or even consumed in terms of commodities, but as a world of objects (things and spaces) that have to be interacted with" (p. 366) ignore the fact that the individual is in "dynamic interaction" with his or her specific environment in any case. They ignore the fact, that environments are experienced in different ways – in other words, that they mean different things to different persons. The authors themselves underscore this fact when, with regard to the child's experience of the environment, they state that "such affordances are not the ones adults look for . . . They either do not notice them or they experience them as aggravating or inhibiting circumstances of their daily activities" (p. 362). For this reason, too, environmental planners and others often encounter the seemingly amazing problem that the environments are used "against the grain," that is, in ways not intended by those who planed them.

On the whole, the elaboration of urban and environmental design for children is very general, a shortcoming not confined to this approach, however.[5] Nonetheless, the special nature and strength of a phenomenological approach in ecological psychology as compared to other approaches is its insistence on "meaning and experience" as the point of departure for any psychological analysis.

3 Methodological implications of a phenomenological approach

Aside from the reference to "some methodological consequences" as one of the "main features" (p. 357) of a phenomenological approach and a few usually rather general remarks, the authors devote comparatively little attention to methodological and procedural implications. They systematically call for the world to "be accounted for as it is, within the limits in which it is experienced and acted upon by a given individual or group of persons" (p. 358). Applied to the study of children's environments, this means that one must "describe and assess a given environment strictly from the perspective of the child, or rather of children of different ages" (p. 361).

The emphasis that perception and experience must in principle be considered from the subject's own perspective and the related claim that scientific research should begin above all with a reconstruction or description of perspectives involves profound methodological problems. It seems important to mention in this context that the point of a phenomenological research approach is not to achieve the "pseudo ideal" of avoiding or suspending all presumptions when it comes to the question of how the researcher is to succeed in describing an environment "strictly from the perspective" of other subjects. It is rather a matter of "describing a given [environment] with as little bias as possible" (Graumann & Métraux, 1977, p. 28). Researchers using a phenomenological approach are thus called upon to examine their own presuppositions, "of which [they] must become aware by reflecting on methods" (p. 29).

But what is meant "by reflecting on methods"? The text does not clarify to what extent the authors adopt, say, Husserl's program of *epoché* and where they do not. Nor does it indicate where they do or do not follow its extension by Schütz, who tries to avoid subjectivist interpretations and to establish a common basis for understanding science and everyday life by assuming that individual experience and action is socially embedded in a collective store of knowledge.[6] But as Meinefeld (1995) correctly notes, Schütz, too, accounted for the possibility of understanding but did not go beyond a merely "voluntarist concept" that would help the researcher grasp it. Hence,

the reference to the '*epoché* of the scientific mindset' . . . , the belief that it can be achieved, that daily ties and orientations can be excluded, feeds the illusion that 'direct knowledge' is possible. By [leading one to] presume that interpretations are sound solely because of the 'resolve to adopt the disinterested attitude of a scientific observer,' it distorts what has just been gained from analyzing the constitutive character of any piece of knowledge – the inevitability that the researcher will determine what it is. (pp. 60-61)

Our objection in no way means that we will or can deny the perspectivity of experience or intentionality. Rather, we accept intentionality also as a characteristic of the relation between the researcher and the object of research. That acceptance necessitates a more active stance in addressing the problems posed by the fact that "the researcher does not adopt patterns of interpretation in the form that they have been worked out by the actors involved. Instead, he understands them by relating them to the patterns of interpretation with which he himself is familiar" (Meinefeld, 1995, p. 286). In this sense, it seems important, but not sufficient, to stress that "taking several perspectives, not just one, should be the rule, not the exception, for understanding meaning" (Graumann, Métraux, & Schneider, 1991, p. 96). Precisely because perspectivity and situatedness of experience apply to research as well, the perspectives of scientists, too, need to be seen in relation to each other. This kind of reflection can be done through collaboration in interpretation teams, for example. "Not until I engaged in lively interaction was I able to get wise to myself, only when I sensed my interlocutor's perplexity, which perplexes me" (Krauß, 1996, p. 98). In terms of personal experiences with qualitative research groups, which are classified somewhere between a colloquium, research supervision, and an interpretation team, it became clear that it is only through cooperation with others that the variability of subjective perspectives can come to a person's attention at all so that one can then integrate them by expanding and validating interpretational patterns. (For further details, see Mruck & Mey, 1998; and even this way of working is certainly not going to "bring to light" any scientific truths that are valid and irrefutable across persons, times, and situations.)

As far as children's environments are concerned, these methodological observations mean that one must go beyond resorting to participatory procedures simply for the sake of legitimacy. Only through their increased use can the special nature of children's experience of the environment find its way into psychological studies. All the same, the "magic word" *participation* is intended as a constant reminder: Whatever ultimately comes of participatory investigation of children's environments, it can never be identical with the perspective of children themselves. It will always consist of an intentional relation – a reconstruction mediated by the researchers involved. This indissoluble relation between researcher and the object of research is made clear by Lewin's film *The child and the world*, which in Graumann and Kruse's opinion enables adults to see the world "as it looks from inside the crib" (p. 362). On the one hand, the creative significance of Lewin's attempt to establish film as a scientific tool should be acknowledged, as should the possibility that this way of working provides for calling attention to the variability of perspectives and the special nature of children's perspectives in the first place (see also Görlitz, 1993). On the other hand, what adults take as evident variability (e.g., the size of objects) lures them into a simplification. The view afforded by the camera's mechanical eye, whose main contribution is to show the world that adults presume children to see, runs the risk of being confounded with the perceiving, valuing, emotional experience of the world from the child's perspective.

4 Concluding remarks

The methodological and procedural problems indicated above arise for every psychological research approach in which the attempt is made to explore the meaningfulness and perspectivity of experience. They cohere with the view that all "interpretations . . . are tentative; they are given by subjects who speak from a particular position and who are prepared to recognize certain things but not others" (Rosaldo, 1984, p. 383). Because this localization of perspective applies to science as well, it would be desirable to counteract the "psychologist's aversion to interaction" (Graumann, 1979) even in the context of specific action taken in research. In this respect, the importance of a phenomenological approach lies especially in the fact that its concept of intentionality, among other things, provides valuable opportunities to reconceptualize the relation between the researcher and the object of research.

As for ecological psychology and the study of children's environments, a phenomenological research approach permits one to distinguish between the world of children and the world of adults, between the environments used by children and environments planned for children by experts (with or without children in mind). Clearly, the "discovery" of environments has ended the phase when psychology went without them. Ignoring the insight that environments are always intentional environments of social and historically situated subjects would ultimately pose what some indications show to be the opposite risk – that of ecological psychology going without subjects.

Acknowledgement

We thank our colleagues – especially this book's three other editors and Jarg B. Bergold and Arnim Stüwert – for reading an earlier version of this contribution. The challenging and valuable discussions with them brought out not only the common aspects of certain points but also the differences in the reception and comments associated with the very dissimiliar positions and views of knowledge (including for example a phenomenological, social-constructivist, and realist) that exist in the scientific system.

Notes

1 The cursory nature of our familiarity with phenomenology is also a reflection of psychology as a university subject. Its roots are passed on, handed down, and cut back from generation to generation, and all too often interpretive approaches remain consigned to the realm of private preferences. Without the aid of an objectively accepted arsenal of methods, the "mainstream majority still has trouble trusting the description of experience and behavior and the analytical

potential of personal reflection. The fear of subjectivity still probably lies too deep."
(Graumann, 1991, p. 39)

2 Further explanation here would go beyond the scope of our commentary. For treatment of
"situational analysis" as "structural analysis," see Graumann and Métraux (1977), for example. A helpful exploration of the concepts of "intentional description" and "intentional analysis" as well as a differentiation between various dimensions of understanding meaning, is presented in Graumann, Métraux, and Schneider (1991).

3 There are similar shifts in the concept of "Wesen" (essence), which is central in phenomenological tradition as well. According to Herzog (1993), it has meanwhile lost "its transphe-
nomenality, which stands 'behind' the empirically ascertainable and which is accessible only
to a metaphysical 'Wesensschau'. It has become modified into a concept for the invariant
structures of phenomena. . . . Wesen is thus not the (a priory) required point of departure but
the (never conclusively established) end product of scientific knowledge." (pp. 50-51)

4 But even where the authors spell out their understanding of appropriation as a social process,
their treatment sometimes tends to come across as rather passive and unidirectional despite
explicit emphasis on an active process of appropriation. This effect is surely due in part to a
tacit adoption of what in our opinion are problematic or simplified sociopsychological concepts of learning.

5 According to Mey, Hinding, and Görlitz at the end of the comments made by the moderator
of the working group on "street" during the Herten conference "City as a Frame of Children's
Development" in July 1992, this impression "may be due to the interdisciplinary split between
the social science faction and the physical-planning faction. . . . Among the planners, [the
moderator] discerns defensiveness about their position of having to discuss on the basis of
pragmatism, social standing, and the limits of financial and local political feasibility, which
makes them forget that their own occupational status obliges to come up with more than just
'solutions to problems'. Among the social scientists, by contrast, he sees that they do succeed
in making the leap from their professorships into daily experience with 'practical suggestions'
but that it usually means sacrificing precision for the problem at hand." (Mey, Hinding, &
Görlitz, in press)

6 Herzog and Graumann's (1991) survey of phenomenological methods in the human sciences
does not help answer these questions, either, though it does offer some interesting ideas. In
this respect the lack of a tie with phenomenological positions and persistent misunderstandings "among the majority of psychologists" (Graumann, 1991, p. 23) seem to indicate not
only the previously mentioned fears of subjectivity (see note 1), but communicational problems produced by phenomenologically oriented researchers as well. "As *the* psychologist . . .
does not exist any more than *the* phenomenologist does", and "the more the relation is burdened by actual or presumed misunderstandings," the more urgent it is also for phenomenologically oriented psychologists "to take perspectivity into account." (p. 23)

References

Görlitz, D. (1993). Es begann in Berlin. Wege einer entwicklungspsychologischen Stadtforschung [It began in Berlin: Paths of developmental kind of urban research]. In H. J. Harloff
(Ed.), *Psychologie des Wohnungs- und Siedlungsbaus. Psychologie im Dienste von Architektur und Stadtplanung* (pp. 92-120). Göttingen: Verlag für Angewandte Psychologie.

Graumann, C. F. (1979). Die Scheu des Psychologen vor der Interaktion. Ein Schisma und seine Geschichte [The psychologist's aversion to interaction: A schism and its history]. *Zeitschrift für Sozialpsychologie, 10*, 284-304.

Graumann, C. F. (1990). Der phänomenologische Ansatz in der ökologischen Psychologie [The phenomenological approach in ecological psychology]. In L. Kruse, C. F. Graumann & E.-D. Lantermann (Eds.), *Ökologische Psychologie: ein Handbuch in Schlüsselbegriffen* (pp. 97-104). Munich: Psychologie Verlags Union.

Graumann, C. F. (1991). Phänomenologie und Psychologie – ein problematisches Verhältnis [Phenomenology and psychology: A problematic relationship]. In M. Herzog & C. F. Graumann (Eds.), *Sinn und Erfahrung. Phänomenologische Methoden in den Humanwissenschaften* (pp. 22-42). Heidelberg: Asanger.

Graumann, C. F. & Métraux, A. (1977). Die phänomenologische Orientierung in der Psychologie [The phenomenological orientation in psychology]. In K. A. Schneewind (Ed.), *Wissenschaftstheoretische Grundlagen der Psychologie* (pp. 27-53). Munich: Reinhardt.

Graumann, C. F., Métraux, A., & Schneider, G. (1991). Ansätze des Sinnverstehens [Approaches to understanding meaning]. In U. Flick, E. v. Kardorff, H. Keupp, L. v. Rosenstiel, & S. Wolff (Eds.), *Handbuch qualitative Sozialforschung* (pp. 67-77). Munich: Psychologie Verlags Union.

Herzog, M. (1993). Phänomenologie und Experiment in der Psychologie [Phenomenology and experiment in psychology]. *Journal für Psychologie, 1*(4), 44-54.

Herzog, M. & Graumann, C. F. (1991). Hundert Jahre phänomenologische Forschung: Rückblick, Status und Ausblick [One hundred years of phenomenological research: Retrospective, status, and outlook]. In M. Herzog & C. F. Graumann (Eds.), *Sinn und Erfahrung. Phänomenologische Methoden in den Humanwissenschaften* (p. IX-XVI). Heidelberg: Asanger.

Krauß, T. (1996). Die Schimäre der Gegenübertragung [The chismeras of countertransfer]. *Journal für Psychologie,* [double issue] *3*(4) and *4*(1), 96-98.

Meinefeld, W. (1995). *Realität und Konstruktion. Erkenntnistheoretische Grundlagen einer Methodologie der empirischen Sozialforschung* [Reality and construction: Epistemological foundations of a methodology for empirical social research]. Opladen: Leske + Budrich.

Mey, G., Hinding, B., & Görlitz, D. (in press). Lebensraum Stadt. Ein Arbeitsbericht über die Herten-Tagung "Stadt als Rahmen kindlicher Entwicklung" [Urban living space: A report on the Herten-Conference, "The city as a frame of children's development"]. In M. Beck & S. Chow (Eds.), *Kinder in Deutschland. Realitäten und Perspektiven.* Tübingen: DGVT.

Mruck, K. & Mey, G. (1998). Selbstreflexivität und Subjektivität im Auswertungsprozeß biographischer Materialien – zum Konzept einer "Projektwerkstatt qualitativen Arbeitens" zwischen Colloquium, Supervision und Interpretationsgemeinschaft [Self-reflexivity and subjectivity in the process of analyzing biographical materials – On the concept of a "Project workshop for qualitative work" bridging colloquium, supervision, and interpretative teams]. In G. Jüttemann & H. Thomae (Eds.), *Biographische Methoden in den Humanwissenschaften* (pp. 288-310). Weinheim: Psychologie Verlags Union / Beltz.

Rosaldo, R. (1984). Der Kummer und die Wut eines Kopfjägers. Über die kulturelle Intensität von Emotionen [The worries and rage of a head hunter: On the cultural intensity of emotions]. In E. Berg & M. Fuchs (Eds.), *Kultur, soziale Praxis, Text. Die Krise der ethnographischen Repräsentation* (pp. 375-401). Frankfurt on the Main: Suhrkamp. (Ausgabe 1993)

Authors' response: Reading a text –
A case study in perspectivity

Carl F. Graumann and Lenelis Kruse

Communication, oral or written, is successful only to the degree that the recipient's understanding matches the sender's intention. Mruck and Mey's reading of our chapter, as evidenced in their comment, indicates a deplorable case of miscommunication, if not misunderstanding. In the eyes of our critics, we have failed to communicate whatever we consider essential for a phenomenological approach. What we had *intended* in our brief chapter was the explication of our phenomenological approach in relation to the topic of children's environments. Mruck and Mey (in the following M&M), (mis)taking our text as "an approach against environmentalism" (a term we never used and an issue we never discussed), certify that we have failed to explicate our conception. This overall grade of F is followed by a whole series of particular Fs, namely with respect to all the essential features by which we had intended to explicate our approach. Intentionality, the four categories of a structural analysis of situations (the bodily subject, materiality/spatiality, historicity, sociality), and the concept of appropriation have (for M&M) remained "rather general," "vague," if not "misleading." They are even "a source of confusion," to cite only some of our critics' red marks. These marks and a set of other critical objections signify that our intention to explicate, however briefly, our phenomenological approach as it pertains to the study of children's environments has failed to be matched by M&M's understanding.

What has happenend? Psychologically speaking, a text is a product of interaction and perspective. Hence, on re-reading our text, where we found most of the explications that M&M have missed, we felt we should raise two questions: (1) What is the deficiency of our text? (2) What may be the difficulty readers (like M&M) would have with a text like ours?

The first question is easily answered. The rationale underlying most of M&M's more than a dozen objections is lack of explication. Here we tend to agree with the critics and to apologize with like-minded readers. Within a volume on "Children, Cities, and Psychological Theories," there is only limited space for the latter, and our theoretical approach is only one of a dozen. Therefore, we had to be brief. Brevity, however, though it may be the soul of wit, is certainly not beneficial to a quick and easy understanding of complex theoretical statements. Consequently, many theoretical propositions were not "spelled out explicitly," as we had done elsewhere. That is why we added about a dozen pertinent sources in the list of references for further reading *if* anyone is really interested in a phenomenological approach to environmental problems.

As for our second question, readers who expect our chapter to tell them everything about phenomenology that they always wanted to know but never dared to read will be disappointed. By the same token, readers who are in need of an elementary introduction to the phenomenological orientation in psychology should not expect to find such a primer in a special volume on children in cities. For both types of reader, our text will be inappropriate, that is, as deficient as M&M find it to be. The chapter – here we change perspective again – was, maybe mistakenly, written for readers who have some knowledge of how the interrelationship between children and their lived urban environment may be conceptualized and who are interested in comparing different theoretical perspectives. If we fail to reach these readers the blame is all ours.

P.S. Since space is limited for responses as well, we have had to refrain from refuting in detail, from stating *explicitly* what we consider to be misreadings of our text.

Commentators' reply: Seductive sciences

Katja Mruck and Günter Mey

Because the advice to beware of possible biases of "environmentalism" is (unfortunately) not our idea (see Graumann & Métraux, 1977, p. 29) and because we are a little surprised at the blame-seeking dimension of the authors' model of communication – for we believe that misunderstandings involve at least two parties (see note 6 in our comment) – the question remains: What has happened? We had an inkling of the answer upon reading Adorno's observation that it takes very great effort

not to think in black and white, but an even greater effort to avoid thinking gray . . . and . . . not to insist on the absoluteness of one's own ego and position; for the driving forces to which we . . . are liable are so determined by what Freud called narcissism that the temptation to put yourself in the right and the other in the wrong is almost prohibitive for thinking. (1974, p. 204)

Despite all good intentions, Adorno, too, occasionally succumbs to this temptation. It happens to us again and again, and perhaps phenomenologists – epoché here, *Wesensschau* there – are not immune to it either.

References

Adorno, T. W. (1974). *Philosophische Terminologie* [Philosophical terminology]. Vol. 2. Frankfurt on the Main: Suhrkamp.
Graumann, C. F. & Métraux, A. (1977). Die phänomenologische Orientierung in der Psychologie [The phenomenological orientation in psychology]. In K. A. Schneewind (Ed.), *Wissenschaftstheoretische Grundlagen der Psychologie* (pp. 27-53). Munich: Reinhardt.

Behavior settings in macroenvironments: Implications for the design and analysis of places

John L. Cotterell

1 Behavior settings as units of the environment

Barker and Wright applied Lewin's topological psychology to the analysis of the environmental structure of whole communities and, while the field of environmental psychology was in its infancy, "discovered" behavior settings as the basic unit of the ecological environment. Barker (1979) wrote "if a satellite (had its) cameras focused on a particular town, they would show that human activities are not uniformly or randomly distributed but are concentrated in bounded regions. These are *behavior settings*, an important class of ecological regions because they form the proximal environments of most molar actions" (pp. 69-70). Behavior-setting theory has evolved from this work into one of the most original and systematic theories of environment-behavior relations in the social sciences. The implications of behavior-setting research for urban design and planning are profound and far-reaching. Schoggen (1989) underlines the following aspects: "several disciplines converge in behavior settings. All roles are played in them. All organisations are composed of them . . . and they appear to be ideal units for describing and modelling social processes" (p. 300).

1.1 Extending the range of ecological units

However, as Schoggen (1989) notes, behavior settings are a mid-range entity "within a hierarchy of topological entities" (p. 367). Ecological research based upon behavior-setting analysis can deal with only a fraction of the vastness that constitutes the environment of human behavior. Barker and Wright and their colleagues, by concentrating their energies upon the behavior-setting unit, gave far less attention to larger units of the ecological environment, and consequently their features remain far less elaborated. Kaminski (1989) acknowledges that Barker's ecobehavioral approach has much to offer in describing reality but comments that "if one expects reality articulation 'above' the level of behavior-setting units, then Barker's approach is a disappointment" (p. 15). Thus the larger potential of Barker's ecological psychology has not yet been fully exploited. Its application to the broader aspects of the environments of cities is the subject of this chapter.

My task is to retrieve the behavior-setting concept from behavior-setting theory; link it to other relevant concepts in the field; relate those concepts to the study of planning problems in the public environments of schools, zoos, hospitals, museums, and so on; and emerge with new urban forms such as shopping malls and theme parks. As I do so, the aspects of Barker's theory[1] pertaining to environment-behavior *synomorphs* may become accessible to the current generation of researchers and practitioners in those fields concerned with the creation and management of environments in our cities.

1.2   Macroenvironments

In urban locations, many of the environments that people enter and occupy outside the home occur as *clusters* of behavior-settings and other smaller environment-behavior units rather than as isolated entities. These complexes, which Barker termed "multiple-setting synomorphs," and which I prefer to call *macroenviron-ments*, are recognizable as coherent environment-behavior systems. They occur as host environments to other settings, to comprise churches, schools, factories, court-houses, and universities. Their forms are manifest in urban redevelopments of precincts, seen in the waterfront areas of Oslo, Toronto, and Sydney, in the rebuilding of inner Birmingham and Berlin, in the designs of World Expos and Olympic villages, in the planning of modern shopping malls (e.g., Flanigan, 1989), and in the creation of theme parks as "entertainment architecture" (e.g., An architects' forum, 1990).

The structures and operation of macroenvironments demand serious attention from environmental psychologists, first, because of their diversity and significance in modern cities as environment-behavior systems; and second, because researchers have not been at the forefront in the design of human environments and have left the running to architects and property developers. Admittedly, the existence of broad environments that are host to a number of smaller environment-behavior systems is not new. In the research of Barker and his coworkers, these broader forms were described and included in their community surveys, but their *system* properties as macroenvironments were not investigated in any great detail. Instead, attention was focused on the component settings of schools, such as music classes, home economics classes, and graduation ceremonies; and the component settings of the annual county fair, such as tractor-pulling contests and horseshoe pitching competitions, rather than on the way in which the school or the fair itself operated as an eco-behavioral system with interconnected parts.

Macroenvironments may be categorized in terms of their different habitats as shown in Table 1. They vary in size, duration, and complexity. For example, recreation environments like circuses and fairs tend to be short-lived and seasonal, whereas educational environments have greater duration and continuity. The greater longevity of the macroenvironments in groups I and II means that the majority of their settings are located inside specifically designed buildings or built spaces. They may be contrasted with those listed in group IV, which rely more strongly on time boundaries and their human components to define them.

Table 1: Macroenvironments grouped by habitat type

	Examples of macroenvironment
I. Education	Museums, zoos, schools
II. Physical health	Hospitals
III. Business	Farmer's markets, shopping malls
IV. Entertainment, recreation	Folk festivals, county fairs, circuses rodeos, theme parks

Macroenvironments emerge inevitably as important urban forms where planning is conceived of at broader levels of the environment than that of individual behavior settings in a small community. They may be *designed* as multisetting systems, which is common in educational, health, and commercial types of habitat, or they may *evolve* from simple to more complex systems. For example, a church may begin as a single-setting system: a worship service conducted in a public hall. Gradually the settings attached to the church authority system may increase, to include a Thursday choir practice, a Sunday school, a Tuesday evening Bible class, and a monthly elders' meeting. Recreational macroenvironments may evolve in similar fashion. An example comes from Paranella Park, in Tropical Queensland, where a Spanish settler in the 1930s purchased a tract of land that included a small waterfall. Using the falls as a tourist attraction and as a source of electric power, he designed the first theme park in the state, gradually differentiating the park environment from a waterfall and swimming pool into a complex of settings and situations. These included the pool and its bathing sheds, picnic areas, a tennis court and pavilion, a grassy playing field, nature walks, and a mystery tunnel, as well as a main building containing a ballroom and large dining room. All of these areas and spaces were linked by common architectural forms and served a similar function – that of leisure, which catered to the needs and interests of different age groups. Macroenvironments can emerge, then, through increasing differentiation of component action patterns and of the objective physical environment into separate but complementary synomorphic structures.

2 Retrieving the behavior-setting concept

Behavior settings are specific environment-behavior systems within which people carry out purposeful social activities. They contain temporal, physical, and behavioral elements and function as a cultural or behavioral template in society through what Barker called "the program" of the behavior setting, which guides each inhabitant concerning the roles and general patterns of behavior that are appropriate to the setting. Because of the size of the behavior-setting unit, which gives it a visible unity, the program of the setting can readily be understood by the setting's inhabitants. The characteristics are summarized:

- The unit has spatial and temporal boundaries.
- The environment of the unit totally surrounds its component elements.
- The behavior and physical elements have pattern and organization.
- The action pattern within the unit is easily distinguished from that outside the boundary of the unit.
- The behavior within the unit cannot be greatly changed without destroying the unit's integrity.
- The unit exists when it is occupied by people.

Behavior-setting research adopts a topological approach to identifying units in the ecological environment. Many disciplines, such as architecture, geography, political science, public health, urban sociology, and social psychology find it valuable to identify sociospatial structures for the purpose of systematic enquiry. In the Barker school, the environment was viewed as being composed of assemblies of nested structures, where each entity in the nested assembly is contained within another structure. Relations between the structures are mutual. Schoggen (1989, p. 165) explained it in terms of constraints exerted on an entity by the outside unit that surrounds it, and on the inside unit that it in turn surrounds. The research undertaken at the field station at Oskaloosa and in other small communities was concerned with determining the "synomorphic structure" of a community, that is, the behavior-milieu configurations (synomorphs) in the ecological environment that occur where two attributes – physical and behavioral – fit together, and the research also sought to describe the processes by which synomorphy (the fit between behavior and environment) is achieved.

2.1 Determining structures in the environment

In determining all the synomorphs in a community that might qualify as behavior settings, Schoggen (1989) suggested that "[t]he best way to begin is to walk the streets and halls of the community or institution and observe and record the walled, fenced, and otherwise bounded areas" (p. 49). The resulting list of environmental "parts" is then subjected to a structure test and a dynamic test. The structure test requires that the part display five characteristics. It must be (a) a standing pattern of behavior that is (b) attached to a physical and geographical boundary having (c) a particular time-space locus that is (d) enclosed within a milieu, with (e) the behavior and milieu fitting together. With the dynamic test (known as K-21), one assesses the degree of interdependence among the synomorphs and examines whether it is greater than their relatedness to parts of other settings, according to seven aspects (see Fuhrer, this volume) that deal with the spillover of molar actions across synomorphs, their populations, leadership, occupation of space, time of operation, use of objects, and kind of behavior mechanism fostered. Researchers like Luke, Rappaport, & Seidman (1991) have been critical of behavior-setting theory's reliance upon "a purely structural method" of classifying behavior settings. They have been equally skeptical of using the "structure test", which leads some milieu to be excluded as behavior-setting units although they are places, and some group activities and organisations to be excluded because there is no standing pattern of behavior. Their criticism is misplaced, and it assumes a dualism that Barker and Wright sought to overcome. The two tests described here underline the fact that behavior settings are not only structural entities; they are social-behavioral units as well. Four of the seven scales of the K-21 test devised by Barker and Wright are people-based, focusing, for example, on molar actions, population, leaders, and behavior mechanisms (see Barker, 1968; Schoggen, 1989).

Vigorous application of the topological approach for identifying "the texture" of the environment and the boundedness of social-spatial units is characteristic of the research on behavior settings (e.g., Barker, 1987; Gump, 1987; Luke et al.,1991; Schoggen, 1988). It may be more easily appreciated when it is remembered that for many years Barker travelled on trains across the prairie as part of his administrative and teaching responsibilities as a professor of Psychology at the University of Kansas. Barker's writings are replete with images from geography, which is primarily a topological discipline concerned with broad spatial relations. Use of superordinate units to describe the ecological environment comes easily to a train traveller seeing the homesteads and towns on the prairie from his carriage window; and Barker writes of the clear demarcation between town and country noted by the train traveller entering and leaving a prairie town. The topological approach anchors the methods of behavior-setting research in the ecological environment. Insofar as the units of analysis in behavior-setting theory capture the persistent characteristics of settings rather than their variations, they are less wedded to seeking explanations of individual patterns of behavior, and the research is better positioned than more psychologically based approaches to contribute to design and planning, which tend to be normative and prescriptive in nature.

2.2 Environments as active systems

A further distinctive aspect of behavior-setting theory is its conception of the environment in terms of systems rather than in terms of variables. The transactional nature of behavior-environment relations is preserved in the units of analysis themselves, which include behavior *and* milieu. A behavior setting is not just a place: *it behaves*. People are components of environmental systems through their actions, an obvious fact at a rock concert or football match. A consequence of the Barker approach is that environmental influences are considered in terms of their general "extra-individual" effects as coercive forces on the inhabitants rather than in terms of the differential effects of the environment on individual occupants. A lengthy discussion is found in Barker (1968) and Schoggen (1989) concerning the distinction between the ecological environment (*Ee*) which is the observable, preperceptual environment, and the psychological environment (*Eψ*), which surrounds the lifespace of the individual. behavior-setting theory recognizes that a person experiences forces from *Eψ* as well as forces from *Ee* but chooses to concentrate on the nonpsychological sector (which includes the physical environment and the molar actions of others present) to examine the relation between environment and behavior, inasmuch as this sector "has a durable existence . . . independent of the psychological processes of any particular person" (Schoggen, 1989, p. 3).

2.3 Environments and development

Human environments are usually studied as separate entities, as if they existed as isolated islands of behavior, with little reference made to their interconnections. Psychologists' knowledge of normal child behavior and developmental processes is confined to a few selected settings. For researchers, when a child occupant of a setting moves out of the setting, in many cases he or she also moves out of range of the observer, although development presumably continues when the child is out of range. McCall (1977) asserted that "we lack a substantial science of natural developmental processes" (p. 333). There are few studies of the natural habitats of children of the kind that document their behavior and experiences across a range of settings, and some of the best work on children's environments has been done by those who were initially trained as geographers (e.g., Hart, 1979). There is considerable potential for behavior-setting theory to contribute to the understanding of the influences of the ecological environment on children's social and personality development (e.g., self-control, competence, leadership, and social responsibility). In fact, a concern with children's development was central to the original focus of the Kansas school. It was continued in the studies of school size (Barker & Gump, 1964; Schoggen & Schoggen, 1988) but became obscured by the empiricism of behavior setting research. Barker and Wright even illustrated how the behavior of the same child may change across the different behavior settings she entered in the school, but they avoided any discussion of the notion that traces of her experiences in each setting remained in her behavior repertoire and contributed to the development of her competence.

A study of macroenvironments would enable the *habitat* concept in behavior-setting theory to be exploited more in terms of linking environments and development. In biology, habitat refers to the sum of the environmental niches utilized by a species. These niches contain resources that are species-specific and relate to all aspects of the organism's functioning. In behavior-setting theory habitat is viewed similarly as sectors of the environment that provide opportunities for people to participate in various kinds of activity. It is measured as the sum of behavior settings that contain "resources for molar actions" (Schoggen, 1989, p. 85), these actions being defined in terms of eleven kinds of "action patterns." Furthermore, settings may be specified in terms of their contribution to particular types of habitat (for example, education, recreation). Unfortunately, despite its appearance in various publications of the Barker school, the term habitat has failed to gain wider acceptance. A likely reason is the excessively empiricist approach to its measurement. "Habitat extent" was measured through *cu* (centi-urb), a composite score based on the number, occurrence, and duration of behavior settings in a community. Perkins, Burns, Perry, and Neilsen (1988) believed this measure is inadequate; and Schoggen (1988, p. 382) appeared to accept the validity of their criticism.

What appears to have been overlooked in devising these crude measures of habitat extent at the community level is that a community contains several "species," subgroups of inhabitants with species-specific habitats. Moreover, a species may utilize certain habitats for different purposes. For example, the recreation habitat of adolescents is distinctive to that age-group. Thus, a local park may have utility for young children and older adults but lack any kind of appeal to adolescents, who prefer to congregate outside a local store or on a vacant piece of land. Like the geography concepts of territory and roaming space, habitat captures the behavioral diversity as well as the range of environments inhabited by individuals. More attention to the ecological niches utilized by groups differing in age or gender would enable the habitat concept to be refined in ways that remain consistent with an ecobehavioral rather than an individual-based approach, and along the lines already indicated by research on children's roaming space and studies of territory (e.g., Anderson & Tindall, 1972; Berg & Medrich, 1980; Cotterell, 1991; Hart, 1979; van Vliet--, 1983). The approach could assist in answering an important question asked by Lynch (1977), "[w]hat interchange between people and their environment encourages them to grow into fully realised persons?" (p.1)

2.4 Associated concepts

Many of the concepts and tools of enquiry needed for fruitful investigation into macroenvironments already exist in behavior-setting theory, but analyses at the level of macroenvironments must extend beyond traditional behavior-setting analysis. Accordingly, certain associated concepts become relevant, particularly *the concept of place* in behavioral geography and architectural psychology, and *the concept of situation* as understood in social psychology.

"Place" is used by Canter (1977, 1986) and Sime (1986) to define a unit that has "geographical, architectural, and social connotations" (Canter, 1977, p. 6) and that exists independently of the observer. Barker's interest in geography made him particularly aware of the issue of place-dependencies in behavior. In his clearest essay on ecological psychology, Barker (1987) asked "what is a place?" and commented that the ecological environment "contributes to the place-specificity of behavior not only by selecting appropriate people but by regulating the behavior that occurs in places" (p. 1420). The problem of the place concept is that behavior is not consistently place-specific. Several entirely different sets of actions may occur at different times within the same physical place. Variations in behavior associated with particular places led Barker to conclude that mere geography and time are insufficient to establish a connection between behavior and environment, at least with the consistency and degree of boundedness that he was seeking. Barker's distinction between the coerciveness of behavior settings and the neutral influence of places in respect of human behavior is captured in his comment that "[b]ehavior settings are not neutral places where people congregate for their own purposes; they are superordinate, self-regulating, dynamic entities that manipulate the behavior of their human components toward an equilibrium state for the setting" (Barker, 1987, p. 1421).

Barker's dismissal of places seemed, however, to be made from the outside; they seemed to disregard the meanings attached to particular places and the activities that are understood to occur there. These meanings are surely attached to behavior settings as well; people plan to go to a baseball game because of the expectations they hold for the events in such a setting. Behavior settings have a continuing existence beyond their operating hours, and Fuhrer (this volume) is justified in describing them as "collective or cultural memories." Thus, Barker's interpretation of places as neutral does not do full justice to Canter's (1986) description of places as "units of environmental experience" (p. 215) comprising a physical structure, associated activities and roles, and a set of feelings and meanings attached to them. Whereas Barker's emphasis is on the system-like program characteristics that distinguish physical places such as the baseball grounds from the setting of the baseball game, Canter focuses more on the social and psychological processes that enable a person to distinguish one place from another in memory, as well as to "read" the physical and social characteristics of a place that are relevant to functioning within it.

Admittedly, Canter's emphasis is on *the individual* acquiring meaning of place in order to perform effectively in it, according to the place rules associated with each location (Canter, 1986). His idea of place rules and roles resembles the concept of "program" in behavior settings, in focusing on the actions of people as they adjust their behavior to the social conventions that operate in that setting.

The concept of "situation" in social psychology has been applied to actions situated within particular places by Silbereisen, Noack, and Eyferth (1986) in the Berlin Longitudinal Study on Adolescent Development. Situations are described as "clusters of social and physical aspects with a pattern of activities being a central feature" (Silbereisen et al., pp. 92-93). From observations in shopping centers, swimming pools, and discos, they identified a set of "situation types" occurring within the broader leisure places they had chosen. For example, discos contained the situations of dancing, hanging out at the bar, game playing, and couple interaction. Swimming pools contained the situations of socializing, sports, roughhousing, and couple interaction. The situation concept is promising, and could be linked to the concept of behavior-milieu synomorphs, but it is not developed in a systematic fashion in their research. Although the authors table "behavior profiles" for situation types, these types are, unfortunately, not linked in the observations to milieu characteristics, so they become behavioral rather than ecobehavioral. The shift is reflected in the report by Silbereisen et al., where the authors move to discussing the behaviors of individuals related to the concept of developmental tasks rather than to the developmental contribution flowing from the influences of extraindividual action patterns associated with the various situations.

3 Issues in applying behavior-setting theory to the study of macroenvironments

Macroenvironments are not simply hosts to a set of highly similar behavior settings and other synomorphs such as situations. They may contain a diverse array of environment-behavior units, and, as a consequence, the application of the two principles for defining behavior-setting units (the structure test and the dynamic test; see Schoggen, 1989) may pose some difficulty. It will be necessary, for example, to resolve differences in the pattern of operation of the component synomorphs, for they may not all co-occur. In short-term systems like farmers' markets and fairs, the duration of all synomorphs is likely to be identical with the duration of the macroenvironment; but in other macroenvironments, some settings may not operate as frequently as others. The question then arises of how interdependent the component settings should be for them to be regarded as parts of the macroenvironment. In a school, the regularly occurring settings and setting-genotypes have similar operating hours, and when school finishes for the day, so do its component student-occupied settings, although not all its administrative ones. In a university, the pattern is different. Bounded areas like libraries may be open at night but closed on weekends; lectures have shorter durations, and their lifespans as a series are fitted around terms and semesters. Clearly, the university is not only operating when all of its key components are "open for business." But when a setting is not operating, is it a place? If no people are present, Barker would argue that its physical space is merely an "exoskeleton" of a setting. To resolve the differences between settings and places requires knowledge of the molar actions that contribute to their programs, knowledge that can only be obtained from careful observation.

3.1   Outline of an analysis procedure

In a coarse-grained taxonomy of ecological units, macroenvironments will usually appear either as *genotypes* (classes of behavior settings with similar programs) or as *authority systems* (settings with power to control their own behavior patterns and those of other settings). Macroenvironments are less behaviorally diverse than a community; apart from physical or temporal boundaries, they derive their unity from a distinctive habitat (e.g., education, health, business) and a single authority system (Kenmore High School, Beenleigh District Hospital, FM104 Sky Show). In identifying and analyzing macroenvironments, three stages of analysis are envisaged:

Stage 1: *Topological Analysis.* Discover the separate host environments, referring to the aspects of structural boundaries, authority system, and habitat, and confirm the existence of component settings.
Stage 2: *Component Analysis.* Identify and list the component settings and other environment-behavior units and describe their physical features, the social rules governing their existence, and the nature of participants' inputs.
Stage 3: *Intersetting Analysis.* Describe how the separate units are related to one another within the broad macroenvironment structure and note the behavior flows across the separate component settings.

To illustrate the analysis procedure, let us consider Kenmore High School as a macroenvironment structure under a single immediate authority system (the Principal, Mr. Shepherd). This environment contains physical places (classrooms), behavior objects (books, chalk), synomorphs (lab benches), situations (class debate in Mr. Lock's ninth-grade English class), groups (A-grade [varsity] girls hockey team), and both regularly occurring behavior settings (swimming team training) and occasional behavior settings (swim meet).

  The macroenvironment as an ecobehavioral system consists of several separate but interlocking functions, with designated settings and key operatives in each. They include administration, teaching, guidance and counseling, student supervision, and recreation management. Each of these functions affects students and each determines certain aspects of the programs in the component settings. The action patterns associated with these functions are linked with particular settings within the school. Some of the settings are openly entered by students and teaching staff; others are restricted to teachers or to specialist personnel. The various settings that comprise the school are behaviorally interconnected; regular connections between the settings may be made by *transfer of messages* (the school intercom or teacher reports), by *transfer of persons* (a class moves from its regular room to the library), or by the *transmission of behavior* (classroom instruction on resuscitation is followed up by practice in life-saving at the school pool).

The features of the school macroenvironment may be further considered in terms of their effects on inhabitants by conducting a detailed examination of the extent of compatibility between component settings. Central to behavior-setting theory is the concept of synomorphy, or fit between environment and behavior, which may also be interpreted as fit between the goals of the setting and those of its inhabitants. The separate programs and goals of the component settings within a school macroenvironment may be expected to display a high degree of complementarity. Katz and Kahn (1978) noted that social systems emphasize "maintenance inputs which sustain the system" (p. 69). The school's maintenance inputs are complex and include the structuring of time and space (through timetables and allocation of teachers and students to classes and classrooms) and constant regulation of these two mechanisms through a system of rules and surveillance. Where there is lack of fit or the danger of incompatibility between component settings within the school, the central authority system will activate further control mechanisms of various kinds to keep the component parts working together. These resemble the "deviation-countering circuits" brought into play in behavior settings. Examples where they may be mobilized are (a) the actions in one setting may be interrupted by competing calls on student attention flowing from another setting (e.g., noise from the music recital disturbs the concentration of the tenth-grade history class; the math teacher sets an exam for a day on which some students are away from school on biology fieldwork); (b) setting A may restrict students to passive levels of performance (penetration zones 2 and 3), whereas setting B promotes greater levels of performance in students (penetration zones 5 and 6), leading students in setting A to express discontent. These aspects of high school life indicate the considerable environmental and organizational complexity that is encountered.

3.2   *Evolution of Southbank as a recreation macroenvironment*

The staging of a World Expo in Brisbane in 1988 stimulated my interest in macroenvironment systems as ecological environments that are less complex than whole communities yet physically larger and behaviorally more varied than single behavior settings. Unlike other World Trade Fairs, the Brisbane Expo was relatively small, confined to a 44-hectare (110-acre) site a kilometre (about half a mile), from the city center, and based on a single theme, "leisure in an age of technology" (see Figure 1). Further unity was given by the single authority system, a statutory body called the Expo Authority established to control the preparation of the Expo site, conduct the daily running of Expo for its six-month duration, and oversee the dismantling of the displays upon completion. Thus Brisbane's Expo had a clear space-time locus, a single authority system, a unity of habitat (leisure), and multiple settings and synomorphs. The component settings were able to be identified by a process similar to a behavior-setting survey and resulted in a roster of 62 national and corporate display pavilions, 30 taverns and restaurants, 50 shops, and a series of 11 entertainment "places." These places were so called for convenience because some were behavior settings (the Aquacade diving show, the Waterfalls, the daily Rock-ski water-ski show on the river); others were venues for events that changed daily (the Riverstage with its concert program); and still others were macroenvironments in themselves (the Funpark with its futuristic rides and its restaurants with their discos). More careful definition of the places as individual settings would have been possible using the tools of behavior-setting analysis and would have yielded a comprehensive taxonomy of the Expo macroenvironment. The decision to adopt a general nomenclature for the entertainment venues and the Funpark was made in order to provide a consistent measure of operating settings per day, so that each listed place-unit was available at least for some time during the 12 hours when Expo was open, on each of the 180 days of Expo.

After the Expo macroenvironment had been "mapped" into its component settings and places, patterns of adolescent leisure behavior were examined (Cotterell, 1990, 1991, 1993). Attendance patterns were found to be related to the distinctiveness of the different pavilion settings, including the style of their exhibits, preferences being given to "dynamic" over "static" displays. In addition, it was noted that young people differentiated the texture of the Expo macroenvironment, linking the atmosphere of different places to their own moods and choosing which leisure places to visit according to a process of person-environment fit. They reported, for example, that "[w]hen I go to the Funpark I'm excited; when I'm visiting pavilions I get more relaxed"; and how "the Riverstage always gets you in a good mood" and that "the Pacific Lagoon is primitive and peaceful." Behavior flows were traced between settings within Expo as well as into outside settings, and evidence was found that adolescents replaced their customary haunts by Expo places on the basis of locational convenience and the greater social stimulation of the Expo environment.

Figure 1: Aerial Photograph of Brisbane City and Expo 88 site. *Royal Australian Airforce (reprinted by permission)*

Following the closure of the World Expo in October 1988, a plan was announced by the state government for redevelopment of the Expo Site, and by mid-1989 the draft proposal was put on display and public reactions sought. The "Southbank Redevelopment" sought to link recreational land-use previously found in Expo with urban residential redevelopment in a mix of residential, commercial, and tourism-leisure functions. Its predominant focus was derived from landscape architecture, and unlike Expo, which was a walled enclosure that opened at 10 A.M. and closed at 10 P.M. daily, Southbank would be open for 24 hours each day. The land-use functions were distinguished from one another by means of a "precinct" framework, with different precincts containing their own distinctive mix of components. A feature of the development was a long lake and city beach, with adjoining parkland containing sports areas and children's museums, linked by paths and fronted by a river boardwalk. At one end of the public space would be an international hotel and conference center, and at the other a series of high-rise residential apartments. The precinct notion resembled Canter's concept of place in that activities as well as physical and architectural forms were described. However, limited consideration of behaviorial aspects meant that the draft design did not take into account potential conflicts between different groups of users at points within the environment. For example, the noise and movement generated by users of the swimming cove would be in conflict with the interests of the adjacent residents of apartments on the site; and children visiting the museum, aquarium, and noctarium were likely to cause congestion in the throughways and adjacent spaces reserved for active recreation. The precinct concept captured the notion of contrasting subareas with their own distinctive functions and atmosphere, but conceived of the interstitial areas as landscaped parkland or waterways. A modified design emerged from the period of public discussion and the submissions to the government authority concerning the redevelopment plan.

Figure 2 shows a general map of Southbank 1995, illustrated with descriptions and photos of some contrasting subenvironments. The map shows a series of regions within Southbank, which are generally oriented to be parallel with the Brisbane river to its north. The openness of the separate regions and enclaves means that boundaries are signaled by texture changes and that there is a degree of permeability between separate settings in that molar activities in one setting are transmitted into another. For example, the performers dancing at the end of Stanley Street Plaza were visible to people sitting on the other side of the pool. This location is favored by singing and dancing groups for the very reason of its centrality and adjacency to a variety of other settings. There is a good deal of harmony between the separate landscapes of Southbank. While children play on the slides and climbing frames or paddle in the rock-strewn creek, their parents can socialize and watch from a shaded gazebo next to the playground and the water areas (see Figure 2).

4   Explorations of selected macroenvironments

In summary, analysis of macroenvironments requires the application of a revised approach to behavior-setting research, including modifications to its methods for describing and measuring habitats and the inclusion of individual data on inhabitant behavior. The extent to which macroenvironments are amenable to the kinds of environment-behavior analysis that I have outlined is an empirical question as much as a theoretical one. I now examine issues of planning and design in museums, zoos, and theme parks in order to identify potential areas where the concepts and methods proposed in this chapter may be applied. These explorations are intended as illustrations rather than established procedures, given the lack of a body of established research on the principles advocated here, and given that the research within these environments has been guided by perspectives often remote from ecologically oriented environment-behavior research.

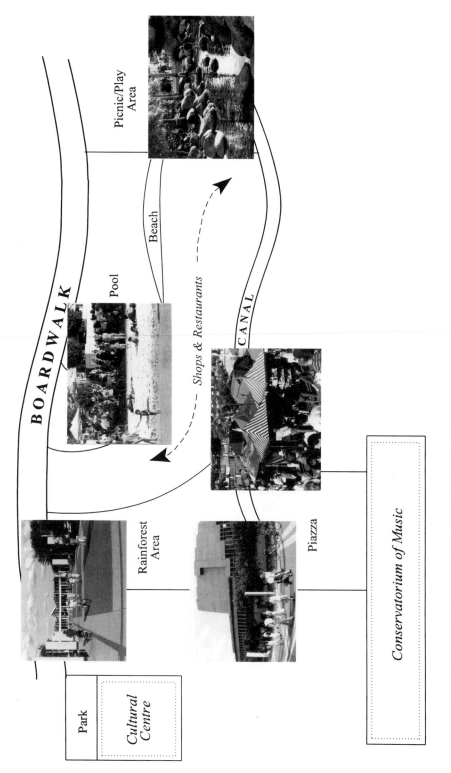

Figure 2: Sketchmap of Southbank and Photos of Selected Settings

4.1 Museums as displays versus interactive environments

A continuing concern of museums is securing visitor satisfaction, maintaining visitor attendance, and devising displays to achieve these goals. A difficulty of traditional museum displays is their "front-on" presentation, which restricts the role of the visitor to that of an onlooker rather than of a participant. In behavior-setting terms, the setting still operates when extraindividual behavior is restricted to watching and listening, but it is also known that satisfactions are increased where more participatory forms of behavior are encouraged. Because visitors are free to choose which exhibits to view, displays that are restricted to front-on formats fall victim to cursory visits, and whole galleries may be dismissed at a glance. While accepting that exploratory searching among the gallery displays plays an important part in museum visits, the concern for curators that arises from such quick tours is that the displays may not successfully engage the attention of visitors.

Diamond (1986) traced the movements of family groups in the Exploratorium in San Francisco and noted that there was a general pattern of rapid search ("shop around") during which a large number of exhibits were visited for very brief periods of time, mixed with longer investments of time being given to a small number of displays. School children who were observed in a Scottish science center (Tuckey, 1992) behaved similarly, with brief visits of less than 15 seconds at exhibits seen in this exploratory phase, although some returned two or three times for increasing periods. Tuckey found that the exhibits pupils remembered best were those that had the greatest interactive claim on them and engaged their attention most. Tracking of visitors was also undertaken by Klein (1993), who related the patterns of movement through a gallery to the display characteristics and sign-posting of the exhibits. Using the concept of coercive forces derived from behavior-setting theory, Klein found that the paths taken by visitors through the gallery could be altered through the simple introduction of clarifying information, which oriented visitors' attention and directed them to particular exhibits.

Science museums have been more inclined than other kinds of museums to develop participatory exhibits and demonstrations. The most successful of these museums is the Exploratorium in San Francisco, which opened in 1969, with the goal of promoting interactive principles of demonstration and experiment in a playful learning environment. Oppenheimer, its founder, argued for a hands-on approach to exhibits so that viewers had "the opportunity to react with them and to explore and manipulate them . . . at a variety of levels" (Danilov, 1989, p. 156). The small number of initial exhibits has now grown to some 750, scattered in the huge hall so that they can be touched and tried with the assistance of a large team of adolescents who act as "explainers." The model of participatory learning that Oppenheimer promoted allows children and adults to become actively involved with the science exhibits, manipulating levers and switches rather than remain onlookers. An additional feature of the Exploratorium is that the displays are not enclosed in rooms or

glassed-in boxes but are scattered around the vast exhibition hall. Interest in exploring any single exhibit is promoted by the visibility of adjoining exhibits and the flow
of behavior from participants at these nearby displays. Although there is synomorphy, the boundaries between exhibits are permeable to certain actions, particularly
those signaling excitement; as a consequence, arousal and persistence is high.

The involvement of explainers in sustaining the "program" of the display is also
important. From his observations in the Ontario Science Centre in Toronto, Parr
(1992) concluded that a key factor in achieving a participatory form of learning is
the enthusiasm and warmth of staff members, who see "showcases, static displays
and working models being supplemented by activities" (p. 73). These explainers
contribute to the setting's coercive forces over visitor behavior because they attempt
to engage the visitor's curiosity and then "make the visitor part of the action" (Parr,
1992, p. 74). In the language of behavior-setting theory, the museum environment is
so structured that the milieu of the display location is circumjacent to the visitor's
behavior, rather than 'front-on', and its coercive forces are enhanced accordingly.

4.2   Applications to the study of zoos

Research on zoos has mainly been concerned with visitor surveys and ratings of
exhibits rather than with ways of managing and assisting visitor movement, including rest points and relief from information overload. The presentation of exhibits has
changed over time, from "first-generation" cages to "third-generation" naturalistic
settings; and there is evidence that visitors prefer the newer formats, spending more
time there and learning more about the animals (see Shettel-Neuber, 1988). Natural
habitats allow animals to engage in normal behavior, and reflect a move away from
an entertainment function for zoos toward an educational function (together with
conservation functions). Although Shettel-Neuber (1988) did not work from an
environment-behavior frame, she acknowledged the system interdependencies of the
various zoo areas with respect to the effects that improvements in layout of one section may have on the presentation of other sections. In their study of selected animal
exhibits at 13 zoos Bitgood, Patterson, and Benefield (1988) identified several constituent elements of zoo exhibits (architectural layout, characteristics of the animals,
and attributes of visitors) and related these to visitor behavior. Among their findings
was the importance of the animal's activity level in sustaining visitor attention, and
the effect of conflicting architectural layouts (visitor viewing was reduced at sites
where exhibits were arranged in such a way that they competed for viewer attention).

Their conclusions (p. 490) could well be considered within the framework of
macroenvironment analysis of the component exhibits in a zoo. Using the "circuitry"
concepts of behavior-setting theory, one could evaluate the impact of various
subenvironments on their intended audiences/customers/inhabitants. Where particu-

lar component units of a macroenvironment are observed to attract and sustain low levels of attention from potential visitors, or few responses from visitors that are appropriate to the unit's "program" or "place rules", these units may need to be replaced, relocated, or remodeled.

Zoo macroenvironments include outdoor elements in their design of landscapes and places within these. Like other park developments, where visitors are required to walk to the various areas, designs are required that cater to three basic patterns of behavior: small-group assembly, large-group assembly, and pedestrian traffic flow. Planning must take account of the flow between different sites, the way in which each site relates to others, and place distinctiveness. Thus, in addition to creating sites that have individual styles, designers attempt to link areas by using creative pathways. Bitgood and Loomis (1993) refer to the need for designs to consider what they term "macroarchitectural factors" (p. 692), so that the overall layout of the environment facilitates visitor navigation and way-finding and also provides opportunities for rest and refreshment of interest.

4.3   Theme parks

Authors have remarked on the power of theme parks to hold their patrons for sustained periods of time, in many cases twelve hours, whereas museums have difficulty coping with visitor fatigue after half an hour. One can examine these issues through environment-behavior research by using aspects of behavior-setting theory to understand the crucial role of setting creation. To appreciate the design process, look at the differences between shopping malls and traditional shopping streets. Flanigan (1989) analyzed the environmental factors involved in attempts to redesign a traditional shopping street into a pedestrian shopping plaza, a phenomenom that became popular in the United States in the 1960s and 70s. He argued that many of these redesigns stagnated because their layouts and spatial structures did not take account of the contributions that people themselves make to the overall environment. He refered to "sense stimulation," which arises when the settings are compact and arranged so as to stimulate and sustain a variety of shopping experiences within the one environment. Shopping malls have high appeal because their total environment approaches the level of sensory stimulation of a bazaar or farmers' market crowded with merchandise and shoppers. Similarly, the sense stimulation of theme parks is assisted by the juxtaposition of contrasting landscapes and rides, the result being that visitors are subjected to the coercive attraction forces of nearby settings before they have the chance to enter them.

The theme park has radically altered the way in which displays are viewed, taking them from the traditional 'hands-off' exhibit to an interactive form, which enlists the visitor as a participant. The mode of engagement tends to be through the use of simulations to captivate the visitor's imagination. Theme parks like Disneyland achieve their wide cross-cultural appeal by embodying what an architects' forum (1990) calls "archetypal settings" such as a journey, by which the separate "lands" are reached (p. 57). The influence of the theme park is detectable in the design of places in historical villages, heritage parks, and world fairs, and it is also setting the standard for the design of modern museums. At the overall design level, "imagineers" assemble physical and behavioral elements in a process of "theming" the lands and settings in the park. King (1991) notes that through the device of theming, and "its shorthand stylisations of person, place and thing," the theme park establishes "an archive of collective memory and belief, symbol and archetype" (p. 6).

Some displays utilize mechanized props that ritualise the behavior of the central actors. For example, in the Disneyland country music display, bears play musical instruments, sing, and dance. Other settings use kinaesthetic means: rides in theme parks, such as Disneyland's Jungle River Cruise and Thunder Mountain roller-coaster ride include the visitor as a participant in the exhibit, although the person is unable to alter the ride in any way. The EPCOT center in Florida enlists technological innovations to provide visitors with simulated space travel, which suggests that physiological experiences of speed, motion, and weightlessness can generate altered psychological states. However, engagement of visitors may also be achieved by social participation. Among the most successful aspects of the World Expo in Brisbane was the waiting lines (yes!). These environmental fragments were transformed into settings by the actions of street entertainers, who created their own rules for interaction with members of the crowd. The settings in the historical theme park at Sovereign Hill in Ballarat, Australia, are driven by social scripts that are highly developed because the history takes on meaning through re-enactment, sustained by staff members who work the settings dressed in the clothing of the time. School children are encouraged to live in a 19th-century gold-mining village and become for a few days a child of the last century, attending school and performing family chores.

5 Conclusion

In this paper, I have argued that Barker's theory of behavior settings will continue to have value where there is a call for broader applications to environmental planning and design, particularly in those fields where environment-behavior relations are considered in terms of people in general, rather than in terms of individual participants. The strategy that I am advocating exploits aspects of behavior-setting theory in identifying the broader structures in the ecological environment but recognizes the value of other approaches, including those that are more psychological, in order to explore the interface between the ecological environment and the life space of the individual.

In environmentally based disciplines that take a molar view of human behavior, it is the nonpsychological emphasis of behavior-setting theory that contributes to its appeal. There is little doubt that consideration of system processes and the behavior of people in general is commonplace for planners. Lang (1991) argues that it is important for architects "to think of the environment as a behavior setting as well as a geometry of surfaces and textures" (p. 92). Design, he adds, is "an argumentative process" (p. 95) in which the behavioral component is important in determining what constitutes "effective environments" for different people. Richards (1990) has recently proposed that an emphasis on molar environments would allow the field of environmental psychology to develop as "a science of settings . . . using settings as the unit of analysis" (p. 315). There are numerous urban environments where such a science could be applied. In short, let's move up a level to macroenvironments.

The test of the applicability of an extension of ecological theory to the level of macroenvironment analysis will, of course, be made in the field and will require close analysis of the various environments and their dynamic interrelations. At times, the approach will require the use of ecological units that are different from behavior settings, but it will remain broadly consistent with behavior-setting theory because many questions relating to urban planning and design can be answered by the methods of ecological psychology.

Like an old boxer, Barker's behavior-setting theory has weathered a lot of punches from critics over the years. But the powers of ecological research are far from spent, as Altman (1990) seems to imply in his review of Schoggen (1989). Insofar as it is only beginning to be applied to larger environments in cities, you ain't seen nothin' yet!

Acknowledgments

In preparing this chapter, I particularly wish to thank each of the editors for their encouragement, patience, and very helpful comments on an earlier draft. Thanks are also due to Phil and Dikkie Schoggen for the wealth of knowledge they shared with me about behavior settings and for their warm friendship over the years. Special thanks also go to Louise Ireland, who has worked on several projects with me. Technical support in the preparation of diagrams was provided by Gaye Bear. The research reported in this chapter was supported by grants from the Brisbane City Council, Capricornia Coal, and the University of Queensland. I also wish to acknowledge the support of the Commanding Officer, Amberley Airforce Base, Australian Department of Defence in supplying photographs of the Expo site and authorizing permission to use them.

Note

1 In this discussion, I employ the term behavior-setting theory to refer to those aspects of Barker's ecological psychology that pertain to behavior settings and the synomorphy of places and behavior.

References

An architects' forum. (1990). Magic and power in the landscape (Discussion). *Landscape Architecture, 80* (6), 56-59.

Anderson, J., & Tindall, M. (1972). The concept of home range: New data for the study of territorial behavior. In W. J. Mitchell (Ed.), *Environmental design: Research and practice* (pp. 111-117). (EDRA Conference Proceedings, EDRA 3). Los Angeles: University of California Press.

Altman, I. (1990). Behavior settings: A revision and extension of Roger Barker's ecological psychology [Book review]. *Environment and Behavior, 22,* 538-541.

Barker, R. G. (1968). *Ecological psychology.* Stanford: Stanford University Press.

Barker, R. G. (1979). The influence of frontier environments on behavior. In J. O. Steffen (Ed.), *The American West: New perspectives, new dimensions* (pp. 61-93). Norman, OK: University of Oklahoma Press.

Barker, R. G. (1987). Prospecting in environmental psychology: Oskaloosa revisited. In D. Stokols & I. Altman (Eds.), *Handbook of environmental psychology* (Vol. 2, pp. 1413-1432). New York: Wiley.

Barker, R. G., & Gump, P. V. (Eds.). (1964). *Big school, small school.* Stanford, CA: Stanford University Press.

Berg, M., & Medrich, E. A. (1980). Children in four neighbourhoods. *Environment and Behavior, 12,* 320-347.

Bitgood, S., & Loomis, R. (1993). Introduction: Environmental design and evaluation in museums. *Environment and Behavior, 25,* 683-697.

Bitgood, S., Patterson, D., & Benefield, A. (1988). Exhibit design and visitor behavior: Empirical relationships. *Environment and Behavior, 20,* 474-491.

Canter, D. (1977). *The psychology of place.* London: Architectural Press.

Canter, D. (1986). Putting situations in their place: Foundations for a bridge between social and environmental psychology. In A. Furnham (Ed.), *Social behavior in context* (pp. 208-239). New York: Allyn and Bacon.

Cotterell, J. L. (1990). Youth leisure patterns and World Expo '88. *Youth Studies, 9* (1), 10-16.

Cotterell, J. L. (1991). The emergence of adolescent territories in a large urban leisure environment. *Journal of Environmental Psychology, 11,* 25-41.

Cotterell, J. L. (1993). Do macro-level changes in the leisure environment alter leisure constraints on adolescent girls? *Journal of Environmental Psychology, 13,* 125-136.

Danilov, V. J. (1989). The Exploratorium of San Francisco twenty years later. *Museum, 41,* 155-159.

Diamond, J. (1986). The behavior of family groups in science museums. *Curator, 29,* 139-154.

Flanigan, N. (1989). Life for traditional shopping streets: Avoiding the quick-fix solution. *Landscape Australia, 11,* (3), 283-294.

Gump, P. V. (1987). School and classroom environments. In D. Stokols & I. Altman (Eds.), *Handbook of environmental psychology* (Vol. 1, pp. 691-732). New York: Wiley.

Hart, R. A. (1979). *Children's experience of place: A developmental study*. New York: Irvington Press.

Kaminski, G. (1989). The relevance of ecologically oriented theory-building in environmental and behavioral research. In E. H. Zube & G. T. Moore (Eds.), *Advances in environment, behavior and design* (Vol. 2, pp. 3-36). New York: Plenum.

Katz, D., & Kahn, R. L. (1978). *The social psychology of organizations*. New York: Wiley.

King, M. J. (1991). 'Never land' or tomorrowland? *Museum, 43*, 6-8.

Klein, H. J. (1993). Tracking visitor circulation in museum settings. *Environment and Behavior, 25*, 782-800.

Lang, J. (1991). Design theory from an environmental and behavioral perspective. In E. H. Zube & G. T. Moore (Eds.), *Advances in environment, behavior and design* (Vol. 3, pp. 53-101). New York: Plenum.

Luke, D. A., Rappaport, J., & Seidman, E. (1991). Setting phenotypes in a mutual help organization: Expanding behavior setting theory. *American Journal of Community Psychology, 19*, 147-167.

Lynch, K. (1977). *Growing up in cities: Studies of the spatial environment of adolescence in Cracow, Melbourne, Mexico City, Salta, Toluca, and Warszawa*. Cambridge, MA: MIT Press.

McCall, R. B. (1977). Challenges to a science of developmental psychology. *Child Development, 48*, 333-344.

Parr, J. (1992). Science museums: Facts or ideas? *Museum, 44*, 73-76.

Perkins, D. W., Burns, T. F., Perry, J. C., & Neilsen, K. P. (1988). Behavior setting theory and community psychology: An analysis and critique. *Journal of Community Psychology, 16*, 355-372.

Richards, J. R., Jr. (1990). Units of analysis and the individual differences fallacy in environmental assessment. *Environment and Behavior, 22*, 307-319.

Schoggen, P. (1988). Commentary on Perkins, Burns, Perry, and Neilsen's "Behavior setting theory and community psychology: An analysis and critique." *Journal of Community Psychology, 16*, 373-386.

Schoggen, P. (1989). *Behavior settings*. Stanford, CA: Stanford University Press.

Schoggen, P., & Schoggen, M. (1988). Student participation and high school size. *Journal of Educational Research, 81*, 288-293.

Shettel-Neuber, J. (1988). Second- and third-generation zoo exhibits: A comparison of visitor, staff, and animal responses. *Environment and Behavior, 20*, 452-473.

Silbereisen, R. K., Noack, P., & Eyferth, K. (1986). Place for development: Adolescents, leisure settings, and developmental tasks. In R. Silbereisen, K. Eyferth, & H. Rudinger (Eds.), *Development as action in context: Problem behavior and normal youth development* (pp. 87-107). Berlin: Springer.

Sime, J. D. (1986). Creating places or designing spaces? *Journal of Environmental Psychology, 6*, 49-63.

Tuckey, C. J. (1992). Schoolchildren's reactions to an interactive science centre. *Curator, 35*, 28-38.

van Vliet--, W. (1983). Exploring the fourth environment: An examination of the home range of city and suburban teenagers. *Environment and Behavior, 15*, 567-588.

Comment: Behavior setting revitalized

Barbara Hinding

Searching for the term "behavior setting" in the data banks on the relevant literature of the last ten years, one does come across it occasionally. It quickly becomes evident, though, that empirical studies relating to the behavior-setting concept can be counted on the fingers of one hand. The approach is not in general use in environmental psychology today.

Cotterell would like to reintroduce Barker's "ecological psychology," particularly the concept of behavior setting, by modifying the approach to make it applicable to the modern city environment. He has two areas of practical relevance in mind: the evaluation of modern architecture in the public sphere, and research on the living conditions of children and adolescents.

1 Basic assumptions: Macroenvironments and behavior settings

Cotterell sees important elements of the modern city environment in certain clusters of behavior settings that he calls "macroenvironments." Macroenvironments are environment-behavior systems that stand out from their surroundings as coherent wholes by virtue of physical and temporal boundaries. They are not merely accumulations of behavior settings, like multiple-setting synomorphs, but a goal-centered assembly that has specific functions to serve.

The behavior settings that a macroenvironment contains can belong to different genotypes and can have varied temporal characteristics. The key point is that they are all oriented to a common goal and that they constitute a single authority system. In addition to the behavior settings, other "fine-grained" environment-behavior units are supposed to be kept in mind at various levels existing either below or at the same level as that of the behavior settings. Within macroenvironments, there are different functions that have impacts on the programs and action patterns of the setting. For that reason there are behavior settings that are specialized in certain functions. A variety of exchange relations between the different behavior settings help maintain those functions. In addition, there also exist maintenance inputs and control mechanisms that preserve the macroenvironmental system and repair breakdowns. The behavior settings thereby retain their special character as those parts of the environment in which day-to-day life itself takes place. They remain the basic unit of analysis. Inclusion of higher order units creates a goal orientation that transcends the program of the behavior setting and points to a cultural context of meaning.

2   Coherence of the assumptions

The assumptions are coherent as far as the metaphors of general systems theory or biological ecology are concerned. The assumption that there are transactions between behavior settings makes these settings open systems. They receive inputs that get processed, and they produce outputs that become inputs for other settings. The postulated regulatory processes also make it possible for behavior settings to change, for existing ones to disappear, or for new ones to emerge. Such changes occur through a process inherent to the system, without individual motives or goals having to be assumed. The focus of interest is the observable, preperceptual environment, not the experiential world of individuals. Subjective perspectives are to be taken into consideration as goals of action, but they are not integrated and are not readily combinable with the ecobehavioral orientation.

Cotterell's proposal, however, is little more than a declaration of intent. The hierarchical arrangement of the environmental system is not worked out in a consistent manner. The kind of environment-behavior units that are also to be included with the macroenvironments and behavior settings basically remains as unclear as their relations to each other. A few examples are given, but details are lacking. Further analysis of context or consistency is impossible because key terms are not sufficiently or clearly defined.

The term synomorphy is particularly obscure. To Barker, it is the correspondence between behavior and milieu, which he postulated as given. Only later was the word interpreted normatively and used as a criterion of evaluation in architecture. At that point, the degree to which environmental design and behavior fit together is examined. Cotterell expands this concept of synomorphy in two directions, subsuming both the extent to which different environment-behavior units are compatible and the concordance between the goals of the behavior settings and those of the persons participating in them. These issues may be justified; as interpretations of the concept of synomorphy they are too global in my opinion. "Lack of synomorphy" thus winds up meaning any kind of disturbance, and the original thought of the unity of behavior and milieu is abandoned for the sake of whatever dualisms happen to surface.

The term macroenvironment, too, still seems unclear. A defining feature of a macroenvironment is, for example, the existence of a single "authority system", which is defined as a behavior setting that controls other behavior settings. In the rest of the chapter, however, the expression serves more as a synonym for power or authority pure and simple, a usage that considerably broadens the scope of interpretation. The other defining features of the macroenvironment are handled similarly. It seems arbitrary to categorize macroenvironments as habitat types. Their meaning and origin are not explained.

Moreover, the demand to make such assignability a criterion for the demarcation of macroenvironments excludes from the definition many clusters of behavior settings that would otherwise be accessible to behavior-setting theory. For example, dwellings, the immediate vicinity, and the street are precluded as objects for research although they are spheres in which urbanites, especially children and adolescents, spend a large part of their everyday lives.

3   The concept and conception of development

Behavior-setting theory is not a theory of development. Forecasts about individual changes are impossible if only because of the special perspective taken on the ecological environment – one in which individuals play no role.

Cotterell brings in development by proposing a change of perspective. The idea is to explore the natural habitats of different species (groups) by documenting their behavior across different environment-behavior units. The result is a kind of inventory of "species-specific habitats." The word habitat thus refers to all those environment-behavior units that offer, say, 10- to 12-year-old girls the opportunity to take part in different activities outside the parental dwelling. It thereby becomes possible to record what children and adolescents actually do during their daily lives, for the range of behavior and the settings that are sought out are recorded simultaneously.

"Setting" in this sense means not only the physical aspect; behavior settings always include the social environment as well. Development takes place as adaptation to the demands of the habitat. Psychological processes entailed by that adaptation remain reduced to the assumption that participation in behavior settings leaves traces in the person. Human behavior and development thus appear as a relatively passive product of behavior settings. The fact that human beings in their telic action also actively shape the behavior setting into which they enter, that they initiate new ones and dissolve others, is not initially acknowledged in Cotterell's chapter. Activity is confined to the selection of appropriate behavior settings.

One should not belabor this point, however, for the investigation into the question of who has what environmental contacts is of some heuristic merit. It could lead to ideas and assumptions about how developmental processes take place under everyday conditions. Comparing different age groups could give clues about how differently small children, school-age children, adolescents, and adults use the environment and about which age-specific ends and means are involved. This comparison could then open a holistic view of the underlying processes, one that embraces all areas of development: motoric, cognitive, social, and so forth.

What this access offers most is a framework, a guide, for observing in new and different ways, in a wider, more encompassing sense than has been the case thus far, and for developing hypotheses about change processes over entire life spans, not about existing or directly derivable assumptions about development.

4 Application of behavior-setting theory for children in the city

Working directly from the approach, one cannot draw recommendations about how the environment of children or adolescents is to be shaped so that they feel good there and so that their development is likely to be enhanced. The possibilities lie instead with its application to practical issues surrounding the use of these age groups.

The main concern in behavior-setting theory is to describe environmental quality, that of a city, for instance. The concept of habitat enables one to ascertain a city's or district's resources at different levels of generality for each group. Comparisons with other cities can reveal shortcomings and special qualities, much as they do in different planning disciplines. The very listing, counting, and summarizing of the macroenvironments accessible to children in a city or district – according to, say, types of habitat – could convey an impression of the variety of alternatives. Macroenvironments contain several behavior settings on whose basis a characterization is feasible. Such inventories of macroenvironments would necessarily be very general because much of what children and adolescents do simply cannot be captured by a chart or grid. Nevertheless, they are a way to describe what happens and to compare it to what is going on elsewhere. Taking behavior setting theory into account gives an advantage over mere lists of existing places or facilities at which children are typically encountered. One finds out not only how many places or specific facilities there are of one habitat type but also which behavioral options are associated with them. Unlike the case with a theory of development, the focus is not inevitably on developmental conduciveness but rather on the richness of current options, without thought necessarily being given to what they may mean for the future.

Little is known about the significance of macroenvironments in the everyday lives of children and adolescents, especially about units from the leisure habitat (facilities such as recreation centers, department stores, swimming pools, museums, and discotheques). How much time is spent by which age groups, where, and how frequently? What do they do there and with whom? Are there differences between boys and girls? Answers to such questions could lead to an idea about what functions these and other facilities have for each of their young users or how the different environment-behavior units are linked with subcultures and life styles. In contrast to mere observation, the proposed inclusion of a subjective perspective would cast additional light upon the motives that the subjects have for seeking out or not seeking out these places and upon the corresponding experiences, perceptions, and connotations. With this added dimension, one arrives at a picture of the demands being made on settings as a function of age, a picture detailing the changes in claims on the environment beyond childhood and adolescence. It could be an important stimulus not only for developmental psychology but especially for the planning disciplines and for the management of children's or leisure facilities, which could improve the degree to which their designs and regulations of use (i.e., the programs of the setting) match the needs of these age groups.

Most theories about the person-environment relation lead one to consider only the individual in his or her physical surroundings. But planners design spaces in which widely varied groups of users are present simultaneously. Behavior-setting theory takes this aspect into account by turning attention to what is going on in general. It is thereby possible to explore conflicts between different groups of users, between adolescents and adults, for example. Because the interaction of different behavior systems is systematically investigated, it is likely that conflicts and contradictions will surface clearly and that they can be analyzed precisely. In this manner one will find where discrete environment-behavior units are incompatible and must be separated in space or time or where improvements can be made with organizational measures. Whereas some exponents of ecological psychology have a tendency to segregate functions spatially (a response that would lead to the demarcation of special areas for people of a given age), the investigation of transactions between environment-behavior units, especially transactions involving regulation processes, can help answer the question of where additional integration and networking is desirable and how to achieve them.

5   Merits of the approach

The strength of the behavior-setting theory lies in its application to practical issues of environmental design. The intention behind environmental planning is to make spaces available for behavior. It is oriented primarily to technical and economic aspects. The planner does not deal with individuals but with mostly anonymous user groups. Traditional approaches centered on the individual cannot contribute much in this respect. By contrast, behavior settings are environment-behavior units in which behavior and milieu are regarded as almost inextricably intertwined with each other. Attention focuses simultaneously on the physical and social milieu on the one hand and the molar behavior of the users as a whole on the other. How the individual behaves, and even what the individual experiences, is not a matter of consideration. This special feature is precisely what makes the approach particularly attractive as an interface between psychology and planning disciplines.

Behavior-setting theory can be used to ascertain the richness of behavioral options that a city offers its different groups of inhabitants and to evaluate individual design elements at the macrolevel. A major focus of studies on individual macroenvironments is on the transactions between the different subsystems, with special attention being given to the search for symptoms that indicate a lack of synomorphy, or fit. It is necessary to forgo theoretically derivable hypotheses serving as preliminary assumptions. It is not possible to make predictions of behavior for an individual architectonic design, that is, the arrangement of behavior settings. The resulting indeterminacy of the approach ultimately allows the researcher to choose from one case to the next which features of complex action will be recorded. Granted, one can thereby respond flexibly to the demands of the object at hand. After all, the example of Southbank Redevelopment shows that such factors as noise, commotion, the view, and the chance to observe others can be included. But without more exacting methodological precepts, there is the danger of moving scarcely beyond a common-sense understanding of what is going on.

At the moment, the reader is left with little more than the concept of behavior setting as a basic unit and some aspects of general systems theory as a metaphor. Systemic family therapy, in which the new look at deviant behavior has led to new explanations and new practices, shows that interesting developments can result from it.

Behavior settings as vehicles of children's cultivation

Urs Fuhrer

1 A plea for a cultural view of development

One tends to feel almost confused by the diversity of research on the psychology of the child that have been and are still being carried out. Some studies, spurred by psychoanalysis, are primarily devoted to the blossoming of the child's affective life. Others, extending Piaget's epistemology, attempt to provide better descriptions, if not explanations, of children's mental and moral development (see Seiler, in this volume). One may also define a third trend, of mixed origins, in which the developing child is conceptualized in the context of his or her interrelationships with the external environment. This alternative to the more person-centered developmental models of psychoanalysis and epistemology, and often labeled as ecological (see Bronfenbrenner & Crouter, 1983; Bronfenbrenner, Kessel, Kessen, & White, 1986; Lang, 1988; Bronfenbrenner, 1989; Bronfenbrenner, in this volume), stems mainly from the work of Kurt Lewin and his intellectual followers such as Roger Barker, Herbert Wright, and Urie Bronfenbrenner. Although the evidence is still meager and most of it indirect, another conceptual line of theorizing of long standing is beginning to be adopted in investigations of human development. I refer to the emerging revolution in psychology that culture and human development are an integral unity, such that culture and human development mutually define one another and that, indeed, one cannot literally understand a developmental phenomenon without studying culture and development as a single unit of analysis (see for example Super & Harkness, 1986; Valsiner, 1989; Bruner, 1990; Cole, 1995).

Since the mid-1980s the focus on the role of culture in development has been significantly influenced by the writings of Russian psychologists associated with the cultural-historical school of Vygotsky, Luria, and Leont'ev (see Valsiner, 1987, or Cole, 1995, for a summary of this line of thought in relation to human development). Central to their formulations is the notion that human beings are distinct from other creatures in that they live in an environment transformed by the artifacts (mediators) of prior generations. The basic function of these artifacts is to coordinate human beings and their development with the environment and each other (Fuhrer & Josephs, in press).

Aside from the efforts of a still growing number of scholars relating their work to the Vygotskyian tradition, a prominent example of a cultural view of development was largely neglected – *the concept of cultivation* as it was introduced by the German sociologist Georg Simmel in 1908 (see also Levine, 1971). His main assumption is that the development of the psyche is based on the cultivation principle, whereby psychologically constituted realities and reality-constituted psyches are mutually adjusted to one another until some attractive equilibrium is reached. It is obvious that cultivation as human-environment transaction (Fuhrer, 1993) is familiar to the transactional paradigm of development (see Wapner, in this volume). Cultivation, however, is not synonymous with transaction.

The theoretical perspective described in this chapter is based on the cultural developmental thinking of both Georg Simmel and the Lewinian scholar Roger G. Barker. The two approaches, however, have developed separately; each has attracted attention, but no one has tried to incorporate the contribution of the other to create an account of human developmental processes that recognizes the essential relation between individuals and their cultural settings. I therefore start this chapter by outlining Simmel's role as intellectual innovator of social sciences and his view of development as cultivation. I then present the conceptual cornerstone of the Barker school, the behavior setting concept. Thereafter, I elaborate this concept in terms of cultivation. From this kind of viewpoint, behavior settings, individuals, and their development are interpreted as interrelated processes that constitute each other, and social scientists' delimitations between components parts of persons, their development, and the world are intentionally blurred. This attempt to rethink development as cultivation leads to the question of what makes behavior settings attractive vehicles for the study of children's cultivation. I tackle this question by using data from diaries of 184 children aged 10, 12, and 14 years who lived in a rural Swiss town in 1992. Lastly, I outline future avenues for a cultural developmental psychology.

2 Form in culture and personality

Of those who created the intellectual capital used to launch the enterprise of professional sociology, Georg Simmel was perhaps the most original and fecund. In search of subject matter that would distinguish from all other social sciences and humanistic disciplines, he charted a new field for discovery and proceeded to explore a world of novel topics in works that have guided and anticipated the thinking of generations of sociologists. For example, the influence of Simmel on Max Weber, other German sociologists, some of the most famous representatives of the Chicago school of sociology such as Robert Ezra Park and Ernest Burgess was direct and enduring (see Frisby, 1981); and his affinity to the cultural view of both the American pragmatism and the symbolic interactionist school is obvious (see Rochberg-Halton, 1986).

The starting point of Simmel's (1908) theory of culture is the distinction between form and content. Contents are those aspects of existence that are determined in themselves, but as such contain neither structure nor the possibility of being apprehended by humans in their immediacy. Forms are the synthesizing principles that select elements from the raw stuff of experience and shape them into determinate unities. In this respect forms are identical with Kant's a priori categories of cognition, but they differ from the latter in two important respects. They inform not only the cognitive realm, but any and all dimensions of human experience. And they are not fixed and immutable, but emerge, develop, and perhaps disappear over time.

Along this lines of reasoning, Simmel assumes that the experiencing self divides into a self-conscious subject and a confronted object. The forms that come into being at this stage are fragmentary and preliminary in character. At this stage of "protoculture," they are bound by the pragmatic interests and adaptive exigencies of the immediate situation. As soon as elements of protoculture have been created for specific practical reasons, they take on an existence of their own. While still rooted in subjective purposes, they become objectified. Sooner or later the forms can be liberated from their connection with practical purposes and become objects of cultivation in their own right. For example, moral regulations designed to regulate human relationships become transformed into autonomous ethical standards. This is the movement from "protoforms" to objective forms.

Beyond any particular realization of "objective culture," there is a *third level of cultural formation*, which Simmel refers to as that of "worlds" (Simmel, 1908). Each of the main types of formative capacity of the human mind is able to shape the totality of contents into a self-contained, irreducible world of experience. The so-called real world consists of that complex of representations needed for one to act adaptively in accord with the psychobiological requirements of the human species. Equally valid as ways of organizing all the contents of life are the worlds of art, theoretical knowledge, values, religion, and so on.

From the many contents that offer themselves as means for individual development, the self selects circumspectly. Its receptive capacity is limited by the degree of unity and closure it has already attained and by the limitations of time and energy of each individual life. The development of objective culture, on the other hand, knows no such limits. It can draw on the contributions of innumerable individuals over many generations.

The elaboration of a given body of culture may then proceed in either of two directions, depending on the relation between cultural forms and the self. To understand this choice properly one must first digress for a brief consideration of Simmel's structural theory of personality; it, too, is based on the distinction between form and content. Just as concrete cultural products are only finite and imperfect realizations of the ideality of some "world," so individual persons are only limited realizations of their ideal selves; ideal not in the sense of what they should be according to some external criteria, but ideal in the sense of a projection of the actual tendencies and syntheses manifested in each individual's own existence. The attainment of individuality is thus not a matter of arbitrary subjectivity, but rather a movement toward realization of a determinate objective form.

In the course of reflecting on this topic over many years, Simmel (1908) produced a number of profound questions and observations including the different forms in which individuality may be attained, the social conditions that favor the attainment of individuality, and the individualities manifested in outstanding historic personalities (see Wolff, 1950). In the present chapter, I am concerned with only one aspect of this vast topic: the relation between "subjective culture" and "objective culture," i.e., cultivation.

3   Culture and human development considered as cultivation

Simmel's (1908) work on culture refers to the cultivation of individuals through the agency of external forms that have been externalized from individual minds in the course of history. This objectified environment, however, refers to only one side of cultivation. The other side, the extent to which individuals assimilate and make use of this objective culture for their personal growth, is the domain of subjective culture. Cultivation, therefore, is a transactional process involving the refinement of both subjective culture *and* objective culture; each one is mediated by the other, and they therefore presuppose each other (Fuhrer, 1993).

The importance of subjective culture derives from the fact that individuals like children or adolescents, unlike any other known creature, carry within themselves the need to be "cultivated." Along these lines of reasoning, human development as cultivation can be conceptualized as a process of developing in a creature a state of being that would not come about naturally, but for which that creature has a natural propensity, by utilizing objects or settings external to it. The capacity for cultivation is inseparately bound up with the human psyche. The process requires that these contents be relevant to and integrated into the central core of the self. Cultivation, therefore, exists only in the process of the psyche's self-development, provided that this self-development relies on external, objective means (Simmel, 1908). Individuals are more or less active centers of a drive toward individuality. As such, they are consumers of cultural objects in accord with the needs of their developing subjective culture. Thus, cultivation considered from the perspective of the self is that development of meaning that follows the inherent proclivities of the being and as such may be called culture (Simmel, 1908).

Simmel was not trying to claim that the self is absolutely determined in advance, only that there is a unique configuration of determining factors in every individual that give the individual unique potentials. Thus, cultivation is not simply the unfolding of inner stages of development, in which the objects of experience do not make a qualitative difference in development (as someone like Piaget might hold). Instead, Simmel made a strong claim for the otherness of interaction as constitutive. One can then postulate that in every act of transforming certain components of the culturally structured environment, one "consumes" or "reproduces," at least in part, the behavioral "footprints" of others (see Vygotsky's (1978) cultural-historical approach for a similar view). Metaphorically speaking, one's own footprints and those of others make up each other (see Fuhrer, 1993). That is, culture calls attention to the transaction of the individual with the culturally structured environment that becomes a product of the transaction and emphasizes how individual and external environment cultivate each other.

Following my own discussion of Simmel's cultivation principle (see Fuhrer, 1993), one finds that the overarching goal of culturally structured environments remains internally oriented cultivation. Along the same lines of reasoning, to Rochberg-Halton (1986) cultivation means the web of meaning that is the medium for the self and that is not merely a noun (culture) but an active process of interpretation requiring both care and inquiry. In applying Oerter's (1991; this volume) theorizing on the development of self-object relations to the transactional relationship between objective culture and subjective culture, one finds that cultivation is constituted by the combination of four different processes: internalization, externalization, subjectivation, and objectivation. Both internalization and externalization are intertwined with subjectivation and objectivation. For example, Piaget's (1959) epistemological interest (see Seiler, in this volume) focused almost exclusively on internalization, that is the process of both adapting the action possibilities of the culture into an internal schema (assimilation) and adapting an internal schema toward the culturally structured environment (accommodation).

Within the tradition of Piaget, the process of internalization during child development was explored by many psychologists; the corresponding process of externalization, however, was rarely studied. With regard to externalization, the environment is constructed, reconstructed, and even co-constructed (e.g., by other children who transact with the same setting) according to the children's own internal psychic structures toward an increase of new action possibilities, such as girls' and boys' personalization of their rooms or their use of playgrounds "against the rules," as happens quite often in children's play. In contrast to Piaget's view, Valsiner (1988) introduced both concepts in connection with his theoretical approach to development within culturally structured environments. In a similar vein, and from the perspective of cultural action theory, both concepts belong together and have to be treated as compensatory processes (see Boesch, 1991).

Objectivation, in turn, as an equivalent of Piaget's accommodation, focuses on the change of the culturally structured environment according to the external conditions governing actions in a given culture. An example is building an adventure playground or modifying the natural landscape in whatever manner children choose. In this sense, the self develops only when culturally structured environments become internalized. Becoming a self, therefore, means becoming an "object" of one's own interpretation. In terms of the cultivation principle, it is correct to say, then, that the self is a transaction between the interpretation of internal structures and external structures and that in this sense the self is in two places (Rochberg-Halton, 1986; Fuhrer, 1993).

Overall, cultivation can be understood as being composed of all four facets, whereby one combination might be more accentuated than the other depending on the nature of both internal and external structures. In contrast to many other contextualized developmental approaches, cultivation as a paradigm for development involves much more than the mere assimilation of cultural contents. Above all, it requires that those contents be relevant and integrated into the central core of the self.

4   A new perspective of human behavior

In psychology, both Lewin's (1936) and Barker's (1968) theorizing exemplify many aspects of a transactional perspective. Lewin considered psychological processes to be embedded in physical and social settings, forming a "life space" or "psychological field." He departed from a strict transactional perspective by assuming quasi-stationary equilibrium states toward which life spaces develop. Although readily accepted in principle, these ideas have not always been translated into theoretical and empirical work. An exception, however, is the ecological research by Barker and his associates (see Schoggen, 1989). Ecological psychology, or ecobehavioral science, as Barker later named the discipline, had its beginning in 1947, when Roger Barker and Herbert Wright opened the Midwest Psychological Field Station at the down-home farming community of Midwest (code name), Kansas. The original modest purpose was to study the development of children in a town small enough to observe and measure. Barker and Wright's (1955) studies moved from an attempt to characterize behavior settings in one community to comparisons of settings across several communities. In the 1960s, Barker opened a counterpart to Midwest in Yoredale (code name), England, and over a decade compared the demise and rise of behavior settings in the sister towns (see Barker & Schoggen, 1973). The Midwest-Yoredale comparative research was undertaken in the hope that the similarities and differences identified in the public life of the two towns might reflect differences in both social opportunities and social obligations of the larger U.S. and English cultures.

4.1 Behavior settings as "natural" human-environment systems

Along with the application of naturalistic methods, there evolved a new perspective on human behavior according to which behavior and environment were seen as occurring in inseparable units called behavior settings. In Barker's terms, these behavior settings are natural phenomena with both specific, denotable space-time locus and people displaying regularly occurring behavior patterns. There is a similarity in structure (called "synomorphy") between these behavior patterns that occur within the arrangement of the physical objects; and these patterns exist independent of any particular person's perception of them, i.e., they are preperceptual ecological entities (Barker, 1968).

Rather than record all human actions in a particular town, Barker and Wright (1955) discovered that places like villages, towns, or cities can be studied in small-scale environments, that is, in the format of behavior settings. Whether one considers neighborhoods, small towns, or metropolitan centers, they are assemblies of behavior settings where people are essential components. Barker and his co-workers discovered that it is easier to predict children's behavior on the basis of what behavior settings they entered than from behavior profiles of the individual children.

While much of developmental psychology viewed children's environments as passive arenas and handled them (conceptually) as a kind of black box, Barker and Wright proposed that behavior settings lead dynamic lives, governed by their own sets of rules, opening goal opportunities, and capable, however, of coercing certain behavior from the people who enter them. Crowded streets, a playground, a shopping mall – each has its own imperatives. This linking of behavior with environment has led to the claim that the psychological field station gave birth to an ecologically oriented psychology.

Barker and his co-workers discovered that human habitats consist of a series of nested ecological units, ranging from single synomorphs to more complex assemblies of synomorphs (see Figure 1). They began experimenting with ways to measure these attributes and came up with a series of scales, which became the principal units of measurement in ecobehavioral science (see Barker, 1968).

4.1.1 Synomorphs
Synomorphs consist of single behavior-milieu parts, that is, they encompass physical and behavioral attributes that are similar in structure (e.g., a child sitting at the school desk, a teacher writing on the blackboard). Synomorphs are the smallest human-environment units, and they have a greater degree of interdependence between themselves than with parts of other behavior settings. Two or more synomorphs form a behavior setting.

4.1.2 K-21 behavior settings

While most behavior settings such as playgrounds, grocery stores, and school classes are easily identified, it is often difficult to know intuitively whether, for example, the lunch counter at a drug store is a separate behavior setting from the pharmacy counter. Thus, the scale was developed to determine whether two putative behavior settings are actually separate or whether they constitute a single setting. The K-21 scale consists of seven subscales (7-point Likert scales) that are added together. The K-test of interdependency is based upon ratings of the degree to which (a) the same people enter both settings, (b) the same leaders are active in both settings, (c) both settings use similar spaces, (d) both settings use similar behavior objects, (e) the same molar action units span the two settings, (f) both settings occur at the same time, and (g) the same kinds of behavior mechanisms occur in the settings. A rating of 1 represents the greatest similarity, a rating of 7 the least similarity between synomorphs on the measure in question; if the sum is 21 or more, the behaviors are considered separate behavior settings. If it is below 21, they are deemed too interdependent to be separate.

4.1.3 Multi-setting synomorphs

If a certain part of a community contains synomorphs with less than the specified degree of interdependence, that is if any of these synomorphs are too independent of other synomorphs of a certain community part, or too independent of the whole bunch of synomorphs, then this community part is, by definition, more than a single behavior setting. This criterion serves to exclude as behavior settings such synomorphs as churches, schools, and many other institutions. These behavior-milieu structures are not behavior settings, but clusters of behavior settings, that is, multi-setting synomorphs.

4.1.4 Macrosystems

Lastly, synomorphs, behavior settings, and multi-setting synomorphs are embedded in sociogeographical contexts. These largest human-environment systems can be described in terms of Bronfenbrenner's (1979) macrosystem. Within Barker's work there is no term for these largest systems, which are defined by cultural boundaries. Although there is no concept that captures contexts larger than multi-setting synomorphs, Barker's work recognizes on such "cultural macrocontexts" (see Barker & Schoggen, 1973; Schoggen, 1989).

Contrasting social interaction in the behavior settings of an American town (Midwest) and a town of similar size in Great Britain (Yoredale), Barker and Schoggen (1973) reported differences not only between the two towns but also between the two macrocontexts in which they are located. For example, behavior settings designed especially for the benefit of children increased substantially in Midwest but decreased slightly in Yoredale, whereas the reverse relation occurred in the behavior settings where children benefit members of other age groups (Barker & Schoggen, 1973).

In contrast to Bronfenbrenner's (1979) work, however, Barker and most of his co-workers do not draw much attention to either multisetting influences on development nor to "ecological transitions" that take place whenever a person undergoes a change in role within a setting or in a different setting during the life course. However, Allan Wicker (1987, 1992) has focused on ways to account for changes in the level of functioning of behavior settings and for setting growth and decline.

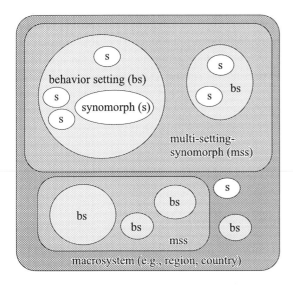

Figure 1: Behavior settings and their relations to smaller and larger ecological contexts

4.2   Behavior settings reconsidered: Cultural human-environment systems

The fact that a behavior setting is typically both located in a man-made environment (i.e., the milieu) and regulated by social norms and rules (i.e., the setting program) says that behavior settings are cultural rather than "natural" settings. I thus suggested that behavior settings be regarded as cultural constructions whose structure can be understood in terms of "life-spaces" that were collectively shared among setting occupants within a particular cultural group or community (Fuhrer, 1990). In accord with Wicker's (1987, 1992) theoretical reformulation of Barker's "pre-psychological" view of behavior settings, the revised framework also recognizes an additional level of analysis beyond that of the person and the behavior setting, that is, the larger cultural environment that constitutes the context of behavior settings (Fuhrer, 1990). Thus, both behavior settings and the larger cultural world in which these behavior settings are embedded are of a culturally structured environment (see also Valsiner, 1988, for a similar view).

Generally, cultural events have an intrinsic double aspect. They give meaning, that is, objective conceptual form, to the social and physical environment both by shaping themselves to it and by shaping it to themselves. Actions, things, places, and temporal dynamics are interlocked in such a way that actions gain meaning by virtue of the actors and actions that exist within it. Thus, it is not surprising that there is remarkable consensus among cultural communities in describing person/group-environment transactions in terms of behavior settings (Stokols & Shumaker, 1981).

However, doubts have often been raised about these assertions, specifically about whether behavior settings can be validly described as kinds of "collectively shared life spaces" in the face of individual variation (Fuhrer, 1990, p. 533). For example, a behavior setting like a market place or a volleyball game has more than a collectively shared meaning, that is, the denotative setting qualities as captured by Barker's K-21 scale. It is important to recognize that behavior settings are full of personal and group-specific experiences; and these "connotations" are not expressed by the denotative level of the K-21 setting analysis. Although this symbolism of settings on the connotative level is extremly complex, it merits considerable attention (see Boesch, 1991).

5   Children cultivate behavior settings to cultivate themselves

In the most general terms, the present endeavor is an effort to integrate the theoretical perspectives of Kurt Lewin, especially of Roger G. Barker, and Georg Simmel. The cultivation paradigm of the present theory is explicitly structuralistic. In other words, it emphasizes the fact that both the developing child and his or her environment are structurally organized. That structured nature of the child and the child's environment is not static and immutable; it is dynamically transformed as the child develops in transaction with the behavior settings in the surrounding culturally structured environment. However, a number of basic notions on which this theory is built must be made more explicit.

5.1   The "using" versus the "cultivation" paradigm of development

In applying Simmel's (1908) view of cultivation to Barker's ecobehavioral science, one notes that children do not simply use behavior settings to take part in some more or less prescribed behavior patterns. Rather, they transact with behavior settings as vehicles to cultivate themselves. That is, they externalize their ideas, goals, and plans when they act, more or less, in accord with the behavior setting. However, by changing either the standing behavior patterns or the physical milieu, children, to varying degrees, transform a behavior setting; they cultivate the behavior setting. For example, kids often engage in alterability play, involving modification either of the physical milieu, the play objects, or the playing rules. The contrast between changing (cultivating) the behavior setting by self-specific actions à la Simmel and just using it à la Barker illuminates the basic difference between the two approaches.

Bringing these two theoretical perspectives together, however, one sees that "settings as vehicles of cultivation" denotes a model of development that entails two critical issues. First, development is seen as the outcome of an individual's own potential for self-specific development aimed at cultivating external environments to make them a part of the self. Second, such externally oriented self-specific actions produce not only change in the environmental context of development, but change in the individual as well; behavior settings as culturally structured environments become vehicles for cultivation. Thus, it is cultivation that links the changing individual and the changing environment (see Fuhrer & Josephs, in press).

This view of development corresponds closely with "development as action in context" as a paradigm for developmental research (see Silbereisen, Eyferth, & Rudinger, 1986). The cultivation model of development, however, differs from this paradigm with respect to the central role of the self as a manifestation of subjective culture and objective culture (in the sense used by Simmel, 1908). In fact, if one views development as cultivation, then the overarching goal of development is the continued growth and concretization of the self, a process that is reached only in transaction with purposively created objects, settings, and other components of the culturally structured environment. For example, a musical child may need a piano lesson to enact his or her musical talent, just as others need a football game or an adventure playground to activate aspects of their selves.

Moreover, development as cultivation within a given behavior setting can be part of a larger socialization process providing necessary elements for aspects of the self. For the child, being socialized into school (as a multi-setting synomorph) also means being socialized in school lessons (as behavior settings). Thus, it may not seem so far-fetched to say that behavior settings can be actual manifestations of the self. However, children differ significantly on how behavior settings become relevant vehicles for the definition of their selves (see Fuhrer, Kaiser, & Hangartner, 1995).

In the absence of more extensive research by developmental psychologists on the qualities of behavior settings for children's cultivation, I refer instead to Muchow and Muchow's (1935) interesting precursor of this approach (see also Wohlwill, 1985). Martha Muchow's work on the life space of children was among the earliest and is still one of the most outstanding approaches concerning children's experiences of urban environments. Consistent with frequent observations by others, the children Muchow observed made use of public spaces intended primarily for pedestrian and vehicular traffic – notably city streets – for their play, while avoiding areas specifically set aside for them such as developed parks. Similarly, they spontaneously selected undeveloped areas in a city block, adapting them for their play activities, while avoiding developed areas. Particularly intriguing is Muchow's comparison between adults' and children's uses of an area serving as a relatively little-used loading and unloading facility for canal ship traffic. Of similar interest are the observations of children's exploration of a large department store, including the analysis of stratagems employed to slip past the guard at the gate in order to gain access into it.

This type of study, combining an ecological focus with an naturalistic approach, has been all too infrequent in this area. Notable exceptions are, for example, Hart's (1979) studies of children in a small Vermont village, Herb Wright's city project on children's activity range in two Kansas towns (1970), and the work that a few German developmental psychologists have done with children in Berlin and, especially, Herten (see Görlitz, 1993; Görlitz & Schröder, 1994). Muchow's work nicely illustrates the significant role of vacant lots and undeveloped areas for children's play. These milieus are used not only for ballplay and other games but also for activities such as climbing and digging. In a similar vein, certain research on child behavior in the outdoor environment points to the significance of settings that are not highly structured in terms of the physical layout and arrangement of significant elements and the behavior appropriate to and supported by these settings (see Wohlwill & Heft, 1987). The work that Hayward, Rothenberg, and Beasley (1974) have done on children's behavior play settings of different types is illustrative in this regard. The study provides useful information, notably on the use of adventure playgrounds, which designers have favored for some time. Hayward et al. (1974) pointed out the value of the adventure-type playground, with its openness and lack of fixed structure for creative and imaginative, as opposed to purely physical, play and thus its suitability for children beyond the preschool level. Generally, the common refrain in the research on children's outdoor play has been that children, particularly of school age, and boys more than girls, tend to prefer physical milieus such as streets, empty lots, quarries, and undeveloped natural areas for their play, as opposed to more structured, designed, and equipped playgrounds (see Wohlwill & Heft, 1987). With regard to adolescents, the work by Silbereisen, Noack, & Eyferth (1986) also illuminates the relevance of behavior settings that are characterized by a loose relation between the physical layout and the behavior patterns of the setting. They pointed out the significant role of "niches" that open opportunities for actions toward "unofficial" goals. These kinds of informal functions are exemplified by such actions as hanging out in shopping centers or roughhousing at swimming pools.

In sum, I assume that a series of self-specific transactions is initiated by children either to transform existing behavior settings or to look for congenial ones. Here again, the distinction between cultivating and using is important. The latter seems dominant in the environmental psychology literature on child development (see Weinstein & David, 1987; Wohlwill & Heft, 1987). In other words, if one likes behavior setting X to act in (and selects it), then one prefers it to others, whereas the cultivation idea links preference with the opportunity for self-specific transactions

with the environment. Thus, the development-as-cultivation paradigm has fundamental implications for both theory (e.g., children's transactions with behavior settings to self-cultivate along lines not foreseen by adults' understanding of "what
children want") and application (i.e., frustration of many efforts by city planners to
design "developed areas"; Hart, 1987).

5.2   Urban children's access to their town's behavior settings

Of course, cultivation will vary with the availability of behavior settings, especially
with the degree to which behavior settings are segregated by age. One might assume
that small villages or rural towns have both different sorts of settings and different
rules of segregation among age groups from metropolitan areas (Barker & Wright,
1955). For example, behavior-setting surveys done at Midwest in the early 1950s
showed that the town was remarkably open to the coming and going of children.
Some 60 percent of all behavior settings were open to children, whereas adolescents
could enter 79 percent of them. The analysis of the number and type of behavior
settings frequented by individuals at all periods of the life span provides a good
illustration of this type of study. The changes are documented with age in both type
and number of settings occupied by the residents of Midwest. Above all the major
shift from family to community settings occurs after preschool, peaking in adolescence and reversing in adulthood and old age.

These data mean that a child who lived to adulthood in Midwest would at some
time during childhood and adolescence have an opportunity to become acquainted
with most of the community settings of the town. In most settings, a Midwest child
associated with people of a wide age range. He or she therefore continually experienced the ways and roles of younger and older persons. Thus, living in Midwest
brought continually expanding action opportunities. Growing up was an advantage
to the children of Midwest. This was not as true for children of other Midwestern
communities or for children in other cultures (cf. Barker & Schoggen, 1973).

In terms of cultivation, behavior settings are thus useful in demonstrating that
opportunities within a more or less stable environment are limited. Within larger
contexts, however, such as neighborhoods and towns, children can select from
among a broad range of settings that fit their "developmental tasks" (Havighurst,
1972), such as learning both a variety of cultural techniques (e.g., reading, writing)
and age-specific social skills (e.g., playing and working in groups). Thus, I assume
that the selection of behavior settings depends on age- and self-specific developmental orientations of the self.

Along these lines of theorizing, the qualities of both the physical milieu and the
setting program are important aspects of behavior settings in terms of their attractiveness to children's self-specific needs. In terms of cultivation, at least two qualities of behavior settings are important: variability and openness. The former is

viewed as the potential that the physical milieu and its props offer for physical manipulation and alteration. The latter refers to the number of different action opportunities that a setting program offers to potential users. On the one side, a physical milieu of low variability is, for example, a play unit without any possibilities for alteration. On the other side, setting programs with high openness are typical, for example, for shopping centers, with their wide range of action opportunities. One can assume that children's cultivation is nourished by such qualities as variability and openness of behavior settings and that their social development is fostered. There is also ample evidence that low-structured or medium-structured places are "preferred" to well-structured ones; the latter provide almost no challenges (see Wohlwill & Heft, 1987).

6   Microscope on children's daily life in a rural Swiss town

Environments on the urban scale are not very readily dealt with by psychologists. This state of affairs is even more obvious when we turn to the work on children's experience in urban settings. In much of the earlier work by Barker and Wright, small towns were chosen because they lent themselves to analysis in terms of behavior settings, which were relatively few in number. A notable advance in this regard, however, is represented by the work of Gump and Adelberg (1978), who presented an analysis of preadolescents in a neighborhood within a large city in terms directly comparable to that employed for Midwest.

   In the present investigation, among other goals, I attempt to describe children's outdoor activities in terms of behavior settings (see Marty & Stucki, 1994, for a more extended version of the whole study). In contrast to the extended outline on behavior settings and cultivation, however, the focus in the study reported here is narrowed down from dynamics to residuals.

6.1   *Location of the study and the population*

The methodological approach adopted for the present study required an identifiable environmental behavior unit, that is, a spatially compact unit so that the children would reside relatively close together. The members of my team and I chose to look for a medium-sized rural town that exhibited as many urban traits as possible. Such requirements would seem to contradict each other, but Midland (code name) was ideal. Midland is a fairly typical rural town located in the Bernese Mittelland with a population size of 10,100. The railway divides the town into two parts. In the center of the town is the expected dense group of stores and schools. The train station, small industries, apartment houses, and a large public swimming pool extend southwards and detached family houses and apartment houses extend northwards. Socioeconomically, 2 percent of the inhabitants are farmers; 25 percent, blue-collar work-ers; and 68 percent, white-collar workers. A total of 184 Midland school children aged 10, 12, and 14 years participated in the study. The sample included 93 girls and 91 boys.

6.2   Research design

We selected the children by controlling variables cristallized from the literature review as being potentially significant factors in terms of leisure activities (see Wohlwill & Heft, 1987): age, sex, and socioeconomic status (SES). The SES (medium-low vs. medium-high) was defined by the type of school in which the chil-dren were enrolled. Children who attended primary school were classified into the lower SES group, whereas those who were enrolled in secondary school were part of the higher SES group. This distinction, however, was possible only for the 12- and 14-year-old children because the 10-year olds all attended the same type of school, primary school.

During August 1992, the children filled out a self-administered diary for seven consecutive days during their entire waking time. Each child was given a form as physically compact as possible on which to record the day's activities, the time when each was begun and ended, the location in which the activity was embedded, and the people who accompanied the child. The major dependent variable was the time that children spent in particular types of public behavior settings.

With regard to the cultivation model of development, the behavior settings were then categorized along the two dimensions described above: the variability of the physical milieu and the functional openness of the setting program. That is, all behavior settings were assessed for both variability and openness on a three-point rating scale (low, medium, high) by two independent raters. Interrater reliabilities for the coding of the behavior settings mentioned in the time budgets were kappa = .68 for variability and kappa = .65 for openness. Behavior settings with low variability were the two large food stores, several restaurants, and the disco. Settings charac-terized as medium variable were streets, youth meetings, and club festivities. A set-ting of high variability was that of cooking on a open fire in the woods. Behavior settings with low program openness were theaters, cinemas, and restaurants. Exam-ples of settings with medium program openness were public festivities and youth meetings. Lastly, behavior settings with high openness were the public swimming pool and several small neighborhood streets.

6.3 Results

6.3.1 The most preferred settings in terms of variability and openness

I first give a short overview of the mean percentage of time that Midland children spent in behavior settings differing in both physical variability and program openness (see Figure 2). The corresponding standard deviations (minutes per week) for physical variability (PV) were: low PV (SD = 3.54), medium PV (SD = 5.13), and high PV (SD = .21). The variability indices for program openness (PO) were: low PO (SD = 1.18), medium PO (SD = 1.84), and high PO (SD = 4.81).

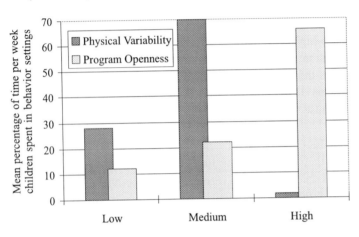

Figure 2: *Mean percentage of time per week that children spent in behavior settings differing in physical variability (low, medium, or high) and program openness (low, medium, or high)*

Figure 2 shows that children spent most of their times in behavior settings that are characterized by either medium variability of the physical milieu or a high openness of the behavior patterns that are prescribed by the setting program. Thus, the Midland children did not prefer completely changeable spaces as often claimed in the developmental literature. Rather, they used spatial milieus that are not totally physically changeable. To these children, behavior settings are most attractive when their physical variability is neither very high nor very low and their programs are highly open.

6.3.2 The impact of the predictor variables (age, sex, and SES)

Second, we tested the relations between the predictor variables and the time that children spent in settings differing in both variability and openness. Because the requirements for multivariate analyses of variance were not given in the study, Wilcoxon matched-pairs signed-ranks tests were performed for either variability or openness, sex and SES being used as predictors. Then a Kruskal-Wallis one-way analysis of variance by ranks was performed for either variability or openness, age being used as predictor. Post-hoc tests were performed when significant age effects were revealed. The major dependent variable was the time (in minutes per week) that children spent in behavior settings differing in both physical variability and program openness.

Table 1: Results of Wilcoxon and Kruskal-Wallis tests regarding the time that children spent in behavior settings differing in both physical variability and program openness as a function of sex, age, and socioeconomic status (SES)

Predictor variables	Sex			Age			SES		
	df	z	p	df	z	p	df	z	p
Dependent variables: *Time spent in settings of*									
Low variability	1	-2.00	.05	2	2.01	.37	1	-.78	.44
Medium variability	1	-1.83	.07	2	2.84	.24	1	-2.51	.01
High variability	1	-.73	.47	2	10.37	.01	1	-.37	.71
Low openness	1	-2.14	.03	2	.15	.93	1	-.77	.48
Medium openness	1	-.21	.83	2	9.77	.01	1	-2.58	.01
High openness	1	-2.06	.04	2	11.42	.01	1	-1.88	.06

Table 1 summarizes the main results of these nonparametric statistical tests. Binomial tests were then performed to check whether the significant effects were random among all other effects. The three binomial tests revealed that the significant univariate effects for each predictor variable were not random ($p < .05$ for each analysis).

Thus, age, sex, and SES are related to the time that children spent in behavior settings differing in both variability and openness. The sex effects indicate that (a) girls spent more time in settings of low variability (mean = 210 min) than did boys (mean = 180 min); (b) girls spent more time in settings of low openness (mean = 95 min) than did boys (mean = 20 min); and (c) boys spent more time in highly open settings (mean = 510 min) than did girls (mean = 390 min). The age effects showed that (a) 10-year olds spent significantly more time in settings of high variability (mean = 30 min) than did both 12- and 14-year olds (mean = less than 3 min for each of these age groups); (b) 14-year olds spent significantly more time in settings of medium openness (M = 280 min) than did both 12- (mean = 140 min) and 10-year olds (mean = 100 min); and (c) both 10- (mean = 490 min) and 12-year olds (mean = 535 min) stayed significantly longer in highly open settings than did 14-year olds (mean = 300 min). Lastly, the SES effects indicate that (a) children of lower SES spent more time (mean = 540 min) in settings of medium variability than did children of higher SES (mean = 360 min); and (b) they also stayed in settings of medium openness significantly longer (mean = 220 min) than did children of higher SES (mean = 100 min).

6.4 Discussion

In accord with studies of both child behavior in the outdoor environment (see Wohlwill & Heft, 1987) and adolescents' preferred leisure-time settings (Silbereisen, Noack, & Eyferth, 1986), the findings showed that children generally go to transact with behavior settings of high program openness, that is, settings that do not prescribe any setting-specific actions. I assume that highly open behavior settings are exactly the kind of settings in which many children, although they may differ in their self-specific needs, can cultivate themselves in transaction with the particular setting. Highly open behavior settings therefore, have exactly the qualities of social gathering places for children.

The children in the present study, however, did not prefer the physically most flexible behavior settings but rather mostly used settings of medium variability. It is assumed that the reason children have for preferring settings of medium variability is the medium potential that such settings have for complexity, challenge, and novelty. These "collative" variables (Berlyne, 1960) do not refer to the visual complexity but rather to the behavioral complexity of the behavior settings. With regard to physical variability, this finding is quite in accord with the research on curiosity and the often observed finding of an inverted U-function between environmental complexity and the intensity of exploratory behavior (see Görlitz & Wohlwill, 1987).

In contrast, children prefer settings of high program openness with which they might compensate their search for functionally complex settings by the desire for physically less complex settings. More or less stable physical environmental prerequisites can be seen as a complexity-reducing orientation context (Kaminski, 1986). In fact, physically more restricted behavior settings might be precisely the settings that give a certain level of security that, in turn, children need to test program-specific rules, or to "break" the "official line" of the setting program as a means to cultivate themselves (e.g., Muchow & Muchow, 1935). With regard to program openness, therefore, the present findings are not consistent with the inverted U-function as it is mentioned above.

Furthermore, the analyses revealed a sex effect on the time that children spent in settings differing in both variability and openness. Obviously, girls prefer settings that are of low variability and of low openness as well. One can only speculate about the reasons why girls spent more time in physically less challenging settings than did boys. Research on sex differences in environmental exploration indicates that boys explore larger territories than girls do (see Wohlwill & Heft, 1987). Parental restraints and environmental fears (relating to security problems in public places) have generally been suggested as responsible for sex differences. Whether these arguments are valid interpretations or not, girls, unlike boys, either preferred or were encouraged to use behavior settings in which their actions were highly supported by both the physical milieu and the setting program. I would speculate that girls, in general, show a lowered self-confidence when coping with environmental challenges than boys do.

In a similar vein, Hart (1987) describes differences between the kinds of settings that boys and girls create for themselves. Boys tend to "build" the settings (e.g., forts), whereas girls concentrate on the furnishings and arrangement to elaborate the interior spaces of these settings. Hart also rejects a psychodynamic explanation for these differences as too simplistic and argues that they reflect sex-related social roles that boys and girls are encouraged to adopt. Among adolescence, however, the gender-typic needs for visiting particular leisure places is more complicated (see Cotterell, in this volume).

In contrast to the sex differences mentioned above, the age effects are less consistent. Moreover, the results are not completely in accord with previous findings that children prefer more challenging settings as they grow older (see Wohlwill & Heft, 1987). However, if one interprets behavior settings as "places for development" (Silbereisen, Noack, & Eyferth, 1986) then the age differences make some sense. As children grow older they may favor settings that facilitate social interaction with peers. For adolescents, meeting their peers, especially affiliating with peers of the opposite sex, can be a "risky" thing. Thus, taking into account that learning to interact with peers of the opposite sex is a challenging process one finds it understandable that 14-years olds spent more time in settings that are neither very open nor highly variable than did 10- and 12-years olds. Again, semiopen settings can be seen as a complexity-reducing orientation context that encourage novel social encounters of older children.

In contrast to the differences of both age and sex, influence of SES on the time that children spent in settings of both medium variability and medium openness are less clear. In the literature, effects of SES are usually explained by differences in parental restraints on children's use of outdoor places (e.g., Hart, 1979). Settings of both medium variability and medium openness are shopping centers, youth meetings, and all kinds of festivities. Thus, among other action opportunities, social interaction with all kinds of people represents a common goal of these settings. One could speculate why children of lower SES spent more time in these types of settings than children of higher SES. I would assume that parents of higher SES are more concerned about protecting their children from negative social conduct than parents of the lower SES are. Moreover, higher SES parents are more restrictive with their children than lower SES parents are with theirs when it comes to the use of settings in which their children run great risk of meeting unknown, perhaps "undesirable" people.

7 Conclusions and directions for future research

Kurt Lewin was certainly among the first psychologists who emphasized the power
of the immediate environment in steering the child's development. His theoretical
conceptions were then translated into research operations by Barker, Wright, and
their colleagues of the Kansas School. They have provided impressive evidence in
support of their thesis that children's behavior can be better predicted and perhaps
even understood by looking at places instead of just children.

With Simmel's concept of cultivation, I introduced a cultural developmental model
that seems fruitful to elaborate Barker's behavior-setting concept with regard to its
potential for human development. That is, cultivation is seen as the outcome of a
person's self-oriented transactions aiming at changing behavior settings to the needs
of specific developmental orientations of the self, and these transactions not only
alter the specific behavior setting but change the individual as well. In contrast to
other contextualized developmental approaches (cf. Silbereisen, Eyferth, & Rudinger, 1986; Wohlwill & Heft, 1987), cultivation as a paradigm for development
points to the significance of children's self-specific transactions with their behavior
settings; above all, it requires that these settings be relevant for the central core of
the self.

Along this line of theorizing, it is my impression that several areas are potentially
valuable directions for further research. First, a multisetting perspective would be
useful in examining links between behavior settings cultivated by children. The
external environment as a context for development is not simply an array of separate
and isolated behavior settings. Children move from setting to setting, and it is likely
that their experiences in one setting will influence their cultivation in another.

Second, interesting questions arise concerning the impact that rapid societal and
environmental change has on how the availability of behavior settings in certain
towns, regions, or countries is altered. For example, the concept of developmental
phases, one growing to some extent upon another, implies that there are progressions
from, say, more restricted to less restricted settings. There could also be progressions
in the other direction. That is, it could be that children and youths in cities of rapid
sociophysical transformations such as those occurring in countries of Eastern Europe
are increasingly and rapidly cut off from transacting with their "old" behavior settings in a self-related manner. The question arises of how these rapid alterations of
children's outdoor environments either facilitate or inhibit their cultivation (see
Fuhrer, 1995).

Third, despite the emerging interest in an ecological view of child development,
less than five percent of the studies were empirically based (Moore, 1987) and no
general theory had emerged that presents child-environment links in a sociophysical
context. All major developmental theories such as those of Stern, Piaget, Vygotsky,
and Bronfenbrenner, point to the need that children have to act in an environment
rich in resources, to explore, or test, and learn from feedback on their entire actions.

Thus, to facilitate personal growth, the opportunity to explore rich, varied, and open settings appears related to cognitive, social, and motor development. Unfortunately, existing behavior settings for children are totally inadequate in many cases, often consisting of physically fixed milieus and setting programs that do not accommodate the self-specific needs of children's transactions with them. The question is what the consequences are for the developing child when the physical environment in which he or she grows up does not fit his or her need for cultivation.

Fourth, some evidence is available to support the suggestion of a link between specific environmental experiences and intellectual abilities (e.g., Webley, 1981). Aside from the differences between the sexes in their territorial range (see Wohlwill & Heft, 1987), the present study also revealed differences between girls and boys with regard to their opportunities to transact with settings differing in both variability and openness. I hypothesize that transactions with behavior settings may be one of several unintended learning experiences that contribute to the differential development of intellectual abilities (e.g., Webley, 1981) and even of independence and self-certainty in males and females. Along these lines of theorizing, it is therefore not surprising to find males so disproportionately represented in such fields as the physical sciences, engineering, and architecture, where, for example, spatial ability is an important element in successful performance (see Quaiser, 1990).

Fifth, there seem to be only a few published findings on historical, intergenerational change of behavior settings for children (e.g., Gaster, 1991; Zeiher & Zeiher, 1994; Zinnecker, 1979; in this volume). However, relating Bronfenbrenner's (1989) ideas on the significance of chronosystem models for developmental research with Wicker's work on the life-cycle of behavior settings would open a highly promising avenue for future research on culture and human development (see Wicker, 1992). Along these lines of reasoning, development may best be described as the sum of self-specific transactions that people, from childhood to adulthood, undertake over relatively long periods of time and across multiple settings as means for cultivating the self. I am convinced that analyzing the person-environment transactions of particular individuals as they work toward specific, concrete, distant goals that they regard as centrally important to themselves would be a highly promising undertaking for a cultural developmental psychology.

Lastly, I hope that the perspective emerging from the thinking behind the cultivation-as-development paradigm has begun to demonstrate significant features of person-environment transactions that help one to understand children. However, there is much to learn on how behavior settings and children make each other up.

Acknowledgments

I am grateful to Allan W. Wicker, and the editors for their helpful comments, clarifications, and suggestions.

References

Barker, R. G. (1968). *Ecological psychology*. Stanford, CA: Stanford University Press.

Barker, R. G. (1987). Prospecting in environmental psychology: Oskaloosa revisited. In D. Stokols & I. Altman (Eds.), *Handbook of environmental psychology* (pp. 1413-1432). New York: Wiley.

Barker, R. G., & Wright, H. F. (1955). *Midwest and its children*. New York: Harper & Row.

Barker, R. G., & Schoggen, P. (1973). *Qualities of community life*. San Francisco: Jossey-Bass.

Berlyne, D. E. (1960). *Conflict, arousal, and curiosity*. New York: McGraw-Hill.

Boesch, E. E. (1991). *Symbolic action theory and cultural psychology*. Berlin: Springer.

Bronfenbrenner, U. (1979). *The ecology of human development*. Cambridge, MA: Harvard University Press.

Bronfenbrenner, U. (1989). Ecological systems theory. *Annals of Child Development, 6,* 187-249.

Bronfenbrenner, U., & Crouter, A. C. (1983). The evolution of environmental models in developmental research. In P. H. Mussen (Ed.), *Handbook of child psychology* (pp. 357-414). New York: Wiley.

Bronfenbrenner, U., Kessel, F., Kessen, W., & White, S. (1986). Toward a critical social history of developmental psychology. *American Psychologist, 41,* 1218-1230.

Bruner, J. S. (1990). Culture and human development: A new look. *Human Development, 33,* 344-355.

Cole, M. (1995). Culture and cognitive development: From cross-cultural research to creating systems of cultural mediation. *Culture & Psychology, 1,* 25-54.

Frisby, D. (1981). *Sociological impressionism: A reassessment of Georg Simmel's social theory*. London: Methuen.

Fuhrer, U. (1990). Bridging the ecological-psychological gap: Behavior settings as interfaces. *Environment and Behavior, 22,* 518-537.

Fuhrer, U. (1993). Living in our own footprints – and in those of others: Cultivation as transaction. *Schweizerische Zeitschrift für Psychologie, 52,* 130-137.

Fuhrer, U. (1995). Stadt als Entwicklungsrahmen [The city as a framework for development]. Magdeburger Wissenschaftsjournal (Heft 1). Magdeburg: Otto-von-Guericke-Universität.

Fuhrer, U., Kaiser, F. G., & Hangartner, U. (1995). Wie Kinder und Jugendliche ihr Selbstkonzept kultivieren: Die Bedeutung von Dingen, Orten und Personen [How children and adolescents cultivate their self-concept: The meaning of things, places, and persons]. *Psychologie in Erziehung und Unterricht, 1,* 57-64.

Fuhrer, U., & Josephs, I. E. (in press). The cultivated mind: From mental mediation to cultivation. *Developmental Review, 18.*

Gaster, S. (1991). Urban children's access to their neighboorhood. Changes over three generations. *Environment and Behavior, 23,* 70-85.

Görlitz, D. (1993). Es begann in Berlin – Wege einer entwicklungspsychologischen Stadtforschung [It began in Berlin – Avenues of developmental urban research]. In H. J. Harloff (Ed.), *Psychologie des Wohnungs- und Siedlungsbaus* (pp. 97-120). Göttingen: Verlag für Angewandte Psychologie.

Görlitz, D., & Schröder, R. (1994). Urban development for children – reexploring a new research area. In H. Keller, K. Schneider, & B. Henderson (Eds.), *Curiosity and exploration* (pp. 307-331). Heidelberg: Springer.

Görlitz, D., & Wohlwill, J. F. (Eds.) (1987). *Curiosity, imagination, and play: On the development of spontaneous cognitive and motivational processes*. Hillsdale, NJ: Erlbaum.

Gump, P. V., & Adelberg, B. (1978). Urbanism from the perspective of ecological psychologists. *Environment and Behavior, 10*, 171-191.

Hart, R. (1979). *Children's experience of place.* New York: Irvington.

Hart, R. (1987). Children's participation in planning and design: Theory, research, and practice. In C. S. Weinstein & T. G. David (Eds.), *Spaces for children* (pp. 217-239). London: Plenum Press.

Havighurst, R. J. (1972). *Developmental tasks and education.* New York: Davis McKay.

Hayward, D. G., Rothenberg, M., & Beasley, R. R. (1974). Children's play and urban playground environments. *Environment and Behavior, 6*, 131-168.

Kaminski, G. (Ed.) (1986). *Ordnung und Variabilität im Alltagsgeschehen* [Order and variability in everyday happenings]. Göttingen: Hogrefe.

Lang, A. (1988). Die kopernikanische Wende in der Psychologie steht noch aus [Still waiting for the Copernican turn in psychology! Ideas towards an ecological developmental psychology]. *Schweizerische Zeitschrift für Psychologie, 47*, 93-108.

Levine, D. N. (Ed.) (1971). *Georg Simmel. On individuality and social forms.* Chicago: University of Chicago Press.

Lewin, K. (1936). *Principles of topological psychology.* New York: Harper.

Marty, I., & Stucki, W. (1994). *Raumaneignung von Kindern und Jugendlichen* [The appropriation of space by children and adolescents]. Unpublished master's thesis, University of Berne, Switzerland.

Moore, G. T. (1987). The physical environment and cognitive development in child-care centers. In C. S. Weinstein & T. G. David (Eds.), *Spaces for children* (pp. 41-72). London: Plenum Press.

Muchow, M., & Muchow, H. H. (1935). *Der Lebensraum des Großstadtkindes.* Hamburg: Martin Riegel.

Oerter, R. (1991). Self-object relation as a basis of human development. In L. Oppenheimer & J. Valsiner (Eds.), *The origins of action* (pp. 65-108). New York: Springer.

Piaget, J. (1959). *Plays, dreams, and imitation.* New York: Norton.

Quaiser, C. (1990). *Die Fähigkeit zur räumlichen Vorstellung. Kognitive und motivationale Faktoren als mögliche Ursachen für geschlechtsspezifische Unterschiede* [The ability to imagine space: Cognitive and motivational factors as possible causes for gender-specific differences]. Unpublished master's thesis. University of Bonn, Federal Republic of Germany.

Rochberg-Halton, E. (1986). *Meaning and modernity.* Chicago: University of Chicago Press.

Schoggen, P. (1989). *Behavior settings.* Stanford, CA: Stanford University Press.

Silbereisen, R. K., Eyferth, K., & Rudinger, G. (Eds.) (1986). *Development as action in context.* New York, Berlin: Springer.

Silbereisen, R. K., Noack, P., & Eyferth, K. (1986). Places for development: Adolescents, leisure settings, and developmental tasks. In R. K. Silbereisen, K. Eyferth, & G. Rudinger (Eds.), *Development as action in context* (pp. 87-107). New York, Berlin: Springer.

Simmel, G. (1908). *Soziologie. Untersuchungen ueber die Formen der Vergesellschaftung* [Sociology: Studies on the forms of socialization]. Leipzig: Duncker & Humblot.

Stokols, D., & Shumaker, S. A. (1981). People in places: A transactional view of settings. In J. H. Harvey (Ed.), *Cognition, social behavior, and the environment* (pp. 441-488). Hillsdale, NJ: Erlbaum.

Super, C. M., & Harkness, S. (1986). The developmental niche: A conceptualization of the interface of child and culture. *International Journal of Behavioral Development, 9*, 545-569.

Valsiner, J. (1987). *Culture and the development of children's action.* New York: Wiley.

Valsiner, J. (1988). Ontogeny of co-construction of culture within socially organized environmental settings. In J. Valsiner (Ed.), *Child development within culturally structured environments* (pp. 283-297). Norwood, NJ: Ablex.

Valsiner, J. (1989). *Human development and culture.* Lexington, MA: D. C. Heath.

Vygotsky, L. S. (1978). *Mind in society: The development of higher psychological processes.* Cambridge, MA: Harvard University Press.

Webley, P. (1981). Sex differences in home range and cognitive maps in eight-year old children. *Journal of Environmental Psychology, 1,* 293-302.

Weinstein, C. S., & David, T. G. (1987). *Spaces for children.* London: Plenum.

Wicker, A. W. (1987). Behavior settings reconsidered: Temporal stages, resources, internal dynamics, context. In D. Stokols & I. Altman (Eds.), *Handbook of environmental psychology* (pp. 613-653). New York: Wiley.

Wicker, A. W. (1992). Making sense of environments. In W. B. Walsh, K. H. Craik, & R. H. Price (Eds.), *Person-environment psychology* (pp. 157-192). Hillsdale, NJ: Erlbaum.

Wohlwill, J. F. (1985). Martha Muchow, 1892-1933: Her life, work, and contribution to developmental and ecological psychology. *Human Development, 28,* 198-224.

Wohlwill, J. F., & Heft, H. (1987). The physical environment and the development of the child. In D. Stokols & I. Altman (Eds.), *Handbook of environmental psychology* (pp. 281-328). New York: Wiley.

Wolff, K. H. (1950). *The sociology of Georg Simmel.* Glencoe, IL: Pelican.

Wright, H. F. (1970, November). Urban space as seen by the child. Paper presented at the International Children's Center, Paris.

Zeiher, H., & Zeiher, H. (1994). *Orte und Zeiten der Kinder. Soziales Leben im Alltag von Großstadtkindern* [Places and times of children: The everyday social life of city children]. Weinheim: Juventa.

Zinnecker, J. (1979). Straßensozialisation [Street socialization]. *Zeitschrift für Pädagogik, 5,* 727-746.

Comment: Behavior settings forever!

Hans Joachim Harloff

1 Basic assumptions of the approach

Fuhrer links the points of departure of Simmel's cultivation theory and Barker's behavior-setting theory and shapes them into a new developmental concept of the self that is worth pursuing and checking against reality as a rival to other approaches. Behind it is a particular view of cultural and human development. Like Valsiner, Fuhrer assumes that both are integral units, that is, that they define each other and cannot be studied separately.

Simmel's principle of cultivation fits this assumption. According to Simmel, psychologically based realities and reality-based psyches are adapted to each other until a balance is reached. This adaptation takes place, by virtue of the fact that, among other things, a culture provides means for human development and the individual actively and teleologically selects from them, thereby developing his or her individuality and changing the culture. The development of the individual is not predetermined by physical environment and cultural objects, nor is the culturally structured social and physical environment something historically given and established. To the degree that individuals interact with other people and objects and thereby continue developing their unique, inherent configurations of determining factors, they "consume" and "reproduce" that which is culturally given and are shaped and adapted in the process, but never irrevocably and totally. The same interaction process also always effects changes in other people and objects, depending on the unique impacts that individuals have. Through the reciprocal, simultaneous, active effect of the two sides (transaction), something new continuously originates, individuals and culture develop. In other words, they cultivate each other in an abiding, open process.[1]

Fuhrer answers the question of how this transaction process works by drawing on Barker's ecological psychology (Barker, 1968), or eco-behavioral science (Barker, 1978). It revolves around the concept of the behavior setting, defined as "standing patterns of behavior" and a corresponding milieu (a physical environment) bounded by time and space. Barker spoke also of extraindividual environment-behavior units, such as worshipping in church, attending class at school, walking or traveling on the street, and telephoning from a public telephone booth. The standing patterns of behavior and the respective milieu are matched with each other (the assumption of synomorphy). The persons taking part in a behavior setting (the inhabitants) perform certain tasks necessary for it to function. The number of persons can be too small in relation to the tasks to be done, can be optimal, or can be too large (the manning assumption). Under certain circumstances institutions or organizations consist of numerous interlinked and matched behavior settings; they are multiple-setting synomorphs. Examples are schools, church parishes, and hospitals. The sum of the behavior settings in a community and the number of its genotypes (behavior settings of the same kind) characterize the scope and richness of its public life (Harloff, 1986). These behavior settings and genotypes contain options for action in the public space of a place.

2 Coherence of the assumptions

The assumptions of this theoretical approach are largely coherent. They are impressive for their ability to describe and explain the development of individuals and culture as a part of the same ongoing transaction processes.

At this point one may ask how much Barker's ecological psychology is really capable of doing what Fuhrer imputes to it. First, Barker confines himself to describing *public space*. He does not say so explicitly, but it becomes absolutely clear if one looks at the list of genotypes (Barker, 1968) or studies how behavior setting surveys are conducted. Barker does not record the synomorphs within dwellings and industrial plants (Harloff, 1986). He analyzes behavior settings in dwellings and industrial plants only insofar as the public (persons outside the family or plant) has access to them (as with homecoming parties or bridge games at home or behavior settings in companies serving private customers). But the development of individuals does take place within dwellings and production plants as well. This flaw in the theoretical approach can be eliminated relatively easily. It is true that appropriate proof (results of Barker's K-21 test for interdependence) is lacking for households, but it is almost certain that they are either behavior settings or multi-setting synomorphs. A K-21 for interdependence has been conducted repeatedly in plants and public administrations, and they have usually proven to be multi-setting synomorphs (Wicker, 1987). Household transactions that involve children and influence children's development need not be left unconsidered in Fuhrer's cultivation approach. It would be bad otherwise, for the synomorphs of the household domain are of paramount importance to infants and small children (as they are later to aging persons, too).

Second, all transactions involve cultivation. Yet even if the behavior-setting approach is expanded in the manner just outlined, it does not record all transactions. Many critics (including Cotterell in this volume) have pointed out that "divergent" behavior occurs, that is, behavior not part of the standing patterns of behavior intended by the culture or the initiators (e.g., smoking by school students in the restrooms, sex in the office). Under certain circumstances such deviant actions can become the main thing in a milieu, leading to the eclipse of old behavior settings and the origination of new ones (Wicker, 1987). Moreover, there are transactions that occur outside existing behavior settings. Examples would be a child picking flowers next to a brook or on the edge of a footpath, boys building a tree house, and cross-country hikers traversing only meadows, fields, and scrub (suitable hiking paths would constitute a behavior setting). Spontaneous action, behavior that occurs for the first time, and the generation of new milieus or the transformation of old ones are transactions that do not take place within but rather outside behavior settings. Neither divergent transactions within existing behavior settings nor transactions outside them can be depicted, but they do represent cultivation and mean that the theoretical approach under discussion here needs to be broadened.

The final inconsistency that I see is actually unnecessary. In Fuhrer's view, the child (the individual) involved in a behavior does not have a role or function in the context of the standing pattern of behavior. Instead, the children "externalize their ideas, goals, and plans" and act only "more or less in accord with the behavior set-ting" (Fuhrer, p. 420). This view runs the risk of destroying one of Barker's basic assumptions, namely, that behavior is shaped by the behavior setting (Barker, 1968, 1978). A child taking part in a school theater production (a behavior setting) in the gymnasium does so as a member of the audience, a ticket seller, a stage hand, or an actor in the play. The child's action is standardized and determined by the function being carried out. Of course, that does not prevent the child from actively shaping his or her role somewhat.[2]

Doing away with the behavior setting's character as something that shapes action would, in my opinion, eliminate one of the main advantages of the developmental theory being discussed here. The fascinating thing about the theory is precisely its ability to show that cultivation occurs mostly along socially and culturally defined lines, that is, in behavior settings. Fuhrer overemphasizes the active participation and free choice of the individual. He asserts that the behavior setting is something that not only forms the individual but that is simultaneously formed by every one of its inhabitants.[3] The following considerations about the development of and calls for child-centered urban research make it clear what Fuhrer's assertion is meant to achieve.

3 The contribution that Fuhrer's theory makes to the topic of urban children's development

In Fuhrer's theory, children develop by taking part in a wide variety of behavior set-tings during their lives. Individuality comes about through the fact that they do so with their unique potential for development.[4] By assuming that children constantly and actively intervene in their behavior settings, Fuhrer dynamizes the person-environment relation, which in Barker's theory is static because it is defined by standing patterns of behavior. Under certain circumstances children in behavior settings do something other than what adults expect.

Such a great change in the original concept of behavior settings is unnecessary in my opinion and entails more disadvantages than advantages. It is true that action not belonging to the standing pattern of behavior can occur in behavior settings. Besides, there are actions that occur as it were outside existing behavior settings. In particular, people are often busy creating milieus for planned standing patterns or new patterns of behavior. Consequently, the behavior-setting "terrain" of communities changes even without one having to assume continuous change within the separate behavior settings as such.

When considering early developmental processes, one should be particularly careful not to overemphasize the degree to which the environment is actively influenced by children and their choice of behavior setting as a function of their potential for development and the decisions they make based on their own free preferences. Instead, one should emphasize the control that other people, especially adults, and preexisting action programs and milieus exert on the developmental process of the child. For all the activity that children themselves bring to the environment, their development is a function of *more* than just their inherent dynamics. Obviously, infants, toddlers, and small children in particular are developed essentially by forces and processes emanating from, and controlled by, their social and physical environment. But even among school-age youngsters, it is rare that children choose their behavior settings or determine within them which functions they will assume. The parents and other adults do that for the child. Barker's concept of the penetration zone (1968) makes it clear that the inhabitants of behavior settings have different degrees of power over and in them (six-level hierarchy ranging from the single leader to the onlooker). In most cases children do not inhabit behavior settings alone or only with other children. They inhabit behavior settings together with adults, in which case the adults are the leaders and the child is at best a "member or customer" or possibly only an "onlooker." The external environment is cultivated by children (a) rather by chance outside a behavior setting, (b) by participation in behavior settings, which are thereby perpetuated, and, of course, (c) together with all other inhabitants of the behavior setting through practice of its standing patterns of behavior. Children rarely, if ever, cultivate the external environment by altering behavior settings themselves.

Fuhrer's approach allows the assertion that an urban environment is positive for children's development insofar as it will usually contain a higher number of genotypes and, hence, a greater variety of possibilities for action than a rural environment (see Harloff, 1986). A negative aspect of small rural communities in particular arises when entire authority systems are absent (such as churches or schools), that is, when their synomorphs are not available as possibilities for action, making appropriate action impossible or requiring long journeys to larger neighboring communities.

Fuhrer's approach does not pick up on disadvantages of cities, especially large cities. Even within city limits, for example, many highly specific behavior settings (e.g., those for special treatment in major hospitals or for very rare sports and leisure facilities) often require long journeys to reach. Nor does it seem to me that Fuhrer's cultivation approach can reflect instances in which noise, excessive traffic, and general overstimulation stemming from the urban setting interfere with development.

Lastly, Fuhrer raises the important question of how urban behavior settings should be structured so that they are attractive for children and conducive to their development (see Fuhrer, pp. 423-424). In this context, in addition to Fuhrer's considerations, Barker and his followers have shown the manning of the behavior settings (p. 435) to be one of the significant factors influencing children's development (Gump, 1987). Both undermanning and overmanning are suboptimal for the functioning of behavior settings but can have both positive and negative effects on the development of the self. In a comparison between large and small schools, for example, one of the many effects that Gump (1987) found was that handicapped and less intelligent children in undermanned behavior settings (which were often in small schools) experienced a significant boost to their egos by the fact that they left the onlooker position and were allowed to assume functions that were relatively important to the success of the behavior setting. Conversely, a great many children in the overmanned behavior setting of large schools found themselves in the position of onlookers, which corresponded with low self-esteem and poor identification with the school. Such contexts suggest that large cities may have another negative effect (in addition to noise, excessive traffic, and stimulus overload). The number of behavior settings and genotypes of the public space and, ultimately, their location within the urban area are to be seen in relation to the resident population. Individual city districts can have an undersupply of them, others, an oversupply. And the behavior settings of major cities, like those of large multiple-setting synomorphs as opposed to small ones, may tend toward overmanning.

4   Research gaps and further comments

First, it is extremely important to keep in mind the view that child development is seen in relation not only to individual behavior settings but also to the sum of all behavior settings in which the child takes part (and to some extent also those in which it *could* take part). The behavior settings affect each other – especially, of course, if they are a part of the same multiple-setting synomorph and/or authority system and if they are interlinked through the affiliation of the same individuals. These reciprocal relations of behavior settings have yet to be investigated from developmental points of view.

Second, as indicated above, it should be considered whether household syno-morphs are not to be included in the cultivation approach that Fuhrer presents. With Barker and most of his disciples (Wicker, too, for example), the families, their action programs, and the milieu of the dwelling are excluded from consideration. I propose bringing synomorphs of the domestic setting into the picture from the outset. What happens in bedrooms, bathrooms, kitchens, and so on has the character of standing patterns of behavior, is framed by milieu, and both the frame and the standing pat-terns of behavior are mutually reconciled, as is the case in restaurants, classroom instruction, or other public behavior settings. The temporal and spatial boundary is present as well. It thus appears that households are behavior settings or multiple-setting synomorphs.[5]

Third, it would therefore be important to bring developmental research perspec-tives to bear on the interaction of household synomorphs among themselves and in relation to those of public life. Much that has emerged from work done on the basis of other theoretical approaches can be tapped for this effort. A fair amount is known, for example, about how dwellings should be arranged parallel to children's devel-opmental phases (Pollowy, 1977), and there are at least intelligent speculations about the connection between different forms of households (e.g., communes with several children as opposed to small-family households) and child development. In relation to public synomorphs, the significance that private, domestic synomorphs have for development is especially great in early childhood, later declines, but increases again in old age.

Lastly, I strongly emphasize what Fuhrer says about the demands on future research about the relation between child (and more generally, human) development and sociocultural change. For the latter, divergent actions within a behavior setting and actions that take place outside any behavior setting seem especially salient (see Wicker, 1987, in particular). They give the decisive pushes toward change, whereby the personality factors of the participating individuals as well as the rank in the "penetration-zone" hierarchy are important for physical and sociocultural change to prevail. Further research on this subject is urgently required. It must also be kept in mind that cultivation is a multilevel phenomenon. It takes place not only in transac-tions between individuals and a sociophysical environment but also between groups and their associated milieus, between several behavior settings, between multiple-setting synomorphs, and between authority systems. Cultivation of the next lowest level is decisively affected by cultivation at higher levels. That is, cultivation in the individual classroom is influenced by school-wide cultivation, which, in turn, is affected by cultivation in the ministry of education.

Within transactionalism, the kind of cultivation theory that Fuhrer advocates is a variant that has not only great value as a descriptive and explanatory tool for devel-opmental interrelationships but also important practical implications for increasing the living quality of children in the city.

Notes

1 The title of Fuhrer's chapter refers to children. However, it is very clear that the described assumptions are also compatible with the concept of life-long human development.
2 As a member of the audience, one can sit still or slide restlessly back and forth on the seat. One can listen or be absorbed in one's thoughts. Similar options also exist for the persons having other functions. It remains role-acting nevertheless. An inhabitant of the behavior setting who, for whatever reason, "steps out of the role" is compelled by the other inhabitants to conform or is removed from the behavior setting.
3 Wicker (1987) was a precursor of this view. He distinguished between several developmental stages of behavior settings and asserted that the phase of "continued existence" was the only one in which behavior settings had the power to determine action. According to Wicker, however, the behavior setting can be changed even in that phase, say, by newcomers who assume the central functions.
4 In addition, individuals in behavior settings assume different roles, actively choosing the behavior settings in which they do or do not wish to take part. Each individual is thus also characterized by a unique mix of behavior settings and executed functions.
5 Bechtel (1987) may be seen as the precursor for this assumption. He disassociated himself early from the complicated data-gathering procedures of ecological psychology (behavior-setting surveys), has implicitly assumed that people are always in behavior settings, has used a questionnaire to collect information on such settings within households, and has treated household synomorphs as behavior settings as a matter of course.

References

Barker, R. G. (1968). *Ecological psychology: Concepts and methods for studying the environment of human behavior.* Stanford, CA: Stanford University Press.
Barker, R. G. (1978). Behavior settings. In R. G. Barker (Ed.), *Habitats, environments, and human behavior: Studies in ecological psychology and eco-behavioral science from the Midwest Psychological Field Station, 1947-1972* (pp. 29-35). San Francisco: Jossey-Bass.
Bechtel, R. B. (1987). Ecological psychology. In R. B. Bechtel, R. W. Marans, & W. Michelson (Eds.), *Methods in environmental and behavioral research* (pp. 191-215). New York: Van Nostrand Reinhold.
Gump, P. V. (1987). School and classroom environments. In D. Stokols & I. Altman (Eds.), *Handbook of environmental psychology* (Vol. 1, pp. 691-732). New York: John Wiley and Sons.
Harloff, H. J. (1986). Das Behavior-Setting-Konzept Barkers im Dienst der Umweltgestaltung [Barker's behavior-setting concept in the service of environmental design]. In G. Kaminski (Ed.), *Ordnung und Variabilität im Alltagsgeschehen* (pp. 230-250). Göttingen: Hogrefe.
Pollowy, A.-M. (1977). *The urban nest.* Stroudsburg, PA: Dowden, Hutchinson & Ross.
Wicker, A. W. (1987). Behavior settings reconsidered: Temporal stages, resources, internal dynamics, context. In D. Stokols & I. Altman (Eds.), *Handbook of environmental psychology* (Vol. 1, pp. 613-653). New York: John Wiley and Sons.

Integration: Ecological psychology and phenomenology – Their commonality, differences, and interrelations

Hirofumi Minami

After reading this section's three main articles and the commentaries on them, one comes away enriched by learning experiences and also puzzled by the complex interlacing of the two theoretical approaches that the authors have dealt with, namely, behavior-setting theories and a phenomenological perspective. When read separately, each approach proves to have internal consistency and heuristic power in understanding children's transaction with the surrounding environment in the urban context. Yet, when the approaches are put together, a new dimension of the theoretical horizon emerges, one perhaps aptly described by a metaphor coined by the German philosopher Gadamer (1976): a "fusion of horizon." However vague it may appear at the moment, such fusion is anticipated in the interface of the two original and distinctive perspectives.

In this integrative article, I try to discern commonalities as well as differences between the two theoretical approaches in the particular context of the present volume – their applicability to studies of children in cities. After clarifying coordinates underlying the two theories, I attempt to search for integrative dimensions for furthering transactional orientation in this field.

1 Modification of behavior-setting theory

Among researchers working in the framework of behavior-setting theories, there is a fair degree of consensus that "the approach is not in general use in environmental psychology today" despite its initial impact on the field of environmental psychology (Hinding, p. 405). This disuse is partially attributed to the "excessively empiricist approach to its measurement" (Cotterell, p. 389) As the behavior-setting theory attained maturity and scientific sophistication, there was a tendency toward increased exactitude in defining and measuring units of behavior settings, as exemplified by the K-21 scale. Such theoretical sophistication, however, resulted in rigidity or something like "trained incapacity" (Burke, 1966, p. 189), with the result that potentially significant parts of the environment were excluded from behavior-setting studies.

Modifications and elaborations of behavior-setting theory are therefore proposed by Cotterell and Fuhrer in order to reactivate the theory's potential for present research and practice. In brief, the two authors (a) broaden the environmental scale from a mid-range scope to that of a "macroenvironment" that contains a hierarchical system of interconnected subordinate behavior-setting units (Cotterell), (b) link environment and development by differentiating age-specific habitats (Cotterell), and (c) incorporate sociocultural dimensions with redefinition of behavior settings as cultural constructions (Fuhrer).

Enlarging the scale of ecobehavioral units to macroenvironments is necessary when one deals with cities, especially big cities. Behavior-setting theory was originally derived from the "modest purpose" of studying "the development of children in a town *small enough* to observe and measure" (Fuhrer, p. 416), my emphasis). As pointed out by Cotterell (p. 384), even though a higher order of interrelations among behavior settings was recognized in Barker's notion of "multi-setting synomorphs," "*system* properties as macroenvironments were not investigated in any great detail" (emphasis mine). However, Cotterell's attempt to formulate "the nested assembly" of behavior settings is not found by Hinding to be complete enough, for "the hierarchical arrangement of the environmental system is not worked out in a consistent manner" (p. 406). Hinding suggests that the "coherent whole" is not a mere accumulation of behavior settings but "a goal-centered assembly that has specific functions to serve" (p. 405). A detailed and finer elaboration of this process poses a major challenge for psychologists ascribing to the behavior-setting approach. Some suggestions in this respect are provided in the final section of this article.

Developmental conceptualization is needed so that researchers and theorists not only focus on children in behavior-setting studies but also "dynamize the person-environment relation" by assuming that children constantly and actively intervene in their behavioral settings (Harloff, p. 438). This modification will compensate the rather static nature of the behavior-setting notion as traditionally conceived by Barker and his associates.

Through such modifications, behavior-setting theory might be "revitalized" as Hinding suggests, and with Harloff one may regain faith in this theory and interest in claiming its usefulness in the field "forever!" Yet, further creative leaps might be possible through its hybrid encounter with another ambitious theoretical approach in this filed, the phenomenological perspective.

2 The experiential world versus ecobehavioral systems

By browsing through such key concepts of phenomenology as intentionality, bodily subject, perspectivity, historicity, and appropriation, Graumann and Kruse elucidate experiential processes that a child has through transaction with his or her *Umwelt*. Their stress on the "basic perspectivity of a person's cognition" (Graumann & Kruse,

p. 359) might be diametrically opposed to the basic assumptions made in the behavior-setting theory, in which the focus is on "environment-behavior systems that stand out from their surroundings as coherent wholes by virtue of physical and temporal boundaries" and in which the issue of "how the individual behaves, and even what the individual experiences, is not a matter of consideration" (Hinding, pp. 405 and 409).

In the phenomenological approach the subject in his or her perspectivity or "corporality" is the foundation for any theoretical or empirical investigation. "Hence, the perspective of the child in a given society or community does not mean the environment as an adult expert (architect, planner, or educator) thinks that a child sees it, but the given setting just as the child experiences it" (Graumann & Kruse, p. 361). Is not the demarcation of behavior settings just another example of the perception of adult experts?

If one keeps in mind the rigorous definition and measurement of behavior settings as devised by Barker and his associates in their original works, it seems inevitable that the behavior-setting and the phenomenological approaches will be incompatible in their conceptions of the environment. Yet, when the recent modification of behavior-setting theory by Cotterell and Fuhrer described above are taken into account, several possibilities and common ground for mutual dialogue arise. First, it is interesting and notable that behavior-setting theorists and phenomenologists both mention the heritage of and their affiliation with Kurt Lewin's works. A close look into the theoretical make-ups of the two approaches, however, reveals that behavior-setting theory was derived from Lewin's conceptions of Ecological environment (Ee), "which is the observable, preperceptual environment" (Cotterell, p. 388), whereas the kinship between the phenomenological approach and Lewinian theory derives from the phenomenological approach's linkage to Psychological environment (EΨ), "which surrounds the life-space of the individual" (p. 388). The apparent enigma, then, is understood as two ramifications of the double-sided conceptions of environment in original Lewinian theory.

In applying Simmel's concept of "cultivation" to behavior-setting theory, Fuhrer poses a wonderful twist in this apparent contradiction between behavior-setting theory and the phenomenological approach. Through his elaboration of the concepts of "externalization" ("objectivation") and "internalization" ("subjectivation"), Fuhrer succeeds in redefining the environment by means of a dialectical and transactional formulation that contains both ecological and psychological domains as Lewin originally conceived.

Another piece of common ground between behavior-setting theory and the phenomenological approach is found in their reference to Muchow and Muchow (1935). Fuhrer regards that work as a precursor of his "cultivation" paradigm and describes it as "one of the most outstanding approaches concerning children's experiences of urban environments" (p. 421). Graumann and Kruse cite the Muchows' work as a "study of the life space of the city child differentiated phenomenologically between 'the space in which the child lives', the 'space that the child experiences', and 'the space that the child lives'" (p. 361). In that earlier study, one finds a concrete paradigm of the investigation, and it is compatible with both behavior-setting theory, at least Fuhrer's version of it, and to the phenomenological approach.

Going back to one of the most original works by Barker and Wright, *One boy's day* (1966), one finds an almost phenomenological description of a boy's transaction with his everyday surroundings, albeit in strictly behavioral terms. Although the subjective perception of the boy is not dealt with in that publication, the detailed description of his conduct and the environmental context reveals what the world is like from his point of view. As phenomenologists always warn, subjective versus objective distinction is not a proper conceptualization. Thus, classifying phenomenology into a category called the subjective domain and ecobehavioral science into one called the objective domain, as is commonly done, may not be a valid representation of the two approaches. Instead, Fuhrer's and Grauman and Kruse's characterization of behavior-setting theory and the phenomenological approach provides new ground for fertilization of previously unrelated areas.

3   A conceptual framework to locate the two approaches

While acknowledging that the two approaches interlace, I find it useful to distinguish differences in their orientation and emphasis on conceptual and empirical manifestations. Reviewing the articles in this section, I came up with two coordinates, or dimensions, that locate each theoretical approach (see Figure 1).

The first dimension, macroscopic and microscopic, refers to the level of the "scope and precision" (Pepper, 1942) that a theory presupposes in the selection of phenomena and the use of measurement. A focus on macroenvironments, as in Cotterell's modification of behavior-setting theory, exemplifies a macroscopic orientation. By contrast, Fuhrer's study as a "microscope on children's daily life in a rural Swiss town" (Fuhrer, p. 424), uses detailed and precise measurement to achieve a microscopic view of a child's everyday transactions. Harloff's proposal to have investigations of domestic settings include "household synomorphs" such as bedroom, bathroom, and kitchen is another move toward microscopic investigation. In current developmental and cultural psychology (e.g., Valsiner, 1988), a detailed observation of everyday life settings, such as mealtime, is a further example of microscopic studies of the child's transaction with the immediate ecological environment.

The second dimension, environmental setting and individual experience, pertains to a theory's relative emphasis on either the objectivized or the subjectivized pole of person-environment transactions. Cotterell's descriptions and analyses of recreational environments and other institutional settings, such as museums, zoos, and theme parks, are examples of the environmental-setting pole of this dimension. As

Hinding noted, such emphasis has merits. It facilitates the interface between psychology and planning disciplines, the latter of which deals mainly with physical settings. The phenomenological approach, which is distinctive in "its insistence on *meaning and experience* as the point of departure for any psychological analysis" (Mruck & Mey, p. 374), constitutes the opposite pole in this dimension. Phenomenologists emphasize that "perception and experience *must in principle be considered from the subject's own perspective*" (Mruck & Mey, p. 375, my emphasis). Adherents of this approach call attention to individual characteristics and differential consideration in the planning and management of domestic and public environments. Various populations whose voices are not often represented in the design process and who constitute minorities in terms of age, gender, social class, ethnicity, or handicaps of various kinds are a particular focus of this approach.

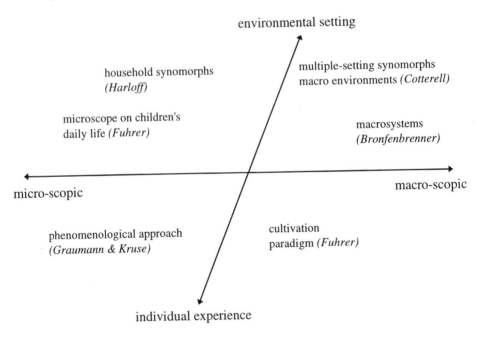

Figure 1: *Two dimensional representation locating ecological and phenomenological approaches in the study of child-environment transaction*

4   A "sociocultural turn" in person-environment transaction studies

There is a dialectical relation between the two poles of individual experience and environmental settings as discussed above. It becomes more evident when sociocultural perspectives are adopted, as in Fuhrer's integration of cultural developmental thinking and behavior-setting theory. As an attempt to develop interpretations of behavior-setting theory that are more dynamic than its original form, Fuhrer focuses on regulations of social norms as abiding forces of behavior settings. He arrives at a new conception of behavior – behavior settings as "cultural construction," which are embedded in a culturally structured environment (Valsiner, 1988).

This "sociocultural turn" of behavior-setting theory makes it more compatible with the phenomenological approach because of mutual emphasis on the shared meaning of social settings and "historicity of place" (Graumann & Kruse). Collective as well as individual construing of the living environment becomes a basis for the "cultivation" and construction of places. In this regard, subject-relatedness, sociality, and historicity attain equal importance as "relevant dimensions of analysis in eco-psychological work" (Mruck & Mey, p. 373). In the attempt to redefine concepts in behavior-setting theory, Cotterell also comes up with a "place" notion that contains not only geographical and architectural aspects but also "social connotations" and the "concept of situation." Here again, one sees the linkage between behavior-setting theory and phenomenology, which is characterized by Graumann and Kruse as a "situation-centered approach." A revised behavior-setting theory as envisioned by Cotterell might profit from the phenomenological approach's elaborated "structural analysis of situations."

5 A new challenge

The review of behavior-setting theory and the phenomenological approach in this section of the book leaves new challenges to be met by future researchers who aim at a creative integration of various approaches in the field of developmental psychology. One of the challenges concerns the multisetting synomorphs initially conceived by Barker but left unfinished. The authors in this section of the book make several suggestions for furthering the idea of this "coherent whole," as Hinding terms it. She characterizes the multisetting synomorph as "a goal-centered assembly that has specific functions to serve" (p. 405) with "hierarchical arrangement" (p. 406). These characterizations remind me of a "holistic, developmental, systems-oriented perspective" developed by Wapner (in this volume). The assumptions made in this theoretical perspective facilitate hierarchical differentiation and increasing integration among system components having teleological, or means-ends, dynamics. Moreover, the developing theory of "self-organization" (Prigogine & Sterngers, 1984) might cast additional light on the actual process of systems formation, which is particularly important in the study of the behavior settings of developing children.

Another challenge for environmental psychologists studying and practicing with children in the modern urban environment lies in the revolutionary changes that technological development has wrought in the sociocultural milieu. What are the effects of newly developing telecommunication, which is characterized as "virtual" in a system of present-day children's macroenvironments? Can behavior settings mediated by TVs and personal computers be analyzed with traditional behavior-setting theory? This area may be one in which a more novel and unbiased approach is needed.

References

Barker, R. G., & Wright, H. F. (1966). *One boy's day: A specimen record of behavior*. Hamden: CT, Archon Books.

Burke, K. (1966). *Language as symbolic action*. Berkeley: University of California Press.

Gadamer, H.-G. (1976). *Philosophical hermeneutics*. Berkeley: University of California Press.

Muchow, M., & Muchow, H. H. (1935). *Der Lebensraum des Großstadtkindes* [The life world of the city child]. Hamburg: Riegel.

Pepper, S. C. (1942). *World hypotheses: A study in evidence*. Berkeley: University of California Press.

Prigogine, I., & Sterngers, I. (1984). *Order out of chaos: Man's new dialogue with nature*. New York: Bantam Books.

Valsiner, J. (1988). *Cultural development within culturally structured environments: Social co-construction and environmental guidance in development*. Norwood: Ablex.

D. Sociobiology, attachment theory, and ecological psychology – Marching towards the city

Introduction

Jaan Valsiner

The part of the book that the reader is about to encounter deals with a series of traditions of a directly interdisciplinary nature. Sociobiology imports notions of evolutionary thought into its coverage, the attachment perspective is based on psychodynamic approaches, and the ecological-psychological point of view is an examination of human actors as environment-dependent automations.

All of these perspectives are hybrids; they link psychological concerns with terminologies from neighboring disciplines. They share an interesting oversight: the loss of the active role of the person as an agent who relates with the environment. The notions of survival, exploration, relationship, and affordance divert attention from the issue at hand: *Who* are the ones who 'survive', 'relate', 'explore', and 'act' within the environment.

1   Dialogue between positions

Much of the discussion that emerges from the overviews of the three positions is of the kind that suggests an enlargement of the scope of the issues addressed by the main presenters (Keller, Charlesworth, and Heine & Guski). Flade points to the differences between agents who explore the environment and happen to be of different gender, Legendre wonders if in sociobiology the images of the 'Pleistocene' are to continue forever to guide applications of this theory to contemporary human conditions, and Munz brings out the need to widen the narrow focus of the affordance concept by reintroducing an agent. All these extensions become part of a dialogue about the positions of the original presenters. The readers can see for themselves how different positions are defended, and they can discover that most of this dialogue bypasses the question of children's lives in the city. Gärling's integration brings the story back to issues of central relevance to the book.

2   What is in a city?

Concern about cities (and children in the cities) is an everyday phenomenon about which any person might have rather fixed personal opinions. These opinions are undoubtedly based on common sense. At the same time, theoretical concepts imported from selected "margins" of psychology – sociobiology, attachment theory, and discourse about affordances – are recent inventions at psychology's common borders with other disciplines. They bring a disconcerting moment of fearful fresh-ness to the discourse about common-sense presuppositions of what living in the city is like. The result is that the theoretical positions are not equally applicable to differ-ent aspects of the *whole* complex of city living. The focus on the "survival of the fittest" – a catchphrase imported from evolutionary vocabulary and put to general-ized use by sociobiologists – is in principle applicable to the acts of walking up or down the staircase or crossing a street (see Heine & Guski as opposed to Charles-worth). Yet it is not easily applied in those microcontexts (where the adherents of the affordance concept find the highly convenient place to apply it). It might instead be applicable to the *macro*context of the city as a whole. As Legendre aptly points out, the assumption that modern city life is another version of the Pleistocene may dramatize people's thinking about living in the cement jungles of everyday life, but do that assumption do much more for people's understanding? It leads to an eclectic blend of common-sense understanding and terminology that is applicable only at the level of the species. Surely, the question of whether I will survive my day in the dangerous traffic jungles of Carrboro City or whether I will have time enough to pass on my genes to my offspring before becoming extinct because a car runs over me might cross my sociobiologist's mind as I leave home in the morning and prepare myself for the exploratory activities of my day. Yet such application of species-level concepts at the level of an individual actor in particular contexts is merely a humor-ous story rather than knowledge-creating analysis. Furthermore, it is conceivable that finding a place in the city, and becoming attached to that place, allows me to relate to it with all the fullness of the affordances present in my relation to the place, without fear of predators – another example of mixing the terminologies of the three perspectives described in this section. The making of a place in the environment may be a personally pleasing survival tactic or merely a reflection of our common-sense descriptions. It does not mean that I belong to the fittest; I might be just one of the fortunate (or unfortunate) renegades who have avoided the business of fighting for survival!

The story here becomes somewhat humorous (a characteristic of many socio-biological stories about human conditions; Valsiner, 1989), yet the problem remains: Do such dramatizations do anything more than sensitize human beings to the dan-gers of living in general, be that in a cement "jungle" or a real one? Readers will hopefully find their own answers by reading through the expositions and mutual criticisms included in this section. Yet it is wortwhile to emphasize that a mere cocktail or simple mixing of terminologies from the three (or more) perspectives, does not engender explanatory power. Instead, it complicates efforts to make sense of the phenomenon of how children develop within their environments.

Reference

Valsiner, J. (1989). On the glory and misery of sociobiological perspectives on human development: A selfish book review. *Developmental Psychobiology, 22*, 413-417.

Figure 1: *Marc Chagall (1887-1985): Moi et le village [I and the village] (1911/12) © VG Bild-Kunst, Bonn 1997*

Exploratory behavior, place attachment, genius loci, and childhood concepts: Elements of understanding children's interactions with their environments

Heidi Keller

The focus of this book is on children in cities. Addressing this topic is an especially challenging task because the adaptivity of behavioral patterns cannot be traced back to the history of humankind. Although the conceptions presented here should be applicable to different environments, the consideration of urban living poses a unique challenge to any theoretical approach. The unpredictability of the constant developmental processes and changes in city life makes it difficult to interpret behavioral adaptations as functional responses to specific demands. City life asks for completely different strategies for survival and adaptation than those that have been evolved for small group life in natural surroundings. The surprising result is that humans are obviously not primarily adapted to the human-made environment.

The aim of this chapter falls within the framework of efforts to bring together different domains of psychological research that contribute to the understanding of human-environment interaction. Although these considerations are concentrated on children as primary targets, the focus is on a developmental perspective defining childhood as a lifelong concern. The experiences that children undergo during the life stage defined as childhood shape basic characteristics of personality that function in terms of defining possibilities and constraints for later actions. But childhood not only represents an antecedent condition for later outcomes but remains lively as a domain of any individual's biographic past. Interestingly enough, one's own childhood remembering is often not the foil against which adults adjust their behavior towards children but the childhood conceptions that are elaborated within specific cultural and historical contexts. Without discussing the adaptational value of those ethnotheories here (see Keller, 1996), one can state that in so-called modern (i.e., mostly westernized) societies there is an increasing gap between societal standards in defining childhood conceptions and the desires and plans that actually guide children's behavior.

The argument presented here offers one perspective for a conception of individual-environment interaction. The building blocks comprise exploration, place attachment, genius loci, and childhood concepts. *Exploration* refers to the behavioral architecture of the child. It constitutes a behavioral system that enables the individual to interact with the environment, acquire information, and build up knowledge systems. It is part of the individual's behavioral repertoire from the beginning and, as such, it never disappears during the life span. It is generally acknowledged that exploratory behavior has unique importance during early and middle-childhood years. After mastering the first developmental task of establishing an emotional attachment to the primary caregiving persons, the child has the next challenge to master during the developmental course – to acquire competence in the physical surroundings. This is only possible if information about the self, the environment, and the self-environment interaction is integrated into a meaningful representational system. Developing attachment to a place (*place attachment*) results from these interactions and constitutes a vital part of the self-concept defining the identity of a person. This part is conceptually the most difficult one because its constituents need theoretical clarification as well as empirical underpinning.

The environment itself has to be specified according to different dimensions. In this chapter, I would like to concentrate especially on the symbolic value of the environment. I refer briefly to an aspect that concerns intersubjective qualities: the meaning of a place as its own special quality is expressed in the concept of *genius loci*.

The culturally and historically localized *conceptions of childhood* regulate the action possibilities and constraints. I consequently present different examples for conceptions of childhood and try to apply a present-day perspective on defining children's life spaces. Lastly, I discuss specific applications of these conceptions for the urban environment.

1 Exploratory behavior and its genesis during childhood

Children explore the social and physical environment from birth on. Exploratory behavior thus obviously constitutes an inborn behavioral system that has acquired adaptational value during phylogenesis (Fagan, 1974; Lorenz, 1969). It can be regarded as a genetically based system having curiosity as its motivational foundation (see Berlyne, 1960). Exploratory behavior can be defined as perceptual motor examination of a situation, an object, or a person. Play stresses repetitive variation and improvement of those exploratory activities. Both form a functional unit for the acquisition of knowledge in order to gain action competence. Exploratory behavior enables human beings to interact with the social and physical environment, to manipulate it and to adapt to it (Keller, 1992; Keller & Schneider, 1991; Schölmerich, 1994). It can be concluded that the exploratory system serves the important purpose of transforming novelty and ambiguity into familiarity and predictability, thus setting the stage for competent functioning. Those basic processes correspond to what Piaget described as "accommodation" and "assimilation" as processes by which to strive for equilibrium (Piaget, 1953). They are not a specific human behavioral repertoire; primates and higher vertebrates also exhibit exploratory behavior. Although young mammals expose themselves to dangerous situations while exploring and playing, the selection advantage obviously seems to superimpose the disadvantages. The basic forms of exploration and play are restricted to juvenile animals. Although exploratory capacities exist as part of, say, intelligent behavior and problem-solving strategies in humans as long as they live, exploration and play can be regarded mainly as a major children's activity. This view allows the conclusion that exploration and play have socialization functions.

The exploration system comprises a variety of behaviors that change during the developmental course. The first exploratory system during ontogeny concerns distal exploration, such as visual attention, visual scanning, hearing, and listening. The attentional systems operate differentially from birth on. Later in life, verbal exploration, that is, mainly question-asking, constitutes a third component of the distal exploratory system. During childhood the main venue of exploration certainly is manipulation. Manipulation comprises tactile behaviors, such as touching, testing surfaces, and executing other movements that allow the child to comprehend the function of objects. During the course of development, the differing modalities combine into complex behavioral strategies that form the exploratory process in detail.

Different models have been formulated in order to describe the exploratory process (see Schölmerich, 1994). The most common view is that the encounter with a stimulus object or situation leads to differential arousal of attention. Part of the attentional process is the evaluation of information according to a continuum of novelty and complexity, which are considered the main elicitors of exploratory behaviors. If novelty or complexity is in an optimal distance to existing schemes, perceptual cognitive activities will begin leading to tactual and manipulatory behaviors. The different systems occur in different combinations until enough information is acquired to assimilate or accommodate. Then, existing schemes are changed or new ones established in order to enhance the mental representation of the world. Emotional appraisal is part of the ongoing perceptual cognitive activity. This course of exploratory behavior is regarded as arousal increasing and is expressed in neutral or attentional interest in faces. After the system has reached an arousal peak, it is directed to release motor activity or emotional reactions. The resulting adaptation and integration forms the basis of balance or equilibrium. The child can then secure newly acquired information by eliciting effects under different conditions by variation and modification that form playful activities. This state of equilibrium or balance, which might result from those activities, can turn into boredom when the system is not confronted with further informational events or confronted again by ongoing stimulation (Berlyne, 1960, 1978).

As has been mentioned, novelty and complexity and also surprise (Charlesworth, 1969) have been identified as the highly potent dimensions for eliciting exploratory activities. Kagan (1970) has formulated a discrepancy hypothesis based on Piaget's (1953) conception of cognitive development. This hypothesis focuses on the discrepancy check outlined briefly in the description of the exploratory process. It says

that the organism confronts the stimulus situation and innately compares and evaluates the information with existing schemas. If the discrepancy is too small, the
organism will not engage in activities, for there is no informational need. If the discrepancy is too great, the organism will avoid the new situation because the
information might be overwhelming, thus arousing anxiety or fear and leading to
avoidance reactions. Only in an intermediate or optimal range of discrepancy will
the organism become active in order to seek information, which then further builds
up the cognitive structures. Thus, the discrepancy hypothesis proposes an inverted
U-shaped function for the elicitation of exploratory behaviors.

So far, mainly small-range exploratory activities have been addressed. With
increasing environmental competence and the experience of mastering environmental challenges from the immediate surroundings, children strive to explore on
larger scales. They extend their exploratory activities from the home as a point of
departure to the neighborhood. Similar to the notion of the mother as a secure base
for the one- to two-year-old child, the home becomes a reference point in the mental
representations and cognitive organizations that three- to six-year olds have of their
environments (Biel, 1982). The ontogenetic step from regulation by others to self-
regulation also develops during this period (Wertsch, 1985). After the age of five
years, the free range of children generally becomes extended beyond what is visually accessible from their homes (Hart, 1979). Girls in their early school years
doubled the distance they could travel from their homes, whereas boys nearly tripled
theirs. The concept of active exploration is crucial in this respect. It refers to the
motor activity of an individual and the extent to which decisions about where to
explore are made by the individual or are guided by an other person. Active self-
guided exploration has an impact on the quality of spatial representations. Different
studies have demonstrated that if kindergarteners and preschool children freely
move across an area or a building, they can remember or reconstruct the environment more precisely than if they were guided or only allowed to look at it (Cohen,
Wetherford, & Bird, 1980; Herman, 1980; Herman & Sigel, 1978).

Tremendous contextual and interindividual differences in exploratory performance
have been described (Keller, 1992). Contextual factors are related to the cultural
appropriateness of children's activities. Fostering individually guided self-centered
exploratory actions and early onsets of competence seem to constitute a western
view of children (Keller & Chasiotis, 1994). This argument demonstrates that childhood concepts are important in defining the range of allowed activities (see below).
Interindividual differences occur mainly in the interconnection of exploration and
the emotional attachment or relationship quality between an infant and primary
caregivers (Ainsworth, Blehar, Waters, & Wall, 1978; Keller, 1991). If the attachment or relationship quality can be described as secure, the infant is expected to
explore its surroundings actively and consequently build up environmental representations. If the relationship is insecure, the child might be afraid to engage in

novel and unfamiliar activities and surroundings (see Hazen & Durrett, 1982; Hazen & Pick, 1985; Keller, 1992).

In any case, the exploratory system provides human beings with the facilities and possibilities of acquiring information about their environments and becoming familiar with the social and physical aspects of their developmental niches.

2   The development of place attachment

Personal attachment of people to geographical places has been discussed in the literature under different labels. Place identity (Proshansky, 1978; Proshansky, Fabian, & Kaminoff, 1983), sense of place or rootedness (Buttimer & Seamon, 1980; Relph, 1976; Tuan, 1980), place dependence (Stokols & Shumaker, 1981), all address the epistemic acts directed to locating oneself in the geographical ecology.

Different perspectives can be identified in these approaches. The cognitive approach concentrates on individual-environmental representations as subjective active constructivistic processes. The focal point is cognitive aspects of human representations of the environment, such as people's cognitive maps in terms of spatial representational arrangements (Tolman, 1932), or the orientation function, such as the legibility and imaginability of the environment (Lynch, 1975).

The self-concept perspectives consider place identity as part of the self's subjective representation, which is a result of social differentiation processes. As Mead (1934) has elaborated, objects and places have meanings that are shared by individuals belonging to reference groups leading to intersubjectivity of meaning. The environment acquires meanings through the potential of uses. Action traces become visible and constitute external memories. Because these traces are usable for many persons, they represent a supraindividual, social, and cultural memory. However, environments are not imposed on people; they are experienced in individual and social terms.

Biological perspectives have also been applied to the understanding of place identity. The personal relevance that the environment has to the individual is stressed in terms of basic adaptational patterns. Territoriality as a process of defending or controlling resources against the interest of competing members of the species has been outlined (Krebs & Davies, 1991). Archetypical space definitions, such as sheltering or clear lines of sight, can be seen as part of the human being's psychobiologically based behavioral repertoire.

Applying the psychoethological attachment paradigm to the attachment of places allows an integration of cognitive as well as emotional components of place identity (see Keller & Leyendecker, 1989).

Attachment signifies an emotional-affective bond, an emotional state of belongingness of two persons. Human beings are equipped from birth with a behavioral repertoire for developing attachments to social partners, attachments that have acquired adaptational values during ontogenesis. Perceptual competencies in different modalities and social behaviors such as looking, smiling, and vocalizing are most prominent. Obviously, the early exploratory competencies serve the function of acquiring information about significant persons.

Developing specific attachment to one or a few caregivers seems to constitute the first major developmental task of the child. Attachment development is organized in different phases (see Ainsworth et al., 1978). In a preparatory phase, the child is susceptible to specific cues, for which a biological predisposition seems to exist. Interactional experiences help organize the flow of information into what is familiar and what is strange. Familiarity builds the basis for affective bonding, which can have different qualitative characteristics (generally speaking, secure or insecure) and which then influences other developmental domains such as social behavior or exploration of the physical surroundings.

Applied to the development of place attachment, the developmental course can be described as follows. Environmental cues are first perceived. These attentional perceptional processes, including the recognition of stimulus configurations, lead to cognitive representations that form the basis of familiarity. Exploratory behavior is the means of action. Consecutive evaluations qualify familiar perceptions as emotionally positive. Next, familiarization can lead to identification; identification to attachment. One aspect of attachment, then, is belongingness, expressing action competence and responsibility.

Analogous to the internalization of the attachment quality developed toward a person as an internal working model (Bowlby, 1969), place attachment in terms of existential security becomes part of the self-concept, the identity of a person.

3   The identity of place (genius loci)

Mainly phenomenological views have concentrated on the intuitive experiencing of the environmental qualities themselves as targets of person-environment interactions. The experience of reality is defined as the experience of meaning. Intuition is a different aspect of mental activity, one that is important to experience the essence of things. In this respect, place identity is an unselfconscious, unreflective state (Relph, 1976; Tuan, 1980). This view has found its most popular expression in the concept of genius loci, the ghost of a place, the guardian of geographical areas. This quality can be traced back to ancient Greek and Roman times (see Dovey, Downton, & Missingham, 1985) and is understood as animating the place as well as the person.

Genius loci concerns the identity of a concrete geographical area, the inherent value of nature, the surplus meaning of a place as compared with its surroundings (Neddens, 1986). It consists of the totality of concrete things, material substance such as form, surface, and color, which constitute the atmosphere, the spirit of a place (Norberg-Schulz, 1982). Markers of an identity of a place become apparent to the person (Mitscherlich, 1971). People experience the spirit of a place intuitively as an emotionally based evaluation. Feelings of peace or threat, familiarity and intimacy, or anonymity are, thus, experienced. The concept of genius loci mainly refers to interindividual qualities as expressed in sacred places or other socially relevant denotations of place, as opposed to individually, biographically rooted sensations.

Although this conception might be highly difficult to realize in empirical research, it is highly an aspect that must not be neglected when one tries to understand human-environment interaction.

4 Conceptions of childhood

Even when compared to nonhuman primates, human beings have an extremely long period of childhood and adolescence among the species. These prolonged life stages are a consequence of the increased complexity of the human socioecological niche (Chasiotis, 1990; Chasiotis & Keller, 1995). Consequently, human childhood and adolescence are mainly an apprenticeship. A person must acquire knowledge in order to become a competent adult. The definition of competence in adulthood may differ depending on the theoretical perspective one takes on development. A detailed psychological analysis would certainly stress mental health, social competence, and a professional orientation in terms of self-maintenance.

4.1 A glimpse into history

The segmentation of the life cycle into socially meaningful units has been a subject of artistic representation across history and cultures (see Joerissen & Will, 1983). Its most pronounced expression is the staircase of life. Similary, conceptions of the child's nature, all stemming from philosophical-ethical issues, vary across cultures and history. Only a few sketchy accounts can be presented here.

The Middle Ages are usually cited as the oldest source of different childhood conceptions. At that time little importance was placed upon childhood as a separate phase of the life cycle. Children were viewed as infants until the age of about 6 years, at which point they were able to be independent from their mothers and other caretakers. Children from that age on were regarded as miniature adults and where treated to adult conversation, jokes, music, and food. As can be inferred from paintings of that period, children were pictured with the same clothing, hair styles, and activities as adults. Children could be recognized as children only by their size (e.g., Ariès, 1960; Berk, 1989; Craig, 1989; Plumb, 1971).

A change in the conception of childhood occurred during the sixteenth century through ideas stemming from Christian religion. Children were seen as carrying original sin, which meant that they were born evil and stubborn and had to be socialized or, better, civilized through restrictive Puritan child-rearing practices. Through formal schooling with moral training as an essential feature – which was allowed only for middle-class boys – the period of childhood was prolonged (Ariès, 1960; Berk, 1989; Moran & Vinovskis, 1986; Suransky, 1982). This view was opposed by natural philosophers, who saw children as guardians of redeeming innocence. In particular, the conception of the *tabula rasa* by the Enlightenment philosopher John Locke (1632-1704) basically expressed that a vast array of experiences shape children, transforming them from a blank slate into their actual characters. His treatise, *Some Thoughts Concerning Education* (1690/1892), recommended repetition, imitation, reward, and punishment as parents' tools for tutoring their children. These ideas form the basis of ideas introduced by later behaviorists. Locke definitely emphasized positive experiences rather than punishment and advocated that parents not reward children with money or candy but with praise and approval (Berk, 1989).

During the eighteenth century, a natural theory of childhood became very popular when Jean-Jacques Rousseau (1712-1778) published his novel *Emile* (1762/1955), which described the upbringing of a fictitious boy as the unfolding of a natural plan. Children were conceived as noble savages who are equipped with inborn senses of right and wrong. The caretaker was supposed to be responsive in watching the natural growth during different developmental stages. Rousseau stressed the conception of development as maturational, self-directed processes (Berk, 1989; see also Kessen, 1969).

Although childhood has become an important life stage over the centuries, it obviously does not have great inherent value in the modern western view. Childhood is a temporary state, and children are considered mistake-prone individuals who do not yet understand the logical structure of the world surrounding them. This view is prevalent not only in folk wisdom but also in science, especially in developmental theories (see Keller, 1989). Only recently, the *theory-of-mind* approach has made visible that children's reasoning and thinking form holistic world views that are sensitive to specific contexts and developmental domains (Sodian, 1991). Thus, stressing the uniqueness and developmental logic in specific developmental stages would have a tremendous impact on the goals and values of socialization. I will come back to this point later.

4.2 A further glimpse on cross-cultural views on childhood

Because of contextual demands, life stages have been quite differently defined from one culture to the next. In western terms, which sound rather technical, the life course is divided into the embryonic stage, childhood, youth, adulthood, and old age. The transitions between these phases are defined by biological markers (birth), legal action (childhood ends with 14 years), or differentiation by researchers (old age begins at 60 years). Ethnologists have given important descriptive accounts of different life periodizations in different cultures and societies. It is obvious that spiritual references points are prevalent in many nonwestern classifications. For example, Nsamenang (1992, p. 148) has identified nine socioontogenetic stages among the Nso of Northwest Cameroon, namely, spiritual self-hood, period of the newborn, social priming, social apprenticing, social entree, social induction or internment, adulthood, old age (and death), and ancestral selfhood.

The social character of the life stages is especially stressed, an aspect that might find its equivalent in the relational definition of the adult personality as opposed to individuality as a main feature of western adult functioning (Keller, 1996).

These sociocultural conceptions of childhood are mirrored in educational ideologies. One obvious behavioral difference between western and nonwestern views is the way physical proximity is regulated. The cultural patterns of care in three societies from the traditional world – the Ainu of Japan, the Trobrianders of Melanesia, and the Gusii of East Africa as described by Munroe and Munroe (1994) – all stress physical proximity between infants and their primary careproviders for the first years of life. Small children in these societies are expected to remain close to home. A slow and gradual appropriation of the physical surroundings should be a consequence.

Western children, especially those living in cities, are exposed to early separations from their mothers or other primary caregivers. Because their lives are segmented into different educational activities from early age on, they must cover larger distances than children in the three societies just described. Thus, western children experience less continuity in environmental features. They must adopt single characteristics from different locations, which only much later might form a mental map.

The most common cultural differentiation is that between the more individualistic, competitive, independent model of personality and an interdependent, socially organized personality type (Keller & Chasiotis, 1994; Trommsdorff, 1993). Accordingly, children's upbringing and training is concentrated on fostering individuality and independence as opposed to promoting a close relationship with the caregiving persons and the home base.

Consequences for the childhood conception of the western child can be formulated with respect to three major constituents:

1. Promoting early independence and development of self-reliability
2. Segmentation of life spaces and segregation from adult life
3. Impact on educational goals

5   Integration of the concepts

It has been argued that conceptions of childhood as adopted in a culture by the parents and translated into socialization practices play an important role in shaping the
developmental niche of children and, in turn, their development (see also Super &
Harkness, 1986). Within the constraints placed on exploratory action, children
acquire environmental representations forming mental images that have the quality
of attachment relationships. The experiences with space, especially places, however,
are also influenced by the inherent value of physical locations.

An integration of these conceptions is very difficult. One of the major problems is
the emergence of the feeling of belongingness as a constituent of the self-concept.
Different approaches to the definition of place identity mainly stress the process of
appropriation. What is usually neglected is the specification of the environment and
the inclusion of the environmental characteristics themselves. Obviously, the first
place that is important to children in the cultural environment of the western world is
the parental dwelling (see Proshansky, Fabian, & Kaminoff, 1983). It is regarded as
the kernel of children's reality; it expresses the externalization of the personal culture, a personalized environment (see Heidmets, 1985; Valsiner, 1988). The house
of the parents is usually the first place where a child experiences familiarity and
security outside the relationship to significant others.

As pointed out earlier, the range is extended during the preschool years, and
external environmental representations become important complements. With few
exceptions (see, for example, Muchow & Muchow, 1935/1980; Hart, 1979), there is
not much empirical evidence on these processes. It is also unclear how early experiences finally form the reference point for preferences for specific physical structures
over others. One can conclude only from deficiencies such as homesickness, and
feelings of homelessness that these processes must have occurred. Assessment of a
person's geographic biography would be helpful in this respect, as would emphasis
on the emotional tones and qualities that have been experienced with respect to specific places.

The city as a geographical, architectural, and behavioral setting (see Stokols,
1981) forms an experiential base with its own challenges. The archetypical environmental needs for an overview and shelter are not accessible per se; they have to
be constructed individually as the personal city.

As a socialization niche for citizens of all ages, the city where permanent developments and changes are vital, represents an element of strangeness and danger
because actions and processes are uncontrolled and uncontrollable to some extent

and present a dimension that extends human standards. In this sense, the city is often evaluated as artificial and threatening, even destructive.

To facilitate environmental appropriation processes, urban planning and design should not be guided solely by one concept of childhood that restricts children to specific places with a uniform appearance (e.g., playgrounds) and mainly educational impact. Accepting the existence of different world views across developmental stages could be an opportunity to open urban spaces from their usually monopolistic functions.

As has been argued, familiarity is an important prerequisite for attachment. To become familiar with environmental outlets, a person must be induced to direct attention to them. Through moderate doses of unfamiliarity and unpredictability, those processes could be instigated. Temporarily installed artifacts (statues, symbols, and so forth) are potent elicitors of attention. Permanent structures in this respect could become salient landmarks (e.g., Acredolo & Evans, 1980; Bremner & Bryant, 1977). As a consequence, prolonged stays outside the home are to be expected by the researchers. This situation reflects the problematic relationship between inside (children's rooms) and outside in western societies (Keller, 1993). The danger posed by traffic is a popular reason given for withdrawing from outdoors, but the many other reasons commonly cited seem dubious when cross-cultural evidence of city life is considered. In many parts of the world, traffic is chaotic, multitudes of people, including children, are in the streets, and sometimes, as in India, animals roam the road as well, yet the accident rates are lower than in the western world.

These considerations point to different loci where conflicts are inherent in the socialization process. Stressing independence and the acquisition of early competence through exploration as a goal of socialization while restricting possibilities of exploratory acquisition by defining spatial and social segments where children are allowed is one example of those developmental conflicts. But more serious consideration of the aspects presented here in a rather associationistic way could influence theorizing about child development as well as practical consequences for child-inclusive urban planning.

References

Acredolo, L. P., & Evans, D. (1980). Developmental changes in the effects of landmarks on infant spatial behavior. *Developmental Psychology, 16*, 312-318.

Ainsworth, M. D. S., Blehar, M. C., Waters, E., & Wall, S. (1978). *Patterns of attachment: A psychological study of the strange situation.* Hillsdale, NJ: Erlbaum.

Ariès, P. (1960). *Centuries of childhood* (Trans., R. Baldick). New York: Knopf.

Berk, L. E. (1989). *Child Development.* Boston: Allyn & Bacon.

Berlyne, D. E. (1960). *Conflict, arousal, and curiosity.* New York: McGraw-Hill.

Berlyne, D. E. (1978). Curiosity and learning. *Motivation and Emotion, 2*, 97-175.

Biel, A. (1982). Children's spatial representation of their neighbourhood: A step toward a general spatial competence. *Journal of Environmental Psychology, 2*, 193-200.

Bowlby, J. (1969). *Attachment and loss. Vol. 1: Attachment.* New York: Basic Books.

Bremner, J. G., & Bryant, P. E. (1977). Glance versus response as a basis of spatial errors made by young children. *Journal of Experimental Child Psychology, 23*, 162-171.

Buttimer, A., & Seamon, D. (Eds.). (1980). *The human experience of space and place.* London: Croom Helm.

Charlesworth, W. R. (1969). The role of surprise in cognitive development. In D. Elkind & J. H. Flavell (Eds.), *Studies in cognitive development* (pp. 257-314). Oxford, Eng.: Oxford University Press.

Chasiotis, A. (1990). *Soziobiologie und Entwicklungspsychologie der frühesten Kindheit* [Sociobiology and developmental psychology of early infancy]. Unpublished master thesis, University of Osnabrueck.

Chasiotis, A., & Keller, H. (1995). Kulturvergleichende Entwicklungspsychologie und evolutionäre Sozialisationsforschung [Culturally comparative developmental psychology and evolutionary socialization research]. In G. Trommsdorff (Ed.), *Kindheit und Jugend in verschiedenen Kulturen* (pp. 21-42). Weinheim: Juventa.

Cohen, R., Wetherford, D. L., & Bird, D. (1980). Distance estimates of children as a function of acquisition and response activities. *Journal of Experimental Child Psychology, 30*, 464-472.

Craig, G. J. (1989). *Human development* (5th ed.). Englewood Cliffs, NJ: Prentice-Hall.

Dovey, K., Downton, P., & Missingham, G. (Eds.). (1985). Place and placemaking. *Proceedings of the PAPER-85 Conference*, Melbourne: People and Physical Environment Research Association.

Fagan, J. F. (1974). Infant recognition memory: The effects of length of familiarization and type of discrimination task. *Child Development, 45*, 351-356.

Hart, R. (1979). *Children's experience of place.* New York: Irvington.

Hazen, N. L., & Durrett, M. E. (1982). Relationship of security of attachment to exploration and cognitive mapping abilities in 2-year-olds. *Child Development, 4*, 751-759.

Hazen, N. L., & Pick, H. L. Jr. (1985). An ecological approach to the development of spatial orientation. In T. D. Johnston & A. T. Pietrewicz (Eds.), *Issues in the ecological study of learning* (pp. 201-243). Hillsdale, NJ: Erlbaum.

Heidmets, M. (1985). Environment as the mediator of human relationships: Historical and ontogenetic aspects. In T. Gärling & J. Valsiner (Eds.), *Children within environments: Toward a psychology of accident prevention* (pp. 217-227). New York: Plenum.

Herman, J. F. (1980). Children's cognitive maps of large-scale spaces: Effects of exploration, direction, and repeated experience. *Journal of Experimental Child Psychology, 29*, 126-143.

Herman, J. F., & Sigel, A. W. (1978). The development of cognitive mapping of the large-scale environment. *Journal of Experimental Child Psychology, 26*, 389-406.

Joerissen, P., & Will, C. (1983). *Die Lebenstreppe. Bilder der menschlichen Lebensalter* [The staircase of life: Pictures of human ages]. Cologne: Rheinland-Verlag.

Kagan, J. (1970). The determinants of attention in infants. *American Scientist, 58,* 289-306.

Keller, H. (1989). Kontinuität und Entwicklung [Continuity and development]. In H. Keller (Ed.), *Handbuch der Kleinkindforschung* (pp. 163-180). Heidelberg: Springer.

Keller, H. (1991). A perspective on continuity in infant development. In M. E. Lamb & H. Keller (Eds.), *Infant development: Perspectives from German-speaking countries* (pp. 135-150). Hillsdale, NJ: Erlbaum.

Keller, H. (1992). The development of exploratory behavior. *The German Journal of Psychology, 16*, 120-140.

Keller, H. (1993). Entwicklungspsychologische Überlegungen zur Funktion von Kinderzimmern [Developmental considerations about the function of children's rooms]. In H. J. Harloff (Ed.), *Psychologie des Wohnungs- und Siedlungsbaus. Psychologie im Dienste von Architektur und Stadtplanung* (pp. 123-130). Göttingen: Verlag für Angewandte Psychologie.

Keller, H. (1996). Evolutionary approaches. In J. W. Berry, Y. H. Poortinga, & J. Pandey (Eds.), *Handbook of cross-cultural psychology, Vol. I. Theory and method* (pp. 215-255). Boston: Allyn & Bacon.

Keller, H., & Chasiotis, A. (1994, April). *A psychobiological conceptualization of ethnotheories.* Lecture delivered at the International Congress "Education, famille et dévelopment en Afrique," Abidjan, Ivory Coast.

Keller, H., & Leyendecker, B. (1989). Ortsidentität und Genius Loci als Konzepte der Mensch-Umwelt-Interaktion. Das Verständnis von Regionalität des Osnabrücker Kulturzentrums Kind (OKKI) [Place identity and genius loci as concepts of person-environment interaction: The understanding of regionality at the children's Cultural Center in Osnabrueck]. In C. Salzmann & W. D. Kohlberg (Eds.), *Modelle des regionalen Lernens und der Umwelterziehung in Europa* (pp. 453-469). Heinsberg: Agentur Dieck.

Keller, H., & Schneider, K. (1991). Entwicklung und Prozeß explorativen Verhaltens [Development and the process of exploratory behavior]. In F. J. Mönks & G. Lehwald (Eds.), *Neugier, Erkundung und Begabung bei Kleinkindern* (pp. 22-39). Munich: Ernst Reinhardt.

Kessen, W. (1969). *The child.* New York: Wiley.

Krebs, J. R., & Davies, N. B. (Eds.) (1991). *Behavioural ecology: An evolutionary approach.* London: Blackwell Scientific Publications.

Locke, J. (1892). Some thoughts concerning education. In R. H. Quick (Ed.), *Locke on education* (pp. 1-236). Cambridge, Eng.: Cambridge University Press. (Original work published 1690)

Lorenz, K. (1969). Innate bases of learning. In K. H. Pribram (Ed.), *On the biology of learning* (pp. 13-93). New York: Harcourt.

Lynch, K. (1975). *Das Bild der Stadt* [The image of the city]. Brunswick: Nieweg. (Original work published 1960)

Mead, M. (1934). *Mind, self, and society.* Chicago: University of Chicago Press.

Mitscherlich, A. (1971). *Die Unwirtlichkeit unserer Städte* [The desolation of our cities]. Frankfurt on the Main: Suhrkamp.

Moran, G. F., & Vinovskis, M. A. (1986). The great care of godly parents: Early childhood in Puritan New England. *Monographs of the Society for Research in Child Development, 50* (Serial No. 211).

Muchow, M., & Muchow, H. H. (1980). *Der Lebensraum des Großstadtkindes* [The life space of the urban child]. Bensheim: päd. extra. (Original work published 1935)

Munroe, R. L., & Munroe, R. H. (1994). *Cross-cultural human development.* Prospect Heights: Waveland Press.

Neddens, M. C. (1986). *Ökologisch orientierte Stadt- und Raumentwicklung* [Ecologically oriented urban and regional development]. Wiesbaden: Bauverlag.

Norberg-Schulz, C. (1982). *Genius loci: Landschaft, Lebensraum, Baukunst* [Genius loci: landscape, life space, architecture]. Stuttgart: Klett-Cotta.

Nsamenang, A. B. (1992). *Human development in cultural context: A Third World perspective.* Newbury Park, CA: Sage.

Piaget, J. (1953). *The origins of intelligence in children.* London: Routledge.

Plumb, J. H. (1971, winter). The great change in children. *Horizon,* 4-12.

Proshansky, H. M. (1978). The city and self-identity. *Environment and Behavior, 10,* 147-169.

Proshansky, H. M., Fabian, A. K., & Kaminoff, R. (1983). Place identity: Physical world socialization of the self. *Journal of Environmental Psychology, 3,* 57-83.

Relph, E. (1976). *Place and placelessness.* London: Pion.

Rousseau, J. J. (1955). *Emile.* New York: Dutton. (Original work published 1762)

Schölmerich, A. (1994). Process and result of manipulative exploration. In H. Keller, K. Schneider, & B. Henderson (Eds.), *Curiosity and exploration* (pp. 241-258). Heidelberg: Springer.

Sodian, B. (1991). The development of deception in young children. *British Journal of Developmental Psychology, 9,* 173-188.

Stokols, D. (1981). Group x place transactions: Some neglected issues in psychological research on settings. In D. Magnusson (Ed.), *Towards a psychology of situations* (pp. 393-415). Hillsdale, NJ: Erlbaum.

Stokols, D., & Shumaker, S. A. (1981). People in places: A transactional view of settings. In J. H. Harvey (Ed.), *Cognition, social behavior, and the environment* (pp. 441-488). Hillsdale, NJ: Erlbaum.

Super, C. M., & Harkness, S. (1986). The developmental niche: A conceptualization at the interface of child and culture. *International Journal of Behavioral Development, 9,* 545-569.

Suransky, V. P. (1982). *The erosion of childhood.* Chicago: University of Chicago Press.

Tolman, E. C. (1932). *Purposive behavior in animals and men.* New York: Appleton-Century-Crofts.

Trommsdorff, G. (1993). Entwicklung im Kulturvergleich [A cultural comparison of development]. In A. Thomas (Ed.), *Kulturvergleichende Psychologie. Eine Einführung* (pp. 103-137). Göttingen: Hogrefe.

Tuan, Y. F. (1980). Rootedness versus sense of place. *Landscape, 24,* 3-8.

Valsiner, J. (1988). Ontogeny of co-construction of cultures within socially organized environmental settings. In J. Valsiner (Ed.), *Child development within culturally structured environments* (Vol. 2, pp. 283-297). Norwood, IL: Ablex.

Wertsch, J. V. (1985). *(Lev Semenovich) Vygotsky and the social formation of mind.* Cambridge, MA: Harvard University Press.

Comment: Gender are two

Antje Flade

1 Basic assumptions

The goal of Keller's chapter is an integration of different perspectives. The resulting integrative view should give new insights into the process of "development in its ecological context," as formulated by Bronfenbrenner (1986, p. 63). Studying development in its ecological context means integrating developmental and environmental psychology. The building blocks or elements called *place attachment* and *genius loci* reflect the integration of environmental psychology in thinking about developmental processes. Besides these two elements, there are two others for a conception of an individual's interaction with the environment: exploration and childhood concepts. Each of these four elements is described, especially exploration and the conceptions of childhood. Conceptions of the child's nature differ from culture to culture and period to period, so the element called *childhood concepts* is described through comparison of cultures over history. The purpose is to widen the horizon for the childhood concept.

The basic assumptions are:
(a) Exploration is a behavioral system that enables the individual to interact with the environment, acquire information, and build up knowledge systems. Through exploration, strange environments are changed into familiar ones. Familiarity builds the basis for affective bonding.
(b) Attachment signifies an emotional/affective bond. Developing attachments to care-giving persons constitutes the first major developmental task of the child. Analogous to the internalization of the quality of attachment to a person, place attachment as existential security becomes part of the self-concept, the identity of a person.
(c) The environment must be specified according to different dimensions. As Rapaport (1985) noted, it is difficult to think about environments. If there are neither models nor theories, one needs at least conceptual frameworks. Such frameworks are not completely arbitrary; some fit evidence better than others. Keller's chosen framework is the symbolic value of the environment, that is, the meaning of a place as its own special quality, which is expressed in the concept of *genius loci*.

(d) The conceptions of childhood regulate the action possibilities and constraints. The promotion of early independence and the segmentation of the life spaces of children from the life spaces of adults are characteristics of the conditions in which children live in western culture.

2   Coherence of the assumptions

Whereas the three components called exploration, place attachment, and childhood concepts together yield an integrative view, the fourth element of Keller's framework, genius loci, does not seem to be integrated as well. The relation between it and the other elements in the interaction processes remains indistinct. Second, the issue is children's interactions with their environments over a fairly long time, so the transactional approach (see Altman & Rogoff, 1987) seems to be more suited than Keller's is for describing the ongoing processes over the many years of childhood and youth.

3   The underlying concept of development

The underlying concept of development stresses uniqueness and developmental logic in specific developmental stages. To make this focus more distinct, Keller cites two comparisons, one in the form of a glimpse into history, the other in the form of a glimpse into nonwestern cultures. Keller rejects the view taken in the modern western societies, which conceive of childhood as a temporary state and children as dull individuals who do not yet understand the world surrounding them compared to adults. Keller prefers the "theory-of-mind" approach, according to which children's reasoning and thinking are regarded as forming holistic world views. The developmental goals are different in western and nonwestern cultures. This fact is reflected in children's upbringing and training. Early separations from primary care-givers is typical in western cultures in contrast to a physical proximity between infants and care-givers in nonwestern cultures. Two different personality types result: a more individualistic, competitive, and independant personality in the western world and an interdependent, socially oriented personality in nonwestern societies.

4   Performance of the approach with regard to children in cities

Keller assumes that the fit between man and the human-made environment is fairly bad. In consequence the consideration of urban living poses a unique challenge to any theoretical approach. The fact that city life requires completely different strategies for survival and adaptation than have been evolved in natural settings is reflected in the research topics of environmental psychology (see, for example, the chapter entitled "The City" in Bell, Fisher, Baum, & Greene, 1990, and the considerations of Graumann, 1990). Keller's four-part framework is more apt for the description of developmental processes in general than for children living in cities or in such specific urban regions as inner cities or disadvantaged areas.

The four elements are described in a general way and then put together in an integrative view. Keller does not conceal the exploratory nature of this endeavour and its sketchy, speculative character, there are no empirical data to test or elaborate the framework. Yet there is no doubt that exploratory behavior must be promoted independently of whether the children are living in cities or in more rural areas. It has to be investigated whether exploration will be restricted through a concept of childhood that emphasizes segmentation of life spaces and segregation from adult life. Such segmentation probably occurs. The possible consequences must be elucidated in more detail than that offered in Keller's chapter.

5   General comments

On the whole the approach is gender-neutral. The gender perspective is, however, quite important with regard to three points. First, western culture is characterized as one that stresses individualism, competence, and independence, whereas nonwestern cultures emphasize social relations and bondedness to the home base. The western culture seems to be a male world; nonwestern cultures, female worlds based on the image of the typically male and the typically female person (see Trautner, 1991). In western cultures, for example, women who have to care for children are considerably dependent. Therefore, it is not the western culture but male dominance in the western culture that is described as a society with individualistic and independent persons. Second, the issue of segmentation of life spaces and segregation from adult life in the conception of childhood is formulated without the gender of the adult person being taken into account. Segregation of children from adult life occurs in that mothers and fathers work at places other than the home throughout the day. This is the case especially for fathers but only partially for mothers, who, after all, spend a great deal of time with their children. Adult life consists not only of professional activities but to a large extent of activities in the family. Third, children's upbringing and training is concentrated on fostering individuality and independence especially for boys and promoting the maintenance of a close relation with the home base especially for girls.

In the context of analyzing and comparing childhood conceptions across history and cultures, the lack of the gender perspective is striking. Maccoby (1988) noted that "gender is ubiquitous as a social category. All known languages include terms to distinguish boys from girls and men from women" (p. 755). She spoke of "distinctive cultures of boys' and girls' groups" (p. 758). The separation of the sexes into distinct social groupings is explained with the different play styles and influence patterns of girls and boys in social groups. Maccoby (1990) summarized that gender segregation is a widespread phenomenon found in all cultural settings. Accordingly, children in cities are always girls and boys in cities (see Flade & Kustor, 1995, 1996; Flade, 1993). Gender differences are salient for exploration and childhood. That salience, however, means that human-environment interactions have to be specified according to gender.

The challenge to meet during the course of development, the aquisition of competence in the physical surroundings is quite different for girls and boys. Different childhood concepts regulate the action possibilities and constraints that ultimately determine the life spaces of boys and girls.

Keller's assumption is that exploration and play have socializing functions because both can be regarded as major children's activities. Maccoby (1988, 1990), Hart (1978, 1979), and Saegert and Hart (1978), for example, have shown that socialization is different for girls and boys, especially in the later years of childhood. From about the age of 8 years on (see Webley, 1981, for example), the differences in home range increases. Richards and Larson (1989) called this phenomenon *gender intensification* (p. 620). On the average, girls have a smaller home range, and boys need more space for the rough-and-tumble play and football games typical for them. My own research, for example, has shown that 10- to- 13-years-old boys bicycle more often than do girls of the same age. For example, boys in the city take the bicycle on 38 percent of their everyday routes, whereas girls, who prefer walking, take it on 26 percent of theirs. Further results are that boys are more outside, girls stay more inside. The games of boys are more "room-consuming," those of girls do not need so much room. Girls have to be at home earlier in the evening (see Flade & Kustor, 1995). The faster means of transport is an important factor determining the extension of the life space. Girls attach much less value to the car than boys do. Girls see themselves as future car drivers more rarely than boys do (Flade, 1994). Martha Muchow already found 60 years ago that the life space of boys is much greater than the life space of girls (Muchow & Muchow, 1935/1978).

At only one point does Keller address the matter of gender differences. She noticed that, during the early school years, girls doubled the distance they could travel from their homes, whereas boys nearly tripled theirs. But the importance of this difference is not subsequently recognized or mentioned by Keller. Webley (1981), for example, found that the home-area cognitive maps of the 8-year-old boys in his study were 40 percent larger than those of the 8-year-old girls because the boys had more extended home ranges.Therefore, the following sentence by Keller is more true for boys than for girls: "With increasing environmental competence and the experience of mastering environmental challenges from the immediate surroundings, children strive to explore on larger scales" (see Keller, p. 458).

The elements in the framework that Keller describes constitute a system; each element interacts with every other. For example, gender differences regarding exploration produce gender differences regarding place attachment. The results reported by Saegert and Winkel (1980) are convenient for this consideration. They found that the meaning of home was different for females and males and that the dwelling was a more central part of the self-concept defining the identity of female persons than it was in the case of males. That is, place attachment and place identity are different for males and females.

Keller describes western culture in comparison to culture in nonwestern societies. The difference between them is implicitly related to gender. Western cultures seem to be male-dominated. Keller assumes that the most common cultural differentiation can be subsumed under the more individualistic, competitive, independent model of personality as opposed to an interdependent, socially oriented personality type. Accordingly, children's upbringing and training is concentrated on fostering individuality and independence as opposed to promoting the maintenance of close relations with the care-giving persons and the home base. Obviously, this picture of socialization is that of male persons in western cultures. Promoting early independence is an important goal in this context. On the other hand, there are more constraints for girls. Saegert (1987) described women's worlds as a challenge to the environment.

Environmental psychology had nothing to say about women. This field, like others, was about 'the person', and the person did not seem to be a women nor to be identified overtly as a man. . . . Women appear as a special category and men as the general person. (p. 119)

Therefore, future efforts to bring together different domains of psychological research that contribute to the understanding of human-environment interactions during childhood and youth should include the gender perspective.

References

Altman, I., & Rogoff, B. (1987). World views in psychology: Trait, interactional, organismic, and transactional perspective. In D. Stokols and I. Altman (Eds.), *Handbook of environmental psychology* (pp. 7-40). New York: Wiley.

Bell, P. A., Fisher, J. D., Baum, A., & Greene, T. C. (1990). *Environmental psychology* (3rd ed.). Fort Worth, TX: Holt, Rinehart and Winston.

Bronfenbrenner, U. (1986). Recent advances in research on the ecology of human development. Technical University of Berlin, *Dokumentation Kongresse und Tagungen, 31*, 63-101.

Flade, A. (1993). Platz für Jungen *und* Mädchen im öffentlichen Raum [Space for boys *and* girls in the public sphere]. In Ministerium für Arbeit, Gesundheit und Soziales des Landes Nordrhein-Westfalen (Ed.), *Kinderfreundlichkeit – das Prüfverfahren* (pp. 39-54). Düsseldorf.

Flade, A. (1994). Der Straßenverkehr aus der Sicht von Schulkindern. In A. Flade (Ed.), *Mobilitätsverhalten, Bedingungen und Veränderungsmöglichkeiten aus umweltpsycho-logischer Sicht* (pp. 185-194). Weinheim: Psychologie Verlags Union.

Flade, A., & Kustor, B. (1995). *Mädchen und Jungen in der Stadt* [Girls and boys in the city]. Wiesbaden: Hessisches Ministerium für Wirtschaft, Verkehr und Landesentwicklung.

Flade, A., & Kustor, B. (Eds.) (1996). *Raus aus dem Haus. Mädchen erobern die Stadt.* Frankfurt on the Main: Campus.

Graumann, C. F. (1990). Ansätze zu einer Psychologie der Großstadt [Approaches to urban psychology]. In G. Lensch (Ed.), *Möglichkeiten der Analyse von natürlichen und kultürlichen Regelsystemen und ihren Verknüpfungen im städtischen Lebensraum* (pp. 64-75). St. Ingbert, Germany: W. J. Röhrig.

Hart, R. (1978). Sex differences in the use of outdoor space. In B. Sprung (Ed.), *Nonsexist early childhood curriculum development (pp.* 101-109). New York: Teachers College Press.

Hart, R. A. (1979). *Children's experience of place.* New York: Irvington Press.

Maccoby, E. E. (1988). Gender as a social category. *Developmental Psychology, 24,* 755-765.

Maccoby, E. E. (1990). Gender and relationships: A developmental account. *American Psychologist, 45,* 513-520.

Muchow, M., & Muchow, H. H. (1978). *Der Lebensraum des Großstadtkindes* [The life space of the urban child]. Bensheim: päd. extra. (Original work published 1935)

Rapaport, A. (1985). Thinking about home environments: A conceptual framework. In I. Altman and C. M. Werner (Eds.), *Home environments* (pp. 255-286). New York: Plenum Press.

Richards, M. H., & Larson, R. (1989). The life span and socialization of the self: Sex differences in the young adolescent. *Journal of Youth and Adolescence, 18,* 617-626.

Saegert, S. (1987). Environmental psychology and social change. In D. Stokols and I. Altman (Eds.), *Handbook of environmental psychology* (Vol. 1, pp. 99-128). New York: Wiley.

Saegert, S., & Hart, R. (1978). The development of environmental competence in girls and boys. In M. Salter (Ed.), *Play: Anthropological perspectives* (pp. 157-176). Cornwall, NJ: Leisure Press.

Saegert, S., & Winkel, G. (1980). The home: A critical problem for changing sex roles. In G. R. Wekerle, R. Peterson, & D. Morley (Eds.), *New space for women* (pp. 41-63). Boulder, CO: Westview.

Trautner, H. M. (1991). *Lehrbuch der Entwicklungspsychologie* [Textbook of developmental psychology]. Vol. 2. Göttingen: Hogrefe.

Webley, P. (1981). Sex differences in home range and cognitive maps in 8-year-old children. *Journal of Environmental Psychology, 1,* 293-302.

Author's response: . . . but different ones

Heidi Keller

My chapter is meant to stimulate the thinking about children in cities by focusing on the emergence of place attachment through exploration of the surroundings, including the sense of place itself (genius loci) within the framework of historical and culturally defined conceptions of childhood in, as I wrote, a rather "associationistic way." In that vein, it is a theoretical contribution that proposes the integration of developmental conceptions (place attachment and exploratory behavior) with implicit categories (genius loci) and implicit ethnotheries (childhood conceptions). It is assumed that the explication of hidden assumptions that also form implicit conceptions of the researcher might be helpful in understanding developmental processes. The gender variable is especially prone to the ideological boundaries often found in empirical research. There is no psychological theory about gender differences. The fact that, say, "boys in the city take the bicycle on 38 percent of their everyday routes, whereas girls . . . take it on 26 percent of theirs" (Flade, p. 472) neither surprises me nor increases understanding of gender differences or children-environment interactions. Inferring "a male [Western] world" from such a fact and other empirical accounts is pure speculation. It is exactly this approach that I wanted to avoid in my account. Granted, the broad framework presented in my chapter needs to be elaborated in greater detail, and its differential aspects and interactions have to be spelled out. In this respect, as in many others, gender is a central category. However, if one wants to go beyond self-evident knowledge, predictions have to be specified according to perspectives of developmental theory. It is necessary to understand why boys develop preferences for larger scale movements as compared to girls. Simple reward schedules are not enough. It is necessary to understand what these preferences imply for the development of place attachment. Simply stating that it might be different is not enough, either. Only when these avenues of understanding are explored can environmental conditions be improved, especially in urban settings that allow boys and girls to develop their individual conceptions of place identity.

Children in cities:
An ethological/sociobiological approach

William R. Charlesworth

The important task of investigating the problems and opportunities facing children in cities should not be left up to one theoretical approach or one scientific discipline. For this reason, the decision to have the present volume include ethology and socio-biology, biological disciplines traditionally devoted to understanding animal behavior from an evolutionary perspective, is especially welcome.

Evolutionists believe that biological laws established millions of years ago now govern key aspects of contemporary human behavior, such governance being genetically mediated in an unbroken fashion across generations. This belief, however, does not necessarily imply that humans are predetermined to behave in specific ways, for all forms of life have alternative ways of behaving depending upon conditions. Nevertheless, the number of alternative behaviors available to humans is not infinite, nor are the consequences of behavior. For purposes of analysis, consequences can be divided into three categories – those behaviors that contribute positively to survival and reproduction (both obligatory goals of all animals), those that contribute negatively, and those that do not contribute at all. Connecting behavior and the conditions of its occurrences to its consequences, then, is the major task of those seeking to understand the origins and functions of animal behavior, including that of humans.

Before expanding on the concepts guiding this task, two reminders are in order. First, it should not be forgotten that Darwin constructed a theory of animal (and plant) behavior, not a theory of human behavior and mind. Although some of his ideas have significance for psychologists (Darwin, 1872/1965), Darwin was not a psychologist. He was well-aware of the dangers of entering areas where he lacked scientific expertise and of extrapolating across species.

Those who did study the human mind during his time were enthusiastic about his theory, but with few exceptions, such as Ekman's (1973) study of facial expressions, the vast bulk of research in psychology was carried out independently of Darwin's specific contribution to evolutionary thinking (Charlesworth, 1992). The reasons for this are now apparent. Darwin's theory, unlike other evolutionary theories, rests on two key principles, genetic variation and natural selection. Both principles, which must be examined in combination (Darwin's unique contribution), received virtually no attention by most psychologists over the century following Darwin (Costall,

1986; Ghiselin, 1986; Morss, 1990). Those studying genetics seldom, if ever, connected their findings with variables of natural selection; those studying environmental factors associated with health, disease, and mortality seldom connected them with genetics. This lack of attention to Darwin's unique contribution, of course, does not imply that Darwinian thinking has no relevance for the study of human behavior. It does, but in ways not anticipated, for the most part, by traditional research in human behavior.

The second reminder is that interest in human biology and its origins in understanding human behavior and culture is certainly not limited to ethologists and sociobiologists. Much thinking has been expended on this topic over the centuries (Degler, 1991). Rousseau, Freud, Durkheim, Levi-Strauss, Malinowski, and many others were well aware of the human's biological nature and the various consequences that resulted as it interacted with cultural demands. It is to be hoped that their insights, although frequently at variance with modern evolutionary theory, will not be neglected in drawing up an evolutionary picture of human behavior. Such a complex species as Homo sapiens needs to be viewed from as many different perspectives as possible.

At present, much of what ethology and sociobiology have to offer to the understanding of modern human behavior, in my estimation, is still in the form of a promissory note. This note is persuasive (containing much hard evolutionary reasoning as well as speculation), and its message is increasingly being converted into empirical research. Representing many different disciplines, researchers are building a broad and interesting data base that will greatly help expand our ways of thinking about human behavior (see the journals *Evolution and Human Behavior* [formerly *Ethology and Sociobiology*] and *Human Nature*).

1 Two approaches

Having somewhat different histories and foci of interest, ethology and sociobiology represent two approaches within evolutionary biology. In current practice, however, differences between them are rapidly fading. Nevertheless, in order to highlight two important points in evolutionary theory, these differences will be emphasized in the present paper. These differences consist of asking two contrasting questions concerning causality, one proximate and one ultimate. Both are discussed below. Combining the questions in a single empirical study, while difficult, is viewed in this chapter as the key to testing evolutionary thinking as it applies to human behavior.

1.1 Ethology

Early ethologists focused their efforts primarily on animal behavior per se – orienting, motor/perceptual, and social behaviors – in a wide range of species. They did so by means of naturalistic field observation and experiment as epitomized in the classical efforts of the pioneer ethologists Karl von Frisch (1914), Konrad Lorenz (1939), and Niko Tinbergen (1951). Since their achievements, ethology has grown rapidly as a major science of animal behavior (Eibl-Eibesfeldt, 1975; Hinde, 1970).

In the last several decades ethology has been expanded to include humans (Hinde, 1983; Eibl-Eibesfeldt, 1989). Because their interest was on the phylogenetic (evolutionary) origins, much of the early empirical work of human ethologists (e.g., Blurton Jones, 1972a; Eibl-Eibesfeldt, 1972) as well as evolutionary anthropologists with ethological orientations (e.g., Chagnon, 1974) focused on hunter-gatherer populations inhabiting environments of considerable distances from urban and suburban areas. Very rapidly, however, human ethologists expanded their empirical efforts to children living in more modern urban conditions. Nursery schools, school playgrounds, laboratories, and living rooms became primary sites of empirical investigation in the 1970s (Blurton Jones, 1972a; McGrew, 1972). Since then research on human ethology has been carried out in many settings touching upon a wide variety of content areas – social, motivational, emotional, cognitive, and developmental (see Hinde, 1974, 1983; Cranach, Foppa, Lepenies, & Plogg, 1979; and Archer, 1992, for comprehensive and critical treatments).

Only recently, however, have ethologists (inspired by concerns for more urban ethological research – see Eibl-Eibesfeldt & Hass, 1985) begun taking a systematic look at children and adults in urban environments (hereafter UE). The Ludwig-Boltzmann Institute for Urban Ethology in Vienna (Atzwanger, 1995; Grammar, 1992, 1993, and 1994; Schaefer, 1994; Schmitt & Atzwanger, 1995) was recently formed in direct response to the need for ethological research in cities. The institute's main efforts so far have been in areas dealing with crowding and aggression, defensible space for apartment dwellers, stranger meetings, walking speed as a function of city size, automobile-driving behavior, territorial marking, identification with the habitat, and other variables directly associated with urban life and factors contributing to levels of satisfaction with it.

1.2 Sociobiology

Also having its roots in the study of animal behavior, sociobiology originally distinguished itself from main stream behaviorism and comparative psychology by applying evolutionary theory to understanding the role social behavior played in animal survival and reproduction. Sociobiology began formally with Wilson's (1975) volume entitled *Sociobiology: The new synthesis*. Wilson's primary aim was to synthesize the realm of animal social behavior by focusing primarily upon the adaptive significance that everyday behavior (to answer proximate questions) has for survival and reproductive success (to answer ultimate questions). Shortly after Wilson's volume appeared, he and others included humans in their formulations (Alexander, 1979; Barash, 1982; Chagnon & Irons, 1979). Application of evolutionary thinking to specific domains of human behavior include the evolution of sexuality, Symons (1979); biology and culture, Bonner (1980); developmental psychology, MacDonald (1988); learning and evolution, Bolles and Beecher (1987); morality and moral systems, Alexander (1987); sex and social status, Barkow (1989); cognitive processes, Barkow, Cosmides, and Tooby (1992); education, Charlesworth (1994); psychology, Buss (1995); evolutionary medicine, McGuire and Troisi (1995); and Darwinian medicine, Nesse and Williams (1995).

2 Distinguishing features

At least two general features distinguish both approaches from that of traditional human behavior sciences. One feature is the combination of causal concepts (proximate and ultimate) that constitute evolutionary theory. The other feature is the combination of empirical methods required to identify and explicate these causes.

2.1 Causal concepts

Proximate causes consist of the immediate causes – neurophysiological, psychological, and external environmental factors – that initiate and control behavior. A standard proximate question would be how and under what conditions a particular behavior occurs and what its immediate consequences are? Ultimate causes, in contrast, consist of features external to the individual – climate, resource availability, predator pressure, intraspecies competition, genetic and biological factors – that historically have been directly implicated in the evolutionary process itself. A standard ultimate question is what, in the evolutionary history of this species, makes this behavior currently function in this particular way?

In empirical research the task of linking proximate and ultimate factors (connecting the smaller to the larger picture) is achieved by asking two related "function" questions: What immediate survival function and what long-term reproductive function does this particular behavior serve? For example, the hypothesized proximate/ultimate functions of a particular social behavior is that it not only serves proximate needs for social contact but also ensures that individuals can cooperate in order to have access to resources as well as to mates for ultimate reproductive success. Similarly, one could ask why humans live in UE settings and what long-term impact these settings have upon them. Such a question is hardly trivial in light of the fact that millions of years of human evolution have taken place in environments very unlike cities. Answering function questions is no easy task, not only because of the complexity of human behavior and the time lag between it and its consequences for survival and reproduction but also because of the limits on the understanding that humans have of their evolutionary past.

An additional causal factor (frequently subsumed under the category of proximate factors) is that of life-span development, or ontogeny. This factor, which was added to ethology by Tinbergen (1963) in order to deal with the construction and operation of behavior over the life of the individual, took a longer time entering the picture among sociobiologists and evolutionary biologists in general (Stearns, 1976). As Gould (1977) has pointed out, ontogeny long posed challenging conceptual problems for Darwin and for evolutionary theory in general.

The significance of including the development of behavior for the understanding of children in cities is obvious. During the span of time between conception and death, the complex interactions of innate (genetic controlled instinctual) processes and experiential (learning) processes take place and become organized to serve both immediate life and growth needs as well to lay down abilities to meet such needs in the future. The collective outcomes of such interactions for individual children have consequences for their reproduction and, thereby, consequences for the human gene pool of succeeding generations.

2.2   Methods

Incorporating the aforementioned elements into a satisfactory account of a particular behavior is a very big order. It requires mastery of, or at least acquaintance with, a wide range of methodological approaches, such as DNA mapping, biochemical assays, karotype analysis and genetic comparison, direct observation, interview and questionnaire methods, cross-sectional comparisons and longitudinal follow-ups, archival records, documented evidence of lineages and life-history events, demographic data, measures of environment and climate, and population densities. Evolutionary theory requires that a good portion of this range must be familiar to ethologists and sociobiologists. The combination of proximate and ultimate questions they ask invariably requires more than just passing acquaintance with various disciplines such as paleontology, anthropology, genetics, ecology, economics, and psychology. As Darwin learned early, understanding evolution required a vast amount of interdisciplinary knowledge.

It should be noted that traditionally interdisciplinary efforts have not been frequent in the behavioral sciences, particularly in the biobehavioral sciences. For example, combining knowledge gained from quantitative behavior genetics with the evolutionary emphasis on natural selection is, surprisingly, a new scientific concern.

Similarly, combining knowledge of neurotransmitters with human social dominance (McGuire & Troisi, 1998) is a relatively recent phenomenon.

The distinctive contribution of ethologists and sociobiologists, then, is to ask proximate/ultimate questions within the evolutionary framework. This effort requires studying species-universal everyday behaviors, identifying individual variations among them, making comparisons with other species, and determining the long-term consequences of the behavior for survival and reproduction. Much time is usually spent in defining behaviors and observing them in natural everyday settings (Blurton Jones, 1972a; Colgan, 1978; Lehner, 1979). In many respects, such efforts are similar to those of ecological psychologists. However, they differ from the latter in their emphasis upon behavior functions and their long-term biological consequences.

3 Conceptual framework

To guide their research into proximate/ultimate causes, ethologists and sociobiologists rely on the total conceptual framework offered by evolutionary theory. The theory and some of its concepts that are relevant for understanding children in cities are as follows.

3.1 Evolution

For biologists, evolution is defined as gene-frequency changes in the gene pools of successive generations. Changes can be due to at least two major factors – to natural and to sexual selection involving physical and social environmental agents that have differential effects upon individuals such that some individuals reproduce their genes in successive generations and others do not. In addition to the operation of selection agents, random processes produce gene-pool changes, some processes favoring some genes over other in a stochastic manner independent of environmental factors (genetic drift). In either case, genetic mutations and variations in mutations constitute the basic material upon which forces of selection or chance operate. Such operation acts directly upon the phenotypes of individuals – that is observable physical, personality, and cognitive characteristics – and indirectly upon the genes that underlie them.

For most evolutionary researchers the process of evolution is understood in terms of a relation between phenotypic (indirectly genotypic) variability and environmental variability, the latter having a positive or negative impact on the former. For example, selective factors responsible for prereproductive death or disability in children due to parental neglect or abuse, accident, disease, or social disorder (war, crime) must have occurred repeatedly over history. Whether such selection pressures are currently changing the human gene pool in any significant manner is too early to determine. For certain, the changes that accompany the mass movement of popula- tions from hunter-gatherer conditions into UE settings has had an enormous behav- ioral and cultural impact, both negative and positive (Graves & Graves, 1974). Whether there are any significant long-term genetic effects remains to be seen.

Today Darwin's theory has been expanded to become the "synthetic theory of evolution," which includes the numerous advances in Mendelian (i.e., population and molecular) genetics, mathematical modeling, and ecology that followed Dar- win's 19th-century achievements (Mayr, 1982; Purves, Orians, & Heller, 1992). Associated with such advances have been numerous methodological developments that, by themselves, have become virtually a world of subdisciplines, many of which have to be mastered in order to test the theory.

3.2   Adaptation

Studying adaptation has been the central problem in evolutionary thinking. "It has been considered one of the major tasks of the evolutionist to demonstrate that organisms are indeed reasonably well adapted, and that this adaptation could be caused by no other agency than natural selection" (Mayr, 1983, p. 324). Adaptation has at least two related meanings: (a) the process of adjusting to an environment, that is, crying when hungry, making friends, solving problems in the classroom, joining gangs, earning money, and (b) morphological structures – mouths for crying, limbs for movement, neurological mechanism that make social behavior and solving problems possible. The quality of adaptation (as both a process or product) is often viewed in ultimate terms of health, longevity, and reproductive success or fitness (that is, number of genetic offspring) (Williams, 1966). Behavioral adaptation, in particular, can be divided into two categories, instinct and learning. Such a division, long discussed and often misunderstood, is still useful in determining the origins and functions of behavior and their relation to environment (Bowlby, 1971; McFarland, 1982; Schiller, 1957).

3.2.1   Instinct

Because many features of every species's environments change little over time, each individual has at birth a behavioral equipment to adapt to such environments (Mayr, 1974, refers to the brain mechanisms responsible for them as *closed programs*). Such equipment (e.g., anatomical structures, brain functions), as shaped by specific proteins under the control of DNA, make it possible for the individual to perform adaptive behaviors rapidly and efficiently. Adaptive behaviors include taxes (orienting movements), reflexes and fixed action patterns (more complex fixed responses), and instincts (complex organizations of taxes, reflexes, and learned behaviors, as well as stimulus preferences and motivational states). Web-making in spiders, prey-avoidance in fish, sucking in mammals, sexual behavior in primates, preferences for certain food sources, stimuli, habitats, and sex objects are instinctual in that they are species universal adaptations that serve vital functions that every species member must have in order to survive and reproduce.

Despite the logic of early Darwinian researchers, instinct theory, when applied to humans, has elicited much fruitless debate often ending in its rejection. It was often thought too imprecise to be of any scientific utility or was considered simply incorrect (Degler, 1991). That opinion was unfortunate, for Darwin's rationale for developing instinct as a working concept was hardly arbitrary. The biological construction of humans has a history of continuous material connection with prehuman species. This history reflects millions of interactions between gene mutations and environmental conditions. The results of these interactions are in the form of DNA, molecules whose identity predates the existence of individuals and at the same time still has some causal control over them.

In short, whatever one wants to call them, instincts exist in virtually all species and need to be recognized. To identify instincts in humans, researchers seek cultural universals (e.g., the incest taboo) that, while varying in intensity or magnitude across individuals, share at least three general characteristics: They aid survival and reproduction; are difficult or impossible to alter without paying a biological cost; and appear to have few, if any, functional substitutes. As a biological species, children living in UE settings have to be recognized as having instincts that can both aid and undermine their ability to survive and ultimately reproduce.

3.2.2   Learning

The picture of adaptation, however, is only half accounted for by instincts. Aspects of most species' environments change constantly in unpredictable ways. As a result, each species member must be equipped with the ability to deal with such changes. Ethologists (e.g., Lorenz, 1965) came to recognize early that the ability to learn and retain what was learned evolved over time to become an important adaptation for species inhabiting environments whose features changed in unpredictable ways. Today, such an ability is commonly referred to as *plasticity*. Bolles and Beecher (1987), as well as many others, see plasticity as a major consequence of natural selection affecting animal adaptation. In addition, culture has come to be viewed by the great majority of evolutionists as a major product of human learning and as a key determinant of human behavior (Bonner, 1980; Boyd & Richerson, 1985; Dawkins, 1976).

As for studying adaptations in children in UE settings, evolutionary researchers are first required to establish connections between behavior and certain environmental variables, to ascertain whether and how they vary across individuals, and then to test the generalizability of these connections with children in other cities.

Addressing questions of the "selective" nature of such behavior/environment corre-lations (that is, how they relate to survival and reproduction) is a much more com-plicated task requiring longitudinal as well as multigenerational research.

As is true of all biological functions, questions of adaptation also require an understanding of its economics, that is, the costs and benefits of a particular behav-ioral adaptation relative to the organism's environment and available resources (Ghiselin, 1974). Costs and benefits, which include energy output, developmental progress, and reproductive outcome, are often very difficult to identify and measure but are essential to include in any test of an evolutionary hypothesis regarding a spe-cific class of behavior.

3.3   Genes

When children enter a city, through birth or immigration, they bring with them a vast genetic heritage, one formed over millions of years of evolution that took place far removed from urban environments. As modern genetics shows us, every cell of the newborn contains an enormous amount of DNA, a store of information that over embryogenesis (and even later during development) dictates a major portion of the child's physical nature. This nature is not only expressed in anatomy and physiology but also in terms of certain needs, emotions, motivations, specific behaviors (reflexes), and certain perceptual and cognitive dispositions, all of which have evolved to make it possible for the child to survive, grow and develop, and ulti-mately reproduce. The long-term function of DNA is to execute a series of devel-opmental steps that will raise the probability that the DNA itself will be replicated in future generations, at least in the child's own children and grandchildren (Dawkins, 1976, 1982). To be able to attach to parents, explore and manipulate objects, make friends with sibling and peers, acquire cognitive and social skills necessary for sur-vival, attract members of the opposite sex, bond with a mate, have and raise children – all these life span abilities, though vulnerable to life events such as abandonment, abuse, accident, and predation that might destroy them, are necessary phenotypic projections of DNA activity. The logic of the evolutionary argument of material continuity requires that this major function of DNA be accepted as axiomatic.

Because humans share much active DNA with chimpanzees and gorillas (Jones, Martin, & Pilbeams, 1992), it is not surprising that many similarities in phenotypes between the three species can be found. These similarities make it possible to extrapolate across species, not only anatomically but behaviorally as well. A good example of extrapolations relevant for those interested in children can be found in Bernhard's (1988) *Primates in the classroom*, a primer for helping educators antici-pate what to expect from children in terms of emotions and motivations when they are placed into classrooms of peers under adult authority. A similar primer of much greater scope, could be written for those planning UE settings for children (Geist,

1978). In addition to general species-characteristic DNA, each child is also made up of a unique configuration of specific DNA to which no single plan will totally do justice. Individual differences make natural selection possible and research difficult.

Apropos the genetic constitution of each child, evolutionists reason that humans exist today because their ancestors acted genetically selfishly, that is, they behaved in the interest of their own genes (Dawkins, 1976; Hamilton, 1964, 1972; Trivers, 1971). Acting in their own genetic interest ensured not only that our ancestors survived daily challenges but that they would be reproductively more successful (genetically more fit) compared to other members of their own species. Fitness can be achieved in several ways, by (a) having one's own offspring and supporting their offspring as well ("individual fitness"), (b) supporting the genetic offspring of genetic relatives ("inclusive fitness"), and (c) acting altruistically to others that act altruistically in return ("reciprocal altruism"). All three strategies raise the probability of passing one's genes into the future gene pool. Failing to have offspring can be compensated for by supporting nieces and nephews and other relatives who carry at least a portion of one's genes (nepotism). In view of this argument, then, virtually all of behavior must be motivated to some extent by selfishness. The complexity of human social interactions generates a wide range of behavioral strategies that are employed contingent on environmental conditions to maximize one's fitness in the most economical way possible.

3.4 Environment

From the evolutionary point of view, today's environment is one part of the adaptational story. The other part of the story deals with the environment in which humans evolved, the environment of evolutionary adaptedness (hereafter, EEA). The idea of the EEA was best developed and explicated by Bowlby (1971): "the environment in terms of which the adaptedness of man's instinctive equipment must be considered is the one that man inhabited for two million years" (p. 59). The human EEA has been characterized primarily in terms of Pleistocene conditions, an epoch during the first half of the Quaternary consisting of varying periods of intense cold, dryness, and glacial activity, especially in northern latitudes, alternating with extreme wetness. Such conditions prevailed for over one million years. During this period humans showed their greatest evolutionary advance – they separated completely from other primates, developing in the process those characteristics (large brain, bipedal gait, care of offspring, etc.) that all members of all Homo sapiens share today.

The behavior adaptations that characterized humans at that time consisted of hunting; gathering; shelter-finding and shelter-building skills; relatively sophisticated group interactions made possible by sophisticated communication skills; ways of protecting the young and food sources; and tool, utensil, and weapons manufacturing (Coon, 1971; Jones et al., 1992). Today, ethologists and sociobiologists seek contemporary analogs of Pleistocene cultures (as do others interested in human origins) (Foley, 1992). For the most part this interest means studying current hunter-gatherer populations in remote regions, hoping to find them in a "pristine" state similar to that of our ancestors. Unfortunately, the 200 million or so present-day tribal peoples that approximate such populations are not isolated from pastoralists, farmers, or the various masses of humanity living in cities (Luling, 1992).

The great majority of modern populations have come to live in, or physically close to, UE settings. There is no consensus when the transition from hunter-gatherer (and later pastoral-agricultural) to UE adaptations begun. Estimates for the establishment of cities range from 4,000 to 5,000 years ago, approximately 5,000 years after agriculture was discovered and practiced on a wide scale. Over subsequent millennia, migrations to the UE have increased and show no signs of abating. During this time humans (as well as other animal species) have been making adaptations to city living. Such plasticity apparently has paid off biologically in the sense that humans over a relatively very short period have become the world's dominant species, rapidly controlling, displacing, and eliminating other species and altering the physical face of the globe.

4   The pleistocene versus the present

The transition from a hunter-gatherer existence during the Pleistocene to the establishment of UE existence can be characterized by a number of general changes that have a direct or indirect effect upon human adaptation. Hunter-gatherer bands during the Pleistocene appeared to have ranged from 30 to 100 members. When organized into tribes or through alliances, they probably numbered no more than 1,000 members. Such band sizes had advantages in that group members could cooperate more efficiently because all members knew each other and could, therefore, trust each other and detect cheaters more quickly than if they were strangers. As will be seen below, small group size also has advantages for children.

4.1   Population size

Beginning approximately 65,000 years ago, the humans subsisting under the conditions of the Pleistocene Ice Age probably numbered fewer than 100,000 individuals (Gibbons, 1993). Roughly 15,000 years later, as a climate warm-up began, their numbers began increasing very rapidly. Today, there are approximately 5.4 billion humans alive, and their habitats range from tropical areas to Arctic regions and lowlands to high mountains. Obvious major physical and cultural changes have occurred during this interval. Such changes include a dramatic impact on human health and, hence, longevity (from 20 to 30 some years to 70 to 100 years) and possibly an effect on the composition of the human gene pool.

Ethologists such as Geist (1978) and Eibl-Eibesfeldt (1989) and others such as Galle, Gove, and McPherson (1972) point out that the increase in population density appears very likely to be causally responsible for increase in infectious and stress-related diseases and social and economic conflict due to competition for scarce resources. However, anthropologists (see Colby, 1987) studying conditions that have affected human well-being since the shift of populations to UE living point out that benefits of high population density also exist – increased protection from non-human predators, improved protection from physical threats or hardships posed by severe weather and rough terrain, and greater access to vital resources (food, water, raw materials) and health facilities made possible by the technological and organizational efforts of masses of cooperating individuals (Graves & Graves, 1974). Today, population density is a major topic of ecologists and others interested in the human future. Residential density of children, in particular, has become an important focus of attention (Wohlwill, 1985).

4.2 Population diversity

The increase in population diversity usually associated with an increase in population size also has risks and benefits. The greatest risk appears to be social in that an increase in the number of strangers usually means an increase in the number of persons who do not share the individual's personal goals and values. Strangers pose a wide range of novel threats to individuals who are accustomed to the familiar minor threats of small group living. From the evolutionary point of view, xenophobia may well have ancient roots in the form of a generalized innate uncertainty and fear about the unfamiliar (whoever is unfamiliar may be a predator). Several topics related to population diversity will be discussed below under the topics of children and strangers and mating choices.

With the increase in individual diversity associated with the shift from Pleistocene to city living, ethnic diversity usually also increases and, along with it, ethnic nepotism, ethnic membership being the main criterion governing social interactions involving resources. This connection is currently true in India, where struggles over scarce resources frequently involve various groups unified on grounds of ethnicity only (Vanhannen, 1991). Large cities that contain ethnic enclaves are generally faced with endemic ethnic conflict resulting from attempts both to settle past grievances and to compete more successfully for scarce resources.

From an evolutionary point of view, ethnic conflicts are explainable in terms of the kin/nonkin distinction and its relevance for inclusive fitness. In early childhood, ethnic distinctions are probably not very important: self-interest overides group membership. By the time children reach school age, however, the influence of culture, as mediated by parents and other adults, increases, and group membership (social class, racial, religious) becomes more important for defining one's identity. In many cultures, the practical value of prosocial behavior in general and the need for ethnic negotiation and compromise are instilled in young children to avoid wasteful and dangerous conflict with peer friends and strangers. Also, it is known from anthropological research that the fusion of tribes into coalitions of nonkin is a common way of overcoming local problems caused by resource shortages, predators, and enemies. Such fusion can only be achieved by assurances on both sides that all members will reciprocate honestly where resources, broadly defined, are involved.

Benefits also accompany the ethnic and cultural diversity that usually result when population sizes increases. The enrichment associated with interactions with persons of different cultures comes not only from the various excitements associated with stimulus novelty per se but also from novel ideas and criticisms that make possible and reinforce creativity in the full range of cultural activities. The same applies to diversity in educational activities. Students are frequently beneficiaries of exotic, challenging ideas from the outside. Another, perhaps not so obvious benefit of diversity is the increase in the probability of meeting friends and possible mates more akin to one's own personality. In many hunter-gatherer societies, exogamy has frequently (if not always) been viewed as a complementary strategy to endogamy. A purely biological benefit of diversity results from the mixture of previously separate gene pools, which reduces homozygosity of harmful mutations.

4.3   Surplus stimulation

The shift from living in hunter-gatherer groups to living in cities has been largely made possible by enormous technological advances in most areas of human existence – agriculture, transportation, industry, water supply, hygiene, medicine, and communication. Such advances not only contribute to physical well-being but also enormously increase the amount of stimulus information available to every human. This surplus of information poses an especially novel problem to adaptation because for the first time in human history, individuals have almost immediate access to a superabundance of information and images far removed (spatially, temporally, and culturally) from their everyday environments. The stimulation, whether recreational or informational, is all-pervasive, sudden and brief, usually novel, and often advertised aggressively as vital for the individual's well-being, health, and pleasure.Television, motion pictures, telecommunications, and inexpensive printed material supply parents and children with an enormous amount of often distracting and conflicting as well as useless stimulation. Information necessary for adaptation, unlike that transmitted by elders and parents in hunter-gatherer societies, is now supplied in UE settings by strangers, many with more selfish than altruistic motives. It is not surprising, then, if most parents today are uncertain about how to raise children, whom or what to believe, and where to obtain useful and inexpensive information. Likewise, it is not surprising that some children in UE settings are uncertain about what to believe and what to learn. Additionally, formal education has become increasingly difficult, given the plethora of information available.

Apart from wasting time watching advertising and consuming resources, time otherwise used for general adaptive purposes, children in UE settings are also distracted by surplus stimulation from acquiring competitive economic skills. The pleasures associated with satisfying needs for novel stimulation can preempt ultimate needs associated with reproduction because the temporal window of opportunity for reproduction is much smaller than that for the proximate joys of recreation. A society that fails to restrain total recreation life styles runs the risk of reduced fertility and, consequently, population stability, which, in turn, undermines successful competition with other societies.

4.4   Match or mismatch

As noted above, the clash of biological needs with cultural controls has elicited much attention from centuries of thinkers. Today, the same issue is revisited, but less in terms of confrontation than in terms of the extent to which Pleistocene living conditions match or mismatch current cultural conditions. Many researchers see the mismatch, especially as it is manifested in cities by crowding, as creating serious psychological and social problems for modern humans (Galle et al., 1972). Others specifically ask to what extent evolved Pleistocene emotional, cognitive, and behavioral adaptations match the demands of current UE living. For example, Crawford and Anderson (1989) inquired whether some adaptations such as male physical aggression, originally useful for establishing dominance, for hunting, or for warfare, are no longer useful. In many UE settings they are socially disruptive as well as individually maladaptive. In contrast, others such as Tooby and Cosmides (1989) and Cosmides (1989), while aware of mismatches, argued that many key rules of modern social interaction regarding reciprocation and control of cheating are not substantially different from those governing our distant ancestors. The possibility that modern living conditions may have already exceeded the potential of human behavior for plasticity was explored by Bailey (1995), who took a "paleopsychopathological" view. This view is based on the fact that the cultural and technological changes that have occurred recently differ so greatly from our hunter-gatherer ancestral environments that psychopathology, in the form of excessive fear of and aversion to strangers, now characterizes many human social interactions.

Despite negative effects of a mismatch, it must be acknowledged that, for the several thousands of years that humans have been living under UE conditions, they have, as a group, made very successful cultural adaptations. Although there exists no absolute scale by which to judge the success of human adaptation, and although the story of such adaptation is not finished, the population explosion of Homo sapiens that has resulted from the invention of agriculture and cities certainly does not suggest that UE living has been biologically inadequate.

5   Children and evolution

Combining the two causal concepts, ultimate and proximate, can serve as an entry point to studying children in cities from an evolutionary point of view in terms of the shift from Pleistocene to current living conditions. The evolutionary answer (hypothesis to be more exact) to the question of the ultimate function of early infant-parent attachment is that it ensures that the helpless infant survives and is thereby able to move closer to a more independent existence. Achieving independence, in turn, raises the child's chances of reaching adulthood, mating, and reproducing. To verify this answer empirically, researchers study various parenting behavior styles and infants' reactions to them during the attachment process. The impact of this process on the future adaptational capacities of infants is then followed up in later developmental periods.

As noted above, because UE living is removed in many significant ways from the hunter-gatherer experiences of human, the question of evolved life-span biological functions becomes especially pertinent. As Hill (1993) points out, life histories that lead to higher genetic fitness than other life histories are products of natural selection. Given this, one can ask the question of the extent to which evolved life history requirements are still well-served by the conditions of UE living. One can seek an answer to this question by first identifying species-universal features that characterize the life-span development of children and then examining them in terms of how well proximate factors surrounding them serve the ultimate function of reproduction.

5.1   Nursing

As a mammalian adaptation to providing the newborn with food and protection, nursing must have universally characterized the early life-span experience of ancestral human infants. Benefits to the infant are obvious – nutrition (accompanied by important antibodies) and maternal protection, as well as tactile, cognitive, and emotional stimulation. Benefits to the mother are genetic (she increases her fitness). They are also psychosocial, for breast-feeding is emotionally rewarding, and it enhances social status. Costs to the infant are probably zero or close to it. Genetic costs to the mother may result if nursing seriously interferes with caring for other offspring. Personal adaptational costs to her may also exist if the process of nursing is unduly stressful.

One would guess from studies of existing hunter-gatherer societies that breast-feeding is more prevalent in them than in UE settings, where bottle-feeding has become (or is rapidly becoming) the norm. Because of the multitude of factors involved, there is no satisfactory way to test the hypothesis that breast-feeding is superior to bottle-feeding. As apparent from common contemporary experience, bottle-fed infants do not seem to be negatively affected. However, other aspects of feeding (namely, parent-child interactions associated with it) most likely contribute more significantly to infants' developmental outcomes than feeding per se.

5.2   Infant attachment and child care

As members of a species born very immature, human infants require extensive care for several years. This care, usually provided by parents or close relatives, usually leads to a close attachment between infants and caretakers. As Bowlby (1971); Ainsworth, Blehar, Waters, and Wall (1978); Sroufe, Fox, and Pancake (1983); and others have shown, attachment plays a major role not only in the daily life of the infant but also in later development. Like nursing, good parental care serves both a survival function for the infant and reproductive function for the parent.

Today, there is growing concern that infants in UE settings may not be getting as much care as they need and may be more abused than in former times. To examine this concern scientifically is obviously impossible because of the lack of reliable comparative information from former times. From our knowledge of contemporary hunter-gatherers, it is quite clear that most infants and young children growing up in such societies have virtually around-the-clock contact with parents and other caring adults (Blurton Jones, 1972a; Konner, 1972). It can be assumed that this arrangement was also the case with our hominid ancestors and with primates in general (Goodall, 1986; Jolly, 1985). One can thus conclude that parent-infant contact is most likely a very old evolutionary adaptation whose primary function has been to keep young infants alive and whose secondary function has been to equip them for later successful adaptation. It can also be argued that, because human populations began expanding during the late Pleistocene to the point of being enormously successful in colonizing the world, the early parental care lavished (in a very costly fashion) on infants during hunter-gatherer times most likely contributed much to their adaptational skills as adults, thereby lavishly benefiting parents genetically.

An example of possible specific effects of close parent-child contact and care has to do with sleeping patterns. In most non-UE settings, infants and parents sleep together, either in the same bed or close proximity. In UE setting this is often not the case. Sudden Infant Death Syndrome (SIDS), observed in the past several decades to occur "unexpectedly" in young infants sleeping alone (usually in their own rooms), may be due to respiratory problems the signs of which parents did not detect (Chavez, Ostrea, Stryker, & Smialek, 1979). In hunter-gatherer times, infants slept

close to their parents and, hence, were periodically jostled awake by parent movements. If breathing momentarily stopped, as is the case with SIDS babies, parents
were immediately present to notice it.

Today, neglect and abuse are being closely scrutinized and measured. Currently
their various manifestations have been studied and given more refined definitions
(Biringen & Robinson, 1991; Egeland & Erickson, 1987). It appears that, apart from
strict and specific socialization practices and rituals, contemporary hunter-gatherers
as a rule do not regularly abuse and neglect their children, at least when resources
are in abundance. When resources are in short supply, however, it can be a very different story (Turnbull, 1971).

If there has been an increase in neglect and abuse since hunter-gatherer times, it
may simply reflect secular changes rather than changes attending the shift to UE
living. Today, failing to nurse may be part of the bigger picture of child neglect for
the simple reason that many parents, especially those in UE settings, are exposed to
more diversionary stimuli than was the case for hunter-gatherers. Most modern
mothers, for example, have numerous opportunities for nonchild oriented activities
and distractions inside the home (television, radio, telephone) as well as outside
social stimulation. They also may have outside jobs that markedly reduce the time
they spend with their children and, hence, dilute the attachment process.

To add to mother's (as well as father's) absence, surrogate care of UE children also
seems to be a relatively modern practice. Paying others to care for one's children
raises the question of whether being in the care of nonkin adolescents or adults puts
children at higher risk for neglect and abuse. If so, not only the child's future development is at risk but the parents' genetic fitness. It can be recalled from the discussion above on genetic selfishness that investing in genetic kin (kin selection) is one
of the great motivators of much of human (and animal) behavior. Nonkin, especially
if they are children, are hardly given equal treatment. As simply demonstrated by
Daly and Wilson (1985), for example, children (as victims of "discriminative parenting") are at much greater risk for abuse at the hands of stepparents than at the
hands of biological parents.

In general, then, modern deviations in nursing and child care from what appear to
be evolved hunter-gatherer adaptive patterns continue to pose challenging tests of
functional hypotheses about the early years of life-span development.

5.3 Family

In all societies (early and contemporary) the family, defined broadly as genetic kin
living together in the same dwelling or circumscribed area, constitutes the key
reproductive unit because it serves genetic selfishness better than alternative units.
Communes, known today as *intentional communities*, usually contain more nongenetic than genetic relatives. This circumstance may pose problems for such commu-

nities. As Greenberg's (1993) recent survey suggests, the expenses associated with raising and educating children are often sources of discord in such communities. In most hunter-gatherer societies, though there were probably many other sources of discord, conflict over investment in known biological children was probably not one of them, for most members were kin. In many UE societies today, the family, though still the key reproductive unit, is experiencing great stress. Most of this stress appears to be due to divorce, infidelity, absent fathers, limited income, and substance abuse. It is too early to predict the long-term reproductive effects of such stress on children. Short-term effects that divorce has on children are well-known (Hetherington & Arasteh, 1988). Such effects ultimately may reduce fitness in that such children, on reaching adulthood, do not marry or, if they do, abstain from having children or, if they have children, put them at risk for abuse and neglect.

The effect of family stress on the greater society is currently more visible in the form of taxpayer concerns about welfare payments and biological parents who do not pay for child care and education. In addition, reproductive issues in general that affect population density appear to be problematic for some societies where cultural and ethnic differences account for some groups having large families that make smaller economic contributions to the society than small families.

It should be kept in mind that there exist many contemporary societies worldwide in which biological family (the clan, tribe) is the most important social and economic unit. In such societies nepotism is a long tradition, as are alliances or arrangements with nonfamily groups. Both practices appear to be adaptations to competitive situations resulting from resource shortages. Today, as anthropologists have amply demonstrated, concern for kinship is a universal characteristic found wherever there are humans. Defining, classifying, identifying, and establishing rules for dealing with kin as distinct from nonkin are major human adult tasks that have to be mastered, not only for regulating their own behavior but for educating their children as well. Such a cross-cultural universal suggests the operation of underlying genetic mechanisms that operate across thousands of generations and societies regardless of how technologically advanced or unadvanced each generation is.

5.4 Peer interactions

Children in all cultures interact with each other in various ways, as do nonhuman primate children. Peer play, being the most dominant form of interaction, appears to serve the functions of acquiring knowledge of the physical world and of learning social skills necessary in later development (Smith, 1982; Sutton-Smith, 1981; MacDonald, 1993). Peer friends are necessary as cooperators in obtaining and defending resources as well as mates for the satisfaction of sexual desires and, ultimately, for reproduction. Early positive peer relations have been demonstrated to contribute to people's later social adaptation as adolescents and adults (Hartup,

1983). As expressions of inadequate social skills, persistent aggressiveness or social withdrawal may well ultimately reduce an individual's mating opportunities and, hence, lower that person's fitness.

In current hunter-gatherer societies children spend much time with a few peers, probably with a very small number compared to most UE children. UE conditions usually bring children (especially public school children) into wide contact with many different peers. Such contact, made possible for example, by large schools and improved transportation, increases the chances of children meeting other children with similar as well as dissimilar preferences. Such encounters could improve peer adaptation but also threaten later development, such as when children with emotional or behavioral problems are exposed to antisocial peers. In many cities today youth gangs constitute a major threat to society and to the individual child's development and education. Gangs frequently interfere with traditional education, thereby jeopardizing the child's future ability to engage in useful employment. On the positive, short-term proximate side, gangs are often substitutes for family and provide children with emotional support and street skills to survive in child-unresponsive communities. In short, early peer interactions appear crucial for later genetic fitness, but how crucial has not yet been determined.

Two critical aspects of peer development that span virtually all levels of development are social dominance and sex. Both play major roles in all primate life, both human and nonhuman (Barkow, 1989). Hunter-gatherer, as well as the most technologically sophisticated modern, societies usually have codes governing the expression of dominance and sex-appropriate behavior. Starting at least in very early childhood, if not late infancy, children are exposed to these codes and socialized directly or indirectly to conform to them.

The functions of social dominance have been studied widely by ethologists and sociobiologists (Bernstein, 1981; Omark, Stryer, & Freemann, 1980). Among other functions, social dominance appears to stabilize group activities by reducing male aggression and provides leadership to organize various group economic activities. Sex-role differentiation apparently has evolved to maximize reproductive success. Females carry, nurse, and care for their young and in return are protected from outside dangers and provisioned with resources by males. Males, in order to perform their part of this arrangement, have to defend resource-holding territory and must hunt and fight. Such collaboration has ensured that both Pleistocene females and males succeeded in getting their genes represented in the next generation. In many current UE settings collaboration is often seen as unnecessary as other means of reproducing and raising children are being explored.

Currently, traditional codes governing dominance and sex roles are being vigorously challenged in many societies. Whether such challenges will lead to the elimination of such codes remains to be seen. From the evolutionary point of view, dominance and sex codes reflect adaptational problems that have confronted social mammals for millions of years. Hence, their total abolition in humans is most unlikely. If they are significantly reduced, it is conceivable that their effects will be socially disruptive and/or will reduce fitness.

5.5 Children and strangers

With the increase in world population and social interactions between normally widely separated groups, dealing with strangers has become a major social issue. In small hunter-gatherer societies strangers were relatively few in number, slow to get to know outside of highly ritualized encounters, and rarely involved in resource reciprocations until carefully tested. Today, UE settings are vastly different. In large and even moderate-size cities strangers are more often encountered than distant relatives or friends. Consequently, children have to be explicitly taught how to deal with them, for a stranger, by definition is a potential nonreciprocator or exploiter. Avoiding strangers, being suspicious of their motives, and resisting their overtures in general seem to be good advice for the younger child whose main source of support is from family and friends. With older children, whose task is to relinquish parental support and seek it elsewhere, different advice is required. Strangers are potential allies, friends, sources of valuable information, and friends as well as enemies. How older children come to distinguish between them and act accordingly is a major social development task.

In evolutionary thinking, dealing with strangers is part of a more generic problem for many species. Strangers are usually avoided, deceived, or attacked. Friends and acquaintances are another matter: Learning how to deceive and cheat others and to detect deception and cheating is a common human behavior (Rue, 1994). It is understandable in light of the bigger picture of evolution. The maximization of one's fitness is the primary biological goal of all organisms, and that maximization requires resources. Given that resources are never in ample supply (because members of the same group also need them), learning how to compete for them is a very important developmentally contingent adaptational task (Charlesworth, 1988). Since aggressive forms of competition disrupt social interactions and are potentially dangerous, other means of competition, such as deception and cheating, must be learned early in life. Deception and cheating range from white lies, big lies, and manipulation to fraud and covert economic exploitation. Though publicly frowned upon and punished when serious enough, deception and cheating nevertheless persist during virtually all developmental phases of the life span, all economic levels, and within governing bodies established to control and eliminate them.

If one can go by tourists' experiences in economically deprived countries, deceiving or cheating strangers does not appear to be frowned upon as much in many societies. It is often recognized as acceptable and necessary when the societies lack adequate resources. The assumption underlying the tolerance of cheating is that, without knowledge of a stranger's ultimate intentions, playing it safe by making a "preemptive attack" on the latter's resources is the wisest policy. Depriving strangers of some of their resources is one way to redress real or imaginary economic and social inequities and to improve one's survival chances. As noted above, reciprocating services and goods can only take place among those who know each other well. Strangers, especially, being unknown, are not within reciprocation circles. However, being unreciprocated or abandoned is always a distinct possibility even with kin, so deception and cheating are major adaptational skills every child needs to possess just in case.

5.6 Mate selection and retention

Meeting members of the opposite sex and establishing friendships that lead to sexual bonding (usually culturally verified by some form of marriage rite) that, in turn, is followed by having children is an obviously important series of life-span adaptations. Sexual bonding takes place sometime during postpubescence (in most societies during adolescence; Savin-Williams, 1987; Weisfeld, 1979) and represents the first step towards genetic replication. The parenting that follows constitutes the long and often arduous phase of protecting the genetic investment. In societies where parents lived long enough to be grandparents, this additional phase of protecting the genetic investment may be considerably protracted, especially when grandparents have time and good health.

Mate selection is usually based on such factors as physical appearance, related to attractiveness and health, as well as genetic distance and social mores (arranged marriages, romantic love, and so on). Recent studies suggest that mate selection in males is based heavily on female physical appearance related to health and childbearing and child-caring capacity, whereas mate selection in females is based more on male resource-holding and resource-acquiring capacity (Buss & Schmitt, 1993). Such sex differences are predicted by evolutionary theory on the basis of differential investments that females and males make in reproducing their genes (Daly & Wilson, 1983).

In hunter-gatherer societies mate selection most likely was limited to a much smaller number of potential mates than that of young people in UE settings. In UE settings, the opportunity to meet mates is enormous: potential mates can be met face-to-face through personal advertisements in newspapers, magazines, or computer networks. The advantage of such availability is that the opportunity of finding a mate compatible at more that one level (economic, personality, interests, values, sexual proclivities, etc.) is very great.

One would think that the increased compatibility achieved by matching so many variables would enhance mate retention. Given current divorce rates in industrialized societies, this expectation does not seem to be the case. High availability of potential mates combined with the human need for novelty through extra-pair bond romances may encourage many to seek more mates, simultaneously or sequentially. In many highly industrialized societies divorce and remarriage are very common, so one can predict that parenting itself would be negatively affected. Investing time and emotional and material resources in stepchildren at the expense of one's own may be experienced as burdensome and may result in discriminative parenting.

Bonding outside of marriage for sexual purposes only has long been a common occurrence in human populations in general. Though usually viewed as socially disruptive, it most likely has occurred sufficiently to affect both the gene pool (e.g., males and females with certain characteristics having higher representation than others) and, more likely, the lives and, hence, adaptational capacities of unwanted children.

5.7 Comment

These areas of children's lives, then, are some of the ones likely to show the impact of UE living on life-span adaptations that have evolved in EEA settings over a million or so years of human evolution. Despite the great changes in population density, population diversity, and information availability that have occurred since the Pleistocene, evolution appears to have left the human brain with rigid legacies of various life-span developments. Such legacies have to be obeyed in some way or other at the risk of losing fitness. It is important, then, to understand the proximate mechanisms that govern them, especially if one wishes to improve the lives of children. It appears that human plasticity has already been considerably stretched by UE living. So far, though, humans do not show any signs of biological diminution, at least as expressed in morbidity and population loss. But this condition could change. The earth's diminishing capacity to tolerate the consequences of many human activities associated with the recent population explosion, and rapid growth of megacities accompanied by high-energy demands, the spread of diseases, pollution, and the potential for social unrest could put large numbers of humans, if not the whole species, at risk.

6 Conclusion

Out of concern for children in cities, it would be naive to assume that, because cities depart in many ways from the evolutionary environment of humans, they are intrinsically inimical to children's development and long-term human survival. City living has long been attractive, so it must be meeting some basic human needs that may or may not be traceable to evolutionary adaptations. Whatever stresses cities impose, most humans learn how to deal with them, at least in the short term.

Conversely, it would be naive to assume that humans, as a species with great adaptational abilities, will eventually succeed in circumventing biological laws that govern survival and reproduction. Penalties associated with "going against nature" do exist. Loss of fertility due to infectious diseases or delayed child-bearing, or health hazards due to uncontrolled industrial pollution most likely will have long-term disruptive impacts upon human populations.

In their concern for children in particular, planners of future cities should be familiar with the conditions characterizing human evolutionary history. Working toward optimal conditions for child development must stress the value of intact families and small community living conditions in which children can grow up physically safe and emotionally secure. Ideally, such conditions should conform as much as possible to the ancestral social (but obviously not physical) conditions in which human children evolved their emotional, cognitive, and behavioral adaptations. We can improve our ideas about these conditions by studying and taking seriously the life adaptations of the few hunter-gatherer societies that still exist.

Future cities should also provide community-based health and educational opportunities that make it possible for all children (according to their abilities and interests) to adapt socially and economically to local life requirements as well as to the larger life around them. Social, educational, and economic inequities, evident in most of today's cities, have historically undermined social stability and, ultimately, the well-being of every individual. It should never be forgotten that genetic selfishness and the social conflict it invariably engenders does not cease with technological and cultural achievement. Selfishness is a powerful biological adaptation and, hence, will continue as before. Controlling social conflict will have to be a major task of local as well as global governments.

Perhaps more difficult to control will be the excessive appetite for consuming nonrenewable resources. This effort will have to start early with the socialization of children. How this will be done, especially because it goes against genetic selfishness and the evolved proximate mechanisms that maximize the pleasure accompanying success, in my estimation, is the biggest socialization and educational problem of the next century.

Cutting a diamond requires a very close study of its physical structure before putting the blade to it. Designing new environments for optimizing child health and development requires an understanding of both the evolutionary character of human nature and the manner in which environmental and cultural factors interact with it over the course of development. An interdisciplinary effort is necessary to seek this understanding because human life is far more complex and more interesting than any diamond.

Acknowledgement

Thanks go to Richard Rodgerson, Marion Heinrichs, and Art Sesma, Graduate Students at the University of Minnesota, for their comments on the first draft of this paper; and special thanks to LuJean Huffman-Nordberg for her secretarial help in preparing this manuscript for publication.

References

Ainsworth, M. D. S., Blehar, M. C., Waters, E., & Wall, S. (1978). *Patterns of attachment*. Hillsdale, NJ: Erlbaum.

Alexander, R. D. (1979). *Darwinism and human affairs*. Seattle: University of Washington Press.

Alexander, R. D. (1987). *The biology of moral systems*. New York: Aldine de Gruyter.

Archer, J. (1992). *Ethology and human development*. Hemel Hempstead: Harvester Wheatsheaf.

Atzwanger, K. (1995, June). *Biological aspects of aggressive driving behavior*. Paper presented at the Seventh Annual Meeting of the Human Behavior and Evolution Society, Santa Barbara, CA.

Bailey, K. G. (1995, June). *Mismatch theory and paleopsychopathology*. Paper presented at the Seventh Annual Meeting of the Human Behavior and Evolution Society, Santa Barbara, CA.

Barash, D. P. (1982). *Sociobiology and behavior* (2nd ed.). New York: Elsevier.

Barkow, J. (1989). *Darwin, sex, and status: Biological approaches to mind and culture*. Toronto: University of Toronto Press.

Barkow, J., Cosmides, L., & Tooby, J. (Eds.) (1992). *The adapted mind*. New York: Oxford University Press.

Bernhard, J. G. (1988). *Primates in the classroom: An evolutionary perspective on children's education*. Amherst, MA: The University of Massachusetts Press.

Bernstein, I. S. (1981). Dominance: The baby and the bathwater. *Behavior and Brain Sciences, 3,* 419-458.

Biringen, Z., & Robinson, J. (1991). Emotional availability in mother-child interactions: A reconceptualization for research. *American Journal of Orthopsychiatry, 61,* 258-271.

Blurton Jones, N. (1972a). Comparative aspects of mother-child contact. In N. Blurton Jones (Ed.), *Ethological studies of child behavior* (pp. 305-328). Cambridge: Cambridge University Press.

Blurton Jones, N. (Ed.) (1972b). *Ethological studies of child behavior*. Cambridge: Cambridge University Press.

Bolles, R. C., & Beecher, M. D. (Eds.) (1987). *Evolution and learning*. Hillsdale, NJ: Erlbaum.

Bonner, J. T. (1980). *The evolution of culture in animals*. Princeton, NJ: Princeton University Press.

Bowlby, J. (1971). *Attachment and loss*. Harmondsworth, England: Penguin Books.

Bowlby, J. (1973). *Attachment and loss: Vol. 2. Separation*. New York, NY: Basic Books.

Boyd, R., & Richerson, P. J. (1985). *Culture and the evolutionary process*. Chicago: University of Chicago Press.

Buss, D. M. (1995). Evolutionary psychology: A new paradigm for psychological science. *Psychological Inquiry, 6,* 1-30.

Buss, D., & Schmitt, D. (1993). Sexual strategies theory: An evolutionary perspective on human mating. *Psychological Review, 100*, 204-232.

Chagnon, N. A. (1974). *Studying the Yanomano*. New York: Holt, Rinehart and Winston.

Chagnon, N. A., & Irons, W. (Eds.) (1979). *Evolutionary biology and human social behavior: An anthropological perspective*. North Scituate, MA: Duxbury Press.

Charlesworth, W. R. (1988). Resources and resource acquisition during ontogeny. In K. B. MacDonald (Ed.), *Sociobiological perspectives on human development* (pp. 24-77). New York: Springer.

Charlesworth, W. R. (1992). Charles Darwin and developmental psychology: Past and present. *Developmental Psychology, 28*, 5-16.

Charlesworth, W. R. (1994). Evolutionary theory: Ethological and sociobiological aspects. In T. Husen & T. N. Postlethwaits (Eds.), *International Encyclopedia of Education* (2nd ed.) (Vol. 4, pp. 2167-2172). Elmsford, NY: Pergamon Press.

Chavez, C. J., Ostrea, E. M., Stryker, J. C., & Smialek, Z. (1979). Sudden infant death syndrome among infants of drug-dependent mothers. *Journal of Pediatrics, 95*, 407-409.

Colby, B. N. (1987). Well-being: A theoretical program. *American Anthropologist, 89*, 879-895.

Colgan, P. W. (Ed.) (1978). *Quantitative ethology*. New York: Wiley.

Coon, C. C. (1971). *The hunting peoples*. Boston: Little, Brown and Company.

Cosmides, L. (1989). The logic of social exchange: Has natural selection shaped how humans reason? Studies with the Wason selection task. *Cognition, 31*, 187-276.

Costall, A. (1986). Evolutionary gradualism and the study of development. *Human Development, 29*, 4-11.

Cranach, M. von, Foppa, K., Lepenies, W., & Plogg, D. (Eds.) (1979). *Human ethology: Claims and limits of a new discipline*. Cambridge: Cambridge University Press.

Crawford, C. B., & Anderson, J. L. (1989). Sociobiology: An environmentalist discipline? *American Psychologist, 44*, 1449-1459.

Daly, M., & Wilson, M. I. (1983). *Sex, evolution, and behavior* (2nd ed.). Boston: Willard Grant Press.

Daly, M., & Wilson, M. I. (1985). Child abuse and other risks of not living with both parents. *Ethology and Sociobiology, 6*, 197-210.

Darwin, C. (1965). *The expression of emotions in man and animals*. Chicago: University of Chicago Press. (Original work published 1872)

Dawkins, R. (1976). *The selfish gene*. Oxford: Oxford University Press.

Dawkins, R. (1982). *The extended phenotype: The genes as the unit of selection*. Oxford: Oxford University Press.

Degler, C. N. (1991). *In search of human nature: The decline and revival of Darwinism in American social thought*. Oxford: Oxford University Press.

Egeland, B., & Erickson, M. F. (1987). Psychologically unavailable caregiving. In M. R. Brassard, R. Germain, & S. N. Hart (Eds.), *Psychological maltreatment of children* (pp. 110-120). New York: Pergamon Press.

Eibl-Eibesfeldt, I. (1972). *Die !Ko-Buschmanngesellschaft: Gruppenbildung und Aggressionskontrolle* [The !Ko Bushman society: Group formation and control of aggression]. Munich: Piper.

Eibl-Eibesfeldt, I. (1975). *Ethology: The biology of behavior* (rev. ed.). New York: Holt, Rinehart and Winston.

Eibl-Eibesfeldt, I. (1989). *Human ethology*. New York: Aldine de Gruyter.

Eibl-Eibesfeldt, I., & Hass, H. (1985). Sozialer Wohnbau und Umstrukturierung der Städte aus biologischer Sicht [Public housing and reorganization of cities from a biological perspective]. In I. Eibl-Eibesfeldt, H. Hass, K. Freisitzer, E. Gehmacher, & H. Glück (Eds.), *Stadt und Lebensqualität* (pp. 49-84). Stuttgart: Deutsche Verlagsanstalt.

Ekman, P. (Ed.). (1973). *Darwin and facial expression: A century of review.* New York: Academic Press.

Foley, R. (1992). Study in human evolution by analogy. In S. Jones, R. Martin, & I. Pilbeam (Eds.), *The Cambridge encyclopedia of human evolution* (pp. 335-340). Cambridge: Cambridge University Press.

Frisch, K. von (1914). Der Farbensinn und Formensinn der Biene [The sense of color and shape in bees]. *Zoologisches Jahrbuch der zoologischen Physiologie, 35,* 1-182.

Galle, O. R., Gove, W. R., & McPherson, J. M. (1972). Population density and pathology: What are the relations for man? *Science, 176,* 20-23.

Geist, V. (1978). *Life strategies, human evolution, environmental design: Toward a biological theory of health.* New York: Springer.

Ghiselin, M. T. (1974). *The economy of nature on the evolution of sex.* Berkeley: University of California Press.

Ghiselin, M. T. (1986). The assimilation of Darwinism in developmental psychology. *Human Development, 29,* 12-21.

Gibbons, A. (1993). Pleistocene population explosions. *Science, 262,* 27-28.

Goodall, J. (1986). *The chimpanzees of Gombe: Patterns of behavior.* Cambridge, MA: The Belknap Press of Harvard University Press.

Gould, S. J. (1977). *Ontogeny and phylogeny.* Cambridge, MA: The Belknap Press of Harvard University Press.

Grammer, K. (1992, 1993, 1994). *Zwischenberichte des Ludwig-Boltzmann-Instituts für Stadtethologie* [Interim reports of the Ludwig Boltzmann Institute for urban ethology]. Vienna.

Graves, N. B., & Graves, T. D. (1974). Adaptive strategies in urban migration. *Annual Review of Anthropology, 3,* 117-151.

Greenberg, D. B. (1993). *Growing up in community: Children and education within contemporary U.S. intentional Communities.* Unpublished doctoral dissertation, University of Minnesota, Minneapolis.

Hamilton, W. D. (1964). The genetical evolution of social behavior, I and II. *Journal of Theoretical Biology, 7,* 1-52.

Hamilton, W. D. (1972). Altruism and related phenomena, mainly in social insects. *Annual Review of Ecology and Systematics, 3,* 193-232.

Hartup, W. W. (1983). Peer relations. In P. H. Mussen (Series Ed.) & E. M. Hetherington (Vol. Ed.), *Handbook of child psychology: Vol. 4. Socialization, personality, and social development* (4th ed., pp. 103-196). New York: Wiley.

Hetherington, E. M., & Arasteh, J. D. (Eds.). (1988). *Impact of divorce, single parenting, and step parenting on children.* Hillsdale, NJ: Erlbaum.

Hill, K. (1993). Life history and evolutionary anthropology. *Evolutionary Anthropology, 2,* 78-88.

Hinde, R. A. (1970). *Animal behavior: A synthesis of ethology and comparative psychology* (2nd ed.). New York: McGraw-Hill.

Hinde, R. A. (1974). *Biological bases of human social behavior.* New York: McGraw-Hill.

Hinde, R. A. (1983). Ethology and child development. In P. H. Mussen (Series Ed.), M. M. Haith & J. J. Campos (Vol. Eds.), *Handbook of child psychology: Vol. 2. Infancy and developmental psychobiology.* (4th ed., pp. 27-93). New York: Wiley.

Jolly, A. (1985). *The evolution of primate behavior* (2nd ed.). New York: Macmillan.

Jones, S., Martin, R., & Pilbeam, D. (Eds.) (1992). *The Cambridge encyclopedia of human evolution*. Cambridge: Cambridge University Press.

Konner, M. J. (1972). Aspects of the developmental ethology of foraging people. In N. Blurton Jones (Ed.), *Ethological studies of child behavior* (pp. 285-304). Cambridge: Cambridge University Press.

Lehner, P. N. (1979). *Handbook of ethological methods*. New York: Garland STPM Press.

Lorenz, K. (1939). Vergleichende Verhaltensforschung [Comparative behavioral research]. *Verhandlungen der Deutschen Zoologischen Gesellschaft. Zoologischer Anzeiger Supplement, 12,* 69-102.

Lorenz, K. (1965). *Evolution and modification of behavior*. Chicago: The University of Chicago Press.

Luling, V. (1992). Tribal peoples in the modern world. In S. Jones, R. Martin, & D. Pilbeam (Eds.), *The Cambridge encyclopedia of human evolution*. Cambridge: Cambridge University Press.

MacDonald, K. B. (1988). *Social and personality development: An evolutionary synthesis*. New York: Plenum.

MacDonald, K. (Ed.) (1993). *Parent-child play: Descriptions and implications*. Albany: State University of New York Press.

Mayr, E. (1974). Behavior programs and evolutionary strategies. *American Scientist, 62,* 650-659.

Mayr, E. (1982). *The growth of biological thought: Diversity, evolution, and inheritance*. Cambridge, MA: The Belknap Press of Harvard University Press.

Mayr, E. (1983). How to carry out the adaptationist program? *The American Naturalist, 121,* 324-334.

McFarland, D. (Ed.) (1982). *The Oxford companion to animal behavior*. New York: Oxford University Press.

McGrew, W. C. (1972). *An ethological study of children's behavior*. London: Academic Press.

McGuire, M., & Troisi, A. (1998). *Evolutionary psychiatry*. Cambridge: Harvard University Press.

Morss, J. R. (1990). *The biologizing of childhood: Developmental psychology and the Darwinian myth*. Hillsdale, NJ: Erlbaum.

Nesse, R. M., & Williams, G. C. (1995). *Why we get sick: The new science of Darwinian medicine*. New York: Random House.

Omark, D. R., Strayer, F. F., & Freeman, D. G. (Eds.). (1980). *Dominance relations: An ethological view of human conflict and social interaction*. New York: Garland STPM Press.

Purves, W. K., Orians, G. H., & Heller, H. C. (1992). *Life: The science of biology*. Sunderland, MA: Sinauer Associates.

Rubin, K. H., Fein, G. G., & Vandenberg, B. (1983). Play. In P. H. Mussen (Series Ed.) & E. M. Hetherington (Vol. Ed.), *Handbook of child psychology: Vol. 4. Socialization, personality, and social development* (4th ed., pp. 752-774). New York: Wiley.

Rue, L. (1994). *By the grace of guile: The role of deception in natural history and human affairs*. Oxford: Oxford University Press.

Savin-Williams, R. C. (1987). *Adolescence: An ethological perspective*. New York: Springer.

Schaefer, K. (1994, August). *Kommunikation und Zufriedenheit in Wohnanlagen* [Communication and satisfaction in housing projects]. Paper presented at the 12th Congress of the International Society for Human Ethology, Toronto, Canada.

Schiller, C. H. (Ed.) (1957). *Instinctive behavior: The development of a modern concept.* New York: International Universities Press.

Schmitt, A., & Atzwanger, K. (1995). Walking fast – ranking high: A sociobiological perspective on pace. *Ethology and Sociobiology, 16,* 451-462.

Smith, P. K. (1982). Does play matter? Functional and evolutionary aspects of animal and human play. *Behavioral and Brain Sciences, 5,* 139-184. (Commentaries included)

Sroufe, L. A., Fox, N. E., & Pancake, V. R. (1983). Attachment and dependency in developmental perspective. *Child Development, 54,* 1615-1627.

Stearns, S. C. (1976). Life-history tactics: A review of ideas. *Quarterly Review of Biology, 51,* 3-47.

Sutton-Smith, B. (1981). *A history of children's play.* Philadelphia: University of Pennsylvania Press.

Symons, D. (1979). *The evolution of human sexuality.* New York: Oxford University Press.

Tinbergen, N. (1951). *The study of instinct.* Oxford: Oxford University Press. (Revised 1989)

Tinbergen, N. (1963). On the aims and methods of ethology. *Zeitschrift für Tierpsychologie, 20,* 410-433.

Tooby, J., & Cosmides, L. (1989). Evolutionary psychology and the generation of culture. *Ethology and Sociobiology, 10,* 29-49.

Trivers, R. L. (1971). The evolution of reciprocal altruism. *Quarterly Review of Biology, 46,* 35-57.

Turnbull, C. M. (1971). *The mountain people.* New York: Simon and Schuster.

Vanhannen, T. (1991). *Politics of ethnic nepotism: India as an example.* New Delhi: Sterling.

Weisfeld, G. E. (1979). An ethological view of human adolescence. *Journal of Nervous and Mental Disease, 167,* 38-55.

Williams, G. C. (1966). *Adaptation and natural selection.* Princeton: Princeton University Press.

Wilson, E. O. (1975). *Sociobiology: The new synthesis.* Cambridge, MA: The Belknap Press of Harvard University Press.

Wohlwill, J. F. (1985). Residential density as a variable in child development research. In J. F. Wohlwill & W. van Vliet-- (Eds.), *Habitats for children: The impacts of density.* Hillsdale, NJ: Erlbaum.

Comment: And ethology?

Alain Legendre

1 Basic assumption of the approach

The theoretical perspective presented by Charlesworth centers on the basic assumption that the biological laws established throughout phylogenesis "govern key aspects of contemporary human behavior" (p. 476) and that there are risks associated with going against these biological laws. The genetic heritage of human phylogenesis shapes human behavior and somehow limits its adaptive plasticity. Charlesworth tempers this fundamental assumption by pointing out that such a perspective does not imply a determinist approach to human behavior. He specifies that humans, like other forms of life, have alternative ways of behaving, depending upon conditions. Nevertheless, the former consideration rather than the latter one is developed throughout the text. Charlesworth emphasizes the "ultimate function" of behavior – survival and reproduction – framed in the long-term phylogenetic perspective rather than the "proximal function" in relation to environmental conditions. The stress is put on the sociobiological perspective rather than the ethological approach.

2 Coherence of the assumptions

Assumptions and explanations derived from sociobiological perspectives on human behavior have given rise to numerous debates and criticisms (see Valsiner, 1989). In this commentary, the focus is on how child development, environment, and the relations between them are conceptualized within the theoretical framework of sociobiology. However, Charlesworth's chapter provides a broad presentation of evolutionary theory in sociobiology and warrants a few preliminary general observations.

2.1 Extrapolating proneness in sociobiology

In the introduction, Charlesworth presents cautious reminders of elementary scientific precautions that, once stated, are no longer considered in the chapter's subsequent discussion and speculation about human behavior and societies. For instance, although Charlesworth (1994) specified that "the distinction between biological and psychological phenomena reveals the limits of applying evolutionary theory in a reductionist manner to all features of Homo sapiens" (p. 7* [1]), he also claimed that "the laws and concepts constituting evolutionary theory can be applied as productively to humans as to ants or elephants" (p. 3*). Similarly, it is underlined that "Darwin constructed a theory of animal (and plant) behavior, not a theory of human behavior and mind" (p. 476, in this volume) and that "[h]e was well-aware of the dangers of entering areas where he lacked scientific expertise and of extrapolating across species" (p. 476). Later in the text, however, it is explained that "[b]ecause humans share much active DNA with chimpanzees and gorillas . . . it is not surprising that many similarities in phenotypes between the three species can be found" (p. 484) and that "[t]hese similarities make it possible to extrapolate across species" (p. 484). Because one might argue that the slightest modification in the DNA structure has tremendous consequences in a given species, this fact should instill one with the greatest caution when extrapolating across species (Jacquard, 1978).

2.2   Function and causality in sociobiology:
A shift toward an evolutionary goal-directed view of behavior

A short, but explicit, presentation of the evolutionary process is given in the chapter's section on conceptual framework. Evolution appears as a dynamic process in which intervene the interaction between environmental changes and the species's responses designed to cope with those changes. The adaptive responses are seen as optimizing the species's chances to survive and to reproduce. More specifically, at a given period in the evolutionary history of a peculiar species, the interaction of a particular behavior with the given environmental conditions – selective factors – may enhance the reproductive success of the species's members exhibiting that behavior. Therefore, the genes related to this particular behavior, which fulfill an adaptive function, are likely to be transmitted to the future gene pool of the species.

However, as the reader goes further into the development of the perspective, a double shift creeps into the sociobiological reasoning, a shift that confounds functions and causes, as well as the species-level and individual-level of discourse. For instance, it is suggested that the behavior contributing positively to the long-term reproductive success of the species is "obligatory goals of all animals" (p. 476). This assertion gives the impression that the evolutionary process has been reversed. The long-term consequences of a behavior in the evolutionary history of species seems to become what motivates the behavior of the individual! Namely, passing one's genes into the future gene pool is presented as the ultimate goal of the individual. It is specified that "humans exist today because their ancestors acted genetically selfishly, that is, they behaved in the interest of their own genes" (p. 485). In view of this argument – which appears tautological – Charlesworth adds that "then, virtually all behavior must be motivated to some extent by selfishness" (p. 485). The qualification of selfishness applied to intraspecies competition may appear tendentious, but the main point is that an overwhelming emphasis is placed on those intraspecies competitions. Whether it concerns relations between individuals or between groups, the adopted behavior is not systematically competition. Cooperation is frequently encountered as active participation in the survival and reproductive success of populations. This cooperation has essentially ensured the success of bacterium for several billion years. Intraspecies competition is only one of many factors in the complex systems of interaction contributing to evolutionary processes (see the journal *Theoretical Population Biology*).

2.3   Future evolution in retrospect

Perusal of the chapter by Charlesworth also suggests that, in the sociobiological perspective, the intermingled dynamics of adaptation and evolution are somehow frozen. Past processes that have participated in anterior evolution of humankind are applied in a prospective way, without much attention to the major changes that occurred in the cultural and physical environment of humans. More specifically, it seems those behaviors that have (or are supposed to have) fulfilled a critical function in the adaptation and evolution of humans must be preserved. Otherwise, the human species might be exposed to "[p]enalties associated with 'going against nature'" (p. 498). In Charlesworth's view this is the case for such behavior as dominance and sex role. However, the first law issuing from phylogenetic studies is that species must adapt to new conditions. It is a fact that evolution proceeds under the pressure of these conditions and of the contradictions they generate with inherited behavior, including social behavior.

3   Implied environmental and developmental concepts

In the sociobiological perspective, two types of environments must be considered. The first, and apparently the most important one, is the environment of evolutionary adaptedness (EEA), which is characterized primarily in terms of the Pleistocene conditions in which humans evolved. The second type, urban environment (UE) settings, refers to modern living conditions. The implied concept of environment is quite hazy. For instance, the terms *UE settings, UE living,* and *UE society* are successively used. Both types of environment are apprehended as broad and general living contexts, with UE being defined mainly as a contrast to EEA. The contrast supports a polarity between hunter-gatherer societies and modern societies. However, from the adopted evolutionary point of view, it might have been expected that cities and urban settings encompass a broad geographical and historical perspective.

This is not the case. As compared to hunter-gatherer living conditions described in very general – and perhaps idealistic – terms, the UE settings essentially refer to current occidental societies, more particularly, to North American living conditions. Nevertheless, cities appear as abstract entities in the discourse, regardless of their concrete environmental features (such as size or spatial organization).

3.1 Pleistocene forever

The tenet of evolutionary thinking in urban planning is that in future cities "conditions should conform as much as possible to the ancestral social (but obviously not physical) conditions in which human children evolved their emotional, cognitive, and behavioral adaptations" (p. 498). The ideal will be to return to social organizations attributed to the hunter-gatherer ancestors, but in modern urban settings provided with all the facilities resulting from technological progress. Insofar as Charlesworth acknowledges that in today's urban environment things are radically different" from Pleistocene conditions, this proposal is very astonishing. First, it rests upon the assumption that social organizations and interindividual relations developed in hunter-gatherer societies are the best for humankind. Second, it seems to assimilate the developmental process (children as individuals) to the evolutionary process (Homo sapiens). Third, it insinuates that interindividual relations and group organizations could be independent to a large extent from the physical and technological features of the living conditions.

Primary biological drives may be relatively independent from environmental and cultural factors, but social relations, and even parent-child interactions are not reducible to their ultimate biological function. Furthermore, the adaptive function of a behavior might change if the particular environmental conditions in which it appeared are substantially modified. Even if genetic predispositions for certain social interaction were differentially shaped by demands of Pleistocene conditions, they might not match modern urban settings and might thereby become *residues of adaptation*.[2] On several occasions, Charlesworth raises the critical question of potential changes in the function of behavior in relation to radical transformations of human living conditions. In his chapter, however, modifications in behaviors are seldom presented as possible adaptations to new environmental conditions, but rather as modern "deviations" (e.g., in nursing, child care, and the sex role).

3.2 Childhood, a preparatory stage toward mating and reproducing

Different aspects of the relations that children establish with their environment during childhood are discussed by Charlesworth: nursing, infant attachment and child care, family, peer interactions, children and strangers, and mate selection and reproduction. The latter point might appear out of place if the reader does not keep in mind that, in the sociobiological perspective, the behavior is framed as a function of its contribution to survival and reproduction. Similarly, child development is framed in a manner that might sometimes appear reductionist. The evolutionary point of view adopted by Charlesworth is explicitly summarized in the two following sentences:

The evolutionary answer (hypothesis to be more exact) to the question of the ultimate function of early infant-parent attachment is that it ensures that the helpless infant survives and is thereby able to move closer to a more independent existence. Achieving independence, in turn, raises the child's chances of reaching adulthood, mating, and reproducing. (p. 490)

Such a perspective may prompt one to consider primarily – if not exclusively – those behaviors, functions, and learning involved in the "construction" of the future adult. It could lead one to overlook that children have to adapt to the immediate environment at every stage of their development. In contrast to this perspective, promoting child-oriented planning implies that one ought to research primarily those behaviors that are meaningful and highly adaptive for children at each period of development. That proposition may lead one to consider even those behaviors that are transitory[3] and that do not play any critical role in the achievement of ultimate functions.

No thorough cost-benefit analysis of the human individual's particularly long period of development has been undertaken in Charlesworth's chapter. This omission is surprising, for childhood's long duration seems particularly significant from both environmental and evolutionary perspectives. If "children . . . have to be recognized as having instincts," (p. 483) it also has to be recognized that those instincts do not provide children with an effective program of specific behavior that allows a rapid access to an independent existence. Adaptation in humans might be less than "half accounted for by instincts" (p. 483). In return for infants' helplessness and children's prolonged dependence, the human being gains a high degree of adaptive plasticity. This adaptability is achieved in the extensive developmental period through the acquisition of cultural knowledge, which enables humans to master complex situations in a wide range of environmental settings. The outstanding increase in plasticity, the acquisition of adaptive behavior via culture – and not as extensively via DNA as in most other species – permitted Homo sapiens to settle in nearly all parts of the earth, customizing the different biotopes and creating their own environments. The major evolutionary advance afforded by the extensive developmental period certainly provides Homo sapiens with a large degree of liberty with regard to past behavioral adaptations in general, particularly ancestral social behavior. Sociobiologists seem well aware that the plasticity of Homo sapiens has biologically paid off. Thus, it is unclear why, when discussing the significance of everyday behavior, they lessen the importance of human behavioral plasticity and emphasize the human's instinctive equipment. Charlesworth pointed out that "ontogeny long posed challenging conceptual problems . . . for evolutionary theory in general" (p. 480), so perhaps child development still poses problems for sociobiologyical theory in particular.

4 The relevance and usefulness of the ethological/sociobiological approach

4.1 Explicatory terms

Whatever criticisms may be leveled at the sociobiological theory, the value of Charlesworth's contribution is to raise the question of the limits of human adaptive plasticity as regards the constraints of modern urban settings. The usefulness of the approach is to draw the reader's attention to the manner in which the contemporary adaptation to the urban environment can still be influenced (negatively or positively) by prior adaptations to the living conditions in which human species evolved. Do children have sufficient plasticity to be raised in cities without suffering negative consequences – damage to their physical health, reduction of their sense of well-being, threats to their comfort, restriction in opportunities for their social and emotional development, and deprivation in educational opportunity?

At least for some of these aspects, such as comfort, educational opportunity, and health, particularly with respect to infants' mortality, the response is not completely negative, even in cities of Third World countries. One might also regret that contemporary living conditions and the associated behavioral changes are discussed from a conservative point of view. There is no reason to be particularly optimistic about present and future living conditions in cities. On the other hand, there are no definite arguments to support the view that the important behavioral and cultural changes that accompany movement of populations into cities jeopardize the future evolution of humankind. Charlesworth recognizes that "[w]hether there are any significant long-term genetic effects remains to be seen" (p. 482). Threats become more pointed and convincing when Charlesworth shifts from an evolutionary to an ecological perspective and raises the question of access to nonrenewable resources.

4.2 Descriptive terms

The major regret I had in reading this chapter on an ethological/sociobiological approach is that sparse attention has been given to the ethological perspective. Urban ethological research is only evoked but not developed. More specifically, the potential contribution of ethological methodology to child-oriented urban planning is not tackled. Nevertheless, the observational technique developed in ethology could yield effective and productive improvements both for practice and theory in urban planning.

Designing a playground relies on a set of hypotheses about the population that will use it, the attraction of the play equipment, the choice of its location, its integration into the surrounding environment, and so forth. This remark underlines the fact that architectural or urban realizations – buildings, playgrounds, street layouts – are the results of successive implicit or explicit hypotheses that should call for an evaluation process. The development of field methods of investigation in ethology could help in this evaluation task. For instance, particularly for young children, observation could be useful in determining whether a playground fits their needs and what kind of activities (duration, diversity) or social encounters (nature) occur in that playground. In short, it could help to determine reliably whether the playground corresponds to what was planned and if there is any misconceived feature. Such investigations could be beneficial to both applied and basic research.

4.3 Prescriptive terms

From a practical point of view, Charlesworth's recommendations remain at a very general level. However, as an architect I think that some of the recommendations need to be made more specific to avoid harmful interpretations. This is the case for the recommendation to plan private spaces for communities. Even with permeable barriers, such a recommendation can lead one to plan urban apartheid. An opposite direction is being currently adopted in France to promote a cultural mixing through urban planning integration. This urban policy is supported by a strong economic incentive: Each municipality must accommodate disfavored populations, otherwise a share of the taxes collected from the district is used for the development of urban facilities in poorer districts.

Although trivial, the basic species-universal needs to which Charlesworth points are, unfortunately, not always satisfied, and sensitivity to individual differences still has to be promoted.

Notes

1 Citations tagged with a "*" were found in the first version of Charlesworth's chapter.
2 The term was proposed by Charlesworth in an earlier version of his chapter.
3 An example of transitory behavior playing a highly adaptive role in peer contexts (day-care centers) at the end of the second year of life can be found in immediate imitation (Nadel & Fontaine, 1989). It enables young peers to engage and sustain social interactions. However, this effective means of communication for two-year olds will play a very minor role in future social interchanges, for the verbal competence will develop.

References

Charlesworth, W. R. (1994). Evolutionary theory: Ethological and sociobiological aspects. In T. Husen & T. N. Postlethwaits (Eds.), *International Encyclopedia of Education* (2nd ed.) (Vol. 4, pp. 2167-2172). Elmsford, NY: Pergamon Press.

Jacquard, A. (1978). *Eloge de la différence: la génétique et les hommes*. Paris: Edition du Seuil.

Nadel, J., & Fontaine, A. M. (1989). Communicating by imitation: A developmental and comparative approach to transitory social competence. In B. H. Schneider, G. Attili, J. Nadel, & R. P. Weissberg (Eds.), *Social competence in developmental perspective* (pp. 277-291). Dordrecht: Kluwer Academic Publishers.

Valsiner, J. (1989). On the glory and misery of sociobiological perspectives on human development: A selfish book review. *Developmental Psychobiology, 22*, 413-417.

Author's response: Adaptive variations and the individual

William R. Charlesworth

Alain Legendre's point that my chapter puts more stress on the sociobiological (evolutionary) perspective than the ethological approach is well taken. This was intended. It is clear that ethology has the methodological tools and concepts to examine empirically the effect of city living on human evolutionary adaptations. However, such an examination has not yet produced a solid foundation of data upon which to claim any successful test of evolutionary theory, and it is certainly not broad-based enough to offer city planners iron-clad suggestions how to proceed to make cities "biologically" more acceptable to children. Evolutionary theory, as it is now articulated by sociobiologists, needs to be stressed at this point in city planning because it has developed a very persuasive rationale for predicting effects of city living on humans. In my opinion those using ethological methods are best qualified to test these predictions.

If there is a tentative tone to much of what I say about biological constraints and plasticity, it is not because I think ethologists and sociobiologists are barking up the wrong tree. To the contrary, I think they are on to something very important, but they still have to prove it. And they can only do this if they deal with the enormous variation in adaptation associated with urban living. So far this has not been done. Until such variation is dealt with, I think it premature to make responsible pronouncements on the pros and cons of city living for human health, survival, and reproduction. The same applies to nonbiological (environmental or cultural) theories and predictions.

I share somewhat Lengendre's concern that city planners might inadvertently create "urban apartheid" (p. 510) if they rested their decisions solely upon evolutionary theory. However, I am not convinced that city planning per se is very efficacious in dealing with ethnic problems. As I see it, apartheid (as we know it from pre-1991 South Africa) was first a state of mind that developed out of historical interactions between white colonists and indigenous peoples in the area. Once it became apparent that blacks and whites were economically dependent upon each other, this state of mind became codified into residential laws, the Group Areas Act (repealed in 1991), that led to segregated living arrangements such as townships. If the state of mind of today's various ethnic groups leads many of its members to choose to live with each other on a daily basis (because they want to ensure that their children learn their group's cultural values, marry group members, and so on), they will try to do so regardless of city planning. Those who do not care for ethnicity and group membership will choose to live in "mixed" areas. So be it. Legendre and I both agree: individual differences are important, as is individual autonomy.

Street traffic, children, and the extended concept of affordance as a means of shaping the environment[1]

Wolf-D. Heine and Rainer Guski

In the domain of environmental psychology, most readers are familiar with the concepts of people-environment relations proposed by Barker (e.g., 1968), Proshansky (e.g., 1973), Altman (e.g., 1975), Bronfenbrenner (e.g., 1977), and Altman and Rogoff (1987) to name but a few. They are also quite familiar with the stress theory of the Berkeley group (Lazarus & Launier, 1978), which neatly fits the contention of many environmental psychologists that it is not the physical world that constrains behavior of offers and opportunities to behave, but the perceived and (cognitively appraised) world. This perspective usually reflects the historic concept of perception as being mainly conscious, deficient, related to cultural traditions, and in need of augmentation via inference.

In recent years, this traditional view has been challenged both by new empirical problems and new theoretical concepts. In the empirical realm, it has been shown that severe environmental health effects can exist without being consciously perceived (and appraised) by the affected people (e.g., radon effects, or hearing impairments caused by loud music). In the theoretical realm, a growing amount of perception research includes analyses of the ecological information contained in the physical world, that is, information that is picked up by organisms with distinctive perception-action capabilities. This theoretical shift is due to the work of James J. Gibson (1966, 1979) and is reflected in an increasing amount of experimental work published in journals of general psychology. This shift has recently been reflected in other fields too, as demonstrated by the paper of Lazarus (1991), who discussed how meaning is generated. It is in that contribution that automatic processing without awareness is contrasted with deliberate and conscious processing and that the concept of resonance between an animal's needs and what is encountered in the environment is discussed. At the end, Lazarus advanced the idea that there is more than one way in which meaning is achieved, allowed for unconscious or preconscious appraisal, and considered J. J. Gibson's concept of "affordance" to be very similar to preconscious appraisal.

We will try to show how environmental psychology can profit from the ecological psychology proposed by Gibson. However, within the bounds of this chapter, the theoretical framework of our perspective is outlined only insofar as it is necessary for the study of children in urban contexts. Furthermore, we restrict ourselves to a specific problem of urban environments, that of traffic.[2]

1   The reciprocity of perception and action

J. J. Gibson (1966, 1979) criticized the unrelated use of physical concepts to describe the environment and of psychological principles to explain the awareness of the world. In Gibson's view, one should first refrain from articulating anything about the nature of perceptual processes until the environment in which perception and action take place is described. This is even more important if perceiving is assumed to be an active process of searching for information in order to be able to act in an environment and if acting is assumed to generate perceivable information about properties of the environment. Thus, there is a reciprocity between perceiving and acting. An organism and its environment, such as children and streets they use, cannot be studied as unrelated entities (section 1.1). After the environment has been described one should, second, ask what kind of information the environment offers for behaving in this environment, that is, what kind of information a child can perceive if it walks forward (section 1.2). Third, one should look for environmental properties that can be identified if the reciprocity of organism and environment is taken seriously. That is, are there any properties of a street that fit the behavioral capabilities of children? It is here that the concept of affordances comes in (section 1.3).

1.1   The environment (to be perceived)

A description of the environment must not be confused with a physicist's description of physical reality. A level of physical description is needed that is appropriate to organisms and their relation to their environment, and to the environment and its relation to its organisms. Instead of using organism-neutral terms like space and bodies in space, Gibson suggested that the terrestrial environment consists of substances, medium, and surfaces. Substances are matter in the solid or semisolid state. Matter (in the sense of solids) does not freely transmit energy or permit motion; it is "substantial" (Gibson, 1979, p. 19). These substances tend to be opaque to light, resistant to deformation, and permanent in shape. They make a variety of behaviors possible for organisms. Properties of the earth's gaseous atmosphere are the transmission and reverberance of energy (e.g., light and sound) and the nonresistance in relation to motions of solid bodies. It is thus a medium for perception and animal locomotion. The interfaces between substances and medium are surfaces. Surfaces are structured, that is, they have texture and a particular characteristic layout. For a behavior-oriented description of the environment, surfaces are of special relevance.

Surfaces are the basis for all action. They are the environmental properties that are perceived.

What does it mean for children and an urban environment? A street, for example, is a persisting substance with a surface. Different substances (concrete, grit, or tar) have different surfaces. Any surface has a characteristic texture (depending on the composition of the substance). Textures are important to the generation of specific information about the environment to be perceived (see below). The surface of a street is the basis for all action of street users, such as children and car drivers. Information about this environmental property is perceived and used to guide action. If one takes organism and environment as independent from each other, then a street is nothing other than a street, irrespective of the organism as a child or a car driver. If one takes an ecological stance, that is, if one assumes that organism and environment are related entities, then a street as a surface layout offers distinct actions for street users with different behavioral capabilities (e.g., car drivers and children). The latter viewpoint might become clearer in section 1.3.

1.2   Information (about the environment to be perceived)

"Due to a textural difference, . . . each different surface modifies light idiosyncratically" (Turvey, 1975, p. 167, see Fig. 1). It can therefore be assumed that light is structured by surface in a specific mode and that light contains information about the layout of surfaces. This ambient light surrounding a point of observation is the ambient optic array, which consists "of a finite (closed) set of visual solid angles with a common apex at the point of observation" (Turvey, 1975, p. 168). The hierarchically structured environment (nested layouts of surfaces) corresponds to the hierarchically structured optic array. A visual stimulus ecologically reassessed means that ambient light (structured by surfaces of substances in the environment and carried in the medium), which is "informative about the sources of its structure by virtue of being lawfully specific to those sources of structure" (Mace, 1986, p. 139), is available to the perceptual system or is encountered by the perceptual system (to emphasize the active role of a perceiving organism). The optic array can be detected by a stationary or "moving point of observation" (Gibson, 1979, p. 308). If the observer is in motion then the array changes. Everything in the array flows; however, with a flowing optic array, some optical relations persist. These relations (invariants) are specific to the persisting features of the environment. The changing properties are specific to the moving animal relative to the environment. In order for an organism to guide its behavior, it has to pick up this specific information about the environment. In other words, an organism has to perform an exploratory activity in order to detect the invariants in the optic array. Thus, the act of perceiving means detecting this information in the optic array, which is generated by the layout of environmental properties and which, in turn, specifies the layout of environmental surfaces (Turvey & Carello, 1986; for comments about the term information in the domain of ecological acoustics, see Heine, 1994, pp. 62-74).

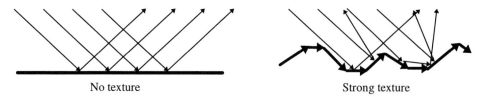

No texture   Strong texture

Figure 1: Because of textural difference, light is reflected in a structured way

A child who moves forward to cross a street generates the outflow of the optical array. This outflow specifies an approach by entailing magnification (of the other side of the street), whereby the center of outflow specifies the direction of locomotion in the street. Take another example for the informational basis of the perception of events on a street. An approaching car is specified to a child as a "looming" object. That is, as the car nears the eye, there is an accelerating magnification of the visual solid angle of the car. For a child, this magnification specifies an impending collision with the car (for basic research concerning progressive magnification, see Schiff, Caviness, & Gibson, 1962; Schiff, 1965).

1.3   Affordances (as organism-referential properties of the environment to be perceived)

1.3.1   The ecological niche

If properties of the environment are specified by invariants in the ambient optic array, and if these invariants are detected by the activities of the perceiving organism, then perceiving is a reciprocal function of the organism and its environment. However, this formulation might be not sufficient to describe this relationship.

The behavior-relevant environment of any organism cannot be described straight away. Instead, the analysis must be limited to an environment for a particular class of organisms that share some degrees of functional equivalence. Functional equivalence includes physiological, biomechanical, biochemical, and epistemic functioning. The environmental context in which organisms with the same functional equivalence can successfully function is the ecological niche. Within the ecological approach proposed by Gibson (1979, chap. 8), this organism-referential concept was further specified as a "set of affordances" (Gibson, 1979, p. 128), or a specific "affordance structure" (Johnston & Turvey, 1980, p. 152). As far as affordances are concerned, an econiche means environmental properties in terms of the activities it can support for functionally equivalent organisms. An affordance can be defined as the functional utility that an environmental object has for an organism with certain properties.[3]

What does that mean for the topic of children and traffic? An organism perceives its traffic environment in terms of the functional utilities the environment has for the organism, and the organism does so in a way commensurate to its behavioral capability. In other words, users of different transport modes (e.g., feet, bicycle, or car) have distinct behavioral capabilities. Therefore, they extract particular kinds of information about affordances from the ambient optic array. One must thus ask what kind of activity a main street offers a child and a car driver, respectively. It is probably not too polemic to state that modern urban streets are collections of functional utilities for car drivers. To be precise, a street is an affordance structure for car drivers and their extended behavioral apparatus, the cars. By contrast, what could the affordance structure of streets mean for children? In a nutshell, properties of the street environment are altered with reference to the developing perception and action capabilities of children. That is, policy-makers have traffic environments adapted to children's abilities and "deficits" rather than have children trained in road safety (see section 2 of this chapter).

1.3.2   Perceiving the affordance of stair-climbing

To be able to determine whether given environmental properties afford a particular action, one must analyze the behaviorally relevant properties of the environment in relation to relevant properties of the organism and its behavior-executing system. This abstract formulation becomes clearer when illustrated by the now almost classical example of studying the affordance of stair-climbing (Warren, 1984; for other examples of the same topic, see Warren & Whang, 1987, or Mark, 1987, for an extension of Warren's work). Warren studied the perception of whether stairs afforded ascending. According to Warren's biomechanical model, the relevant body characteristic for the activity of stair-climbing is leg length (see, however, Konczak, Meeuwsen, & Cress, 1992). He analyzed leg length in its relation to riser height (the behaviorally relevant property of the environment). It is obvious that tall people can climb higher riser heights than short people can. But it is not obvious that both short and tall people can perceive beforehand whether they could climb the riser comfortably. Subjects were presented with different riser heights and were asked to categorize them as optimally or nonoptimally climbable. Only risers whose heights are of a particular relation to leg length were perceived to be optimal. Moreover, subjects were asked to use different stairs in a treadmill while their energy expenditure was measured. It could be shown that the riser heights perceived as optimally climbable were also those where the lowest oxygen consumption of the subjects was recorded. Again, if dimensions of the environmental property (stair riser) and dimensions of a person are compatible, then the environmental object affords the specific activity. If one uses the basic unit of length in physics, the meter, organisms with different legs show different preferences for riser heights. However, if one applies an intrinsic (i.e., body-scaled) metric by scaling riser height against leg length in the unit of leg length (thereby constructing a dimensionless number), then measurements will show that a riser with the height of a quarter of any leg length is perceived as optimal for ascending (see Fig. 2). Risers of the height of a quarter of the animal's leg length afford the activity of stair-climbing.

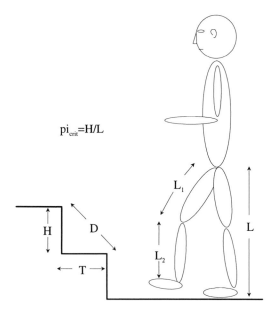

$pi_{crit}=H/L$

Figure 2: *If body-scaled metrics are applied, then the critical riser height (H) shows an invariant relation (pi_{crit}) to leg length (L)*

1.3.3   Reflecting the reciprocity of organism and environment
This empirically derived statement documents a distinctive feature of the notion of affordance, which reflects the reciprocity of animal and environment. From a traditional point of view, a riser height has certain objective properties such as a particular height and width. An individual has certain subjective properties such as a particular body mass, length, and metabolism. The concept of affordance, however, is a relational one that cuts across the dichotomy of subjective-objective, and overcomes the classic organism-environment dualism. (For specific criticisms of organism-environment dualism, see Turvey & Shaw, 1979; Shaw & Turvey, 1981; Turvey, Shaw, Reed, & Mace, 1981; Shaw, Turvey, & Mace, 1982; and Turvey & Kugler, 1984.) As Gibson (1979) stated,

an affordance is neither an objective property nor a subjective property; or it is both if you like. . . . It is equally a fact of the environment and a fact of behavior. It is both physical and psychical, yet neither. An affordance points both ways, to the environment and to the observer. (p.129)

A critic from the faculty of town- or transportation-planning may object to the concept of affordance, saying, on the one hand, that it is too specific to be of value for topics of planning. What can be transferred from examples like the affordance of stair-climbing to the task of planning an urban setting that responds to the needs and desires of children? On the other hand, a critic could contend that the concept of affordance is too general to be applicable in planning. A town with one million inhabitants has a much more complex structure than a rural village with a population of one thousand. A street in a town and in a village differ from each other with respect to many features. Is not this concept of affordance in urgent need of differentiation? First, the example of the stair-climbing was used for the sake of simplicity. In chapter 2.4 it appears in parts of the new concept of affordance analysis for large-scale environmental properties. Second, the strength of the concept of affordance is its specificity and generality, depending on the purpose of analysis. One can use it in a specific sense to differentiate between towns and villages by looking for the affordance of "playability" of streets. Parents perceive the automobile-centered affordance structure of modern urban streets for their children and act by forbidding them to play there. Parents in rural areas allow their children to play in streets because these still have the functional utility for playing. The concept of affordance has the advantage of generality, too. From the perspective of performance it does not make any difference whether a child likes to cross a street in a town or in a village or whether that child likes to jump a brook. The crucial point is that an environmental property affords an activity for an organism if certain compatibility relations between an environmental property and an organism exist. Thus the notion of affordance can be a guiding principle of generalized validity to evaluate environments for an organism or for a particular class of organisms that share some degree of functional equivalence.

This ecological approach to perceiving and acting shares one common axiom with most well-known approaches to environmental psychology (e.g., those of Barker, Altman, and Stokols): Places and other environmental objects offer and restrict the behavior of humans (see the comparison between Barker and Gibson in Heft, 1988). Unlike Barker, who stresses social and cultural traditions as important influences on human behavior in places during the ontogenetic development (see Fuhrer or Cotterell, this volume), Gibson stresses the human action capabilities that have evolved during phylogenetic development. This perspective does not exclude individual developments, as the work of E. J. Gibson (e.g., 1982, 1988) and her followers show, but it does favor individual attunements to terrestrial information instead of adaptations to social and cultural symbols. In this sense, Gibson's approach to environmental psychology may be seen as an extended instrumental view of people-environment relations, as contrasted with a spiritual view (cf. Stokols, 1990).

2   The ecological approach and traffic

Let us turn now to the possibilities and problems of the ecological approach to one of the most serious challenges for children in our modern world: how to survive and behave in an automobile-dominated society.

Today it is generally agreed that motorized traffic has a tremendous impact on the environment. Walking and bicycling are dangerous travel modes. Referring to conditions in Great Britain, Tolley (1990, p. 18) stated that "walking is the most dangerous travel mode next to motor cycling." In 1993 85.5 percent of all road accidents in Germany were caused by drivers of motorized vehicles (Bundesminister für Verkehr, 1994). Some people are more likely to have an accident than others, with the young and elderly being particularly vulnerable. Environmental problems associated with traffic in housing areas affect a great many people. They are annoyed and disturbed by noise, dirt, fumes, and vibration (see Koelega, 1987). Air pollution and the effect of lead compounds on children and other emissions on human health in general are well known today. Traffic also has many social impacts. As Appleyard and Lintell (1972) showed, the privacy of residents is diminished in heavily congested streets, and their communication is reduced. Parents in particular are concerned about the social consequences of traffic. Their residential satisfaction is affected by their cognitions of children's accident risk (Gärling & Gärling, 1990), which prompts parental restrictions on children's environmental activities. Such responses are crucial for children's development of space perception and action because "parental restrictions [have] the most influence on how the children [use] their neighborhood" (Torell & Biel, 1985, p. 117; see also Hart, 1979). That is, children's opportunities to explore their surroundings are fundamentally reduced by the effects of traffic. It should be added that parents' risk perception is not the epitome of hysterical imagination but a good estimation of what is happening on streets within home range (Malek, Guyer, & Lescohier, 1990). After all, 50 percent of all accidents with child pedestrian injuries occur within a radius of 500 m from home (Pfafferott, 1993 according to Limbourg, 1994).

In the following sections we examine the common approaches to improving the probability that children will survive the modern traffic environment. We present an example of traffic research committed to the ecological approach (2.1), discuss whether children should (and could) be adapted to traffic environments by measures like road-safety training (2.2), and suggest how the ecological approach should be developed as a research strategy to promote an environmentally friendly traffic infrastructure (section 3). We conclude this chapter with examples of intuitively affordance-oriented measures of area-wide traffic calming.

2.1 *Traffic safety for children*

There are three strategies to increase traffic safety for children: institute road-safety training, try to modify the behavior of motor-vehicle drivers, and change the physical properties of the traffic environment. In the past the ecological approach could explicitly contribute to the first strategy only (see below).

A prominent field within the ecological approach is time-to-contact research (or time-to-arrival, for a short overview, see Schiff & Arnone, in press). It is assumed that there is information in the optic array (called tau) that enables a person to perceive the time remaining before contact with another surface layout (another person, a vehicle, etc.). Tau is derived by considering the relative velocities of optical texture elements (see Bruce & Green, 1990, pp. 261-265, for a short introduction). In traffic a driver can use this visual information to avoid collisions by knowing when to start braking (Lee, 1976) and how to maintain the direction of a vehicle on the road (Lee & Lishman, 1977). Pedestrians have to estimate whether the gap between two moving cars is sufficient to cross a street. That is, they have to perceive the difference between the time of arrival of the vehicles on either side of this gap, and they have to relate this difference to their own crossing time (distance to be walked divided by walking speed). They have to combine information about an environmental situation and information about their own action capability. To put it in more formal terms, if the temporal size of the gap is smaller than the crossing time, it means unsafe crossing. If it is larger, then crossing is safe. The typical crossing behavior of adults differs from the crossing behavior that is taught to children (Füsser, Jakobs, & Steinbrecher, 1993). Adults do not wait until the first car has crossed their projected path (the crossing line). They start walking at a moment that will allow the first car to reach the crossing line just before the would-be point of collision. Adults are thereby able to use even small gaps between two cars to cross a street. By contrast children are taught to wait until the first car has passed them, then use information about the collision time of the second car in relation to their own walking velocity. If children apply this strategy, they have to wait for larger gaps between two cars to be able to cross a street. If children are in a hurry or if they see an attractive object or situation on the other side of the street (Limbourg & Gerber, 1978), they may also try to use the smaller gaps, increasing the probability of an accident. However, it is known from the literature in developmental psychology that children have this general visuo-motor timing ability (see, for example, von Hofsten, 1983).

Thus it would be beneficial for younger children if one could use this ability to teach them special timing skills for road crossing. Lee, Young, and McLaughlin (1984) and Young and Lee (1987) developed and applied the "pretend road crossing task" for training children. They told a child that a stretch of side walk beside a road is the road itself (see Fig. 3 for the two-way road crossing task in Young & Lee, 1987). Children were to stand at the edge of the pretend road. They had to imagine that for each real car (car with straight lines in Fig. 3) coming along the road there was one in a corresponding position on the pretend road (car with dotted lines). The children had to cross the pretend road in the direction of the barrier, but they were not allowed to cross the pretend road when a car passed the barrier. Thus they were to use the particular gaps. The children were thereby able to practice their crossing skills and could check their performance by themselves. The authors showed that even five-year-olds became more efficient in exploiting gaps in traffic by adequate training of perceiving and acting. In single-lane crossing they reached almost adult standard. They developed a consistent crossing speed, but they were also able to adjust their walking speed to the time available before the next car arrived. Obviously, they were able to detect and apply time-to-contact information available in the optic array.

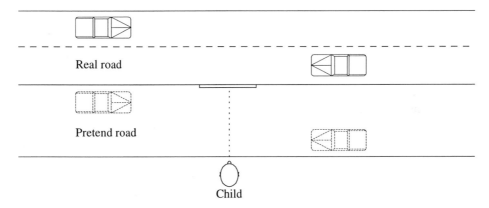

Figure 3: *The pretend road crossing task*

2.2   Road-safety training or alteration of the traffic environment?

Certainly the crossing strategy based on time-to-contact information might be more useful than the traditional one taught to children. Clearly, an approach to perception and action can be turned to problems of identifying important perceptual information and acting in an efficient and safe way in traffic environments. The question arises, however, whether the ecological approach should focus on this kind of research to improve the quality of children's lives in towns. Before promoting this application of tau information as a contribution that training can make to the improvement of traffic safety for children in general and as a contribution that the ecological approach can make to the improvement of traffic safety in specific, we should discuss the value of road-safety training for children in principle.

2.2.1 Traffic behavior of children

Before crossing a road, child pedestrians orient themselves in a superficial way compared to adults (Füsser et al., 1993). As a function of age, their crossing behavior can be influenced easily by distracting stimulus information (Limbourg & Gerber, 1978). Cohen and Fischer (1982) showed that a motor vehicle's form and function generate distinct expectancies of its particular velocity. In other words primary school children's perception of vehicles moving with a certain velocity can be influenced by these expectancies. During a crossing task, children are therefore at higher risk if they encounter moving cars whose velocities are expected to be lower because they do not look as if they can travel quickly. At least preschool children have more trouble finding safe places to cross the road, if they are in unknown surroundings than if they are in their familiar environments (Füsser et al., 1993). Furthermore, children perform secondary activities (games) while moving on a sidewalk (Grayson, 1975). According to Sandels (1975), children walking along a sidewalk behave with more risk when accompanied by other children than when walking alone. For them a street is experienced not only as a connection mode from A to B but as a location that offers the space they need for social communication (Köhler, 1983, summarizing a study of Peter-Habermann, 1974). They show an unstable behavior in the traffic environment, that is, they do not perform the same or similar behavior in the same situation over time (Limbourg & Günther, 1977). Basner and de Marées (1993) documented that child bicyclists have difficulty with their visual orientation (at least until the age of eight) if, for example, they have to look in a direction deviating from the direction in which they are riding. They change between sidewalk, bicycle path, and the carriageway. Young bicyclists use their bikes sometimes as "horses" or "motor cycles" on the road and eventually behave in that way.

2.2.2 An initial conclusion

To sum up, children behave differently than adults. One can label children's behavior as deficient. However, it might be more neutral to see the actions of children as behavior commensurate to their developmental status. Indeed, children do behave unsafely in the traffic environment. Allenbach (1995) documented that 20.6 percent of all child pedestrian accidents (five to six year olds) in Switzerland were caused by "unsafe crossing" and 55.9 percent by "darting out." However, what kind of response is appropriate? Children could be forbidden to play outside or to walk on the streets alone. If the idea of restricting children's possibilities to explore their surroundings is rejected, one can think about road-safety training. It is not our intention to evaluate the particular effectiveness of such approaches, but we would like to show some of the problems that could impede the success of programs based on them. Successively we present problems from the perspective of developmental, social, and clinical psychology.

2.2.3 Problems for road-safety training

Off-road cycle training of children (i.e., training given in a school yard or classroom instruction) has been shown to be less effective than roadside training at places where children perform their activities (for a short overview, see Limbourg, 1994). Moreover, Limbourg (1994) has asserted that roadside training is more effective if younger children practise at junctions and streets that they use during their daily activities (e.g., cycling to school). According to Piaget, she explained, children have to take the behavior they have acquired in one surrounding and generalize it to other surroundings. They fail to manage that generalization before reaching the formal operational stage (eleven years and up). From a Gibsonian point of view, one could argue that children are not able to show appropriate behavior because they still have not learned to detect the invariant information that specifies traffic events. In any case, road-safety training must be conducted in the surroundings relevant to the particular child. Are these efforts defensible if other less person-specific solutions exist?

Without going into detail, we note that the development of perception is not complete after the first year of life (although most textbooks of developmental psychology suggest that it is). The ecological approach to perceiving and acting has always emphasized that visually guided exploratory activities

become increasingly specific and systematic with age. Exploratory skills develop along with the development of knowledge of what has utility for a task and of differentiation of relevant from irrelevant information. This development is particularly evident when children attempt to perform tasks set for them by others, such as to compare two objects or scenes, to follow one event and ignore another, or to find an object in a cluttered scene. (E. J. Gibson & Spelke, 1983, p. 9)

In other words, road-safety training must be adapted to the behavioral capabilities of children as a function of their status of perceptual development.

As mentioned above, children's attention can be influenced easily by distracting information even despite road-safety training (Limbourg, 1994). Does it do much good to optimize the use of information and perceptual learning in a traffic environment? Children's attention (in ecological terms, their control of detection, see Michaels & Carello, 1981) might be not compatible with the adult's notions about detecting the necessary traffic-related information. In other words, adults think that a child's attention, say, to an injured cat in the middle of the road is the exact opposite of attention. For a child, however, the cat's circumstances are the most important information available. Is it not more useful to accept the incompatibility of children's and adults' attention as such? Should one not look for an alternative that does not suffer from this incompatibility?

Children up to the age of seven have difficulty taking the perspective of other persons; there is an inability to distinguish viewpoints of others from their own. They believe that everyone else perceives what they do (egocentrism in terms of Piaget's approach to cognitive development). For the present topic that means they are not able to put themselves in a car driver's position. In fog or twilight a child perceives a car's headlights earlier than the driver detects the child. A child with an egocentric frame of reference may think: I see the headlights shining. Thus, the driver can see me. Therefore, I can cross the street. Examples of the ways in which children put themselves in danger by egocentric reasoning can be found in Blendermann (1987). Can road-safety training change such a developmental phase?

For road safety it is essential to understand road signs and other traffic regulations. Sandels (1975) showed that children's comprehension of terms relevant for road-safety training differs especially with respect to age. Words that adults assessed as easy for children were misinterpreted by children, a result that reflects adults' lack of knowledge about what is comprehensible for children in the domain of road-safety training. This interpretation is supported by van Schagen and Brookhuis's study (1994) on different psychological methods for teaching application of the rules of right-of-way. A 'byproduct' of their analysis was that children's decisions often deviated from what is expected on the basis of the formal priority rule system. They seemed to behave according to their own rules, which are defensive in nature. They used information about environmental properties such as approaching speed and motor noise to decide whether to wait or not. Did they learn to apply a set of intrinsic rules generated by their previous encounters with the traffic environment? Did they perceive the functional significance of the automobile traffic relative to their behavioral capabilities? If so, one should not discuss children's lack of ability to integrate formal rules of road safety into their cognitive framework of schemes but should instead recognize that these children behaved correctly on the basis of the information they used provided by the environment. How can road-safety training handle this problem?

Planners should also be aware of facts from developmental biomechanics that have an impact on children's road safety (in this paragraph we refer to Basner and de Marées, 1993). Around six years of age, a child's head size has reached 90 to 95 percent of an adult's. That is, the head is disproportionately large at that stage of development, destabilizing the child's state of equilibrium when riding a bicycle. The child's efforts to keep equilibrium are further complicated by the fact that children clearly have proportionately less muscle mass than body height and body mass. For example, posturographic analysis has shown that the stability of posture of primary school children is three to six times lower than that of adults. Given that posture is the basis for behavior, the implications for children's road safety are clear. Lastly, primary school children are shorter than adults. As trivial as that may sound, it, too, has tremendous consequences for the safety of children in the traffic environment. They can be hidden by parked cars. In average children do not reach the average height of a car, 1.40 m, before nine years of age. The drivers of approaching motor vehicles have only a reduced possibility to detect them. These parked cars restrict the field of vision for children as well, reducing the possibility that they will detect approaching cars. In other words, even if perceptual information strategies are available to children, they must often go unused because the relation between children's body heights and cluttered sidewalks reduces visibility in traffic environments. Second, the lower body height of children shortens their stride in comparison to an adult's, meaning that children despite their higher pace need a longer time to cross the carriageway than an adult does. It might be hard for road-safety training to alter these adverse facts.

Socioeconomic factors need to be recognized also (see Bagley, 1992, for an outline of methodological problems in this research). Accident frequency correlates with such indicators of the family situation as income, familiy structure, and housing conditions (Bagley, 1992). Three- to five-year-old children of parents with fairly low social status are less supervised by their parents than same-aged children of parents with higher social status, even after interventions by a traffic club (West, Sammons, & West, 1993). Vormweg (1989), who analyzed the possible influence that residential area structures (and related factors) had on accidents of children in Hamburg over a period of four years (1984 through 1987), found that accident rates of preschool children were high in areas of low social status (as measured by the average income of the residents) and high traffic volume inside the particular area. This disproportionate injury rate is consistent with that reported in studies from other countries (Pless, Verrault, Arsenault, Frappier, & Stulginskas, 1987; Rivara & Barber, 1985). In Germany foreign preschool children have an accident rate two to three times higher than German preschool children (statistical basis: 15 cities; Hohenadel, Porschen, & Seliger, 1985). Although all these socioeconomic factors have something to do with child safety in traffic environments, are they not far beyond the scope of road-safety training?

Lastly Köhler's clinical work (1983) has a bearing on road-safety training for children. His diagnostic analysis showed two distinct types of "accident children." Type-1-children showed a more cognitive-impulsive style of behavior and higher scores on an extraversion scale. Köhler's type-2-children suffered from stress from different sources and had above-average scores on a neuroticism scale. Both types of disposition can indicate above-average traffic risk. One can question whether clinical or differential properties of children can be influenced by road-safety training.

2.2.4 A second conclusion

In the previous section we presented some of the problems that should be solved, or at least reduced, if an intervention based on road-safety training is intended. However, the developmental and social nature of those problems prevent them from being solved by safety training. Obviously, there is only so much one can do to adapt children to their automobile-dominated surroundings (leaving aside the question whether it would be desirable). And why should the issue of children's accident prevention be anchored within the developing child? Why should a specific group of persons, children in this case, be expected to change their behavior, while other road-users are left to behave as they behaved before? It is difficult to understand why researchers suggest changing the behavior of persons who did not cause the problem of traffic safety. Researchers should instead address the problem at its roots. Those who do not like to restrict children's independent mobility could support two strategies, (a) development of behavior modifying measures for drivers of motor vehicles, and (b) alteration of the traffic environment. Despite different campaigns, despite the legal requirement to pay regard to weaker road users, motor vehicle drivers who were observed in various studies did not change their behavior decisively, if at all, when a child was playing on a sidewalk close to the road (Kockelke & Steinbrecher, 1983; Oude Egberink, Lourens, & van der Molen, 1986; Reichardt & Hehlen, 1980). Drivers' actions in the presence of a child pedestrian who enters the roadway is virtually never defensive, so there is one strategy left: the alteration of the traffic environment. Given what we have presented in the preceding sections, the traffic environment should be designed to direct motor-vehicle drivers to a behavior that accommodates the behavioral capabilities of children and – maybe even more effective – to an intelligent choice of transport mode guided by mobility management (Fiedler & Thiesies, 1993; Heine, 1995). That is, one has to identify and analyze the particular action-guiding utilities of the traffic environment as perceived by drivers. The traffic environment also has to be designed with the behavioral properties of children in mind. One must analyze how children perceive their environment, must anticipate the locations at which problems may occur, and must then design or redesign the traffic environment to allow for the behavioral apparatus of children. To sum up, one needs an approach, a program that facilitates the diagnosis of properties of an environment and its organisms, and permits the intervention and evaluation of organism-related environmental design. Based on the presentation and discussion thus far this chapter, our conclusion is that an elaborated ecological approach like that by James J. Gibson may serve such a purpose suitably. This approach will be outlined in the next section.

3   The future of an ecological approach to traffic

The reasoning in this chapter has been that the ecological approach should use the concept of affordance especially to alter the modern traffic environment so that it has functional utilities for all road users. However, it must be conceded today that the ecological approach has optimized only certain components of the present traffic system. Since Gibson and Crooks's (1938) analysis of the perceptual and control characteristics of driving, ecological researchers have developed a tradition in dealing with problems of egomotion and vehicular egomotion and have tried to optimize the information needed for appropriate action (see Warren & Wertheim, 1990). Berthelon, Mestre, and Peruch (1991), Landwehr (1991), Schiff, Arnone, and Cross (1994), and Schiff and Arnone (1995) are exclusively concerned with automobile traffic and problems of ecological optics. In our opinion, however, the theoretical framework of the ecological approach has the potential to improve the urban contexts of children (and people in general) by changing the traffic environment.

3.1 The challenge

In the framework of the ecological approach, one should, first, try to develop actor-referential descriptions of the traffic environment. Second, one should generate hypotheses about possible affordances of the traffic environment and should analyze them. If these steps are successful, then the identified affordance structure can be applied as a diagnostic instrument to ascertain the shortcomings of the traffic environment relative to the particular road user. That is, the knowledge about the affordances necessary for a street to be defined as an affordance structure for an urban child can be used to analyze whether the existing design of traffic environment X affords an activity Y for a child Z. Furthermore, listings of identified affordance structures can be used for anticipatory and retrospective evaluations. During the planning phase one can estimate which functional utilities (in terms of activities permitted by the designed environment) will be perceived by particular road users in the absence of certain components of the affordance structure. This instrument can also be used for retrospective evaluation. Suppose, for example, that one were to design a sidewalk with the intended utility X for senior citizens. If the utility X is not detected by a sample of pedestrians with those action capabilities but is detected by a sample with different action capabilities, one can possibly explain the error by comparing the measure (the sidewalk) with the standard postulated by the affordance structure checklist.

These thoughts are simply a prospect of the potential that the ecological approach has for the design of traffic environments. Before pursuing these ideas, one should focus on the further clarification and development of the concept of affordance. To advance this concept for the designing of environments, it is necessary to ask, first, what the criteria are for the successful design of affordances and, second, how an analysis of affordances should be conducted. We now attempt to outline one direction that the ecological approach could take.

3.2 An actor-referential description of a street

Gibson (1979, p. 2) emphasized "first, the environment must be described, since what there is to be perceived has to be stipulated before one can even talk about perceiving it." In section 1.1 of this chapter the environment (to be perceived) was described in the basic terms of substance, medium, and surface. In section 1.2 it was shown that light carries information for the perception of surfaces. In section 1.3 it was shown that there is information for the perception of what surfaces and layouts of surfaces afford. On this necessary logical basis, it is possible to describe environments in terms of what they afford, or may afford, the organism. Space precludes the actor-referential descriptions of the traffic environment that are actually called for in this chapter, so we confine ourselves to presenting a conceptual framework of an affordance-guided approach to environmental description and outline a child- and driver-referential description of streets as an example of the traffic environment.

Taking an ecological point of view, that is, an affordance perspective, Heft (1988) analyzed descriptive studies of children's outdoor play, including Barker and Wright (1951). His work revealed an alternative to the standard classification of environmental features and a set of functional properties of children's environments. First, as Heft maintained, environmental features should in principle be described in terms of their functional significance for an organism, that is, in terms of their relational specification instead of their independence from a particular organism. Thus, a street's affordances for a child differ from those for a driver. Second, there is an "experiential primacy of the functional significances" (Heft, 1988, p. 31). Therefore, environment should not be described in abstractions derived from immediate experience. Instead of talking of a "street," one should note the "ride-on-able surface." Third, an environmental property can have multiple affordances, whereas standard classifications of environmental features are mutually exclusive. From an ecological point of view, a tree near the curb can be perceived as a "hide-behind-able feature" or as a "climb-on-able feature." However, a "tree" cannot be a transformer booth. Both tree and booth can afford, however, "hide-behind-ability." Fourth, an ecological description of environmental properties reflects the fact that they have a developmental dimension. A "swing-on-able feature" for a four-year old becomes a "break-and-fall-down-able feature" for the child at the age of seven. In terms of standard classification, though, the particular feature does not change; it remains a "tree limb."

Bearing in mind Heft's ideas about a functional approach to environmental description and Gibson's nomenclature for surface layout (1979, pp. 33-42), we now offer a description of an environmental feature that has been called a street in the pre-Gibsonian age. For a child (depending on his or her visuo-motor development as a basis of behavioral capabilities), a street has a flat, relatively smooth surface that affords walking, running, cycling, skateboarding, and so on. A street may have climbable and hide-behind-able features near the curb. They afford looking out from and going out of sight. At its transversal edges a street may have a distinctive surface with a specific texture that affords safe walking or children's games. A street may have temporary attached objects close to the distinctive surface with a specific texture. These objects (parked cars) afford non-detectability of information for safe crossing and walking-through-ability as apertures between them in a cluttered traffic environment. On the street there move detached objects that afford non-walkability, non-cycle-ability, non-cross-ability, vulnerability, etc., in short: non-act-on-ability.

For a car driver a street has a flat, relatively smooth surface that affords moving. If this flat surface allows drivers an unobstructed line of sight, it affords fast driving. A street may have information-impedable features near the curb. They afford non-detectability of detached objects that may appear to cross the street. These features may afford slower move-ability. On the street there move detached objects that cause an optical magnification in the driver's optic array at the eye and thus afford braking. Other detached objects may move across the street, affording temporary barriers for fast moving. In general all surface layouts on the street that produce slopes, narrowings or lateral dislocations reduce the functional utilities of this environmental property for fast moving.

Certainly, this list could be continued with the necessary scientific seriousness. For the present purpose it might be more relevant to draw conclusions from this unusual description. This, and only this, functional approach makes evident that a single environmental feature (defined in an organism-neutral frame of reference) has particular functional significance for a given actor. (That is, it is more than one environmental feature from the ecological point of view.) Second, this mode of description shows that a single environmental feature can have multiple affordances. One street feature provides a utility for either good or ill, depending on the actor. Third, functional utilities for a class of actors can eliminate functional utilities for another class of actors. Fourth, functional descriptions can give initial clues to conflicts that must be considered. For instance, an even ground surface is known to afford very rapid movement for car drivers and young cyclists or skateboarders. If both groups of users act on this information for their respective affordances, a conflict between them cannot be avoided. This situation might become more complicated if one recognizes that this kind of surface simultaneously affords playing and exploration by still other children. Lastly, this approach serves as a heuristic. By functionally describing the environment from the point of view of a particular organism, one can generate hypotheses about possible affordances that can alter the traffic environment by design. Thus, one can now ask what the criteria are for the successful design of affordances.

3.3   Four criteria for the design of affordances

3.3.1   Criteria 1 and 2

Two criteria (see Warren, 1985) can be deduced easily from the presentation of the affordance concept so far. First, the design of the environmental property must fit the behavioral capabilities of the person participating in the traffic. Second, the affordance has to be perceptually specific to the organism. This fact has implications for city and transportation planning. Planners must know the person's action-guiding informational basis if they are to design the traffic environment successfully. The significance to be perceived in environmental properties has to stem from their design, which must be in keeping with the action they offer. Here the design of a traffic environment can be enriched by knowledge from product-design research. The everyday things that are easiest to use are those that do not require processes of problem-solving thinking. In other words, design for traffic environments should be self-explanatory (for theory and examples see Smets, 1994, and Norman, 1988).

3.3.2   Criterion 3

The first two criteria were functional (and functionalistic) in nature. However, from product-design research, it is known that the use of a product is conditioned by both functionability and the product's emotional components. What is relevant, in other words, is not only the interrelated criteria of fitting the action capabilities and the self-explanatory quality but also the user's, or potential user's, emotion that is associated with the design. Thus, the third criterion for successful design of affordances is the affective interaction between the person and the designed environmental property. Following Smets (1994), we call this criterion the "expressivity of design." It can be illustrated by the implementation of play streets in residential areas. In these streets, which give the right of way to pedestrians, especially to children, it is not sufficient to reduce the functional utility for car drivers by physical measures like humps, narrowings, and lateral dislocations to enforce a speed limit of 7.5 km/h. The design of this surface layout should generate emotions like "being unwelcome" for car drivers and "fit for fun" for children, too.

3.3.3   Criterion 4

Affordance researchers (e.g., Warren, 1985) confined themselves to the analyses of singular and well-defined activities. The primacy of functional optimizing of organism-environment systems was an intuitive homage to Ostwald's energetic imperative "do not waste energy, utilize it" (Schmale, 1983). In this sense one obtains perfect perceiving-acting cycles that are desired explicitly by the first two criteria. While emphasizing the optimization of functional utilities for an individual or a class of functional equivalent organisms, affordance researchers did not address the social and/or environmental consequences of their scientific results. "Teleological guidelines" (Schmale, 1983) for the relationship between organism and environment had not been introduced. Such guidelines may be irrelevant for sitting (Mark, 1987), walking through apertures (Warren & Whang, 1987), or any other activity that has no social or environmental impact. However, traffic is different. As everybody knows, motorized traffic has tremendous social and environmental impacts. Hüttenmoser's (1994) studies on the social incompatibility of today's traffic have shown that social and psychomotor development, such as autonomy and the ability to keep balance, is reduced in children who are not allowed to play outside alone because of traffic conditions, thus making traffic a threat to the development of children. It is evident from the tenets of developmental psychology within the ecological approach that children should have the possibility to explore their environment in order to differentiate their perceiving-acting cycles. Thus there are theoretical reasons and external reasons (social and environmental impacts of motorized traffic) to introduce a fourth criterion for the successful design of affordances: the assessment of a designed affordance's social and environmental impact. It should serve as a correction factor of possible consequences of the first three criteria. Together the four criteria will contribute to the successful design of the traffic environment by helping planners focus on the functional utilities of environmentally and socially compatible transportation systems.

3.4 The affordance analysis

To determine whether the required four criteria for the successful design of affordances are met, one must analyze the task-specific variables of the particular organism-environment system. As noted earlier in this chapter, affordance analysis has to take into account, first, that any environmental property has to be measured relative to the organism and, second, that the consideration of the organism-referential must not reduce the measurement to the generation of idiosyncratic values or outcomes of subjective experience.

3.4.1 Criteria 1 and 2

To assess whether a designed environmental property fits the behavioral capabilities of a road user, one has to perform measurements based on the principles of intrinsic metrics (Warren & Shaw, 1981). This procedure facilitates a physical description of the environment and takes into account the functional significance of the environment relative to the organism. The particular task-specific variable of the organism's action system is defined as standard. If one applies this body-scaled metric by scaling the environmental property against the organism's variable in the unit of the task-specific organismic property, a dimensionless number (Buckingham, 1914; McMahon & Bonner, 1985) will result. The value of this dimensionless number indicates the fit between the environmental property and the organism. For the purpose of environmental design it is fruitful to compute optimal and pessimal values of this organism-environment fit. The pessimal point is obtained if a phase transition from the original behavior to a different behavior begins. The optimal point is defined by the most task-specific efficiency (operationalized, for example, in terms of energetics, as in Warren, 1985). Because those intrinsic values are dimensionless, optimal and pessimal points are constants for organisms of a functionally equivalent class. The first criterion is met if the designed environmental property is compatible with the optimal or pessimal point (depending on the task).

In the next step the perceptual specification of the functional utility for the user of the particular environmental property has to be analyzed. That is, one must ask whether the pessimal and optimal points are identified as such by means of perceptual analysis. From a pragmatic perspective one can perform this task by simple estimation. From a basic perspective of the ecological approach, one should be interested in the modal information an organism uses. Thus, one has to search for the particular transformational and structural invariants that are detected in the ambient optic array by the individual (Shaw, McIntyre, & Mace, 1974).

3.4.2   Criterion 3

When it comes to the analysis of the third criterion for successful environmental design, the expressivity of design, the ecological approach seems to encounter problems. The third criterion has not yet been a focus of empirical affordance analysis. Within the ecological approach, however, there is knowledge from another area of research that might be fruitful for analysis of the affective interactions between a person and an environmental property. Based on the results of ecological face perception (Alley, 1988; for comments see Heine, 1990), a concept for the analysis of the expressivity of affordances is outlined.

Since the 1970s Shaw and his colleagues (e.g., Pittenger & Shaw, 1975) have developed a morphogenetic model of craniofacial growth. Orthodontists use this model to anticipate growth effects in children with craniofacial anomalies. Pittenger, Shaw, and Mark (1979) applied cardioidal transformations not only to face profiles but also to drawings of a Volkswagen bug. The researchers showed that the application of this transformation had a consistent effect on the perceived age of the car. Close inspection of particular forms of the car shows that they are associated with different emotions. Further empirical support for this outline of the analysis of the expressivity of affordances is provided by Alley (1983), whose subjects responded with more or less emotion to protect a child after presentation of cardioidally transformed displays with children's heads (Alley, 1988, cites similar examples). What does that mean for the third step of affordance analysis? An object's particular appearance, generated by application of a transformational invariant, can contain a particular emotion. Distinct appearance can, therefore, lend distinct expressivity to the designed object (Smets, 1994, advocates the application of form semantics to achieve the same purpose).

3.4.3   Criterion 4

How can one conduct the assessment of a designed affordance's social and environmental impact? Previous empirical research within the framework of the ecological approach offers little to go by. Generally speaking, one has to determine whether the current state of affordances or the implementation of a designed environmental property is causing intolerable social and environmental impacts.

In this vein, then, the question is whether the environmental properties of urban contexts support some activity of children. What kind of activity is offered by a main street? Because modern urban streets are collections of functional utilities for drivers, are not children being required to function successfully in an environmental context that provides them with nothing to serve this purpose? These issues are the starting point for the fourth step of affordance analysis. One can examine the distribution of functional utilities across the classes of road users, noting whether the current or planned affordance can help redistribute action capabilities to the benefit of environmentally and socially compatible transportation systems. In this procedure it is taken for granted that the functional approach to environmental description (see section 3.2) will be optimized. The status of motor development (see Hüttenmoser, 1994) in children living in the area (whose streets should be analyzed for their functional utilities) can be another indicator of whether criterion 4 is fulfilled.

3.5   Area-wide traffic calming

We have now outlined a direction that the ecological approach can follow in the future if it is not aimed at adapting children's behavior to the demands of motorized traffic but at adapting traffic to the needs of children (and pedestrians, cyclists, users of public transport, and so forth). To fill in this picture somewhat, we conclude with examples of intuitively affordance-oriented measures of area-wide traffic calming in Buxtehude (Germany). As mere illustrations of changes that can be made in the physical properties of traffic environments, however, they must not be understood as measures that satisfy the requirements discussed in the previous sections of this chapter.

Measures for alteration of the traffic environment were pursued in Buxtehude to improve the safety, speed, and comfort of pedestrian and bicycle traffic as a basis for the mobility of nonmotorized persons. Furthermore, neighborhood recreation and local environmental conditions should be enhanced. To achieve these goals, planners modified environmental properties to diminish the functional utilities of streets for motor-vehicle locomotion. That is, they reduced affordances for drivers and created affordances for pedestrians, especially for children, and cyclists. They made public space usable again by reducing the number of cars in the town center, lowering the speed of cars to 30 km/h (approximately 20 mph), and reclaiming areas for walking and cycling.

These improvements in the quality of the urban environments stemmed, first, from planners' recognition that the bicycle network was not sufficient. Because of serious discontinuities in bicycle routes (e.g., one-way streets), unsafe intersections, and other drawbacks, the bicycle network as an environmental property did not have enough perceivable functional utility for cyclists. Then, among other things, routes important for bicycle traffic were designed as "bicycle streets," where cyclists have the right of way. Cars and trucks are only tolerated. They are not allowed to pass bicycles. Despite the "no passing" signs posted in these areas, however, cars still overtake cyclists, crowding them to the edge of the road if it widens slightly. To reduce the utility for motor-vehicle locomotion, engineers have narrowed the streets to a point that cars can move, but cannot pass a cyclist. This measure thus reduces an affordance for car drivers while increasing the functional utility of the route network for cyclists. In streets with heavy traffic, cycle paths on both sides were built in space taken from the main carriageway. Posting a road sign prescribing, say, a speed limit merely adds symbolic information that would be nothing more than a single contradictory item for car drivers. It is unlikely to influence their behavior much at all because the affordance of fast movement still exists. Research in area-wide traffic calming has shown that automobile traffic can be slowed only through radical change in the whole setting.[4] Thus, actual and optical road narrowings, raised pavings, 10 percent ramps at crossing points, and redesign of the free right-turn lanes for cars successfully reduced the motor-vehicle affordance structure of Buxtehude. These and other measures (for full documentation see Krause, 1989) augmented the functional utilities of the urban environment for pedestrians and cyclists in terms of their mobility and possibilities to use public space again. Many of these measures could be optimized by applying tools that were developed by the ecological approach. For example, the affordance concept could be especially helpful for determining the spatial dimensions necessary for cyclists (proposed in Heine & Guski, 1994). And using the knowledge of ecological optics to narrow streets might increase the effect of lowered speed.

Certainly, it is by no means easy to apply the concept of affordances to traffic and urban planning, and, in turn, it poses new theoretical problems for Gibson's kind of ecological psychology. However, we hope that we have shown it is possible to reduce the disparity between the impacts of street traffic and the behavioral capabilities of children (among other nonmotorized road-users) by applying the concept of affordances as a means of shaping the environment.

Notes

1 This manuscript is part of the first author's post-doctoral thesis submitted in partial fulfillment of the requirements for a German professorship.
2 Full documentation of the ecological approach and further developments elaborated since 1979 goes beyond the scope of this chapter. The reader is referred for further reference to the eleven volumes of the book series entitled Resources for ecological psychology, edited by Shaw, Mace, and Turvey.
3 The interested reader might see certain similarities to the concept of valence (Lewin, 1935) or that of demand character (Koffka, 1935). When discussing the origin of the concept of affor-

dances, J. J. Gibson (1979, p. 138) stated "the concept of affordance is derived from these concepts of valence, invitation, and demand." However, he stressed a "crucial difference" between the concept of affordance and the others: "The affordance of something *does not change* as the need of the observer changes" (Gibson, 1979, pp. 138-139; italics by Gibson). An affordance may be selectively attended to. E. J. Gibson listed as an antecedent of the concept of affordance Tolman's "manipulanda" as a case of "behavior supports", too. She stated: "None of these predecessors carries the entire meaning of affordance, but each emphasizes some aspect of it" (1982, p. 62).

4 In a regression model identifying the most significant factors that influence speed change, Engel and Thomsen (1992) showed that the height of a hump is of greatest relevance for speed change. They also included two examples of how to calculate the expected influence on speed as a function of the implementation of a specific type of countermeasure.

References

Allenbach, R. (1995). Verkehrssicherheit auf Schulwegen [Traffic safety on school routes]. *Zeitschrift für Verkehrssicherheit, 41*, 87-91.

Alley, T. R. (1983). Growth-produced changes in body shape and size as determinants of perceived age and adult caregiving. *Child Development, 54*, 241-248.

Alley, T. R. (Ed.). (1988). *Social and applied aspects of perceiving faces.* Hillsdale, NJ: Erlbaum.

Altman, I. (1975). *The environment and social behavior.* Monterey, CA: Brooks/Cole.

Altman, I., & Rogoff, B. (1987). World views in psychology: Trait, interactional, organismic, and transactional perspectives. In D. Stokols & I. Altman (Eds.), *Handbook of environmental psychology* (Vol. 1, pp. 1-40). New York: Wiley.

Appleyard, D., & Lintell, M. (1972). The environmental quality of city streets: The resident viewpoint. *Journal of the American Institute of Planners, 38,* 84-101.

Bagley, C. (1992). The urban setting of juvenile pedestrian injuries: A study of behavioural ecology and social disadvantage. *Accident Analysis & Prevention, 24,* 673-678.

Barker, R. G. (1968). *Ecological psychology: Concepts and methods for studying the environment of human behavior.* Stanford, CA: Stanford University Press.

Barker, R. G., & Wright, H. F. (1951). *One boy's day: A specimen record of behavior.* New York: Harper.

Basner, B., & Marées, H. de (1993). *Fahrrad- und Straßenverkehrstüchtigkeit von Grundschülern* [Bicycle and road fitness of grade-schoolers]. Münster: Gemeindeunfallversicherungsverband Westfalen-Lippe.

Berthelon, C., Mestre, D., & Peruch, P. (1991). Perception of a moving vehicle when approaching an intersection. In A. G. Gale, I. D. Brown, C. M. Haslegrave, I. Moorhead, & S. Taylor (Eds.), *Vision in vehicles III* (pp. 127-133). Amsterdam: Elsevier.

Blendermann, K.-A. (1987). Gefährliche Denkhaltungen junger Fußgänger – Erfahrungen aus der Schulpraxis zum Thema: Gesehenwerden [Hazardous attitudes of young pedestrians. Experiences from practices at school on the subject of being seen]. *Zeitschrift für Verkehrssicherheit, 33,* 36-39.

Bronfenbrenner, U. (1977). Toward an experimental ecology of human development. *American Psychologist, 32,* 513-531.

Bruce, V., & Green, P. R. (1990). *Visual perception: Physiology, psychology and ecology* (2nd ed. Hillsdale, NJ: Erlbaum.

Buckingham, E. (1914). On physically similar systems: Illustrations of the use of dimensional equations. *Physical Review, 4*, 345-376.

Bundesminister für Verkehr. (1994). *Verkehr in Zahlen 1994* [Traffic statistics, 1994]. Bonn: n. p.

Cohen, A. S., & Fischer, H. (1982). Wie sich Kinder die Fahrgeschwindigkeit von Fahrzeugen in Abhängigkeit von deren Merkmalen vorstellen [How children imagine the speed of moving vehicles as a function of their characteristics]. *Zeitschrift für Verkehrssicherheit, 28*, 177-180.

Engel, U., & Thomsen, L. (1992). Safety effects of speed reducing measures in Danish residential areas. *Accident Analysis & Prevention, 24*, 17-28.

Fiedler, J., & Thiesies, M. (1993). Mobilitätsmanagement – Was ist das? [What is mobility management?] *Nahverkehrspraxis, 41*, 223-225.

Füsser, K., Jakobs, A., & Steinbrecher, J. (1993). *Sicherheitsbewertung von Querungshilfen für den Fußgängerverkehr* [Assessment of the safety of pedestrian crossing facilities]. Bergisch Gladbach: Bundesanstalt für Straßenwesen.

Gärling, A., & Gärling, T. (1990). Parents' residential satisfaction and perception of children's accident risk. *Journal of Environmental Psychology, 10*, 27-36.

Gibson, E. J. (1982). The concept of affordances in development: The renaiscence of functionalism. In W. A. Collins (Ed.), *The concept of development* (pp. 55-81). Hillsdale, NJ: Erlbaum.

Gibson, E. J. (1988). Exploratory behavior in the development of perceiving, acting, and the acquisition of knowledge. *Annual Review of Psychology, 39*, 1-41.

Gibson, E. J., & Spelke, E. S. (1983). The development of perception. In P. H. Mussen (Ed.), *Handbook of child psychology* (Vol. 3, pp. 1-76). New York: Wiley.

Gibson, J. J. (1966). *The senses considered as perceptual systems*. Boston, MA: Houghton Mifflin.

Gibson, J. J. (1979). *The ecological approach to visual perception*. Boston, MA: Houghton Mifflin.

Gibson, J. J., & Crooks, L. E. (1938). A theoretical field-analysis of automobile-driving. *American Journal of Psychology, 51*, 453-471.

Grayson, G. B. (1975). *Observations of pedestrian behaviour at four sites* (Research Rep. No. 670). Crowthorne (GB): Transport and Road Research Laboratory.

Hart, R. A. (1979). *Children's experience of place*. New York: Irvington.

Heft, H. (1988). Affordances of children's environments: A functional approach to environmental description. *Children's Environments Quarterly, 5*, 29-37.

Heine, W.-D. (1990). Gesichtswahrnehmung als Beispiel der ökologischen Herangehensweise (sensu Gibson) an einen sozialpsychologischen Gegenstand [Perception of faces as an example of the ecological approach (in Gibson's sense) to a sociopsychological object]. *Zeitschrift für Sozialpsychologie, 21*, 143-146

Heine, W.-D. (1994). *An ecological consideration of stimulus-response compatibility*. Münster: Waxmann.

Heine, W.-D. (1995). Verhaltenswissenschaft und Mobilitätsmanagement [Behavioral science and mobility management]. In mobilité (Ed.), *Mobilitätsberatung – Erfahrungen und Perspektiven* (pp. 45-60). Cologne: mobilité.

Heine, W.-D., & Guski, R. (1994). Aspekte des Verkehrsverhaltens aus Sicht des ökologischen Ansatzes von J. J. Gibson [Aspects of traffic behavior from the viewpoint of J. J. Gibson's ecological approach]. In A. Flade (Ed.), *Mobilitätsverhalten – Bedingungen und Veränderungen aus umweltpsychologischer Sicht* (pp. 65-80). Weinheim: Beltz, Psychologie Verlags Union.

Hofsten, C. von (1983). Catching skills in infancy. *Journal of Experimental Psychology: Human Perception and Performance, 9,* 75-85.

Hohenadel, D., Porschen, K. M., & Seliger, A. (1985). Verkehrssicherheit ausländischer Kinder [The traffic safety of foreign children]. *Zeitschrift für Verkehrssicherheit, 31,* 133-135.

Hüttenmoser, M. (1994). Auswirkungen des Straßenverkehrs auf die Entwicklung der Kinder und den Alltag junger Familien [Effects of road traffic on the development of children and the everyday life of young families]. In A. Flade (Ed.), *Mobilitätsverhalten – Bedingungen und Veränderungsmöglichkeiten aus umweltpsychologischer Sicht* (pp. 171-181). Weinheim: Beltz, Psychologie Verlags Union.

Johnston, T. D., & Turvey, M. T. (1980). A sketch of an ecological metatheory for theories of learning. In G. H. Bower (Ed.), *The psychology of learning and motivation* (Vol. 14, pp. 147-205). London: Academic Press.

Kockelke, W., & Steinbrecher, J. (1983). Sicherheit von Kindern und älteren Menschen im Verkehr [The safety of children and the aged in traffic]. *Zeitschrift für Verkehrssicherheit, 29,* 10-14.

Koelega, H. S. (Ed.). (1987). Environmental annoyance: Characterization, measurement, and control. *Proceedings of the International Symposium on Environmental Annoyance.* Amsterdam: Elsevier.

Köhler, G. (1983). *Unfall ist kein Zufall* [Accidents are not pure chance]. Heidelberg: G. Schindele.

Koffka, K. (1935). *Principles of gestalt psychology.* New York: Harcourt Brace.

Konczak, J., Meeuwsen, H. J., & Cress, M. E. (1992). Changing affordances in stair-climbing: The perception of maximum climbability in young and older adults. *Journal of Experimental Psychology: Human Perception and Performance, 18,* 691-697.

Krause, J. (1989). *Modellvorhaben Flächenhafte Verkehrsberuhigung* [Pilot project on area-wide traffic calming] (Vol. 1, Maßnahmendokumentation Teil Buxtehude). Bergisch Gladbach: Bundesanstalt für Straßenwesen.

Landwehr, K. (1991). Optical guidance revisited. In A. G. Gale, I. D. Brown, C. M. Haslegrave, I. Moorhead, & S. Taylor (Eds.), *Vision in vehicles III* (pp. 187-194). Amsterdam: Elsevier.

Lazarus, R. S. (1991). Cognition and motivation in emotion. *American Psychologist, 46,* 352-367.

Lazarus, R. S., & Launier, R. (1978). Stress-related transactions between person and environment. In L. Pervin & M. Lewis (Eds.), *Perspectives in interactional psychology* (pp. 1-67). New York: Plenum.

Lee, D. N. (1976). A theory of visual control of braking based on information about time to collision. *Perception, 5,* 437-459.

Lee, D. N., & Lishman, R. (1977). Visual control of locomotion. *Scandinavian Journal of Psychology, 18,* 224-230.

Lee, D. N., Young, D. S., & McLaughlin, C. M. (1984). A roadside simulation of road crossing for children. *Ergonomics, 27,* 1271-1281.

Lewin, K. (1935). *A dynamic theory of personality.* New York: McGraw-Hill.

Limbourg, M. (1994). *Kinder im Straßenverkehr* [Children in street traffic]. Münster: Gemeindeunfallversicherungsverband Westfalen-Lippe.

Limbourg, M., & Gerber, W. D. (1978). Das Verhalten von drei- bis siebenjährigen Kindern bei der Straßenüberquerung unter Ablenkungsbedingungen [Street-crossing behavior of 3- to 7-year olds under distracting conditions]. *Zeitschrift für Verkehrserziehung, 28,* 10-13.

Limbourg, M., & Günther, R. (1977). Erleben und Verhalten von vier- bis neunjährigen Kindern im Straßenverkehr [The experience and behavior of 4- to 9-year olds in road traffic]. *Zeitschrift für Verkehrserziehung, 27*, 3-8.

Mace, W. (1986). J. J. Gibson's ecological theory of information pickup: Cognition from the ground up. In T. J. Knapp & L. C. Robertson (Eds.), *Approaches to cognition: Contrasts and controversies* (pp. 137-157). Hillsdale, NJ: Erlbaum.

Malek, M., Guyer, B., & Lescohier, I. (1990). The epidemiology and prevention of child pedestrian injury. *Accident Analysis & Prevention, 22*, 301-313.

Mark, L. S. (1987). Eyeheight-scaled information about affordances: A case study of sitting and stair-climbing. *Journal of Experimental Psychology: Human Perception and* Performance, 13, 361-370.

McMahon, T. A., & Bonner, J. T. (1985). *Form und Leben* [Form and life]. Heidelberg: Spektrum Akademischer Verlag.

Michaels, C. F., & Carello, C. (1981). *Direct perception*. Englewood Cliffs: Prentice Hall.

Norman, D. A. (1988). *The psychology of everyday things*. New York: Basic Books.

Oude Egberink, H., Lourens, P. F., & van der Molen, H. H. (1986). Driving strategies among younger and older drivers when encountering children. *Accident Analysis & Prevention, 18*, 315-324.

Peter-Habermann, I. (1974). *Motorisierte Verkehrsteilnehmer im Erleben von Kindern* [Motorized road users as experienced by children]. Bergisch Gladbach: Bundesanstalt für Straßenwesen.

Pittenger, J. B., & Shaw, R. E. (1975). Aging faces as viscal-elastic events: Implications for a theory of nonrigid shape perception. *Journal of Experimental Psychology: Human Perception and Performance, 1*, 374-382.

Pittenger, J. B., Shaw, R. E., & Mark, L. S. (1979). Perceptual information for the age level of faces as a higher order invariant of growth. *Journal of Experimental Psychology: Human Perception and Performance, 5*, 478-493.

Pless, I. B., Verrault, R., Arsenault, L., Frappier, J. Y., & Stulginskas, J. (1987). The epidemiology of road accidents in childhood. *American Journal of Public Health, 77*, 358-360.

Proshansky, H. M. (1973). Theoretical issues in "environmental psychology." *Representative Research in Social* Psychology, 4, 93-107.

Reichardt, P., & Hehlen, P. (1980). Verhalten von Automobilisten gegenüber Kindern im Straßenverkehr [Behavior of drivers when encountering children on the road]. *Zeitschrift für Verkehrssicherheit, 26*, 81-82.

Rivara, F. P., & Barber, M. (1985). Demographic analysis of childhood pedestrian injuries. *Pediatrics, 76,* 375-381.

Sandels, S. (1975). *Children in traffic*. London: Paul Elek.

Schagen, I. N. L. G. v., & Brookhuis, K. A. (1994). Training young cyclists to cope with dynamic traffic situations. *Accident Analysis & Prevention, 26*, 223-230.

Schiff, W. (1965). Perception of impending collision: A study of visually directed behavior. *Psychological Monographs: General and Applied, 79,* Whole No. 604.

Schiff, W., & Arnone, W. (1995). Perceiving and driving: Where parallel roads meet. In P. A. Hancock, J. M. Flach, J. K. Caird, & K. J. Vicente (Eds.), *Local applications of the ecological approach to human-machine systems* (pp. 1-35). Hillsdale, NJ: Erlbaum.

Schiff, W., Arnone, W., & Cross, S. (1994). Driving assessment with computer-video scenarios: More is sometimes better. *Behavior Research Methods, Instruments, & Computers, 26*, 192-194.

Schiff, W., Caviness, J. A., & Gibson, J. J. (1962). Persistent fear responses in rhesus monkeys to the optical stimulus of "looming." *Science, 136,* 982-983.

Schmale, H. (1983). *Psychologie der Arbeit* [Psychology of work]. Stuttgart: Klett-Cotta.

Shaw, R. E., Mace, W. M., & Turvey, M. T. (Eds.). (1982-1995). *Resources for ecological psychology* (11 vols.). Hillsdale, NJ: Erlbaum.

Shaw, R. E., McIntyre, M., & Mace, W. (1974). The role of symmetry in event perception. In R. B. MacLeod & H. L. Pick (Eds.), *Perception: Essays in honor of James J. Gibson* (pp. 276-310). Ithaca, NY: Cornell University Press.

Shaw, R. E., & Turvey, M. T. (1981). Coalitions as models for ecosystems: A realist perspective on perceptual organization. In M. Kubovy & J. R. Pomerantz (Eds.), *Perceptual organization* (pp. 343-421). Hillsdale, NJ: Erlbaum.

Shaw, R. E., Turvey, M. T., & Mace, W. (1982). Ecological psychology: The consequence of a commitment to realism. In W. Weimer & D. Palermo (Eds.), *Cognition and the symbolic processes II* (pp. 159-226). Hillsdale, NJ: Erlbaum.

Smets, G. (1994). Industrial design engineering and the theory of direct perception and action. In R. Guski & W.-D. Heine (Eds.), *Third European Workshop on Ecological Psychology: Program and Proceedings* (pp. 72-102). Bochum: Ruhr-Universität.

Stokols, D. (1990). Instrumental and spiritual views of people-environment relations. *American Psychologist, 45,* 641-646.

Tolley, R. (1990). A hard road: The problems of walking and cycling in British cities. In R. Tolley (Ed.), *The greening of urban transport: Planning for walking and cycling in Western cities* (pp. 13-33). London: Belhaven.

Torell, G., & Biel, A. (1985). Parental restrictions and children's acquisition of neighborhood knowledge. In T. Gärling & J. Valsiner (Eds.), *Children within environments: Toward a psychology of accident prevention* (pp. 107-118). New York: Plenum.

Turvey, M. T. (1975). Perspective in vision: Conception or perception? In M. Rawson & D. D. Duane (Eds.), *Language, perception and reading* (pp. 131-194). Baltimore, MD: York.

Turvey, M. T., & Carello, C. (1986). The ecological approach to perceiving-acting: A pictorial essay. *Acta Psychologica, 63,* 133-155.

Turvey, M. T., & Kugler, P. N. (1984). An ecological approach to perception and action. In H. T. A. Whiting (Ed.), *Human motor actions--Bernstein reassessed* (pp. 373-412). Amsterdam: North-Holland.

Turvey, M. T., & Shaw, R. E. (1979). The primacy of perceiving: An ecological reformulation of perception for understanding memory. In L.-G. Nilssen (Ed.), *Studies of memory: In honor of Uppsala University's 500th anniversary* (pp. 167-222). Hillsdale, NJ: Erlbaum.

Turvey, M. T., Shaw, R. E., Reed, E. S., & Mace, W. M. (1981). Ecological laws of perceiving and acting: In reply to Fodor and Pylyshyn (1981). *Cognition, 9,* 237-304.

Vormweg, K. (1989). Verkehrsunfälle mit Kindern in Hamburg, 1984-1987 [Traffic accidents with children in Hamburg, 1984-1987]. *Zeitschrift für Verkehrssicherheit, 35,* 138-145.

Warren, R., & Wertheim, A. H. (Eds.). (1990). *Perception and control of self-motion.* Hillsdale, NJ: Erlbaum.

Warren, W. H., Jr. (1984). Perceiving affordances: Visual guidance of stair-climbing. *Journal of Experimental Psychology: Human Perception and Performance, 10,* 683-703.

Warren, W. H., Jr. (1985). *Environmental design as the design of affordances.* Paper presented at the Third International Conference on Event Perception and Action, Uppsala, Sweden.

Warren, W. H., Jr., & Shaw, R. E. (1981). Psychophysics and ecometrics. *The Behavioral and Brain Sciences, 4,* 209-210.

Warren, W. H., Jr., & Whang, S. (1987). Visual guidance of walking through apertures: Body-scaled information for affordances. *Journal of Experimental Psychology: Human Perception and Performance, 13*, 371-383.

West, R., Sammons, P., & West, A. (1993). Effects of a traffic club on road safety knowledge and self-reported behaviour of young children and their parents. *Accident Analysis & Prevention, 25*, 609-618.

Young, D. S., & Lee, D. N. (1987). Training children in road-crossing skills using a roadside simulation. *Accident Analysis & Prevention, 19*, 327-341.

Comment: Children as perceivers and actors – The view from ecological realism

Christian Munz

W. Heine and R. Guski link environmental psychology with J. J. Gibson's ecological approach to visual perception *primarily* by means of an experimental paradigm (Warren, 1984) that belongs to the ecological theory of affordances (Gibson, 1979; Turvey & Shaw, 1979). This paradigm is used as a descriptive device for showing what an affordance is and, "in part," for analyzing the affordances of a street. But that is not all. It is also used as a device for showing how to design an affordance. Holding that the reciprocity of perception and action is the founding principle of the ecological approach and/or ecological psychology (p. 515), the paradigm implies a special understanding of J. J. Gibson's ecological psychology. The authors link J. J. Gibson's ecological approach with environmental psychology also by pointing out the "challenge[ ] for children in our modern world: how to survive and behave in an automobile-dominated society" (p. 521).

This problem is discussed under the issue of strategies to increase traffic safety for children. The authors detail an ecological study by Lee, Young, and McLaughlin (1984), which deals with the most dangerous task for young children, crossing the street. In this study children are taught to detect optical information that specifies time to collision with cars and to use this information adaptively. Do such studies conducted in the spirit of ecological psychology follow the best strategy? Do studies from environmental psychology referred to by the authors? The authors doubt it. They list the characteristic shortcomings of all approaches to road-safety training, but they claim that even the strategy aiming to alter the behavior of car drivers is not good enough. The best strategy instead seems to be one inspired by the goal of altering the whole traffic environment by redesigning it in the interest of all participants, especially children. With this definition of the problem, the authors come back to Gibson's ecological approach, particularly to an extended concept of affordances, which appears now as a means of shaping the environment for solving problems of environmental psychology.

The challenge is, first, to develop actor-referential descriptions of the traffic environment. These descriptions based on naturalistic observations "can generate hypotheses about possible affordances that can alter the traffic environment by design. Thus, one can now ask what the criteria are for the successful design of affordances" (p. 531). The authors describe four criteria for the design (or *successful*

design?) of affordances. The first and second criteria follow Warren's (1984) paradigm in concept and methodology, the third incorporates the expressivity of
affordance design, and the last criterion concerns the social and environmental
impact of the affordance. The third and fourth criteria are extensions of the concept
of affordance (as used in Warren's experiment). The authors claim to refer to an
unpublished programmatic paper by Warren (1985) concerning the successful
design of affordances in all four criteria. With these criteria in mind, they say, one
should analyze affordances. "To determine whether the required four criteria for the
successful design of affordances are met, one must analyze the task-specific variables of the particular organism-environment system" (p. 533). The relevant questions seem to be which tasks children or car drivers have in principle and how these
tasks in principle have to be described. The authors give no further information
about this essential theoretical point. Analyzing the task, one can ask about a
designed property's actional and informational "fit" (Warren, 1985, p. 8)[1] to the
behavioral capabilities of a road user. One might also ask about the users' emotions
relative to expressive qualities of designs. The final criterion concerns the negative
or positive impacts that designs can have, especially on children as traffic participants, impacts that result partly from side effects of designed surface layouts. The
authors' interpretation of area-wide traffic calming in Buxtehude is in line with the
approach taken in the chapter.

1   The ecological approach

At the beginning of the section on the ecological psychology of J. J. Gibson, the
authors present the reciprocity of action and perception as its main assumption or
principle. One may argue that this principle gives ecological psychology semantic
closure (Mace, 1986). But as the most general assumption of the ecological
approach as the authors depict it, it points in the wrong direction. This principle or
assumption is dangerously unecological – even a Piagetian psychologist could agree
with it. From the outset the definition lacks the basic assumption of the reciprocity
of animal and environment (Gibson, 1979; Munz, 1989) or of perceiver and environment (Lombardo, 1987). Of course, the authors refer to the reciprocity of animal
and environment, but only in the sense of it being subordinated to the reciprocity of
perception and action, which in Gibson's account is derived from (Gibson, 1979,
p. 223) "the mutuality of animal and environment" (Gibson, 1979, p. 2).

"A child who moves forward to cross a street generates the outflow of the optical
array. This outflow specifies an approach by entailing magnification (of the other
side of the street)" (p. 517). What the authors call the "magnification (of the other
side of a street)" is not a magnification of the other side of the street but a magnification of the *optical contours* of the ambient optic array, in which the other side of
the street gets projected. These optical contours specify the other side of the street

not as a magnifying layout of the other side of the street (what could that be?) but as a *constant* layout to which the perceiver is directed in a process of locomotory approach. Therefore, the perceptual experience is not an experience of its optical basis, as the authors' statement implies, but an experience of the substantial environment. "Although we pick up optical structure whenever we see anything at all, we do not see that structure itself. Instead, we see what it specifies. This means that the underlying basis of direct perception is not available in phenomenal experience or to systematic introspection" (Neisser, 1991, p. 20).

2   The concept of affordances ill-defined

How do the authors define their core concept of an affordance? They do not use the original Gibsonian concept of an affordance but a concept that defines an affordance as a relationship of compatibility between an animal and an environmental component, or so it seems. Reading this definition, I first thought it would refer to the Neo-Gibsonian concept of compatibility presented by Turvey and Shaw (1979). In that account compatibility explains why an environment is meaningful to an animal. It is meaningful because it is compatible with the effectivities of an animal. To Turvey and Shaw compatibility is an ontological concept stating that if the environment is meaningful to an animal it cannot be meaningful in any other way than through compatible relationships between animal and environment.

But this does not seem to be the definition that Heine and Guski have in mind. If it were, their definition of an affordance would be prescisely inconsistent when they define affordances not only as compatibilities with an "activity for an organism" (p. 520) but also as relationships incompatible with an activity such as an affordance of "non-walkability" of a detached object in relation to a child (p. 530). By definition, this kind of incompatible relationship cannot constitute an affordance! Maybe the authors define affordances implicitly as *properties* that characterize environmental components as compatible *or* not compatible with the activity of an animal. This would be a new definition of what affordances are. Compatibility relationships would involve one set of properties, noncompatibility relationships would involve a different set. Both sets of properties would define the whole set of affordances of an environment for an animal. But what would be a definitional criterion for noncompatibility? The authors would say "non-act-on-ability" (p. 530). The example they give is a driven car, which affords non-act-on-ability for the child as pedestrian. But the child can act upon the car, say, by throwing something at it. In my opinion one cannot even imagine properties of the environment that would define non-act-on-ability. Further, what would be the optimal and pessimal values of the car as an affordance of non-act-on-ability? What would be the expressive qualities? In my opinion these questions do not make any sense. The concept of negative affordances in Gibson's original definition of affordances may be far more powerful here because one would have a robust design criterion, at least in the case of negative affordances for children: Make the set of an environment's negative affordances as small as possible.

There is at least one remaining option: to define noncompatibility of environmental components – be it as non-act-on-ability or otherwise – not in terms of real ecological properties but in terms of lacking action-related reciprocities that one cannot execute because the actions have no environmental and informational support. But this definition would make the affordance concept entirely empty. No meaningful relationship would be excluded through an environmental component, for nothing that one could do with the component would belong to its affordances. The definition would lead out of the realm of affordance theory because affordances have to be informationally specified. To conclude, I do not believe that the authors have a working definition of their core concept. Their affordance concept is inconsistently defined or empty or inconsistent with the assumption that affordances are perceived directly.

3   Environmental psychology: An application of the ecological approach or a theoretical part of it?

Let me assume now that the usage of the term affordance can be restricted to the original – ontological – sense employed by Turvey and Shaw (1979). This version does not include negative affordances, an omission that seems a severe restriction on traffic environments in particular. Nor is this version up to date. Turvey (1992) has revised the concept, but I cannot discuss the change here. So what is the message for the design of traffic environments if one follows Warren's (1984) concept of an affordance and the principles of intrinsic metrics? For the sake of simplicity, assume there are reasons – derivable from observational studies like that of Heft (1988) – that a provision of a stairway for pedestrians is lacking in a distinctive traffic environment. Would the provision of a manufactured stairway be a shaping of an environment through the concept of affordances? Each stairway would also have other affordances as a surface layout. The authors may subsume this fact under their fourth criterion, but it may be more reasonable to speak of shaping the environment through alteration of surfaces, substances, and events. From this perspective the affordance would be more a goal of design, and substances, surfaces, and events would be more the means to achieve this goal. But the provision of a stairway surely has to be evaluated in the spirit of the design of the authors' fourth criterion, and perhaps also the third. I will discuss only the first criterion to single out the crucial points.

What would be reasonable to expect if an environmental psychologist used the design criteria? That person would have a methodology that makes it possible to measure the degree to which environmental components fit with action characteristics of an observer – measures known as phi numbers. Warren's (1984) experimental paradigm has shown this possibility on a conceptual and methodological level. In my opinion this methodology would conceptualize what one does and has done if one alters the environment. But the authors claim additionally that pessimal and optimal values also give criteria for what one *should* do for successful design. One criterion for success may be therefore a functioning stairway. In terms of this methodology this criterion at least means creating a riser height that does not belong to the pessimal values of potential users or user groups such as children. These criteria do in fact capture a criterion of success: One has designed a stairway if what one has designed is at least a stairway for the ascent of potential would-be-climbers. Although this point seems trivial, it describes ecopsychological reality for possible evaluation.

In the same manner, one can argue for the optimal values. In the case of stairs those optimal values may be one of energy expenditure. It would have been extremely helpful if the authors had stated what other measurable criteria of optimality they had in mind, especially for children. Think, for example, of a child playing on a stairway. Maybe the child's play is best characterized by surplus energy expenditure, which has training effects. The optimal values in the sense of the authors would surely not be applicable in this case. But even optimal energy expenditure of ascending and *descending* users of the same stairs may vary, not to speak of persons carrying loads, of physically impaired users, and so on. It would be important to know whether the methodology could in principle deal with these cases, or at least some of them.

Would the optimal values that Warren has found for the energy expended by ascending climbers successfully capture design criteria of a stairway? I think they would, but only if there is a critical constraint. The optimal values would have to be different at least for tall and small people. A tall man's optimal stairway cannot be the same as a small man's. Most existing stairways are surely not optimal for children, for most stairways have modal character. Of course, it is hard to imagine what this modal character would mean in a practical sense, but in my opinion it would be wrong for the results of Warren's study to be deemed irrelevant or idiosyncratic. Heine and Guski's ecological approach allows a basic and perhaps unique distinction that seems relevant for environmental psychology in general: the distinction between a *theoretical* and an *applied* environmental psychology. Warren's studies show that, in relation to optimal energy expenditure, most people do not live in a world of stairways that are optimal for them.

This statement belongs, in my opinion, to a theoretical environmental psychology. Whether the statement can indeed be used for applications would be another matter and would belong to the conventional understanding of environmental psychology as an applied discipline. The authors do not actually make this distinction. But if they do not want to follow merely common-sense criteria of what an optimal traffic environment would be – traffic calming in Buxtehude, for example – they may extend their approach not only to "practical" problems of environmental psychology but also to a basic theoretical environmental psychology, which is indeed envisaged by J. J. Gibson (1979):

Why has man changed the shapes and substance of his environment? To change what it affords him. He has made more available what benefits him and less pressing what injures him. . . . Over the millenia, he has made it easier for himself to get food, easier to keep warm, easier to see at night, easier to get about, and easier to train his offspring (p. 130).

In this perspective the project of "successful design of affordances" belongs to the way we are in the world. It would point in the wrong direction to speak here of an application of the ecological approach. But the authors do not do that. With their methodology of successful affordance design, they offer a new perspective on how people can make their lives or the lives of their children easier, less pressing, and so forth. It is not an application of the ecological approach, but it is the processing of this approach, a widening of its scope. In this case, it is presumably how an environment would look if successfully designed for distinct affordances. It might be the discovery that the human individual does not live in an environment that is optimally designed for humans. Talking about the successful design of affordances is therefore entirely different from talking about problems that are defined as practical ones, problems that, in my opinion, belong to a branch of *traffic* psychology. What would be the design of a stairway in this respect? It might be a problem to design a stairway that helps meet all the demands potential user groups can have. One design strategy may be to make the stairway adaptible to different users, say, in terms of riser height. Another strategy might be to construct a stairway more optimal in one or more ways for most of the users, more optimal than an alternative stairway would be. But in each case, the choice of the strategy would be *contingent* on the practical problem and not on the problems of theoretical environmental psychology in the sense of successful affordance design. Perhaps it will be the task (or one task) and unique competence of an environmental psychologist of the future to define as much as possible practical problems as problems of successful affordance design. This seems to me an exciting interdisciplinary perspective.

4   Summary and conclusion

Although the authors present an ill-defined notion of affordance that will not do what it claims to do, their approach is not invalid if attention is confined to conceptualizing only compatible relationships as affordances. Furthermore, there seems to be no consensus on what a complete definition of the affordance concept is among the Gibsonians. The authors cannot be blamed for that. If one is convinced that the environment is not in the head – as Wohlwill would say – and if one is also convinced that it is an ecologically based psychology that should give environmental psychology a theoretical basis, the new approach of the authors is impressive. It is impressive because it gives an overall account with distinct descriptive concepts stemming from Gibson's ecological psychology. In combination with naturalistic observational studies, the outline of a methodology for what they call successful affordance design seems to point in the right direction. The approach would be far more convincing if one could be certain that the methodology of successful affordance design would indeed be applicable. Perhaps one more way to convince environmental psychologists would have been for the authors to contrast their own strategy with a different strategy of affordance design (i.e., Mark, Dainoff, Moritz, & Vogele, 1991). As far as I see, the authors also give no argument for the *general* applicability of their approach. This omission is true at least for their first design criterion, especially the optimal values. One does not see how the observer moving in a traffic environment would be constrained to such criteria for the optimal values the authors have in mind. Another matter is the relevance of their approach to environmental problems of traffic psychology. Criteria for successful affordance design may well have no usable implications here. The authors must therefore be asked how their criteria actually help solve such problems. If they do help, the perspective is unique and in the interest of all children concerned.

Note

1 The paper by Warren (1985) has been recently published in an extended version.

References

Gibson, J. J. (1979). *The ecological approach to visual perception.* Boston, MA: Houghton Mifflin.

Lee, D. N., Young, D. S., & McLaughlin, C. M. (1984). A roadside simulation of road crossing for children. *Ergonomics, 27,* 1271-1281.

Lombardo, T. J. (1987). *The reciprocity of perceiver and environment: The evolution of James J. Gibson's ecological psychology.* Hillsdale, NJ: Erlbaum.

Mace, W. (1986). J. J. Gibson's ecological theory of information pickup: Cognition from the ground up. In T. J. Knapp & L. C. Robertson (Eds.), *Approaches to cognition: Contrasts and controversies* (pp. 137-157). Hillsdale, NJ: Erlbaum.

Mark, S. L., Dainoff, M., Moritz, R., & Vogele, D. (1991). An ecological framework for ergonomic research and design. In R. R. Hoffman & D. S. Palermo (Eds.), *Cognition and the symbolic processes: Applied and ecological perspectives* (pp. 477-505). Hillsdale, NJ: Erlbaum.

Munz, C. W. (1989). Der ökologische Ansatz zur visuellen Wahrnehmung: Gibsons Theorie der Entnahme optischer Information [The ecological approach to visual perception: Gibson's theory of optical information pickup]. *Psychologische Rundschau, 40,* 63-75.

Neisser, U. (1991). Direct perception and other forms of knowing. In R. R. Hoffman & D. S. Palermo (Eds.), *Cognition and the symbolic processes: Applied and ecological perspectives* (pp. 17-30). Hillsdale, NJ: Erlbaum.

Turvey, M. T. (1992). Affordances and prospective control: An outline of the ontology. *Ecological Psychology, 4*(3), 173-187.

Turvey, M. T., & Shaw, R. E. (1979). The primacy of perceiving: An ecological reformulation of perception for understanding memory. In L. G. Nilssen (Ed.), *Studies of memory: In honor of Uppsala University's 500th anniversary* (pp. 167-222). Hillsdale, NJ: Erlbaum.

Warren, W. H., Jr. (1984). Perceiving affordance: Visual guidance of stair climbing. *Journal of Experimental Psychology: Human Perception and Performance, 10,* 683-703.

Warren, W. H., Jr. (1985). *Environmental design as the design of affordances.* Paper presented at the Third International Conference on Event Perception and Action, Uppsala, Sweden.

Authors' response: Environmental design means the design of affordances

Wolf-D. Heine and Rainer Guski

In contrast to Munz's insinuation, we did not link environmental psychology with the ecological approach by means of an experimental procedure by Warren (1984). First, we criticized traditional road safety training for children because of its shortcomings. From these shortcomings we deduced that shaping the traffic environment has a behavior-guiding potential (a) to avoid consequences, especially lethal ones of children's nonadaptable behavior toward automobile-dominated traffic, and (b) to alter the behavior of motorized road users. Second, we did not suggest that one change the traffic environment by applying planning rules of thumb. Instead, we postulated a theoretically guided procedure based on the ecological approach, according to which environmental design should be the design of affordances. To be able to decide whether this design is successful, we introduced four design criteria and outlined an affordance analysis to test whether the designed environment meets the criteria. In a nutshell this analysis was the core of our manuscript.

To achieve this aim, we did not refer to Warren's stair-climbing experiment (1984), as Munz insinuated, but to an unpublished theoretical paper from 1985, which was followed by Warren (1995). We indicated that fact at the beginning of section 3.3. To enable readers to follow our programmatic suggestions, we introduced them to the basic ideas of the ecological approach and placed special emphasis on the concept of affordance. Within that introduction we indeed used Warren's stair-climbing studies (1984) because we stressed them at the beginning of section 1.3.2: "This abstract formulation becomes clearer when illustrated by the now almost classical example of studying the affordance of stair-climbing" (p. 518). Thus, we took Warren's experiments as an example and not as an "experimental paradigm" (Munz) for affordance research. The attentive reader will already have noticed that we used just 25 lines of 27 pages for reporting stair-climbing studies. Comparing this relation with Munz's focus on such experiments to criticize our approach, readers can work out things for themselves.

Munz wrote that our work "lacks the basic assumption of the reciprocity of animal and environment" (p. 544). May we venture to ask how it was possible for Munz to overlook the corresponding lines in section 1 (especially 1.1), where we stressed that "[a]n organism and its environment, such as children and streets they use, cannot be studied as unrelated entities" (p. 515)? How is it possible that Munz missed an entire section (1.3.3) on this point? Gibson's postulation of the necessity of the reciprocity of organism and environment can probably not be made clearer than in section 1.3.3, where we quoted a central notion of Gibson himself (1979) concerning this ecological principle.

Concerning the compatibility problem that Munz has raised in the second section of his commentary, we refer the interested reader to Turvey and Shaw (1979, p. 206), who wrote: "An environmental event or situation X affords an activity Y for an animal Z if and only if certain mutual compatibility relations between X and Z obtain."

It is always a problem if one tries to criticize something out of context. Of course, it might be possible that children "can act upon the car, say, by throwing something at it" (p. 545). In section 3.2, however, we wished to show that children cannot act on a street as pedestrians, bicyclists, street-crossers, and so forth for cars (detached objects in Gibsonian terms) dominate the space of a street and thereby reduce the functional utility of a street as public space for children as road users. Children as representatives of vandalism against motorized affordance structures may be an interesting research topic, but it was not ours.

In his introduction Munz criticized that we did not specify "which tasks children or car drivers have in principle and how these tasks in principle have to be described" (p. 544). According to the ecological principles presented in our chapter, it should be clear that one cannot talk about tasks of organisms, of road users in this case, without outlining an actor-referential description of the particular environment in question. In principle, this procedure has to imply already task-specific variables. The attentative reader will notice that we tried to address this point in section 3.2: "An actor-referential description of a street" (p. 529).

At the end of section 3 Munz labeled our work as a component of traffic psychology. If one knows about the traditions and the current state of traffic psychology, one should know that the subject of traffic psychology has always been the improvement of the conditions for car drivers. The needs of other road users have been ignored or they have been analyzed only as problems for the safety of car-driving. Certainly, we did not aim to do so. At the end of section 2.2 in our chapter, we proposed the notion of "mobility management" (p. 528) as an alternative strategy. Most recently, the notion and an initial concept of "mobility psychology" was developed to stress a road-user-centered approach to traffic as well as to outline the shortcomings this approach would have if it were to be subsumed into environmental psychology (Heine, 1997).

We could continue responding to Munz's commentary in much more detail. However, we think we have already provided readers with the information needed for deciding whether one can criticize our chapter by stating that its core concept, affordance, is "ill-defined" (p. 545) or whether the direction of the commentary by Munz was ill-defined because he focused on a stair-climbing experiment instead of discussing whether the first ecologically principled strategy to alter the traffic environment might be fruitful in the future.

References

Gibson, J. J. (1979). *The ecological approach to visual perception.* Boston, MA: Houghton Mifflin.

Heine, W.-D. (1997). Mobilitätspsychologie und Mobilitätsmanagement [Mobility psychology and mobility management]. In B. Schlag (Ed.), *Fortschritte der Verkehrspsychologie 1996* (pp.127-134). Bonn: Deutscher Psychologen Verlag.

Turvey, M. T., & Shaw, R. E. (1979). The primacy of perceiving: An ecological reformulation of perception for understanding memory. In L.-G. Nilssen (Ed.), *Studies of memory: In honor of Uppsala University's 500th anniversary* (pp. 167-222). Hillsdale, NJ: Erlbaum.

Warren, W. H., Jr. (1984). Perceiving affordances: Visual guidance of stair climbing. *Journal of Experimental Psychology: Human Perception and Performance, 10,* 683-703.

Warren, W. H., Jr. (1985). *Environmental design as the design of affordances.* Paper presented at the Third International Conference on Event Perception and Action, Uppsala, Sweden.

Warren, W. H., Jr. (1995). Constructing an econiche. In J. M. Flach, P. A. Hancock, J. K. Caird, & K. J. Vicente (Eds.), *Global perspectives on the ecology of human-machine systems* (Vol. 1, pp. 210-237). Hillsdale, NJ: Erlbaum.

Commentator's reply: The extended concept reconsidered

Christian Munz

"On the street there move detached objects that afford non-walkability . . . in short: non act-on-ability" (p. 530). The authors may have noticed that this false 'facon de parler' reduces Gibson's concept of affordance to a caricature – without future.

Integration: The path to integration is not straight

Tommy Gärling

Impressive progress has been made toward understanding child development. Does this mean that psychologists are in a position to answer socially urgent questions such as how the urban conditions under which a majority of children live affect their development? If not, what desirable features should a theory have to be able to answer such questions?

In this integrative commentary, I try to judge the extent to which the three preceding theoretical contributions, individually or collectively, achieve the goal of increasing the understanding of the role of cities in child development. Let me say immediately that I feel this goal is too ambitious. More realistically, and perhaps more useful, is to aim at low-level theories or facts. Why not leave it to societal decision-makers, planners, and architects to make the best they can out of the limited, although reliable and valid, knowledge that I think developmental and environmental psychology are sometimes capable of offering?

I start with some observations concerning what cities are. Then I try to specify some of the things psychologists may want to know. The extent to which the theories contribute to this effort is finally noted.

1 Cities

Cities are said to have existed for thousands of years. Whether this is true or not depends, I guess, on what the definition of a city is. And that definition is clearly of importance for how a city is thought to affect child development. Traffic congestions, air pollution, vandalism, and crowding are examples of urban phenomena that have existed for only a short time.

Regional scientists study urban systems. They know that such systems develop. Thus, not only people living in cities but the cities themselves undergo changes. These changes both interrelate at different levels of aggregation and depend on environmental influences. When speculating about the future, confining oneself to human evolution is not sufficient. How cities evolve is also an issue.

Even if the focus is on present-day cities, there are national and regional differences to be considered. Are there any features common to almost all cities (such as dense population), or should the concern be with important characteristics (such as population size) that distinguish different cities?

Another important general question, in particular from a practical point of view, is to what extent it is possible to affect the development of a city and at which level – that of individual actors, policy, legislation, planning, or design?

2   Things one may want to know

In very general terms one may want to know whether the development of children is affected by growing up in cities and, if so, whether they are affected in good or bad ways. A difficulty is, of course, to define what are good or bad ways. Is the short or long run meant? The words good and bad also imply value judgment. From an evolutionary perspective, survival and reproduction are important criteria in both the short and long run. From other perspectives, however, quality of life is a greater, or at least additional, concern.

In my opinion the task of research cannot be to define what quality of life is. What research may be able to do is to uncover and explain invariants. At a distal level such invariants include how developmental outcomes depend on sociophysical characteristics of cities. At a proximal level they include how children with different characteristics are affected by such sociophysical characteristics.

Complications arise because few simple cause-and-effect relationships may exist. Furthermore, the goal of research is to reveal processes or mechanisms that are not directly observable.

In the absence of an integrated developmental theory, another issue is whether the focus should be on children's development with respect to experience, behavior, or performance?

3   Failure to integrate the theoretical contributions

The three theoretical chapters differ in both focus and scope. The broadest scope focusing on developmental outcomes over generations is the evolutionary perspective proposed by Charlesworth. The intention is to provide a conceptual framework broad enough to offer suggestions for how to make cities biologically more suitable to children. Evolutionary theory as developed by sociobiologists is said to have a persuasive rationale for predicting effects that urban living has on humans. Based on the observation that modern urban living differs in several respects from living in those environments where evolutionary adaptedness evolved, the rationale is, briefly stated, that these effects are claimed to be negative for the long-term survival of the species. However, we do not know. The theory is therefore offered as a heuristic tool for ethological research on the effects of urban living on how children develop.

The second theoretical chapter, by Keller, has a similarly broad scope but quite a different, cognitivist focus. Here, childhood is the target, not only its role for development but also well-being during childhood. Thus, quality of life is highlighted rather than survival in the short or long run. The relation to urban environments is developed in analyses of the concepts of behavioral exploration, the experience of place attachment resulting from behavioral exploration, and the meaning of places and conceptions of childhood that develop both individually and collectively. The chapter's main contribution is that it integrates these concepts, highlighting the role of environmental characteristics. In the latter respect an important factor is the degree of independence in children's behavioral exploration and the resulting exposure to environmental features. The influence that conceptions of childhood have on parental practice is emphasized rather than regulations, planning, or design aimed at safety and security. In contrast to the evolutionary perspective and research in environmental psychology (Hartig & Evans, 1993), no analysis is made of differences between living in urban and natural environments. The role that conceptions of childhood play in behavioral exploration of environments relative to, for instance, salience of environmental cues is not spelled out in great detail.

The third theoretical chapter, by Heine and Guski, differs markedly from the others in its narrow focus on the role that environmental features have for children's traffic safety. Both survival and quality of life are important criteria. The concept of affordance is borrowed from Gibsonian ecological psychology (Gibson, 1979; Turvey, 1992), perhaps in a way that, strictly speaking, is open to criticism. Yet, the general message is clear: Places offer directly perceivable opportunities for behavior as well as restrictions on it. A knowledge of what information individual actors use to guide their behavior might make it possible, through environmental design, to reduce dangerous aspects of the traffic environment. However, the road to this goal is neither straight nor safe.

Do the different foci and scopes of the three different theoretical chapters under discussion mean that they are complementary? If they were, that fact would be a first step to integration. Unfortunately, the question is not easy to answer. Whereas Charlesworth's evolutionary theory is an attempt to specify the relation between certain target behaviors and environmental conditions, Keller's cognitivist theory is centered on experiences and Heine and Guski's ecological theory on performance. There is little explicit basis for inferring any connections.

The ecological theory is applied to the problem of increasing traffic safety for children. Since a perceptual analysis is the starting point, the role of active behavioral exploration proposed in the cognitivist theory should fit into the ecological conceptual framework. To go further than this would require more specific hypotheses. For instance, is novelty-familiarity a dimension that is important to introduce? How does the ecological theory deal with a concept that seems so obviously important in child development?

The role of parental supervision cannot be ignored in any approach to child safety (Gärling, Svensson-Gärling, & Valsiner, 1984). Another issue is, therefore, how the role of parents can be accommodated by the ecological theory. An obvious part of the answer to this question should be the realization that affordances are learnt, quite plausibly in part through parents. Conversely, the effect of designing environments to increase traffic safety for children may affect parents. If parents as well as children perceive environments as safe, then independent behavioral exploration might increase, with beneficial effects in both the short and long run.

Since injuries are a dominant cause of death in young children (Roberts & Brooks, 1987), it should be of interest to analyze them from an evolutionary perspective. Is affordance a useful concept in such an analysis? It may simply be that environments are designed in a way that limited perceptual (and cognitive?) capabilities are strained. Although this possibility is a simplification of the evolutionary and ecological theories, it appears to be one that they may have in common. However, the explanation of why environments are designed in such a way does not seem to be equally simple. Human factors certainly contribute to this asymmetry at many different levels. Politicians, planners, designers, and parents alike, individually or collectively, acting in a dynamic environment, make faulty decisions or sometimes fail to make decisions at all. Not even the evolutionary theory seems broad enough to incorporate this fact.

4   Things one may still know

Despite failing to provide an integrated view, each theory may still contribute something valuable to the understanding and predictabilty of the outcome for children of urban living. A distinction can be made between direct effects and effects of the physical environment that are mediated by the social environment. Another distinction can be made between short- and long-term effects.

Claims based on cognitivist theory are potentially relevant for the issue at hand. An important role is assigned to behavioral exploration of the environment for place attachment. Both direct effects that the environment has on exploration and indirect effects that ensue from parental supervision are hypothesized. However, it is also believed that there are large interindividual differences in explorative behavior, depending on culture and context. Place attachment still appears to be a general phenomenon, as do place identity and conceptions of childhood. It is, however, difficult to strictly state any implications for urban living. Will children living in certain kinds of cities explore their everyday environments differently than comparable children living in other environments? Will their attachment to place consequently be less, more, or different? How will their place identity eventually emerge? And what conceptions of childhood do they develop? This set of questions appears to be too simplistic for the theory to address. Yet, such questions are asked by politicians, planners, designers, and laypeople.

By contrast, the evolutionary theory has perhaps too many definite answers to immensely important questions about urban life. Not surprisingly, the main factor defining urban life is population density. Few observers would deny its importance, as attested by the many hundreds of human studies on the phenomena of personal space, crowding, and territoriality (Stokols & Altman, 1987). Obviously, there are many other, more profound effects of population density on children that are mediated by mainly long-term changes of the social environment. Unfortunately, hard evidence is lacking for these effects and their causal mediation. What seems to be most striking about urban living is the adaptiveness people show. A major research task is, in fact, to study human adaptation to urban environments. Scientists other than psychologists (Gärling & Golledge, 1993) assigned themselves this task long ago.

In line with my introductory suggestion, a narrow scope such as that chosen in the ecological theory appears to be the most manageable solution. Through the concept of affordance, which relates an individual to his or her environment, a starting point is provided for both a theoretical and applied analysis. In the chapter by Heine and Guski, the latter tends to dominate. How may a theoretical analysis proceed? Probably, the existence of cognitive structures such as schemata directing and being changed by exploration cannot be ignored. Furthermore, systems of structures constituting environmental knowledge would account for differences in experiences and behavior, depending on the type of environment in which the child lives (Spencer, Blades, & Morsley, 1989). Of course, there will be individual differences as well. In order to be useful, however, the theoretical analysis should not be focused on them but on invariances across individuals, exactly as done through analysis in which affordances are taken as the point of departure.

5   Things one still want to know

Although there are many things developmental psychologists still want to know and understand, I will only point out here that the theoretical chapters under discussion seem in particular to have difficulty in accommodating possible positive effects of urban living. Population diversity, physical well-being, and complex stimulation counteracting boredom are believed to be positive consequences of urban living. Which is the evolutionary role, if any, of such positive consequences?

6   Conclusion

The evolutionary, cognitivist, and ecological perspectives represented in the three preceding theoretical contributions have something in common that should eventually make it possible to integrate them. At present, however, there are too many gaps for this to be possible. Yet, each of these perspectives provides valuable insights. By virtue of the concept of affordance the ecological perspective is perhaps the most manageable one and the one that at least has the potential to tie child development closest to urban environments. Theoretically, however, there is far to go before any thorough understanding of how urban living affects child development is achieved.

References

Gärling, T., & Golledge, R. G. (1993). Understanding behavior and environment: A joint challenge to psychology and geography? In T. Gärling & R. G. Golledge (Eds.), *Behavior and environment: Psychological and geographical approaches* (pp. 1-15). Amsterdam: Elsevier/North-Holland.

Gärling, T., Svensson-Gärling, A., & Valsiner, J. (1984). Parental concern about children's traffic safety in residential neighborhoods. *Journal of Environmental Psychology, 4*, 235-252.

Gibson, J. J. (1979). *The ecological approach to visual perception.* Boston: Houghton Mifflin.

Hartig, T., & Evans, G. W. (1993). Psychological foundations of nature experience. In T. Gärling & R. G. Golledge (Eds.), *Behavior and environment: Psychological and geographical approaches* (pp. 427-457). Amsterdam: Elsevier/North-Holland.

Roberts, M. C., & Brooks, P. H. (1987). Children injuries: Issues in prevention and public policy. *Journal of Social Issues, 43*, 1-12.

Spencer, C., Blades, M., & Morsley, K. (1989). *The child in the physical environment.* Chichester, UK: Wiley.

Stokols, D., & Altman, I. (Eds.) (1987). *Handbook of environmental psychology* (Vol. 1). New York: Wiley.

Turvey, M. T. (1992). Affordances and prospective control: An outline of the ontology. *Ecological Psychology, 4*, 173-187.

Reflections: What has happened in treading the path toward a psychological theory of children and their cities

Günter Mey

> ... if our thinking were to take form as a
> city, we would necessarily get a labyrinth.
> Nietzsche (in Kamper, 1987, p. 21)

As editors, we intended the presentation of psychological theories in this volume to address a particular topic and task, the goal being to improve the understanding of children's development in urban settings. Not only were the principles of different theoretical positions to be outlined, but possibilities for their further development within urban contexts were to be elaborated upon in subsequent comments, and the conceptualizations were then to be compared for ways to integrate them (see the introduction to this part). That was what we had in mind. But before proceeding to the finale, including a personal outlook (see the final chapter in Part III), we must first ask what has happened in treading the path toward a psychological theory of children and their cities.

In this closing chapter of Part II, the steps taken along the way (or rather, along very different ways) are to be roughly retraced. Individual chapters are no longer discussed; no microanalytic observations are or even can be attempted in these pages. The authors and readers may judge for themselves which of the following points pertain to which approach or contribution. Instead, rather general impressions that have emerged during our editorial work on the many manuscripts of this book are pointed out to invite further dialogue. The main purpose is to highlight some of the peculiarities of the manners in which the authors of the various chapters have tackled the thematic complex we have called children, cities, and psychological theories and how – whether in the theoretical expositions, the comments, or the effort to integrate both – they have gone about their job of envisaging developing relationships.

It is worth noting at the very outset how sincerely all the authors have tried to solve this difficult problem of giving a commensurate overview of the wide field between a rather amorphous macrocontext (city) and elusive, real human beings (children). It is hoped that this book's diverse interdisciplinary discussion, which displays very different styles of treatment, thought, and presentation, will be taken as a challenge and be pursued in the future.

It is precisely in the desire for such continuation that this chapter dwells mostly on the complications that arose during this project. Above all, the following remarks reflect a few of the sometimes almost inevitable dilemmas that have sprung from the tension between theory and practice and between the aspiration and the reality of research. These passages also delve into some specific and occasionally not unproblematic aspects that can be associated with the dialogue between academics. We have decided on this critical perspective primarily in the hope that it will offer possible points of reference for future discourses of the kind we have undertaken.

1   Theoretical convergence and exhaustion and ensuing dilemmas

It is apparent first that all the authors, whose disciplinary moorings in environmental or developmental psychology are at times clearly recognizable, avoid a simple person-vs.-environment dualism and seek to balance out this relation conceptually. In this context one can speak of what Lerner and Spanier (1980) refer to as "weakly" or "strongly" interactional or transactional approaches. That is, dealing with the topic "children in the city" has been taken as an invitation to go beyond (and at times well beyond) the original assumptions of the particular approaches and to fall back on terms used in other areas and subdisciplines of science. As much as Wohlwill encouraged this kind of borrowing (see the note in the introduction to Part II), the attempt to reformulate the original theory often makes it unclear how compatible such extension is with the basic assumptions involved. The resulting terminological vagaries to which some of the commentators call attention are probably bound to arise when "old" theories are "enriched" by "new" and "modern" loans. A few of these enrichments seem so far-reaching that one is compelled at times to ask how much more a theory can be stretched without its character changing so fundamentally that it begins to function more as a trade name than as a helpful heuristic tool.

The brevity imposed by the space available for these reflections (a constraint that may, however, also help put some problems in bolder relief than would otherwise be the case) ultimately makes one aware of specific quandaries how children's environments are actually to be shaped, how the settings to be considered were selected, and how the theoretical explications can be translated into empirical work. These issues are examined a bit in the following paragraphs.

One problem is the vast gap between the heavenly heights of theory and the abysses of practice. Although the presentation of the basic assumptions about the relation between person and environment are quite thorough in most instances, with the authors sometimes delineating the boundaries to neighboring approaches and providing an outline of relevant research work, many statements remain quite general. As previously mentioned, that *explicit* references to this book's central topic area, "children in the *city*," are attempted, but by and large they are rather rare and scant compared to what we initially expected (see also the observation by Bronfenbrenner in his foreword). In relation to the presentations of the various theoretical approaches, the city as an object of study seems, to put it metaphorically, to have too many edges for it to have fit precisely enough into the theories. Most of the authors give it only general treatment and leave it at that, a sketch from which they often draw only equally general suggestions and recommendations regarding the desired composition of an urban environment designed to promote children's development (or at least not inhibit it). Given the great theoretical aspirations, the "practical" inferences sometimes come across as simplistic, an impression that one has particularly when general aspects such as the variability and flexibility of environmental conditions enter the discussion. Some of the proposals formulated in this manner occasionally seem to fall from the theory's sky (and at times, so it seems, only from thin air). Such is the case when they contain generalizations that are well meant but, strictly speaking, hard to reconcile with the antecedent theoretical assumptions or underivable from the respective starting assumptions. This incompatibility occurs, for example, when authors emphasize the active role of children yet put forward a catalogue of measures implying that children are understood to be fairly passive, defenseless objects of what is going on around them.

As presented in this volume, psychological theories entail abstractions and thus cannot be claimed to correspond exactly to mental and physical reality. Hence, it should not be especially surprising that some of the authors' inferences remain abstract. Nonetheless, because theories are also a researcher's constructions (and simultaneously reconstructions) based on dissimilar assumptions about human beings, there is sometimes the impression that "the scientist's social and political beliefs can be especially biasing in a field such as psychology, in which people are studying people. The psychologist holds a mirror rather than a telescope" (Miller, 1983, p. 17; see Mruck & Mey, 1996, for additional considerations). And perhaps a few of the accents in the "practical" proposals can be explained in light of these personal inclinations and disinclinations, which figure reflected in the theoretical statements without actually being explicit.

A second issue concerns contemplative environments and developmental psychology as nondevelopmental psychology. Quite different urban environments have been invoked and described in the theoretical discussions. For instance, such special forms of urban living as rituals and celebrations are handled, and it is suggested that children be included in the surrounding social world so that they can experience and conquer it in new and different ways. Overviews of different everyday places frequented by children are also offered, with the authors referring to relevant daily worlds (e.g., schools, and children's homes), spelling out ideas for regulating and calming road traffic, and discussing the city as a space for children's adventure and leisure. The facets they thereby take up usually mean that the town and the city are dealt with in a friendly, though not unexciting, atmosphere in small-scale, personally significant regions – say, individual settings or secondary territories. The socio-communicational modalities of development in the city are thereby underlined, but there is little thorough discussion of the city as a complex entity of signs and things. Much of the description in the book has a sentimental and contemplative tone far removed from all main traffic arteries and high-rises. The city as a human grave, the city with its potential for enticement/seduction and alarm/menace is not denied, but it is not illuminated in its own right, either. Seen from this angle, children's appropriation of the city usually occurs within a manageable space, and attention is often directed to the question of whether development has succeeded. By contrast, the authors are far less occupied with what is actually going on in that development, less intent on the developmental process itself. As critiqued by Valsiner (1997), developmental psychology often actually appears to be *non*developmental psychology.

Third, one notes a tendency toward grand focuses but small conclusions and small focuses but grand conclusions. Although the basic theoretical assumptions and the presentations of individual metropolitan segments are usually quite rich, in many cases they forfeit that richness in the attempt to spell out a research program and, what is more, when it comes to translating the research into action. This loss may sometimes be due to the fact that the richness of the dynamic and diversity of the relation between the child and the city threatens, in many works of developmental psychology, to vanish behind static (read: statistical) methodology when the course of children's development in context is abbreviated to variables, just as the articulation of man-made environments as urban environments seems too wan to capture the impact of the urban context.

These contradictions become clear especially when the empirical dimension of the main theoretical chapters includes only narrowly circumscribed aspects and leaves others out altogether. As a result, the authors can formulate only highly specific statements about the necessary nature and structure of children's environments. At such points, those edges that earlier could not be fit into theory become pivotal. It seems almost as though the researchers seek footing in order to protect themselves against the ephemerality of the city as an object of study by dissecting and analyzing discrete "materialized" places – without urban life thereby slipping into the picture. In this respect the recourse to general principles and the listing of the previously mentioned and quite global suggestions for shaping children's environments can acquire a different connotation. It could be presumed that some of the researchers themselves feel their narrow focuses to be inadequate, with the grand conclusions tacitly serving as a possible counterweight.

2   Problems with the dialogue: An unwieldy object of research, environmental and developmental psychologists who resist development, and the question of "must there be an integration?"

Let us turn from the presentations of theoretical approaches and cast an eye on the comments, whose authors had the job of pursuing the theoretical discussion and narrowing it down to children's development in urban environments. They pointed out additional, sometimes neglected matters: the emphasis on the active or passive role of children (depending on the approach), the importance of gender-specific differences, the relativity of the research perspectives, the concentration on settings typical of cities, and so forth.

Yet a theory of the city and its children all but defies attempts to outline it in this dialogue between commentators and the contributors of the main theoretical chapters. Like the latter contributors, who bring their own vantage points to bear on specific environments and children's development as they present their respective theoretical positions, the commentators, too, write from *one* salient stance drawn from their individual understanding of the research they are speaking about. The striking thing in this regard is that the questions raised (and the answers offered) often do not relate specifically to the approaches under discussion. As calls and demands, they could have been directed at other approaches as well.

The commentators certainly did not intend to show their "own" points of view, at least not exclusively. They did always also uncover a critical issue in the theory they were dealing with. That they largely failed to take the discussion further, as desired, may indicate how difficult it is to orient a theory to an object of study, or to incorporate what in this case was a rather unwieldy object of study into the building, critique, and further development of theory. It is perhaps in this sense that one must understand the initially vexing fact that the admittedly limited space reserved for responses to the commentators was used by most of the main presenters, if they used it at all, to "salvage" their own positions rather than take advantage of critical comments as an opportunity to elaborate upon their theories. The responses consist largely of rebuttals to the effect that the critique missed the point, that the supposedly missing explications were given but not given their due, that lack of space precluded the explanations needed for presenting the theory, and so on. Theories, or their proponents, seem hard to move, and there is much to suggest that theories do have a certain *resistance to development* (Görlitz, 1981). It acquires its own dynamics in the dialogic conception of this book when, for example, contributors of the main theoretical chapters resort to protecting their views. Attempts to explain the paths taken are coupled above all with the "*technique of reinterpretation*, by which one tries to neutralize the explosive effect of a contradictory (frequently also annoying) stance or event by labeling it 'irrelevant'" (Görlitz, 1981, p. 54).

Consider now the integrators, whose primary task was to plumb groups of theories for the potential they have for the topic of children's development in the city, to interrelate those groups, and delineate possible new ways of looking at the issue. In their contributions, the question of "what is city" becomes precise. Moreover, they direct attention to specific conditions of life faced by, say, street children, conditions that did not or could not really figure in light of the sometimes genial, contemplative way in which urban realities had been dealt with earlier in the book.

In addition, the integrators put some things into a different perspective. They caution against rashly speaking of "good" or "bad" environments. They remind one that nomenclature can have unlike connotations, depending on the surrounding culture. They also stress the difference between the focuses of a developmental outlook and those of an environmental one. This kind of probe allows for a more stringent evaluation of inferences for the applied disciplines. Contrastive analysis of approaches not only allows sharper delineations to be drawn and conceivable linkages between different theories to be pointed but also occasionally enables the shortcomings of those theories to surface more clearly. It demonstrates that the theoretical conceptualizations require far greater precision than they now have and that the positions based on them cannot easily be integrated unless that precision is achieved.

3   Oversized cities, traditional discussions, and the trouble with synoptic theory

Despite the problems and criticism already mentioned, the triadic structure of this book – the presentation of a theory followed by a comment on it and a comparison or integration of a group of theories – offers an enlightening slant on a psychology centered on the this volume's complex of topics, child and city. It shows that theories can (and must) be made useful in very different ways. On the whole, however, psychological theory of the city and its children is still underdeveloped. Despite all we have done, this synoptic theory still does not exist. These efforts could not have sufficed for more than a draft outline. Why?

Perhaps certain idiosyncrasies of the topic "children in the city" play a role that we editors and the other contributors have vastly underestimated. As previously intimated, a detailed and systematic consideration of urban environments runs the risk of not seeing the forest for all the trees. After all, the urban, the very object of our study, consists of more than individual settings. In only a few contributions has the configuration of buildings and signs, of social and historical elements been described in a way would commensurately convey this sense of what is urban in all its temporal restrictions and forms and its complexly intermeshed sequences of action. For in addition to the utter pervasiveness of its abidingly material reality, its massive concentration of buildings, it must be remembered that those buildings change. They become rent with cracks, are restored, and get replaced. They tower up from the historical past, for "the temporal atmosphere of the town is more than a reflection of its actual age" (Strauss, 1976, p. 26). They are comprehensible in themselves in today's conglomerate of dizzily swirling traffic and the perpetual illumination that turns night into day and gives the impression that it is always daytime (see Métraux, 1992). This overt coexistence of past and present, movement and quiescence, thing and meaning bears witness to an otherwise scarcely perceivable simultaneity of the nonsimultaneous.

But this peculiarity is not readily apparent, for the often quite extensive effort that most of the authors make to come to grips with the topic by focusing on particular settings, be they schools, recreational areas, or some other venue, obscure the specifics of these places in their relation to this urban quality. On the other side, global statements are frequently made about urban environments, with the matter-of-fact aspect characterizing them remaining unconsidered. In that sense, possibilities for the analysis and evaluation of distinct (commonly familiar) places are provided, but the reciprocal linkages between the individual places are missing in the approaches. What usually remains are definite places without the city or cities without definite places.

In addition to these problems inherent in the nature of the city itself, scholarly dialogue seems to follow its own laws – a matter touched on above. To be fruitful, to have a bearing on the task and topic at hand, which is to advance a theory of children's development in urban environments, such dialogue requires the willingness to rethink one's own theory and, perhaps even more far-reaching, to put it on the line. This call appears to be at odds with academia's rules of the game, however, as when the question arises as to whether the proponents of a theory take the commentator(s) seriously and about how much actual collaboration is permitted at all by university etiquette that remains committed to the ideal of originality (including the rivalries and territorial imperatives entailed; see Merton, 1963/1985) rather than to the credo of interdisciplinarity and teamwork.

Despite these difficulties rooted in the object of study and the scientific system, we consider it worthwhile to continue pursuing the path taken thus far. This conviction is borne out by the many initiatives to be found in this volume, though it has not been possible in these reflections to accord them all the recognition they deserve. But with this long and winding road now having been tread, the question still remains whether psychology even needs a theory about the city and, if so, whether it should be a specifically and exclusively city-oriented theory that also includes the dimension of children's development.

One possible answer: Towns and cities demand attention not only because they are the daily life world of many children. Such attention would be the "practical" necessity. Towns and cities demand it also because there has not yet been a theoretical debate that could move beyond particularizing delimitations on the one hand and general person-environment statements on the other. A question to clarify, for example, would be how knowledge of the city forms in children as they grow up. Included in this regard are the conventional meaning of common knowledge, beginning with the sketch of networks relating to concepts that can later be translated into mental theories about objects, events, and the properties of both. An answer to this question would be a reconstruction that starts out from an individual's idiosyncratic knowledge but does not stop there. In genuinely developmental approaches, however, the city must then not be allowed to slip from sight so easily. Using such a theory, one might have to refrain from confining analysis to consistent, harmonizing aspects and would have to try to acknowledge and portray the city as a complex, self-contradictory entity. (Interesting perspectives on a debate of this sort is found in postmodern discourse in which an attempt is made to dispense with the notion of integrity; see Kamper, 1987). Herein lies the opportunity to take what is special, what is genuinely urban, and make it more visible and, hence, more understandable. Herein lies the chance to construct (and reconstruct) that dimension's developmental significance to children growing up in a big city (as opposed to rural settings) in order to arrive, step-by-step, at a "phenomenology" of places frequented by children.

In psychology, it still remains to determine even more precisely the theoretical coordinates of the path indicated in Muchow and Muchow's *The life world of the city child* (1935/1980), that early trail-blazing empirical work frequently cited by the authors in this volume. It is the path made "visible" in Lewin's film *The child and the world* (see Lück & van Elteren, 1988) and depicted so realistically in Whyte's more rarely cited studies on the *Street corner society* (1943/1996) and in Barker and Wright's *One boy's day* (1951) that readers feel they are experiencing it personally. These works are not only pioneering in their character but also important as guide-posts showing the way toward a psychological theory of children and their cities. By laying foundations in this manner for a psychological theory that both centers on and includes cities, our hope has been to go beyond a mere description of places, to make the urban experience of children and their comprehension of the city more understandable, and, ultimately, to express in words and concepts something of the animation of cities as well as of their bleakness. To achieve this goal, perhaps we should – and must – first do what Benjamin (1992) reminds himself of: learn how to get lost in the city.

Acknowledgement

These reflections draw on discussions among the editors. I am indebted to my coeditors for their comments and especially to Dietmar Görlitz for his insights and additions. Sincere thanks also go to my partner and colleague, Katja Mruck, for her helpful critique and suggested revisions.

References

Barker, R. G., & Wright, H. F. (1951). *One boy's day: A specimen record of behavior*. New York: Harper.

Benjamin, W. (1992). *Städtebilder* [Images of cities]. Photographed by Anna Blau. Frankfurt on the Main: Suhrkamp.

Görlitz, D. (1981). *Entwicklungsresistenz von Theorien und Alltagsmeinungen* [Theories, every-day opinions, and resistance to development]. In H. J. Fietkau & D. Görlitz (Eds.), *Umwelt und Alltag in der Psychologie* (pp. 41-65). Weinheim: Beltz.

Kamper, D. (1987). Der Körper der Stadt. Reflexionen über das ganze Bewußtsein und die zer-stückelte Wahrnehmung [The body of the city: Reflections on whole consciousness and frag-mented perception]. In *Mythos Berlin. Zur Wahrnehmungsgeschichte einer industriellen Metropole. Eine szenische Ausstellung auf dem Gelände des Anhalter Bahnhofs* [exhibition catalogue] (pp. 21-26). Berlin: Ästhetik und Kommunikation.

Lerner, R. M., & Spanier, J. V. (1980). *Adolescent development*. New York: McGraw-Hill.

Lück, H. E., & van Elteren, M. (1988). Eine wichtige Wiederentdeckung. Kurt Lewins Film 'Das Kind in der Welt' (1931) [An important rediscovery: Kurt Lewin's film *The child and the world* (1931)]. *Berichte aus dem Arbeitsbereich Psychologie* (Nr. 24). Hagen: FernUniversität-Gesamthochschule.

Merton, R. K. (1985). Die Ambivalenz des Wissenschaftlers [The ambivalence of scientists]. In R. K. Merton, *Entwicklung und Wandel von Forschungsinteressen. Aufsätze zur Wissenssoziologie.* Frankfurt on the Main: Suhrkamp. (Original work published 1963)

Métraux, A. (1992). Lichtbesessenheit. Zur Archäologie der Wahrnehmung im urbanen Milieu [Obsession with light: On the archeology of perception in the urban milieu]. In M. Smuda (Ed.), *Die Großstadt als 'Text'* (pp. 13-35). Munich: Fink.

Miller, P. H. (1983). *Theories of developmental psychology.* New York: W. H. Freeman.

Muchow, M., & Muchow, H. H. (1980). *Der Lebensraum des Großstadtkindes* [The life world of the city child] (2nd ed.). Bensheim: päd.-extra. (Original work published 1935)

Mruck, K., & Mey, G. (1996). Qualitative Forschung und das Fortleben des Phantoms der Störungsfreiheit [Qualitative research and the persistence of the phantom of reactivity-free research settings]. *Journal für Psychologie, 4*(3), 3-21.

Strauss, A. L. (1976). *Images of the American city.* New Brunswik, NJ: Transaction Books.

Valsiner, J. (1997). *Culture and the development of children's action. A theory of human development* (2nd ed.). New York: Wiley.

Whyte, W. F. (1996). *Die Street Corner Society. Die Sozialstruktur eines Italienerviertels* [Street corner society: The social structure of an Italian slum]. Berlin: Walter de Gruyter. (Original work published 1943)

Part III
The Finale

Integrating youth- and context-focused research and outreach: A developmental contextual model

Richard M. Lerner and Alexander von Eye

Over the course of this century the study of child and adolescent development has not ordinarily been linked to assessments of changes in the complex and multilevel context comprising the ecology of human development (Bronfenbrenner, 1979, in press; Hagen, Paul, Gibb, & Wolters, 1990; Lerner, 1995). In fact, most studies of child development have involved controlled, experimental assessments of white, middle-class children (Bronfenbrenner, 1977; Graham, 1992; Hagen et al., 1990). Thus, neither the diversity of individual differences among youth nor the variation in their context has been a prominent focus of developmental research (Lerner, 1995). Even less prominent have been studies of the *relations over time* between the developing youth and his or her changing context.

In this chapter, we argue that the omission of scientific concern with diversity and with changing youth-context relations has been associated with a lack of adequate theoretical understanding of the dynamic and relatively plastic character of human development (Baltes, 1987; Baltes & Baltes, 1980; Brim & Kagan, 1980; Lerner, 1984). In addition, this omission has been concerned with a data base that cannot adequately address the burgeoning needs and problems of the diverse youth, families, and communities of the world (Hamburg, 1992; Lerner, 1995; Little, 1993). Furthermore, the omission has been linked to a failure to understand the synthetic relation that exists in regard to basic and applied research pertinent to diverse youth studied in the context of the ecologically valid settings of their lives.

We also argue that a "developmental systems" view of human development (Ford & Lerner, 1992; Smith & Thelen, 1993; Thelen & Smith, in press), and in particular one that has crystallized over the course of the last two decades – a perspective termed "developmental contextualism" (Lerner, 1986, 1991, in press; Lerner & Kauffman, 1985) – provides theoretical and empirical means to redress these problems with the extant human development literature. We note that over the last two decades the study of human development has evolved in at least three significant directions. These trends involve: (a) changes in the conceptualization of the nature of the person, (b) the emergence of a life-span perspective about human development, and (c) stress on the contexts of development. These trends were both products and producers of developmental contextualism, and we will explain how this perspective promotes a synthesis of research and "outreach," that is, the generation, transmission, or application of knowledge to address problems of human behavior and development, as these problems are defined by members of the youth, families, and communities experiencing these problems (Lerner, 1995).

1 An overview of developmental contextualism

Developmental contextualism stresses that bidirectional relations exist among the multiple levels of organization involved in human life (e.g., biology, psychology, social groups, and culture) (Bronfenbrenner, 1977, 1979; Lerner, 1986, 1991, in press). These dynamic relations provide a framework for the structure of human behavior (Ford & Lerner, 1992). In addition, this system is itself dynamically interactive with historical changes; this temporality provides a change component to human life (Dixon, Lerner, & Hultsch, 1991). In other words, within developmental contextualism a changing configuration of relationships constitutes the basis of human life – of behavior and development (Ford & Lerner, 1992).

Developmental contextualism is thus a perspective on human development that takes an integrative approach to the multiple levels of organization presumed to comprise the nature of human life. That is, "*fused*" (Tobach & Greenberg, 1984) *and changing relations* among biological, psychological, and social contextual levels comprise the process of developmental change. Rather than approach variables from these levels of analysis in either a reductionistic or a parallel-processing way, the developmental contextual view rests on the idea that variables from these levels of analysis are dynamically interactive – they are reciprocally influential over the course of human ontogeny.

If the course of human development is the product of the processes involved in these dynamic interactions (Lerner, 1978, 1979, 1984) among integrative levels, then the processes of development are more plastic than often previously believed (cf. Brim & Kagan, 1980). Within this perspective, the context for development is not seen merely as a simple stimulus environment but rather as an "ecological environment ... conceived topologically as a nested arrangement of concentric structures, each contained within the next" (Bronfenbrenner, 1979, p. 22) and including variables from biological, psychological, physical, and sociocultural levels, all changing interdependently across history (Riegel, 1975, 1976a, 1976b).

It is accurate to say that since the 1970s developmental contextual conceptions have been increasingly prominent bases of scholarly advances in human development theory and methodology (Dixon & Lerner, 1992; Dixon et al., 1991; Lerner, Hultsch, & Dixon, 1983; Riegel, 1975, 1976a, 1976b; Sameroff, 1975, 1983). Indeed, the three above-noted trends in the study of human development define the place of developmental contextualism in theory and research over the last two decades. Accordingly, it is useful to discuss each of these trends in some detail.

1.1 Children's influences on their own development

Children have come to be understood as active producers of their own development (Bell, 1968; Lerner & Spanier, 1978; Lewis & Rosenblum, 1974; Thomas, Chess, Birch, Hertzig, & Korn, 1963). These contributions primarily occur through the reciprocal relations individuals have with other significant people in their context, such as children with family members, caregivers, teachers, and peers.

The content and functional significance of the influences that people have on others and, in turn, on themselves, occur in relation to people's characteristics of individuality (Schneirla, 1957). Individual differences in people evoke differential reactions in others, reactions that provide feedback to people and influence the individual character of their further development (Schneirla, 1957). Accordingly, individuality – diversity among people – is central in understanding the way in which any given person is an active agent in his or her own development (Lerner, 1982, 1991; Lerner & Busch-Rossnagel, 1981). In other words, diversity has core, substantive meaning and, hence, implications for all studies of human development.

To illustrate, the specific and often special characteristics of a particular child influence parents, other adults, and peers in very unique ways. How parents behave toward children depends quite a lot on how they have influenced parents to behave. Such child influences are termed *child effects*. By influencing the parents that are influencing him or her, the child is shaping a source of his or her own development. In this sense, children are producers of their own development (Lerner, 1982), and the presence of such child effects constitutes the basis of *bidirectional* relations between parents and children.

However, the effect of a youth's stimulation of others, for instance, the parent, depends in part on the parent's own characteristics of individuality. However, to explain this point it is useful to consider the second trend in the literature that helped crystallize the developmental contextual view of human development.

1.2 Development as a life-span phenomenon

The emergence of interest during the 1970s and 1980s in a life-span perspective about human development led to the understanding that development occurs in more than the childhood or adolescent years (Baltes, 1968, 1987; Block, 1971; Brim & Kagan, 1980; Elder, 1974, 1980; Featherman, 1983; Riley, 1979; Schaie, 1965). Parents as well as children develop as distinct individuals across life (Lerner & Spanier, 1978). Parents develop both as adults in general and, more specifically, in their familial and extrafamilial (for example, vocational or career) roles (Vondracek, Lerner, & Schulenberg, 1986). Indeed, the influence of a child on his or her parents will depend in part on the prior experience the adult has had with the parental role and on the other roles in which the parent is engaged (e.g., worker, adult-child, and caregiver for an aged parent) (Hetherington & Baltes, 1988). Thus, a person's unique history of experiences and roles, as well as his or her unique biological (e.g., genetic) characteristics, combine to make him or her unique – and with time, given the accumulation of the influences of distinct roles and experiences, increasingly more unique across the course of life (Lerner, 1988). This uniqueness is the basis of the specific feedback a parent gives to his or her individual child.

Parents who are stimulated differentially may be expected to differentially react to, or process (for example, think and feel about), the stimulation provided by their child. The individuality of these parental reactions underscores the idea that parents are as individually distinct as are their children. However, at the same time, parental individuality underscores the uniqueness of each child's context. This observation is related to the third above-noted trend in the human development literature.

1.3   Development in its ecological context

The study of children and their parents became increasingly "contextualized," or placed within the broader "ecology of human development," during this period (Bronfenbrenner, 1977, 1979; Elder, 1974; Garbarino, 1992). This focus has involved a concern with the "real life" situations within which children and families exist. This focus has led also to the study of the bidirectional relations between the family and the other social settings within which children and parents function, for instance, the work place, the welfare office, the day care, and the formal and the nonformal educational and recreational settings present in a neighborhood or a community (Lewis & Fiering, 1978; Lewis & Rosenblum, 1974).

One approach to the conceptualization of these relations that we see as particularly useful has been proposed by Bronfenbrenner and his colleagues (e.g., 1979; Bronfenbrenner & Crouter, 1983; Garbarino, 1992). These scholars have been major catalysts in promoting the contextualization of human development and in helping scholars understand why the study of development must move beyond its status during the 1970s as "the science of the strange behavior of children in strange situations with strange adults for the briefest possible periods of time" (Bronfenbrenner, 1977, p. 513).

Bronfenbrenner (1977, 1979, 1983) has argued that human development needs to be understood as it occurs in its real-world setting, or *ecology*. He believes that this ecology of human development is composed of four distinct although interrelated systems, or types of settings (the microsystem, the mesosystem, the exosystem, and the macrosystem). Thus, Bronfenbrenner's model of the ecology of human development allows one to devise a means to represent the idea that the bidirectional socialization that occurs between children and parents is embedded in a still more complex system of social networks and of societal, cultural, and historical influences. It is useful to discuss this embeddedness in more detail.

1.4   Levels of embeddedness in the ecology of human development

The core idea in developmental contextualism is that the organism (organismic attributes or, most generally, biology) and context cannot be separated (Gottlieb, 1991, 1992; Lerner, 1984; Tobach, 1981). Both are fused across all of life, and thus across history. One way to begin to illustrate just what is involved in this relation, even for one person, is to consider the diagram presented in Figure 1 (see Lerner, 1984, 1986). Here, multiple dimensions of individuality are used to represent a child and parent. The mutual influence between child and parent, their fusion with each other, is represented in the figure by the bidirectional arrows between them.

It is important to indicate at this point that one may speak of dynamic interactions between parent and child that pertain to either *social* or *physical* (for instance, biological or physiological) relations. For example, in regard to social relationships, the parent "demands" attention from the child, but the child does not show it; this "lights" the parent's "short fuse" of tolerance; he or she scolds the child, who then cries; this creates remorse in the parent and elicits soothing behaviors from him or her; the child is calmed, snuggles up to the parent, and now both parties in the relationship show positive emotions and are happy (see Tubman & Lerner, 1994, for data pertinent to such parent-child relationships).

One may also illustrate dynamic interactions that involve not only the exchange of "external" social behaviors but also biological or physiological processes. For example, parental religious practices, rearing practices, or financial status may influence the child's diet and nutritional status, health, and medical care. By the same token, the contraction of an infectious disease by either parent or child can lead to the other member of the relationship contracting the disease. Moreover, the health and physical status of the child influences the parent's own feelings of well-being and his or her hopes and aspirations regarding the child (Finkelstein, 1993).

Thus, the child's physiological status and development are not disconnected from his or her behavioral and social context (in this example, parental) functioning, and development (e.g., see Finkelstein, 1993; Ford & Lerner, 1992; Howard, 1978). The inner and outer worlds of the child are fused and dynamically interactive. In addition, of course, the same may be said of the parent and, in fact, of the parent-child relationship. Each of these foci – child, parent, or relationship – is part of a larger, enmeshed *system* of fused relations among the multiple levels that compose the ecology of human life (Bronfenbrenner, 1979).

For instance, Figure 1 illustrates the idea that both parent and child are embedded in a broader social network and that each person has reciprocal relations with this network. This set of relations occurs because both the child and the parent are much more than just people playing only one role in life. As already emphasized, the child may also be a sibling, a peer, and a student; the parent may also be a spouse, a worker, and an adult child. All of these networks of relations are embedded within a particular community, society, and culture. Finally, all of these relations are continually changing across time, across history. Simply fomulated, for all portions of the system of person-context, or biology-environment, relations envisioned in developmental contextualism, change across time is an integral, indeed inescapable, feature of human life.

Figure 1 illustrates that within and among each of the networks depicted one may conceive of bidirectional relationships existing among the people populating the network. Also, events in settings lying far beyond the child-parent relationship can influence it. For instance, a community's resources for child daycare during the parent's working hours, the laws (e.g., regarding tax exemptions) or social programs available in a society supporting daycare and the cultural values regarding families who place their infants in daycare all exert an impact on the quality of the parent-child relationship.

In this regard, for instance, the cultural level of organization depicted in Figure 1 is important to consider. For example, in reference to the issue of child care, key variations in facilities, in parental leave policy, and in values regarding daycare exist between Sweden and the United States (Andersson, 1989). Assessment of the differential impact of child care experiences in Sweden versus the United States can elucidate the impact of culture on child and family behavior and development in ways that are not possible if one maintained only a national focus.

Similarly, cross-national comparisons involving other European countries can provide insight into the ways that child development is influenced by cultural variation in health care policies and delivery systems (e.g., involving Great Britain and the United States), in educational paths available to youth (e.g., involving Germany and the United States), in the impact of war on child development (e.g., involving areas of the former Yugoslavia), and in historical changes from socialist to market-oriented economies (e.g., involving countries from central and eastern Europe).

Moreover, as we have just noted, the child-parent relationship and the social networks in which it is located are embedded in still larger community, societal, cultural, and historical levels of organization. These relations are also illustrated in Figure 1. Time – history – cuts through all the systems. This feature of the figure is introduced to remind one that, as with the people populating these social systems, change is always occurring. Diversity within time is created as change across time (across history) introduces variation into all the levels of organization involved in the system depicted in Figure 1.

In other words, people develop, the family changes from one having infants and young children to one having teenagers, to an "empty nest:" The children have left the home of their parents to live elsewhere and very likely to start their own families. Similarly, communities, societies, and cultures change, too (Elder, 1974; Elder, Modell, & Parke, 1993; Garbarino, 1992; Hernandez, 1993). In addition, each of these multiple "levels" is embedded in the natural and human-designed physical ecology, a physical world that of course changes also. Changes at one or more of these levels produce changes in the other levels as well, given their bidirectional connections.

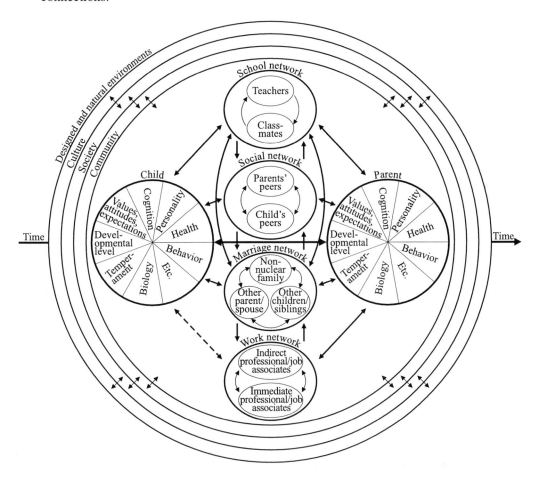

Figure 1: The developmental contextual view of human development: Parent-child relations and interpersonal and institutional networks are embedded in and influenced by particular community, societal, cultural, and designed and natural environments, all changing across time (across history)

Urban settings provide excellent illustrations of how the physical and social ecology of the context within which children and their families are embedded can texture and direct the course of their lives. The population density of cities can affect the quality of family interaction. For instance, in high-density settings the probability of child abuse is increased (Parke & Collmer, 1975). Moreover, cities may provide children and their caregivers with more and more propinquitous social services, recreational and cultural activities, and educational resources than might be available in suburban and/or in rural settings.

Furthermore, urban settings are more likely than rural settings to be the homes of people from diverse cultural, ethnic, and racial backgrounds. Although there are few longitudinal data sets tracing the impact that development in the midst of such diversity has on children's personal and social characteristics, it may be hypothesized that a richer understanding of the variation in customs, mores, and values that exist in the world will develop in children embedded in communities characterized by such diversity.

Finally, as we have noted, all changes are embedded in history (Baltes, 1987; Elder, 1974; Elder et al., 1993); that is, time "cuts through" all levels of organization. As such, the nature of parent-child relations, of family life and development, and of societal and cultural influences on the child-parent-family system are influenced by both "normative" and "nonnormative" historical changes (Baltes, 1987) or, in other words, by "evolutionary" (i.e., gradual) and "revolutionary" (i.e., abrupt; Werner, 1957), historical changes. This system of multiple, interconnected, or "fused" (Tobach & Greenberg, 1984) levels comprises a complete depiction of the integrated organization involved in the developmental contextual view of human development (Lerner, 1986, 1991).

1.5   Implications of developmental contextualism for research and application

In essence, (a) individuality (diversity); (b) change, involving both the individual and the context; and, as a consequence, (c) further individuality are the essential features of human development within developmental contextualism. Given that the multiple levels of change involved in person-context relations may involve individuals at any point in their lives – whether they are infants or young children on the one hand or adults (and acting in roles such as parents, spouses, or teachers) on the other – it is possible to see why a developmental contextual perspective provides a useful frame for studying development across the life span.

The possibility that bidirectional relations exist across the life span among all the levels shown in Figure 1 represents a formidable state of complexity, but one that behavioral and social science theory and research must address. If scholarship does not cope with this complexity, then neither research nor application will be adequate. Research inattentive to the complexity of person-context relations will be deficient in that it will fail to appreciate the substantive nature of individual, familial, or relationship variation and/or will mistakenly construe variation around some potentially specifically inapplicable mean level as, at best, error variance (Lerner, 1991, in press). In turn, applications – policies and/or programs that are at least ideally derived from research (Lerner & Miller, 1993) – will be insufficiently fit with the needs of the specific people intended to be served by these interventions (e.g., regarding the promotion of positive or healthy development), *if* these activities are insufficiently informed by knowledge about the specific characteristics of individuality of these groups (e.g., their values, goals, and assets).

However, developmental contextualism offers an alternative to this situation. It does so by stressing the importance of a focus on diversity and context for integrated research and outreach.

2   An integrative vision of human development – research and outreach

Developmental contextualism emphasizes the bidirectional connections between the individual and the actual ("ecologically valid") settings within which he or she lives. This emphasis has brought to the fore of concern in the social and behavioral sciences both *diversity* (individual differences) and *context* (of peoples and their sociocultural institutions). In addition, developmental contextualism stresses the relation between the individual and his or her context. This stress has resulted in the recognition that a synthesis of perspectives from multiple disciplines is needed to understand the multilevel (e.g., person, family, and community) integrations involved in human development. Furthermore, there has been a recognition that, in order to understand the basic process of human development – the process involved in the changing relations between individuals and contexts – both descriptive and explanatory research must be conducted within the actual ecology of people's lives.

Descriptive research involves the depiction, or representation, of development as it exists for a given person or group, in one or more contexts, at one or more points in time. Explanatory research involves the introduction (through manipulation or statistical modeling) of independent variation into such person-context relations. These planned variations in the course of human life are predicated on (a) theoretical ideas about the source of particular developmental phenomena (for specific combinations of people and contexts); or (b) theoretically guided interests about the extent to which a particular developmental phenomenon (e.g., cognitive development in old age) may show systematic change in structure and/or function, i.e., *plasticity*, across the life span (Baltes, 1987; Lerner, 1984). In the case of either "a" or "b," such researcher-introduced variation is an attempt to simulate the "natural" variation of life; if theoretical expectations are confirmed, the outcomes of such investigations provide an explanation of how developmental change occurs within a person or group.

Given the developmental contextual focus on studying person-context relations within the actual ecology of human development, explanatory investigations by their very nature constitute intervention research. In other words, the goal of developmental contextual explanatory research is to understand the ways in which variations in ecologically "valid" person-context relations account for the character of actual or potential trajectories of human development, that is, life paths enacted in the "natural laboratory" of the "real world." Therefore, to gain understanding of how theoretically relevant variations in such person-context relations may influence actual or to-be-actualized developmental trajectories, the researcher may introduce policies and/or programs as, if you will, "experimental manipulations" of the proximal and/or distal natural ecology. Evaluations of the outcomes of such interventions thus become a means to bring data to bear on theoretical issues pertinent to changing person-context relations and, more specifically, to the plasticity in human development that may exist, or that may be capitalized on, to enhance human life (Lerner, 1988). The housing projects, the restoration activities, and the other construction measures associated with urban planning and urban design may be seen as instances of contextual "manipulations" intended to alter people's relations with the settings within which they live. In other words, a key theoretical issue for explanatory research in human development is the extent to which changes in the multiple, fused levels of organization comprising human life can alter the structure and/or function of behavior and development.

Of course, the naturally occurring events experienced by people constantly shape, texture, and help direct the course of their lives independent of any researcher-imposed attempts to intervene in the course of human development. The accumulation of the specific roles and events a person experiences across life – involving normative age-graded events, normative history-graded events, and non-normative events (Baltes, 1987; Baltes, Reese, & Lipsitt, 1980) – alters each person's developmental trajectory in a manner that would not have occurred had another set of roles and events been experienced. The interpersonal differences in intrapersonal change that exist as a consequence of these naturally occurring experiences attest to the magnitude of the systematic changes in structure and function – the plasticity – that characterizes human life (Lerner, 1984).

Explanatory research is necessary, however, to understand what variables from what levels of organization are involved in particular instances of plasticity that have been seen to exist. In addition, such research is necessary to determine what instances of plasticity may be created by science or society. In other words, explanatory research is needed to ascertain the extent of human plasticity or, in turn, the limits of plasticity (Lerner, 1984). From a developmental contextual perspective, the conduct of such research requires the scientist to alter the natural ecology of the person or group he or she is studying. Such research may involve either proximal and/or distal variations in the context of human development (Lerner & Ryff, 1978), but, in any case, these manipulations constitute theoretically guided alterations of the roles and events a person or group experiences at, or over, a portion of the life span.

These alterations are indeed interventions. They are planned attempts to alter the system of person-context relations constituting the basic process of change; they are conducted in order to ascertain the specific bases of, or to test the limits of, particular instances of human plasticity (Baltes, Dittmann-Kohli, & Dixon, 1984; Baltes, Smith, & Staudinger, 1992). These interventions are a researcher's attempt to substitute designed person-context relations for naturally occurring ones, a substitution done in an attempt to understand the process of changing person-context relations that provides the basis of human development. In short, then, basic manipulative research in human development is intervention research.

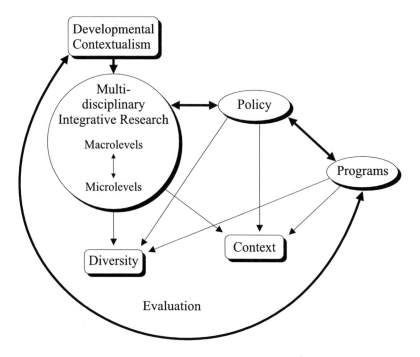

Figure 2: *A developmental contextual model of the integration of multilevel, multidisciplinary research, aimed at diversity and context, with policies, programs, and evaluations*

In this view, policy and program endeavors do *not* constitute secondary work, or derivative applications, conducted after research evidence has been complied. Quite to the contrary, policy development and implementation, and program design and delivery, become integral components in a developmental contextual vision for research. The evaluation component of such policy and intervention work provides critical feedback about the adequacy of the conceptual frame from which this research agenda should derive. This conception taking multidisciplinary research endeavors centrally aimed at diversity and context and integrating them with policies, programs, and evaluations is illustrated in Figure 2. As depicted in this figure, intervention research becomes a means to test basic propositions about process of human development. To test theoretically predicated ideas about how the differences in person-context relations lead to diverse developmental trajectories, developmental contextual researchers introduce (or select) variations in these relations and appraise whether this variance is associated with predicted differences in development. Such person-context variation may involve contrasts in levels of urbanization, differences in the services present in particular urban neighborhoods, or differences in living density in various parts of a city. In any case, and dependent on the level of organization involved in the induced (or simulated) person-context variation, these "manipulations" represent interventions into, that is planned alternations of, the nature of the relations that individuals have with the settings within which they live.

It should be noted that the developmental contextual perspective about the integration between developmental research and policies and programs is consistent with the vision of this relation articulated more than two decades ago by Bronfenbrenner (1974). He argued that engagement with social policy not only enhances developmental research but, consistent with the developmental contextual perspective, also augments understanding of key theoretical issues pertinent to the nature of person-context relations. As Bronfenbrenner (1974) noted:

In discussions of the relation between science and social policy, the first axiom, at least among social scientists, is that social policy should be based on science. The proposition not only has logic on its side, but what is more important, it recognizes our proper and primary importance in the scheme of things. The policymakers should look to us, not only for truth, but for wisdom as well. In short, social policy needs science.

My thesis in this paper is the converse proposition, that, particularly in our field, science needs social policy – needs it not to guide our organizational activities, but to provide us with two elements essential for any scientific endeavor – vitality and validity (p. 1). . . . I contend that the pursuit of [social policy] questions is essential for the further development of knowledge and theory on the process of human development. Why essential? (p. 2). . . . [Because] issues of social policy [serve] as points of departure for the identification of significant theoretical and scientific questions concerning the development of the human organism as a function of interaction with its enduring environment – both actual and potential (p. 4).

In short, with Bronfenbrenner (1974), we believe that the cutting-edge of theory and research in human development lies in the application of the conceptual and methodological expertise of human-development scientists to the "natural ontogenetic laboratory" of the real world. Multilevel and, hence, qualitatively and quantitatively multivariate, and longitudinal research methods must be used by scholars from multiple disciplines to derive, from theoretical models of person-context relations, programs of research that involve the design, delivery, and evaluation of interventions aimed at enhancing – through scientist-introduced variation – the course of human development.

In developmental contextualism there is a stress on ontological (and on epistemological, we would add) relationism and contextualization. These emphases have brought to the fore of scientific, intervention, and policy concerns issues pertinent to the functional importance of diverse person-context interactions. Examples are studies of the effects of variations in inner-city mothers' employment on infant, child, and young adolescent development; the importance of differences in quality day care for the immediate and long-term development in urban children of healthy physical, psychological, and social characteristics; and the effect ways that the healthy development of children and adolescents are affected by variations in marital role strain, marital stability-instability, and other aspects of urban family life.

2.1   The substantive importance of a focus on diversity in research and outreach

As greater study has been made of the actual contexts within which people live, behavioral and social scientists have shown increasing appreciation of the diversity of patterns of individual and family development that exist and that comprise the range of human structural and functional characteristics. We have noted that such diversity – including racial, ethnic, gender, physical handicap, national, and cultural variation – has not been a prime concern of empirical analysis (Fisher & Brennan, 1992; Hagen et al., 1990) to the detriment of the knowledge base in human development.

For instance, content analyses of articles that appeared from 1930 through 1990 in in *Child Development,* the flagship journal of the Society for Research in Child Development and arguably the most prestigious publication outlet for scientific scholarship about children, indicate that little attention was paid to either diversity of people or variation in their contexts (see Hagen et al., 1990).

Indeed, across that 60-year period since *Child Development* began publication in 1930, only a very small percentage of the articles in the journal focused on the context of the child, and that number continued to decrease. From 1930 through 1969, the share of articles in which the child was the only focus of measurement varied from about 80 to 90 percent. From 1970 through 1990, it was about 95 percent or more. From 1930 through 1964, the share of articles in which the environment, or context, of child development was the focus of measurement varied about 10 to 15 percent, but from 1969 through 1990 it varied from about 2 to zero percent. Obviously, with this low percentage of articles involving the measurement of context, the percentage of studies involving the measurement of child-context *relations*, that is, the focal unit of analysis stressed in developmental contextualism (Lerner, 1991), would be even lower.

And who was the child focused on in the research reported in the pages of *Child Development*? Was the absence of attention to the context of child development, an omission that therefore precluded any focus on the role of contextual *variation* (diversity) in children's development, associated with concern with the individual differences (diversity) that existed among the children participating in the research reported in the journal? Unfortunately, the answer to this question is "no."

According to the analyses of Hagen et al. (1990) the participants in the studies published in *Child Development* were either middle-class, European-American children or were children whose racial and socioeconomic status were not even mentioned. Considering only the 1980s, for example, one finds that about 50 percent of all articles did not specify the socioeconomic status of the children who were studied and, if socioeconomic status was noted, over 30 percent of the articles were about children from the middle class. About 55 percent of all studies published in *Child Development* in the 1980-1984 period did not specify the race of the children participating in the research. From 1984 through 1989, this percentage *increased* to about 65 percent! Moreover, in the minority of articles wherein the race of participants was indicated, most articles were about European-American children. This was the case with about 29 percent of the articles in the 1980-1984 period and about 25 percent of the articles in the 1984-1989 period. Clearly, with such a predominant focus on these American children, not only were other groups of U.S. youth not extensively studied but there was little attention given to the children of Europe, South America, and Asia.

This omission of concern with diversity was not just a characteristic of articles published in *Child Development*. Assessing the share of articles about African-Americans published from 1970 through 1989 in the four major journals of the American Psychological Association that pertain to human behavior and development – the *Journal of Personality and Social Psychology*, the *Journal of Educational Psychology*, the *Journal of Consulting and Clinical Psychology*, and *Developmental Psychology* – Graham (1992) found that only about 5.5 percent of the articles published in the 1970-1974 period pertained to African-Americans. From 1985 through 1989 – the end of the 20-year period assessed by Graham (1992) – the share of articles about African-Americans published across the four journals *decreased* to about 1.5 percent. Moreover, rates of publication about non-U.S. individuals would have been even lower than those associated with African-Americans.

Thus, researchers publishing in the best disciplinary and multidisciplinary journals pertinent to research about child behavior and development appear to be increasingly *less* concerned about studying the diversity of people that comprise the youth of the United States and of the world. In other words, scholars publishing in the best journals in the field of human behavior and development have as a group acted either (a) as if they were studying the "generic child," a child whose individual and contextual characteristics were of such little importance that even mention of some of the relatively easily accessible instances of these characteristics (e.g., race and/or socioeconomic status) was not necessary, or (b) as if the only characteristics worth mentioning were European-American, middle-class ones.

It may be deemed by some people as impolite or impolitic to note this shortcoming of scientific inquiry. However, such lack of sensitivity to human individual and contextual diversity cannot continue. The absence of sensitivity to diversity is, clearly, morally repugnant to many people *and*, at least equally important in this context, such lack of sensitivity is simply bad science (Lerner, 1991, in press).

From a developmental contextual perspective, there are several reasons why diversity should become a key focus of concern in the study of human development (Lerner, 1991, Lerner, 1992, in press). Over the course of the next decade, 1.5 billion new children will be born in the world, and most of these births will occur in Third World countries (Lerner, 1994). The pressures these young people will place on the economic, energy, employment, and ecological dimensions of their countries, and the world as a whole, cannot be fully appreciated; knowledge about the different cultural, religious, ethnic, and historical backgrounds of these diverse young people and about their specific developmental needs and potential will need to be generated by developmental scientists if they are to contribute relevant information to the global community.

Diversity exists within countries as well as across nations, and the pressures that this variation imposes on developmentalists to provide new knowledge relevant to the different groups of youth living in a country will increase as the racial and/or ethnic composition of a nation becomes more diverse over the next decade. Trends in the United States may be used to illustrate this point. As noted by McLoyd (1994), about 25 percent of all U. S. citizens had African, Asian, Hispanic, or Native American ancestry by 1990. Moreover, the proportion of U.S. citizens from other than European backgrounds will continue to grow. For example, more than 80 percent of legal immigrants to America continue to be from non-European backgrounds (Barringer, 1991). Furthermore, McLoyd (1994) noted that higher fertility rates among minority groups continue to contribute to the increasing proportion of the American population that is comprised by groups that are now considered minorities. By the end of this century the Hispanic population in America will increase by about 21 percent, the Asian-American population by about 22 percent, and the African-American population by about 12 percent. By contrast, the European-American population will grow by only about 2 percent (Barringer, 1991; McLoyd, 1994; Wetzel, 1987). Accordingly, by about the year 2000 approximately 33 percent of all U.S. children and youth will be from "minority" groups and, in some states (e.g., California, Texas, and New Mexico), the majority of young people are already, or by the year 2000 will be, from "minority" groups (Dryfoos, 1990; Henry, 1990; McLoyd, 1994).

Given these demographic trends, it is not appropriate – and, in fact, it might be disastrous for the future health and welfare of America – for the diversity of America's children to be ignored in scientific research or outreach. As stressed by McLoyd (1994, pp. 59-60):

In view of these demographic changes, rendering minority children virtually invisible in the annals of knowledge about the conditions that facilitate and disrupt development is indefensible ethically. That some of the most pressing problems now facing America affect, disproportionately, children and youth from ethnic minority backgrounds makes it all the more so. It is also inimical to the long-term self-interests of the nation because minority youth's fraction of the total youth population is increasing precisely at a time when the proportion of youth in the total population is dwindling. . . . Consequently, the proportion of youths in the total population will continue to fall, reaching a low of 13 percent in 1996, down from 19 percent in 1980. The implications of this trend are far-reaching. The decline in the number of youth, and ultimately, the number of entrants into the labor force, means that the ratio of workers to retirees will shrink. The economic and social well-being of the nation will depend even more than at present on its ability to enhance the intellectual and social skills of all its youth, as these will be crucial for maximum productivity in the workplace.

Evidence for the presence and substantive and societal importance of individual diversity is coupled with similar information relevant to the significance of contextual variation in human development. A key instance here, especially insofar as it pertains to building outreach programs that address the problems of youth developing in poor or low-income urban neighborhoods, involves the needs and assets of such communities.

2.2 Diversity in the characteristics of poor urban communities

Given the historical record in child development research of insensitivity to the general environment, or context, within which children develop (Bronfenbrenner, 1977, 1979; Hagen et al., 1990), it is not surprising that little attention has been paid to the variation that exists *within* any given setting. After all, if the context in general has not been of particular concern to child development researchers, then it is understandable that even less interest has been shown about the potential importance for development of either variation across or variation within contexts (Elder, Modell, & Parke, 1993).

One instance of a lack of attention to important contextual diversity occurs with respect to poor or low-income urban communities (Kretzmann & McKnight, 1993), that is, neighborhoods where the majority of the families live at or below the poverty line, defined (at least as far the United States is concerned) with regard to levels of income associated with families of a given size. In the United States it is often the case that these neighborhoods are seen to be exclusively characterized by needs and deficiencies. For instance, Kretzmann and McKnight (1993) noted that such settings may be often aptly characterized as being comprised of slum housing, crime gangs, drug abuse, and the other neighborhood needs depicted in the "map" presented in Figure 3.

However, while these needs are in fact often all present in such communities, a sole focus on such problems will result in a significant underestimation of the community's capacity for marshalling the human, and even fiscal, resources necessary for the design and implementation of programs promoting positive features of human development. Kretzmann and McKnight (1993) noted that poor neighborhoods have assets such as cultural and religious organizations, public schools, citizen associations, and the other assets depicted in the "map" presented in

Figure 4. Unless attention is paid to these assets, that is, to the fact that there is diversity involving needs as well as resources, only a deficit model of poor communities will be available to contribute to ideas for policies and programs pertinent to the people living in such settings. If that happens, both research and outreach will underestimate the human capital that exists and that may be enhanced in poor and low income urban communities.

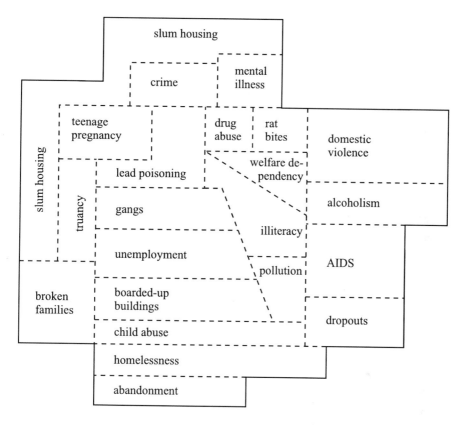

Figure 3: An example of a "neighborhood needs" map (from Kretzmann & McKnight, 1993)

In sum, diversity of people and their settings means that one cannot assume that general rules of development either exist for, or apply in the same way to, all children. Even if only small portions of the total variance in human behavior and development reflect variance that is unique to an individual or group, one cannot assume that this nonshared variance is not the most salient information available when attempting to understand or enhance the quality of life for the person or group. Accordingly, a new research agenda is called for. This agenda would focus on diversity and context while attending to individual development, contextual changes, and the mutual influences between the two.

In addition, however, scholars involved in such research would have at least two other concerns, ones deriving from the view, noted above, that basic, explanatory research in human development is, in its essence, intervention research.

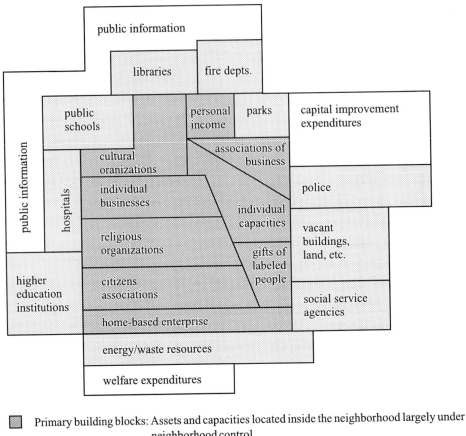

Primary building blocks: Assets and capacities located inside the neighborhood largely under neighborhood control

Secondary building blocks: Assets located within the commuity, but largely controlled by outsiders.

Potential building blocks: Resources originating outside the neighborhood, controlled by outsiders.

Figure 4: An example of a "neighborhood assets" map (from Kretzmann & McKnight, 1993)

3 Implications for policies and programs

In developmental contextualism the variation in settings within which people live means that studying development in a standard (e.g., "controlled") environment does not provide information pertinent to the actual (ecologically valid) developing relations between individually distinct people and their specific contexts (e.g., their particular families, schools, or communities). This point underscores the need to conduct research in real-world settings and highlights our view that (a) policies and programs constitute natural experiments, that is, planned interventions for people and institutions; and (b) the evaluation of such activities becomes a central focus in the developmental contextual research agenda we have described.

However, we must emphasize that, to be successful, these developmental, individual differences and this contextual/ecological view of an integrated agenda of research, policy, and programs for human development require not only collaboration across disciplines. In addition, two other types of collaboration are required. It is useful to discuss these collaborative activities in relation to themes that might organize the future activities of the individuals involved in studying and enhancing human development in the urban context.

A new research and outreach agenda is brought to the fore by a developmental contextual perspective. This agenda should focus on individual diversity and contextual variation and on the mutual influences between the two. Simply stated, integrated multidisciplinary and developmental research and outreach devoted to the study of diversity and context must be moved to the fore of scholarly concern.

Second, this integrative research and outreach must be synthesized with two other foci. First, as just implied, this research must be integrated with policies and programs. Second, this research must involve collaboration among disciplines and between scholarly and community interests.

With regard to the first focus, we have just noted that human development research that is concerned with one or even a few instances of individual and contextual diversity cannot be assumed to be useful for understanding the life course of all people. Similarly, policies and programs derived from research insensitive to diversity and context cannot hope to be applicable, or equally appropriate and useful, in all settings or for all individuals. Accordingly, developmental and individual differences-oriented policy development and program design and delivery must be integrated with the new research base (Lerner & Miller, 1993; Lerner et al., 1994). Indeed, when attempts are made to explain the diversity of changing person-context relations that characterizes the human life course, then research-derived outreach becomes a means to test developmental contextual models of change processes. To be successful, these endeavors require more than collaboration across disciplines. In addition, two other types of collaboration are necessary.

First, multiprofessional collaboration is essential. Colleagues in the research, policy, and intervention communities must plan and implement their activities in a synthesized manner in order to develop and extend this vision successfully. All components of this collaboration must be understood as equally valuable, indeed as equally essential. The collaborative activities of colleagues in university extension and outreach; in program design and delivery; in elementary, middle (or junior high), and high schools; in urban policy planning, development, and analysis; and in academic research are vital to the success of this new agenda for science and outreach for children, adolescents, parents, and their contexts, for example, their extended families, their schools, their workplaces, and their communities.

Second, given the contextual embeddedness of these synthetic research and outreach activities, collaboration must occur with the people developmental researchers are trying both to understand and to serve. Without incorporating the perspective of the urban community into our work, without this community's sense of ownership, value, and meaning for these endeavors, research and outreach activities cannot be adequately integrated into the lives we are studying.

From a developmental contextual perspective, research that "parachutes" into the urban community from the heights of the academy (i.e., research done in a community without collaboration with the members of the community) is fatally flawed with regard to its ability to understand the process of human development. The reason is that human development does not just happen at the general level (Lerner, 1988, 1991); it does not occur in a manner necessarily generalizable across diverse people and contexts. Development happens in particular urban settings as they exist in particular nations and at specific periods of history, and development involves the attempts of specific children and families to relate to the physical, personal, social, and institutional situations found in their communities and cultures. Without bringing the perspective of the urban community into the "plan" for research, the scholar may very likely fail to address the correct problems of human development, the ones involved in the actual lives of the people he or she is studying. And if the wrong problem is being addressed, any "answers" that are found are not likely to be relevant to the actual lives of people. Not surprisingly, these "answers" will be seen all too often (and quite appropriately) as irrelevant by the community.

However, if the community collaborates in defining the problems of development that they and their collaborators are confronting, and if they participate in the construction of the research process, then answers that are obtained will more likely be the ones that they wish to know. The answers will be ones more apt to be used to build community-specific policies and programs. Moreover, building community empowerment and capacity is a collaborative process wherein the community places value and meaning on, and participates in, the research and outreach being conducted within its boundaries (Dryfoos, 1990, 1994; Schorr, 1988).

In sum, a developmental contextual perspective promotes collaboration *with* communities (and not just research or outreach *in* communities). By linking the academy's scholarship with an empowered community, developmental contextualism provides theoretically innovative, methodologically rigorous (von Eye, 1990a, b, c), but complex and arduous, means to build relevance into the study of how human development occurs in urban settings.

References

Andersson, B.-E. (1989). Effects of public day care: A longitudinal study. *Child Development, 60*, 857-866.

Baltes, P. B. (1968). Longitudinal and cross-sectional sequences in the study of age and generation effects. *Human Development, 11*, 145-171.

Baltes, P. B. (1987). Theoretical propositions of life-span developmental psychology: On the dynamics between growth and decline. *Developmental Psychology, 23*, 611-626.

Baltes, P. B., & Baltes, M. M. (1980). Plasticity and variability in psychological aging: Methodological and theoretical issues. In G. E. Gurski (Ed.), *Determining the effects of aging on the central nervous system* (pp. 41-66). Berlin: Schering.

Baltes, P. B., Dittmann-Kohli, F., & Dixon, R. A. (1984). New perspectives on the development of intelligence in adulthood: Toward a dual-process conception and model of selective optimization with compensation. In P. B. Baltes & O. G. Brim, Jr. (Eds.), *Life-span develop-ment and behavior* (Vol. 6, pp. 33-76). New York: Academic Press.

Baltes, P. B., Reese, H. W., & Lipsitt, L. P. (1980). Life-span developmental psychology. *Annual Review of Psychology, 31*, 65-110.

Baltes, P. B., Smith, J., & Staudinger, U. M. (1992). Wisdom and successful aging. In T. B. Sonderegger (Ed.), *Nebraska Symposium on Motivation, 39* (pp. 123-167). Lincoln, NE: University of Nebraska.

Barringer, F. (1991, March 11). Census shows profound change in racial makeup of the nation. *The New York Times*, pp. 1, A12.

Bell, R. Q. (1968). A reinterpretation of the direction of effects in studies of socialization. *Psychological Review, 75*, 81-95.

Block, J. (1971). *Lives through time*. Berkeley: Bancroft Books.

Brim, O. G., Jr., & Kagan, J. (Ed.). (1980). *Constancy and change in human development*. Cambridge: Harvard University Press.

Bronfenbrenner, U. (1974). Developmental research, public policy, and the ecology of childhood. *Child Development, 45*, 1-5.

Bronfenbrenner, U. (1977). Toward an experimental ecology of human development. *American Psychologist, 32*, 513-531.

Bronfenbrenner, U. (1979). *The ecology of human development*. Cambridge, MA: Harvard University Press.

Bronfenbrenner, U. (1983). The context of development and the development of context. In R. M. Lerner (Ed.), *Developmental psychology: Historical and philosophical perspectives* (pp. 39-83). Hillsdale, NJ: Erlbaum.

Bronfenbrenner, U. (in press). The ecology of developmental processes. In W. Damon (General Ed.) & R. M. Lerner (Vol. Ed.), *Handbook of Child Psychology: Vol 1. Theoretical models of human development* (5th ed.). New York: Wiley.

Bronfenbrenner, U., & Crouter, A. C. (1983). The evolution of environmental models in developmental research. In P. H. Mussen (Series Ed.) & W. Kessen (Vol. Ed.), *Handbook of child psychology: Vol. 1: History, theories, and methods* (4th ed., pp. 39-83). New York: Wiley.

Dixon, R. A., & Lerner, R. M. (1992). A history of systems in developmental psychology. In M. H. Bornstein & M. E. Lamb (Eds.), *Developmental psychology: An advanced textbook* (3rd ed., pp. 3-58). Hillsdale, NJ: Erlbaum.

Dixon, R. A., Lerner, R. M., & Hultsch, D. F. (1991). The concept of development in individual and social change. In P. Van Geert & L. P. Mos (Eds.), *Annals of theoretical psychology* (Vol. 7, pp. 279-323). New York: Plenum.

Dryfoos, J. G. (1990). *Adolescents at risk: Prevalence and prevention.* New York: Oxford University.

Dryfoos, J. G. (1994). *Full service schools: A revolution in health and social services for children, youth and families.* San Francisco: Jossey-Bass.

Elder, G. H. (1974). *Children of the Great Depression: Social change in life experiences.* Chicago: University of Chicago Press.

Elder, G. H., Jr. (1980). Adolescence in historical perspective. In J. Adelson (Ed.), *Handbook of adolescent psychology* (pp. 3-46). New York: Wiley.

Elder, G. H., Modell, J., & Parke, R. D. (1993). Studying children in a changing world. In G. H. Elder, J. Modell, & R. D. Parke (Eds.), *Children in time and place: Developmental and historical insights* (pp. 3-21). New York: Cambridge University Press.

Featherman, D. L. (1983). Life-span perspectives in social science research. In P. B. Baltes & O. G. Brim, Jr. (Eds.), *Life-span development and behavior* (Vol. 5, pp. 1-57). New York: Academic.

Finkelstein, J. W. (1993). Familial influences on adolescent health. In R. M. Lerner (Ed.), *Early adolescence: Perspectives on research, policy, and intervention* (pp. 111-126). Hillsdale, NJ: Erlbaum.

Fisher, C. B., & Brennan, M. (1992). Application and ethics in developmental psychology. In D. L. Featherman, R. M. Lerner, & M. Perlmutter (Eds.), *Life-span development and behavior* (Vol. 11, pp. 189-219). Hillsdale, NJ: Erlbaum.

Ford, D. L., & Lerner, R. M. (1992). *Developmental systems theory: An integrative approach.* Newbury Park, CA: Sage.

Garbarino, J. (1992). *Children and families in the social environment* (2nd ed.). New York: Aldine de Gruyter.

Gottlieb, G. (1991). The experiential canalization of behavioral development: Theory. *Developmental Psychology, 27,* 4-13.

Gottlieb, G. (1992). *Individual development and evolution: The genesis of novel behavior.* New York: Oxford.

Graham, S. (1992). "Most of the subjects were white and middle class": Trends in published research on African Americans in selected APA journals, 1970-1989. *American Psychologist, 5,* 629-639.

Hagen, J. W., Paul, B., Gibb, S., & Wolters, C. (1990, March). Trends in research as reflected by publications in *Child Development:* 1930-1989. In *Biennial Meeting of the Society for Research on Adolescence,* Atlanta, GA.

Hamburg, D. A. (1992). *Today's children: Creating a future for a generation in crisis.* New York: Time Books.

Henry, W. (1990, April 9). Beyond the melting pot. *Time,* pp. 28-31.

Hernandez, D. J. (1993). *America's children: Resources from family, government, and the economy.* New York: Russell Sage Foundation.

Hetherington, E. M., & Baltes, P. B. (1988). Child psychology and life-span development. In E. M. Hetherington, R. M. Lerner, & M. Perlmutter (Eds.), *Child development in life-span perspective* (pp. 1-19). Hillsdale, NJ: Erlbaum.

Howard, J. (1978). The influence of children's developmental dysfunction on marital quality and family interaction. In R. M. Lerner &. G. B. Spanier (Eds.), *Child influences on marital and family interaction: A life-span perspective* (pp. 275-298). New York: Academic Press.

Kretzmann, J. P., & McKnight, J. L. (1993). *Building communities from the inside out: A path toward finding and mobilizing a community's assets.* (Available from the Center for Urban Affairs and Policy Research, Northwestern University, 2040 Sheridan Road, Evanston, IL 60208.)

Lerner, R. M. (1978). Nature, nurture, and dynamic interactionism. *Human Development, 21,* 1-20.

Lerner, R. M. (1979). A dynamic interactional concept of individual and social relationship development. In R. L. Burgess & T. L. Huston (Eds.), *Social exchange in developing relationships,* (pp. 271-305). New York: Academic.

Lerner, R. M. (1982). Children and adolescents as producers of their own development. *Developmental Review, 2,* 342-370.

Lerner, R. M. (1984). *On the nature of human plasticity.* New York: Cambridge University.

Lerner, R. M. (1986). *Concepts and theories of human development* (2nd ed.). New York: Random House.

Lerner, R. M. (1988). Early adolescent transitions: The lore and the laws of adolescence. In M. D. Levine & E. R. McArarney (Eds.), *Early adolescent transitions* (pp. 1-40). Lexington, MA: D. C. Heath.

Lerner, R. M. (1991). Changing organism-context relations as the basic process of development: A developmental-contextual perspective. *Developmental Psychology, 27,* 27-32.

Lerner, R. M. (1992). Diversity. *SRCD Newsletter,* pp. 2, 12.

Lerner, R. M. (1994). Addressing the problems of youth through the promotion of positive youth development: A developmental contextual model. In Korea Institute for Youth Development, *Adolescent development and community participation* (pp. 2-61). Seoul, Korea: Korea Institute for Youth Development.

Lerner, R. M. (1995). *America's youth in crisis: Challenges and options for programs and policies.* Thousand Oaks, CA: Sage.

Lerner, R. M. (in press). Diversity and context in research, policy, and programs for children and adolescence: A developmental contextual perspective. In G. K. Brookins & M. B. Spencer (Eds.), *Ethnicity & diversity: Implications for research policies.* Hillsdale, NJ: Erlbaum.

Lerner, R. M., & Busch-Rossnagel, N. A. (Eds.). (1981). *Individuals as producers of their development: A life-span perspective.* New York: Academic.

Lerner, R. M., Hultsch, D. F., & Dixon, R. A. (1983). Contextualism and the character of developmental psychology in the 1970s. *Annals of the New York Academy of Sciences, 412,* 101-128.

Lerner, R. M., & Kauffman, M. B. (1985). The concept of development in contextualism. *Developmental Review, 5,* 309-333.

Lerner, R. M., & Miller, J. R. (1993). Integrating human development research and intervention for America's children: The Michigan State University model. *Journal of Applied Developmental Psychology, 14,* 347-364.

Lerner, R. M., Miller, J. R., Knott, J. H., Corey, K. E., Bynum, T. S., Hoopfer, L. C., McKinney, M. H., Abrams, L. A., Hula, R. C., & Terry, P. A. (1994). Integrating scholarship and outreach in human development research, policy, and service: A developmental perspective. In D. L. Featherman, R. M. Lerner, & M. Perlmutter (Eds.), *Life-span development and behavior* (pp. 249-273). Hillsdale, NJ: Erlbaum.

Lerner, R. M., & Ryff, C. D. (1978). Implementation of the life-span view of human development: The sample case of attachment. In P. B. Baltes (Ed.), *Life-span development and
behavior, 1* (pp. 1-44). New York: Academic.

Lerner, R. M., & Spanier, G. B. (Eds.). (1978). *Child influences on marital and family
interaction: A life-span perspective.* New York: Academic.

Lewis, M., & Fiering, C. (1978). A child's social world. In R. M. Lerner & G. B. Spanier (Eds.),
Child influences on marital and family interaction (pp. 47-66). New York: Academic.

Lewis, M., & Rosenblum, L. A. (Eds.). (1974). *The effect of the infant on its caregivers.* New
York: Wiley.

Little, R. R. (1993, March). *What's working for today's youth: The issues, the programs, and the
learnings.* Paper presented at an ICYF Fellows' Colloquium, Michigan State University, East
Lansing.

McLoyd, V. C. (1994). Research in the service of poor and ethnic/racial minority children: A
moral imperative. *Family and Consumer Sciences Research Journal, 23,* 56-66.

Parke, R. D., & Collmer, C. (1975). Child abuse: An interdisciplinary review. In E. M.
Hetherington (Ed.), *Review of child development research* (Vol. 5, pp. 509-590). Chicago:
University of Chicago Press.

Riegel, K. F. (1975). Toward a dialectical theory of development. *Human Development, 18,* 50-
64.

Riegel, K. F. (1976a). The dialectics of human development. *American Psychologist, 31,* 689-
700.

Riegel, K. F. (1976b). From traits and equilibrium toward developmental dialectics. In J. K.
Cole (General Ed.) and A. W. Landfield (Vol. Ed.), *Nebraska symposium on motivation: Vol
24. Current theory and research in motivation: Personal construct psychology* (pp. 348-408).
Lincoln: University of Nebraska.

Riley, M. W. (Ed.). (1979). *Aging from birth to death.* Washington, DC: American Association
for the Advancement of Science.

Sameroff, A. (1975). Transactional models in early social relations. *Human Development, 18,*
65-79.

Sameroff, A. J. (1983). Developmental systems: Contexts and evolution. In P. H. Mussen
(Series Ed.) & W. Kessen (Vol. Ed.), *Handbook of child psychology: Vol. 1. History, theory
and methods* (pp. 237-294). New York: Wiley.

Schaie, K. W. (1965). A general model for the study of developmental problems. *Psychological
Bulletin, 64,* 92-107.

Schneirla, T. C. (1957). The concept of development in comparative psychology. In D. B. Harris
(Ed.), *The concept of development* (pp. 78-108). Minneapolis: University of Minnesota.

Schorr, L. B. (1988). *Within our reach: Breaking the cycle of disadvantage.* New York:
Doubleday.

Smith, L. B., & Thelen, E. (Eds.). (1993). *A dynamic systems approach to development:
Applications.* Cambridge, MA: MIT Press.

Thelen, E., & Smith, L. B. (in press). Dynamics systems theories. In W. Damon (General Ed.) &
R. M. Lerner (Vol. Ed.), *Handbook of Child Psychology: Vol. 1. Theoretical models of human
development* (5th ed.). New York: Wiley.

Thomas, A. T., Chess, S., Birch, H. G., Hertzig, M. E., & Korn, S. (1963). *Behavioral
individuality in early childhood.* New York: New York University.

Tobach, E. (1981). Evolutionary aspects of the activity of the organism and its development. In
R. M. Lerner & N. A. Busch-Rossnagel (Eds.), *Individuals as producers of their development: A life-span perspective* (pp. 37-68). New York: Academic.

Tobach, E., & Greenberg, G. (1984). The significance of T. C. Schneirla's contribution to the concept of levels of integration. In G. Greenberg & E. Tobach (Eds.), *Behavioral evolution and integrative levels* (pp. 1-7). Hillsdale, NJ: Erlbaum.

Tubman, J. G., & Lerner, R. M. (1994). Stability of affective experiences of parents and their children from adolescence to young adulthood. *Journal of Adolescence, 17,* 81-98.

von Eye, A. (1990a). *Introduction to configural frequency analysis: The search for types and antitypes in cross-classifications.* Cambridge: Cambridge University.

von Eye, A. (Ed.). (1990b). *Statistical methods in longitudinal research: Principles and structuring change.* New York: Academic.

von Eye, A. (Ed.). (1990c). *Statistical methods in longitudinal research: Time series and categorical longitudinal data.* New York: Academic.

Vondracek, F. W., Lerner, R. M., & Schulenberg, J. E. (1986). *Career development: A life-span developmental approach.* Hillsdale, NJ: Erlbaum.

Werner, H. (1957). The concept of development from a comparative and organismic point of view. In D. B. Harris (Ed.), *The concept of development* (pp. 125-148). Minneapolis: University of Minnesota.

Wetzel, J. (1987). *American youth: A statistical snapshot.* New York: William T. Grant Foundation.

The young and the old in the city: Developing intergenerational relationships in urban environments

Frieder R. Lang

The benefits and costs of living in the city have been debated since the beginnings of modern urbanism. A central issue of this debate refers to the impact of urbanization on the life quality of those who grow up and become old in the city. Urbanization has been associated with a predominance of cosmopolitan as opposed to traditional values and changes of age-specific social roles (Cowgill, 1974). The city has also been described as patronizing the individual, whose mobility and social ties are kept in leading-strings (Mitscherlich, 1971). This chapter addresses the role of urban environments for the life-span development of social and intergenerational relationships. More specifically, the constraints and opportunities of urban contexts are discussed in relation to the development of social relationships between young and old urban residents.

At least two interwoven perspectives need to be differentiated in this realm. The first one refers to the city as a context of development in general, and of personal relationships in specific. The social embeddedness and social interactions of the individual are viewed as being regulated by the specific constraints of urban life. The second perspective focuses on social relationships as a context of development within the constraints and potentials of the city. Both perspectives are closely connected. Depending on whether the functions and processes of social relationships are conceptualized as antecedent or consequent conditions of urban development, one might find oneself skipping repeatedly from the one perspective to the other. In this chapter, both the development of relationships within the urban context and the specific relationships in the city as a context of development are discussed within a general framework of adaptive life-span development, that is, the model of selective optimization with compensation (Baltes & Baltes, 1990; Marsiske, Lang, Baltes, & Baltes, 1995). This means that the respective costs and benefits of intergenerational relationships are discussed with respect to the age-specific developmental demands and potentials of the urban context.

Adults living in a city all know it from their adult perspective. In their minds, then, they may represent "their" city as a coherent "life space" rather than as an incoherent collection of diverse opportunities, events, and places (see Downs & Liben, 1993; Lynch, 1963; Muchow & Muchow, 1935/1978). As the contributions in this volume suggest, the child's perspective on the city may be different from that of an adult. One may even speculate that the city is clustered around "small worlds" that are age-specific in their nature (e.g., Fischer, 1982; Lynch, 1977).

For example, the city of a child might be structured around places such as the home and playgrounds in the neighborhood. While some areas such as the immediate vicinity of the child's home may provide a sense of security and reliability to the child, other places, such as unknown areas beyond the limits of these "secure areas" may stimulate and help unravel the child's curiosity, imagination, and play (see Görlitz & Wohlwill, 1987; see also Keller, in this volume) beyond the parents' or caregivers' zone of influence on the child. Playgrounds, sidewalks, traffic signs, fields in the neighborhood, courtyards of public schools, and all other urban places offer their particular and unique opportunities to the developing child and point to some of the unique potentials and dangers that characterize child development in the city (see, for example, Proshansky & Fabian, 1987). It has been argued that the city of the child consists of a number of insular spaces for particular activities (Zeiher, 1990). Thus, it is the subjective coherence of these "islands of activity" in the city that determines the child's development of an inner map of the city (Downs & Stea, 1977; Matthews, 1992; Muchow & Muchow, 1935/1978). Note, though, that it cannot be the pretension of this chapter to provide an extensive discussion of the mechanisms and processes by which urban environments may affect or determine child development. Rather, this chapter addresses specifically the impact of urban contexts on the child's social world and the child's developing relationships with older people as well as the interrelatedness between the child's and the older individual's social worlds in the city.

But what about the older adults living in the city? Obviously, older adults live in the same city as the child. The elderly individual walks along the same sidewalks as the child; lives in the same living quarters or apartment house; refers to the same public buildings, greens, and public parks; and uses the same stairways, malls, galleries, public transportation, and other facilities. However, the older individual's subjective representation of his or her urban neighborhood differs in many ways from that of the child. For example, the old person's perspective on the city is affected by her or his biography as well as by the historical events that have occurred during the individual's lifetime. Although such influences may also have affected the child's perspective on the city, the older person may have developed a sense that one's own life story in the city and the city's history are quite distinct and separate concepts, a developmental task that lies ahead for the young child. For example, the old person may have lived most of his or her life in the city while performing social roles that may have helped turn urban life into what it has become today (Rubinstein & Parmelee, 1992). Additionally, the city's geography may have changed completely so that an older resident may not even be able to recognize a formerly well-known place. Finally, as age increases and mobility decreases, the old individual's activities might be increasingly restricted to the vicinity of his or her home or apartment (Brim, 1988; Rowles, 1981). The opportunity structure of this vicinity, then, becomes crucial in determining the everyday life of older people (Friedrichs, 1990). Accordingly, such facets of urban life in old age will be referred to in this chapter as *the city of late life*, that is, the subjective and idiosyncratic perspective that an older individual has on the specific demands and resources of his or her urban context.

Thus, the city of childhood and the city of late life differ with respect to the constraints and opportunities that they entail for their respective age-graded subpopulations. The city of the late life, for example, might be constrained by the individual's experience of loss of physical capacities, of sensory deficits, or of age-specific needs and wishes (Altman, Lawton, & Wohlwill, 1984; Carp, 1980; Lawton, 1987, 1989). In contrast, the city of childhood depends on the child's cognitive and behavioral development as well as on the regulatory influence of the child's primary caregivers (Valsiner, 1987; Vygotsky, 1978). As a matter of fact, the child's and the old person's social and physical worlds overlap considerably. Such overlap of the child's and the older adult's city will be referred to here as the *urban zone of intergenerational contact*. However, before turning to a description and discussion of such intergenerational zones in the city, it needs to be clarified how the concept of urban environment (or city) is defined in contrast to the nonurban environment.

Many models of environment (see Bronfenbrenner & Crouter, 1983) contribute to understanding the specific characteristics of urban environments. For example, the city has been defined as a concentration of population, that is, the density of people who live in the same area (Fischer, 1982). From a second perspective the urban context is conceived rather in terms of its morphological or architectural – nonagricultural – characteristics that constitute specific behavior settings (e.g., Bechtel, 1987). In this latter perspective, social space is seen as both the origin and the target of the urban environment: The city is man- and woman made, and the city determines and influences the everyday lives of men and women as well as their life cycle (Bosselmann & Craik, 1987). Both perspectives on the urban environment are relevant to understanding the age-specific adaptiveness of intergenerational relationships in the city.

1. The concentration of population in the city brings together different generations from all ages. Intergenerational relations in the city are therefore not restricted to intergenerational contact within the family or kinship. The city provides an opportunity to see and meet individuals of all age strata and, thus, to learn about the different characteristics of other life phases. Such intergenerational contact might have the character of weak ties rather than of strong ties (see Granovetter, 1973).

2. Urban life is a product of human society, not just a static environment. It changes over time, so urban residents are typically confronted with much change and fluctuation in the characteristics of their environment (Wachs, 1987). The inter-

generational nexus carries on the development and simultaneously preserves the continuity of the city environment.

3. The architecture and design of the city is constructed around the socially desired and normatively determined requirements of all generations living in the city. Thus, in all phases of life, urban citizens are constantly confronted with the architectural and institutional manifestations of the many generations that live and used to live in the city.

In the first section of this chapter, the developmental zones and intergenerational spaces of urban environments are discussed within a framework of life-span development. Particularly, the contextual influences on the adaptive development of intergenerational relationships across the life span are discussed in relation to demographic change and migration in urban environments. In the second section, I discuss selected theoretical considerations and empirical findings that focus on the city of childhood and on the development of intergenerational relationships in urban environments. In the third section of the chapter, selected theoretical and empirical notions pertaining to the city of late life are discussed. That section focuses on the potential adaptive functions of intergenerational relationships in later adulthood. In the fourth section, the age-specific developmental potentials and constraints of an urban zone of intergenerational contact are discussed in relation to a general model of successful development across the life span.

Throughout this chapter, the term *intergenerational relationships* will be used in its broadest sense, meaning all kinds of relationships and transactions between the members of different generations inside and outside the family context. In this sense, all aspects of social contact or interaction between the young and the old are implied, from the most casual contact in the street to the most enduring and close relationship between a grandchild and a grandparent.

1   Development of intergenerational relationships across the life span: contextual influences and theoretical models

In most general terms, life-span developmental psychology views development as a life-long process (P. Baltes, 1987) in which no single life phase assumes priority over others (Marsiske et al., 1995). One of the fundamental perspectives common to most scholars of life-span developmental psychology is contextualism (P. Baltes, 1994; see also Lerner & von Eye, in this volume; Overton, in this volume). According to Baltes (1987; P. Baltes, Reese, & Lipsitt, 1980) at least three interacting sources of contextual influences (i.e., biological or environmental) on ontogenetic development can be differentiated:

1. Age-graded influences relate to factors that are mostly determined by an individual's chronological age. Age-graded influences, for example, pertain to the age-
specific positions of the developing individual in intergenerational relationships as
he or she moves from the position of the youngest (e.g., grandchild) to the position of the oldest generation (e.g., great-grandparent).
2. History-graded influences reflect change in the frame of historical time. For
example, demographic changes reflect history-graded influences that have a direct
effect on the structure of intergenerational relationships.
3. Nonnormative influences, by contrast, reflect those idiosyncratic influences on the
development of some individuals that are, in addition, not timed by chronological
age or historical time. Examples of nonnormative influences are traffic accidents,
diseases and injuries or social losses such as the death of close friends. Obviously,
nonnormative influences can occur at any phase in the life cycle, but there is also
a likelihood that the experience of nonnormative influences accumulates over the
life span. Consequently, nonnormative events may also affect intergenerational
relationships because the older individual reacts to and evaluates the child's
behavior from the perspective of having lived through his or her life story. For
example, a grandmother who has lost a grandchild in a traffic accident might react
quite idiosyncratically upon seeing her neighbor's child play in the street. The
child, in turn, might have trouble understanding the old neighbor's specific reaction.

The three sources of contextual influence are neither static nor mutually independent. As P. Baltes (1987) states, the dynamic interplay of age-graded, history-graded,
and nonnormative influences implies that individuals who are at different phases in
the life span (e.g., grandparents and children) co-develop within "different segments
of the streams of influences" (p. 621). The interplay of age-graded, history-graded,
and nonnormative influences on the development of intergenerational relationships
in the city becomes most obvious when the consequences of demographic change
are taken into consideration.

History-graded influences. The demographics of western industrialized societies are
shifting toward a greater number of elderly people and a smaller number of children
as a result of increased life expectancy and reduced fertility and migration (Ahmed
& Smith, 1992; Deutscher Bundestag, 1994; Myers, 1990). In Germany, for
example, the share of people older than 60 years is expected to increase from
20 percent in 1992 to 34 percent in 2030, whereas the share of those younger than
20 years will decrease from 22 to 16 percent in the same period (Felscher, Gahlen-
Klose, & Neubauer, 1995). The consequences of such changes are reflected in the
city more rapidly and dramatically than in small towns. For instance, there is some
indication that fertility in densely populated areas is even lower than in smaller cities
or towns (Bertram & Dannenbeck, 1991). One consequence of such change is a

relatively high percentage of people above 60 years who live in urban regions (Deutscher Bundestag, 1994), whereas the percentage of children younger than 15 years will decrease in these areas (e.g., Myers, 1990).

Social and demographic changes are affecting the intergenerational structure within the family as well (Aizenberg & Treas, 1985; De Vos & Ruggles, 1988; Hagestad, 1989). In Germany, for example, the birth rate decreased from more than 2 children in 1920 to about 1.5 children in 1990. That is, approximately 75 percent of parents have one or two children (Deutscher Bundestag, 1994). That is, in 1994 an average grandparent with two adult children has three grandchildren. In other words, there are four grandparents who have approximately three grandchildren. In addition, these grandparents are very likely to experience their grandchild's adolescence during their lifetime (Bengtson & Allen, 1993; Kovar & Stone, 1992). Another consequence may be that some grandparents are still involved in professional activities when their grandchildren are born.

On the other side, the share of households with more than five persons (i.e., children, parents, older family member, or older nonfamily person) has been reduced from 44.4 percent in 1900 to 5.3 percent in 1990 (Bretz, 1992). Note, however, that this reduction is mostly due to lower fertility and increased divorce rates and does not indicate a neglect of older generations in the family. Typically, the percentage of older people who live in households with more than two persons increases among people who are older than 80 years (e.g., Lang & Schütze, 1992). However, demographic changes in urban regions are not just a consequence of reduced fertility or prolonged life expectancies but also of age-graded and nonnormative influences.

Age-graded influences. Preferences for the place of residence change as a function of an individual's life phase, social status, and education (Deutscher Bundestag, 1994; Wagner, 1989, 1990). Childless urban professionals and retired older people tend to move downtown in order to minimize distances to their working places, shops, institutions, or other urban facilities, most of which are located in the inner city. Families with young or middle-aged children, however, move out of the inner city into suburban areas or the countryside (Wagner, 1990). It becomes quite clear that there is consequently some loss of opportunity for extrafamilial intergenerational contact in the city when the age homogeneity of a neighborhood increases as a function of such age-graded mobility.

Nonnormative influences. Moreover, the increase of divorce rates, which are even higher in urban areas than in rural ones (Bertram & Dannenbeck, 1991), and remarriage are leading to "step-grandparenthood" (i.e., parents of a step-parent) as a new pattern of intergenerational relationship in addition to biological grandparenthood (e.g., Booth & Dunn, 1994; Kennedy & Kennedy, 1993; Trygstad & Sanders, 1989; Wilk, 1993). That is, a child may have four step-grandparents in addition to four biological grandparents. Obviously, relationships and interaction with older family members can become a ubiquitous and complex aspect of everyday family life for children, depending on whether older family members live in the same city. Although no detailed statistics on the percentages of grandparents living in the same city as their grandchildren have been available to the author, there is clear indication that geographical distance is the most influential predictor of contact frequency between generations (Frankel & DeWit, 1989).

The demographic, familial, and migration-related changes in the age structure of urban life have two implications for intergenerational development in the city. (a) When grandparents live near their childrens' family, urban context creates opportunity structures that promote the development of strong intergenerational ties within the family. (b) In the everyday life of an urban child, contact or interaction with old and very old people who are not acquainted with the child is a rather typical event. This fact clearly enhances the likelihood of casual everyday contact with older people on streets, on public transportation, in shops, and in other public places, for example. Thus, urban children might have a greater number of "weak ties" with older individuals than rural children do. However, the context of such intergenerational ties is restricted to a selected and structured set of particular events or daily activities. Some of these intergenerational encounters might be confined to formal interaction with neighbors (e.g., saying hello to each other, having a small talk in the courtyard) or to informal exchanges such as giving help in exchange for "a dime" or some sweets. The city offers a great variety of opportunities for such casual intergenerational contact. It is still an open question to what extent such encounters actually affect the child's social cognition and perceptions of age and old age and to what extent such contact serves to enhance the social adaptivity of older adults living in the city (e.g., to prevent feelings of loneliness). For example, while there is no doubt about the crucial role that relationships with grandparents and other older adults have for the developing child (e.g., Krappmann, 1997; Schmidt-Denter, 1996), it is still an open question through which mechanisms intergenerational contact can enhance social adaptivity in later life. Which mechanisms characterize adaptive development of social embeddedness and social behavior across the life span (Baltes & Carstensen, in press; P. Baltes, 1994; Marsiske et al., 1995)? Drawing on the concepts and empirical findings of life-span developmental psychology, Paul and Margret Baltes (1990) have developed a metamodel of successful development, namely, the model of selective optimization with compensation that describes processes and mechanisms that lead to positive developmental outcomes.

1.1   The model of selective optimization with compensation

The model of selective optimization with compensation describes a dynamic system of three interacting components that lead to successful life-span development, that is, selection, compensation, and optimization (P. Baltes & Baltes, 1980, 1990). The broader framework and the components of the model of selective optimization with compensation have been described and elaborated elsewhere (e.g., Baltes & Carstensen, in press; P. Baltes & Baltes, 1990; Heckhausen & Schulz, 1993; Marsiske et al., 1995). In the context of this chapter, selective optimization with compensation is related to the domain of social and intergenerational development (Lang & Baltes, 1997; Lang & Carstensen, 1994; Lang & Tesch-Römer, 1993) and discussed in relation to influences of the urban context. As the most fundamental developmental process, *selection* refers to a developmental narrowing of contextual (i.e., biological and environmental) resources. Selection relates to the process by which the individual comes to display a specific unit of behavioral or cognitive performance, thus, excluding some other unit. For example, from the perspective of action theory the process of selection refers predominantly to goal management (Marsiske et al., 1995). Selection is manifest in the urban context, for cities offer a specific set of opportunities and restrictions to the individual. Unlike rural areas, the city offers a greater variety of casual or weak ties to developing individuals. As a consequence, selection in the domain of social functioning might be a relatively salient process in urban areas, where individuals at all ages might have to know with whom, when, where, and how they want to interact before an actual interaction takes place. For instance, the child who wants to meet a friend on the street or in the neighborhood needs to arrange a meeting point and time. Otherwise, there is small likelihood of meeting friends in the city. It seems obvious that children who live in the city need to be quite selective when creating social networks; the number of potential social partners is overwhelming and only a finite number of social relationships can be maintained at the same time. Thus, most neighbors in the city will remain totally unknown to the young or old urban resident. In this sense, selection refers to the individual's specific social goals and preferences when choosing social partners (e.g., Carstensen, 1991).

Compensation refers to a loss-based process of adjustment or recuperation. Compensation means that the individual acquires new resources or uses new means in response to a loss of previously available resources or means. Compensation is manifest in many recreational urban settings where individual's recover from work or urban life. Examples are urban parks or fitness studios, where the city offers facilities pertaining to specific needs and demands of the young and the old in their respective life phases (i.e., playgrounds, benches, quiet zones in the park).

Compensation in intergenerational relationships is most obvious, for example, in the case of a grandparent who gets involved in child-care or child-rearing activities after the parents have divorced (e.g., Werner, 1991). Intergenerational relationships per se may be seen as general compensatory resources, as when grandparents support their adult child by baby-sitting the grandchild or when grandparents receive social support from their grandchild (e.g., Antonucci & Akiyama, 1991; Kennedy, 1992; Lehr & Kruse, 1990; Oyserman, Radin, & Benn, 1993; Sticker, 1991; Tinsley & Parke, 1987).

Optimization refers to the process of enhancing the adaptive value of available or acquired means or resources. Optimization, in this sense, relates to the ensuring and management of energetical resources necessary for performing specific tasks. More generally, optimization implies a refinement or enhancement of means or resources that fit the specific demands or requirements of developmental goals or tasks (P. Baltes & Baltes, 1990; Marsiske et al., 1995). For example, an older person may seek intergenerational contact in order to share or pass on his or her life experience and knowledge to the younger generation, thus pursuing the goal of generativity (Lang & Baltes, 1997).

Optimization, selection, and compensation are manifest in urban life, for it provides manifold institutions and facilities giving specific and adequate education, training, and practice that are in line with the developmental potentials and needs of different individuals. Moreover, the individual who grows up in the city might have experienced interactions with a large variety of different persons. The urban individual develops and trains particular social skills that are required for an adaptive mastery of daily life in the city. As noted above, this means that selection of social partners (e.g., differentiating weak ties from strong ties) is a salient aspect of dealing with others in urban environments. Consequently, there is some need to discuss the age-specific influences and determinants of how people choose their social interaction partners. One model that addresses the motivational and emotional determinants of social contact behavior across the life span is socioemotional selectivity theory.

1.2 Socioemotional selectivity theory and contextual influences

Socioemotional selectivity theory (Carstensen, 1991, 1993a) has been proposed as a motivational model of social interaction behavior across the life span. According to the theory, individuals seek and maintain social contact and social interaction for different purposes or goals that are specific to the individual's phase of life. Although there is a fundamental constellation of goals for social contact related to basic needs of the organism at all ages (e.g., social affiliation, instrumental needs), there are also age-specific and age-dependent goals of social interaction that are determined by past learning experiences, psychological perceptions of the future, and opportunity structures in the environment (Carstensen, 1993a; Carstensen & Lang, 1997). Carstensen (1991, 1993a) distinguishes between three examples of age-specific goals of social interaction: (a) the regulation of emotion, (b) the acquisition of information and (c) development of self-definitions and identity.

The theory contends that, very early in life, children seek social stimulation in order to learn about themselves and about the world. The child is motivated to seek contact even with more unfamiliar social partners. In this sense, intergenerational relationships within the family may be highly important for pursuing self-development and finding out about one's roles and potentials. By contrast, intergenerational relationships outside the family (e.g., with teachers, friends of the family, friends' grandparents, and so forth) might be important informational sources for learning about the world and others. Here, the opportunity structure of the city is unique for the urban child because it offers a great variety of relationships in different contexts. The urban environment seems to match with some of the salient motivations for social contact in childhood.

In old age, by contrast, the individual perceives his or her remaining life time to be limited, and self-definitions and knowledge structures have been stabilized and specialized, so novel social partners become less attractive than social relationships with familiar people who are emotionally meaningful (Carstensen, 1993; Lang & Carstensen, 1994). Moreover, because many relationships in old age have a long history, contact and interaction with familiar social partners also entail many opportunities for reminiscence and life review as well as an expert knowledge about the social partner's biography. Thus, long-term relationships are characterized by high predictability and control of relational outcomes such as emotional rewards or empathy (Carstensen & Lang, 1997). Carstensen (1993a; Carstensen & Lang, 1997) argues that according to socioemotional selectivity theory, the interplay of social motives operates throughout the life span. That is, different social motives and preferences are always present. However, depending on the specific developmental context of the individual, the salience of specific motivation for developing or maintaining a social relationship differs. According to socioemotional selectivity theory (Carstensen, 1993a), this developmental context is mostly determined by the individual's subjective construal of the future. When the future is perceived as limited, short-term gratifications that are predominantly related to emotional aspects of relationships become more salient. The salience of specific social motivations is also determined by characteristics of the individual's social and physical environment. When the external environment is perceived as threatening to the self or when environmental or social resources are insufficient or lacking, the salience and adaptivity of emotional regulation as a social motive seems to increase. For example, Lang, Staudinger, and Carstensen (in press) found in an urban sample of old people aged 70 to 103 years that the adaptivity of socioemotional selectivity increased when nuclear family members were *not* available as compared to when nuclear family members were available in the network.

To summarize, the old and the young interact with each other in the face of differential age-graded, history-graded, and nonnormative influences on their age-specific social motivations and social preferences. I have argued so far that city contexts differ *psychologically*, that is, with respect to their developmental functions depending on the individual's specific life phase. Moreover, the preference for social or intergenerational partners is also closely associated with the specific future orientations and demands of the individual's respective life phase. Thus, the adaptive influence of the urban zone of intergenerational relationships is very different for the child as compared to the old individual. In the following sections, the differential opportunities and constraints of intergenerational relationships (a) in the city of childhood and (b) in the city of later life are discussed.

2   The city of childhood – Developing intergenerational relationships

Although there are no obvious associations, the emergence of childhood as a distinct phase of the life cycle and the formation of urban cities seem to share some common facets and historical parallels. In central Europe, for example, the city had its first great migration boom during the end of medieval times, when freedom and liberation from bondage and serfdom were promised to the peasants and their families who moved to and settled in the city. In Germany, this association is still reflected in an old proverb: "*Stadtluft macht frei*" (City air sets you free). The formation of the city as a geographical region with high population density has been associated with the advent of utopian ideas about freedom and equality for every citizen at the close of the Middle Ages; ideas and values that were subsequently achieved in the course of the civil revolutions in France and Italy and in the war of independence in Britain's American colonies in the late 18th century and the 19th century.

Similarly, although somewhat later, ideas about childhood or adolescence as a distinct life phase emerged with dissemination of modernity and enlightenment. As Ariès (1962) illustrated, children or adolescents during the Middle Ages were not perceived as being different from adults in any way. Public spaces and streets were used by children and adults equally, thus creating many opportunities for intergenerational contact (Görlitz, 1995). Beginning with early pedagogical ideas in the 17th and 18th century, namely, with the writings of John Amos Comenius (1592-1670), John Locke (1632-1704), and Jean-Jacques Rousseau (1712-1778), ideas about the course of child development with its specific needs and potentials began to spread. Simultaneously, the institutionalization of childhood was advanced in the course of urbanization and with the growing self-confidence of urban middle-class families. Child-labor laws and compulsory education reflect this sociocultural development in most industrialized societies. However, until the mid-20th century, streets and public places in the city continued to function as predominant spaces for children's play. Only in the course of the technical revolution and traffic explosion after World War II did streets and sidewalks lose most of their function as extended living spaces of work and family life (Ledig & Nissen, 1987). Simultaneously, the creation of particular spaces for children in the city further underscored the process of institutionalization of childhood (Zeiher, 1990). For example, playgrounds and fields in the city were fenced in and thus separated from traffic and street life. In addition, the city of childhood is no safe place for the child, for environmental pollution, traffic, and crime are factors that are typically more prevalent in urban than in rural areas and that affect daily contact and the management of social relationships.

In sum, three phases in the emergence of the city of childhood may be distinguished: (a) the development of the city as a context of self-actualization and self-realization of a new class of urban citizens, (b) the institutionalization of childhood as a distinct phase in the life course began but without any segregation of children, and (c) the city of childhood, which has emerged as a separate and delimited space within the larger urban context. The evolution of the "city of childhood" may thus be seen as reflecting a history-graded influence on the selective optimization of developmental outcomes in childhood (Marsiske et al., 1995). The separate space for children restricts the child's life space or zone of free action to those activities that are in the zone of proximal development (Valsiner, 1987; Vygotsky, 1978) and thus optimizes the speed and outcomes of development. In this respect, urban zones of intergenerational contact do play an important role for the urban child's development.

2.1   Intergenerational development in the city of childhood

Consequently, the development of intergenerational relationships in the city can only occur when there is opportunity for intergenerational contact. Bronfenbrenner's (1979) epochal work on the ecology of development described childhood development as a slow expansion from a microsystemic environment to the progressive integration of mesosystemic, exosystemic, and macrosystemic environments. The child's development is also determined by an additional ecological system that entails age-graded as well as history-graded influences on development. Bronfenbrenner (1986, 1993a) has called it a chronosystem of ecological development that comprises life-course transitions as well as the mutual influences of successive generations across historical time. The city of childhood seems to be organized hierarchically around the child-caregiver dyad and is stepwise extended to the family, the vicinity of the family's home, the kindergarden and the school as a public institution, the homes and families of friends, parks and playgrounds, shops and malls, streets and playgrounds (Muchow & Muchow, 1935/1978; Zeiher, 1990), and, finally, to the generational nexus and an integration of sociohistorical concepts about the city and the environment. In this respect, urban zones of intergenerational development operate as manifestations and socialization agencies of the chronosystemic influence on development.

Bronfenbrenner (1993b) states that an "educating city" needs to provide opportunities for intergenerational contact that allows mutual and reciprocal interactions, "an escalating psychological ping-pong game between two people who are crazy about each other and who play regularly over extended periods of time" (p. 279). The playground of this developmental ping-pong game is the city, and, of course, the players involved in this game are not just two or three people (i.e., mother and child, father and child). The game involves the extended family, grandparents, and old people who live in the city and who determine what kind of intergenerational contact and interaction the child experiences. However, where do urban children meet and interact with older people? The city provides a variety of circumscribed sets of opportunities for intergenerational contact. At least two major opportunity structures for intergenerational contact can be distinguished: (a) intergenerational relationships within the family, and (b) intergenerational relationships in public spaces or outside the family.

2.2   Inside and outside the family – Urban contexts of children's contact with older people

Hartup (1989) described the social worlds of the child as age-graded and consisting of "vertical relationships," that is, child-caregiver bonds on the one hand and "horizontal relationships," that is, peer relationships on the other hand. Whereas vertical relationships serve to guide the child in developing basic social skills and knowledge, horizontal relationships are characterized by reciprocity and mutuality between peers and might thus serve to elaborate and train these acquired skills. In this respect, intergenerational relationships between young and old individuals might play an intermediate role because the child's relationship to the old individual may be seen as horizontal with respect to the mutuality of the relationship. That is, social contact between the child and an old adult is typically based on a deliberate agreement between both partners, the child and the old individual, to interact with each other. However, when it comes to the life expertise and interpersonal knowledge of the old individual, intergenerational relationships are vertically structured and characterized by the old individual's advantage in knowing about the pragmatics of life (e.g., P. Baltes, 1993). Analogously, Hart (1979) has proposed to distinguish between three separate zones of the child's life space, (a) the zone of free range, (b) the zone of range with permission and (c) the zone of range with other children. In this respect, the urban zone of intergenerational contact combines the horizontal and the vertical social worlds of children. Urban zones of intergenerational contact contribute to the child's zone of free range, as in the case of extrafamilial intergenerational contact in the street, and to the zone of range with permission, as when older family members accompany or guide the child in the city.

2.2.1   Intergenerational relationships within the family

There is some empirical evidence that available grandparents do play an influential role in the development of children and adolescents (Clingempeel, Colyar, Brand, & Hetherington, 1992; Creasey & Koblewski, 1991; Ponzetti & Folkrod, 1989; Sanders & Trygstad, 1993; Sticker, 1991; Werner, 1991) and that most intergenerational contact occurs within the family, that is, with grandparents or with great-grandparents (Feiring & Lewis, 1984; Schmidt-Denter, 1984). Moreover, the child's family context is also determined by relational characteristics of the parent-grandparent relationship (Lehr & Kruse, 1990; Sticker, 1991; Troll, 1983; Werner, 1991).

Thus, the grandparents' developmental influence on children and adolescents may be related to a number of situational or contextual determinants. As noted above, a major determinant of intergenerational family contact is geographical proximity (Frankel & DeWit, 1989). Consequently, when grandparents live nearby, the grandchild is more likely to have a close relationship with his or her grandfather or grandmother. However, there is some evidence that the frequency of contact with grandparents decreases with increasing population density in an urban area (Schmidt-Denter, 1984). Moreover, socioeconomic status was shown to have some influence on both the quantity and quality of grandchild-grandparent relationships (e.g., Hurme, 1991; Schmidt-Denter, 1996). It may be concluded that many aspects of urban environments such as population density, lower living standards, and crime rates actually restrict the urban zones of intergenerational contact to the family context.

The functions of grandparents also change as children move from early childhood to adolescence. During early childhood, the grandparent has mostly caring and playing functions for the child (Sticker, 1991). Grandchildren in middle childhood often report supportive relationships with grandparents (Creasey & Kaliher, 1994; Gottlieb & Sylvestre, 1994). When grandchildren reach puberty and adolescence, though, the tie with grandparents becomes less important and less influential (Clingempeel et al., 1992; Sanders & Trygstad, 1993). However, despite the fact that adolescent grandchildren do not report intimate or confidential relationships with their parents, they continue to perceive their grandparents as emotionally meaningful social partners or important attachment figures (Creasey & Koblewski, 1991).

It can be concluded that the grandchild-grandparent dyad prevails in the development of intergenerational relationships between young and old. Social development in childhood has been characterized as a continuous expansion and differentiation of social worlds from primary relationships within the family to relationships outside the family (Krappmann, 1993; Röhrle, 1994).

2.2.2 Intergenerational relationships outside the family

Intergenerational relationships outside the family seem to be rare in childhood (Blyth, Hill, & Thiel, 1982). In the course of childhood development, however, as children and adolescents develop a sense of social competence, their interest in relationships with adults and more knowledgeable people seems to increase (e.g., Gottlieb & Sylvestre, 1994; Hamilton & Darling, 1989). Further empirical research on children's intergenerational relationships with persons outside the family is needed. At least three social contexts of extrafamilial intergenerational contact in the city can be distinguished. One central context of extrafamilial intergenerational relationships pertains to parents and grandparents of friends and peers of children. In urban settings, these relationships might be of particular relevance in early and middle childhood, when children cannot visit or walk alone to their friend's home but need to be transported by their parents (e.g., Zeiher, 1990). It is therefore more likely that the urban child often spends time and stays overnight in another family's home.

A second context of extrafamilial intergenerational relationships is older friends of the child's parents, that is, senior colleagues, mentors, or family friends (Fischer, 1982). Although there is a large body of empirical work on the social networks and family relationships in mid-life, that is, the "sandwich generation" (e.g., Richards, Bengtson, & Miller, 1989; Schaller, 1992; Schlesinger, 1989), the role of parents' extrafamilial relationships with older adults on the social and intergenerational development of their children is a neglected research topic (see Bronfenbrenner & Crouter, 1983). However, from the perspective of the social-convoy model of personal relationships, some reported findings suggest at least some intergenerational transfer of social relationships from generation to generation (Antonucci & Akiyama, 1994). It has also been suggested that extrafamilial intergenerational relationships might become important to children in times of personal crises or when parents are absent (e.g., Galbo, 1983; Gottlieb & Sylvestre, 1994).

A third context for extrafamilial intergenerational contact in the city pertains to the child's everyday life outside the family home, that is, the context of playing or socializing with peers on public playgrounds; in the street; or in the courtyard, in the entrance hall or on the staircase of an apartment house. Such intergenerational contact with older people is often just casual and restricted to short interaction sequences. For example, older neighbors or other old people on the street may urge the child to show considerate behavior such as not being too loud or not disruptive. A rather typical situation of such intergenerational contact is one in which the child is rebuked for not having complied with social rules or normative expectations. The urban child might learn about the differential perspectives and constraints of city life and the manifold needs and desires of different people living in the city. For example, there is evidence that positive beliefs about old people and about aging increase as a function of contact and interaction with older individuals (Aday, Sims, & Evans, 1991; Chapman & Neal, 1990; Kühne, 1992). Children growing up in city environments might therefore have a better understanding of age-specific perspectives and needs than rural children of the same age. Public places in the city may thus contribute to the child's personality development (see also Carr, Francis, Rivlini, & Stone, 1992). In this vein, Proshansky (1978) characterized the development of self in childhood as a function of interacting with others in public spaces, where negotiation about individual places, space, and rights occur.

To sum up, intergenerational relationships seem to play an important role in the city of childhood and, vice versa, the urban environment seems to affect the structural and functional properties of children's intergenerational relationships. However, empirical knowledge about the child's intergenerational zones in the city of childhood is still rather general and rough. Therefore, more detailed research about the developmental processes and mechanisms of such contextual implications of intergenerational relationships is needed.

3   The city of late life – Adaptive functions of intergenerational relationships

Both old age as a distinct phase of life and the aging process have been of interest to philosophers, artists, and authors since classical antiquity. In particular, the issue of intergenerational relationships has occupied many philosophers and scholars, stimulating many ideas and theories about the nexus of generations living together in one society (see P. Baltes & Baltes, 1994). However, the reasoning about intergenerational relationships in old age is also, implicitly or explicitly, very much influenced by specific social myths about old age. For example, one of the most dominant and invincible social myths about old age contends that in preindustrialized societies, old people typically lived together with their families in multigenerational households, whereas the family in modern times is breaking apart and leaving the older generations alone and isolated, particularly in urban environments (Hagestad, 1987; Shanas, 1979). This myth also swears to the feigned idyll of a preindustrial, rural society in which old and young generations are said to have lived together in peace and harmony on one farm. As Borscheid (1994) illustrates, the contrary was apparently the case. Old people were often quite reluctant to give their farm to the next generation, and there were many quarrels and disputes about the rights and duties of the old parents who continued to live on the farm after handing over their property to the younger generation. In preindustrial cities, similarly, old and young generations did not cohabit but typically lived in separate households within the city (Borscheid, 1994; Mitterauer & Sieder, 1982). This way, friction between the young and the old generation was less apparent and family ties were more harmonious in the urban family than in the rural family.

Such separated housing of generations was given up during the transitional period of early industrialization and urbanization in the late 19th century and the first half of the 20th century, when poverty and a deficient social insurance system forced the family generations to move together into one household (Borscheid, 1994; Ehmer, 1990). Since then, the number of persons living in one household has decreased steadily (e.g., Deutscher Bundestag, 1994; Lang & Schütze, 1992). Therefore, some caution may be necessary when interpreting increases in the proportion of old people living alone in the city in contrast to rural areas (e.g., Arbeitsgruppe Gesundheits-analysen und soziale Konzepte an der FU Berlin und Interdisziplinäre AG für Angewandte Soziale Gerontologie an der GHS Kassel, 1991) as evidence for the "breaking apart" of the family in the course of modernization, urbanization, and increased individualization in urban societies. Separate housing in late life more likely points to the traditional ways in which generations used to live together in the city. Moreover, separate housing of generations reflects the increasing wealth of "urban" societies, where older family members can afford to run a household on their own (Schütze, 1997). A crucial question in this context is, however, to what extent the separation of families or the segregation of generations in the city actually adds to increased adaptivity in late life.

3.1 Theories on the city of late life and the adaptiveness of intergenerational contact

Indeed, most theories of social aging spark controversial discussions about the adaptiveness or adequacy of separated living of generations and of intergenerational relationships within and outside the family. For example, disengagement theory emphasized that withdrawal from social roles "results in a shift in the quality of relationships in the remaining roles" (Cumming & Henry, 1961, p. 217). The old individual is expected to become affectively neutral, turn inward, and be indifferent to most aspects of daily life except for the most intimate aspects of the environment (Cumming & Henry, 1961). Consequently, intergenerational relationships with grandchildren are seen as being more of a burden and are therefore less important to old people. When living separated from other generations, the old individual is expected to disengage from social roles more easily and prepare him- or herself better for the process of dying.

In contrast, activity theory emphasized the adaptiveness of being socially active and engaged in a variety of social roles within and outside the family (Havighurst, Neugarten, & Tobin, 1968; Lemon, Bengtson, & Peterson, 1972). Intergenerational contact thus refers to just one of many social activities that enhances social adaptivity in late life. Living separately, in this respect, is seen to protect the old individual from social expectations of the younger generations and to ensure maximal freedom from the needs and desires of one's children or grandchildren in order to develop those activity patterns and styles that provide the most satisfaction to the older individual.

According to continuity theory (Atchley, 1977, 1993), old people prefer activities that allow elderly people to experience continuity in their self and their life circumstances. Therefore, old people prefer to do activities that build on existing competencies and experiences and pertain to role identities of the previous life. For example, grandparenthood draws on experiences that were made during early parenthood.

In contrast to continuity theory, social integration theory focuses on the loss of social roles in late life (Rosow, 1974, 1982). This prevailing role loss in old age requires old people to find and define new social roles. Rosow (1974) argues that intergenerational contact might impede the process of developing new, age-specific, and age-adequate roles in late life. When being together with people of the same age, the old individual can identify with others and thereby develop an in-group identity of old age. Thus, age-segregated environments protect old people against interference and intrusion of the younger generation. For example, satisfaction with the quality of the neighborhood has been found to be higher in age-segregated blocks than in nonsegregated living quarters (e.g., Messer, 1967; Sherman, 1975). As a result, feelings of security among old people are reduced in age-heterogeneous quarters because of the presence of adolescents hanging around and fear of victimization. However, there is evidence that the positive association between living satisfaction and age homogeneity in the neighborhood is only valid for low-quality neighborhoods. Vaskovics (1990) reports that in urban regions with good infrastructure and a high-quality living standard the age concentration in the neighborhood is unrelated to living satisfaction. It seems that the life quality of old people is not affected by the presence of children or adolescents if the younger generations are not experienced as physically threatening.

Finally, the city of late life also differs from the city of childhood with respect to other age-specific characteristics. Most old people who live in urban regions have spent a large portion of their lives in the city in which they live. This means that old people do not only know "their" city very well, they also hold a chronological knowledge about how the city has changed over the years or decades and thus develop a specific place attachment to their city (Rubinstein & Parmelee, 1992). Sometimes, though, cities change so rapidly that older people are the only ones who know about the way the city looked in earlier times. In such cases, the older individual's place attachment to his or her city will be seriously challenged. By the end of World War II, for example, many European cities had been devastated and reconstruction changed their appearance dramatically.

Moreover, the old individual's life space shrinks with age, mostly because of reduced mobility (Brim, 1988; Rowles, 1981). It would be misleading, though, to interpret such contraction of life space in old age as a reversal to the expansion of life space in childhood. Whereas, in Lewin's (1946) terms, the child's psychological reality just begins to extend beyond the child's actual life space, the old person often continues to have a differentiated psychological reality even though his or her actual zone of influence diminishes. That is, the old individual's life space is constrained by physical and biological conditions rather than by psychological or cognitive determinants.

The composition of social networks in old age is also influenced by decisions made throughout life concerning romantic relationships, family, and friendships. In other words, the social worlds of the elderly individual reflect not only current social preferences and demands but also choices and decisions that were made decades earlier. Such life-long accumulated social attachments to social networks have been elaborated in the convoy model of social relationships introduced by Robert Kahn and Toni Antonucci (Kahn & Antonucci, 1980; Antonucci, 1985a, 1985b, 1990; Antonucci & Akiyama, 1994, 1997). According to the social-convoy model, social networks are organized as a hierarchy that is very much determined by contextual influences such as physical or socioemotional needs of the individual, duration of relationships, and the age and gender of social partners. Social roles and functions of the convoy members also determine how close they are to the developing individual. The convoy metaphor underscores the interplay of continuity and discontinuity in life-long social relationships. Whereas some ties endure across the life span, some relationships drop out of the social convoy and other social partners enter the convoy and take over specific functions. The latter aspect is highly relevant to the development of intergenerational relationships in late life. By definition, relationships with members of younger cohorts emerge in later phases of life, at which point the individual's social convoy has already been formed. A new tie with a child, for example, requires the old person to restructure the social convoy. That tie may, hence, depend greatly on the old individual's personal and life context (Antonucci & Jackson, 1987). It is therefore not surprising that most intergenerational contact in late life, as in childhood, occurs within the family context, that is, with adult children and grandchildren (e.g., Carstensen, 1993b; Field & Minkler, 1988, 1993; Fischer, 1982). Because of the great diversity and variety of potential social partners in the city, urban contexts further promote such constraints on intergenerational contacts.

3.2   Children in the everyday life of old people living in the city

In the city of late life, as in the city of childhood, interactions between young and old are largely restricted to the family and the role of grandparenthood. However, there is also extrafamilial contact, which is mostly related to everyday activities such as errands or shopping.

3.2.1 Intrafamilial relationships with children

Becoming a grandparent actually is a unique developmental task of late life, for it requires the older person to learn a new social role as well as integrate a new member into his or her network (Kivnick, 1982). Idiosyncratic adjustments to this new social role might partly account for reports on differential styles of grandparenting, such as fun-seeking, formal, or distant (e.g., Sticker, 1991). The differences in grandparenting styles, to a certain extent, might also be associated with specific characteristics of the social convoy, depending on the specific social motivations, preferences, and needs of the older individual. For example, preadolescent grandchildren are only rarely mentioned as support providers of their grandparents.

Moreover, the process of integrating relationships with young people depends on contextual influences. As mentioned before, for example, contact frequencies between younger and older family members are greatly determined by geographical proximity (Frankel & DeWit, 1989). Consequently, when grandparents live in the same city as their grandchildren, the likelihood that they will become active grandparents is somewhat higher. However, there is also some empirical evidence suggesting that contact frequencies between grandchildren and grandparents are lower in urban than in rural areas (Schmidt-Denter, 1984). The city offers a great variety of opportunities for leisure activities that are of specific interest to children (e.g., going to zoos, museums, or the resident circus). Such "active" grandparenting in the city confronts the old individual with many activities that require physical mobility as well as cultural knowledge (Friedrichs, 1990; Kaiser, 1993; Sticker, 1991).

3.2.2 Extrafamilial relationships with the young

Outside the family context, there are few opportunities for the old individual to become acquainted and interact with children in the city. Just as with the city of childhood, as described above, different contexts of intergenerational relationships outside the family can be distinguished for the city of late life: (a) friends of grandchildren, (b) children and grandchildren of friends, and (c) children in the neighborhood. There is no available empirical material or data on any of these aspects of developing intergenerational relationships.

Empirical research on childless old people suggests that friends take over some social functions that are typically associated with family interactions (Lang, 1994). There is also some indication that older people who have no contact with nuclear family members have more relationships with friends, acquaintances, and neighbors (Lang & Carstensen, 1994). Although there is no empirical data available, it can be assumed that extrafamilial relationships with younger people are more likely when no grandchild is present. However, further research on the consequences of "grandchildlessness" in late life is needed.

In everyday life elderly people are typically confronted with children who live in their immediate neighborhood. In these contexts, an old individual's extrafamilial interactions with children might be restricted mostly to those situations in which children may be experienced as a source of annoyance, excessive noise, or physical threat (Vaskovics, 1990).

4   The urban zone of intergenerational contact – Potentials and constraints

Throughout this chapter I have argued that, from the perspective of developmental psychology, the city of childhood and the city of late life differ with respect to the demands and potentials of intergenerational relationships for the developing individual. I have tried to discuss some of the possible reasons for such age-specific developmental functions of intergenerational relationships. One reason lies in the differential adaptive functions of intergenerational contact in childhood and late life. In addition, such differences even seem to be enlarged by the differential demands and constraints of urban environments on development in childhood and old age.

It seems that ideas about intergenerational contact in the city are often fed by the seeming idyll of an urban neighborhood as a place of recreation, self-verification, social participation, and mutual intergenerational contact and support (Garms-Homolová, 1987). Such ideas are reminiscent of naive paintings that picture the city in light colors without any shadow or gray zones. In reality, though, the immediate developmental demands of children and old people may indeed be quite different at times. What is "good" for the young may not be "good" for the old and vice versa.

Indeed, as Garms-Homolová (1987) notes, the meaning of intergenerational relationships and neighborhood networks might be overstated in the social sciences. Palliative ideas about the old and the young living together, joyfully interacting with each other, deliberately exchanging their respective resources and thus developing mutual understanding in their city might be in danger of failing to reflect the developmental demands and needs of children and those of older people. Moreover, such ideas risk neglecting the fact that there is actually not much empirical certainty about the mechanisms and processes that determine adaptive person-environment transactions from early to late phases of the life cycle (e.g., Carp, 1987; Wapner, 1981).

As shown above, both theory and research on social development across the life span suggest that adaptive demands and potentials of intergenerational relationships in the city are quite different in childhood and in late life. Whereas childhood might be characterized by the dynamics between security in the relationship with a caregiver and the need to develop autonomy and independent social functioning, the prevailing developmental task of late life is to balance the increasing dependencies on others with the individual's available competencies and goals (M. Baltes & Silverberg, 1994).

For example, in early childhood an individual may prefer to play close to his or her home, thus causing noise in the family's neighborhood. Such noise as well as other behaviors that cause annoyance to older adults are often an unavoidable or even integrative part of the child's play. That is, children at times experience as joyful what causes stress reactions in adults and older people. The child's exploration and play is also targeted at learning about the world, acquiring and training skills or competencies in different life domains. Traffic, streets, squares, parks, or other urban characteristics might all serve as hallmarks in the child's developing understanding of the world and of his or her connectedness with others. In contrast, the older urban resident needs to match his or her competence and available resources with the environmental demands of the city (Lawton, 1989). Thus, traffic, crowds, groups of adolescents, or other facets of urban life might be experienced as severe stressors or even as mortal threats to the old individual. Moreover, when city environments undergo rapid constructional change, older people will experience increased stress in the management of daily life.

In sum, knowing about the developmental needs and potential of children is a necessary condition for understanding the functions and adaptiveness of intergenerational relationships in late life and vice versa. In this respect, the model of selective optimization with compensation describes some of the mechanisms and processes of adaptive intergenerational development in the city. For example, from the perspective of socioemotional selectivity theory, an adaptive mechanism of *selection* in the social domain is determined by age-specific motivations for social contact and social interaction. In early childhood, contact or interaction with older people is mostly related to information-seeking needs, that is, learning about the risks and opportunities of living in the city. For the child, intergenerational relationships may be informational bridges to another social world (Krappmann, in press). In contrast, an old individual may have completely different needs because she or he perceives her time as coming to an end. Therefore, the old person may prefer to have contact with those young people who are emotional meaningful to them.

It has also been argued that because there is greater variability of potential social partners in the city, the social ties might be less strong and interwoven than those in small towns. One consequence may be that the functions of particular relationships in the city (e.g., intergenerational relationships versus peer friendships) are more distinct in urban contexts than in rural ones. For example, in the city a child's contact with an elderly social partner may be restricted to specific activities such as playing or learning, whereas other functions such as child-care or support are taken over by other social partners. It is the city context that determines in what way age-specific social preferences can be met within intergenerational relationships. For example, when the older person can satisfy socioemotional needs while the young individual can profit from the contact in terms of finding out about the self and the world, intergenerational relationships are very likely.

Mechanisms of *optimization* pertain directly to the impact of the urban context on developing intergenerational relationships. The city as a rapidly changing context of development is kept together through the intergenerational zones in the city, which also preserve and enhance the continuity of the city environment. The elderly urban resident may thus be seen in the role of the "keepers of meaning" (Vaillant & Milofsky, 1980; Lang & Baltes, 1997) who preserve and optimize cultural identity across generations. The old individual gives further knowledge and expertise to the young individual who, in turn, may pick up the thread and proceed. It is the intergenerational nexus, the young and the old together, that optimizes the face and character of their urban environment.

Compensation is the most obvious mechanism of an adaptive development within intergenerational relationships in urban contexts. For example, intergenerational relationships provide resources to both the young and the old when other resources are not available. An illustration that is relatively specific to urban contexts relates to the phenomenon of latchkey children, who spend most of their day unsupervised at home while their parents are at work (e.g., Chawla, 1991). Intergenerational relationships also provide compensatory resources. For example, grandparents or other old people in the neighborhood who are retired might take over responsibilities in caring for the child. It is an open question, however, whether the urban context might not even be characterized by a loss of these compensatory functions of intergenerational relationships in contrast to rural areas.

To conclude, what characterizes intergenerational relationships in an urban environment as opposed to other contexts? The social world of the city has been characterized as offering social bonds that are more diverse and less strong than those of rural towns. Such diversity of potential social relationships makes it necessary to be rather selective with social partners. Such "selectivity pressure" of social contact behaviors in the city, however, may not favor contact between young and old. For example, children might expect older people to display wisdom and to function as informational guides in the city. However, the child may not be interested very much in other social transactions with the older individual, such as supportive exchanges or instructions about how to behave according to specific social norms. On the other hand, the older person might prefer contact with children with whom emotionally meaningful relationships exist. In grandchild-grandparent dyads, for example, there may be a perfect match between different age-graded social motivations. Thus, intrafamilial intergenerational contact satisfies the age-specific developmental needs and goals of grandchildren and grandparents alike. By contrast, whereas urban areas impede the development of emotionally close extrafamilial intergenerational relationships, casual extrafamilial contact between the young and the old seem to prevail in the city. One consequence of the differential developmental benefits of urban intergenerational relationships directly relates to urban planning. One requirement in order to enhance the adaptivity of urban zones of intergenerational contact is to find a balance between age-homogenous and separated areas for childrens' and older people's age-specific needs on the one hand and, on the other hand, age-heterogenous areas that serve to promote and enhance contact between young and old in the city.

References

Aday, R. H., Sims, C. R., & Evans, E. (1991). Youth's attitudes toward the elderly: The impact of intergenerational partners. *Journal of Applied Gerontology, 10,* 372-384.

Ahmed, B., & Smith, S. K. (1992). How changes in components of growth affect the population aging of states. *Journals of Gerontology: Social Sciences, 47,* S27-S37.

Aizenberg, R., & Treas, J. (1985). The family in late life: Psychosocial and demographic considerations. In J. E. Birren & K. W. Schaie (Eds.), *Handbook of the psychology of aging* (2nd ed., pp. 169-189). New York: Van Nostrand Reinhold.

Altman, I., Lawton, M. P., & Wohlwill, J. F. (Eds.) (1984). *Elderly people and the environment.* New York: Plenum Press.

Antonucci, T. C. (1985a). Personal characteristics, social support, and social behavior. In R. H. Binstock & E. Shanas (Eds.), *Handbook of aging and the social sciences* (2nd ed., pp. 94-128). New York: Van Nostrand Reinhold.

Antonucci, T. C. (1985b). Social support: Theoretical advances, recent findings and pressing issues. In I. G. Sarason & B. R. Sarason (Eds.), *Social support: Theory, research and application* (pp. 21-37). Dordrecht, Netherlands: Nijhoff.

Antonucci, T. C. (1990). Social supports and social relationships. In R. H. Binstock & L. K. George (Eds.), *Handbook of aging and the social sciences* (3rd ed., pp. 205-226). San Diego: Academic Press.

Antonucci, T. C., & Akiyama, H. (1991). Convoys of social support: Generational issues. *Marriage and Family Review, 16,* 103-123.

Antonucci, T. C., & Akiyama, H. (1994). Convoys of attachment and social relations in children, adolescents, and adults. In F. Nestmann & K. Hurrelmann (Eds.), *Social networks and social support in childhood and adolescence* (pp. 37-52). Berlin: de Gruyter.

Antonucci, T. C., & Akiyama, H. (1997). Social support and the maintenance of competence. In S. Willis, K. W. Schaie, & M. Hayward (Eds.), *Societal mechanisms for maintaining competence in old age* (pp. 182-206). New York: Springer.

Antonucci, T. C., & Jackson, J. S. (1987). Social support, interpersonal efficacy, and health: A life course perspective. In L. L. Carstensen & B. A. Edelstein (Eds.), *Handbook of clinical gerontology* (pp. 291-311). New York: Pergamon Press.

Arbeitsgruppe Gesundheitsanalysen und soziale Konzepte an der FU Berlin und Interdisziplinäre AG für Angewandte Soziale Gerontologie an der GHS Kassel (1991). *Alte Menschen in der Stadt und auf dem Land* [Old people in the city and in the countryside]. Berlin: Deutsches Zentrum für Altersforschung.

Ariès, P. (1962). *Centuries of childhood: A social history of family life.* New York: Vintage Books.

Atchley, R. C. (1977). *The social forces in late life.* Belmont, CA: Wadsworth.

Atchley, R. C. (1993). Continuity theory and the evolution of activity in later adulthood. In J. R. Kelly (Ed.), *Activity and aging* (pp. 5-16). Newbury Park: Sage.

Baltes, M. M., & Carstensen, L. L. (in press). The process of successful aging. *Aging and Society,* in press.

Baltes, M. M., & Silverberg, S. B. (1994). The dynamics between dependency and autonomy: Illustrations across the life span. In D. L. Featherman, R. M. Lerner, & M. Perlmutter (Eds.), *Life-span development and behavior* (Vol. 12, pp. 41-90). Hillsdale, NJ: Erlbaum.

Baltes, P. B. (1987). Theoretical propositions of life-span developmental psychology: On the dynamics between growth and decline. *Developmental Psychology, 23*, 611-626.

Baltes, P. B. (1993). The aging mind: Potential and limits. *The Gerontologist, 33*, 580-594.

Baltes, P. B. (1994, 13 August). *Life-span developmental psychology: On the overall landscape of human development.* Invited Address, Division 7, American Psychological Association. Los Angeles, CA.

Baltes, P. B., & Baltes, M. M. (1980). Plasticity and variability in psychological aging: Methodological and theoretical issues. In G.E. Gurski (Ed.), *Determining the effects of aging on the central nervous system* (pp. 41-66). Berlin: Schering.

Baltes, P. B., & Baltes, M. M. (1990). Psychological perspectives on successful aging: The model of selective optimization with compensation. In P. B. Baltes & M. M. Baltes (Eds.), *Successful aging: Perspectives from the behavioral sciences* (pp. 1-34). New York: Cambridge University Press.

Baltes, P. B., & Baltes, M. M. (1994). Problem "Zukunft des Alterns und gesellschaftliche Entwicklung" [The problem of "the future of aging and the development of the society"]. In P. B. Baltes, J. Mittelstraß, & U. M. Staudinger (Eds.), *Alter und Altern: Ein interdisziplinärer Studientext zur Gerontologie* (pp. 1-34). Berlin: de Gruyter.

Baltes, P. B., Reese, H. W., & Lipsitt, L. P. (1980). Life-span developmental psychology. *Annual Review of Psychology, 31*, 65-110.

Bechtel, R. B. (1987). Ecological psychology. In R. B. Bechtel, R. W. Marans, & W. Michelson (Eds.), *Methods in environmental and behavioral research* (pp. 191-215). New York: Van Nostrand Reinhold.

Bengtson, V. L., & Allen, K. R. (1993). The life course perspective applied to families over time. In P. G. Boss, W. J. Doherty, R. LaRossa, W. R. Schumm, & S. K. Steinmetz (Eds.), *Sourcebook of family theories and methods: A contextual approach* (pp. 469-497). New York: Plenum.

Bertram, H., & Dannenbeck, C. (1991). Familien in städtischen und ländlichen Regionen [Families in urban and rural regions]. In H. Bertram (Ed.), *Die Familie in Westdeutschland* (pp. 79-110). Opladen: Leske + Budrich.

Blyth, D. A., Hill, J. P., & Thiel, K. S. (1982). Early adolescents' significant others: Grade and gender differences in perceived relationships with familial and nonfamilial adults and young people. *Journal of Youth and Adolescence, 11*, 425-450.

Booth, A., & Dunn, J. (Eds.) (1994). *Stepfamilies: Who benefits? Who does not?* Hillsdale, NJ: Erlbaum.

Borscheid, P. (1994). Der alte Mensch in der Vergangenheit [The old individual in the past]. In P. B. Baltes, J. Mittelstraß, & U. M. Staudinger (Eds.), *Alter und Altern: Ein interdisziplinärer Studientext zur Gerontologie* (pp. 35-61). Berlin: de Gruyter.

Bosselmann, P., & Craik, K. H. (1987). Perceptual simulations of environments. In R. B. Bechtel, R. W. Marans, & W. Michelson (Eds.), *Methods in environmental and behavioral research* (pp. 162-190). New York: Van Nostrand Reinhold.

Bretz, M. (1992). Veränderungen in Größe und Struktur von Haushalten – Eine Analyse der vergangenen 150 Jahre [Changes in size and structure of households – An analysis of the past 150 years]. Bundesinstitut für Bevölkerungsforschung (Ed.), *Materialien zur Bevölkerungswissenschaft Nr. 75* (pp. 221-240). Wiesbaden: Bundesinstitut f,r Bevölkerungsforschung.

Brim, G. (1988). Losing and winning. *Psychology Today, 9*, 48-52.

Bronfenbrenner, U. (1979). *The ecology of human development: Experiments by nature and design*. Cambridge, MA: Harvard University Press.

Bronfenbrenner, U. (1986). Ecology of the family as a context for human development. *Developmental Psychology, 22*, 723-742.

Bronfenbrenner, U. (1993a). Generationenbeziehungen in der Ökologie menschlicher Entwicklung [Intergenerational relations in the ecology of human development]. In K. Lüscher & F. Schultheis (Eds.), *Generationenbeziehungen in "postmodernen" Gesellschaften* (pp. 51-73). Konstanz, Germany: Universitätsverlag Konstanz.

Bronfenbrenner, U. (1993b). Cities are for families. In D. Görlitz, H. J. Harloff, J. Valsiner, & G. Mey (Eds.), *Entwicklungsbedingungen von Kindern in der Stadt. Praxisbeiträge der Herten-Tagung*. Unpublished manuscript. Technical University, Berlin, Germany.

Bronfenbrenner, U., & Crouter, A. C. (1983). The evolution of environmental models in developmental research. In P. H. Mussen & W. Kessen (Eds.), *Handbook of child psychology: Vol. 4, History, theory, and methods* (pp. 357-414). New York: Wiley.

Carp, F. M. (1980). Environmental effects upon the mobility of older people. *Environment and Behavior, 12*, 139-156.

Carp, F. M. (1987). Environment and aging. In D. Stokols & I. Altman (Eds.), *Handbook of environmental psychology* (pp. 329-360). New York: Wiley.

Carr, S., Francis, M., Rivlin, L. G., & Stone, A. M. (1992). *Public space*. Cambridge, Eng.: Cambridge University Press.

Carstensen, L. L. (1991). Socioemotional selectivity theory: Social activity in life-span context. *Annual Review of Gerontology and Geriatrics, 11*, 195-217.

Carstensen, L. L. (1993a). Motivation for social contact across the life span: A theory of socioemotional selectivity. *Nebraska Symposium on Motivation* (pp. 209-254). Lincoln, NE: University of Nebraska Press.

Carstensen, L. L. (1993b). Perspective on research with older families: Contributions of older adults to families and to family theory. In. P. Cowan, D. Field, D. Hansen, A. Skolnick, & G.E. Swanson (Eds.), *Family, self, and society: Toward a new agenda for family research* (pp. 353-359). Hillsdale, NJ: Erlbaum.

Carstensen, L. L., & Lang, F. R. (1997). Social relationships in context and as context: Comments on social support and the maintenance of competence in old age. In S. Willis, K. W. Schaie, & M. Hayward (Eds.), *Societal mechanisms for maintaining competence in old age* (pp. 207-222). New York: Springer.

Chapman, N. J., & Neal, M. B. (1990). The effects of intergenerational experience on adolescents and older adults. *Gerontologist, 30*, 825-832.

Chawla, L. (1991). Homes for children in a changing society. In E. H. Zube & G. T. Moore (Eds.), *Advances in environment, behavior, and design* (Vol. 3, pp. 187-228). New York: Plenum.

Clingempeel, W. G., Colyar, J. J., Brand, E., & Hetherington, E. M. (1992). Children's relationships with maternal grandparents: A longitudinal study of family structures and pubertal effects. *Child Development, 63*, 1404-1422.

Cowgill, D. O. (1974). Aging and modernization: A revision of the theory. In J. F. Gubrium (Ed.), *Late life: Communities and environmental policy* (pp. 123-146). Springfield, IL: Charles C. Thomas.

Creasey, G. L., & Kaliher, G. (1994). Age differences in grandchildren's perceptions of relations with grandparents. *Journal of Adolescence, 17*, 411-426.

Creasey, G. L., & Koblewski, P. J. (1991). Adolescent grandchildren's relationships with maternal and paternal grandmothers and grandfathers. *Journal of Adolescence, 14*, 373-387.

Cumming, E., & Henry, W. E. (1961). *Growing old: The process of disengagement.* New York: Basic Books.

De Vos, S., & Ruggles, S. (1988). The demography of kinship and the life course. In P. B. Baltes, D. L. Featherman, & R. M. Lerner (Eds.), *Life-span development and behavior* (Vol. 8, pp. 259-279). Hillsdale, NJ: Erlbaum.

Deutscher Bundestag (Ed.) (1994). *Zwischenbericht der Enquete-Kommission "Demographischer Wandel" – Herausforderungen unserer älter werdenden Gesellschaft an den einzelnen und die Politik* [Interim report of the commission of enquiry on "demographic change" – Challenges of an aging society to the individual and to politics]. Bonn: Deutscher Bundestag, Referat Öffentlichkeitsarbeit.

Downs, R. M., & Liben, L. S. (1993). Mediating the environment: Communicating, appropriating, and developing graphic representations of place. In R. H. Wozniak, & K. W. Fischer (Eds.), *Development in context: Acting and thinking in specific environments* (pp. 155-181). Hillsdale, NJ: Erlbaum.

Downs, R. M., & Stea, D. (1977). *Maps in minds.* New York: Harper and Row.

Ehmer, J. (1990). *Sozialgeschichte des Alters* [Social history of old age]. Frankfurt on the Main: Suhrkamp.

Feiring, C., & Lewis, M. (1984). The child's social network from three to six years: The effects of age, sex, and socioeconomic status. In S. Salzinger, J. Antrobus, & M. Hammer (Eds.), *Social networks of children, adolescents, and college students* (pp. 93-112). Hillsdale, NJ: Erlbaum.

Felscher, H., Gahlen-Klose, A., & Neubauer, E. (Eds.). (1995). *Fakten und Felder der freien Seniorenarbeit. Ältere Menschen in Deutschland* [Facts and domains of senior work: Older people in Germany]. Bonn: Bundesarbeitsgemeinschaft der Senioren Organisationen (BAGSO).

Field, D., & Minkler, M. (1988). Continuity and change in social support between young-old and old-old or very-old age. *Journal of Gerontology: Psychological Sciences, 43,* P100-P106.

Field, D., & Minkler, M. (1993). The importance of families in advanced old age: A family is "forever." In P. Cowan, D. Field, D. Hansen, A. Skolnick, & G. E. Swanson (Eds.), *Family, self, and society: Toward a new agenda for family research* (pp. 331-351). Hillsdale, NJ: Erlbaum.

Fischer, C. S. (1982). *To dwell among friends: Personal networks in town and city.* Chicago: The University of Chicago Press.

Frankel, B. G., & DeWit, D. J. (1989). Geographical distance and intergenerational contact: An empirical examination of the relationship. *Journal of Aging Studies, 3,* 139-162.

Friedrichs, J. (1990). Aktionsräume von Stadtbewohnern verschiedener Lebensphasen [Activity spaces of urban inhabitants in different phases of life]. In L. Bertels & U. Herlyn (Eds.), *Lebenslauf und Raumerfahrung* (pp. 161-178). Opladen: Leske + Budrich.

Galbo, J. J. (1983). Adolescents' perceptions of significant adults. *Adolescence, 18,* 417-427.

Garms-Homolová, V. (1987). Entfaltungsraum oder Idylle im Kiez? Zur Bedeutung räumlich-sozialer Verankerung alter Menschen [Developmental spaces or idyll in the neighborhood? On the meaning of spatial-social moorings of old people]. In Deutsches Zentrum für Altersfragen (Ed.), *Die ergraute Gesellschaft* (pp. 378-386). Berlin: Deutsches Zentrum für Altersfragen.

Görlitz, D. (1995, September). *Präsentation von Themen in Kind-Stadt Beziehungen: 2. Remembering some parts of history.* Paper presented at the 12th German Conference for Developmental Psychology, Leipzig.

Görlitz, D., & Wohlwill, J. F. (Eds.) (1987). *Curiosity, imagination, and play.* Hillsdale, NJ: Erlbaum.

Gottlieb, B. H., & Sylvestre, J. C. (1994). Social support in the relationships between older adolescents and adults. In F. Nestmann & K. Hurrelmann (Eds.), *Social networks and social support in childhood and adolescence* (pp. 53-73). Berlin: de Gruyter.

Granovetter, M. (1973). The strength of weak ties. *American Journal of Sociology, 78,* 1360-1380.

Hagestad, G. O. (1987). Parent-child relations in later life: Trends and gaps in past research. In J. B. Lancaster, J. Altmann, A. S. Rossi, & L. R. Sherrod (Eds.), *Parenting across the life span* (pp. 405-433). New York: Aldine de Gruyter.

Hagestad, G. (1989). Familien in einer alternden Gesellschaft: Veränderte Strukturen und Beziehungen [Families in an aging society: Changing structures and relationships]. In M. M. Baltes, M. Kohli, & K. Sames (Eds.), *Erfolgreiches Altern. Bedingungen und Variationen.* (pp. 42-46) Bern: Huber.

Hamilton, S. F., & Darling, N. (1989). Mentors in adolescents' lives. In K. Hurrelmann & U. Engel (Eds.), *The social world of adolescents* (pp. 121-139). Berlin: de Gruyter.

Hart, R. (1979). *Children's experience of place: Environmental psychology program.* New York: Irving Publishers.

Hartup, W. W. (1989). Social relationships and their developmental significance. *American Psychologist, 44,* 120-126.

Havighurst, R. J., Neugarten, B., & Tobin, S. (1968). Disengagement and patterns of aging. In B. Neugarten (Ed.), *Middle age and aging* (pp. 161-172). Chicago: University of Chicago Press.

Heckhausen, J., & Schulz, R. (1993). Optimisation by selection and compensation: Balancing primary and secondary control in life-span development. *International Journal of Behavioral Development, 16,* 187-303.

Hurme, H. (1991). Dimensions of the grandparent role in Finland. In P. K. Smith (Ed.), *The psychology of grandparenthood: An international perspective* (pp. 19-31). London: Routledge.

Kahn, R. L., & Antonucci, T. C. (1980). Convoys over the life course. Attachment, roles and social support. In P. B. Baltes & O. G. Brim (Eds.), *Life-Span Development and Behavior* (pp. 254-283). New York: Academic Press.

Kaiser, P. (1993). Beziehungen in der erweiterten Familie und unterschiedliche Familienformen [Relationships in the extended family and different types of family]. In A. E. Auhagen & M. v. Salisch (Eds.), *Zwischenmenschliche Beziehungen* (pp. 143-172). Göttingen: Hogrefe.

Kennedy, G. E. (1992). Quality in grandparent/grandchild relationships. *International Journal of Aging and Human Development, 35,* 83-98.

Kennedy, G. E., & Kennedy, C. E. (1993). Grandparents: A special resource for children in stepfamilies. *Journal of Divorce and Remarriage, 19,* 45-68.

Kivnick, H. Q. (1982). *The meaning of grandparenthood.* Ann Arbor, MI: UMI Research Press.

Kovar, M. G., & Stone, R. I. (1992). The social environment of the very old. In R. M. Suzman, D. P. Willis, & K. G. Manton (Eds.), *The oldest old* (pp. 303-320). New York: Oxford University Press.

Krappmann, L. (1993). Die Entwicklung vielfältiger sozialer Beziehungen unter Kindern [The development of manifold social relationships among children]. In A. E. Auhagen & M. v. Salisch (Eds.), *Zwischenmenschliche Beziehungen* (pp. 37-58). Göttingen: Hogrefe.

Krappmann, L. (1997). Brauchen jüngere Menschen ältere Menschen. [Do young people need older people?]. In L. Krappmann & A. Lepenies (Eds.), *Alt und Jung: Beziehungen und Probleme zwischen den Generationen* (pp. 185-204). Frankfurt: Campus.

Kühne, V. S. (1992). Older adults in intergenerational programs: What are their experiences really like? *Activities, Adaptation and Aging, 16*, 49-67.

Lang, F. R. (1994). *Die Gestaltung informeller Hilfebeziehungen im hohen Alter – Die Rolle von Elternschaft und Kinderlosigkeit* [Social support management in late life – The role of parenthood and childlessness]. Berlin: Max Planck Institute for Human Development and Education, Studien und Berichte, Vol. 59.

Lang, F. R., & Baltes, M. M. (1997). Brauchen alte Menschen junge Menschen? Überlegungen zu den Entwicklungsaufgaben der dritten Lebensphase [Do older people need young people? Considerations about the developmental tasks of the third phase of life]. In L. Krappmann & A. Lepenies (Eds.), *Alt und Jung: Beziehungen und Probleme zwischen den Generationen* (pp. 161-184). Frankfurt on the Main: Campus.

Lang, F. R., & Carstensen, L. L. (1994). Close emotional relationships in late life: Further support for proactive aging in the social domain. *Psychology and Aging, 9*, 315-324.

Lang, F. R., & Schütze, Y. (1992). Soziale Beziehungen im Alter [Social relationships in old age]. *Spektrum der Wissenschaft, 1*, 113-116.

Lang, F. R., Staudinger, U. M., & Carstensen, L. L. (in press). Socioemotional selectivity in late life: How personality does (and does not) make a difference. *Journals of Gerontology: Psychological Science.*

Lang, F. R., & Tesch-Römer, C. (1993). Erfolgreiches Altern und soziale Beziehungen: Selektion und Kompensation im sozialen Kontaktverhalten [Successful aging and social relationships: Selection and compensation in social contact behavior]. *Zeitschrift für Gerontologie, 26*, 321-329.

Lawton, M. P. (1987). Methods in environmental research with older people. In R. B. Bechtel, R. W. Marans, & W. Michelson (Eds.), *Methods in environmental and behavioral research* (pp. 337-360). New York: Van Nostrand Reinhold.

Lawton, M. P. (1989). Behavior-relevant ecological factors. In K. W. Schaie & C. Schooler (Eds.), *Social structure and aging: Psychological processes* (pp. 57-78). Hillsdale, NJ: Erlbaum.

Ledig, M., & Nissen, U. (1987). *Kinder und Wohnumwelt* [Children and living environment]. Munich: Verlag Deutsches Jugendinstitut.

Lehr, U., & Kruse, A. (1990). The multigeneration family: Theoretical and empirical contributions. In M. Bergener & S. I. Finkel (Eds.), *Clinical and scientific psychogeriatrics, Vol. 1: The holistic approaches* (pp. 15-34). New York: Springer.

Lemon, B. W., Bengtson, V. L., Peterson, I. A. (1972). An exploration of the activity theory of aging: Activity types and life satisfaction among in-movers to a retirement community. *Journal of Gerontology, 27*, 511-523.

Lewin, K. (1946). Behavior and development as a function of the total situation. In L. Carmichael (Ed.), *Manual of child psychology* (pp. 791-844). New York: Wiley.

Lynch, K. (1963). *The image of the city.* Cambridge: MIT Press.

Lynch, K. (1977). *Growing up in cities.* Cambridge: MIT Press.

Marsiske, M., Lang, F. R., Baltes, P. B., & Baltes, M. M. (1995). Selective optimization with compensation: Life-span perspectives on successful human development. In R. Dixon & L. Bäckman (Eds.), *Psychological compensation: Managing losses and promoting gains* (pp. 35-79). Hillsdale, NJ: Erlbaum.

Matthews, M. H. (1992). *Making sense of place.* Hertfordshire: Harvester Wheatsheaf.

Messer, M. (1967). The possibility of an age concentrated environment becoming a normative system. *The Gerontologist, 7*, 247-251.

Mitscherlich, A. (1971). *Thesen zur Stadt der Zukunft* [Theses on the future of the city]. Frankfurt on the Main: Suhrkamp.

Mitterauer, M., & Sieder, R. (1982). *The European Family*. Oxford: Basil Blackwell.

Muchow, M., & Muchow, H. H. (1978). *Der Lebensraum des Großstadtkindes* [The living space of the urban child]. Bensheim: päd. extra. (Original work published 1935)

Myers, G. C. (1990). Demography of aging. In R. H. Binstock & L. K. George (Eds.), *Handbook of aging and the social sciences* (3rd ed., pp. 19-44). San Diego, CA: Academic Press.

Oyserman, D., Radin, N., & Benn, R. (1993). Dynamics in a three-generational family: Teens, grandparents, and babies. *Developmental Psychology, 29*, 564-572.

Ponzetti, J. J., & Folkrod, A. W. (1989). Grandchildren's perceptions of their relationship with their grandparents. *Child Study Journal, 19*, 41-50.

Proshansky, H. M. (1978). The city and self-identity. *Environment and behavior, 10*, 147-169.

Proshansky, H. M., & Fabian, A. K. (1987). The development of place identity in the child. In C. S. Weinstein & T. G. David (Eds.), *Spaces for children: The built environment and child development* (pp. 21-40). New York: Plenum.

Richards, L. N., Bengtson, V. L., & Miller, R. B. (1989). The "Generation in the middle": Perceptions of changes in adults' intergenerational relationships. In K. Kreppner & R. M. Lerner (Eds.), *Family systems and life-span development* (pp. 341-366). Hillsdale, NJ: Erlbaum.

Röhrle, B. (1994). *Soziale Netzwerke und soziale Unterstützung*. Munich: Psychologie Verlags Union.

Rosow, I. (1974). *Socialization to old age*. Berkeley, CA: University of California Press.

Rosow, I. (1982). Intergenerational perspectives on aging. In G. Lesnoff-Caravaglia (Ed.), *Aging and the human condition* (pp. 40-53). New York, NY: Human Sciences Press.

Rowles, G. D. (1981). Geographical perspectives on human development. *Human Development, 24*, 67-76.

Rubinstein, R. L., & Parmelee, P. A. (1992). Attachment to place and the representation of the life course by the elderly. In I. Altman & S. M. Low (Eds.), *Place attachment* (pp. 139-163). New York: Plenum.

Sanders, G. F., & Trygstad, D. W. (1993). Strengths in the grandparent-grandchild relationship. *Activities, Adaptation and Aging, 17*, 43-53.

Schaller, S. (1992). Die "Sandwich-Generation" [The "sandwich generation"]. In M. Hofer, E. Klein-Allermann & P. Noack (Eds.), *Familienbeziehungen* (pp. 238-249). Göttingen: Hogrefe.

Schlesinger, B. (1989). The "sandwich generation": Middle-aged families under stress. *Canada's Mental Health, 37*, 11-14.

Schmidt-Denter, U. (1984). *Die soziale Umwelt des Kindes: Eine ökopsychologische Analyse* [The social environment of the child: An ecopsychological analysis]. Berlin: Springer.

Schmidt-Denter, U. (1996). *Soziale Entwicklung* [Social development]. Munich: Psychologie Verlags Union.

Schütze, Y. (1997). Generationenbeziehungen: Familie, Freunde und Bekannte [Intergenerational relationships: Family, friends, and acquaintances]. In L. Krappmann & A. Lepenies (Eds.), *Alt und Jung: Beziehungen und Probleme zwischen den Generationen* (pp. 97-111). Frankfurt on the Main: Campus.

Shanas, E. (1979). Social myth as hypothesis: The case of family relations of old people. *The Gerontologist, 19*, 3-9.

Sherman, S. R. (1975). Patterns of contact for residents of age-segregated and age-integrated housing. *Journal of Gerontology, 30*, 103-107.

Sticker, E. J. (1991). The importance of grandparenthood during the life cycle in Germany. In P. K. Smith (Ed.), *The psychology of grandparenthood: An international perspective* (pp. 32-49). London: Routledge.

Tinsley, B. J., & Parke, R. D. (1987). Grandparents as interactive and social support agents for families with young infants. *International Journal of Aging and Human Development, 25*, 259-277.

Troll, L. E. (1983). Grandparents: The family watchdogs. In T. Brubaker (Ed.), *Family relationships in later life* (pp. 63-74). Beverly Hills, CA: Sage.

Trygstad, D. W., & Sanders, G. F. (1989). The significance of step grandparents. *International Journal of Aging and Human Development, 29*, 119-134.

Vaillant, G. E., & Milofsky, E. (1980). Natural history of male psychological health: IX. Empirical evidence for Erikson's model of the life cycle. *American Journal of Psychiatry, 137*, 1348-1359.

Valsiner, J. (1987). *Culture and the development of children's action.* New York: Wiley.

Vaskovics, L. A. (1990). Soziale Folgen der Segregation alter Menschen in der Stadt [Social consequences of segregating older people in the city]. In L. Bertels & U. Herlyn (Eds.), *Lebenslauf und Raumerfahrung* (pp. 35-58). Opladen: Leske + Budrich.

Vygotsky, L. S. (1978). *Mind in society: The development of higher psychological processes.* Cambridge, MA: Harvard University Press.

Wachs, T. D. (1987). Developmental perspectives on designing for development. In C. S. Weinstein T. G. & David (Eds.), *Spaces for children: The built environment and child development* (pp. 291-307). New York: Plenum.

Wagner, M. (1989). Spatial determinants of social mobility. In J. van Dijk, H. Folmer, H. W. Herzog, & A. M. Schlottmann (Eds.), *Migration and labor market adjustment* (pp. 241-264). Dordrecht: Kluwer.

Wagner, M. (1990). Wanderungen im Lebensverlauf [Migration in the life cycle]. In K. U. Mayer (Ed.), *Kölner Zeitschrift für Soziologie und Sozialpsychologie, Special Issue 31: Lebensverläufe und sozialer Wandel* (pp. 212-238). Opladen: Westdeutscher Verlag.

Wapner, S. (1981). Transactions of persons-in-environments: Some critical transitions. *Journal of Environmental Psychology, 1*, 223-239.

Werner, E. E. (1991). Grandparent-grandchild relationships amongst US ethnic groups. In P. K. Smith (Ed.), *The psychology of grandparenthood: An international perspective* (pp. 68-82). London: Routledge.

Wilk, L. (1993). Großeltern und Enkelkinder [Grandparents and grandchildren]. In K. Lüscher & F. Schultheis (Eds.), *Generationenbeziehungen in "postmodernen" Gesellschaften* (pp. 203-214). Konstanz: Universitätsverlag Konstanz.

Zeiher, H. (1990). Organisation des Lebensraums bei Großstadtkindern – Einheitlichkeit oder Verinselung [Organization of the living space among urban children – Uniformity or insularization?]. In L. Bertels & U. Herlyn (Eds.), *Lebenslauf und Raumerfahrung* (pp. 35-58). Opladen: Leske + Budrich.

Where we are – A discussion

Bettina Koböck
interviewing Dietmar Görlitz, Hans Joachim Harloff,
Günter Mey, and Jaan Valsiner

Editing a book has a life course of its own. We, the editors of this admittedly long book, realized that fact during our discussions, which went on over a five-year period. We were at times elated by new ideas the contributors brought to our book and at other times desperate about the ease with which the realities of lives in cities seemed to disappear from focus. We disputed how much of the dialogue between theoretical positions (and their presenters) would benefit the book as a whole and arrived, largely by trial and error, at a solution: more rather than less dialogue is better for the ideas involved. The dialogical character of this subject matter, of course, was already present right from the beginning (the period of the Herten conference in the summer of 1992), where different participants talked about practical issues of applying psychology in city-planning contexts. Yet we underestimated the potential value of it for a theoretical integration, which is the topic of the present book. Fortunately, the dialogue reemerged as the book took on form (and grew longer), as different contributors eagerly seized the opportunity to respond to others' criticisms of their positions.

Thus, when we arrived at the point where the parts of this volume needed to be integrated by us, it was consistent with the whole nature of the book to bring out the voices of the editors, to have us speak on our topic. Thanks to the participation of Bettina Koböck, a joint interview was organized in which these voices were made publicly audible. The lively dialogue was added to later, with the interviewees elaborating their perspectives, all of which are now included in the following summary interview. We think it brings the polyphonic treatment of the issues in the book to an appropriate, multivoiced ending. It could be a starting point for further inquiries. The content of our book and the necessities of contemporary urban life call out for constructive syntheses of psychology and lives in cities.

Koböck: Do you think your view of children living in cities has changed as you edited this book?

Görlitz: I think something peculiar happened in these years of dealing with the book. Interest in the subject was there long before the Herten conference and grew out of specific encounters with the urban setting, the interdisciplinary work on the topic, and particularly Lewin's film.[1] What happened in the course of our work on the book is that I had to forget about the city so that I could see it, just as it was also necessary to forget about theories in order to assimilate them, although it was enjoyable and sometimes even intriguing to work through the individual theories carefully. Quite unintentionally, my outlook on the topic changed. Towns, and especially major cities, have become something else, something infinitely exciting to me: metropolitan environments as a very special way of life, as a life setting notable for the fact that it is incomprehensible in principle. Earlier times also lived with things that are incomprehensible, many of which, like the existence of God and His workings, perhaps no longer plague us today as much as they used to, but the big city is an incomprehensibility of a new dimension.

Koböck: What is new about it?

Görlitz: It has a new dimension. In sociology, the modern city was already regarded as a special place shortly after it emerged. Robert E. Park, for example, has stated that the city is a place where you can see "the good and evil in human nature in excess" and that "human nature and social processes" can be studied especially well there.[2] Artists – perhaps I will miss a few genres if I say painters, novelists, and poets – have also said that, given this reality, we are not managing our canon, we need a different language, a different canon, to be able to deal with this complex. That is how a new interest originated in the work on this book, the interest in ways to present the city environment, particularly the big city. In the 18th century there was the attempt in painting to depict urban reality in an almost documentary sort of way. In that sense, the painting in metropolitan centers was quite different. It was not just urban; something entirely new happened. It was precisely the same with photography, and film was born along with the modern metropolis as it were. And it is said that film is a medium especially fitting for the metropolitan setting. In the course of the work on this book and through the discussions among us editors, the phenomenality of this field has become much clearer, much more urgent and engaging for me. My critique frequently gained scope as I read the various contributions to this book. It became clear to me that we modern psychologists still have not "grasped" this special form of existence. In a manner of speaking, we do not "have" big cities. It became clearer to me, too, that a theory on children's development was needed especially in the metropolitan setting.

Koböck: And that we have to forget theory in order to build it?

Görlitz: Yes, although the ideas in the widely divergent viewpoints presented in this book are highly fruitful and I became increasingly sure that we were on the right path. Our topic brings together two incomprehensibilities, the city and temporality, both of which are difficult for our discipline to come to terms with. And above all there is the child, with wide-eyed wonderment, with others, with parents. And my view of children in the city has changed.

Koböck: In what way?

Görlitz: The idea of adapting theories to Herten, or rather parts of Herten, and of evaluating the city according to what is conducive and what is less conducive to the development of children was presumably a harmless way to initiate dialogue at that time. In combing through the contributions that we were so fortunate to receive, I noticed that these clear parameters could not be derived from that approach. Instead, they are orientations, stylistic recommendations, for how to listen to the world, in this context meaning cities in which children live, too. This manner of viewing children's lives in cities has stimulated me and increased my confidence. My perspective has changed, as have the questions I ask myself. I wouldn't do it today the way it was done in Herten. I look more at what we do we cross the threshold of a city, what I'm doing when I go from the Oderbruch to Berlin. The Oderbruch is the most solitary area in these parts. What happens when I come back from there to this city familiar to me? That is one kind of threshold. Another is the literal threshold of the door to the house. And how is it when children slowly get to know a city? What significance does it have, say, for the formation of identity? What does it mean to say, "I am a Berliner?" I'm increasingly interested in what things do with us, not what we do with things.

Koböck: So more and more questions are surfacing that way?

Görlitz: Yes, but as I've said, more and more confidence is building by way of asking questions, particularly when I think of the different chapters in the book.

Koböck: What are the most astonishing or interesting chapters to you?

Harloff: There are four chapters I remember best, but for different reasons. One is Charlesworth's chapter about sociobiology; the others are the explicitly transactional approaches – the chapters by Werner and Altman, Oerter, and the one by Fuhrer.

Koböck: What are the different reasons that you remember those chapters best?

Harloff: In Charlesworth's case, I found the attempt interesting to take something from such remote historical epochs and relate it to today, especially the topic of child and city. I was surprised that it could be done at all. The transactional approaches appeal to me most. They are the most developed in environmental psychology, they have the most practical possibilities, and in my view they are the best suited to depicting and explaining person-environment relations.

Koböck: What connection do you think children and city have to psychological theories?

Valsiner: When I think of psychologists in the world, I see a topic enlarging our theme of children in the city. I sometimes have the image of us four editors driving in a landrover on an African safari, looking at different wild animals in the natural habitat, and trying to make sense of the noises they are making. We have a nice little or big animal shouting about transactionalism or interactionalism. And then there is a little group of animals talking about affordance, and so on. And sometimes a big lion tries to attack our car, and we have to escape. So it goes. What seems to me most interesting is how difficult it is to bring psychologists to discuss seriously any issue of an applied kind, particularly when the issue is extremely complex like a city. The matter may be doubly complex if we think of children in the city. It would be crystal clear if we were to talk about waste in the city. There the task is simple: to get rid of it, so to say. But in the case of children the task is far more complicated. "To get rid of them"? No. If we look at the city, we will somehow find exactly the same issues about children as will arise in any environment, be it rural, urban, or superurban. The same questions exist, and psychologists have not asked them in very advanced ways. They have asked them in accordance with traditions. The result is that psychologists are good at presenting their positions and arguing for them but are not good at all at linking their positions with concrete life environments such as those in the city. My opinion is that if we had studied children in the *Dorf* (rural context),[3] the difficulties would have been very similar. It is not the particular issue of the city. Nevertheless, I think we have succeeded in bringing some order, contrastive order, into this dialogue of psychologists. It will be interesting to see how that is actually read by people who think about cities as cities and not as psychological objects.

Koböck: Do you think psychological theories can kind of capture the life of children in a city?

Mey: I don't because I'm generally unable to really share the epistemological hope of creating realistic constructs, regardless of their disciplinary origins. In particular, I consider it impossible in principle to do justice to the phenomenon, if I may call it that, of development in all its aspects. In that sense, theories are bound to fail if I take seriously what Dietmar mentioned as the incomprehensibility of development, with which the incomprehensibility of the city is associated. In a theory, certain aspects are focused on and others are ignored. For that reason it may be more meaningful than it has been thus far to focus on what a theory, or perhaps more correctly and accurately, what a theory's proponent does and does not do. In this context it would have been more frequently desirable to do what we permit ourselves to do as private persons: to take in and just dwell a while on the phenomenon. In other words, perhaps we have to do what Dietmar Görlitz mentioned at the beginning of this discussion – to forget theories so that we can see in the city something other than what is already known to us.

Koböck: In that case, Dietmar, let me ask again what it is we see if we forget theories?

Görlitz: In the literary documents of our century, cities figure as "schools of perception." It is clear that cities confront us adults, as urbanites, with the familiar experience of being confronted with the unknown. One's view of the sky is hardly ever unobstructed, and contact with direct natural light is reduced, but the streets are almost always artificially illuminated by means of streetlamps, signs, or the lights of houses and apartment buildings. The different lights can also create the impression that it is possible to make night into day. In traveling from one region to the next in quick succession there are usually asphalted surfaces whose use changes rapidly. The horizon is truncated by a curtain of man-made, sign-bearing, prefabricated, transported, or not-quite finished objects such as houses, squares, and streets.

Moreover, we have the uncomfortable guarantee of continuous visibility and audibility corresponding to constant lines of sight from buildings, the oppressively anonymous presence of others, and constant, though changing, background noise. This is all supplemented by indirect experience from a wide variety of sources such as newspapers, television, images, and stories. If we consider what is included in a theory about the city and the development of children, if we think about what it would have to take into account, it is clear that the task is very difficult.

In addition to everything I've mentioned so far, there are many different interwoven time patterns. Despite the ubiquity of the city's enduring physical features, young city-dwellers develop in an urban environment that is constantly changing. And nowhere are courses of events as complexly interlinked as they are in the city. That is the stimulating thing I see in development – complex systems that each have a certain unique duration and both synchronous and asynchronous facets. Theories may no doubt often have no adequate answer for that, but our book enables the reader to ask more informed questions than we could before.

Harloff: I'd like to expound a bit on what you just said about complex systems, Dietmar. The main thing in future theory-building will not be to tear complex systems apart but to preserve their unity. "Child in the city" mustn't be broken down into "child" over here and "city" over there but must be kept together as a whole. The dwelling, for example, then means either carpeting or a stone floor with a child on it, and we observe the difficulties or ease with which the child moves on it at various ages and stages of development. With that approach, the child and the nature of the floor's surface remain linked.

Furthermore, Dietmar, I often find that it makes more sense to talk of change rather than development, which is always seen as something special. What you meant by the linkages of many different processes can be grasped better that way. Everything develops constantly and everywhere, not just organisms but the physical environment, too. That's how things wear out, for example. The world consists of a great many processes running at the same time: physical, economic, social, individual, and so on. The special aspect therefore doesn't have to be change; more exciting is if something does *not* change when an object or a relation remains as it is.

Görlitz: Given the change we are constantly experiencing, what strategies of determining and asserting identity do we have? How do individuals reduce this complexity of the everyday world and make the city something manageable? Do they stay on the block they know and where people know them? Or do they use symbolic reductions to manage the complexities of what in principle can never be known in its entirety? The simplest symbolic reduction is to say, "I am a Berliner," "I'm from Hamburg," or "I'm from New York." Pictorial symbols standing for a metropolis are also simple – the Brandenburg Gate, Bremen's Roland, and the skyline of Manhatten or Frankfurt on the Main. Visitors to a city reduces its complexity by means of travelogues, guidebooks, city maps, a view from the television tower, and, of course, the choice of places they go to. How can we model the development of children in a big city? How does it start, and where does it go?

Mey: Perhaps quite a contrasting train of thought is what I, as a village kid, remember experiencing on the trips my family and I used to take to the neighboring city about once a year. It was always something special. To me, a city was a place in which a lot of people were going every which way, a place with big display windows, toys, ice cream cones, and a jungle of buildings. This city, which would probably be a village to me today, began with the city gates and extended from there through many corridors in a vast maze of buildings. It was much the same for me when I came to Berlin, which I visited for the time when I was 18 years old – infinite rows of buildings, huge streets, traffic, neon lights, street life. In those memories from childhood and adolescence, the thought seems to have coalesced that the city presented itself to me as something holistic. That idea has remained with me to this day. I'll end this excursion into my past with the question of whether this image of the unitary, the vast, the continuous is at all adequate or whether it doesn't seem more likely that it expresses the desire for the coherent, whole, because it is difficult to think in terms of fragments, it is hard to endure them. Interestingly enough, I see analogies. For instance, the development of Potsdamer Platz[4] is intended to close the gap between the two halves of the city. The city is supposed to be reunified. Is it all a façade for creating a new – coherent? – Berlin and underscoring Berlin's status as a metropolis? Berlin's heterogeneity – Kreuzberg and Ku-damm, punk and opera, currywurst and lobster[5] – is not regarded as a sum of opposites. The idea is to give it a corporate identity as "Berlin is all of it," which dissolves the contradiction. We don't seem to be able to bear what Dietmar has called the incomprehensibility of the city, the diversity of phenomena. Instead, we always seem to have to make them smaller, have to corral the contrasts. In earlier discussions, Jaan repeatedly mentioned the city as a village. That hits it more or less on the head, I think.

Koböck: How can a city be a village?

Valsiner: We create our person-centered worlds in different environments, whatever their physical characteristics may be: a cave, a suburban home, a forest, an apartment building, a tent during camping trips, or, among the homeless, a particular street corner to sleep on. Following this line of argument, one can say that every person in a large city creates his or her idiosyncratically personal village that selectively borrows from the ever increasing physical and informational possibilities of the city. The city is rich in resources exactly because it provides for a variety of possibilities for different persons to create their "personal villages," however much outside their home territory it may be extended into the real city environment. So if we look from the perspective of a person, one is always a "villager" whether one lives in an actual village or in a large city. The person constructs his or her village anywhere. But if we look at it from the perspective of a city, there is a complex whole that necessarily transcends the capacities of any particular city dweller to use all of that richness in his or her personal construction. For the latter reason, persons can only construct their personal villages in a large city; they can't embrace the whole of that city.

Mey: As we look at the development of children and adolescents in cities, a quite different example leads me to a similar idea. In towns, and particularly in cities, these young people leave their marks on site as graffiti and tags,[6] which communicate something beyond the action areas of their writers and sprayers. Their markers can be taken as an attempt to appropriate space, to make it their own. And graffiti has the potential to reshape the urban environment. They have always been interpreted as the attempt to lend urban monotony a new face and to underscore one's individuality amid the monotony. But are they really an expression of the desire for individuality? A city planner once asked me why, if the thesis of personal impact and appropriation holds, all places look equally defaced. I didn't have any proper answer then, but today I would say, "Could it be that graffiti perhaps do not express the need for special appropriation of space as much as the tendency to parade mile for mile through the city – a sprayed cord that holds the city together and tries to do what the city planner are also attempting: to build a unified city."

Koböck: So most, if not all, people apparently have the need to think of a city as something whole. But how does that affect the theory-building of psychologists?

Mey: That is the key question, the one I ask myself. May we, as psychologists, think in terms of the *one* city that children conquer bit by bit? Doesn't the reconstruction of children's development under such conditions have something of the experiments of city planners and sprayers? I believe we must seriously learn to think in terms beyond the integrated, holistic dimension. In my mind, to pursue this metaphor, it is otherwise undecided whether psychology plays the role of the city planners inspired by the idea of closing gaps and breaches, in which case they are the constructors, or the role of the sprayers, who "only" paint over the gaps and breaches, in which case they are reconstructors.

Koböck: But how can we preserve the openness being called for if human need apparently speaks against it?

Mey: We can only try and try again, and I think discussions like this one, in which we generate and pick up different ideas, are essential for that effort. For the moment, I can say something more easily about how we can*not* tackle this problem – an idiosyncrasy I have of stating things in the negative instead. The special features of different urban places and the individual significance each feature has for people can't be measured and counted. I "experienced" this boundary in various studies on this topic because what lies behind exactitude is only an ostensibly conveyed certainty, not "actual" meaning, which in a novel, for example, comes through to me more between the lines than in any specific word. In terms of this book, it has sometimes been sort of the same for me as it has been for Dietmar. Although grappling with different theories has certainly not quenched my curiosity about understanding a phenomenon, my question about that phenomenon nevertheless remains unanswered in a sense. But maybe this skepticism also has to do with my preference for "qualitative psychology," which leans more toward interpretation, allows more room for metaphors, and necessitates a certain desired affinity to the autobiographical by virtue of its "reflexive" conceptual mode. This stance, incidentally, also brings up the question of the boundary between novelists and scientists. It is rather odd that most of the authors of this book are city-dwellers but that their experience does not find its way into the book, at least not explicitly.

Görlitz: To me, the worst thing a person can say about cities is "urban environment," and the worst thing one can say about metropolises is "metropolitan area." When you do that, everything that makes up a city or metropolis disappears.

Harloff: But it can be the other way around, too. I find this discussion very engaging. You know that I'm both a psychologist and an economist by training, and the worst thing that can happen to an economist is to hear phrases such as the "city as a phenomenon," "what do I take 'city' to mean," "approaching and gradually entering the city," and formulations like those being used in our discussion right now. You have to see these terms from the perspective of the corresponding discipline. "Urban environment" or "metropolitan area" are quite specific and understandable things that say a lot from the angle of the relevant discipline.

Mey: But do these concepts help one better understand what constitutes life in a city or metropolis?

Harloff: Yes, of course, but only in the context of one's discipline. The problem is that the topic of the child's development in the city is so complex that it cannot be captured by any single theory, especially not a purely psychological one. It is an interdisciplinary topic. When you, Dietmar, speak of the "incomprehensibility of cities" or of the "incomprehensibility of development in cities," it is to me nothing other than a sign of our topic's complexity, which cannot be grasped by a single discipline. And unfortunately, there are no all-round scientists any more who can do justice to the multidisciplinary nature of this subject.

Koböck: If we also consider this discussion and Günter's comments, it naturally becomes harder and harder to answer a question that has come up repeatedly, one that Dietmar has touched on as well, namely, do we need a specific theory when we look at people's development in cities? Is there an answer?

Mey: I don't have an answer to it yet, but I do have a pointed, thought-provoking question. Does a person who grows up in a world of round corners manage well in a world with sharp corners? If so, that person wouldn't need a special theory. In other words, is the metropolis versus the city versus the village something special?

Harloff: I would definitely say "yes." Let me spin the idea to a somewhat greater extreme, as when children become separated from human contact and are brought up, like Romulus and Remus, by animals. Or when we think of African pygmies, for instance, who live in a predominantly phytogenetic environment as opposed to a man-made environment, then I do think different theories are needed because the environments are so different. An example of the fact that a person who grows up in a world of round corners and does not seem to manage all that well in one with sharp corners is illustrated by the problems that migrants have, those of culture shock.

Koböck: On the other hand, the amazing thing about that is how flexible human beings can also be. A further question is whether the many theories about the wide variety of environments can be reconciled? Can we, as Europeans, propose *any* kind of theory about development in Africa, for example? Before delving into that issue, though, I'd like to ask Dietmar a question that he himself has brought up again and again. In what way does the city exist for children as developing beings? In what way does its existence change and what does it bring about in children?

Görlitz: To answer that question, I'd first like to outline a general framework of human development. It can be understood as the transformation of structures of the individual's cognitive action and active cognition. It is stimulated, guided, constrained, or suppressed to varying degrees by persons and things and by persons who use, who are assisted by, or who are represented in things. This exchange is governed by explicit or implicit rules for regulating, promoting, or suppressing behavior and action with regard to motivationally significant or hidden needs. It takes place in a certain flow or sequence, with different degrees of consistency and variety, and covering regions of different size, providing different degrees of freedom for action and being embedded in larger cultural value systems. Moreover, development of individually different children occurs in sufficiently familiar, sociospatially confined regions inside and outside the home through and in a changing kaleidoscope of socially symmetrical and asymmetrical exchange relations directly or indirectly referenced to malleable, reactive, and closed things. So much for a general view of development.

Koböck: How does that perspective relate specifically to cities?

Görlitz: If we look at development in cities, a complementary question arises. Which resources for free mobility, visibility, and audibility do today's major cities offer people growing up in them? How do children develop and experience their nature as physical beings? And how much individual perceptibility, sensuality, and corporeality do cities take away from people developing there? What do cities do to enrich and expand them? The thesis I'd like to posit is that major cities, even before modern media began linking places to each other, offer a different kind of school for seeing, hearing, and moving. They call upon the people growing up in them to develop different kinds of mobility, flexible hierarchies of knowledge and control, and reflexive styles of presentation and representation. Cities take children and adolescents and fit them into an ever more obviously paradoxical quasi-stationary entity that is saturated with signs and zones. And the interpersonally graduated exchange in which they do that is increasingly malleable.

Koböck: That is an exciting thesis with which to close the theoretical part of the book, which certainly sets forth an interesting program for further research. The final topic I'd like to turn to is the practical section of the book, the applications that Jaan Valsiner has also called for. Do you think you can give, for example, recommendations based on the theories of this book to architects or city planners in order to improve life for children in the cities?

Görlitz: When thinking of the contributions in this book, I believe it is very hard to give *direct* recommendations. That was our original idea at the Herten conference. I think the theories give us stylistic recommendations along the lines of how we can improve the way we see children in the city. That is an essential aspect if we want to promote development.

Harloff: The Herten conference showed us how difficult it is to assess the quality of the networks of child-environment units because they depend on so many different factors. These factors have to do with the child, the caregivers, their material situation, and so forth. And, of course, the specific features of the places and the respective possibilities for compensation afforded by the child-environment units have to be considered. A few recommendations can be given at a very general level, however.

Koböck: What are they?

Harloff: I would distinguish between three areas in which recommendations could be given: the dwelling, the immediate vicinity, and the local neighborhood and greater metropolitan area. It is very important for the dwelling to have a flexible floor plan because the needs of children and their families change as the children develop. It needs, for example, flexible partitions, the possibility for breaking through walls, and the division of large spaces. That way, one can keep the children's bedroom from becoming a multipurpose room in which the children are "locked away." The design and construction of single-family row houses and multistory apartment buildings should provide the possibility of realloting room(s) from one dwelling to an adjacent one so that entire dwellings can be enlarged or reduced. Looking at one dwelling again, I have found that a vertical arrangement over several floors has been more successful in a certain sense than a horizontal organization.

Koböck: So the frequently disparaged row houses are ideal for children?

Harloff: Exactly, because children who have a floor to themselves in a three-, four-, or five-story single-family houses are better at using this space for privacy regulation than are children who live in a dwelling that is set up horizontally. Another recommendation concerns the entrance area. It is best placed at ground level. Better still is to have two ground-level entrances: one at the front, if possible, with a front yard even if it is tiny, and one leading to the back porch and to the back yard beyond. The yard needn't be large, but it offers the opportunity to be outdoors in a private space and to grow up in "nature." In a dwelling located above the ground floor of a building, the yard can be supplanted by a large balcony or terrace, but that is, of course, not the same.

Koböck: Why is a ground-level entrance actually so important?

Harloff: In Herten we had an interesting discussion about that after having addressed the question of why children like so much to sit on the threshold and why children in multistory structures like to play in the entryway so much. We agreed that mechanisms regulating privacy were responsible and that handling them smoothly was important for children's development. A house door that opens to the street gives the children the chance to make contact with the outside under relative protection of the caregivers while keeping open the option to retreat if a threat is perceived. As for the dwelling itself, there is also a recommendation that has become very familiar, namely, that it is best not to build the kitchen as a separate and, if possible, small room. It is better to have a family room in which the kitchen is only a niche or a combined kitchen and living room.

Koböck: What about the immediate vicinity of the dwelling?

Harloff: There it is important above all to have spaces that can be played and lived in, which is salient not only for children but also for the development of positive social relations in neighborhoods. That point came to mind earlier, when Jaan said that each person creates his or her own personal village even in the city. That's the way it is, I think. Each person at least tries it, but under certain conditions the structural framework thwarts it. A wide variety of planning possibilities exist to bring about outdoor areas that can be played and lived in. They include the construction of residential courtyards, the building of row houses, the choice of a dwelling located on streets where motorized traffic has been restricted and slowed. With blocks of multistory buildings it is important to develop inner courtyards with various kinds of play and quiet areas for children as well as adults. With high-rise buildings and free-standing rows of apartment houses a similar measure would be to use walls, hedges, or fences to separate them from the street and, of course, to create areas for play and other activities inside the block. By contrast, free-standing single-family houses are often not at all as good as one thinks, since the housing density may be too low for children to form peer groups easily. I think it would take too long to review and justify each suggestion and measure in detail in this discussion.

Koböck: But please tell us something about planning recommendations for the local neighborhood and the greater metropolitan area.

Harloff: It is extremely difficult to make suggestions for shaping the local neighborhood and the greater metropolitan area so that they meet the development needs of children. A polycentric urban arrangement is certainly an advantage, with local centers in the individual districts. That often results in cases where independent and mutual competing parts grew together to form a city. Under those conditions the separate districts and their boroughs usually have all the facilities conducive to the development of children, so routes to get there are short and parents can decide more easily to let their children go there on their own. In addition, safety is very important, not only in terms of modes of transportation and routes but also as far as personal safety is concerned. If children are assaulted even only occasionally, adults will not be willing to allow children in their care to go unsupervised to public or semipublic areas no matter how good the other factors there may be. And that significantly reduces the positive developmental function of those spaces because the independent, ludic, and self-responsible exploration and appropriation of objects and spaces is absolutely central to development. These recommendations are highly abstract, of course, and what they entail in any given city would have to be spelled out. The complexity we spoke of earlier makes it impossible to give more detailed planning advice for the city as a whole.

Koböck: That brings us back to the topic running throughout this discussion: the complexity of cities. My final question is what you think the tasks are for the future?

Mey: I think we've talked about a great many in the issues that have arisen. Despite the major difficulties I have observed throughout the process of preparing this book and despite the fact that we have made only slight progress at best in coming to terms with the questions that have been posed, I don't think we can afford to tire of examining theories for their practical value. To me that seems necessary so that the planning advice Hans Joachim Harloff just mentioned don't come out of the blue. In addition, I repeat – and I prefer to repeat it in this case – that we must strive for a climate of discourse, the academic sphere included, that allows for surprises and for the chance to question one's own theory and the theories of others, a climate that doesn't just reproduce certainties and ostensibly secure knowledge.

Görlitz: I'd like to illustrate the fruitful thing about a discourse like the one we're having today. Rome, a city thousands of years old, is a good example. Despite all the earthquakes, conflagrations, storms, wars, and other calamities that city has endured, it is still very stable and resilient. With this book we and our colleagues have jointly produced something very fragile as an answer to this durability, something not at all like a city, with its order, district divisions, roads, and concrete buildings. Instead, we have produced something that is in flux, something that changes and perhaps approximates what is initially not so clear – change that occurs in cities. It is something process-oriented directed to something that has become clearer than it used to be, like "heavenly Jerusalem" as a reality of faith.[7]

I also find it interesting that our book may be appearing at a time when cities, even metropolises, are leaving the stage of history, a time when the sedentary tie to places is being supplanted by the simultaneity of places experienced by computer kids in internet villages. What is the nature of the entities and certainties in which future generations will grow up and in which prosperous industry will be interested? In that case, it can be that our book is tantamount to a swan song. Heavenly Jerusalem has become more visible and yet more remote because cities are losing their primacy as a crucial reality of life. Or, as Günter would say, they are becoming an enriched, more comprehensive kind of city, the *telepolis*, or whatever you wish to call it.

Harloff: Telepolis is a fine word . . .

Görlitz: . . . meaning that it acquires a complementary, and not only virtual, dimension that future psychologists will follow our children into. Jaan, you have the final word, for you are the only one of us four editors to have been born in a city.

Valsiner: Look at the result . . .

Görlitz: . . . not as product but as process.

Notes

1 Lewin, K. (1931). *Das Kind und seine Welt* [The child and his world.] [Film]. (Available from the FernUniversität Gesamthochschule Hagen, Germany.)
2 Park, R. E. (1915). The city: Suggestions for the investigation of human behavior in the city environment. *The American Journal of Sociology, 20,* 577-612. Quoted from p. 612.
3 The term used in the original interview was *Dorf* (village). The contrast is between city and noncity environments, hence, the translation *rural contexts* to express the opposite of urban contexts.
4 Before the division of Berlin, Potsdamer Platz was one of the central squares of the city. When the Wall was built, a wide strip along both sides of the structure was cleared, with the houses located there being evacuated and demolished. When Berlin was reunited in 1990, the city therefore had a large undeveloped tract through the middle of it, including Potsdamer Platz, which had lain directly on the boundary between East and West Berlin. This space is now undergoing redevelopment.
5 Kreuzberg is a part of former West Berlin known for its run-down housing and its counterculture of intellectuals and non-German immigrants. Ku-damm (short for Kurfürstendamm) is

the glamorous center of former West Berlin. Berlin likewise owes much of its color to the coexistence of its punk and opera-going publics. *Currywurst* is a fast food popular among busy Berliners on the way to their jobs. (This book's editors confess that some of their work was carried out under the influence of *currywurst*.) Lobster is a delicacy the editors might be able to afford after the publication of this book.

6 Graffiti are understood here in general to refer to all paintings in the form of pictures or inscriptions; tags are the signatures (logos) written with a marker or spray.

7 We learned of this image in a text by Aaron Gurjewitsch about the medieval European conception of the world. As Pastor Jürgen Wehrmann (Berlin) kindly made known to us, the formulation appears in Hebrews 12:22. For the topic of our book, it is perhaps spelled out more specifically in Zechariah 8:4-5. The interested reader may also refer to Werner Müller (1961), *Die heilige Stadt. Roma quadrata, himmlisches Jerusalem und die Mythe vom Weltnabel* [The Holy City: Roma quadrata, heavenly Jerusalem, and the myth of the navel of the world]. Stuttgart: Kohlhammer.

Appendix

Biographical notes

Irwin Altman is Distinguished Professor of Psychology and Professor of Family and Consumer Studies at the University of Utah. His research examines interpersonal relationships by means of a dialectical and transactional perspective, including study of the role of physical and social environments in a cross-cultural perspective. His most recent work addresses husband-wife and wife-wife relationships in American polygamous families (*Polygamous families in contemporary society*, Cambridge University Press, 1996, coauthored with Joseph Ginat). (Mailing address: University of Utah, Department of Psychology, 390 South 1530 East, Room 502, Salt Lake City, UT 84112-0251, USA; E-mail: irwin.altman@m.cc.utah.edu)

Urie Bronfenbrenner is the Jacob Gould Schurman Professor of Human Development and Family Studies and of Psychology at Cornell University. He received a bachelor's degree from Cornell University in 1938, with a double major in psychology and in music. He did graduate work in developmental psychology, completing a master's degree at Harvard and received a doctorate from the University of Michigan in 1942. In his scholarly work, Bronnfenbrenner has pursued three mutually reinforcing themes: (a) developing theory and corresponding research designs at the frontiers of developmental science; (b) laying out the implications and applications of developmental theory and research for policy and practice; and (c) communicating the findings of developmental research. Widely published in all three spheres, he has received many honors and distinguished awards, including that for "Lifetime Contribution to Developmental Psychology in the Service of Science and Society," which is henceforth to be given annually in his name. (Mailing address: Department of Human Development, Cornell University, Ithaca, N.Y. 14853, USA)

William Charlesworth is a recently retired professor from the Institute of Child Development of the University of Minnesota. He received a master's degree from Wesleyan University in comparative psychology and a Ph.D. from Cornell in child development and family relationships. Currently, he is attempting to forge better connections between evolutionary theory and human development. (Mailing address: PO Box 18, Stockholm, Wisconsin, USA, 54769)

John Cotterell is a professor in the Faculty of Social and Behavioral Sciences at the University of Queensland in Brisbane, Australia. His research interests lie in the social and physical environments of young people and in environmental interventions to enhance the leisure activities and educational experiences of children, adolescents, and young adults. (Mailing address: Graduate School of Education, University of Queensland, St. Lucia, Australia, 4072; E-mail: j.cotterell@mailbox.uq.edu.au)

Werner Deutsch was born in 1947 and studied psychology, linguistics, and philosophy at the University of Münster, the University of Marburg, and Stanford University. Since 1987 he has been Professor at the Technical University of Braunschweig. His major interests are in the psychology of language and developmental mechanisms in cognitive, linguistic, and social development. (Mailing address: Institut für Psychologie, TU Braunschweig, Spielmann-straße 19, D-38106 Braunschweig; E-mail: w.deutsch@tu-bs.de)

Cornelia Eybisch is a member of the Environmental and Social Psychology Unit at the Technical University of Berlin. Her thesis examines conflict resolution within the context of a bank's team training. Beyond that she is concerned with environmental conflict mediation. (Mailing address: Technische Universität Berlin, Psychologie im Institut für Sozialwissenschaften, Sekr. HAD 40, Hardenbergstraße 4-5, D-10623 Berlin; E-mail: eybisch@zrzsp3.gp.tu-berlin.de)

Alexander von Eye is Professor of Psychology and Professor of Family and Child Ecology at Michigan State University. His interests are in methodology, statistics, and life-span development. (Mailing address: Michigan State University, Department of Psychology, S-119 Snyder Hall, East Lansing, Michigan 48824-1117, USA, phone: (+1) 517-432 2476; E-mail: voneye@pilot.msu.edu)

Antje Flade received her master's degree in psychology at the University of Hamburg. She has studied the psychology of perception for many years and specializes in environmental psychology. Since 1980 she is working at the Institut Wohnen und Umwelt (the Institute of Dwelling and Environment). Her main research interests are in evaluation research, residential psychology, and gender and the environment. (Mailing address: Institut Wohnen und Umwelt, Anna-straße 15, D-64285 Darmstadt; E-mail: iwu-darmstadt@t-online.de)

Urs Fuhrer is Professor of Developmental and Educational Psychology at the Otto von Guericke University of Magdeburg. His research areas include the cultural mediation of the emerging self, a life-span oriented approach to cultural development addressing questions of stability and change in personal identities under conditions of rapid societal change, the impact of home environments on juvenile delinquency, the relation between classroom design and student-teacher interaction, and the effects of new information technologies on people's mind. (Mailing address: Otto-von-Guericke-Universität Magdeburg, Institut für Psychologie, PF 4120, D-39016 Magdeburg; E-mail: urs.fuhrer@gse-w.uni-magdeburg.de)

Tommy Gärling is currently Professor of Psychology at Göteborg University, Sweden, and head of the Cognitive, Motivational, and Social Psychology Unit of his department. His main areas are cognitive and environmental psychology. His recent research interests include basic principles of individual decision-making and the applications of such principles, to analyses of travel demand and traffic safety, among other areas. (Mailing address: Department of Psychology, Göteborg University, Haraldsgatan 1, S-41314 Göteborg, Sweden; E-mail: tommy.garling@psy.gu.se)

Dietmar Görlitz is Professor of Psychology and has lived in Berlin, Germany, for many years. He teaches developmental psychology at the Technical University of Berlin and social and cultural psychology at the Free University of Berlin. After researching nonverbal communication and speech, he turned to motivation theory and Heiderian psychology. He has since written about developmental aspects of curiosity research and about methodologies used in historically oriented psychology. Together with architects and town planners, he founded the Herten research project to establish an interdisciplinary and urban perspective within developmental psychology. (Mailing address: Technische Universität Berlin, Psychologie im Institut für Sozialwissenschaften, Sekr. HAD 40, Hardenbergstraße 4-5, D-10623 Berlin)

Carl F. Graumann is Professor Emeritus of Psychology at the University of Heidelberg, Germany. He has published widely on the social psychology of cognition and language, the history of social psychology, and environmental psychology. He is a proponent of a phenomenological orientation in psychology. His special research interest has been the role of perspective in knowledge acquisition and in language use. (Mailing address: Psychologisches Institut, Universität Heidelberg, Hauptstraße 47-51, D-69117 Heidelberg; E-mail: graumann@psi-svl.psi.uni-heidelberg.de)

Hartmut Günther is Professor of Psychology. His research and teaching focus on environmental psychology and research methodology, particularly such aspects of the urban quality of life, as sense of neighborhood, traffic safety, and access to recreation and leisure for young people. He studied in Germany and the United States, where he received his Ph.D. from the University of California, Davis. Since arriving in Brazil in 1975, he has taught at the Federal Universities of Rio Grande do Sul and of Paraíba, and, since 1988, at the University of Brasília. (Mailing address: Caixa Postal 4480; 70919-970 Brasília, DF, Brazil; E-mail: hartmut@unb.br)

Isolda de Araújo Günther is a senior research associate in developmental psychology. Her main interests are in adolescent and health psychology. She studied in Brazil and the United States, where she received her Ph.D. from Michigan State University in 1983. She has taught at the Federal University of Paraíba, and, since 1988, at the University of Brasília. (Mailing address: Caixa Postal 4480; 70919-970 Brasília, DF, Brazil)

Rainer Guski is Professor of Psychology at the Ruhr University of Bochum and specializes in human perception and environmental psychology. His main interests are in auditory perception, environmental noise effects, and behavior modification in order to achieve low-energy consuming and low-emission producing behavior. (Mailing address: Fakultät für Psychologie, Ruhr-Universität Bochum, D-44780 Bochum; E-mail: rainer.guski@ruhr-uni-bochum.de)

Hans Joachim Harloff is Professor of Psychology at the Technical University of Berlin and specializes in social and environmental psychology. He also holds a master's degree in economics. His main research interests are in residential psychology, health psychology, and sustainable economic growth. Professor Harloff is married and has four sons. In a project on the Lüneburg Heath (Lower Saxony), he and his wife are converting a former village school building into living quarters and recreation facilities. (Mailing address: Technische Universität Berlin, Psychologie im Institut für Sozialwissenschaften, Sekr. HAD 40, Hardenbergstraße 4-5, D-10623 Berlin)

Roger Hart received a doctoral degree in geography from Clark University in Worcester, Massachusetts. He has since taught at the Graduate School of the City University of New York in Environmental Psychology, with an affiliate position in Developmental Psychology. He was the founder and an editor of the journal *Children's Environments*. His research focuses on children's relationship to the outdoor environment, particularly in low-income families in both the northern and southern hemispheres. He is currently coauthoring a UNICEF book on the implications of the U.N. Convention on the Rights of the Child for the planning and managing of cities.

(Mailing address: Children's Environments-Research Groups, City University of New York Graduate School, 33 West 42nd Street, New York, N.Y. 10036, USA, phone: (+1) 212-6422970, fax: (+1) 212-6422971; E-mail: rhart@email.gc.cuny.edu)

Harry Heft is Professor of Psychology at Denison University, Granville, Ohio 43023, USA. His empirical work has explored human navigation and way-finding, affordances, environmental perception, and effects of home environment conditions on development. His theoretical work has primarily concerned the historical and philosophical foundations of ecological psychology. (E-mail: heft@denison.edu)

Wolf-D. Heine, studied psychology at the Ruhr University of Bochum and the University of Connecticut. Since 1988 he has been with the Division of Cognitive and Environmental Psychology at the Ruhr University. His main interest is in applied research on the coupling of perception and action. Since 1996 he has been manager and partner of ZEUS Ltd, a consulting and research company in the domain of environmental science. At ZEUS his main interest is the psychology of user-friendliness concerning traffic, transportation, and mobility. (Mailing address: ZEUS GmbH, Universitätsstraße 142, D-44799 Bochum; E-mail: zeusgmbh@aol.com)

Barbara Hinding is member of the Environmental and Social Psychology Unit at the Technical University of Berlin. In her dissertation she is concerned with individual, social, and environmental aspects of home energy conservation. She is also interested in residential and in health psychology. (Mailing address: Technische Universität Berlin, Psychologie im Institut für Sozialwissenschaften, Sekr. HAD 40, Hardenbergstraße 4-5, D-10623 Berlin; E-mail: hinding@zrzsp3.gp.tu-berlin.de)

Siegfried Hoppe-Graff is Professor of Psychology at the College of Education, University of Leipzig, Germany. Specialized in several fields of developmental psychology, he began his career with research on methodological and metatheoretical aspects of Piagetian theory (in particular, the concepts of stage and sequence). His recent interests include the social-constructivist approach to development; moral development and education; and the influence of the media on children's moral socialization and play. (Mailing address: Erziehungswissenschaftliche Fakultät, Universität Leipzig, Karl-Heine-Straße 22b, D-04229 Leipzig; E-mail: hoppe@rz.uni-leipzig.de)

Heidi Keller is Professor of Psychology at the University of Osnabrück. Her interests in gender differences, early relationship formation, exploratory behavior, and the impact of cultural conceptions on behavioral development are integrated into an evolutionary-based framework. She has published several books and articles, among them *Handbuch der Kleinkindforschung*, now in its second edition. (Mailing address: Universität Osnabrück, Fachgebiet Entwicklungspsychologie, Seminarstraße 20, D-49069 Osnabrück; E-mail: hkeller@luce.psycho.uni-osnabrueck.de)

Bettina Koböck is member of the Developmental Psychology Unit at the Technical University Berlin. Her main interest is the role of consciousness, emotions, and culture in concept development based on Piagetian theory. At the Technical University Darmstadt she was research associate in several projects dealing with the development of the concept of work, the development of student's psychological concepts, and psychotherapists' concepts of the self. She is now working on the subject of concept development of the city. (Mailing address: Technische Universität Berlin, Psychologie im Institut für Sozialwissenschaften, Sekr. HAD 40, Hardenbergstraße 4-5, D-10623 Berlin; E-mail: koboeck@zrzsp3.gp.tu-berlin.de)

Lenelis Kruse is Professor of Psychology at the FernUniversität Hagen, Germany. Her special interests are in the field of environmental psychology. She has also published in social psychology and the psychology of language. Her current research focuses on human dimensions of global environmental problems and on verbal communication between young and older people. (Mailing address: FernUniversität Hagen, Institut für Psychologie, Postfach 940, D-58084 Hagen; E-mail: lenelis.kruse@ fernuni-hagen.de)

Alfred Lang is Professor of Psychology at the University of Bern, Switzerland. His work is devoted to the ecological problem or understanding of the relation between people and their environment in their coevolution. Because humans largely live in a self-generated environment, he sees psychology as both a cultural and biological science. His semiotic ecology develops tools to conceive that relation on a strictly non-Cartesian basis. (Mailing address: Hostalen 106, CH-3037 Herrenschwanden/Bern; E-mail: alfred.lang@psy.unib.ch)

Frieder R. Lang works as a research scientist in the Department of Gerontopsychiatry at the Free University of Berlin. He received his doctoral degree in 1993 from the Free University of Berlin. Since 1990 he 's a research collaborator of the Berlin Aging Study (BASE). His major research interests are family and social relationships over the life course, successful aging, everyday competence, and adaptive processes in social behaviors across adulthood and old age. (Mailing address: Psychological Gerontology (WE 30), Free University of Berlin, Nussbaumallee 38, D-14050 Berlin, phone: (+49) 30-84458252, fax: (+49) 30-84458289; E-mail: flang@ zedat.fu-berlin.de)

Alain Legendre is a researcher from the French CNRS (National Center for Scientific Research). He holds a diploma of architecture (1978) and received a doctorate in developmental psychology (1983). He first conducted research on the influence of building facilities on young children's social development (e.g., spatial arrangement in day-care centers). His current research deals with the environmental constraints and the biobehavioral processes that lead to stress and disease susceptabilities in young children. (Mailing address: Laboratoire de Psychologie Environnementale, 28, Rue Serpente, F-75720 Paris cedex 06; E-mail: legendre@lpe.msh-paris.fr)

Simone Lehnert is member of the Environmental and Social Psychology Unit at the Technical University of Berlin. Her dissertation focuses on the evaluation of residential situations with regard to sustainability. She is also concerned with the critique of city planning. (Mailing address: Technische Universität Berlin, Psychologie im Institut für Sozialwissenschaften, Sekr. HAD 40, Hardenbergstraße 4-5, D-10623 Berlin; E-mail: lehnert@zrzsp3.gp.tu-berlin.de)

Richard M. Lerner is the Anita L. Brennan Professor of Education at Boston College and the Director of the Boston College Center for Child, Family, and Community Partnerships. He was a fellow at the Center for Advanced Study in the Behavioral Sciences and is a fellow of the American Association for the Advancement of Science. He is also a member of the American Psychological Association, the American Psychological Society, and the American Association of Applied and Preventive Psychology. Lerner is the founding editor of the *Journal of Research on Adolescence* and of the new journal *Applied Developmental Science*. (Mailing address: Center for Child, Family, and Community Partnerships, Boston College, Chestnut Hill, MA 02167, USA; E-mail: lernerr@bc.edu)

Günter Mey is a member of the Developmental Psychology Unit at the Technical University of Berlin. He has worked as a research associate on various projects related to the environment of adolescents and children and has made documentary films about youth cultures. His work focuses on qualitative methodologies and research methods and on social science approaches to youth development. (Mailing address: Technische Universität Berlin, Psychologie im Institut für Sozialwissenschaften, Sekr. HAD 40, Hardenbergstraße 4-5, D-10623 Berlin; E-mail: mey@zrzsp3.gp.tu-berlin.de)

Hirofumi Minami is Associate Professor of Environmental Psychology at Kyushu University. He received his doctorate from Clark University in 1985 and has been a visiting researcher in the Social Ecology Program of the University of California at Irvine. His current research projects include a longitudinal and ethnographic study of urban renewal from the perspectives of elderly residents, environmental designs for developing children, and participant observation studies on early enculturation processes. (Mailing address: Department of Educational Psychology, Faculty of Education, Kyushu University, 6-19-1 Hakozaki, Fukuoka 812 Japan; E-mail: minamedu@mbox.nc.kyushu-u.ac.jp)

Katja Mruck is a member of the Department of Clinical Psychology at the Free University of Berlin. Since working as a research associate in projects on youth unemployment and public health, she has specialized in research methods and evaluation. Her research interests are qualitative methodologies and research methods, psychoanalytic social research, the psychology of science, and philosophy. (Mailing address: Freie Universität Berlin, WE 09, Institut für Klinische Psychologie, Psychologische Diagnostik und Gemeindepsychologie, Habelschwerdter Allee 45, D-14195 Berlin; E-mail: mruck@zedat.fu-berlin.de)

Christian Munz is lecturer on ecological psychology in the Department of Psychology at the University of Tübingen. His 1987 dissertation is about an ecological approach to the psychology of play. He has published on the ecological approach of J. Gibson (1989) and an ecological approach to the psychology of film viewing (1992). In his current research on the ecological perspective, he is exploring and outlining an approach to the psychology of the human observer seen as being embedded in and created by an ecopsychological world of many observers. (Mailing address: Psychologisches Institut, Universität Tübingen, Friedrichstraße 21, D-72072 Tübingen)

Rolf Oerter is Professor of Developmental Psychology and Educational Psychology at the Psychological Institute of the Ludwig Maximillians University in Munich. His main research interests are cultural and ecological psychology as seen from the developmental perspective. One main area of research is the concept of human nature in different cultures, ranging from East Asia and Europe to South and North America. (Mailing address: Institut für Pädagogische Psychologie und Empirische Pädagogik der Universität München, Fakultät für Psychologie und Pädagogik, Leopoldstraße 13, D-80802 München; E-mail: oerter@edupsy.uni-muenchen.de)

Willis F. Overton is Professor of Psychology at Temple University. He specializes in developmental psychology and has written extensively on metatheoretical, theoretical, and methodological models of development. His primary research interests are cognitive development, the development of logical reasoning, and developmental psychopathology. He is a past president of the Jean Piaget Society. (Mailing address: Department of Psychology, 567 Weiss Hall, Temple University, Philadelphia, PA 19122, USA; E-mail: overton@vm.temple.edu)

Hellgard Rauh is Professor of Developmental Psychology at Potsdam University, Germany. She received her Diploma of Psychology degree and doctorate at the University of Bonn. In 1973 she was appointed Professor of Developmental Psychology at the University of Bielefeld and moved to the Free University of Berlin in 1977. In a series of longitudinal research studies, she is observing and analyzing the development of coping behavior in infants and toddlers, comparing the adaptation of school beginners with differing socialization backgrounds, tracking the early developmental courses of infants and children with Down syndrome, and following risk children into their adolescence. (Mailing address: Institute for Psychology, University of Potsdam, Postbox 60 15 53, D-14415 Potsdam; E-mail: rauh@rz.uni-potsdam.de)

Ute Ritterfeld is currently working as an assistant professor at the Department of Social and Environmental Psychology, University of Magdeburg, Germany. She received a degree as a speech and language pathologist and a master's degree in psychology from the University of Heidelberg and, in 1995, a Ph.D. from the Technical University of Berlin. Her research is focused on aesthetic preferences, account episodes, and parent-child interaction. (Mailing address: Otto-von-Guericke-Universität Magdeburg, Institut für Psychologie, Postfach 4120, D-39016 Magdeburg; E-mail: ute.ritterfeld@gse-w.uni-magdeburg.de)

Thomas Bernhard Seiler is Professor Emeritus of Psychology at the Technical University of Darmstadt, Germany. He received degrees in mathematics, physics, botanics, French literature, and psychology. In 1971 he was appointed Professor of Developmental Psychology at the Free University of Berlin and in 1976 went to Darmstadt. His main research in recent years has dealt with the development of concepts and word meanings. (Mailing address: Institut für Psychologie, Arbeitsgruppe Begriffsforschung, Technical University Darmstadt, Hochschulstraße 1, D-64289 Darmstadt)

Noam Shpancer is a doctoral candidate in Clinical Psychology at Purdue University. He is currently on his clinical psychology internship at Indiana University Medical Center. His research focuses on child development, with an emphasis on the home day-care link. His clinical interests involve the treatment of anxiety disorders. He is married and has one daughter. (Mailing address: Department of Psychological Sciences, Purdue University, West Lafayette, IN 47907-1364, USA)

Jaan Valsiner, a native of Estonia, is a developmental and cultural psychologist. He is mostly interested in theoretical issues of human development in cultural contexts. His main books are *Culture and the development of children's action* and *The guided mind.* He was awarded the Alexander von Humboldt Research Prize in 1995. Currently, he is Professor of Psychology at Clark University and a member of the Center for Developmental Science, University of North Carolina at Chapel Hill. (Mailing address: Frances L. Hiatt School of Psychology, Clark University, Worcester, MA 01610-1477, USA)

Theodore D. Wachs is Professor of Psychological Sciences at Purdue University. His research focuses on the role of environmental and nutritional influences upon development and the moderation of environmental influences by individual characteristics such as child temperament. He has authored and coedited a number of books, including *The nature of nurture; Conceptualization and measurement of organism-environment interaction,* and *Temperament: Individual differences at the interface of biology and behavior.* (Mailing address: Department of Psychological Sciences, Purdue University, West Lafayette, IN 47907-1364, USA; E-mail: wachs@psych.purdue.edu)

Seymour Wapner is chair of the Executive Committee of the Heinz Werner Institute for Developmental Analysis, Frances L. Hiatt School of Psychology, Clark University. His programmatic research in perception, development, and environmental psychology has been informed by and instrumental in the development of the sensory-tonic field theory of perception and of the holistic, developmental, systems-oriented theory. (Mailing address: Heinz Werner Institute for Developmental Analysis, Clark University, 950 Main Street, Worcester, MA 01610 1477, USA; E-mail: swapner@clarku.edu)

Carol M. Werner is Professor of Psychology and Director of Environmental Studies at the University of Utah. In her recent research she examines behavior change strategies around such environmental issues as increasing precycling and recycling and reducing household pesticide use. (Mailing address: University of Utah, Department of Psychology, 390 South 1530 East, Room 502, Salt Lake City, UT 84112-0251, USA; E-mail: carol.werner@m.cc.utah.edu)

Subject index

Author index

Italicized page numbers designate cross-references to contributions in this volume.